Readings for Diversity
and Social Justice

Readings for Diversity and Social Justice

edited by

Maurianne Adams

Warren J. Blumenfeld

Rosie Castañeda

Heather W. Hackman

Madeline L. Peters

Ximena Zúñiga

Routledge   New York and London
A member of the Taylor and Francis Group

Published in 2000 by
Routledge
29 West 35th Street
New York, NY 10001

Published in Great Britain by
Routledge
11 New Fetter Lane
London EC4P 4EE

Library of Congress Cataloging-in-Publication Data

Readings for diversity in social justice : an anthology on racism, anti-Semitism, sexism, heterosexism, ableism, and classism / editors, Maurianne Adams, Warren J. Blumenfeld, Rosie Castañeda, Heather W. Hackman, Madeline L. Peters, Ximena Zúñiga.
p. cm.
Includes bibliographical references.
ISBN 0-415-92633-5—0-415-926634-3 (pbk)
1. Prejudices—United States. 2. Racism—United States. 3. Minorities—United States. 4. Social Justice—United States. 5. United States—Race Relations. 6. United States—Ethnic Relations. I. Adams, Maurianne. II. Blumenfeld, Warren J. III. Castañeda, Rosie. IV. Hackman, Heather W. V. Peters, Madeline L. VI. Zúñiga, Ximena.

E184.A1 R386   2000
303.3/85/0973—dc21   00710866

Contents

Section 8: Working for Social Justice: Visions and Strategies for Change

Acknowledgments

The editing team for this volume brings together a range of different perspectives on gender, race, ethnicity and national origin, language, sexual orientation, class, physical and mental ability, and religion. Together, we bring the experience of the dominant and targeted social identities represented in this reader to the selection of the readings—we include men and women; we are gay, lesbian, bisexual, and heterosexual; we include blacks, Latino/as, and whites, Jews and Christians; some of us have learning disabilities or physical disabilities; we were born poor, working class, and middle class. Our academic specializations include ableism, antisemitism, heterosexism, sexism, and racism. We include college faculty and doctoral students who have, among us, many years of experience teaching a variety of undergraduate courses and workshops on each of these social justice issues.

Our work on this volume has been an exciting and challenging collaborative project. We have worked together as an editorial team, valuing the different gifts and perspectives we bring to this work, and reaching consensus on issues concerning the overall scope and organization of this volume. At the same time, we agreed that specific editors would be identified as having primary responsibility for specific section content, for writing the section introductions, and for suggesting further print and video references, based upon our primary areas of expertise and experience. Decisions and agreement were not always easy, but this process has only increased our mutual respect and appreciation for the knowledge and insight, the dedication, energy, and goodwill that each of us has brought to this project. For all of us as coeditors, the time and attention we devoted to the process of coordinating our perspectives has been indispensable to the integrity of this volume.

It is also important for us to acknowledge that our work has depended upon the contributions of others. We appreciate the suggestions made by Social Justice Education course instructors and colleagues at the University of Massachusetts, Amherst, who critiqued our selections and gave us further references: Christopher Lester, Linda McCarthy, Lisa Robinson, Sheri Schmidt, and Teeomm Williams, all doctoral students in the Social Justice Education Program, and Larry Goldbaum, Director of the Office of Jewish Affairs. We appreciate and build upon the work of previous Social Justice course instructors who prepared an earlier reader, published as *Social Diversity and Social Justice: Selected Readings* (Dubuque, Iowa: Kendall/Hunt, 1994, 1997) and edited by Maurianne Adams, Peg Brigham-Alden, Paulette Dalpes, and Linda Marchesani.

We thank Mary McClintock for her resourceful, upbeat, and tireless library support and ingenuity in gaining permissions and in preparing several generations of the manuscript. Leslie Edwards provided valuable editorial support.

We consider ourselves tremendously fortunate to have worked closely with Ilene Kalish as our editor at Routledge. This volume has benefited enormously from her commitment to and enthusiasm for this project, her careful reading of many iterations of the text, her knowledge of the literature of social justice, and her tactful but firm recommendations.

We appreciate and acknowledge the many ways in which Lee Bell, Pat Griffin, Rita Hardiman, Bailey Jackson, Barbara Love, Linda Marchesani, together with generations of social diversity and Social Justice Education course instructors and workshop facilitators from the 1970s through to the present day, have immeasurably enriched each version of the curriculum that underpins this volume, the range of readings, and each other's instructional practice in the growing community of Social Justice Education students and teachers.

Readings for Diversity and Social Justice: A General Introduction

Maurianne Adams

This collection of readings is designed to help students take new perspectives on social diversity and social justice in the United States. We take an approach that emphasizes the interactions among racism, antisemitism, sexism, heterosexism, ableism, and classism. Our selections call attention to the interconnections among these issues as they are part of everyday lived experience. This is the approach we proposed in the earlier *Teaching for Diversity and Social Justice: A Sourcebook*, edited by Maurianne Adams, Lee Anne Bell, and Pat Griffin, which suggests the theoretical orientation, curricula, and teaching approaches that we have found useful in our own social justice educational efforts. This earlier volume assumed an experiential approach to social justice education to be augmented by a volume of readings that focuses upon each of the major issues as well as their interactions. This volume presents the readings we had in mind.

We have selected recent, accessible articles and testimonials that have challenged and informed our own thinking, as well as that of our students, about cultural differences and societal injustice, and we have organized them into eight sections. In each of these sections, except the first, the readings have been divided into three subsections: *Contexts, Personal Voices,* and *Next Steps and Action*. Some of our selections theorize or describe structural inequality and societal oppression in clear and intellectually accessible ways.

These chapters appear in the first section on *Conceptual Frameworks* and in the following subsections labeled *Contexts.* Other chapters give voice to the experience of being different, especially when "difference" signifies inequality as well as "otherness." These appear in subsections labeled *Personal Voices.* Each section concludes with *Next Steps and Action* that suggest or illustrate how we might take action in our own lives and in coalition with others to effect positive social change. The final section, *Working for Social Justice: Visions and Strategies for Change,* further explores these possibilities.

These selections explore aspects of social identity (such as race, gender, or sexuality) and the corresponding dimensions of social inequality and oppression (for example, racism, sexism, and heterosexism) as they are experienced in the contemporary United States. While we explore these human experiences through the distinctive lens of social identity, we also understand these lenses to be socially constructed. In other words, we view categories of social experience not as "essentially" determined by biology or human nature, but rather as creations of specific cultures situated in unique historical contexts. The socially constructed categories of social experience taken up in this volume include race, gender, sexual identity, religion, physical and mental abilities, and socioeconomic class.

In line with our emphasizing the interconnection of multiple social identities in the experience of any one person, it is our belief that all forms of social injustice are equally important for study and consideration. All forms of oppression are equally hurtful and limiting to persons or groups who are targets of that oppression. They also limit the full humanity of persons and groups who are agents and who benefit from inequality, however unintentional their legacy may be.

The interconnectedness of social identity and social inequality informs the selections within the various sections of this volume. Thus, on the one hand, selections describing antisemitism or racism highlight some of the unique histories, dynamics, institutional patterns and practices, social and cultural norms and values that together shape and account for the subordination of Jews or peoples of color. Yet, on the other hand, it is also important to understand that the personal experience of a Jewish or Latino/a or Asian-American man or woman must be understood in relation to other dimensions of his or her social group experience—in relation to the experiences he or she may have as Jewish, Latino/a, or Asian-American; as lesbian, bisexual, gay, or heterosexual; as able-bodied or physically disabled; with a specific class background, experience, age cohort, and religious or spiritual beliefs; in a specific cultural and historical U.S. context. And, while we acknowledge that overt manifestations of oppression surely vary in their intensity or virulence within different historical periods and across different geographical areas, in our selections for this volume we emphasize the common elements in oppression and suggest the overarching phenomenon that stigmatizes some groups, privileges others, and maintains a complex system of domination and subordination.

Principles of Selection

This collection of readings consists of eight sections. The first section presents a conceptual introduction and overview of issues of social justice, understood as generic issues of domination and subordination. The final section presents visions of a more socially just future, and suggests specific ways that we might take action toward social change. The six content sections in between focus upon racism, antisemitism, sexism, heterosexism, ableism, and classism, with emphasis upon their interactions in lived everyday experience. For example, readings in the sexism section include some of the ways in which gender intersects with race and ethnicity, heterosexism, and class. Similarly, selections in the ableism section illustrate specific interactions of physical and mental disabilities with gender, race, and class. The antisemitism section, while focusing mainly upon the history and current examples of antisemitism, includes perspectives on the relations of blacks and Jews, and the intersection of antisemitism with class and gender.

Within each of these six topics of social oppression, we include essays that present conceptual and theoretical approaches and up-to-date descriptive, historical, and statistical information for each issue. We include personal testimonials of people of mainly subordinate social status (women, gay men and lesbians, people with physical and mental disabilities). Wherever possible, we include testimonials and narratives that highlight the interaction among several group statuses (such as accounts of working-class Jews, disabled people of color, Asian-American lesbians, or black female domestic workers) in order to emphasize the coexistence and constant interaction of our multiple identities. Finally, we include pieces that dramatize how these issues play out in contemporary life and the actions that people are taking, or have taken, toward social change.

Despite the broad coverage of these six topics of social justice, this volume cannot presume to be exhaustive. Ageism, which many people consider to be a social justice issue, is not represented as a stand-alone topic here. Similarly, the various ways in which racism is experienced by different communities of color—African Americans, Asian Americans, Latinos, Native Americans—would, if explored fully, require a separate volume. Although we do represent the experiences of different communities of color in order to preclude a narrow black/white representation of racism in the United States, we cannot be exhaustive in a single multi-issue volume. And while treating antisemitism as an issue that crosses religious, ethnic, even racial lines, we note that in this volume we do not propose to treat other forms of combined religious, ethnic, and racial oppression—against Muslims, for example.

How to Use This Book

Many courses utilize an approach to social justice education that looks at the multiple manifestations of social oppression issue by issue, in a sequential approach. The sequential, topical organization of this book supports such an approach, in order to enable students to disentangle the multiple dynamics of inequality by focusing on each topic separately. Nonetheless, while separating the topics into distinct sections, our selections still dramatize the interaction of these issues. For that reason, essays dealing with sexism, classism, or racism (to name just three) will be found throughout the volume and not restricted to sections 2, 4, or 7. Further, since some courses on diversity and social justice take a thematic rather than a topic or "ism-based" approach focusing upon considerations such as social group membership, domination and subordination, institutional and cultural manifestations, historical backgrounds and the like, we have organized a Thematic Table of Contents, which concludes the book (see page 507).

In our own brief introductions to the book's sections—written in each case by that section's editor(s)—we suggest our own approaches to the subject, our sense of the most pressing themes and issues, and the issues we intend to present by way of our selections. In the Further Print and Video Resources section at the back of this volume (see page 499), we offer a list of print and videotape materials that we believe will enrich classroom exposure to these complex subjects.

Teaching Approach

Unlike traditional subject areas in which knowledge often relies primarily upon discipline-specific perspectives, and where delivery is usually transmitted through lectures, readings, and full class discussions, many Social Justice Education courses are now utilizing multi- and cross-disciplinary perspectives and experiential, active, and collaborative teaching/learning approaches. These cross-disciplinary approaches help to capture the nuanced and multilayered experience of social reality, and the interactive approaches enable participants to connect new intellectual insights with changes in their personal attitudes, feelings, and understanding of their daily lived experience.

This is the approach we favor. It is the approach we have already described in *Teaching for Diversity and Social Justice: A Sourcebook*. The *Sourcebook* presents our conceptual analysis of social diversity and social justice; it describes our approach to course design and facilitation; and it presents specific course curricula for each of the major topics addressed in this volume as well. Thus, the selected readings here will complement the approaches adopted by the many educators who have been using the *Sourcebook* and looking for a companion volume of readings. However, this volume of readings can also be used as a freestanding text for any course that incorporates a range of social justice topics into the curriculum. In our own teaching, as described in *Teaching for Diversity and Social Justice: A Sourcebook*, we encourage an experiential rather than a didactic approach to social justice and multicultural courses by incorporating a series of experiential activities or discussion topics related to the course topics. The readings are assigned as homework and discussed in class or in short papers. Because these activities are described at length in the *Sourcebook*, we do not repeat them here.

Conceptual Frameworks

Introduction by Maurianne Adams

As a Black, lesbian, feminist, socialist, poet, mother of two including one boy and a member of an interracial couple, I usually find myself part of some group in which the majority defines me as deviant, difficult, inferior, or just plain "wrong." From my membership in all of these groups I have learned that oppression and the intolerance of differences comes in all shapes and sizes and colors and sexualities; and that among those of us who share the goals of liberation and a workable future for our children, there can be no hierarchies of oppression.

In the words of Audre Lorde quoted above (1983), "There is no hierarchy of oppressions." This statement does not mean that different forms of oppression do not affect people in different ways, or do not vary in their intensity or virulence for different groups across different historical periods or various geographical parts of this country, or that their time frames or impact on whole populations do not differ. However, while acknowledging differences of intensity and degree, our approach claims that all forms of oppression are equally important, that they interact with each other in the lives of individuals and groups in complex ways, and that a fair and just society requires an end to all forms of oppression. It is simply not useful to argue competitive victim status (who has suffered more, or longer). Instead, the approach taken in this section will be to understand the general dynamics of social oppression as they affect us, primarily in the United States, on the basis of our differences and commonalities of race, ethnicity, language, and culture; gender and sexual orientation; physical and mental ability; religion, and class (see Bell 1997 for further discussion).

Second, these social categories or groups, according to which everyone in our society is to some degree privileged or targeted, are socially constructed, which is to say that they are creations of specific cultures situated in specific historical conditions, and therefore are also capable of being changed. This section does not agree with the view that differences in skin color, accented speech, physical gender, or sexual orientation, or the presence or absence of a physical or mental disability, have any "essential" implications for a person's talents, character, intelligence, values, or morality. Social groups as we know them derive from common histories, cultures, and traditions, so that our understandings of what it means to be female or male; gay or straight; white, Latino, or black; or learning disabled or able-bodied are meanings that we take in from our social context with the air that we breathe. Similarly, we understand the stereotypes and prejudices we all learn about members of targeted social groups (such as women; communities of color; those for whom English is not the primary language; gays, lesbians, or bisexuals; Jews; lower- or working-class people) to be attitudes we learn as part of our socialization processes (described by Bobbie Harro in chapter 2), but those learnings at the individual level are reinforced throughout our experience by organizational and societal structures of privilege and of disenfranchisement.

Third, therefore, we pay attention in this section to the ways in which these individual expressions of stereotypes or prejudice, mentioned above, derive from a social system in which *difference* often also means *inequality*. This means that not all people have equal opportunities: some of our needs and interests are empowered, but others are systematically devalued.

In this section's analyses of racism, antisemitism, sexism, heterosexism, ableism, and/or classism in the United States, several key terms appear that are defined and used in different ways by various writers on the basis of their differing social perspectives, conceptual frameworks, and academic disciplines. These key terms include *stereotype, prejudice, discrimination*, and *oppression*, and the various *isms* all understood as forms of structural inequality. Further, some of these analyses examine whether the dynamics that characterize oppression are playing out at the individual, institutional, or societal levels (or some combination of these three) and also whether they can be said to be conscious or unconscious (see Iris Marion Young and Fred L. Pincus in chapters 4 and 5; see also Hardiman and Jackson 1997 for further analysis).

Some of these terms (such as *stereotype* and *prejudice*) are most often used to describe the attitudes of individual people in their personal interactions with other individuals, whereas other terms (*discrimination, oppression*, and the specific *isms)* are generally used to convey the workings of the larger social system. Sometimes these meanings overlap, as when a prejudiced individual, acting on behalf of a governmental agency or an educational organization, implements policies that are discriminatory; other times, individuals who are not aware that they are prejudiced may unconsciously carry out discriminatory practices as part of their "business as usual."

Other key terms, which may be new to readers of this volume, help us to think about our various *social identities* and to differentiate between those social identities that are dominant or *agent* (such as male, white, heterosexual, able-bodied, or upper class) and those that are subordinate or *target* (such as female, black or Latino/a; gay, lesbian or bisexual; physically disabled; working poor or unemployed); (see Miller 1976 for further discussion). This distinction helps us understand social privilege and power, and to think about how we may have internalized dimensions of our agent statuses (*internalized domination*) or our target statuses (*internalized subordination,* sometimes also termed *internalized oppression*). Part of the challenge of the readings in this section has to do with the different ways in which the levels and types of inequality (personal or interpersonal, structural or societal) are presented, given the different perspectives and purposes of various authors.

The terms introduced above convey an approach to social diversity that might be understood to convey two complementary sets of meanings for the term *diversity*. One set of meanings takes the term quite literally to refer to the different experiences, perspectives, worldviews, modes of communication and behavior, and belief systems and values that we all learn as we are socialized within our different social groupings—as girls and boys or women and men who are at the same time also socialized within different ethnic and racial communities; religious communities; socioeconomic class opportunities or limitations; heterosexual, gay, lesbian, or bisexual identities; physical, cognitive, and psychological abilities or disabilities. The nuances of these differences are infinite in their complexity, given our socialization within specific, intersecting social communities and cultures.

Yet, a second set of meanings understands *diversity* also to refer to social groups that are unequal as well as different—groups that are not equally valued, but rather are classifications or categories of persons that occupy different places in a social hierarchy. This second set of meanings leads us to try to build linkages among different groups, not just for better understanding, but also in order to eradicate prejudice, discrimination, inequality and oppression of one group by another.

Readings in this Section

The first two chapters in this volume, by Beverly Daniel Tatum and Bobbie Harro, examine the processes of social identity formation and socialization described above. Tatum defines social identity in a complex, multifaceted way that captures the tensions between dominant and subordinate identities (those systematically advantaged or systematically disadvantaged because of social group memberships) as they interact within the person (a gay or working-class man, or an upper-class or heterosexual woman, for example), or between people or groups of people (students of color and white students, or wealthy and working-class coworkers, for example). She places social identity in the broader context of identity development more generally and describes the ways in which one's identity develops through the interaction between a person's internal sense of who one is (based upon one's social groupings) and the views of oneself and one's group that are reflected back by others in the broader society.

Harro's "The Cycle of Socialization" describes the social processes by which social identities and social roles are learned. This process often includes misinformation or limited or missing information about other social identity groups, especially about targeted or subordinated social groups, in an almost invisible socialization process that takes place continuously in our homes, neighborhoods, communities, schools, places of worship, the range of institutions with which we come in contact, and other conduits of our culture such as the media. This socialization process can be changed and interrupted, or it can be reinforced and perpetuated. Harro's "The Cycle of Liberation" (see section 8, chapter 88 of this volume) picks up the story of socialization where it is left here, to talk about how we can all take steps to break the negative, restrictive features of the socialization process and to transform our understandings of each other and our possibilities for the future.

Chapters 3 and 4—by Warren J. Blumenfeld and Diane Raymond, and by Fred L. Pincus, respectively—introduce and define some of the key terms mentioned earlier, namely *prejudice* and *discrimination, ethnicity* and *race, stereotypes,* and the various *isms.* Pincus distinguishes between different meanings of discrimination at the individual, institutional, and structural levels.

The last two selections, by Iris Marion Young and by Stephanie M. Wildman with Adrienne D. Davis, present useful ways of understanding some of the parallels and commonalities among differing forms of oppression. Young shows why it is not especially helpful to look for a monolithic definition of the various forms of oppression, given the different factors or combinations of factors that operate in the dynamics of racism, sexism, or heterosexism, studied in and for themselves. Her complex and nuanced discussion places the experience of oppression within the context of unequal social groups, for whom the experience of group oppression can best be characterized by the following five "faces" or facets: exploitation, marginalization, powerlessness, cultural imperialism, violence. Young offers examples from a number of social justice issues to show how these five dynamics play out as areas of commonality as well as difference for various social groups in different times and places. Young's analysis also includes a valuable discussion of social groups that can be read in a complementary fashion to the essays by Tatum and Harro.

Wildman presents an extended analysis of the notion of privilege. She offers anecdotal examples of privilege and its absence in order to surface notions of social normality and aberrance, and to explain how they support or hinder people's opportunities and energies on a daily basis. She portrays the workings of privilege in relation to a series of social justice issues and concludes her analysis with a metaphor of how the strands of privilege come together.

Not all of the "conceptual frameworks" offered in this volume appear here in section 1. In section 8, the essay by Patricia Hill Collins presents an important example of how one might consider the interaction of multiple issues, such as the interactive effects of race and class and gender. Collins rejects what she calls an additive analysis of race *and* class *and* gender (*either/or* thinking) in favor of the simultaneous ways we experience our various, interlocking identities (*both/and* thinking). She also presents race, class, and gender at individua, institutional, and symbolic (cultural) levels of analysis, and discussion of power and privilege, thus providing another level of complexity for the analyses presented in this section by Blumenfeld and Raymond, Pincus, and Tatum.

There is an enormous and growing literature on these issues, much of which has been usefully summarized by Lee Anne Bell and Pat Griffin (1997). Rita Hardiman and Bailey Jackson (1997) present a perspective on the dynamics of oppression and their relation to social identity development that complements both the Young and Tatum articles in this section. Other overviews of the dynamics of social oppression that we have found especially useful include Miller 1976; Frye 1983; Pharr 1988; Wildman 1996; Andrzejewski 1996; and Rothenberg 1996; and the historical approaches taken by Steinberg 1989; Takaki 1993; and Zinn 1995. Other readings on specific issues of social justice will be found in the appropriate sections that follow.

References

Adams, M., L.A. Bell, and P. Griffin, eds. (1997). *Teaching for Diversity and Social Justice: A Sourcebook.* New York: Routledge.

Andrzejewski, J., ed. (1996). *Oppression and Social Justice: Critical Frameworks,* 5th ed. New York: Simon and Schuster.

Bell, L. A. (1997). "Theoretical Foundations for Social Justice Education." In M. Adams, L. A. Bell, and P. Griffin, eds., *Teaching for Diversity and Social Justice: A Sourcebook.* New York: Routledge.

Frye, M. (1983). "Oppression." *In The Politics of Reality: Essays in Feminist Theory.* Freedom, Calif.: The Crossing Press.

Griffin, P. (1997). "Introductory Module for the Single Issues Courses." In M. Adams, L. A. Bell, and P. Griffin, eds., *Teaching for Diversity and Social Justice: A Sourcebook.* New York: Routledge.

Hardiman, R., and B. W. Jackson. (1997). "Conceptual Foundations for Social Justice Courses." In M. Adams, L. A. Bell, and P. Griffin, eds., *Teaching for Diversity and Social Justice: A Sourcebook.* New York: Routledge.

Lorde, A. (1983). "There Is No Hierarchy of Oppressions." *International Books for Children Bulletin* 14.

Miller, J. B. (1976). *Toward a New Psychology of Women.* Boston: Beacon Press.

Pharr, S. (1988). "Common Elements of Oppressions." In *Homophobia: A Weapon of Sexism.* Inverness, Calif.: Chardon Press.

Rothenberg, P. S., ed. (1996). *Race, Class, and Gender in the United States: An Integrated Study,* 4th ed. New York: St. Martin's Press.

Steinberg, S. (1989). *The Ethnic Myth: Race, Ethnicity, and Class in America,* updated ed. Boston: Beacon Press.

Takaki, R. (1993). *A Different Mirror: A History of Multicultural America.* Boston: Little, Brown.

Wildman, S. M. (1996). *Privilege Revealed: How Invisible Preference Undermines America.* New York: New York University Press.

Zinn, H. (1995). *A People's History of the United States, 1492–Present,* rev. and updated ed. New York: Harper and Row.

1

The Complexity of Identity: "Who Am I?"

Beverly Daniel Tatum

The concept of identity is a complex one, shaped by individual characteristics, family dynamics, historical factors, and social and political contexts. Who am I? The answer depends in large part on who the world around me says I am. Who do my parents say I am? Who do my peers say I am? What message is reflected back to me in the faces and voices of my teachers, my neighbors, store clerks? What do I learn from the media about myself? How am I represented in the cultural images around me? Or am I missing from the picture altogether? As social scientist Charles Cooley pointed out long ago, other people are the mirror in which we see ourselves.[1]

This "looking glass self" is not a flat one-dimensional reflection, but multidimensional. How one's racial identity is experienced will be mediated by other dimensions of oneself: male or female; young or old; wealthy, middle-class, or poor; gay, lesbian, bisexual, transgender, or heterosexual; able-bodied or with disabilities; Christian, Muslim, Jewish, Buddhist, Hindu, or atheist. . . .

What has my social context been? Was I surrounded by people like myself, or was I part of a minority in my community? Did I grow up speaking standard English at home or another language or dialect? Did I live in a rural county, an urban neighborhood, a sprawling suburb, or on a reservation?

Who I am (or say I am) is a product of these and many other factors. Erik Erikson, the psychoanalytic theorist who coined the term *identity crisis*, introduced the notion that the social, cultural, and historical context is the ground in which individual identity is embedded. Acknowledging the complexity of identity as a concept, Erikson writes,

> We deal with a process "located" *in the core of the individual* and yet also *in the core of his communal culture.* . . . In psychological terms, identity formation employs a process of simultaneous reflection and observation, a process taking place on all levels of mental functioning, by which the individual judges himself in the light of what he perceives to be the way in which others judge him in comparison to themselves and to a typology significant to them.[2]

Triggered by the biological changes associated with puberty, the maturation of cognitive abilities, and changing societal expectations, this process of simultaneous reflection and observation, the self-creation of one's identity, is commonly experienced in the United States and other Western societies during the period of adolescence.[3] Though the foundation of identity is laid in the experiences of childhood, younger children lack the physical and cognitive development needed to reflect on the self in this abstract way. The adolescent capacity for self-reflection (and resulting self-consciousness) allows one to ask, "Who am I now?" "Who was I before?" "Who will I become?" The answers to these questions will influence choices about who one's romantic partners will be, what type of work one will do, where one will live, and what belief system one will embrace. Choices made in adolescence ripple throughout the lifespan.

Who Am I? Multiple Identities

Integrating one's past, present, and future into a cohesive, unified sense of self is a complex task that begins in adolescence and continues for a lifetime. . . . The salience of particular aspects of our identity varies at different moments in our lives. The process of integrating the component parts of our self-definition is indeed a lifelong journey.

Which parts of our identity capture our attention first? While there are surely idiosyncratic responses to this question, a classroom exercise I regularly use with my psychology students reveals a telling pattern. I ask my students to complete the sentence, "I am _____," using as many descriptors as they can think of in sixty seconds. All kinds of trait descriptions are used—friendly, shy, assertive, intelligent, honest, and so on—but over the years I have noticed something else. Students of color usually mention their racial or ethnic group: for instance, I am Black, Puerto Rican, Korean American. White students who have grown up in strong ethnic enclaves occasionally mention being Irish or Italian. But in general, White students rarely mention being White. When I use this exercise in coeducational settings, I notice a similar pattern in terms of gender, religion, and sexuality. Women usually mention being female, while men don't usually mention their maleness. Jewish students often say they are Jews, while mainline Protestants rarely mention their religious identification. A student who is comfortable revealing it publicly may mention being gay, lesbian, or bisexual. Though I know most of my students are heterosexual, it is very unusual for anyone to include their heterosexuality on their list.

Common across these examples is that in the areas where a person is a member of the dominant or advantaged social group, the category is usually not mentioned. That element of their identity is so taken for granted by them that it goes without comment. It is taken for granted by them because it is taken for granted by the dominant culture. In Eriksonian terms, their inner experience and outer circumstance are in harmony with one another, and the image reflected by others is similar to the image within. In the absence of dissonance, this dimension of identity escapes conscious attention.

The parts of our identity that *do* capture our attention are those that other people notice, and that reflect back to us. The aspect of identity that is the target of others' attention, and subsequently of our own, often is that which sets us apart as exceptional or "other" in their eyes. In my life I have been perceived as both. A precocious child who began to read at age three, I stood out among my peers because of my reading ability. This "gifted" dimension of my identity was regularly commented upon by teachers and classmates alike, and quickly became part of my self-definition. But I was also distinguished by being the only Black student in the class, an "other," a fact I grew increasingly aware of as I got older.

While there may be countless ways one might be defined as exceptional, there are at least seven categories of "otherness" commonly experienced in U.S. society. People are commonly defined as other on the basis of race or ethnicity, gender, religion, sexual orientation, socioeconomic status, age, and physical or mental ability. Each of these categories has a form of oppression associated with it: racism, sexism, religious oppression/anti-Semitism,[4] heterosexism, classism, ageism, and ableism, respectively. In each case, there is a group considered dominant (systematically advantaged by the society because of group membership) and a group considered subordinate or targeted (systematically disadvantaged). When we think about our multiple identities, most of us will find that we are both dominant and targeted at the same time. But it is the targeted identities that hold our attention and the dominant identities that often go unexamined.

In her essay, "Age, Race, Class, and Sex: Women Redefining Difference," Audre Lorde captured the tensions between dominant and targeted identities co-existing in one individual. This self-described "forty-nine-year-old Black lesbian feminist socialist mother of two" wrote,

> Somewhere, on the edge of consciousness, there is what I call a *mythical norm*, which each one of us within our hearts knows "that is not me." In america, this norm is usually defined as white, thin, male, young, heterosexual, christian, and financially secure. It is with this mythical norm that the trappings of power reside within society. Those of us who stand outside that power often identify one way in which we are different, and we assume that to be the primary cause of all oppression, forgetting other distortions around difference, some of which we ourselves may be practicing.[5]

Even as I focus on race and racism in my own writing and teaching, it is helpful to remind myself and my students of the other distortions around difference that I (and they) may be practicing. It is an especially useful way of generating empathy for our mutual learning process. If I am impatient with a White woman for not recognizing her White privilege, it may be useful for me to remember how much of my life I spent oblivious to the fact of the daily advantages I receive simply because I am heterosexual, or the ways in which I may take my class privilege for granted.

Domination and Subordination

It is also helpful to consider the commonality found in the experience of being dominant or subordinate even when the sources of dominance or subordination are different. Jean Baker Miller, author of *Toward a New Psychology of Women*, has identified some of these areas of commonality.[6]

Dominant groups, by definition, set the parameters within which the subordinates operate. The dominant group holds the power and authority in society relative to the subordinates and determines how that power and authority may be acceptably used.

Whether it is reflected in determining who gets the best jobs, whose history will be taught in school, or whose relationships will be validated by society, the dominant group has the greatest influence in determining the structure of the society.

The relationship of the dominants to the subordinates is often one in which the targeted group is labeled as defective or substandard in significant ways. For example, Blacks have historically been characterized as less intelligent than Whites, and women have been viewed as less emotionally stable than men. The dominant group assigns roles to the subordinate that reflect the latter's devalued status, reserving the most highly valued roles in the society for themselves. Subordinates are usually said to be innately incapable of performing the preferred roles. To the extent that those in the target group internalize the images that the dominant group reflects back to them, they may find it difficult to believe in their own ability.

When a subordinate demonstrates positive qualities believed to be more characteristic of dominants, the individual is defined by dominants as an anomaly. Consider the following illustrative example. Following a presentation I gave to some educators, a White man approached me and told me how much he liked my ideas and how articulate I was. "You know," he concluded, "if I had had my eyes closed, I wouldn't have known it was a Black woman speaking." (I replied, "This is what a Black woman sounds like.")

The dominant group is seen as the norm for humanity. Jean Baker Miller also asserts that inequitable social relations are seen as the model for "normal human relationships." Consequently, it remains perfectly acceptable in many circles to tell jokes that denigrate a particular group, to exclude subordinates from one's neighborhood or work setting, or to oppose initiatives that might change the power balance.

Miller points out that dominant groups generally do not like to be reminded of the existence of inequality. Because rationalizations have been created to justify the social arrangements, it is easy to believe everything is as it should be. Dominants "can avoid awareness because their explanation of the relationship becomes so well integrated *in other terms;* they can even believe that both they and the subordinate group share the same interests and, to some extent, a common experience."[7]

The truth is that the dominants do not really know what the experiences of the subordinates is. In contrast, the subordinates are very well informed about the dominants. Even when firsthand experience is limited by social segregation, the number and variety of images of the dominant group available through television, magazines, books, and newspapers provide subordinates with plenty of information about the dominants. The dominant worldview has saturated the culture for all to learn. Even the Black or Latino child living in a segregated community can enter White homes of many kinds daily via the media. However, dominant access to information about the subordinates is often limited to stereotypical depictions of the "other." For example, there are many images of heterosexual relations on television, but very few images of gay or lesbian domestic partnerships beyond the caricatures of comedy shows. There are many images of White men and women in all forms of media, but relatively few portrayals of people of color.

Not only is there greater opportunity for the subordinates to learn about the dominants, there is also greater need. Social psychologist Susan Fiske writes, "It is a simple principle: People pay attention to those who control their outcomes. In an effort to predict and possibly influence what is going to happen to them, people gather information about those with power."[8]

In a situation of unequal power, a subordinate group has to focus on survival. It becomes very important for subordinates to become highly attuned to the dominants as a way of protecting themselves. For example, women who have been battered by men often talk about the heightened sensitivity they develop to their partners' moods. Being able to anticipate and avoid the men's rage is important to survival.

Survival sometimes means not responding to oppressive behavior directly. To do so could result in physical harm to oneself, even death. In his essay "The Ethics of Living Jim Crow" Richard Wright describes eloquently the various strategies he learned to use to avoid the violence of Whites who would brutalize a Black person who did not "stay in his place."[9] Though it is tempting to think that the need for such strategies disappeared with Jim Crow laws, their legacy lives on in the frequent and sometimes fatal harassment Black men experience at the hands of White police officers.[10]

Because of the risks inherent in unequal relationships, subordinates often develop covert ways of resisting or undermining the power of the dominant group. As Miller points out, popular culture is full of folktales, jokes, and stories about how the subordinate—whether the woman, the peasant, or the sharecropper—outwitted the "boss."[11] In his essay "I Won't Learn from You," Herbert Kohl identifies one form of resistance, "not-learning," demonstrated by targeted students who are too often seen by their dominant teachers as "others":

> Not-learning tends to take place when someone has to deal with unavoidable challenges to her or his personal and family loyalties, integrity, and identity. In such situations, there are forced choices and no apparent middle ground. To agree to learn from a stranger who does not respect your integrity causes a major loss of self. The only alternative is to not-learn and reject their world.[12]

The use of either strategy, attending very closely to the dominants or not attending at all, is costly to members of the targeted group. "Not-learning" may mean there are needed skills that are not acquired. Attending closely to the dominant group may leave little time or energy to attend to one's self. Worse yet, the negative messages of the dominant group about the subordinates may be internalized, leading to self-doubt or, in its extreme form, self-hate. There are many examples of subordinates attempting to make themselves over in the image of the dominant group—Jewish people who want to change the Semitic look of their noses, Asians who have cosmetic surgery to alter the shapes of their eyes, Blacks who seek to lighten their skin with bleaching creams, women who want to smoke and drink "like a man." Whether one succumbs to the devaluing pressures of the dominant culture or successfully resists them, the fact is that dealing with oppressive systems from the underside, regardless of the strategy, is physically and psychologically taxing.

Breaking beyond the structural and psychological limitations imposed on one's group is possible, but not easy. To the extent that members of targeted groups do push societal limits—achieving unexpected success, protesting injustice, being "uppity"—by their actions they call the whole system into question. Miller writes that they "expose the inequality, and throw into question the basis for its existence. And they will make the inherent conflict an open conflict. They will then have to bear the burden and take the risks that go with being defined as 'troublemakers.'"[13]

The history of subordinate groups is filled with so-called troublemakers, yet their names are often unknown. Preserving the record of those subordinates and their dominant allies who have challenged the status quo is usually of little interest to the dominant culture, but it is of great interest to subordinates who search for an empowering reflection in the societal mirror.

Many of us are both dominant and subordinate. As Audre Lorde said, from her vantage point as a Black lesbian, "There is no hierarchy of oppressions." The thread and threat of violence runs through all of the isms. There is a need to acknowledge each other's pain, even as we attend to our own.

For those readers who are in the dominant racial category, it may sometimes be difficult to take in what is being said by and about those who are targeted by racism. When the perspective of the subordinate is shared directly, an image is reflected to members of the dominant group that is disconcerting. To the extent that one can draw on one's own experience of subordination—as a young person, as a person with a disability, as someone who grew up poor, as a woman—it may be easier to make meaning of another targeted group's experience. For those readers who are targeted by racism and are angered by the obliviousness of Whites, it may be useful to attend to your experience of dominance where you may find it—as a heterosexual, as an able-bodied person, as a Christian, as a man—and consider what systems of privilege you may be overlooking. The task of resisting our own oppression does not relieve us of the responsibility of acknowledging our complicity in the oppression of others.

Our ongoing examination of who we are in our full humanity, embracing all of our identities, creates the possibility of building alliances that may ultimately free us all.

Notes

1. See C. Cooley, *Human Nature and the Social Order* (New York: Scribner, 1922). George H. Mead expanded on this idea in his book *Mind, Self, and Society* (Chicago: University of Chicago Press, 1934).
2. E. H. Erikson, *Identity, Youth, and Crisis* (New York: W. W. Norton, 1968), 22; emphasis in the original.
3. For a discussion of the Western biases in the concept of the self and individual identity, see A. Roland, "Identity, Self, and Individualism in a Multicultural Perspective," in E. P. Salett and D. R. Koslow, eds., *Race, Ethnicity, and Self: Identity in Multicultural Perspective* (Washington, D.C.: National MultiCultural Institute, 1994).
4. *Anti-Semitism* is a term commonly used to describe the oppression of Jewish people. However, other Semitic peoples (Arab Muslims, for example) are also subject to oppressive treatment on the basis of ethnicity as well as religion. For that reason, the terms *Jewish oppression* and *Arab oppression* are sometimes used to specify the particular form of oppression under discussion.
5. A. Lorde, "Age, Race, Class, and Sex: Women Redefining Difference," in P. S. Rothenberg, ed., *Race, Class, and Gender in the United States: An Integrated Study*, 3d ed. (New York: St. Martin's Press, 1995), 446; emphasis in the original.
6. J. B. Miller, "Domination and Subordination," in *Toward a New Psychology of Women* (Boston: Beacon Press, 1976).
7. Ibid., 8; emphasis in the original.
8. S. T. Fiske, "Controlling Other People: The Impact of Power on Stereotyping," *American Psychologist* 48, no. 6 (1993), 621–28.
9. R. Wright, "The Ethics of Living Jim Crow" (1937), reprinted in P. S. Rothenberg, ed., *Race, Class, and Gender in the United States: An Integrated Study*, 3d ed. (New York: St. Martin's Press, 1995).
10. An article in the popular weekly magazine *People* chronicled the close encounters of famous black men with white police officers. Despite their fame, these men were treated as potential criminals. Highlighted in the article is the story of Johnny Gammage, who was beaten to death by white police officers following a routine traffic stop in Pittsburgh. T. Fields-Meyer, "Under Suspicion," *People* (January 15, 1996), 40–47.
11. Miller, "Domination and Subordination," p. 10.
12. H. Kohl, "I Won't Learn from You: Confronting Student Resistance," in *Rethinking Our Classrooms: Teaching for Equity and Justice* (Milwaukee: Rethinking Our Schools, 1994), 134.
13. Miller, "Domination and Subordination," 12.

2

The Cycle
of Socialization

Bobbie Harro

Introduction and Context

Often, when people begin to study the phenomenon of oppression, they start with recognizing that human beings are different from each other in many ways based upon gender, ethnicity, skin color, first language, age, ability status, religion, sexual orientation, and economic class. The obvious first leap that people make is the assumption that if we just began to *appreciate differences*, and *treat each other with respect*, then everything would be all right, and there would be no oppression. This view is represented beautifully by the now famous quote from Rodney King in response to the riots following his beating and the release of the police officers who were filmed beating him: "Why can't we all just get along?" It should be that simple, but it isn't.

Instead, we are each born into a specific set of *social identities*, related to the categories of difference mentioned above, and these social identities predispose us to unequal *roles* in the dynamic system of oppression. We are then socialized by powerful sources in our worlds to play the roles prescribed by an inequitable social system (Hardiman and Jackson 1997). This socialization process is *pervasive* (coming from all sides and sources), *consistent* (patterned and predictable), *circular* (self-supporting), *self-perpetuating* (intradependent) and often *invisible* (unconscious and unnamed) (Bell 1997). All of these characteristics will be clarified in the description of the *cycle of socialization* that follows.

In struggling to understand what roles we have been socialized to play, how we are affected by issues of oppression in our lives, and how we participate in maintaining them, we must begin by making an inventory of our own social identities with relationship to each issue of oppression. An excellent first learning activity is to make a personal inventory of our various social identities relating to the categories listed above—gender, race, age, sexual orientation, religion, economic class, and ability/disability status. The results of this inventory make up the mosaic of social identities (our *social identity profile*) that shape(s) our socialization. (Harro 1986, Griffin 1997).

We get systematic training in "how to be" each of our social identities throughout our lives. The cycle of socialization that follows is one way of representing how the socialization process happens, from what sources it comes, how it affects our lives, and how it perpetuates itself. The "Directions for Change" that conclude this chapter suggest ways for interrupting the cycle of socialization and taking charge of our own lives. For purposes of learning, it is often useful to choose only *one* of our social identities, and trace it through the cycle of socialization, since it can be quite overwhelming to explore seven identities at once.

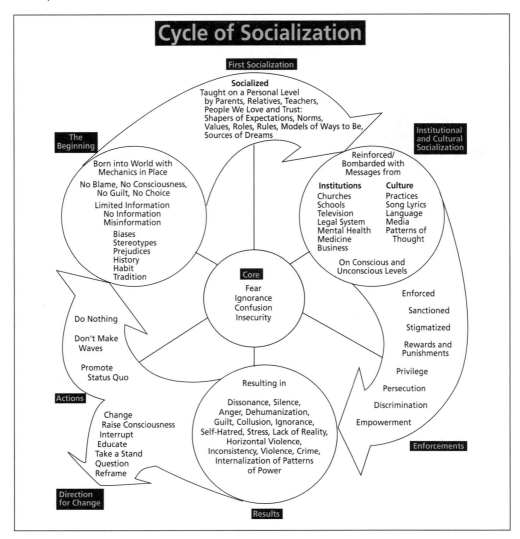

Fig. 2.1. The Cycle of Socialization.

The Beginning (Circle no.1)

Our socialization begins before we are born, with no choice on our part. No one brings us a survey, in the womb, inquiring into which gender, class, religion, sexual orientation, cultural group, ability status, or age we might want to be born. These identities are ascribed to us at birth through no effort or decision or choice of our own; There is, therefore, no reason to blame each other or hold each other responsible for the identities we have. This first step in the socialization process is outside our control. In addition to having no choice, we also have no initial consciousness about who we are. We don't question our identities at this point. We just *are* who we are.

On top of these givens, we are born into a world where all of the mechanics, assumptions, rules, roles, and structures of oppression are already in place and functioning; we have had nothing to do with constructing them. There is no reason for any of us to feel guilty or responsible for the world into which we are born. We are innocents, falling into an already established system.

The characteristics of this system were built long before we existed, based upon history, habit, tradition, patterns of belief, prejudices, stereotypes, and myths. *Dominant* or *agent* groups are considered the "norm" around which assumptions are built, and these groups receive attention and recognition. Agents have relatively more social power, and can "name" others. They are privileged at birth, and ascribed access to options and opportunities, often without realizing it. We are "lucky" to be born into these groups and rarely question it. Agent groups include men, white people, middle- and upper-class people, abled people, middle-aged people, heterosexuals, and gentiles.

On the other hand, there are many social identity groups about which little or nothing is known because they have not been considered important enough to study. These are referred to as *subordinate* groups or *target* groups. Some target groups are virtually invisible while others are defined by misinformation or very limited information. Targets are disenfranchised, exploited, and victimized by prejudice, discrimination, and other structural obstacles. Target groups include women; racially oppressed groups; gay, lesbian, bisexual and transgendered people; disabled people; Jews; elders; youth; and people living in poverty (Baker-Miller 1976; Hardiman and Jackson 1997). We are "unlucky" to be born into target groups and therefore devalued by the existing society. Both groups are dehumanized by being socialized into prescribed roles without consciousness or permission.

First Socialization (Arrow no. 1)

Immediately upon our births we begin to be socialized by the people we love and trust the most, our families or the adults who are raising us. They shape our self-concepts and self-perceptions, the norms and rules we must follow, the roles we are taught to play, our expectations for the future, and our dreams. These people serve as role models for us, and they teach us how to behave. This socialization happens both intrapersonally (how we think about ourselves), and interpersonally (how we relate to others). We are told things like, "Boys don't cry"; "You shouldn't trust white people"; "They're better than we are. Stay in your place"; "Don't worry if you break the toy. We can always buy another one"; "Christianity is the true religion"; "Children should be seen and not heard"; "Don't tell anyone that your aunt is mentally retarded. It's embarrassing"; and "Don't kiss other girls. You're supposed to like boys." These messages are an automatic part of our early socialization, and we don't initially question them. We are too dependent on our parents or those raising us, and we haven't yet developed the ability to think for ourselves, so we unconsciously conform to their views.

It is important to observe that they, too, are not to be blamed. They are doing the best they can to raise us, and they only have their own backgrounds from which to draw. They may not have thought critically about what they are teaching us, and may be unconsciously passing on what was taught to them. Some of us may have been raised by parents who *have* thought critically about the messages that they are giving us, but they are still not in the majority. This could be good or bad, as well, depending on what their views are. A consciously racist parent may intentionally pass on racist beliefs to his children, and a consciously feminist parent may intentionally pass on non-stereotypical roles to her children, so it can go either way.

Regardless of the content of the teaching, we have been exposed, without initial question, to a strong set of rules, roles, and assumptions that cannot help but shape our sense of ourselves and the world. They influence what we take with us when we venture out of our protected family units into the larger world of other institutions.

A powerful way to check out the accuracy of these assertions is to choose one of our social identities and write down at least ten examples of what we learned about being that identity. It's helpful to consider whether we chose an agent or a target identity. We may find that we have thought more about our target identities, and therefore they are easier to inventory. Gender rules are sometimes the easiest, so we might start there. We might also consider doing it for an agent group identity, like males, white people, heterosexuals, gentiles, adults, middle-class people, able-bodied or able-minded people. Most likely, we will find it easier to list learnings for targeted groups than for agent groups.

Institutional and Cultural Socialization (Circle no. 2)

Once we begin to attend school, go to a place of worship, visit a medical facility, play on a sports team, work with a social worker, seek services or products from a business, or learn about laws and the legal system, our socialization sources are rapidly multiplied based on how many institutions with which we have contact. Most of the messages we receive about how to be, whom to "look up to" and "look down on," what rules to follow, what roles to play, what assumptions to make, what to believe, and what to think will probably reinforce or contradict what we have learned at home.

We might learn at school that girls shouldn't be interested in a woodworking shop class, that only white students go out for the tennis team, that kids who learn differently or think independently get put in special education, that it's okay for wealthy kids to miss classes for a family vacation, that it's okay to harass the boy who walks and talks like a girl, that most of the kids who drop out are from the south side of town, that "jocks" don't have to do the same work that "nerds" do to pass, or that kids who belong to another religious group are "weird." We learn who gets preferential treatment and who gets picked on. We are exposed to rules, roles, and assumptions that are not fair to everyone.

If we are members of the groups that benefit from the rules, we may not notice that they aren't fair. If we are members of the groups that are penalized by the rules, we may have a constant feeling of discomfort. We learn that these rules, roles, and assumptions are part of a structure that is larger than just our families. We get consistent similar messages from religion, the family doctor, the social worker, the local store, or the police officer, and so it is hard to not believe what we are learning. We learn that black people are more likely to steal, so store detectives follow them in stores. Boys are expected to fight and use violence, so they are encouraged to learn how. We shouldn't stare at or ask questions about disabled people; it isn't polite. Gay and lesbian people are sick and perverted. Kids who live in certain sections of town are probably on welfare, taking our hard-earned tax dollars. Money talks. White means good; black means bad. Girls are responsible for birth control. It's a man's world. Jews are cheap. Arabs are terrorists. And so on.

We are inundated with unquestioned and stereotypical messages that shape how we think and what we believe about ourselves and others. What makes this "brainwashing" even more insidious is the fact that it is woven into every structural thread of the fabric of our culture. The media (television, the Internet, advertising, newspapers, and radio), our language patterns, the lyrics to songs, our cultural practices and holidays, and the very assumptions on which our society is built all contribute to the reinforcement of the biased messages and stereotypes we receive. Think about Howard Stern, Jerry Springer, *Married with Children*, beer and car advertising, talk radio, *girl* vs. *man*, Christmas vacation, the Rolling Stones' "Under My Thumb," the "old boy's network," and websites that foster hate. We could identify thousands of examples to illustrate the oppressive messages that bombard us daily from various institutions and aspects of our culture, reinforcing our divisions and "justifying" discrimination and prejudice.

Enforcements (Arrow no. 2)

It might seem logical to ask why people don't just begin to think independently if they don't like what they are seeing around them. Why don't we ignore these messages if we are uncomfortable with them, or if they are hurting us? Largely, we don't ignore the messages, rules, roles, structures, and assumptions because there are enforcements in place to maintain them. People who try to contradict the "norm" pay a price for their independent thinking, and people who conform (consciously or unconsciously) minimally receive the benefit of being left alone for not making waves, such as acceptance in their designated roles, being considered normal or "a team player," or being allowed to stay in their places. Maximally, they receive rewards and privileges for maintaining the status quo such as access to higher places; attention and recognition for having "made it" or being the model member of their group; or the privilege that brings them money, connections, or power.

People who go against the grain of conventional societal messages are accused of being troublemakers, of making waves, or of being "the cause of the problem." If they are members of target groups, they are held up as examples of why this group is inferior to the agent group. Examples of this include the significantly higher numbers of people of color who are targeted by the criminal justice system. Although the number of white people who are committing crimes is just as high, those whites are much less likely to be arrested, charged, tried, convicted, or sentenced to jail than are people of color. Do different laws apply depending on a person's skin color? Battering statistics are rising as more women assert their equal rights with men, and the number one suspect for the murder of women in the United States is the husband or boyfriend. Should women who try to be equal with men be killed? The rationale given by some racists for the burning of black churches was that "they were getting too strong." Does religious freedom and the freedom to assemble apply only to white citizens? Two men walking together in a southeastern U.S. city were beaten, and one died, because "they were walking so close, they must be gay." Are two men who refuse to abide by the "keep your distance" rule for men so threatening that they must be attacked and killed? These examples of differential punishment being given to members or *perceived* members of target groups are only half of the picture.

If members of agent groups break the rules, they too are punished. White people who support their colleagues of color may be called "n — — lover." Heterosexual men who take on primary child-care responsibilities, cry easily, or hug their male friends are accused of being dominated by their spouses, of being "sissies," or being gay. Middle-class people who work as advocates on economic issues are accused of being do-gooders or self-righteous liberals. Heterosexuals who work for the rights of gay, lesbian, bisexual, or transgendered people are immediately suspected of being "in the closet" themselves.

Results (Circle no. 3)

It is not surprising that the results of this systematic learning are devastating to all involved. If we are examining our target identities, we may experience anger, a sense of being silenced, dissonance between what the United States stands for and what we experience, low self-esteem, high levels of stress, a sense of hopelessness and disempowerment that can lead to crime and self-destructive behavior, frustration, mistrust, and dehumanization. By participating in our roles as targets we reinforce stereotypes, collude in our own demise, and perpetuate the system of oppression. This learned helplessness is often called *internalized oppression* because we have learned to become our own oppressors from within.

If we are examining our agent identities, we may experience guilt from unearned privilege or oppressive acts, fear of payback, tendency to collude in the system to be self-protective, high levels of stress, ignorance of and loss of contact with the target groups, a sense of distorted reality about how the world is, fear of rising crime and violence levels, limited worldview, obliviousness to the damage we do, and dehumanization. By participating in our roles as agents, and remaining unconscious of or being unwilling to interrupt the cycle, we perpetuate the system of oppression.

These results are often cited as the problems facing our society today: high drop-out rates, crime, poverty, drugs, and so on. Ironically, the root causes of them are inherent in the very assumptions on which the society is built: dualism, hierarchy, competition, individualism, domination, colonialism, and the scarcity principle. To the extent that we fail to interrupt this cycle we keep the assumptions, the problems, and the oppression alive.

A way that we might personally explore this model is to take one of the societal problems and trace its root causes back through the cycle to the core belief systems or patterns in U.S. society that feed and play host to it. It is not a coincidence that the United States is suffering from these results today; rather, it is a logical outcome of our embracing the status quo, without thinking or challenging.

Actions (Arrow no. 3)

When we arrive at the results of this terrible cycle, we face the decision of what to do next. It is easiest to do nothing, and simply to allow the perpetuation of the status quo. We may choose not to make waves, to stay in our familiar patterns. We may say, "Oh well, it's been that way for hundreds of years. What can I do to change it? It is a huge phenomenon, and my small efforts won't count for much." Many of us choose to do nothing because it is (for a while) easier to stay with what is familiar. Besides, it is frightening to try to interrupt something so large. "What does it have to do with me, anyway?" say many agents. "This isn't my problem. I am above this." We fail to realize that we have become participants just by doing nothing. This cycle has a life of its own. It doesn't need our active support because it has its own centrifugal force. It goes on, and unless we choose to interrupt it, it will continue to go on. Our silence is consent. Until our discomfort becomes larger than our comfort, we will probably stay in this cycle.

Some of us who are targets have been so beaten down by the relentless messages of the cycle that we have given up and resigned ourselves to survive it or to self-destruct. We are the victims of the cycle, and are playing our roles as victims to keep the cycle alive. We will probably go around a few more times before we die. It hurts too much to fight such a big cycle. We need the help of our brothers and sisters and our agent allies to try for change.

The Core at the Center of the Cycle

We are blocked from action by the fear and insecurity that we have been taught. We have been kept ignorant and confused by the myths and misinformation that we have been fed, and we lack a core of confidence and vision to guide us. We don't know how to take action against a system so powerful and pervasive. As long as our core is filled with these negative elements, we will be paralyzed and will re-create the same cycle again.

Somehow, however, change and hope still find their way to the surface. Perhaps someone's discomfort or pain becomes larger than her complacency. Perhaps strength, encouragement, determination, love, hope, or connection to other people begin to grow in someone's core, and he decides to take a different direction, and to interrupt this cycle.

Direction for Change

Some of us who are targets try to interrupt the cycle, because for us the discomfort *has* gotten larger than the comfort. If we try this alone, or without organization, we may be kicked back down to our powerless positions. If we begin a new direction, and even work with our agent allies, however, we can create our own hope.

Some of us who are agents may decide to use our power and privilege to try to make change—either out of guilt, moral values, or vision. If our motivation is guilt, we are doomed to fail, but if we operate from a strong moral base and vision, and if we work together with our targeted brothers and sisters, we create hope. We become allies with our target groups, and build coalitions for success.

When groups begin to empower themselves—by learning more about each other, by unlearning old myths and stereotypes, by challenging the status quo—we make the difficult decision to interrupt the cycle of socialization. We begin to question the givens, the assumptions of the society, the norms, the values, the rules, the roles, and even the structures. As we attempt this, it becomes obvious that we cannot do it alone. We must build coalitions with people who are like us and people who are different from us. We will not be the minority if we work in coalitions. We will gain the necessary vision and power to reconstruct new rules that truly are equal, roles that complement each other instead of competing, assumptions that value all groups instead of ascribing value to some and devaluing others, and structures that promote cooperation and shared power instead of power over each other.

For this new direction of action to work, we need education for critical consciousness for all groups. We need to take a stand, reframe our understandings, question the status quo, and begin a critical transformation that can break down this cycle of socialization and start a new cycle leading to liberation for all. This is possible. We *can* change the world (see Harro, "The Cycle of Liberation," chapter 87 of this volume).

References

Baker-Miller, J. (1976). *Toward a New Psychology of Women*. Boston: Beacon Press.

Bell, L. A. (1997). Theoretical foundations for social justice education. In M. Adams, L. A. Bell, and P. Griffin, eds., *Teaching for Diversity and Social Justice: A Sourcebook*. New York: Routledge.

Griffin, P. (1997). Introductory module for the single issue courses. In M. Adams, L. A. Bell, and P. Griffin, eds., *Teaching for Diversity and Social Justice: A Sourcebook*. New York: Routledge.

Harro, R. L. (1986). *Teaching about Heterosexism: A Psychological Education Design Project*. University of Massachusetts, Amherst; unpublished manuscript.

Hardiman, R. and B. W. Jackson. (1997). Conceptual Foundations for Social Justice Courses. In M. Adams, L. A. Bell, and P. Griffin, eds., *Teaching for Diversity and Social Justice: A Sourcebook*. New York: Routledge.

3

Prejudice and Discrimination

Warren J. Blumenfeld
and Diane Raymond

In [Nazi] Germany they first came for the Communists, and I didn't speak up because I wasn't a Communist. Then they came for the Jews, and I didn't speak up because I wasn't a Jew. Then they came for the trade unionists, and I didn't speak up because I wasn't a trade unionist. Then they came for the Catholics, and I didn't speak up because I was a Protestant. Then they came for me—and by that time no one was left to speak up.

—Attributed to Martin Niemoeller, in John Bartlett, *Familiar Quotations* (1982, 824)

Introduction

In many societies, there are groups of people who are denied access to the rights and privileges enjoyed by others on account of physical, biological, social, or other traits. These segments of the population are sometimes called "minorities." There is, however, disagreement over the exact meaning of the term "minority." Some people define it strictly in terms of relative degrees of power irrespective of numbers. For example, black people under the system of apartheid in South Africa would constitute a minority; though they vastly outnumber whites, they had little power to control the course of the country or their own lives. There are others, however, who argue that for a group to constitute a minority it must be placed in a lower position of power and must also be numerically smaller than more powerful groups. . . .

There is evidence that virtually every society has in-groups and out-groups. Minority group members often receive negative treatment, ranging from negative beliefs (which may or may not be expressed), to exclusion, denial of civil and legal protections, and in some cases overt acts of violence directed against them. Though the reasons why certain groups are singled out for such treatment vary, some conditions remain constant.

Two related systems come into operation in keeping some groups on the fringe. The first is *prejudice*. Its Latin root means "prejudgment," and to feel prejudice toward an individual or group is to hold an adverse opinion or belief without just ground or before acquiring sufficient knowledge. For example, a person is said to be prejudiced if he or she believes that all people within a given group—say, redheads—are inherently inferior.

When prejudiced feelings or beliefs move into the realm of behavior, the result is *discrimination*, which denies to individuals or groups of people equality of treatment. Therefore, it is discriminatory for parents not to allow their children to play with red-haired children, and for legislators to vote to deny redheaded people access to certain jobs, such as teaching.

It is sometimes the case that major social institutions—laws, customs, religion, education, and so forth—work to reinforce existing prejudice and discrimination. This is said to constitute *institutionalized discrimination* (Eitzen 1980.) It is obvious that the institutions of society can influence behavior and have enormous power to reward or penalize its members. They can, for example, "reward by providing career opportunities for some people and foreclosing them on others. They reward as well by the way social employment, fair treatment by the law, decent housing, self-confidence, and the promise of a secure future for self and children" (Knowles and Prewitt 1969). Where there exists widescale and deep-seated prejudice, often one of the by-products is a condition known as *segregation*. This is the exclusion or separation of certain groups, usually minorities, by other groups, usually the dominant group. It has been most visible in neighborhood residences, schools, workplaces, and public accommodations.

There are two primary types of segregation: *de jure* and *de facto*. *De jure* segregation is a formalized system of segregation that exists by law. For example, the 1896 Supreme Court decision *Plessy v. Ferguson* ruled that segregated facilities did not constitute a violation of the United States Constitution. It was not until 1954, in *Brown v. Board of Education*, that this was overturned, and the Court decided that "separate but equal" was not truly equal.

De facto segregation exists more informally. For example, when a homeowner and real-estate agency refuse to show a residence to a member of a minority group, the result is that minority members do not attend certain neighborhood schools. Ultimately, there are segregated schools.

Ethnicity and Race

Human beings have a propensity to categorize in an attempt to sort reality into neat and orderly arrangements. Since reality often does not fit this package, definitions may be arbitrary and inconsistent. Such tends to be the case when trying to provide adequate definitions of race and ethnicity.

Ethnic Groups

A standard definition of an *ethnic group* is one that is socially distinguishable from other groups, has developed its own subculture—which can include nationality, religion, and language—and has "a shared feeling of peoplehood" (Gordon 1964). If we walk down the streets of New York, we are apt to see many ethnic groups residing in various parts of the city. We might see Italian Americans in Little Italy, Latinos/as from a variety of Spanish-speaking countries living in Spanish Harlem, Chinese Americans in Chinatown, and so on. Often what distinguishes these groups is their shared culture, including their distinctive cuisine, music, and native language. However, there are also some ethnic groups that do not meet all these criteria. An example is the Jews, who, though they come from many different countries and different cultural backgrounds, constitute an ethnic group because of their shared sense of peoplehood, linking them through centuries of dispersion and migration.

Racial Groups

The concept of race is also problematic. . . . *Race* has been defined as a distinct human type based on inherited physical characteristics (Julian and Kornblum 1983). This definition implies that the concept is easily applied and that the categories we call "racial" are obvious and distinct. But today many sociologists and anthropologists maintain that race is a social or cultural concept rather than an inherent, observable characteristic, for all races are simply variations of a single human species of common prehistoric ancestry. Any differences in our species may have evolved to ensure the survival of people in varying geographic locales. For example, in the evolutionary process a greater amount of skin pigmentation (melanin) and thicker-textured hair developed in people in warmer, sun-drenched lands as a way to protect them from ultraviolet rays.

Often the concepts of ethnicity and race overlap and become confused. . .

Stereotypes

A great many traits go into the physical and psychological makeup of every person. How we look, behave, think, and relate affects the ways we are defined by ourselves and by others. The same is true for how groups are defined: whether a group is linked by race, ethnicity, sex, occupation, physical condition, age, nationality, social rank, or sexual orientation, a myriad of factors go into its essential composition.

Nevertheless, individuals and groups are sometimes defined by others in terms of characteristics called *stereotypes,* which are—more often than not—negative. When this occurs, a network of belief develops around the group in question. The stereotypes may have originally contained some small grain of truth, but that element has since been exaggerated, distorted, or in some way taken out of context. So stereotypes may be based on false generalizations derived from very small samples or even on a unique case. Some stereotypes have no foundation in fact at all. When stereotyping occurs, people tend to overlook all other characteristics of the group. Individuals sometimes use stereotypes to justify the actions taken against members of that group.

Taking up the example of red-haired people, we can see more easily how stereotyping operates. Though every red-haired person is multifaceted, when we call them "hot-tempered," we make redheadedness reducible to a single trait. While some red-haired people may show their temper on occasion, it is not the case that all do. And besides, people with other hair shades, or for that matter, no hair at all, flare up sometimes. Further, stereotypes are self-perpetuating, for once a stereotype is in place, we tend to notice more the behavior consistent with the stereotype and miss that which is not. It is in this way that stereotypes are reinforced regardless of the social realities.

Stereotyping is common in attitudes toward minority group members. Sometimes people stereotype by focusing on a positive quality of a group. However, in most cases, the stereotyping is negative. This can result in the singling out of individuals or groups of people as targets of hostility even though they may have little or nothing to do with the evils for which they stand accused. This is referred to as *scapegoating*. Hitler blamed Jews, Jehovah's Witnesses, gypsies, homosexuals, and others for the collapse of the German economy prior to World War II. African Americans were scapegoated for the deplorable conditions of the Southern states following the American Civil War.

The origin of the scapegoat goes back to the Book of Leviticus (16: 20–22). On the Day of Atonement a live goat was selected by lot. The high priest placed both hands on the goat's head and confessed over it the sins of the people. In this way, the sins were symbolically transferred to the animal, which was then cast out into the wilderness. This process thus purged the people, for a time, of their feelings of guilt.

What conditions are necessary for certain people or groups to be chosen as scapegoats? First, prejudice must already exist against the particular groups or individuals before the scapegoating commences. Second, the individuals in question must appear to be too weak to fight back successfully when attacked. And finally, the society must sanction the scapegoating through its own institutional structures (Saenger 1953).

With scapegoating, there is the tendency to view all members of the group as inferior and to assume that all members are alike in most respects. This attitude often leads to even further discrimination.

Exploring the "Isms"

As a black woman, a lesbian, a feminist, and an activist, I have little difficulty seeing how the systems of oppression interconnect, if for no other reason than that their meshings so frequently affect my life.

—Barbara Smith, "Homophobia: Why Bring It Up?" (1983, 7)

Definitions

There are as many names for the varieties of discrimination as there are minority groups. This in no way means to suggest that all groups experience forms of discrimination similarly. The experiences of victims of racism, for example, are not identical to those who suffer the effects of homophobia. The many strands of discrimination, however, run parallel and intersect at points. All involve negative prejudgments whose purpose is to maintain control or power over others. Discrimination can be the result of a deliberate, conscious act; or it may be unconscious and unintentional, yet have discriminatory results nonetheless.

Typical names used for some of the many forms of discrimination are:

- *Racism:* discrimination on the basis of race;

- *Sexism:* discrimination on the basis of sex, most often by men;

- *Misogyny:* a hatred or distrust of women;

- *Ethnocentrism* or *Ethnic Prejudice:* the belief that one's ethnic group is superior to all others, resulting, at times, in discrimination toward those of different ethnic backgrounds or national origin;

- *Ageism:* discrimination on the basis of age, usually against the elderly and the young;

- *Ableism:* discrimination against the physically or mentally disabled;

- *Xenophobia:* fear and or hatred of strangers or foreigners or anything that appears strange or foreign;

- *Anti-Semitism:* discrimination against Jews (a traditional usage that does not include discrimination against Arabs, who are also Semites);

- *Religious Prejudice:* discrimination on the basis of a particular religious preference;

- *Chauvinism:* originally used to refer to jingoism or excessive patriotism, it has also come to be associated with sexist attitudes, most especially of men toward women;

- *Classism:* Prejudice and discrimination based on socio-economic level or class;

- *Heterosexism:* the system by which heterosexuality is assumed to be the only acceptable and viable life option;

- *Homophobia:* fear, dislike, or hatred of lesbians, gays, and bisexuals often resulting in acts of discrimination (Weinberg 1972). Other terms have been coined to express this condition including *homophilephobia* (Rosan 1978), literally meaning fear of persons of one's own sex; *homoerotophobia* (Churchill 1967); *homosexphobia* (Levitt and Klassen 1974); *homosexophobia* (Boswell 1980); *homosexism* (Lehne 1976); and *homonegativism* (Hudson and Ricketts 1980). Though the term *homophobia* has appeared in revised editions of some dictionaries since the mid-1970s, it is still absent from other standard lexicons.

Prejudice: Functions and Origins

Prejudice (along with its active component, discrimination) seems to be a universal phenomenon that has probably been around since the time of the first human grouping. One may ask, "Why do people hold on to their prejudices?" Beliefs, whether true or false, serve some function. And prejudice, like other beliefs, must meet some sort of need or fulfill a purpose. If this were not the case, prejudice itself would, in all likelihood, cease to exist and be replaced by more functional beliefs. In an attempt to understand what role prejudice plays in human interactions, social scientists have studied how it operates.

Functions

Jaime Wurzel (1986) has identified four basic functions of prejudice, which will be discussed here.

The Utilitarian Function

People maintain prejudicial attitudes to gain certain rewards and to avoid punishment. They generally want to be liked and, therefore, will endorse the prejudices of others, including family members—namely parents—and peers outside the home environment. In doing so, they are consolidating their personal and social relationships, and in turn enhancing their own concepts of self.

Also, when a leader exploits a prejudice widely held by his constituency, group members may experience a heightened sense of purpose and a stronger feeling of community while at the same time solidifying the leader's position.

Self-Esteem, the Protective Function

People often hate that which appears threatening or uncertain, as it reminds them of the fragility of the ego. All of us fail at times, and it is frightening to take responsibility for those failures. Prejudice protects one's sense of self-esteem against conflicts and weaknesses arising from one's limitations (whether internal or external). Thus, scapegoating certain groups shields people psychologically from their own inadequacies and fears. As R. Breslin (1978) explains, "Holding the prejudice protects people from a harsh reality. For instance, a person who is unsuccessful in the business world may believe that members of a certain successful group are a scheming bunch of cheaters" (34).

Value-Expressive Function

People prize their own particular sets of values and modes of living, and there may be some insecurity surrounding anything that is different from those standards. Any difference may be construed as a threat to those frameworks, a threat that would undermine the security social norms provide. Consequently, any group that is perceived as challenging one's values is considered inferior and threatening. Prejudice against people who maintain values different from one's own tends to strengthen the values of those who hold the prejudice. Seeing even imaginary threats to one's shared values may not only increase animosity toward those who are perceived as threats but also make the values appear to be worth defending. For example, Jaime Wurzel (1986) tells us "a religious group may discriminate against members of another religion because their beliefs threaten their notion of God. Or people may engage in atrocities toward out-groups' members in order to retain their own supposed values of a pure social stock."

The Cognitive Function

Cognition, by definition, is an act or process by which people come to know or understand. To comprehend a complex world, people tend to divide reality into distinct categories. In this process, the individual parts lose their uniqueness and are viewed in terms of their supposed similarity to others in the same category. This tendency toward homogeneity may be that which enables us to create concepts and make sense of a world that might otherwise seem overwhelming.

We may do the same with people. That is, we tend to evaluate others in terms of general categories. Stereotypes provide such categories and thus serve to order the world. Prejudice becomes a shortcut means of relating to others and digesting new information.

Origins

Prejudice and discrimination can be tools used by the dominant group to maintain its control or power. Unless and until a minority group challenges this, this treatment may be viewed as being a part of the natural order of things. The origins of prejudice are many and are extremely complex, and include both the psychological makeup of the individual and the structural organization of the society.

Psychological Factors

It is not uncommon for people to feel frustrated occasionally. They may want something but for some reason or other cannot get it. Anger and aggression may arise and find expression in a number of ways. One can, for example, strike out directly at the source of the irritation. Yet this is often difficult, because the source is either unknown or else too dangerous to confront. Therefore, one must find another channel similar enough to the source of the frustration to provide satisfaction.

For instance, a parent may punish a child with a spanking. Unable to hit the parent back, the child turns around and socks a younger sibling, who then runs outside and kicks the family dog. In an organizational setting, aggression may travel down from the president to the vice-president(s), then through the entire chain of command, eventually terminating at the worker with the lowest status. In terms of relative degrees of power, those lower down become the scapegoats in the social pecking order. In a social context, this leads to prejudice if the person transfers this aggression onto members of minority groups. Take, for example, the man who is interviewed for a desirable job but is passed over for the position by a woman who is better qualified. That night on a cab ride home the man may complain to the driver that "unless something is done soon, women will be taking over the country."

Personal insecurity can also give rise to prejudice, which in turn serves the function of building self-esteem and reducing feelings of guilt. People who are insecure about their social standing and expectations often have a great need for conformity (Saenger 1953; Weinberg 1972). By identifying with a dominant group, an insecure person gains a place in society and experiences a sense of importance. Because minorities are often seen as being nonconformist, they are easy targets of aggression.

Some people appear to be more prone than others to highly prejudiced beliefs. Adorno (1950) and other psychologists believed that such people exhibit an "authoritarian personality." Unlike the "democratic personality," the authoritarian personality suffers from repressed feelings of weakness and rejection, where the world appears as a jungle in which everyone is the enemy of everyone else. Further, the authoritarian person values strength and toughness above all else; love and sympathy are signs of weakness; security can be obtained only through domination or submission, not love and cooperation. Distrust of others is coupled with the absence of secure emotional attachments. This person lacks a sense of belonging and is unsure of his or her role and place in society. She or he overrates the power of some people, while exaggerating the weakness of others. Because of insecurity, she or he gives up individuality, and is dependent on a strong person or conforms to the dictates of a group. This denial of self often results in frustration and hostility, which have to be displaced onto those perceived as weaker and nonconformist because the person cannot afford to attack those on whom she or he is dependent.

Very often, highly prejudiced people are impervious to the sorts of logical arguments that could expose the fallacies in their beliefs. Using logic or facts does not usually succeed in changing the opinions of many prejudiced people because they do not play by common rules of reason (Sartre 1965). This may be because their egos are threatened by contradictory evidence or because they recognize (perhaps unconsciously) that to change one's belief might require changing a whole network of beliefs. Rather than sacrifice the prejudiced belief, prejudiced people may find clever rationalizations to accommodate what may be even blatant contradictions of their belief systems. "I don't care *what* you say, I still believe . . . " is a common response to inconsistent data. Anti-gay activist Anita Bryant showed clear signs of this form of reasoning in her Save Our Children campaign during the late 1970s. When directly pressed to give logical arguments for her position, she would rise and sing "The Battle Hymn of the Republic" in an attempt to play on the patriotic sympathies of her audience; reason had no impact on her views.

Most people, from time to time, are either unwilling or unable to look at some of their own undesirable personality traits and may transfer these traits onto others. This process is referred to as *projection*. Gordon Allport (1954) describes three types of projection.

Direct projection involves the projection of attributes which lie *solely* within the person who projects them onto those who are blamed. Women, for example, may be blamed for being "seductive," when in reality it is their accusers who are denying their own sexual desires.

The *mote-beam mechanism* refers to the process of exaggerating a relatively minor negative trait or characteristic in other people that *both* they and we, ourselves, possess, though we may not realize we also possess it. All of us—men and women—are irrational at times. Yet one version of sexism singles out women as irrational and emotional, devalues emotion, and denies the existence of those qualities in men.

Complementary projection explains and justifies one's own state of mind in reference to the imagined intentions and behaviors of others. This has to do with finding causes for one's own troubled emotions in others ("I fear, therefore they threaten"). In the case of many so-called moral zealots, their self-righteousness may be the result of unconscious or even conscious feelings of guilt based on their own repressed sexual desires. This point came to light dramatically in 1987, when, in separate incidents, the TV ministers Jim Bakker and Jimmy Swaggart were accused of engaging in "sexual indiscretions"—the latter with a prostitute—and were forced to suspend their preaching.

Projection thus becomes another justification for aggression against minorities. Such aggression serves to cleanse the person of an undesirable trait. Projection onto an individual or group is used to free oneself of the forbidden thought while at the same time enjoying vicarious gratification of that desire. With respect to homophobia, prejudice against gays may serve to reduce the tension and anxiety aroused by unconscious doubts about one's own sexuality. Sigmund Freud termed this aversion *reaction formation*, which is the mechanism used to defend against an impulse in oneself by taking a firm stand against its expression in others.

The homophobic person is threatened by the mere existence of sexual minorities whom he or she sees as belittling or undervaluing the importance of his or her own sexual qualities (e.g., sexual prowess and the ability to attract members of the other sex). A person's negative feelings toward homosexuals of the other sex may also stem from that person's feeling of rejection as a potential sexual partner. In addition, the person may experience a repressed envy of gays, lesbians, and bisexuals, who are often perceived as enjoying a greater degree of freedom by not accepting rigid gender roles. This can be extremely distressing for those who need to be rewarded for their conformity to rules. Such envy might be translated unconsciously into hostility.

Weinberg (1972) suggests the concept of existence without vicarious immortality as another psychological component of homophobia. Simply stated, homosexuals are generally regarded as people who either do not or cannot bear children. Though in fact this is often not the case, the thought of persons without children awakens in some people a fear of death, often unconscious, since children provide a continuation of the family line after the death of individual members. Any reminder of one's own mortality is threatening to the ego, and this fear translates into homophobia.

Those who have a solid sense of who they are and where they stand in the world are not only less likely to experience prejudice but are also more open to abandon prejudiced beliefs in the face of contrary evidence. Likewise, heterosexual males and females who are genuinely comfortable with their own sexual identities apparently feel far less threatened by homosexuality than those who are insecure (Marmor 1980).

Psychological factors alone, however, do not completely explain the origins of prejudice. In particular, the psychological explanations do not make clear why some attributes are singled out over others, why some attributes are negatively valued, and why some groups and not others bear the brunt of social prejudice. Prejudice is not an individual phenomenon, hence it is important to look at the larger social context in which prejudice occurs and is reinforced.

Competition and Exploitation

Prejudice and discrimination are problems in societies where there are hierarchical structures. In social settings where some have more than others, a belief system develops which justifies the entitlement of those with economic power. In particular, people whose class status is somewhat tenuous may struggle to keep others from ascending the economic ladder. Furthermore, as goods and services become scarcer, there is increasing economic competition. Thus, "prejudice is reversely proportional to the economic climate of a society" (Saenger 1953). When economic times are good, there is more need for inexpensive immigrant labor, which tends to result in a decline of prejudice. However, in a bad economy, the reverse is usually true, and members of different groups may see others as competition for scarce resources.

The myth of inherent racial differences originally justified the institution of slavery and the exploitation of native populations by colonial powers. More recently, discrimination remains to buttress vested economic interests. Landlords can exact high rents and merchants can charge high prices from minorities forced to reside in segregated areas. Employers can get away with paying low wages to minority workers. Management has a stake in turning various groups of workers against each other so that they do not join together against their bosses to push for improved wages and working conditions. . . .

There are, of course, *bona fide* differences in the appearance, religion, social customs, and sexual orientation of various groups. However, many times the threatening nature of the differences is more imagined than real. People who look or sound different will actually appear to be threatening to some individuals. In most instances, however, the negative reputation of a given minority group is not so much earned as it is thrust upon them. Further, it is not clear why some differences appear to be more threatening than others. At times, competition for scarce resources or stressful or poor quality of contact between groups can also bring about hard feelings which can last for generations. This is true in many of our larger cities, where contact between people is often brief and impersonal. Allport terms the condition arising from this situation as "urban insecurity." In addition, prejudice often exists in populations of bordering countries where there is competition for land or natural resources, and where rapid change in population distribution occurs.

The rate at which a population changes its composition often determines how newly entering groups will be treated by the dominant group . As Saenger (1953) explains, "A slow, imperceptible change over years or decades is less likely to create a negative reaction than a sudden increase in minority populations over a short period of time." When individual minority members increase in number, are more visible, or when they begin to gain political or social advances, the dominant group may react unfavorably. Called *backlash*, this may result in increased and intensified incidents of discrimination against the minority group.

Short or unsustained positive experiences with minorities are often unlikely to alter prejudice if the negative stereotypes are strongly ingrained. Sometimes direct contact actually deepens prejudice because of the process of *selection* and *distortion*. The prejudiced individual may select to focus on the negative contacts, thus distorting them to seem worse than they actually are. Prejudice then becomes circular, feeding off itself.

Once again, situational (or contact) theory is relevant to the existence of homophobia. Though homosexuals constitute a significant percentage of the population, most gay people are not visible. As a result, heterosexuals are not always aware of their contact with lesbians and gays. Thus, they may tend to focus on one isolated negative encounter or some lurid headline involving a gay person and generalize from that to all gay people. We frequently hear about murders on the evening news, for example. But when a gay man or lesbian is involved, homophobia encourages singling out this aspect of the case, reinforcing the already existing prejudice. Similarly, positive encounters that may contradict the stereotype are often dismissed as being atypical.

References

Adorno, T. W., E. Frenkel-Brunswick, D. J. Levinson, and R. N. Sanford. *The Authoritarian Personality.* New York: Harper and Row, 1950.

Allport, Gordon. *The Nature of Prejudice.* Reading, Mass.: Addison-Wesley, 1954.

Boswell, John. *Christianity, Social Tolerance, and Homosexuality: Gay People in Western Europe from the Beginning of the Christian Era to the Fourteenth Century.* Chicago: University of Chicago Press, 1980.

Breslin, R. "Structured Approaches to Dealing with Prejudice and Intercultural Misunderstanding." *Journal of Internalized Group Tensions* 8 (1978).

Churchill, Wainwright. *Homosexuality in Males: A Cross-Cultural and Cross-Species Investigation.* Englewood Cliffs, N.J.: Prentice-Hall, Inc., 1967.

Eitzen, D. Stanley. *Social Problems.* Boston: Allyn and Bacon, 1980.

Gordon, Milton M. *Assimilation in American Life: The Role of Race, Religion, and National Origins.* New York: Oxford University Press, 1964.

Hudson, W. W., and W. A. Ricketts. "A Strategy for the Measurement of Homophobia." *Journal of Homosexuality* 5, no. 4 (1980).

Julian, Joseph, and William Kornblum. *Social Problems,* 4th ed. Englewood Cliffs, N.J.: Prentice-Hall, 1983.

Knowles, Louis L., and Kenneth Prewitt, eds. *Institutional Racism in America.* Englewood Cliffs, N.J.: Prentice-Hall/Spectrum Books, 1969.

Lehne, G. H. "Homophobia among Men." In *The Forty-Nine Percent Majority: The Male Sex Role,* edited by D. Davis and R. Brannon. Reading, Mass.: Addison-Wesley, 1976.

Levitt, E. E., and A. D. Klassen. "Public Attitudes toward Homosexuality: Part of the 1970 National Survey by the Institute for Sex Research." *Journal of Homosexuality* 1, no. 1 (1974).

Marmor, Judd, ed. "Overview: The Multiple Roots of Homosexual Behavior." In *Homosexual Behavior: A Modern Reappraisal.* New York: Basic Books, 1980.

Niemoller, Martin, in John Bartlett, *Bartlett's Familiar Quotations,* 15th ed. Boston: Little, Brown and Company, 1982, 824.

Rosan, L. J. "Philosophies of Homophobia and Homophilia." In *The Gay Academic.* Palm Springs, Calif.: ETC Publications, 1978.

Saenger, Gerhart. *The Social Psychology of Prejudice.* New York: Harper, 1953.

Sartre, Jean-Paul. *Anti-Semite and Jew.* New York: Schocken, 1965.

Smith, Barbara. "Homophobia: Why Bring It Up?" *Interracial Books for Children Bulletin* 14, nos. 3–4. (1983).

Weinberg, George. *Society and the Healthy Homosexual.* New York: St. Martin's Press, 1972.

Wurzel, Jaime. "The Functions and Forms of Prejudice." In *A World of Difference: Resource Guide for Reduction of Prejudice.* Boston: Anti-Defamation League of B'nai B'rith/Facing History and Ourselves National Foundation, 1986.

4

Discrimination Comes in Many Forms: Individual, Institutional, and Structural

Fred L. Pincus

Discrimination is a critical term in understanding problems associated with diversity. Historically, of course, discrimination has been a major cause of the *lack* of diversity in higher education and the rest of society. In the 1990s, race and gender discrimination still permeate the institutions and structure of the United States even though most white Americans view discrimination as relatively unimportant.

Several years ago, I wrote that there were three different levels of discrimination—individual, institutional, and structural (Pincus 1994). *Individual discrimination* refers to the behavior of individual members of one race/ethnic/gender group that is intended to have a differential and/or harmful effect on the members of another race/ethnic/gender group. *Institutional discrimination*, on the other hand, is quite different because it refers to the policies of the dominant race/ethnic/gender institutions and the behavior of individuals who control these institutions and implement policies that are intended to have a differential and/or harmful effect on minority race/ethnic/gender groups. Finally, *structural discrimination* refers to the policies of dominant race/ethnic/gender institutions and the behavior of the individuals who implement these policies and control these institutions, which are race/ethnic/gender neutral in intent but which have a differential and/or harmful effect on minority race/ethnic/gender groups.

In these definitions, the term *dominant* refers to groups that have most of the power in society. In the United States, this refers to whites, especially white males. The term *minority* refers to groups that lack power; it does not refer to groups that are small. In the United States, people of color and women are minority groups as are certain non-Christian religious groups like Jews and Muslims. People of color also happen to be a numerical minority, but women are not.

Individual versus Institutional Discrimination

Although both individual and institutional discrimination involve an intention to harm, the level of behavior is quite different. Individual discrimination involves the actions of an individual or small group of individuals. The following are some examples: a lone employer who rejects all Black job applicants, a landlord who refuses to rent an apartment to a single woman, a police officer who beats a Mexican immigrant suspect, a group of teenagers who decide to paint a swastika on a Jewish temple—these are all examples of individuals acting against other individuals because of their group membership.

With institutional discrimination, on the other hand, the discriminatory behavior is embedded in important social institutions. Jim Crow segregation in the South during the first half of the twentieth century is one clear example. State laws mandated the separation of Blacks and Whites in all areas of life. Using any of the one-hour segments of the *Eyes on the Prize* documentary on the Civil Rights movement is an excellent way to illustrate the historical nature of institutional discrimination. . . .

A 1933 Gallup Poll, for example, posed the following question: "How serious a problem do you think discrimination against blacks is where you live?" Almost two-thirds of the Whites said that discrimination was not too serious or not at all serious. Less than one-third said it was somewhat serious or very serious. Black responses were the opposite of the White responses, with two-thirds of the Blacks viewing discrimination as very or somewhat serious and less than one-third viewing it as not serious (Gallup 1993).

The events surrounding the Rodney King beating by five White Los Angeles police officers in 1991 and the resulting riot provide a good vehicle to discuss these issues. If the beating was an isolated incident of several officers brutalizing a Black suspect, we could call it individual discrimination. However, it gradually became clear that leadership of the Los Angeles Police Department tolerated and often condoned antiblack activities. The atmosphere was so lax that officers felt free to use racial slurs on their car radios even though they knew that they were being recorded. The beating, then, becomes an example of institutional discrimination because it involved policies of the entire department.

The 1992 trial and acquittal of the officers involved in King's beating illustrates institutional discrimination in the criminal justice system. The defense requested a change of venue and the trial was moved to a conservative, predominantly white community of Simi Valley. In spite of the documentation of the beating by an amateur photographer, an all-White jury eventually acquitted the officers. It is hard to find a clearer case of how institutional discrimination in the criminal justice system hurts Blacks. The Los Angeles riots broke out immediately after the acquittal.

Ironically, a very similar situation occurred in Miami in 1980 after several White and Hispanic police officers were accused of beating Black motorist Arthur McDuffey to death. This trial was also moved from Miami to a predominantly white area of Florida; the police officers were acquitted and a riot ensued. The events surrounding the Miami riot are documented in one of the *Eyes on the Prize II* segments. . . .

The struggles of women to enter the Virginia Military Institute (VMI) and the Citadel are good examples of institutional discrimination because both state-supported institutions denied admission to women until 1996. Virginia even established a "separate but equal" program for women at Mary Baldwin College, a private women's institution. In June 1996, the U.S. Supreme Court ruled that VMI's all-male policy was unconstitutional because the institution received public funds. Although not directly involved in the decision, The Citadel subsequently announced that it would begin admitting women. VMI administrators and alumni, on the other hand, said that they would explore privatizing the institution to retain its all-male admissions policy (Lederman 1996; Mitchell 1996). This is reminiscent of how many southern states tried to avoid racial integration in the 1950s by closing their public schools and creating private all-White schools.

Institutional discrimination does not just involve the public sector, however. Two large restaurant chains provide examples of how intentional discrimination still exists in the private sector as well. Shoney's Inc., with over eighteen hundred restaurants in thirty-six states, had an unwritten policy of denying employment to Blacks in positions that involved customer contact—including waiters, waitresses, and managers. Exceptions were made for restaurants in black communities. Ray Danner, the founder of Shoney's, felt that this was good business because he believed that Whites would not want to eat at a restaurant where they would have to interact with Blacks. In 1992, Shoney's agreed to a $132.5 million out-of-court settlement to end a lawsuit and agreed to hire more Blacks (Feagin and Vera 1995; Watkins 1993).

In another nationally publicized case, the Denny's chain, with over fifteen hundred restaurants around the country, agreed to a $46 million out-of-court settlement. In 1993, six Black Secret Service officers were denied service at a Denny's restaurant in Annapolis and filed a complaint. This could have been an example of individual discrimination by a single employer. However, after word of the incident got out, more than four thousand other Blacks complained of similar treatment at other Denny's restaurants around the country. This, then, was an example of institutional discrimination because the entire restaurant chain had a "blackout" policy which called for denying service to Blacks when they became "too numerous." Waiters and waitresses also were instructed to ask black customers for payment in advance under certain conditions (Feagin and Vera 1995; Labaton 1994).

Who can practice discrimination? A person from any race/ethnic/gender group can carry out acts of individual discrimination. A woman employer can refuse to hire a man just as easily as a White can refuse to hire a Hispanic. Similarly, a Black can attack an Asian for simply being Asian, just as the Ku Klux Klan can burn a cross in front of a black church. The key issue is the intent to treat unequally or to cause harm because of group membership.

Institutional discrimination, on the other hand, is usually carried out by the dominant group against minority groups because it is the dominant group, by definition, that generally controls the social institutions. Government policies do not discriminate against Whites because Whites developed the policies and often implement them. Large private employers are overwhelmingly White, as are real estate developers and the owners of banks. It is theoretically possible, however, for a minority-run local government to practice institutional discrimination against Whites.

Using these examples of individual and institutional discrimination would be more problematic if one used the term *racism*. Often, racism is defined as a system of beliefs, policies, and practices designed to maintain White superiority. By this definition, Blacks cannot be racist because they lack power and are the victims of racism; that is, the Black who attacks a White is not practicing racism. . . .

The question here is whether or not members of minority groups can act negatively toward members of the dominant group, and the answer is clearly *yes*. Using the term *individual discrimination* allows the focus to be on how both dominant and minority group members can act in nasty ways toward one another. Although it is possible for women and minorities to practice institutional discrimination against White males, it occurs much less frequently than individual discrimination because white males tend to control most of the social institutions.

At some point during the discussion, a student is bound to ask if affirmative action is an example of institutional discrimination against Whites. I generally say no and argue that affirmative action is intended to create a more level playing field by eliminating the unfair (and often illegal) privilege that has been enjoyed—and that is *still* being enjoyed— by many Whites . . . .

Institutional versus Structural Discrimination

Structural discrimination is a more controversial but also a more fascinating concept to discuss because it involves behavior that is race and gender neutral in intent. In fact, the issue of intent is the main distinction between institutional and structural discrimination. Many scholars would not even call this race/gender neutral behavior discrimination. However, I think it is important to emphasize the negative *effects* on minority groups. . . .

Consider the lending practices of banks, for example. There is voluminous evidence that Blacks and Hispanics are less likely than Whites to get loans or home mortgages. There are several explanations for this finding, some of which suggest intentional institutional discrimination. The U.S. Justice Department has sued two banks for denying loans to qualified Blacks and Hispanics—the Decatur Federal Loan Association of Atlanta and the Shawmut National Corporation of New England. Both banks agreed to out-of-court settlements (Labaton 1993).

In addition, the Federal Reserve Bank of Chicago analyzed almost two thousand mortgage applications made in the Boston area in 1990. They found that Blacks and Hispanics with bad credit histories were twice as likely to be rejected for mortgages as Whites with bad credit histories. This was attributed to "the existence of a cultural affinity between white lending officers and white applicants, and a cultural gap between white loan officers and marginal minority applicants" (Bradsher 1995, D18). In other words, the white loan officers didn't trust minority applicants.

However, even if banks act in a race-neutral manner toward each customer by only considering their "creditworthiness," Blacks and Hispanics would *still* be less likely than Whites to get loans because of their lower incomes; that is, their creditworthiness is not as strong as it is for Whites. I call this legal lending policy *structural discrimination* because it has a negative impact on low-income minority groups. . . .

Do banks have any community responsibility other than making a profit and treating people in a color-blind manner? Chicago's South Shore Bank, for example, has a relatively good record of serving several poor communities (Moberg, 1993). . . .

The issue of seniority in employment also brings up the question of structural discrimination. When faced with the need to reduce their workforce, many employers lay off those workers who have been employed for fewer years. However, because minorities often tend to be the last hired, they will be disproportionately represented among those who are laid off. Hence the apparently race-neutral concept of seniority is an example of structural discrimination because it has negative impacts on minority populations.

I would also describe many of the policies of the Contract With America, the Republican Party's 1994 election platform, as structural discrimination. The proposed cuts in Medicaid, food stamps, school lunches, and the Women, Infants, and Children nutrition program would have a disproportionately negative impact on poor people of color and on women. . . .

This can lead to a discussion of the relative values of budget balancing versus providing services to the poor. Are there ways to balance the budget without hurting poor people of color? Perhaps reducing the number of new bombers or submarines would be an alternative method. . . .

Well-intentioned people who carry out structurally discriminatory policies still hurt minority groups. Being gender-blind or color-blind is not enough.

Policy Implications

Some students will ask, "What difference does it make whether something is institutional or structural discrimination?" I respond by saying that there are important policy implications about the distinctions between these two concepts. If one is trying to decide how to combat institutional discrimination, it is necessary to convince the leaders or policymakers of the particular institution that it is wrong (immoral, illegal) to purposely treat minority groups in negative ways—for example, banks refusing to lend to qualified blacks, or Republicans taking food out of the mouths of minority children. In addition, one might try to embarrass the perpetrators for their antiminority actions through publicizing their actions; clearly, neither Shoney's nor Denny's benefited from the publicity.

These arguments, however, are irrelevant to eliminating structural discrimination. For the banks, it is necessary to make the argument that equality is as important as profits or that there should be a better balance between the two. For Republicans, it is necessary to confront the negative consequences of the Contract with America along with the potential gains. The issue for structural discrimination is whether the goals of the race/gender-neutral policies are worth the negative effects.

Though all three types of discrimination are still serious problems, it is harder to deal with structural discrimination than with the other two. After all, structural discrimination is not intentional and it is not even illegal; it is carrying on business as usual. Confronting structural discrimination requires the reexamination of basic cultural values and fundamental principles of social organization. Isn't that what education is supposed to be all about?

References

Bradsher, K. (1995). "A Second Fed Bank Study Finds Disparities in Mortgage Lending." *The New York Times*, July 13, D1, D18.

Feagin, J. R., and H. Vera. (1995). *White Racism*. New York: Routledge.

Gallup, G. Jr. (1993). *The Gallup Poll: Public Opinion 1993*. Wilmington, Del.: Scholarly Resources, Inc.

Labaton, S. (1994). "Denny's Restaurants to Pay $54 Million in Race Bias Suits." *The New York Times*, May 25, A1, A18.

Lederman, D. (1996). "Supreme Court Rejects VMI's Exclusion of Women." *Chronicle of Higher Education*, July 5, A21, A26–27.

Mitchell, P. T. (1996). "VMI Should Go Coed or Go Public." *Chronicle of Higher Education*, January 19, A48.

Moberg, D. (1993). "Banking on the Inner City." *In These Times*, June 28, 21–23.

Pincus, F. L. (1994). "From Individual to Structural Discrimination." In F. L. Pincus and H. J. Ehrlich, *Race and Ethnic Conflict: Contending Views on Prejudice, Discrimination and Ethnoviolence*. Boulder, Colo.: Westview.

Watkins, S. (1993). "Racism du Jour at Shoney's." *The Nation*, October 18, 424–28.

5

Five Faces of Oppression

Iris Marion Young

Many people in the United States would not choose the term *oppression* to name injustice in our society. For contemporary emancipatory social movements, on the other hand—socialists, radical feminists, American Indian activists, black activists, gay and lesbian activists—oppression is a central category of political discourse. Entering the political discourse in which oppression is a central category involves adopting a general mode of analyzing and evaluating social structures and practices which is incommensurate with the language of liberal individualism that dominates political discourse in the United States.

A major political project for those of us who identify with at least one of these movements must thus be to persuade people that the discourse of oppression makes sense of much of our social experience. We are ill prepared for this task, however, because we have no clear account of the meaning of oppression.

In this chapter I offer some explanation of the concept of oppression as I understand its use by new social movements in the United States since the 1960s. My starting point is reflection on the conditions of the groups said by these movements to be oppressed: among others women, Blacks, Chicanos, Puerto Ricans and other Spanish-speaking Americans, American Indians, Jews, lesbians and gay men, Arabs, Asians, old people, working-class people, and the physically and mentally disabled. I aim to systematize the meaning of the concept of oppression as used by these diverse political movements, and to provide normative argument to clarify the wrongs the term names.

Obviously the above-named groups are not oppressed to the same extent or in the same ways. In the most general sense, all oppressed people suffer some inhibition of their ability to develop and exercise their capacities and express their needs, thoughts, and feelings. In that abstract sense all oppressed people face a common condition. Beyond that, in any more specific sense, it is not possible to define a single set of criteria that describe the condition of oppression of the above groups. Consequently, attempts by theorists and activists to discover a common description or the essential causes of the oppression of all these groups have frequently led to fruitless disputes about whose oppression is more fundamental or more grave. The contexts in which members of these groups use the term *oppression* to describe the injustices of their situation suggest that oppression names in fact a family of concepts and conditions, which I divide into five categories: exploitation, marginalization, powerlessness, cultural imperialism, and violence.

In this chapter I explicate each of these forms of oppression. . . .

Oppression as a Structural Concept

One reason that many people would not use the term *oppression* to describe injustice in our society is that they do not understand the term in the same way as do new social movements. In its traditional usage, oppression means the exercise of tyranny by a ruling group.

Oppression also traditionally carries a strong connotation of conquest and colonial domination. The Hebrews were oppressed in Egypt, and many uses of the term oppression in the West invoke this paradigm. . . . New left social movements of the 1960s and 1970s, however, shifted the meaning of the concept of oppression. In its new usage, oppression designates the disadvantage and injustice some people suffer not because a tyrannical power coerces them, but because of the everyday practices of a well-intentioned liberal society. . . .

Oppression refers to systemic constraints on groups that are not necessarily the result of the intentions of a tyrant. Oppression in this sense is structural, rather than the result of a few people's choices or policies. Its causes are embedded in unquestioned norms, habits, and symbols, in the assumptions underlying institutional rules and the collective consequences of following those rules. It names, as Marilyn Frye puts it, "an enclosing structure of forces and barriers which tends to the immobilization and reduction of a group or category of people" (1983, 11). In this extended structural sense, oppression refers to the vast and deep injustices some groups suffer as a consequence of often unconscious assumptions and reactions of well meaning people in ordinary interactions, media and cultural stereotypes, and structural features of bureaucratic hierarchies and market mechanisms—in short, the normal processes of everyday life. We cannot eliminate this structural oppression by getting ride of the rulers or making some new laws, because oppressions are systematically reproduced in major economic, political, and cultural institutions. . . .

I do not mean to suggest that within a system of oppression individual persons do not intentionally harm others in oppressed groups. The raped woman, the beaten Black youth, the locked-out worker, the gay man harassed on the street, are victims of intentional actions by identifiable agents. I also do not mean to deny that specific groups are beneficiaries of the oppression of other groups, and thus have an interest in their continued oppression. Indeed, for every oppressed group there is a group that is privileged in relation to that group. . . .

Racism, sexism, ageism, homophobia, some social movements asserted, are distinct forms of oppression with their own dynamics apart from those of class, even though they may interact with class oppression. From often heated discussions among socialists, feminists, and antiracism activists in the last ten years, a consensus is emerging that many different groups must be said to be oppressed in our society, and that no single form of oppression can be assigned causal or moral primacy (see Gottlieb 1987). The same discussion has also led to the recognition that group differences cut across individual lines in a multiplicity of ways that can entail privilege and oppression for the same person in different respects. Only a plural explication of the concept of oppression can adequately capture these insights.

Accordingly, I offer below an explication of five faces of oppression as a useful set of categories and distinctions which I believe is comprehensive in the sense that it covers all the groups said by new left social movements to be oppressed, and all the ways they are oppressed. I derive the five faces of oppression from reflection on the condition of these groups. Because different factors, or combinations of factors, constitute the oppression of different groups, making their oppression irreducible, I believe it is not possible to give one essential definition of oppression. The five categories articulated in this chapter, however, are adequate to describe the oppression of any group, as well as its similarities with and differences from the oppression of other groups. But first we must ask what a "group" is.

The Concept of a Social Group

. . . A social group is a collective of persons differentiated from at least one other group by cultural forms, practices, or way of life. Members of a group have a specific affinity with one another because of their similar experience (or way of life), which prompts them to associate with one another more than with those not identified with the group. Groups are an expression of social relations; a group exists only in relation to at least one other group. Group identification arises, that is, in the encounter and interaction between social collectivities that experience some differences in their way of life and forms of association, even if they also regard themselves as belonging to the same society.

As long as they associated solely among themselves, for example, an American Indian group thought of themselves only as "the people." The encounter with other American Indians created an awareness of difference; the others were named as a group, and the first group came to see themselves as a group. But social groups do not arise only from an encounter between different societies. Social processes also differentiate groups within a single society. The sexual division of labor, for example, has created social groups of women and men in all known societies. Members of each gender have a certain affinity with others in their group because of what they do or experience, and differentiate themselves from the other gender, even when members of each gender consider that they have much in common with members of the other, and consider that they belong to the same society. . . .

A social group is defined not primarily by a set of shared attributes, but by a sense of identity. What defines Black Americans as a social group is not primarily their skin color; some persons whose skin color is fairly light, for example, identify themselves as black. Though sometimes objective attributes are a necessary condition for classifying oneself or others as belonging to a certain social group, it is identification with a certain social status, the common history that social status produces, and self-identification that define the group as a group. . . .

Groups constitute individuals. A person's particular sense of history, affinity, and separateness—even the person's mode of reasoning, evaluating, and expressing feeling—are constituted partly by her or his group affinities. This does not mean that persons have no individual styles, or are unable to transcend or reject a group identity. Nor does it preclude persons from having many aspects that are independent of these group identities. . . .

A person joins an association, and even if membership in it fundamentally affects one's life, one does not take that membership to define one's very identity, in the way, for example, being Navaho might. Group affinity, on the other hand, has the character of what Martin Heidegger (1962) calls "throwness": one *finds oneself* as a member of a group, which one experiences as always already having been. For our identities are defined in relation to how others identify us, and they do so in terms of groups which are always already associated with specific attributes, stereotypes, and norms.

From the thrownness of group affinity it does not follow that one cannot leave groups and enter new ones. Many women become lesbian after first identifying as heterosexual. Anyone who lives long enough becomes old. These cases exemplify throwness precisely because such changes in group affinity are experienced as transformations in one's identity. Nor does it follow from the throwness of group affinity that one cannot define the meaning of group identity for oneself; those who identify with a group can redefine the meaning and norms of group identity. . . . While groups may come into being, they are never founded.

Groups, I have said, exist only in relation to other groups. A group may be identified by outsiders without those so identified having any specific consciousness of themselves as a group. Sometimes a group comes to exist only because one group excludes and labels a category of persons, and those labeled come to understand themselves as group members only slowly, on the basis of their shared oppression. In Vichy France, for example, Jews who had been so assimilated that they had no specifically Jewish identity were marked as Jews by others and given a specific social status by them. These people "discovered" themselves as Jews, and then formed a group identity and affinity with one another (see Sartre 1948). A person's group identities may be for the most part only a background or horizon to his or her life, becoming salient only in specific interactive contexts.

Some people think that social groups are invidious fictions, essentializing arbitrary attributes. From this point of view problems of prejudice, stereotyping, discrimination, and exclusion exist because some people mistakenly believe that group identification makes a difference to the capacities, temperament, or virtues of group members. This individualist conception of persons and their relation to one another tends to identify oppression with group identification. Oppression, on this view, is something that happens to people when they are classified in groups. Because others identify them as a group, they are excluded and despised. Eliminating oppression thus requires eliminating groups. People should be treated as individuals, not as members of groups, and allowed to form their lives freely with stereotypes or group norms.

This chapter takes issue with that position. While I agree that individuals should be free to pursue life plans in their own ways, it is foolish to deny the reality of groups. Despite the modern myth of a decline of parochial attachments and ascribed identities, in modern society group differentiation remains endemic. As both markets and social administration increase the web of social interdependency on a world scale, and as more people encounter one another as strangers in cities and states, people retain and renew ethnic, locale, age, sex, and occupational group identifications, and form new ones in the processes of encounter (cf. Ross 1980, 19; Rothschild 1981, 130). Even when they belong to oppressed groups, people's group identifications are often important to them, and they often feel a special affinity for others in their group. I believe that group differentiation is both an inevitable and a desirable aspect of modern social processes. Social justice requires not the melting away of differences, but institutions that promote reproduction of and respect for group differences without oppression.

Through some groups have come to be formed out of oppression, and relations of privilege and oppression structure the interactions between many groups, group differentiation is not in itself oppressive. Not all groups are oppressed. In the United States Roman Catholics are a specific social group, with distinct practices and affinities with one another, but they are no longer an oppressed group. Whether a group is oppressed depends on whether it is subject to one or more of the five conditions I shall discuss below. . . .

The Faces of Oppression

Exploitation

The central insight expressed in the concept of exploitation is that this oppression occurs through a steady process of the transfer of the results of the labor of one social group to benefit another. The injustice of class division does not consist only in the distributive fact that some people have great wealth while most people have little (cf. Buchanan 1982, 44–49; Holmstrom 1977). Exploitation enacts a structural relation between social groups. Social rules about what work is, who does what for whom, how work is compensated, and the social processes by which the results of work are appropriated operate to enact relations of power and inequality. These relations are produced and reproduced through a systematic process in which the energies of the have-nots are continuously expended to maintain and augment the power, status, and wealth of the haves. . . .

Feminists have had little difficulty showing that women's oppression consists partly in a systematic and unreciprocated transfer of powers from women to men. Women's oppression consists not merely in an inequality of status, power, and wealth resulting from men's excluding them from privileged activities. The freedom, power, status, and self-realization of men is possible precisely because women work for them. Gender exploitation has two aspects: transfer of the fruits of material labor to men, and the transfer of nurturing and sexual energies to men.

Christine Delphy (1984), for example, describes marriage as a class relation in which women's labor benefits men without comparable remuneration. She makes it clear that the exploitation consists not in the sort of work that women do in the home, for this might include various kinds of tasks, but in the fact that they perform tasks for someone on whom they are dependent. Thus, for example, in most systems of agriculture production in the world, men take to market the goods women have produced, and more often than not men receive the status and often the entire income from this labor.

With the concept of sex-affective production, Ann Ferguson (1984; 1989, chap. 4) identifies another form of the transference of women's energies to men. Women provide men and children with emotional care and provide men with sexual satisfaction, and as a group receive relatively little of either from men (cf. Brittan and Maynard 1984, 142–48). The gender socialization of women makes us tend to be more attentive to interactive dynamics than men, and makes women good at providing empathy and support for people's feelings and at smoothing over interactive tensions. Both men and women look to women as nurturers of their personal lives, and women frequently complain that when they look to men for emotional support they do not receive it (Easton, 1978). The norms of heterosexuality, moreover, are oriented around male pleasure, and consequently, many women receive little satisfaction from their sexual interactions with men (Gottlieb, 1984).

Most feminist theories of gender exploitation have concentrated on the institutional structure of the patriarchal family. Recently, however, feminists have begun to explore relations of gender exploitation enacted in the contemporary workplace and through the state. Carol Brown argues that as men have removed themselves from responsibility for children, many women have become dependent on the state for subsistence as they continue to bear nearly total responsibility of child rearing (Brown 1981; cf. Boris and Bardaglio 1983; and A. Ferguson 1984). This creates a new system of the exploitation of women's domestic labor mediated by state institutions, which Brown calls public patriarchy.

In twentieth-century capitalist economies the workplaces that women have been entering in increasing numbers serve as another important site of gender exploitation. David Alexander (1987) argues that typically feminine jobs involve gender-based tasks requiring sexual labor, nurturing, caring for others' bodies, or smoothing over workplace tensions. In these ways women's energies are expended in jobs that enhance the status of, please, or comfort others, usually men; and these gender-based labors of waitresses, clerical workers, nurses, and other caretakers often go unnoticed and undercompensated.

To summarize, women are exploited in the Marxist sense to the degree that they are wage workers. Some have argued that women's domestic labor also represents a form of capitalist class exploitation insofar as it is labor covered by the wages a family receives. As a group, however, women undergo specific forms of gender exploitation in which their energies and power are expended, often unnoticed and unacknowledged, usually to benefit men by releasing them for more important and creative work, enhancing their status or the environment around them, or providing them with sexual or emotional service. . . .

Is it possible to conceptualize a form of exploitation that is racially specific on analogy with the gender-specific forms just discussed? I suggest that the category of *menial* labor might supply a means for such conceptualization. In its derivation, "menial" designates the labor of servants. Wherever there is racism, there is the assumption, more or less enforced, that members of the oppressed racial groups are or ought to be servants of those, or some of those, in the privileged group. In most white racist societies this means that many white people have dark- or yellow-skinned domestic servants, and in the United States today there remains significant racial structuring of private household service. But in the United States today much service labor has gone public: anyone who goes to a good hotel or a good restaurant can have servants. Servants often attend the daily—and nightly—activities of business executives, government officials, and other high-status professionals. In our society there remains strong cultural pressure to fill servant jobs—bellhop, porter, chambermaid, busboy, and so on—with Black and Latino workers. These jobs entail a transfer of energies whereby the servers enhance the status of the served.

Menial labor usually refers not only to service, however, but also to any servile, unskilled, low-paying work lacking in autonomy, in which a person is subject to taking orders from many people. Menial work tends to be auxiliary work, instrumental to the work of others, where those others receive primary recognition for doing the job. Laborers on a construction site, for example, are at the beck and call of welders, electricians, carpenters, and other skilled workers, who receive recognition for the job done. In the United States explicit racial discrimination once reserved menial work for Blacks, Chicanos,

American Indians, and Chinese, and menial work still tends to be linked to Black and Latino workers (Symanski 1985). I offer this category of menial labor as a form of racially specific exploitation, as a provisional category in need of exploration. . . .

The injustice of exploitation consists in social processes that bring about a transfer of energies from one group to another to produce unequal distributions, and in the way in which social institutions enable a few to accumulate while they constrain many more. The injustices of exploitation cannot be eliminated by the redistribution of goods, for as long as institutionalized practices and structural relations remain unaltered, the process of transfer will re-create an unequal distribution of benefits. Bringing about justice where there is exploitation requires reorganization of institutions and practices of decisionmaking, alteration of the division of labor, and similar measures of institutional, structural, and cultural change.

Marginalization

Increasingly in the United States, racial oppression occurs in the form of marginalization rather than exploitation. *Marginals* are people the system of labor cannot or will not use. Not only in Third World capitalist countries, but also in most Western capitalist societies, there is a growing underclass of people permanently confined to lives of social marginality, most of whom are racially marked—Blacks or Indians in Latin America, and Blacks, East Indians, Eastern Europeans, or North Africans in Europe.

Marginalization is by no means the fate only of racially marked groups, however. In the United States a shamefully large proportion of the population is marginal: old people, and increasingly people who are not very old but get laid off from their jobs and cannot find new work; young people, especially Black or Latino, who cannot find first or second jobs; many single mothers and their children; other people involuntarily unemployed; many mentally and physically disabled people; American Indians (especially those on reservations).

Marginalization is perhaps the most dangerous form of oppression. A whole category of people is expelled from useful participation in social life and thus potentially subjected to severe material deprivation and even extermination. The material deprivation marginalization often causes is certainly unjust, especially in a society where others have plenty. Contemporary advanced capitalist societies have in principle acknowledged the injustice of material deprivation caused by marginalization, and have taken some steps to address it by providing welfare payments and services. The continuance of this welfare state is by no means assured, and in most welfare state societies, especially the United States, welfare redistributions do not eliminate large-scale suffering and deprivation.

Material deprivation, which can be addressed by redistributive social policies, is not, however, the extent of the harm caused by marginalization. Two categories of injustice beyond distribution are associated with marginality in advanced capitalist societies. First, the provision of welfare itself produces new injustice by depriving those dependent on it of rights and freedoms that others have. Second, even when material deprivation is somewhat mitigated by the welfare state, marginalization is unjust because it blocks the opportunity to exercise capacities in socially defined and recognized ways. I shall explicate each of these in turn.

Liberalism has traditionally asserted the right of all rational autonomous agents to equal citizenship. Early bourgeois liberalism explicitly excluded from citizenship all those whose reason was questionable or not fully developed, and all those not independent (Pateman 1988, chap. 3; cf. Bowles and Gintis 1986, chap. 2). Thus, poor people, women, the mad and the feebleminded, and children were explicitly excluded from citizenship, and many of these were housed in institutions modeled on the modern prison: poorhouses, insane asylums, schools.

Today the exclusion of dependent persons from equal citizenship rights is only barely hidden beneath the surface. Because they depend on bureaucratic institutions for support or services, the old, the poor, and the mentally or physically disabled are subject to patronizing, punitive, demeaning, and arbitrary treatment by the policies and people associated with welfare bureaucracies. Being a "dependent" in our society implies being legitimately subject to the often arbitrary and invasive authority of social service providers and other public and private administrators who enforce rules with which the marginal must comply, and otherwise exercise power over the conditions of their lives. In meeting the needs of the marginalized, often with the aid of social scientific disciplines, welfare agencies also construct the needs themselves. Medical and social service professionals know what is good for those they serve, and the marginals and dependents themselves do not have the right to claim to know what is good for them (Fraser 1987a; K. Ferguson 1984, chap. 4). Dependency in our society thus implies, as it has in all liberal societies, a sufficient warrant to suspend basic rights to privacy, respect, and individual choice.

Although dependency produces conditions of injustice in our society, dependency in itself need not be oppressive. One cannot imagine a society in which some people would not need to be dependent on others at least some of the time: children, sick people, women recovering from childbirth, old people who have become frail, depressed or otherwise emotionally needy persons have the moral right to depend on others for subsistence and support.

An important contribution of feminist moral theory has been to question the deeply held assumption that moral agency and full citizenship require that a person be autonomous and independent. Feminists have exposed this assumption as inappropriately individualistic and derived from a specifically male experience of social relations, which values competition and solitary achievement (see Gilligan 1982; Friedman 1985). Female experience of social relations, arising both from women's typical domestic care responsibilities and from the kinds of paid work that many women do, tends to recognize dependence as a basic human condition (cf. Hartsock, 1983, chap. 10). Whereas on the autonomy model a just society would, as much as possible, give people the opportunity to be independent, the feminist model envisions justice as according respect and participation in decision making to those who are dependent as well as to those who are independent (Held 1987b). Dependency should not be a reason to be deprived of choice and respect, and much of the oppression many marginals experience would be lessened if a less individualistic model of rights prevailed.

Marginalization does not cease to be oppressive when one has shelter and food. Many old people, for example, have sufficient means to live comfortably but remain oppressed in their marginal status. Even if marginals were provided a comfortable material life within institutions that respected their freedom and dignity, injustices of marginality would remain in the form of uselessness, boredom, and lack of self-respect. Most of our society's productive and recognized activities take place in contexts of organized social cooperation, and social structures and processes that close persons out of such social cooperation are unjust. Thus, while marginalization definitely entails serious issues of distributive justice, it also involves the deprivation of cultural, practical, and institutionalized conditions for exercising capacities in a context of recognition and interaction.

The fact of marginalization raises basic structural issues of justice, in particular concerning the appropriateness of a connection between participation in production activities of social cooperation on the one hand, and access to the means of consumption on the other. As marginalization is increasing with no sign of abatement, some social policy analysts have introduced the idea of *social wage* as a guaranteed socially provided income not tied to the age system. Restructuring of productive activity to address a right of participation, however, implies organizing some socially productive activity outside of the wage system (see Offe 1985, 95–100), through public works of self-employed collectives.

Powerlessness

As I have indicated, the Marxist idea of class is important because it helps reveal the structure of exploitation: that some people have their power and wealth because they profit from the labor of others. For this reason I reject the claim some make that a traditional class exploitation model fails to capture the structure of contemporary society. It remains the case that the labor of most people in the society augments the power of relatively few. Despite their differences from nonprofessional workers, most professional workers are still not members of the capitalist class. Professional labor either involves exploitative transfers to capitalists or supplies important conditions for such transfers. Professional workers are in an ambiguous class position, it is true, because they also benefit from the exploitation of nonprofessional workers.

While it is false to claim that a division between capitalist and working classes no longer describes our society, it is also false to say that class relations have remained unaltered since the nineteenth century. An adequate conception of oppression cannot ignore the experience of social division reflected in the colloquial distinction between the "middle class" and the "working class," a division structured by the social division of labor between professionals and nonprofessionals. Professionals are privileged in relation to nonprofessionals by virtue of their position in the division of labor and the status it carries. Nonprofessionals suffer a form of oppression in addition to exploitation, which I call *powerlessness.*

In the United States, as in other advanced capitalist countries, most workplaces are not organized democratically, direct participation in public policy decisions is rare, and policy implementation is for the most part hierarchical, imposing rules on bureaucrats and citizens. Thus, most people in these societies do not regularly participate in making decisions that affect the conditions of their lives and actions, and in this sense most people lack significant power. At the same time, domination in modern society is enacted through the widely dispersed powers of many agents mediating the decisions of others. To that extent many people have some power in relation to others, even though they lack the power to decide policies or results. The powerless are those who lack authority or power even in this mediated sense, those over whom power is exercised without their exercising it; the powerless are situated so that they must take orders and rarely have the right to give them. Powerlessness also designates a position in the division of labor and the concomitant social position that allows persons little opportunity to develop and exercise skills. The powerless have little or no work autonomy; exercise little creativity or judgment in their work; have no technical expertise or authority; express themselves awkwardly, especially in public or bureaucratic settings; and do not command respect. Powerlessness names the oppressive situations Sennett and Cobb (1972) describe in their famous study of working-class men.

This powerless status is perhaps best described negatively: the powerless lack the authority, status, and sense of self that professionals tend to have. The status privilege of professionals has three aspects, the lack of which produces oppression for nonprofessionals.

First, acquiring and practicing a profession has an expansive, progressive character. Being professional usually requires a college education and the acquisition of a specialized knowledge that entails working with symbols and concepts. Professionals experience progress first in acquiring the expertise, and then in the course of professional advancement and rise in status. The life of the nonprofessional by comparison is powerless in the sense that it lacks this orientation toward the progressive development of capacities and avenues for recognition.

Second, while many professionals have supervisors and cannot directly influence many decisions or the actions of many people, most nevertheless have considerable day-to-day work autonomy. Professionals usually have some authority over others, moreover—either over workers they supervise, or over auxiliaries or clients. Nonprofessionals, on the other hand, lack autonomy, and in both their working and their consumer/client lives often stand under the authority of professionals.

Though based on a division of labor between "mental" and "manual" work, the distinction between "middle class" and "working class" designates a division not only in working life, but also in nearly all aspects of social life. Professionals and nonprofessionals belong to different cultures in the United States. The two groups tend to live in segregated neighborhoods or even different towns, a process itself mediated by planners, zoning officials, and real estate people. The groups tend to have different tastes in food, decor, clothes, music, and vacations, and often different health and educational needs. Members of each group socialize for the most part with others in the same status group. While there is some intergroup mobility between generations, for the most part the children of professionals become professionals and the children of nonprofessionals do not.

Thus, the privileges of the professional extend beyond the workplace to a whole way of life. I call this way of life *respectability*. To treat people with respect is to be prepared to listen to what they have to say or to do what they request because they have some authority, expertise, or influence. The norms of respectability in our society are associated specifically with professional culture. Professional dress, speech, tastes, demeanor all connote respectability. Generally professionals expect and receive respect from others. In restaurants, banks, hotels, real estate offices, and many other such public places, as well as in the media, professionals typically receive more respectful treatment than nonprofessionals. For this reason nonprofessionals seeking a loan or a job, or to buy a house or a car, will often try to look "professional" and "respectable" in those settings.

The privilege of this professional respectability appears starkly in the dynamics of racism and sexism. In daily interchange, women and men of color must prove their respectability. At first they are often not treated by strangers with respectful distance or deference. Once people discover that this woman or that Puerto Rican man is a college teacher or a business executive, however, they often behave more respectfully toward her or him. Working-class white men, on the other hand, are often treated with respect until their working-class status is revealed.

I have discussed several injustices associated with powerlessness: inhibition in the development of one's capacities, lack of decisionmaking power in one's working life, and exposure to disrespectful treatment because of the status one occupies. These injustices have distributional consequences, but are more fundamentally matters of the division of labor. The oppression of powerlessness brings into question the division of labor basic to all industrial societies: the social division between those who plan and those who execute.

Cultural Imperialism

Exploitation, marginalization, and powerlessness all refer to relations of power and oppression that occur by virtue of the social division of labor—who works for whom, who does not work, and how the content of work defines one institutional position relative to others. These three categories refer to structural and institutional relations that delimit people's material lives, including but not restricted to the resources they have access to and the concrete opportunities they have or do not have to develop and exercise their capacities. These kinds of oppression are a matter of concrete power in relation to others—of who benefits from whom, and who is dispensable.

Recent theorists of movements of group liberation, notably feminist and Black liberation theorists, have also given prominence to a rather different form of oppression, which following Lugones and Spelman (1983) I shall call *cultural imperialism*. To experience cultural imperialism means to experience how the dominant meanings of a society render the particular perspective of one's own group invisible at the same time as they stereotype one's group and mark it as the Other.

Cultural imperialism involves the universalization of a dominant group's experience and culture, and its establishment as the norm. . . . Often without noticing they do so, dominant groups project their own experience as representative of humanity as such. Cultural products also express the dominant group's perspective on and interpretation of events and elements in the society, including other groups in the society, insofar as they attain cultural status at all.

An encounter with other groups, however, can challenge the dominant group's claim to universality. The dominant group reinforces its position by bringing the other groups under the measure of its dominant norms. Consequently, the difference of women from men, American Indians or Africans from Europeans, Jews from Christians, homosexuals from heterosexuals, workers from professionals becomes reconstructed largely as deviance and inferiority. Since only the dominant group's cultural expressions receive wide dissemination, their cultural expressions become the normal, or the universal, and thereby the unremarkable. Given the normality of its own cultural expressions and identity, the dominant group constructs the differences which some groups exhibit as lack and negation. These groups become marked as Other.

The culturally dominated undergo a paradoxical oppression in that they are both marked out by stereotypes and at the same time rendered invisible. As remarkable, deviant beings, the culturally imperialized are stamped with an essence. The stereotypes confine them to a nature which is often attached in some way to their bodies, and which thus cannot easily be denied. These stereotypes so permeate the society that they are not noticed as contestable. Just as everyone knows that the earth goes around the sun, so everyone knows that gay people are promiscuous, that American Indians are alcoholics, and that women are good with children. White males, on the other hand, insofar as they escape group marking, can be individuals.

Those living under cultural imperialism find themselves defined from the outside, positioned, placed, by a network of dominant meanings they experience as arising from elsewhere, from those with whom they do not identify and who do not identify with them. Consequently, the dominant culture's stereotyped and inferiorized images of the group must be internalized by group members at least to the extent that they are forced to react to the behavior of others influenced by those images. This creates for the culturally oppressed the experience that W. E. B. Du Bois called "double consciousness"—"this sense of always looking at one's self through the eyes of others, of measuring one's soul by the tape of a world that looks on in amused contempt and pity" (Du Bois 1969, 45). Double consciousness arises when the oppressed subject refuses to coincide with these devalued, objectified, stereotyped visions of herself or himself. While the subject desires recognition as human—capable of activity, full of hope and possibility—she receives from the dominant culture only the judgment that she is different, marked, or inferior.

The group defined by the dominant culture as deviant, as a stereotyped Other, is culturally different from the dominant group, because the status of Otherness creates specific experiences not shared by the dominant group, and because culturally oppressed groups also are often socially segregated and occupy specific positions in the social division of labor. Members of such groups express their specific group experiences and interpretations of the world to one another, developing and perpetuating their own culture. Double consciousness, then, occurs because one finds one's being defined by two cultures: a dominant and a subordinate culture. Because they can affirm and recognize one another as sharing similar experiences and perspectives on social life, people in culturally imperialized groups can often maintain a sense of positive subjectivity.

Cultural imperialism involves the paradox of experiencing oneself as invisible at the same time that one is marked out as different. The invisibility comes about when dominant groups fail to recognize the perspective embodied in their cultural expressions as a perspective. These dominant cultural expressions often simply have little place for the experience of other groups, at most only mentioning or referring to them in stereotyped or marginalized ways. This, then, is the injustice of cultural imperialism: that the oppressed group's own experience and interpretation of social life finds little expression that touches the dominant culture, while that same culture imposes on the oppressed group its experience and interpretation of social life. . . .

Violence

Finally, many groups suffer the oppression of systematic violence. Members of some groups live with the knowledge that they must fear random, unprovoked attacks on their persons or property, which have no motive but to damage, humiliate, or destroy the person. In American society women, Blacks, Asians, Arabs, gay men, and lesbians live under such threats of violence, and in at least some regions Jews, Puerto Ricans, Chicanos, and other Spanish-speaking Americans must fear such violence as well. Physical violence against these groups is shockingly frequent. Rape crisis center networks estimate that more than one-third of all American women experience an attempted or successful sexual assault in their lifetimes. Manning Marable (1984, 238–41) catalogs a large number of incidents of racist violence and terror against blacks in the United States between 1980 and 1982. He cites dozens of incidents of the severe beating, killing, or rape of Blacks by police officers on duty, in which the police involved were acquitted of any wrongdoing. In 1981, moreover, there were at least five hundred documented cases of random white teenage violence against Blacks. Violence against gay men and lesbians is not only common, but has been increasing in the last five years. While the frequency of physical attack on members of these and other racially or sexually marked groups is very disturbing, I also include in this category less severe incidents of harassment, intimidation, or ridicule simply for the purpose of degrading, humiliating, or stigmatizing group members.

Given the frequency of such violence in our society, why are theories of justice usually silent about it? I think the reason is that theorists do not typically take such incidents of violence and harassment as matters of social injustice. No moral theorist would deny that such acts are very wrong. But unless all immoralities are injustices, they might wonder, why should such acts be interpreted as symptoms of social injustice? Acts of violence or petty harassment are committed by particular individuals, often extremists, deviants, or the mentally unsound. How then can they be said to involve the sorts of institutional issues I have said are properly the subject of justice?

What makes violence a face of oppression is less the particular acts themselves—though these are often utterly horrible—than the social context surrounding them, which makes them possible and even acceptable. What makes violence a phenomenon of social injustice, and not merely an individual moral wrong, is its systemic character, its existence as a social practice.

Violence is systemic because it is directed at members of a group simply because they are members of that group. Any woman, for example, has a reason to fear rape. Regardless of what a Black man has done to escape the oppressions of marginality or powerlessness, he lives knowing he is subject to attack or harassment. The oppression of violence consists not only in direct victimization, but in the daily knowledge shared by all members of oppressed groups that they are *liable* to violation, solely on account of their group identity. Just living under such a threat of attack on oneself or family or friends deprives the oppressed of freedom and dignity, and needlessly expends their energy.

Violence is a social practice. It is a social given that everyone knows happens and will happen again. It is always at the horizon of social imagination, even for those who do not perpetrate it. According to the prevailing social logic, some circumstances make such violence more "called for" than others. The idea of rape will occur to many men who pick up a hitch-hiking woman; the idea of hounding or teasing a gay man on their dorm floor will occur to many straight male college students. Often several persons inflict the violence together, especially in all-male groupings. Sometimes violators set out looking for people to beat up, rape, or taunt. This rule-bound, social, and often premeditated character makes violence against groups a social practice.

Group violence approaches legitimacy, moreover, in the sense that it is tolerated. Often, third parties find it unsurprising because it happens frequently and lies as a constant possibility at the horizon of the social imagination. Even when they are caught, those who perpetrate acts of group-directed violence or harassment often receive light or no punishment. To that extent society renders their acts acceptable.

An important aspect of random, systemic violence is its irrationality. Xenophobic violence differs from the violence of states or ruling-class repression. Repressive violence has a rational, albeit evil, motive: rulers use it as a coercive tool to maintain their power. Many accounts of racist, sexist, or homophobic violence attempt to explain its motivation as a desire to maintain group privilege or domination. I do not doubt that fear of violence often functions to keep oppressed groups subordinate.

On the contrary, the violation of rape, beating, killing, and harassment of women, people of color, gays, and other marked groups is motivated by fear or hatred of those groups. Sometimes the motive may be a simple will to power, to victimize those marked as vulnerable by the very social fact that they are subject to violence. If so, this motive is secondary in the sense that it depends on a social practice of group violence. Violence-causing fear or hatred of the other at least partly involves insecurities on the part of the violators; its irrationality suggests that unconscious processes are at work.

Cultural imperialism, moreover, itself intersects with violence. The culturally imperialized may reject the dominant meanings and attempt to assert their own subjectivity, or the fact of the cultural difference may put the lie to the dominant culture's implicit claim to universality. The dissonance generated by such a challenge to the hegemonic cultural meanings can also be a source of irrational violence.

Violence is a form of injustice that a distributive understanding of justice seems ill equipped to capture. This may be why contemporary discussions of justice rarely mention it. I have argued that group-directed violence is institutionalized and systemic. To the degree that institutions and social practices encourage, tolerate, or enable the perpetration of violence against members of specific groups, those institutions and practices are unjust and should be reformed. Such reform may require the redistribution of resources or positions, but in large part can come only through a change in cultural images, stereotypes, and the mundane reproduction of relations of dominance and aversion in the gestures of everyday life.

Applying the Criteria

Social theories that construct oppression as a unified phenomenon usually either leave out groups that even the theorists think are oppressed, or leave out important ways in which groups are oppressed. Black liberation theorists and feminist theorists have argued persuasively, for example, that Marxism's reduction of all oppressions to class oppression leaves out much about the specific oppression of Blacks and women. By pluralizing the category of oppression in the way explained in this chapter, social theory can avoid the exclusive and oversimplifying effects of such reductionism.

I have avoided pluralizing the category in the way some others have done by constructing an account of separate systems of oppression for each oppressed group: racism, sexism, classism, heterosexism, ageism, and so on. There is a double problem with considering each group's oppression a unified and distinct structure or system. On the one hand, this way of conceiving oppression fails to accommodate the similarities and overlaps in the oppressions of different groups. On the other hand, it falsely represents the situation of all group members at the same.

I have arrived at the five faces of oppression—exploitation, marginalization, powerlessness, cultural imperialism, and violence—as the best way to avoid such exclusions and reductions. They function as criteria for determining whether individuals and groups are oppressed, rather than as a full theory of oppression. I believe that these criteria are objective. They provide a means of refuting some people's beliefs that their group is oppressed when it is not, as well as a means of persuading others that a group is oppressed when they doubt it. Each criterion can be operationalized; each can be applied through the assessment of observable behavior, status relationships, distributions, texts, and other cultural artifacts. I have no illusions that such assessments can be value-neutral. But these criteria can nevertheless serve as means of evaluating claims that a group is oppressed, or adjudicating disputes about whether or how a group is oppressed.

The presence of any of these five conditions is sufficient for calling a group oppressed. But different group oppressions exhibit different combinations of these forms, as do different individuals in the groups. Nearly all, if not all, groups said by contemporary social movements to be oppressed suffer cultural imperialism. The other oppressions they experience vary. Working-class people are exploited and powerless, for example, but if employed and white do not experience marginalization and violence. Gay men, on the other hand, are not qua gay exploited or powerless, but they experience severe cultural imperialism and violence. Similarly, Jews and Arabs as groups are victims of cultural imperialism and violence, though many members of these groups also suffer exploitation or powerlessness. Old people are oppressed by marginalization and cultural imperialism, and this is also true of physically and mentally disabled people. As a group, women are subject to gender-based exploitation, powerlessness, cultural imperialism, and violence. Racism in the United States condemns many Blacks, and Latinos to marginalization, and puts many more at risk, even though many members of these groups escape that condition; members of these groups often suffer all five forms of oppression.

Applying these five criteria to the situation of groups makes it possible to compare the oppressions without reducing them to a common essence or claiming that one is more fundamental than another. One can compare the ways in which a particular form of oppression appears in different groups. For example, while the operations of cultural imperialism are often experienced in similar fashion by different groups, there are also important differences. One can compare the combinations of oppressions groups experience, or the intensity of those oppressions. Thus, with these criteria one can plausibly claim that one group is more oppressed than another without reducing all oppressions to a single scale. . . .

References

Alexander, David. 1987. "Gendered Job Traits and Women's Occupations." Ph.D. dissertation, University of Massachusetts.

Boris, Ellen and Peter Bardaglio. 1983. "The Transformation of Patriarchy: The Historic Role of the State." In Irene Diamond, ed., *Families, Politics and Public Policy*. New York: Longman.

Bowles, Samuel and Herbert Gintis. 1986. *Democracy and Capitalism*. New York: Basic Books.

Brittan, Arthur and Mary Maynard. 1984. *Sexism, Racism and Oppression.* Oxford: Blackwell.

Brown, Carol. 1981. "Mothers, Fathers and Children: From Private to Public Patriarchy." In Lydia Sargent, ed., *Women and Revolution*. Boston: South End Press.

Buchanan, Allen. 1982. *Marx and Justice*. Totowa, N.J.: Rowman and Allanheld.

Delphy, Christine. 1984. *Close to Home: A Materialist Analysis of Women's Oppression*. Amherst: University of Massachusetts Press.

Du Bois, W. E. B. 1969 [1903]. *The Souls of Black Folk*. New York: New American Library.

Easton, Barbara. 1978. "Feminism and the Contemporary Family." *Socialist Review* 39 (May/June), 11–36.

Ferguson, Ann. 1984. "On Conceiving Motherhood and Sexuality: A Feminist Materialist Approach." In Joyce Trebilcot, ed., *Mothering: Essays in Feminist Theory.* Totowa, N.J.: Rowman and Allanheld.

———. 1989. *Blood at the Root.* London: Pandora.

Ferguson, Kathy. 1984. *The Feminist Case against Bureaucracy.* Philadelphia: Temple University Press.

Fraser, Nancy. 1987. "Women, Welfare, and the Politics of Need Interpretation." *Hypatia: A Journal of Feminist Philosophy* 2 (Winter), 103–22.

Friedman, Marilyn. 1985. "Care and Context in Moral Reasoning." In Carol Harding, ed., *Moral Dilemmas: Philosophical and Psychological Issues in the Development of Moral Reasoning.* Chicago: Precedent.

Frye, Marilyn. 1983. "Oppression." In *The Politics of Reality.* Trumansburg, N.Y.: Crossing Press.

Gilligan, Carol. 1982. *In a Different Voice.* Cambridge, Mass.: Harvard University Press.

Gottlieb, Rhonda. 1984. "The Political Economy of Sexuality." *Review of Radical Political Economy* 16 (Spring), 143–65.

Gottlieb, Roger. 1987. *History and Subjectivity.* Philadelphia: Temple University Press.

Hartsock, Nancy. 1983. *Money, Sex and Power.* New York: Longman.

Heidegger, Martin. 1962. *Being and Time.* New York: Harper and Row.

Held, Virginia. 1987. "A Non-Contractual Society." In Marsha Hanen and Kai Nielsen, eds., *Science, Morality and Feminist Theory.* Calgary: University of Calgary Press.

Holmstrom, Nancy. 1977. "Exploitation." *Canadian Journal of Philosophy* 7 (June): 353–69.

Lugones, Maria C. and Elizabeth V. Spelman. 1983. "Have We Got a Theory for You! Feminist Theory, Cultural Imperialism and the Demand for 'the Woman's Voice.'" *Women's Studies International Forum* 6, 573–81.

Marable, Manning. 1984. *Race, Reform and Rebellion: The Second Reconstruction in Black America, 1945–82.* Jackson: University Press of Mississippi.

Offe, Claus. 1985. *Disorganized Capitalism.* Cambridge: MIT Press.

Pateman, Carole. 1988. *The Sexual Contract.* Stanford: Stanford University Press.

Ross, Jeffrey. 1980. Introduction to Jeffrey Ross and Ann Baker Cottrell, eds., *The Mobilization of Collective Identity.* Lanham, Md.: University Press of America.

Rothschild, Joseph. 1981. *Ethnopolitics.* New York: Columbia University Press.

Sartre, Jean-Paul. 1948. *Anti-Semite and Jew.* New York: Schocken.

Sennett, Richard and Jonathan Cobb. 1972. *The Hidden Injuries of Class.* New York: Vintage.

Symanski, Al. 1985. "The Structure of Race." *Review of Radical Political Economy* 17 (Winter), 106–20.

6

Language and Silence: Making Systems of Privilege Visible

Stephanie M. Wildman
with Adrienne D. Davis

In a class I once taught, an African-American student observed, "White people always ask me what they can do to fight racism. My answer to them is, 'Make a friend of color as the first step in this long process.'"

This advice is important, but I worry about it being misunderstood. For many white people, making a friend of color means they are able to convince themselves that they must not be racist, because they have this trophy friend. Another woman of color I know commented that she has many white friends, but avoids discussing race with them. She is afraid of being hurt by her white friends' small stake in issues of race, when her stake is so large. It is easier for her just to avoid the whole conversation.

Given these difficulties, let me say why I am so taken by this simple, yet serious advice—"make a friend." Most of us who are white lead lives that are segregated by race. Race is imprinted on most neighborhood patterns, which means it is transferred to schools. Our lives as straight people are also generally segregated by sexual orientation. Most of us who are heterosexual tend to socialize with other heterosexuals, with couples if we ourselves are part of a couple. The lives we lead affect what we are able to see and hear in the world around us. So if you make a friend across categories of difference, realize that this means working on listening to what is important to your friend. . . .

I begin, first, with an examination of the language that we use to discuss discrimination and subordination. This language makes privilege invisible. Second, I turn to privilege, describing its forms and stressing the importance of addressing privilege as well as oppression. Next, I show that intersectionality can help reveal privilege by reminding us of the complex interactions of the systems of privilege and subordination. Finally, I conclude by considering the importance of looking for the operation of privilege systems in our classrooms. . . .

How Language Veils the Existence of Systems of Privilege

Language contributes to the invisibility and regeneration of privilege. To begin the conversation about subordination we sort ideas into categories such as race and gender. These words are part of a system of categorization, one that we use without thinking and that seems linguistically neutral. Race and gender are, after all, just words. Yet when we learn that someone has had a child, our first question is usually, "Is it a girl or a boy?"

Why do we ask that question, instead of something like, "Are the mother and child okay?" We ask, "Is it a girl or a boy?" according to philosopher Marilyn Frye, because we don't know how to relate to this new being without knowing its gender.[1] Imagine how long you could have a discussion with or about someone without knowing her or his gender. We place people into these categories because our world is gendered.

Similarly our world is also raced, making it hard for us to avoid taking mental notes as to race. We use our language to categorize by race, particularly, if we are white, when that race is other than white. Professor Marge Shultz has written of calling on a Hispanic-American student in her class.[2] She called him "Mr. Martinez," but his name was Mr. Rodriguez. The class tensed up at her error; earlier that same day another professor had called Mr. Rodriguez, "Mr. Hernandez," the name of the defendant in a criminal law case under discussion. Professor Shultz talked with her class, at its next session, about how her error and our thought processes pull us to categorize in order to think. She acknowledged how this process leads to stereotyping, which causes pain to individuals. We all live in this raced and gendered world, inside categories that make it hard to see each other as whole people.

The problem does not stop with the general terms, such as *race* and *gender*. Each of these categories contains the image, like an entrance to a tunnel with different arrows, of sub-categories. Race is often defined as Black and white, even though there are other races. Sometimes it is defined as white and of color; sometimes the categories are each listed, for example, as African-American, Hispanic-American, Asian-American, Native American, and White American, if whiteness is mentioned at all. All of these words, lists of racial sub-categories, seem neutral on their face, like equivalent titles. But however the sub-categories are listed, however neutrally the words are expressed, these words mask a system of power, and that system privileges whiteness.

Gender, too, is a seemingly neutral category that leads us to imagine sub-categories of male and female. A recent scientific article suggested that five genders might be a more accurate characterization of human anatomy, but there is a heavy systemic stake in our image of two genders.[3] The apparently neutral categories *male* and *female*, mask the privileging of males that is part of the gender power system. Try to think of equivalent gendered titles, like king and queen, prince and princess, and you will quickly see that *male* and *female* are not equal titles in our cultural imagination.

Poet and social critic Adrienne Rich has written convincingly about the compulsory heterosexuality that is part of this gender power system.[4] Almost everywhere we look, heterosexuality is portrayed as the norm. In Olympic ice skating and dancing, couples are defined to mean a man partnered with a woman.[5] Rampant heterosexuality is everywhere. What is amazing, says Rich, is that there are *any* lesbians or gay men.[6] Heterosexuality is privileged over any other relationships. The words we use, such as *marriage*, *husband*, and *wife*, are not neutral, but convey this privileging of heterosexuality.

Our culture suppresses conversation about economic class. Although money or access to money is tied to human necessities such as food, clothing, and shelter, those fundamental needs are recognized only as an individual responsibility. The notion of privilege based on economic wealth is viewed as an idiosyncratic throwback to the past, conjuring up countries with monarchies, nobility, serfs, and peasants, or as a radical, dangerous idea. Yet even the archaic vocabulary makes clear that no one wants to be categorized as a have-not. So the economic power system is not invisible in the sense that everyone knows money brings privilege. Rather, the myth persists that all have access to that power through individual resourcefulness. This myth of potential economic equality supports the invisibility of the other power systems that prevent fulfillment of that ideal.

Other words we use to describe subordination also serve to mask the operation of privilege. Increasingly, people use terms like *racism* and *sexism* to describe disparate treatment and the perpetuation of power. -Isms language serves as a way to describe discriminatory treatment. Yet this vocabulary of -Isms as a descriptive shorthand for undesirable, disadvantaging treatment creates several serious problems.

First, calling someone *racist* individualizes the behavior, ignoring the larger system within which the person is situated. To label an individual a racist veils the fact that racism can only occur where it is culturally, socially, and legally supported. It lays the blame on the individual rather than the forces that have shaped that individual and the society that the individual inhabits. For white people this means that they know they do not want to be labeled *racist*. They become concerned with how to avoid that label, rather than worrying about systemic racism and how to change it.

Second, the language of isms focuses on larger categories such as race, gender, and sexual preference. This language suggests that within these larger categories two seemingly neutral halves exist, equal parts in a mirror. Thus, Black and white, male and female, heterosexual and homosexual appear, through the linguistic juxtaposition, as equivalent subparts. In fact, although the categories do not take note of it, Blacks and whites, men and women, heterosexuals and gays/lesbians are not equivalently situated in society. Thus, the way we think and talk about the categories and subcategories that underlie these isms, considering them as parallel parts, obscures the pattern of domination and subordination within each classification.

Similarly, the phase *–Isms* itself gives the illusion that all patterns of domination and subordination are the same and interchangeable. The language suggests that someone subordinated under one form of oppression would be similarly situated to another person subordinated under another form. Thus, someone subordinated under one form may feel no need to view himself/herself as a possible oppressor, or beneficiary of oppression, within a different form. For example, white women, having an –Ism that defines their condition—sexism—may not look at the way they are privileged by racism. They have defined themselves as one of the oppressed.

Finally, the focus on individual behavior, the seemingly neutral subparts of categories, and the apparent interchangeability underlying the vocabulary of –Isms all obscure the existence of systems of privilege and power. It is difficult to see and talk about how oppression operates when the vocabulary itself makes these systems of privilege invisible. *White supremacy* is a phrase associated with a lunatic fringe, not with the everyday life of well-meaning white citizens. *Racism* is something whites define as bad action by others. The vocabulary allows us to talk about discrimination and oppression, but it hides the mechanism that makes that oppression possible and efficient. It also hides the existence of specific, identifiable beneficiaries of oppression, who are not always the actual perpetrators of discrimination. The use of the language of –Isms, or any focus on discrimination, masks the privileging that is created by these systems of power.

Thus, the very vocabulary that we use to talk about discrimination obfuscates these power systems and the privilege that is their natural companion. To remedy discrimination effectively we must make the power systems and privileges they create visible and part of the discourse. To move toward a unified theory of the dynamics of subordination, we have to find a way to talk about privilege. When we discuss race, sex, and sexual orientation, each needs to be described as a power system that creates privileges in some people as well as disadvantages in others. Most of the literature has focused on disadvantage or discrimination, ignoring the element of privilege. To really talk about these issues, privilege must be made visible.

What Is Privilege?

A Merriam-Webster electronic dictionary defines privilege as "a right granted as an advantage or favor." It is true that the holder of a privilege might believe she or he had a right to it, if you tried to take it away. But a right suggests the notion of a deserved entitlement; a privilege is not a right.

The *American Heritage Dictionary of the English Language* (1978) defines privilege as "a special advantage, immunity, permission, right, or benefit granted to or enjoyed by an individual, class, or caste." The word is derived from the Latin *privilegium,* a law affecting an individual, *privus* meaning "single or individual" and *lex* meaning "law."

This definition includes the important root of the word *privilege* in law. The legal, systemic nature of the term has become lost in its modern meaning. And it is the systemic nature of these power systems that we must begin to examine.

What, then, is privilege? We all recognize its most blatant forms. "Men only admitted to this club." "We won't allow African-Americans into that school." Blatant exercises of privilege certainly exist, but they are not what most people will say belongs as part of our way of life. They are also only the tip of the iceberg in examining privilege.

When we look at privilege, we see several elements. First, the characteristics of the privileged group define the societal norm, often benefiting those in the privileged group. Second, privileged group members can rely on their privilege and avoid objecting to oppression. Both conflicting privilege with the societal norm and the implicit choice to ignore oppression mean that privilege is rarely seen by the holder of the privilege.

The Normalization of Privilege

Examining privilege reveals that the characteristics and attributes of those who are privileged group members are described as societal norms—as the way things are and as what is normal in society.[7] This normalization of privilege means that members of society are judged, and succeed or fail, measured against the characteristics that are held by those privileged. The privileged characteristic comes to define the norm. Those who stand outside are the aberrant, or "alternative."

For example, a thirteen-year-old girl who aspires to be a major-league ball player can have only a low expectation of achieving that goal, no matter how superior a batter and fielder she is. Maleness is the foremost "qualification" of major league baseball players. Similarly, couples who are legally permitted to marry are heterosexual. A gay or lesbian couple, prepared to make a life commitment, cannot cross the threshold of qualification to be married.

I had an example of being outside the norm when I was called to jury service. Jurors are expected to serve until 5 P.M. During that year, my family's life was set up so that I picked up my children after school at 2:40 P.M., and made sure that they got to various activities. If courtroom life were designed to privilege my needs, then there would be an afternoon recess to honor children. But in this culture children's lives, and the lives of their caretakers, are the alternative or other and we must conform to the norm.

Even as these child care needs were outside the norm, I was privileged economically to be able to meet my children's needs. My conduct would be described as mothering, not as privilege. My ability to pick them up and be present in their after-school lives was a benefit of my association with privilege.

Members of the privileged group gain many benefits by their affiliation with the dominant side of the power system. This affiliation with power is not identified as such. Often it may be transformed into and presented as individual merit. For example, legacy admissions at elite colleges and professional schools are perceived to be merit-based when this process of identification with power and transmutation into qualifications occurs. Achievements by members of the privileged group are viewed as meritorious and the result of individual effort, rather than as privileged.

Many feminist theorists have described the male tilt to normative standards in law, including the gendered nature of legal reasoning,[8] the male bias inherent in the reasonable person standard,[9] and the gender bias in classrooms.[10] Looking more broadly at male privilege in society reveals that definitions based on male models delineate many societal norms. As Catharine MacKinnon has observed,

> Men's physiology defines most sports, their health needs largely define insurance coverage, their socially designed biographies define workplace expectations and successful career patterns, their perspectives and concerns define quality in scholarship, their experiences and obsessions define merit, their military service defines citizenship, their presence defines family, their inability to get along with each other—their wars and rulerships—defines history, their image defines god, and their genitals define sex.[11]

Male privilege thus defines many vital aspects of American culture from a male point of view. The maleness of that view becomes masked as that view is generalized as the societal norm, the measure for us all. The use of "he" as a generic pronoun stated to include all people, but making women in a room invisible when it is used, is seen as a norm. But a generic "she" is not permitted, and many people become upset when women try to use it. This emotion is not about the grammatically correct use of English, but about the challenge to the system of male privilege, veiled as the norm of using "he."

Choosing Whether to Struggle against Oppression

Members of privileged groups experience the comfort of opting out of struggles against oppression if they choose; this is another characteristic of privilege. Often this privilege may be exercised by silence. At the same time that I was the outsider in jury service, I was also a privileged insider. During voir dire, each prospective juror was asked to introduce herself or himself. The plaintiff's and defendant's attorneys then asked supplementary questions. I watched the defense attorney, during voir dire, ask each Asian-looking male prospective juror if he spoke English. No one else was asked. The judge did nothing. The Asian-American man sitting next to me smiled and flinched as he was asked the question. I wondered how many times in his life he had been made to answer questions such as that one. I considered beginning my own questioning by saying, "I'm Stephanie Wildman, I'm a professor of law, and yes, I speak English." I wanted to focus attention on the subordinating conduct of the attorney, but I did not. I exercised my white privilege by my silence. I exercised my privilege to opt out of engagement, even though this choice may not always be consciously made by someone with privilege.

Depending on the number of privileges someone has, she or he may experience the power of choosing the types of struggles in which to engage. Even this choice may be masked as an identification with oppression, thereby making the privilege that enables the choice invisible. This privilege advantage in societal relationships benefits the holder of privilege, who may receive deference, special knowledge, or a higher comfort level to guide societal interaction. Privilege is not visible to its holder; it is merely there, a part of the world, a way of life, simply the way things are. Others have a *lack*, an absence, a deficiency.

Systems of Privilege

In spite of the common characteristics of normativeness, ability to choose whether to object to the power system, and invisibility that different privileges share, the form of privilege may vary based on the type of power relationship that produces it. Within each power system, privilege manifests itself and operates in a manner shaped by the power relationship from which it results. White privilege derives from the power system of white supremacy.[12] Male privilege[13] and heterosexual privilege result from the gender hierarchy.[14]

Examining white privilege, Peggy McIntosh has found it "an elusive and fugitive subject," and that as a white person who benefits from the privileges, "[t]he pressure to avoid it is great."[15] She defines white privilege as an invisible package of unearned assets which [she] can count on cashing in each day, but about which [she] was "meant" to remain oblivious.[16] White privilege is like an invisible weightless knapsack of special provisions, assurance, tools, maps, guides, codebooks, passports, visas, clothes, compass, emergency gear, and blank checks.

McIntosh identified forty-six conditions available to her as a white person that her African American co-workers, friends, and acquaintances could not count on.[17] Some of these include: being told that people of her color made American heritage or civilization what it is; not needing to educate her children to be aware of systemic racism for their own daily protection; and never being asked to speak for all people of her racial group.

Privilege also exists based on sexual orientation. Society presumes heterosexuality, generally constituting gay and lesbian relations as invisible.[18] Professor Marc Fajer describes what he calls three societal preunderstandings about gay men and lesbians: the sex-as-lifestyle assumption, the cross-gender assumption, and the idea that gay issues are inappropriate for public discussion.

According to Fajer, the sex-as-lifestyle assumption means that there is a "common non-gay belief that gay people experience sexual activity differently from non-gays" in a way that is "all-encompassing, obsessive and completely divorced from love, long-term relationships, and family structure."[19] As to the cross-gender assumption, Fajer explains that many nongay people believe that gay men and lesbians exhibit "behavior stereotypically associated with the other gender."[20] The idea that gay issues are inappropriate for public discussion has received prominent press coverage recently with the military's "don't ask, don't tell" policy.[21] Thus, even if being gay is acceptable, "talking about being gay is not," according to Fajer.[22] One professor I know has a picture of his lover of twenty years, who is also male, on his desk, along with a photo of their son. No one has ever said to him,"What a lovely family you have."

Fajer does not discuss these preunderstandings explicitly in terms of privilege. Nevertheless, he is describing aspects of the sexual orientation power system that allow heterosexuals to function in a world where these assumptions are not made about their sexuality. Not only are these assumptions not made about heterosexuals, but also their sexuality may be discussed, and even advertised, in public.

In spite of the pervasiveness of privilege, it is interesting that antidiscrimination practice and theory has generally not examined privilege and its role in perpetuating discrimination. One notable exception is the work of Kimberlé Crenshaw, who has explained using the examples of race and sex, "Race and sex . . . become significant only when they operate to explicitly *disadvantage* the victims; because the *privileging* of whiteness or maleness is implicit, it is generally not perceived at all."[23]

Antidiscrimination advocates focus only on one portion of the power system, the subordinated characteristic, rather than seeing the essential links among domination, subordination, and the resulting privilege.

Adrienne Davis has explained,

Domination, subordination, and privilege are like three heads of a hydra. Attacking the most visible heads, domination and subordination, trying bravely to chop them up into little pieces, will not kill the third head, privilege. Like a mythic multi-headed hydra, which will inevitably grow another head, if all heads are not slain, discrimination cannot be ended by focusing only on . . . subordination and domination.[24]

Subordination will grow back from the ignored head of privilege, yet the descriptive vocabulary and conceptualization of discrimination hinders our ability to see the hydrahead of privilege. This invisibility is serious because that which is not seen cannot be discussed or changed. Thus, to end subordination, one must first recognize privilege. Seeing privilege means articulating a new vocabulary and structure for anti-subordination theory. Only by visualizing this privilege and incorporating it into discourse can people of good faith combat discrimination.

Visualizing Privilege

For me, the struggle to visualize privilege most often has taken the form of the struggle to see my white privilege. Even as I write about this struggle, I fear that my own racism will make things worse, causing me to do more harm than good. Some readers may be shocked to see a white person contritely acknowledge that she is racist. I do not say this with pride. I simply believe that no matter how hard I work at not being racist, I still am. Because part of racism is systemic, I benefit from the privilege that I am struggling to see.

In an article I wrote with Trina Grillo, we chose to use the term racism/white supremacy to talk about racism.[25] We got this idea from Professor bell hooks who had written, "The word racism ceased to be the term which best expressed for me exploitation of black people and other people of color in this society and . . . I began to understand that the most useful term was white supremacy."[26]

Whites do not look at the world through a filter of racial awareness, even though whites are, of course, a race. The power to ignore race, when white is the race, is a privilege, a societal advantage. The term racism/white supremacy emphasizes the link between the privilege held by whites to ignore their own race and discriminatory racism.

As bell hooks explains, liberal whites do not see themselves as prejudiced or interested in domination through coercion, yet "they cannot recognize the ways their actions support and affirm the very structure of racist domination and oppression that they profess to wish to see eradicated" (hooks 1989, 113). The perpetuation of white supremacy is racist.

All whites are racist in this use of the term because we benefit from systemic white privilege. Generally whites think of racism as voluntary, intentional conduct, done by horrible others. Whites spend a lot of time trying to convince ourselves and each other that we are not racist. A big step would be for whites to admit that we are racist and then to consider what to do about it.[27]

I also work on not being sexist. This work is different from my work on my racism, because I am a woman and I experience gender subordination. But it is important to realize that even when we are not privileged by a particular power system, we are products of the culture that instills its attitudes in us. I have to make sure that I am calling on women students and listening to them as carefully as I listen to men.

While we work at seeing privilege, it is also important to remember that each of us is much more complex than simply our race and gender. Just as I have a race, which is white, and a gender, which is female, I have a sexual orientation (heterosexual) and a religious orientation (Jewish) and thin fingers and I'm a swimmer. The point is that I am, and all of us are, lots of things. Privilege can intersect with subordination or other systems of privilege as well.

Seeing privilege at the intersection is complicated by the fact that there is no purely privileged or unprivileged person. Most of us are privileged in some ways and not in others. A very poor person might have been the oldest child in the family and exercised power over his siblings. The wealthiest African-American woman, who could be a federal judge, might still have racial, sexist epithets hurled at her as she walks down the street. The presence of both the experience of privilege and the experience of subordination in different aspects of our lives causes the experiences to be blurred, further hiding the presence of privilege from our vocabulary and consciousness.

Often we focus on the experience of oppression and act from privilege to combat that oppression without consciously making that choice. An African-American woman professor may act from the privilege of power as a professor to overcome the subordination her white male students would otherwise seek to impose upon her. Or a white female professor may use the privilege of whiteness to define the community of her classroom, acting from the power of that privilege to minimize any gender disadvantage that her students would use to undermine her classroom control. Because the choice to act from privilege may be unconscious, the individual, for example, the white female professor, may see herself as a victim of gender discrimination, which she may in fact be. But she is unlikely to see herself as a participant in discrimination for utilizing her white privilege to create the classroom environment.

Intersectionality can help reveal privilege, especially when we remember that the intersection is multi-dimensional, including intersections of both subordination and privilege. Imagine intersections in three dimensions, where multiple lines intersect. From the center one can see in many different directions. Every individual exists at the center of these multiple intersections, where many strands meet, similar to a Koosh ball.™[28]

The Koosh ball is a popular children's toy. Although it is called a ball and that category leads one to imagine a firm, round surface used for catching and throwing, the Koosh ball is neither hard nor firm. Picture hundreds of rubber bands, tied in the center. Mentally cut the end of each band. The wriggling, unfirm mass in your hand is a Koosh ball, still usable for throwing and catching, but changing shape as it sails through the air or as the wind blows through its rubbery limbs when it is at rest. It is a dynamic ball. . . .

Societal efforts at categorization are dynamic in the same way as the Koosh ball is, changing, mutating, yet keeping a central mass. When society categorizes someone on the basis of race, as either white or of color, it picks up a strand of the Koosh, a piece of rubber band, and says, "See this strand, this is defining and central. It matters." And race might be a highly important strand, but looking at one strand does not really help anyone to see the shape of the whole ball or the whole person. Even naming the experience "race" veils its many facets because race may be a whole cluster of strands including color, culture, identification, and experience.

This tendency to label with categories obfuscates our vision of the whole Koosh ball, where multiple strands interrelate with each other. No individual really fits into any one category; rather everyone resides at the intersection of many categories. Categorical thinking makes it hard or impossible to conceptualize the complexity of an individual. The cultural push has long been to choose a category. Yet forcing a choice results in a hollow vision that cannot do justice.

Justice requires seeing the whole person in her or his social context, but the social contexts are complicated. Complex, difficult situations that are in reality subordinating cannot be adequately described using ordinary language, because that language masks privilege. Language masks privilege by making the bases of subordination, themselves, appear linguistically neutral, so that the cultural hierarchy implicit in words such as race, gender, and sexual orientation is banished from the language. Once the hierarchy is made visible, the problems remain no less complex, but it becomes possible to discuss them in a more revealing and useful fashion.

We are all Koosh balls consisting of many threads coming together. These threads are not all treated the same in our culture. Some of these categories have meanings that resonate and create other assumptions. In 1990s America, race is such a category. For example, I have a friend who is seventeen. She has blond hair and hazel eyes and pale skin. She identifies herself as Hispanic and Black and white, because that is her racial heritage. She is also smart and a swimmer. She was excitedly telling a school friend about her acceptance to UC San Diego, which had awarded her a merit scholarship. Her so-called friend said to her, "Yeah, but what race did you put?"

The use of that category, race, had the power to erase all her accomplishments, her late nights studying to get good grades, and her efforts at swim practice. The use of race in the conversation made her feel unworthy and somehow "less than." Her friend's highlighting of race, implying her non-whiteness, made her feel diminished, even though she is proud of her race.

Power categories such as race, shape our vision of the world and of ourselves. Most of us with white privilege lead pretty white lives. Consider our schools, shops, medical buildings, and neighborhoods. In most places we spend time, we are in white settings, unless we act affirmatively to seek a racially integrated environment.

Our universities are some of the few places where we have a real chance to participate in an integrated community, one that is truly diverse across these many power categories. Building a sense of community across these power categories is our real challenge. Institutions need to acknowledge this ongoing project of building a diverse community as part of the work of the institution. It is important to make this work visible, because it is a continuing process. One white law professor I know asked why she should continue working on racism when she had already spent eight hours, a whole weekend day, at a workshop, and no end to racism was in sight.

Power systems that interfere with building community have no quick fix, but building community needs to be our life—all of our lives. A white person can recede into privilege and not worry about racism whenever she or he chooses. People of color cannot. Men and heterosexuals can ignore the system of gender hierarchy, if they choose. Women and gay men cannot. . . .

Ensuring participation by everyone in the educational process means that we, as teachers and students, members of a community, have to think about how our remarks and comments in class are heard. This is basic politeness, not censorship. If we want a community to include all people within it, we will not talk about "Kikes" when we mean Jewish people or say "chicks" when referring to women. . . .

Also we need to notice who is talking in our classes and who is not. Notice who the professor is calling on, who is being affirmed, who is given longer chances, who is passed over quickly. When women students in my class are doing 10 percent of the talking and they are in fact 50 percent of the class, I have asked them to stay after class and talk about it. These invisible dynamics need to be named and brought out into the open.

My own teaching style is to hear from other people and to listen. The lecture format and the room arrangement grant me the power, privilege me. I understand that this is the art form, but we need to develop better ways to build classrooms. We need to rearrange furniture. And most important, we need to create better ways to communicate with each other for community building. No one is immune from the difficulty of this process. . . .

Share my hope that people of goodwill can change these power systems by looking at them in our own lives. The power of the feminist slogan of the 1970s "The personal is political" needs to be explored in new ways.

Notes

This essay has been abridged from an earlier form of a chapter that currently appears as Chapter 1 in *Privilege revealed: How invisible preference undermines America* (New York: New York University Press, 1996).

1. See Marilyn Frye, *The Politics of Reality: Essays in Feminist Theory* (1983), 19–34, discussing sex marking, sex announcing, and the necessity to determine gender.

2. Angela Harris and Marge Shultz, *"A(nother) Critique of Pure Reason": Toward Civic Virtue in Legal Education*, 45 *Stan. L. Rev.* 1773, 1796 (1993).

3. Anne Fausto-Sterling, "The Five Sexes: Why Male and Female Are Not Enough," *The Sciences*, March/April 1993, 20. (Thanks to Gregg Bryan for calling my attention to this article.) See also Frye, *The Politics of Reality*, 25.

4. Adrienne Rich, "Compulsory Heterosexuality and Lesbian Existence," in *Blood, Bread, and Poetry, Selected Prose 1979–1985* (1986).

5. See Stephanie M. Wildman and Becky Wildman-Tobriner, "Sex Roles Iced Popular Team?" *S.F. Chron.*, Feb. 25, 1994, A23.

6. Rich, "Compulsory Heterosexuality," 57: "Heterosexuality has been both forcibly and subliminally imposed on women."

7. Richard Delgado and Jean Stefancic, "Pornography and Harm to Women: 'No Empirical Evidence?'" 53 *Ohio St. L.J.* 1037 (1992), describing the "way things are." Because the norm or reality is perceived as including these benefits, the privileges are not visible.

8. See Lucinda M. Finley, "Breaking Women's Silence in Law: The Dilemma of the Gendered Nature of Legal Reasoning," 64 *Notre Dame L. Rev.* 886 (1989).

9. See Leslie Bender, "A Lawyer's Primer on Feminist Theory and Tort," 38 *J. Legal Educ.* 1 (1988).

10. See Taunya Banks, "Gender Bias in the Classroom," 38 *J. Legal Educ.* 137 (1988); Stephanie M. Wildman, "The Question of Silence: Techniques to Ensure Full Class Participation," 38 *J. Legal Educ.* 147 (1988).

11. Catharine A. MacKinnon, *Toward A Feminist Theory of The State* (1989), 224.

12. See Cheryl Harris, "Whiteness as Property," 106 *Harv. L. Rev.* 1709 (1993), describing the allocation of societal benefits based on white racial identity. See also Neil Gotanda, "A Critique of 'Our Constitution Is Color-Blind,'" 44 *Stan. L. Rev.* 1, 23–36 (1991), describing the contingent, socially constructed nature of racial categories.

13. See MacKinnon, *Feminist Theory*, regarding male privilege.

14. See Sylvia Law, "Homosexuality and the Social Meaning of Gender," 1988 *Wis. L. Rev.* 187, 197 (1988); Marc Fajer, "Can Two Real Men Eat Quiche Together? Storytelling, Gender-Role Stereotypes, and Legal Protection for Lesbians and Gay Men," 46 *U. Miami L. Rev.* 511, 617 (1992). Both articles describe heterosexism as a form of gender oppression. Yet describing heterosexual privilege as part of another system of oppression, i.e. gender, may ultimately contribute to the maintenance of heterosexism.

15. Peggy McIntosh, "Unpacking the Invisible Knapsack: White Privilege," *Creation Spirituality*, January/February 1992, 33. Martha Mahoney has also described aspects of white privilege in her "Whiteness and Women, In Practice and Theory: A Reply to Catharine MacKinnon," 5 *Yale J. Law & Feminism* 217 (1993).

16. McIntosh, "Unpacking," 33. The quotations around *meant* evidently refer in an unspoken way to the unwritten rules that surround the subject of white privilege.

17. Ibid., 34.

18. See Rich, "Compulsory Heterosexuality."

19. Fajer, "Real Men," 514.

20. Ibid., 515.

21. See, e. g., Michael R. Gordon, "Pentagon Spells Out Rules For Ousting Homosexuals; Rights Groups Vow a Fight," *N.Y. Times*, Dec. 23, 1993, A1.

22. Fajer, "Real Men," 515.

23. Kimberlé Crenshaw, "Demarginalizing the Intersection of Race and Sex: A Black Feminist Critique of Antidiscrimination Doctrine, Feminist Theory and Antiracist Politics," *Chicago Legal Issues Forum* 139, 151 (1989).

24. Adrienne D. Davis, *Toward A Post-essentialist Methodology or a Call to Countercategorical Practice* (1994) (unpublished manuscript on file with the author).

25. Trina Grillo and Stephanie M. Wildman, "Obscuring the Importance of Race: The Implication of Making Comparisons Between Racism and Sexism (or Other -Isms)," 1991 *Duke L.J.* 397.

26. bell hooks, "Overcoming White Supremacy: A Comment," in *Talking Back: Thinking Feminist, Thinking Black* 112 (1989).

27. See also Jerome McCristal Culp, Jr., "Water Buffalo and Diversity: Naming Names and Reclaiming the Racial Discourse," 26 *Conn. L. Rev.* 209 (1993), urging people to name racism as racism.

28. The image of the Koosh ball to describe the individual at the center of many intersections evolved during a working session between Adrienne Davis, Trina Grillo, and me. I believe that Trina Grillo uttered the words, "It's a Koosh ball." San Francisco, California, March, 1992. Koosh ball is a registered trademark of Oddzon Products, Inc., Campbell, CA.

Racism

Introduction by Ximena Zúñiga and Rosie Castañeda

> Now, more than ever, racial discrimination is not only about skin color and other physical characteristics associated with race, it is also about other aspects of our identity, such as ethnicity, national origin, language, accent, religion, and cultural customs. The challenge of America is to ensure that none of these factors continues to affect the quality of life choices so that we can finally treat each other with dignity and respect regardless of our differences.
>
> —The President's Initiative on Race, *The Advisory Board's Report to the President*, (1998, 35)

Many attempts have been made to end racial discrimination in the United States, but, as the quote above suggests, the problems of racism are far from being solved. The civil rights movement of the 1950s and 1960s led to the end of legal segregation and the passage of laws that guarantee equal access and fair treatment for all people. However, racial discrimination, prejudice, and inequality continue to be significant aspects of the U.S. experience. An important lesson learned in the last few decades has been that these problems are too deeply embedded in the history and culture of the United States to be eliminated simply by changing a law.

The rhetoric of "liberty and justice for all" has, until recently, diverted attention away from the fact that the United States was founded on the conquest, removal, and almost total annihilation of the indigenous peoples of North America, and that this nation was built by a constitutionally sanctioned slave system, and cheap labor brought from different shores and from "south of the border." The pattern of domination and economic exploitation that was established by the early colonizers and slaveholders continued throughout the nineteen century, first with the conquest of the Mexican southwest and later with the annexation of such territories as Puerto Rico, Guam, Alaska, and Hawaii. These legacies of genocide, slavery, conquest, and economic exploitation continue to shape the fabric of our social and cultural institutions and the lives of many Americans to this day.

Against the legacy of slavery and the "color line," the lives of African Americans continue to be impacted by subtle and overt forms of racism and racial discrimination in the occupational, educational, health care, police, and legal systems. Overt patterns of discrimination and exclusion are, for example, particularly acute in urban areas, where the loss of job opportunities has resulted in a dramatic decline of social networks and community institutions (Wilson 1997). Subtle manifestations of racism have been identified as barriers to success in corporate America because they hinder professional achievement and undermine self-confidence (Cose 1993).

Although American Indians and Alaskan Natives tribes have geographic land-based boundaries, like any other nation, the federal government continues to challenge indigenous sovereignty by tightly controlling who may qualify as Native Americans. As a result of these policies, indigenous tribes are losing membership, economic assets, and legal rights (Jaimes 1999). Despite their distinctive status, the indigenous people continue to suffer the consequences of racism disproportionately in relation to any other racial/ethnic minority. According to the President's Initiative on Race's findings, American Indians and Alaskan Natives have "the lowest family incomes, the lowest percentage of people ages twenty-five to thirty-four who receive a college degree, the highest unemployment rates, the highest percentage of people living below the poverty line, the highest accidental death rate, and the highest suicide rate" (1998, 39).

The history of Latinos in the United States is also complex. Many Latino families can trace their roots to what are now Arizona, California, Colorado, Nevada, New Mexico and Texas; others are recent immigrants. The impact of racial segregation continues to shape the lives of many Mexican American and Puerto Rican communities, as it did before the civil rights movement, negatively impacting their access to educational opportunities, neighborhoods that secure police and legal protection, or jobs that provide economic security and health insurance. Latinos are the second-largest minority group in the U.S., but as the fastest growing population they are expected to become the largest minority group by the year 2010 (Shinagawa and Jang 1998). The report from the President's Initiative on Race tell us that Latinos constitute close to "12 percent of the labor force, and current projections suggest that they will become almost 40 percent of new labor force entrants; it is estimated that 30.3 percent of Latinos lives in poverty, compared with 29.9 percent of Blacks, and 11.2 percent of whites as of 1990" (1998, 42).

As Takaki (1993) points out most people in the United States believe that Asian Pacific Americans are new to this country, but they have in fact been contributing to the shaping of this nation since the second half of the nineteenth century, despite immigration laws intended to exclude them. Discriminatory laws and informal sanctions during those early years limited the economic opportunities of Asian Pacific Americans, and relegated them to jobs as agricultural or factory work or owners of small businesses such as laundries, restaurants and grocery stores (President's Initiative on Race, 1998). In fact, these practices also limited their ability to become citizens, prohibiting them from owning land, and perpetuating their alien status. New immigrants from south east and central Asia continue to feel the legacy of discrimination against Asian Pacific Americans' largely because they continue to be treated and perceived as foreigners (Presidents' Initiative on Race, 44).

European Americans constitute a large and diverse segment of U.S. society. Although several European origin ethnic groups (e.g., the Irish, Eastern European Jews and Italians) confronted ethnic prejudice as well as racial discrimination during the nineteenth and early twentieth centuries, subsequent generations, particularly after the Second World War, have successfully integrated into legal, political, economic and cultural institutions. As these European ethnic groups "became white" they also benefited from "color-blind" public policies that have actually contributed to the reproduction of systemic inequalities based on race (Lipsitz 1998).

Despite the presence and participation of many different racial/ethnic groups in the history of United States, discussions about racism often have focused on the relationship between blacks and whites, even though other forms of racism were also being practiced (Marable 1995; Takaki 1993). The increased visibility of other groups targeted by racism has challenged people to understand and respond to racism in a more complex way in the post-civil rights era. Changing demographics have also heightened tensions among racially defined "minority" groups, as well as between these groups and the dominant white majority. One response to the changing dynamics of race and race relations has been the re-emergence of "a pan-ethnic phenomena among Asian Pacific Americans, Latinos/as and Native Americans and Alaskan Natives, reconstituting the US racial panorama in a multipolar (as opposed to the former, bipolar) direction" (Omi 1999, p. 18). Another response concerns the backlash against affirmative action, immigration policies, and bilingual education at the state and national levels. Still another set of responses has been a call for a dialogue about race at a national level (The President's Initiative on Race, 1998), and for multi-racial/multi-ethnic organizing at the grassroots level (Anner 1996; Marable 1995). This section focuses on some of these and other forms of contemporary racism and the ways that it is experienced, practiced, and challenged.

In order to understand racism we have to begin by discussing the different ways the concept of "race" has been used, and continues to be understood, in the United States. Quotation marks were used in the previous sentence to alert the reader to the fact that race as a biological category marked by physical differences is not supported by any scientific evidence (Spickard 1992). Many scientists today reject the idea of race as a useful biological concept to classify human beings because it does not correspond with the reality and complexities of human biological variation (Smedley 1999). This argument, though valid, is not helpful to those who continue to grapple with everyday social realities of race in our society. In this respect, we follow Smedley's position that race does indeed exist as a social reality but not "as something biological, tangible, and existing in the outside world that has to be discovered, described and *defined, but as a cultural creation, a product of human invention* (1999, 6; emphasis added).

Even though the construct "race" was used to codify physical and cultural differences by the first waves of English colonists during the early sixteenth century, it only emerged as a worldview, and as an ideology utilized to justify white dominance, during the European colonial expansion to Africa, Asia, and the New World and the creation of slavery as a social system based on race (Smedley 1999). The extent to which the concept of race has changed over time demonstrates that earlier categories based on race (e.g., Negroid, Caucasoid, and Mongoloid) have primarily served to perpetuate or justify systems of privilege and power. For instance, in the United States the "one-drop rule" was established during slavery in order to ensure that anyone who had a remote relative of African descent, even if this heritage was not visible, could be kept in slavery (Spickard 1992). On the other hand, rigid federal standards for who could be considered Native American, based upon "blood quantum" rules have been used to eliminate most "mixed-bloods" from tribal rolls (Jaimes 1999). In both cases the goal was to perpetuate a system of advantages that benefited the white power structure.

It is important to try to disentangle the concept of race from that of ethnicity, even though the two terms are often used interchangeably. Ethnicity is generally considered "the bearer of culture" (Dalton 1995, 107) and refers to "all those traditions, activities, beliefs, and practices that pertain to a particular group of people who see themselves and are seen by others as having distinct cultural features, a separate history, and a specific socio-cultural identity" (Smedley 1999, 31). Add to the elements in this definition of ethnicity, further elements of physical and biological differences that are popularly taken as markers for other less visible differences (for example, of emotional expression, skills, or value orientation) and we can see how unexamined notions of race interact with ethnicity and culture. These concepts evolve to meet changing social and historical conditions and interact with changes in the social environment. For example, changes in the United States census for 2000 enable respondents to claim more than one racial category, whereas earlier census forms required respondents to make an either/or decision about their racial and ethnic heritage. Clearly there is considerable room for progress as we attempt to acknowledge the complexities of racial and ethnic legacies that characterize most people in the United States.

Readings in This Section

In the essay that opens this section, Ronald Takaki reviews the historical factors through which the concept of race as social construction has been utilized to create a structure of domination that has set Native Americans, African Americans, Asian Americans and Chicanos and other Latino groups apart from European immigrant groups. This approach to a historical context for the establishment of racial distinctions draws from the approach outlined by Michael Omi and Howard Winant (1986) in *Racial Formation in the United States: From the 1960's to the 1980's.* They describe racial formation as a socio-historical construct whereby racial categories and the meaning of race are given concrete expression by specific social relations and historical contexts in which they are embedded. There are at least two implications to this socio-political and historical context. First, racial meanings and categories are not based on biological differences but rather on evolving social constructions. Second, it is only possible to understand the meaning of "race" in the context of specific relations between groups. For instance, the meanings associated with "whiteness" have evolved over time. Some immigrant groups of European ancestry such as the Irish and Eastern European Jews were, for example, not considered white by the dominant Anglo-Protestant power structure of the nineteenth century. In fact, Takaki argues, these two ethnic groups of European ancestry were "racialized" and discriminated against, on the basis of physical, cultural, religious and linguistic differences even though they look "white" because of the particular social and economic historical context.

In the second reading of this section, Michael Omi discusses the evolution of racial categories in an U.S. context, particularly as they are reflective of changing federal standards for racial classification. In this article, Omi establishes that census categories have been assigned in response to specific political and social agendas. For, example the first census distinguished "the enfranchised" (those who could vote, namely white male property owners) from the general population. Later, the practice of slavery motivated changes in racial categorization, including the division of blacks into free and slaved populations. More recently, current census categories (American Indian, Eskimo, and Aleut, Asian and Pacific Islander, Black, Hispanic and White) were assigned in response to anti-discriminatory and equal opportunity laws of the 1960s and 1970s. As Omi observes, one of the most striking and problematic aspects of the current set of racial classification utilized by the Census Bureau to sort social groups in the U.S. is that some of the categories are based on "racial" (outwardly physical) differences, some on geographic origin, and some, such as "Hispanics," on cultural or ethnic origins regardless of racial distinctions. As Maria P. P. Root states (see chapter 17), the existing framework is being seriously questioned as a result of shifting meanings of racial and ethnic identification, including the inadequacy of the current categorizations to classify people of multiracial heritage

Beverly Daniel Tatum's essay in this section defines the concept of racism. Tatum draws a clear distinction between prejudice (as a pre-conceived judgement or opinion, often based on limited or misinformation) and racism (as a system of advantages based on racial categorizations). This definition highlights the systemic origin of social inequalities based on racial differences. Thus, racism cannot be adequately understood only as an expression of *individual* prejudice or individual acts of bigotry, but as a *system* of advantages that works to benefit whites as a social group in the United States. Furthermore, this definition allows us to see that racism, like other forms of oppression, "is not only a personal ideology based on racial prejudice, but a system involving cultural messages and institutional practices as well as the beliefs and actions of individuals."

The next two selections present contemporary manifestations of racism in U.S. society. Joe Feagin's article provides a rich description of anti-black discrimination in public places such as restaurants and stores, or when blacks are harassed as pedestrians or drivers. He interviews middle class African Americans to shed light on the dynamics of race in public settings, and the personal costs of coping with persisting racial discrimination. The interviews indicate that middle class African Americans, despite their class status, remain vulnerable targets in public spaces. Marc Cooper, on the other hand, presents a dramatic account of the utilization of immigrant labor (often undocumented) in the meatpacking industry in the Midwest, and the social and economic structures in place for creating a new immigrant underclass. He describes the lives of impoverished workers of Mexican and Laotian background who have worked long hours under unsafe conditions largely because their immigration status, prevents them from having labor protection.

One of the lessons of the Los Angeles riots after the Rodney King trial was the recognition that the United States has become a multi-racial/multi-ethnic society and that race and racism cannot be anymore discussed or addressed in strictly binary terms of white and black. The next selection, by Elizabeth Martinez, argues for a shifting paradigm of race that goes beyond black and white. She provides an overview of U.S. race/ethnic relations from the standpoint of the conquered people of the South West, and the new waves of Latino and Asian Pacific immigrant groups, particularly in the context of California. In her view, these groups challenge us to think more deeply and more complexly about race and race relations in the U.S.

Next we have selected four personal narratives that reflect the impact of race and racism on men and women of different racial/ethnic backgrounds. Cooper Thompson, a white male anti-racist educator, raises a number of controversial questions that in his experience tend to surface, either overtly or covertly, in talking about race and racism with other white men in social gatherings, classrooms, or in the workplace. John Brown Childs, a Native American and African American man traces his multi-racial heritage both to Madagascar and to the Blue Hills of the Massachuseuck Native American nation by using historical material and his own personal recollections growing up in Roxbury, Massachusetts. He highlights the values of remaining connected to "the place between two currents," in order to emerge as a full person. From a different perspective, Richard Rodriguez's "Complexion" explores the dynamics of dark and light complexion within his family of origin and society as he was growing up, and establishes the important connection between complexion and class status. He writes that "what was most intrigued me was the connection between dark skin and poverty. Because I heard my mother so often speak about the relegation of dark people to menial labor, I considered the great victims of racism to be those who were poor and forced to do menial work." C. Allyson Lee investigates "the more concealed form of oppression," internalized racism, by chronicling her own development as an Asian lesbian who grew up in a predominantly white neighborhood. Lee describes fear and hatred of her race growing up, spurred by the need to avoid being stereotyped by whites as "noisy, slanty-eyed rice gobblers." Eventually Lee is able to differentiate herself from her traditionalist father and explores the possibility of incorporating parts of her Chinese heritage into her own individualized experience.

It is important to us as editors of this section to highlight further steps that people can take to challenge the consequences of racism and to bridge racial and ethnic divisions. Within this section, we include selections that either highlight some concrete action steps or introduce new ways of thinking and acting about multi-racial identity or language discrimination. Maria P. P. Root's "Bill of Rights for Racially Mixed People," problematizes the construction of race that has dominated the racial classification system in the U.S. which has oppressed, fragmented, and marginalized the experiences of multi-racial individuals. She proposes a "bill of rights" for bi-racial and multi-racial people. People from the dominant groups (people of European heritage) have identified common barriers in combating racism such as feelings of guilt, remorse, fear, shame, and resentment. We have included Amy Edgington's, "Moving Beyond White Guilt" in order to explore these feelings. Edgington recommends a number of strategies to assist white men and women to break away from guilt and shame: seeking information, taking concrete actions, conversing with other white people, and taking collective responsibility. Next, Nancy Schniedewind and Ellen Davidson's article on "Linguicism" offers a concise definition of discrimination based on language, briefly discussing the importance of the mother tongue for bilingual families and children, the issue of second language acquisition, and the potential benefit in educational policies and practices that support second language for all students. Finally, we include an excerpt from Clyde W. Ford's "Develop Cross-Cultural Communication Skills " to suggest a concrete set of steps that improve communication across racial and ethnic groups. Ford's suggestions are useful in the diverse classroom as well as in multi-racial/ethnic dialogues and coalitions.

A number of further issues are represented by the Further Resources listings on the back of this volume. These include issues of language discrimination, debates over affirmative action, immigration, bi-racial and bi-cultural identities, and inter-racial relationships. The intersection of race with class and economic inequalities appears in section 7 on "Classism."

References

Anner, J. 1996. *Beyond Identity Politics: Emerging Social Justice Movements in Communities of Color.* Boston: South End Press.

Childs B. J. 1999. *Transcommunality: From the Politics of Conversion to the Ethics of Respect.* Santa Cruz, CA: Unpublished manuscript.

Cose. E. 1993. *The Rage of the Privileged Class.* New York: Harper Collins.

Dalton, H. L. 1995. *Racial Healing: Confronting the Fear between Blacks and Whites.* New York: Double Day.

Jaimes, M.A. 1992. *The State of Native America.* Boston: South End Press.

Lipsitz, G. 1998. *The Possessive Investment in Whiteness.* Philadelphia: Temple University Press.

Marable, M. 1995. *Beyond Black and White.* London: Verso.

Omi, M. and H. Winant. 1986. *Racial Formation in the United States.* New York: Routledge.

The President's Initiative on Race. 1998. *One America in the 21st. Century.* The Advisory Board's Report to the President. Washington, D.C: G. P.O

Smedley, A. (1999). *Race in North America: Origin and Evolution of a Worldview.* 2nd. ed. Boulder, Colo.: Westview Press.

Spickard, P. (1992). "The Illogic of American Racial Categories." In *Racially Mixed People in America,* M. Root, ed. Newbury, Calif.: Sage.

Shinagawa, L. H. and Jang, M. 1998. *Atlas of American Diversity.* Walnut Creek, CA: Altamira Press.

Takaki, R. 1993. *A Different Mirror: A History of Multicultural America.* Boston: Back Bay Books.

Tatum, B. D. 1997. *"Why Are All the Black Kids Sitting Together in the Cafeteria?" and Other Conversations about Race.* New York: Basic Books.

Wilson, W. J. 1996. *When Job Disappears: The World of the New Urban Poor.* New York: Alfred A. Knopf.

Contexts

7

A Different Mirror

Ronald Takaki

I had flown from San Francisco to Norfolk, Virginia, and was riding in a taxi to my hotel to attend a conference on multiculturalism. Hundreds of educators from across the country were meeting to discuss the need for greater cultural diversity in the curriculum. My driver and I chatted about the weather and the tourists. The sky was cloudy, and Virginia Beach was twenty minutes away. The rearview mirror reflected a white man in his forties. "How long have you been in this country?" he asked. "All my life," I replied, wincing. "I was born in the United States." With a strong southern drawl, he remarked: "I was wondering because your English is excellent!" Then, as I had many times before, I explained: "My grandfather came here from Japan in the 1880s. My family has been here, in America, for over a hundred years." He glanced at me in the mirror. Somehow I did not look "American" to him; my eyes and complexion looked foreign. . . .

Questions like the one my taxi driver asked me are always jarring, but I can understand why he could not see me as American. He had a narrow but widely shared sense of the past—a history that has viewed American as European in ancestry. "Race," Toni Morrison explained, has functioned as a "metaphor" necessary to the "construction of Americanness": in the creation of our national identity, "American" has been defined as "white."[1] . . .

But how should "we" be defined? Who are the people "stuck here" in America? One of the lessons of the Los Angeles explosion is the recognition of the fact that we are a multiracial society and that race can no longer be defined in the binary terms of white and black. "We" will have to include Hispanics and Asians. While blacks currently constitute 13 percent of the Los Angeles population, Hispanics represent 40 percent. The 1990 census revealed that South Central Los Angeles, which was predominantly black in 1965 when the Watts rebellion occurred, is now 45 percent Hispanic. A majority of the first 5,438 people arrested were Hispanic, while 37 percent were black. Of the fifty-eight people who died in the riot, more than a third were Hispanic, and about 40 percent of the businesses destroyed were Hispanic-owned. Most of the other shops and stores were Korean-owned. The dreams of many Korean immigrants went up in smoke during the riot: two thousand Korean-owned businesses were damaged or demolished, totaling about $400 million in losses. There is evidence indicating they were targeted. "After all," explained a black gang member, "we didn't burn our community, just *their* stores."[2] . . .

African Americans have been the central minority throughout our country's history. They were initially brought here on a slave ship in 1619. Actually, these first twenty Africans might not have been slaves; rather, like most of the white laborers, they were probably indentured servants. The transformation of Africans into slaves is the story of the "hidden" origins of slavery. How and when was it decided to institute a system of bonded black labor? What happened, while freighted with racial significance, was actually conditioned by class conflicts within white society. Once established, the "peculiar institution" would have consequences for centuries to come. During the nineteenth century, the political storm over slavery almost destroyed the nation. Since the Civil War and emancipation, race has continued to be largely defined in relation to African Americans — segregation, civil rights, the underclass, and affirmative action. Constituting the largest minority group in our society, they have been at the cutting edge of the Civil Rights Movement. Indeed, their struggle has been a constant reminder of America's moral vision as a country committed to the principle of liberty. Martin Luther King clearly understood this truth when he wrote from a jail cell: "We will reach the goal of freedom in Birmingham and all over the nation, because the goal of America is freedom. Abused and scorned though we may be, our destiny is tied up with America's destiny."[3]

Asian Americans have been here for over one hundred and fifty years, before many European immigrant groups. But as "strangers" coming from a "different shore," they have been stereotyped as "heathen," exotic, and unassimilable. Seeking "Gold Mountain," the Chinese arrived first, and what happened to them influenced the reception of the Japanese, Koreans, Filipinos, and Asian Indians as well as the Southeast Asian refugees like the Vietnamese and the Hmong. The 1882 Chinese Exclusion Act was the first law that prohibited the entry of immigrants on the basis of nationality. The Chinese condemned this restriction as racist and tyrannical. "They call us 'Chink,' " complained a Chinese immigrant, cursing the "white demons." "They think we no good! America cuts us off. No more come now, too bad!" This precedent later provided a basis for the restriction of European immigrant groups such as Italians, Russians, Poles, and Greeks.

The Japanese painfully discovered that their accomplishments in America did not lead to acceptance, for during World War II, unlike Italian Americans and German Americans, they were placed in internment camps. Two-thirds of them were citizens by birth. "How could I as a 6-month-old child born in this country," asked Congressman Robert Matsui years later, "be declared by my own Government to be an enemy alien?" Today, Asian Americans represent the fastest-growing ethnic group. They have also become the focus of much mass media attention as "the Model Minority" not only for blacks and Chicanos, but also for whites on welfare and even middle-class whites experiencing economic difficulties.[4]

Chicanos represent the largest group among the Hispanic population, which is projected to outnumber African Americans. They have been in the United States for a long time, initially incorporated by the war against Mexico. The treaty had moved the border between the two countries, and the people of "occupied" Mexico suddenly found themselves "foreigners" in their "native land." As historian Albert Camarillo pointed out, the Chicano past is an integral part of America's westward expansion, also known as "manifest destiny." But while the early Chicanos were a colonized people, most of them today have immigrant roots. Many began the trek to El Norte in the early twentieth century. "As I had heard a lot about the United States," Jesus Garza recalled, "it was my dream to come here." "We came to know families from Chihuahua, Sonora, Jalisco, and Durango," stated Ernesto Galarza. "Like ourselves, our Mexican neighbors had come this far moving step by step, working and waiting, as if they were feeling their way up a ladder." Nevertheless, the Chicano experience has been unique, for most of them have lived close to their homeland—a proximity that has helped reinforce their language, identity, and culture. This migration to El Norte has continued to the present. Los Angeles has more people of Mexican origin than any other city in the world except Mexico City. A mostly mestizo people of Indian as well as African and Spanish ancestries, Chicanos currently represent the largest minority group in the Southwest, where they have been visibly transforming culture and society.[5]

The Irish came here in greater numbers than most immigrant groups. Their history has been tied to America's past from the very beginning. Ireland represented the earliest English frontier: the conquest of Ireland occurred before the colonization of America, and the Irish were the first group that the English called "savages." In this context, the Irish past foreshadowed the Indian future. During the nineteenth century, the Irish, like the Chinese, were victims of British colonialism. While the Chinese fled from the ravages of the Opium Wars, the Irish were pushed from their homeland by "English tyranny." Here they became construction workers and factory operatives as well as the "maids" of America. Representing a Catholic group seeking to settle in a fiercely Protestant society, the Irish immigrants were targets of American nativist hostility. They were also what historian Lawrence J. McCaffrey called "the pioneers of the American urban ghetto," "previewing" experiences that would later be shared by the Italians, Poles, and other groups from southern and eastern Europe. Furthermore, they offer contrast to the immigrants from Asia. The Irish came about the same time as the Chinese, but they had a distinct advantage: the Naturalization Law of 1790 had reserved citizenship for "whites" only. Their compatible complexion allowed them to assimilate by blending into American society. In making their journey successfully into the mainstream, however, these immigrants from Erin pursued an Irish "ethnic" strategy: they promoted "Irish" solidarity in order to gain political power and also to dominate the skilled blue-collar occupations, often at the expense of the Chinese and blacks.[6]

Fleeing pogroms and religious persecution in Russia, the Jews were driven from what John Cuddihy described as the "Middle Ages into the Anglo-American world of the *goyim* 'beyond the pale.'" To them, America represented the Promised Land. This vision led

Jews to struggle not only for themselves but also for other oppressed groups, especially blacks. After the 1917 East St. Louis race riot, the Yiddish *Forward* of New York compared this anti-black violence to a 1903 pogrom in Russia: "Kishinev and St. Louis—the same soil, the same people." Jews cheered when Jackie Robinson broke into the Brooklyn Dodgers in 1947. "He was adopted as the surrogate hero by many of us growing up at the time," recalled Jack Greenberg of the NAACP Legal Defense Fund. "He was the way we saw ourselves triumphing against the forces of bigotry and ignorance." Jews stood shoulder to shoulder with blacks in the Civil Rights Movement: two-thirds of the white volunteers who went south during the 1964 Freedom Summer were Jewish. Today Jews are considered a highly successful "ethnic" group. How did they make such great socioeconomic strides? This question is often reframed by neoconservative intellectuals like Irving Kristol and Nathan Glazer to read: if Jewish immigrants were able to lift themselves from poverty into the mainstream through self-help and education without welfare and affirmative action, why can't blacks? But what this thinking overlooks is the unique history of Jewish immigrants, especially the initial advantages of many of them as literate and skilled. Moreover, it minimizes the virulence of racial prejudice rooted in American slavery.[7]

Indians represent a critical contrast, for theirs was not an immigrant experience. The Wampanoags were on the shore as the first English strangers arrived in what would be called "New England." The encounters between Indians and whites not only shaped the course of race relations, but also influenced the very culture and identity of the general society. The architect of Indian removal, President Andrew Jackson told Congress: "Our conduct toward these people is deeply interesting to the national character." Frederick Jackson Turner understood the meaning of this observation when he identified the frontier as our transforming crucible. At first, the European newcomers had to wear Indian moccasins and shout the war cry. "Little by little," as they subdued the wilderness, the pioneers became "a new product" that was "American." But Indians have had a different view of this entire process. "The white man," Luther Standing Bear of the Sioux explained, "does not understand the Indian for the reason that he does not understand America." Continuing to be "troubled with primitive fears," he has "in his consciousness the perils of this frontier continent. . . . The man from Europe is still a foreigner and an alien. And he still hates the man who questioned his path across the continent." Indians questioned what Jackson and Turner trumpeted as "progress." For them, the frontier had a different "significance": their history was how the West was lost. But their story has also been one of resistance. As Vine Deloria declared, "Custer died for your sins."[8]

By looking at these groups from a multicultural perspective, we can comparatively analyze their experiences in order to develop an understanding of their differences and similarities. Race, we will see, has been a social construction that has historically set apart racial minorities from European immigrant groups. Contrary to the notions of scholars like Nathan Glazer and Thomas Sowell, race in America has not been the same as ethnicity. A broad comparative focus also allows us to see how the varied experiences of different racial and ethnic groups occurred within shared contexts.

During the nineteenth century, for example, the Market Revolution employed Irish immigrant laborers in New England factories as it expanded cotton fields worked by enslaved blacks across Indian lands toward Mexico. Like blacks, the Irish newcomers were stereotyped as "savages," ruled by passions rather than "civilized" virtues such as self-control and hard work. The Irish saw themselves as the "slaves" of British oppressors, and during a visit to Ireland in the 1840s, Frederick Douglass found that the "wailing notes" of the Irish ballads reminded him of the "wild notes" of slave songs. The United States annexation of California, while incorporating Mexicans, led to trade with Asia and the migration of "strangers" from Pacific shores. In 1870, Chinese immigrant labor-ers were transported to Massachusetts as scabs to break an Irish immigrant strike; in response, the Irish recognized the need for interethnic working-class solidarity and tried to organize a Chinese lodge of the Knights of St. Crispin. After the Civil War, Mississippi planters recruited Chinese immigrants to discipline the newly freed blacks. During the debate over an immigration exclusion bill in 1882, a senator asked: If Indians could be located on reservations, why not the Chinese?[9]

Other instances of our connectedness abound. In 1903, Mexican and Japanese farm laborers went on strike together in California: their union officers had names like Yamaguchi and Lizarras, and strike meetings were conducted in Japanese and Spanish. The Mexican strikers declared that they were standing in solidarity with their "Japanese brothers" because the two groups had toiled together in the fields and were now fighting together for a fair wage. Speaking in impassioned Yiddish during the 1909 "uprising of twenty thousand" strikers in New York, the charismatic Clara Lemlich compared the abuse of Jewish female garment workers to the experience of blacks: "[The bosses] yell at the girls and 'call them down' even worse than I imagine the Negro slaves were in the South." During the 1920s, elite universities like Harvard worried about the increasing numbers of Jewish students, and new admissions criteria were instituted to curb their enrollment. Jewish students were scorned for their studiousness and criticized for their "clannishness." Recently, Asian-American students have been the targets of similar complaints: they have been called "nerds" and told there are "too many" of them on campus.[10]

Indians were already here, while blacks were forcibly transported to America, and Mexicans were initially enclosed by America's expanding border. The other groups came here as immigrants: for them, America represented liminality—a new world where they could pursue extravagant urges and do things they had thought beyond their capabili-ties. Like the land itself, they found themselves "betwixt and between all fixed points of classification." No longer fastened as fiercely to their old countries, they felt a stirring to become new people in a society still being defined and formed.[11] . . .

Through their stories, the people who have lived America's history can help all of us, including my taxi driver, understand that Americans originated from many shores, and that all of us are entitled to dignity. "I hope this survey do a lot of good for Chinese peo-ple," an immigrant told an interviewer from Stanford University in the 1920s. "Make American people realize that Chinese people are humans. I think very few American peo-ple really know anything about Chinese." But the remembering is also for the sake of the children. "This story is dedicated to the descendants of Lazar and Goldie Glauberman," Jewish immigrant Minnie Miller wrote in her autobiography. "My history is bound up in their history and the generations that follow should know where they came from to know better who they are." Similarly, Tomo Shoji, an elderly Nisei woman, urged Asian Americans to learn more about their roots: "We got such good, fantastic stories to tell. All our stories are different." Seeking to know how they fit into America, many young people have become listeners; they are eager to learn about the hardships and humilia-tions experienced by their parents and grandparents. They want to hear their stories, unwilling to remain ignorant or ashamed of their identity and past.[12] . . .

Through their narratives about their lives and circumstances, the people of America's diverse groups are able to see themselves and each other in our common past. They cele-brate what Ishmael Reed has described as a society "unique" in the world because "the world is here" — a place "where the cultures of the world crisscross." Much of America's past, they point out, has been riddled with racism. At the same time, these people offer hope, affirming the struggle for equality as a central theme in our country's history. At its conception, our nation was dedicated to the proposition of equality. What has given concreteness to this powerful national principle has been our coming together in the creation of a new society. "Stuck here" together, workers of different backgrounds have attempted to get along with each other.

> *People harvesting*
> *Work together unaware*
> *Of racial problems,*

wrote a Japanese immigrant describing a lesson learned by Mexican and Asian farm laborers in California.[13] . . .

Notes

1. Toni Morrison, *Playing in the Dark: Whiteness in the Literary Imagination* (Cambridge, Mass., 1992), 47.
2. Tim Rutten, "A New Kind of Riot," *New York Review of Books*, June 11, 1992, 52–53; Maria Newman, "Riots Bring Attention to Growing Hispanic Presence in South-Central Area," *New York Times*, May 11, 1992, A10; Mike Davis, "In L.A. Burning All Illusions," *The Nation*, June 1, 1992, 744–45; Jack Viets and Peter Fimrite, "S.F. Mayor Visits Riot-Torn Area to Buoy Businesses," *San Francisco Chronicle*, May 6, 1992, A6.
3. Abraham Lincoln, "The Gettysburg Address," in *The Annals of America*, vol. 9, *1863–1865: The Crisis of the Union* (Chicago, 1968), 462–63; Martin Luther King Jr., *Why We Can't Wait* (New York, 1964), 92–93.
4. Interview with old laundryman, in "Interviews with Two Chinese," circa 1924, Box 326, folder 325, Survey of Race Relations, Stanford University, Hoover Institution Archives; Congressman Robert Matsui, speech in the House of Representatives on the 442 bill for redress and reparations, September 17, 1987, *Congressional Record* (Washington, D.C., 1987), 7584.
5. Camarillo, *Chicanos in a Changing Society*, 2; Juan Nepomuceno Seguín, in David J. Weber, ed., *Foreigners in Their Native Land: Historical Roots of the Mexican Americans* (Albuquerque, N. M., 1973), vi; Jesus Garza, in Manuel Gamio, *The Mexican Immigrant: His Life Story* (Chicago, 1931), 15; Ernesto Galarza, *Barrio Boy: The Story of a Boy's Acculturation* (Notre Dame, Ind., 1986), 200.
6. Lawrence J. McCaffrey, *The Irish Diaspora in America* (Washington, D.C., 1984), 6, 62.
7. John Murray Cuddihy, *The Ordeal or Civility: Freud, Marx, Levi Strauss, and the Jewish Struggle with Modernity* (Boston, 1987), 165; Jonathan Kaufman, *Broken Alliance: The Turbulent Times between Blacks and Jews in America* (New York, 1989), 28, 82, 83–84, 91, 93, 106.
8. Andrew Jackson, First Annual Message to Congress, December 8, 1829, in James D. Richardson, ed.), *A Compilation of the Messages and Papers of the Presidents, 1789–1897* (Washington, D.C., 1897), vol. 2, 457; Frederick Jackson Turner, "The Significance of the Frontier in American History," in *The Early Writings of Frederick Jackson Turner* (Madison, Wisc., 1938), 185ff.; Luther Standing Bear, "What the Indian Means to America," in Wayne Moquin, ed., *Great Documents in American Indian History* (New York, 1973), 307; Vine Deloria, Jr., *Custer Died for Your Sins: An Indian Manifesto* (New York, 1969).
9. Nathan Glazer, *Affirmative Discrimination: Ethnic Inequality and Public Policy* (New York, 1978); Thomas Sowell, *Ethnic America: A History* (New York, 1981); David R. Roediger, *The Wages of Whiteness: Race and the Making of the American Working Class* (London, 1991), 134–36; Dan Caldwell, "The Negroization of the Chinese Stereotype in California," *Southern California Quarterly* 33 (June 1971), 123–31.
10. Tomas Almaguer, "Racial Domination and Class Conflict in Capitalist Agriculture: The Oxnard Sugar Beet Workers' Strike of 1903," *Labor History*. 25, no. 3 (summer 1984), 347; Howard M. Sachar, *A History of the Jews in America* (New York, 1992), 183.
11. For the concept of liminality, see Victor Turner, *Dramas, Fields, and Methapors: Symbolic Action in Human Society* (Ithaca, N.Y., 1974), 232, 237; and Arnold Van Gennep, *The Rites of Passage* (Chicago, 1960). What I try to do is to apply liminality to the land called "America."
12. "Social Document of Pany Lowe, interviewed by C. H. Burnett, Seattle, July 5, 1924," 6, Survey of Race Relations, Stanford University, Hoover Institution Archives; Minnie Miller,

"Autobiography," private manuscript, copy from Richard Balkin; Tomo Shoji, presentation, Ohana Cultural Center, Oakland, California, March 4, 1988.

13. Ishmael Reed, "America: The Multinational Society," in Rick Simonson and Scott Walker, eds., *Multi-Cultural Literacy* (St. Paul, 1988), 160.

8

Racial Identity and the State: Contesting the Federal Standards for Classification

Michael Omi

In February 1995, the *Chronicle of Higher Education* carried a feature article on racial classification and the sciences that highlighted an interesting dilemma facing scientists in the United States. On the one hand, they routinely utilize racial categories in their research and regularly make comparisons between the races with respect to health, behavior, and (as the *Bell Curve* controversy reminds us) intelligence. On the other hand, most scientists feel that racial classifications are meaningless and unscientific. In the *Chronicle* article, Kenneth Kennedy of Cornell University is quoted as saying: "In the social sense, race is a reality. In the scientific sense, it is not."

It is the reality of race in the "social sense" that I want to explore by focusing on the racial categories utilized by the federal government and the problems associated with them, highlighting the deeply political character of such categories.

My initial interest in state definitions of race was inspired by a court case in the early 1980s. In 1977, Susie Guillory Phipps, who was then forty-three years old, found herself in need of her birth certificate in order to apply for a passport. As she had believed all her life that she was white, you can imagine her surprise when a clerk at the New Orleans Division of Vital Records showed her that she was designated "colored." Quoting Ms. Phipps:

> "It shocked me. I was sick for three days. I was brought up white, I married white twice." The problem was a 1970 Louisiana state law which allowed for anyone with more than 1/32nd black blood to be defined as "black." Prior to that a black person was defined as anyone who had "any traceable amount" of black ancestry. According to the state's genealogical investigation, Ms. Phipps' great-great-great-great-grandmother was a black woman slave named Margarita. Ms. Phipps was at least 1/32nd black. (Omi and Winant, 1994)

The logic of this racial classification is consistent with what anthropologist Marvin Harris has called the "principle of hypodescent." This descent rule requires us to classify anyone who is known to have had a black ancestor as black. Ms. Phipps went on to sue the state of Louisiana to change her racial designation from "colored" to "white." She lost. In 1983, the state Supreme Court denied her motion and upheld the state's right to classify and quantify racial identity. In 1986, the U.S. Supreme Court refused to review the case and thus let the lower court's decision stand.

The designation of racial categories and the determination of racial identity are not simple tasks. During the past several centuries, these tasks have provoked numerous debates around the country involving matters of natural versus legal rights, such as who should be permitted to become a naturalized citizen, and who should be permitted to marry whom.

State Definitions of Race

Racial and ethnic categories in the United States have historically been shaped by the political and social agendas of particular times. The first U.S. census, conducted in 1790, distinguished holders of the franchise (namely, white male property owners) from the general population. Later, the practice of slavery motivated changes in categorization, including the division of blacks into free and slave populations.

The current census categories were assigned and implemented in response to the antidiscriminatory and equal opportunity laws of the 1960s and 1970s. Established in 1977, OMB Directive Number 15 fosters the creation of compatible, nonduplicated, exchangeable racial and ethnic data by federal agencies for three reporting purposes— statistical, administrative, and civil rights compliance:

Office of Management and Budget (OMB) Statistical Directive No. 15

Race and Ethnic Standards for Federal Statistics and Administrative Reporting

1. Definitions

The basic racial and ethnic categories for Federal Statistics and program administrative reporting are defined as follows:

a. American Indian or Alaskan Native. A person having origins in any of the original peoples of North America, and who maintains cultural identification through tribal affiliation or community recognition.

b. Asian or Pacific Islander. A person having origins in any of the original peoples of the Far East, Southeast Asia, the Indian subcontinent, or the Pacific Islands. This area includes, for example, China, India, Japan, Korea, the Philippine Islands, and Samoa.

c. Black. A person having origins in any of the black racial groups of Africa.

d. Hispanic. A person of Mexican, Puerto Rican, Cuban, Central or South American or other Spanish culture or origin, regardless of race.

e. White. A person having origins in any of the original peoples of Europe, North Africa, or the Middle East.

2. Utilization for Recordkeeping and Reporting

To provide flexibility, it is preferable to collect data on race and ethnicity separately. If separate race and ethnic categories are used, the minimum designations are:

a. Race:

- American Indian or Alaskan Native

- Asian or Pacific Islander

- Black

- White

b. Ethnicity:

- Hispanic origin

- Not of Hispanic origin

Note the problems inherent in this categorization. Some of the categories are racial, some geographic, and some cultural.

The Census Bureau and most government agencies use three different sets of questions and concepts to describe and measure race and ethnicity:

- Race (the 1990 Census question included sixteen categories of race)

- Ethnicity (designed to ascertain whether a person is of Hispanic origin)

- Ancestry (open-ended, with no precoded categories)

The existing framework is being seriously questioned. In February 1994, I participated in a two-day session convened by the National Research Council at the request of the Office of Management and Budget. The purpose of the meeting was to assess the existing racial and ethnic categories (as defined in OMB Statistical Directive Number 15); to note their limitations; and perhaps to suggest more stable and coherent categories for research and administrative purposes. In my opinion, this session—however well intended—was ill founded: any attempt to frame such coherent categories immediately confronts a range of contradictory choices and gaps in understanding.

Gaps Between State Definitions and Individual/Group Identities

First, there is the gap between administrative requirements and popular consciousness. The federal, state, and local agencies involved in compiling and analyzing racial and ethnic data do so with the intent to track socioeconomic progress, assess health trends, and determine patterns of discrimination, as well as to measure other important indicators of well-being and life chances. Agencies want relatively static racial and ethnic categories that can be objectively determined—meaning that they must be conceptually valid, exclusive and exhaustive, measurable, and reliable over time.

Such categories, however, would clash with conceptions of race and ethnicity that stress their dynamic nature and the "slippery" subjective indicators of that dynamism, such as self-identity. Administrative definitions, therefore, might not be meaningful to the very individuals or groups they purport to represent.

Clara Rodriguez's studies of Latinos, which reveal a strong group rejection of the dominant mode of conceptualizing racial categories in the United States, provide evidence of precisely such a disjuncture. More than half of Rodriguez's Puerto Rican respondents answered the race/ethnicity question wrong. Rodriguez's findings are supported by other data: The Census Bureau reported that 40 percent of Hispanic respondents in 1980 and 1990 chose no other racial or ethnic identity. It was also estimated that 95 percent of persons reporting in the "other race" category were Hispanic (Rodriguez 1980).

Part of the problem lies with differences in conceptualizing race. With respect to new immigrant populations, it is important to examine the shifts in racial self-identity as immigrants move from a society organized around specific concepts of race to a new society with a different mode of conceptualization.

Table 8.1. Race and Ethnic Identification and Classification by Life Cycle.

Birth:	by mother
Childhood:	by household head for the decennial census by self, parents, or administrators for school forms by self, parents, or administrators for health forms
Adulthood:	by household head for the decennial census by self or administrators for employment forms by self or administrators for health forms by self or administrators for misc. government and business forms
Death:	by physician or funeral home administrator (perhaps in consultation with relatives of deceased)

Life Cycle Effects

Given the contextual nature of racial and ethnic identification, it may be difficult to achieve the reliability and consistency in time series data and analysis. You are likely to elicit different responses on racial and ethnic identification in different historical periods. You are also likely to elicit different responses from the same individual at different points in her or his life cycle. (See table 8.1.)

Since 1989, births have been categorized by the race of the mother. Racial classification at death, by contrast, is designated by a third party, either a physician or funeral director. This has led to the overassignment of deaths to black and white categories and an underassignment of deaths to American Indian and Asian categories.

In addition to these problems with existing classifications, there is also the temporal effect of evolving racial and ethnic labels. New labels come into vogue, old groups dissolve through assimilation, and new groups emerge as a result of changes in civil status or patterns of immigration.

Changing Self-Identification

A fascinating example of changing self-identification is the dramatic increase in the American Indian population. American Indians increased from 552,000 in 1960 to 1,959,000 in 1990—255 percent in thirty years. This rate of increase is virtually impossible demographically.

Much of the increase is explainable by changes in racial self-identification that are driven by shifts in attitudes toward American Indians, a romanticization of the past, and tangible benefits tied to American Indian identification. There is a very large pool of Americans who claim some degree of American Indian ancestry. In 1980, only 1.4 million chose American Indian as a racial category, whereas 6.8 million noted that they were American Indian on the open-ended ancestry question. In 1990, the number claiming American Indian ancestry increased to 8.8 million.

Panethnicity

The reorganization of old groups and the creation of new groups are features of changing political and social contexts. One dramatic political development in the post-civil rights era is the rise of *panethnic* consciousness and organization. Groups whose previous national or ethnic identities were quite distinct became consolidated into a single racial (or in the case of Latinos, ethnic) category.

Prior to the late 1960s, for example, there were no "Asian Americans." In the wake of the civil rights movement, distinct Asian ethnic groups—primarily Chinese, Japanese, Filipino, and Korean Americans—began to frame and assert their "common identity" as Asian Americans. This political label reflected the similarity of treatment that these groups historically encountered at the hands of state institutions and the dominant culture at large. Different Asian ethnic groups had been subject to exclusionary immigration laws, restrictive naturalization laws, labor market segregation, and patterns of "ghettoization" by a polity and culture that treated all Asians as alike.

The panethnic organization of Asian Americans involved the muting of profound cultural and linguistic differences and significant historical antagonisms that existed among the distinct nationalities and ethnic groups of Asian origin. In spite of diversity and difference, Asian American activists found the political label a crucial rallying point for raising political consciousness about the problems in Asian ethnic communities and for asserting demands on political institutions.

These panethnic formations are not stable. Conflicts often occur over the precise definitions and boundaries of various panethnic groups, and over their adequate representation in census counts, reapportionment debates, and minority aid programs. Panethnic consciousness and organization are, to a large extent, situationally and strategically determined. There are times when it is advantageous to be in a panethnic bloc and times when it is seen as more desirable to mobilize along particular ethnic lines.

However, for researchers and policymakers, lumping various groups together results in a flattening of important distinctions that we might wish to discern and analyze. Specific groups might "all look alike," but they are not homogeneous. How meaningful, for example, is an Asian American category for analysis when both Japanese and Laotian Americans are subsumed under it? Only 28.4 percent of Japanese Americans are foreign born, and only 9 percent do not speak English well. Their median family income is 137 percent of the national average, and their poverty rate is 4.2 percent. By contrast 93.7 percent of Laotians are foreign born, and 69 percent do not speak English well. Their median family income is 26 percent of the national average, and their poverty rate is 67.2 percent. The point is that the conflation of important "differences" is a hazard with the construction and use of particular categories.

The Shifting Meaning of Racial/Ethnic Identification

The meaning of racial/ethnic identification for specific groups and individuals varies enormously. Recent research on white Americans suggest that they do not experience their ethnicity as a definitive aspect of their social identity. Rather, they perceive it dimly and irregularly, picking and choosing among its varied strands, which allows them to exercise, in the words of sociologist Mary Waters (1990), an "ethnic option." Waters found that ethnicity was flexible, symbolic, and voluntary for her white respondents in ways that it was not for nonwhites.

A recent analysis (Petersen, 1997, pp. 315–320) of the open-ended question on ancestry or descent that first appeared in the 1980 Census underscores the fluid nature of white ethnicity. The examples given below the question had a dramatic influence on responses. (See table 8.2.)

Multiracial Category

An important emerging issue is the inability of existing state definitions to deal with people of mixed racial descent. A concerted effort has been made by school boards and organ-

Table 8.2 Selected Ancestry Groups: 1980 and 1990 Censuses

Ancestry	Is the Group Listed as an Example? 1980	1990	Population in Thousands 1980	1990	Percent Change
German	Yes	Yes	49,224	57,986	15
English	Yes	Yes	49,598	32,056	−34
Italian	Yes	Yes	12,184	14,715	21
French	Yes	No	12,892	10,321	−20
Polish	Yes	Yes	8,228	9,336	14
Ukrainian	Yes	Yes	730	741	2
Hungarian	Yes	No	1,777	1,582	−11
Serbian	No	No	101	117	15
Croatian	No	Yes	233	554	115
French Canadian	No	Yes	780	2,167	178
Cajun	No	Yes	<10	668	>6,000
Taiwanese	No	Yes	15	193	1,106
Born in Taiwan	—	—	75	244	225

izations such as Project RACE (Reclassify All Children Equally) to have the category "multiracial" added to the census form. This change has been opposed by many civil rights organizations, including the Urban League and the National Council of La Raza. Some groups fear a reduction in their numbers and worry that a multiracial category would spur debates regarding the "protected status" of groups and individuals. According to various estimates, from 75 to 90 percent of census respondents who now check off the "black" box could check off "multiracial." This is not to say they would, but only to suggest that complex issues of identity would emerge from the institutionalization of a multiracial category.

References

Decker, D., D. Schichor, and R. M. O'Brien. (1982). *Urban Structure and Victimization*. Lexington, Mass.: Lexington Books.

Omi, M., and H. Winant. (1994). *Racial Formation in the United States: From the 1960s to the 1990s*. New York: Routledge.

Petersen, W. (1997). *Ethnicity Counts*. New Brunswick, N.J.: Transaction Books.

Rodriguez, C. E. (1980). Puerto Ricans: Between Black and White. In C. E. Rodríguez and V. S. Korrol, eds. *Historical Perspectives on Puerto Rican Survival in the United States*. Princeton, N.J.: Markus Wiener Publications.

Waters, M. C. (1990). *Ethnic Notions: Choosing Identities in America*. Berkeley: University of California Press.

9

Defining Racism: "Can We Talk?"

Beverly Daniel Tatum

. . . The impact of racism begins early. Even in our preschool years, we are exposed to misinformation about people different from ourselves. Many of us grew up in neighborhoods where we had limited opportunities to interact with people different from our own families. When I ask my college students, "How many of you grew up in neighborhoods where most of the people were from the same racial group as your own?" almost every hand goes up. There is still a great deal of social segregation in our communities. Consequently, most of the early information we receive about "others"—people racially, religiously, or socioeconomically different from ourselves—does not come as the result of firsthand experience. The secondhand information we do receive has often been distorted, shaped by cultural stereotypes, and left incomplete. . . .

Sometimes the assumptions we make about others come not from what we have been told or what we have seen on television or in books, but rather from what we have *not* been told. The distortion of historical information about people of color leads young people (and older people, too) to make assumptions that may go unchallenged for a long time. . . .

Omitted information can have a similar effect. For example, young woman, preparing to be a high school English teacher, expressed her dismay that she had never learned about any Black authors in any of her English courses. How was she to teach about them to her future students when she hadn't learned about them herself? A White male student in the class responded to this discussion with frustration in his response journal, writing "It's not my fault that Blacks don't write books." Had one of his elementary, high school, or college teachers ever told him that there were no Black writers? Probably not. Yet because he had never been exposed to Black authors, he had drawn his own conclusion that there were none.

Stereotypes, omissions, and distortions all contribute to the development of prejudice. *Prejudice* is a preconceived judgment or opinion, usually based on limited information. I assume that we all have prejudices, not because we want them, but simply because we are so continually exposed to misinformation about others. Though I have often heard students or workshop participants describe someone as not having "a prejudiced bone in his body," I usually suggest that they look again. Prejudice is one of the inescapable consequences of living in a racist society. Cultural racism—the cultural images and messages that affirm the assumed superiority of Whites and the assumed inferiority of people of color—is like smog in the air. Sometimes it is so thick it is visible, other times it is less apparent, but always, day in and day out, we are breathing it in. None of us would introduce ourselves as "smog-breathers" (and most of us don't want to be described as prejudiced), but if we live in a smoggy place, how can we avoid breathing the air? If we live in an environment in which we are bombarded with stereotypical images in the media, are frequently exposed to the ethnic jokes of friends and family members, and are rarely informed of the accomplishments of oppressed groups, we will develop the negative categorizations of those groups that form the basis of prejudice.

People of color as well as Whites develop these categorizations. Even a member of the stereotyped group may internalize the stereotypical categories about his or her own group to some degree. In fact, this process happens so frequently that it has a name, *internalized oppression*. . . .

To say that it is not our fault does not relieve us of responsibility, however. We may not have polluted the air, but we need to take responsibility, along with others, for cleaning it up. Each of us needs to look at our own behavior. Am I perpetuating and reinforcing the negative messages so pervasive in our culture, or am I seeking to challenge them? If I have not been exposed to positive images of marginalized groups, am I seeking them out, expanding my own knowledge base for myself and my children? Am I acknowledging and examining my own prejudices, my own rigid categorizations of others, thereby minimizing the adverse impact they might have on my interactions with those I have categorized? Unless we engage in these and other conscious acts of reflection and reeducation, we easily repeat the process with our children. We teach what we were taught. The unexamined prejudices of the parents are passed on to the children. It is not our fault, but it is our responsibility to interrupt this cycle.

Racism: A System of Advantage Based on Race

Many people use the terms *prejudice* and *racism* interchangeably. I do not, and I think it is important to make a distinction. In his book *Portraits of White Racism*, David Wellman argues convincingly that limiting our understanding of racism to prejudice does not offer a sufficient explanation for the persistence of racism. He defines racism as a "system of advantage based on race."[1] In illustrating this definition, he provides example after example of how Whites defend their racial advantage—access to better schools, housing, jobs—even when they do not embrace overtly prejudicial thinking. Racism cannot be fully explained as an expression of prejudice alone.

This definition of racism is useful because it allows us to see that racism, like other forms of oppression, is not only a personal ideology based on racial prejudice, but a *system* involving cultural messages and institutional policies and practices as well as the beliefs and actions of individuals. In the context of the United States, this system clearly operates to the advantage of Whites and to the disadvantage of people of color. Another related definition of racism, commonly used by antiracist educators and consultants, is "prejudice plus power." Racial prejudice when combined with social power—access to social, cultural, and economic resources and decision making—leads to the institutionalization of racist policies and practices. While I think this definition also captures the idea that racism is more than individual beliefs and attitudes, I prefer Wellman's definition because the idea of systematic advantage and disadvantage is critical to an understanding of how racism operates in American society. . . .

The systematic advantages of being White are often referred to as White privilege. In a now well-known article, "White Privilege: Unpacking the Invisible Knapsack," Peggy McIntosh, a White feminist scholar, identified a long list of societal privileges that she received simply because she was White.[2] She did not ask for them, and it is important to note that she hadn't always noticed that she was receiving them. They included major and minor advantages. Of course she enjoyed greater access to jobs and housing. But she also was able to shop in department stores without being followed by suspecting salespeople and she could always find appropriate hair care products and makeup in any drugstore. She could send her child to school confident that the teacher would not discriminate against him on the basis of race. She could also be late for meetings, and talk with her mouth full, fairly confident that these behaviors would not be attributed to the fact that she was White. She could express an opinion in a meeting or in print and not have it labeled the "White" viewpoint. In other words, she was more often than not viewed as an individual, rather than as a member of a racial group. . . .

Understanding racism as a system of advantage based on race is antithetical to traditional notions of an American meritocracy. For those who have internalized this myth, this definition generates considerable discomfort. It is more comfortable simply to think of racism as a particular form of prejudice. Notions of power or privilege do not have to be addressed when our understanding of racism is constructed in that way. . . .

I sometimes visualize the ongoing cycle of racism as a moving walkway at the airport. Active racist behavior is equivalent to walking fast on the conveyor belt. The person engaged in active racist behavior has identified with the ideology of White supremacy and is moving with it. Passive racist behavior is equivalent to standing still on the walkway. No overt effort is being made, but the conveyor belt moves the bystanders along to the same destination as those who are actively walking. Some of the bystanders may feel the motion of the conveyor belt, see the active racists ahead of them, and choose to turn around, unwilling to go to the same destination as the White supremacists. But unless they are walking actively in the opposite direction at a speed faster than the conveyor belt—unless they are actively antiracist—they will find themselves carried along with the others. . . .

It is important to acknowledge that while all Whites benefit from racism, they do not all benefit equally. Other factors, such as socioeconomic status, gender, age, religious affiliation, sexual orientation, and mental and physical ability, also play a role in our access to social influence and power. A White woman on welfare is not privileged to the same extent as a wealthy White heterosexual man. In her case, the systematic disadvantages of sexism and classism intersect with her White privilege, but the privilege is still there. This point was brought home to me in a 1994 study conducted by a Mount Holyoke graduate student, Phyllis Wentworth.[3] Wentworth interviewed a group of female college students, who were both older than their peers and were the first members of their families to attend college, about the pathways that lead them to college. All of the women interviewed were White, from working-class backgrounds, from families where women were expected to graduate from high school and get married or get a job. Several had experienced abusive relationships and other personal difficulties prior to coming to college. Yet their experiences were punctuated by "good luck" stories of apartments obtained without a deposit, good jobs offered without experience or extensive reference checks, and encouragement provided by willing mentors. While the women acknowledged their good fortune, none of them discussed their Whiteness. They had not considered the possibility that being White had worked in their favor and helped give them the benefit of the doubt at critical junctures. This study clearly showed that even under difficult circumstances, White privilege was still operating.

It is also true that not all people of color are equally targeted by racism. We all have multiple identities that shape our experience. I can describe myself as a light-skinned, well-educated, heterosexual, able-bodied, Christian African American woman raised in a middle-class suburb. As an African American woman, I am systematically disadvantaged by race and by gender, but I systematically receive benefits in the other categories, which then mediate my experience of racism and sexism. When one is targeted by multiple isms—racism, sexism, classism, heterosexism, ableism, anti-Semitism, and ageism—in whatever combination, the effect is intensified. The particular combination of racism and classism in many communities of color is life-threatening. Nonetheless, when I, the middle-class Black mother of two sons, read another story about a Black man's unlucky encounter with a White police officer's deadly force, I am reminded that racism by itself can kill.

The Cost of Racism

. . . Why should Whites who are advantaged by racism *want* to end that system of advantage? What are the *costs* of that system to them?

A *Money* magazine article called "Race and Money" chronicled the many ways the American economy was hindered by institutional racism.[4] Whether one looks at productivity lowered by racial tensions in the workplace, or real estate equity lost through housing discrimination, or the tax revenue lost in underemployed communities of color, or the high cost of warehousing human talent in prison, the economic costs of racism are real and measurable.

As a psychologist, I often hear about the less easily measured costs. When I ask White men and women how racism hurts them, they frequently talk about their fears of people of color, the social incompetence they feel in racially mixed situations, the alienation they have experienced between parents and children when a child marries into a family of color, and the interracial friendships they had as children that were lost in adolescence or young adulthood without their ever understanding why. White people are paying a significant price for the system of advantage. The cost is not as high for Whites as it is for people of color, but a price is being paid.[5] . . .

The dismantling of racism is in the best interests of everyone.

Notes

1. For an extended discussion of this point, see D. Wellman, *Portraits of White Racism* (Cambridge: Cambridge University Press, 1977), ch. 1.
2. P. McIntosh, "White Privilege: Unpacking the Invisible Knapsack," *Peace and Freedom* (July/August 1989), 10–12.
3. P. A. Wentworth, "The Identity Development of Non-Traditionally Aged First-Generation Women College Students: An Exploratory Study" (master's thesis, Department of Psychology and Education, Mount Holyoke College, South Hadley, Mass., 1994).
4. W. L. Updegrave, "Race and Money," *Money* (December 1989), 152–72.
5. For further discussion of the impact of racism on Whites, see B. Bowser and R. G. Hunt, eds., *Impacts of Racism on White Americans* (Thousand Oaks, Calif.: Sage, 1981); P. Kivel, *Uprooting Racism: How White People Can Work for Racial Justice* (Philadelphia: New Society Publishers, 1996); and J. Barndt, *Dismantling Racism: The Continuing Challenge to White America* (Minneapolis: Augsburg Press, 1991).

10

The Continuing Significance of Race: Antiblack Discrimination in Public Places

Joe R. Feagin

The Range of Discriminatory Actions

In his classic study, *The Nature of Prejudice,* Allport (1958, 14–15) noted that prejudice can be expressed in a series of progressively more serious actions, ranging from antilocution to avoidance, exclusion, physical attack, and extermination. . . . Allport's work suggests a continuum of actions from avoidance, to exclusion or rejection, to attack. In my data, discrimination against middle-class blacks still ranges across this continuum: (1) avoidance actions, such as a white couple crossing the street when a black male approaches; (2) rejection actions, such as poor service in public accommodations; (3) verbal attacks, such as shouting racial epithets in the street; (4) physical threats and harassment by white police officers; and (5) physical threats and attacks by other whites, such as attacks by white supremacists in the street. Changing relations between blacks and whites in recent decades have expanded the repertoire of discrimination to include more subtle forms and to encompass discrimination in arenas from which blacks were formerly excluded, such as formerly all-white public accommodations. . . .

Middle-class strategies for coping with discrimination range from careful assessment to withdrawal, resigned acceptance, verbal confrontation, or physical confrontation. Later action might include a court suit. Assessing the situation is a first step. Some white observers have suggested that many middle-class blacks are paranoid about white discrimination and rush too quickly to charges of racism (Wieseltier 1989). . . . But the daily reality may be just the opposite, as middle-class black Americans often evaluate a situation carefully before judging it discriminatory and taking additional action. This careful evaluation, based on past experiences (real or vicarious), not only prevents jumping to conclusions, but also reflects the hope that white behavior is not based on race, because an act not based on race is easier to endure. After evaluation one strategy is to leave the site of discrimination rather than to create a disturbance. Another is to ignore the discrimination and continue with the interaction, a "blocking" strategy similar to that Gardner (1980, p. 345) reported for women dealing with street remarks. In many situations resigned acceptance is the only realistic response. More confrontational responses to white actions include verbal reprimands and sarcasm, physical counterattacks, and filing lawsuits. Several strategies may be tried in any given discriminatory situation. In crafting these strategies middle-class blacks, in comparison with less privileged blacks, may draw on middle-class resources to fight discrimination. . . .

"Middle class" was defined broadly as those holding a white-collar job (including those in professional, managerial, and clerical jobs), college students preparing for white-collar jobs, and owners of successful businesses. This definition is consistent with recent analyses of the black middle class (Landry 1987). . . .

Responses to Discrimination: Public Accommodations

Two Fundamental Strategies: Verbal Confrontation and Withdrawal

In the following account, a black news director at a major television station shows the interwoven character of discriminatory action and black response. The discrimination took the form of poor restaurant service, and the responses included both suggested withdrawal and verbal counterattack.

> He [her boyfriend] was waiting to be seated. . . . He said, "You go to the bathroom and I'll get the table. . . . "He was standing there when I came back: he continued to stand there. The restaurant was almost empty. There were waiters, waitresses, and no one seated. And when I got back to him, he was ready to leave, and said. "Let's go." I said. "What happened to our table?" He wasn't seated. So I said. "No, we're not leaving, please." And he said. "No, I'm leaving." So we went outside, and we talked about it. And what I said to him was, you have to be aware of the possibilities that this is not the first time that this has happened at this restaurant or at other restaurants, but this is the first time it has happened to a black news director here or someone who could make an issue of it, or someone who is prepared to make an issue of it.
>
> So we went back inside after I talked him into it and, to make a long story short. I had the manager come. I made most of the people who were there (while conducting myself professionally the whole time) aware that I was incensed at being treated this way. . . . I said, "Why do you think we weren't seated?" And the manager said, "Well, I don't really know." And I said, "Guess." He said, "Well I don't know, because you're black?" I said. "Bingo. Now isn't it funny that you didn't guess that I didn't have any money (and I opened up my purse) and I said, "because I certainly have money. And isn't it odd that you didn't guess that it's because I couldn't pay for it because I've got two American Express cards and a Master Card right here. I think it's just funny that you would have assumed that it's because I'm black." . . . And then I took out my card and gave it to him and said, "If this happens again, or if I hear of this happening again, I will bring the full wrath of an entire news department down on this restaurant." And he just kind of looked at me. "Not [just] because I am personally offended. I am. But because you have no right to do what you did, and as a people we have lived a long time with having our rights abridged." . . .
>
> There were probably three or four sets of diners in the restaurant and maybe five waiters/waitresses. They watched him standing there waiting to be seated. His reaction to it was that he wanted to leave. I understood why he would have reacted that way, because he felt that he was in no condition to be civil. He was ready to take the place apart and . . . sometimes it's appropriate to behave that way. We hadn't gone the first step before going on to the next step. He didn't feel that he could comfortably and calmly take the first step, and I did. So I just asked him to please get back in the restaurant with me, and then you don't have to say a word, and let me handle it from there. It took some convincing, but I had to appeal to his sense of, this is not just you, this is not just for you. We are finally in a position as black people where there are some of us who can genuinely get their attention. And if they don't want to do this because it's right for them to do it, then they'd better do it because they're afraid to do otherwise. If it's fear, then fine, instill the fear.

This example provides insight into the character of modern discrimination. The discrimination was not the "No Negroes" exclusion of the recent past, but rejection in the form of poor service by restaurant personnel. The black response indicates the change in black-white interaction since the 1950s and 1960s, for discrimination is handled with vigorous confrontation rather than deference. . . .

The news director articulates the American dream: she has worked hard, earned the money and credit cards, developed the appropriate middle-class behavior, and thus has under the law a *right* to be served. There is defensiveness in her actions too, for she feels a need to legitimate her status by showing her purse and credit cards. One important factor that enabled her to take such assertive action was her power to bring a TV news team to the restaurant. This power marks a change from a few decades ago when very few black Americans had the social or economic resources to fight back successfully.

This example underscores the complexity of the interaction in such situations, with two levels of negotiation evident. The negotiation between the respondent and her boyfriend on withdrawal versus confrontation highlights the process of negotiating responses to discrimination and the difficulty in crafting such responses. Not only is there a process of dickering with whites within the discriminatory scene, but also a negotiation between the blacks involved.

The confrontation strategy can be taken beyond immediate verbal confrontation to a more public confrontation. The president of a financial institution in a Middle Atlantic city brought unfavorable publicity to a restaurant with a pattern of poor service to blacks.

> I took the staff here to a restaurant that had recently opened in the prestigious section of the city, and we waited while other people got waited on. And decided that after about a half hour that these people don't want to wait on us. I happened to have been in the same restaurant a couple of evenings earlier, and it took them about forty-five minutes before they came to wait on me and my guest. So, on the second incident, I said, this is not an isolated incident, this is a pattern, because I had spoken with some other people who had not been warmly received in the restaurant. So, I wrote a letter to the owners. I researched and found out who the owners were, wrote a letter to the owners and sent copies to the city papers. That's my way of expressing myself and letting the world know. You have to let people, other than you and the owner, know. You have to let others know you're expressing your dismay at the discrimination, or the barrier that's presented to you. I met with the owners. Of course, they wanted to meet with their attorneys with me, because they wanted to sue me. I told them they're welcome to do so, I don't have a thing, but fine they can do it. It just happens that I knew their white attorney. And he more or less vouched that if I had some concern that it must have been legitimate in some form. When the principals came in—one of the people who didn't wait on me was one of the owners, who happened to be waiting on everybody else—we resolved the issue by them inviting me to come again. And if I was fairly treated, or if I would come on several occasions and if I was fairly treated I would write a statement of retraction. I told them I would not write a retraction, I would write a statement as to how I was treated. Which I ultimately did. And I still go there today, and they speak to me, and I think the pattern is changed to a great degree.

This example also demonstrates the resources available to many middle-class black Americans. As a bank executive with connections in the white community, including the legal community, this respondent used his resources not only to bring discrimination to public attention but also to pressure a major change in behavior. He had the means to proceed beyond the local management to both the restaurant owners and the local newspapers. The detailed account provides additional insight into the black-white bargaining process. At first the white managers and owners, probably accustomed to acquiescence or withdrawal, vigorously resisted ending the blatant discrimination. But the verbal and other resources available to the respondent forced them to capitulate and participate in a negotiation process. The cost to the victor was substantial. As in the first incident, we see the time-consuming and energy-consuming nature of grappling with poor-service discrimination. Compared to whites entering the same places, black Americans face an extra burden when going into public accommodations putatively made hospitable by three decades of civil rights law protection. . . .

Discrimination in public accommodations can occur in many different settings. A school board member in a northern city commented on her experiences in retail stores:

> [I have faced] harassment in stores, being followed around, being questioned about what are you going to purchase here. . . . I was in an elite department store just this past Saturday and felt that I was being observed while I was window shopping. I in fact actually ended up purchasing something, but felt the entire time I was there—I was in blue jeans and sneakers, that's how I dress on a Saturday—I felt that I was being watched in the store as I was walking through the store, what business did I have there, what was I going to purchase, that kind of thing. . . . There are a few of those white people that won't put change in your hand, touch your skin— that doesn't need to go on. [Do you tell them that?] Oh, I do. I do. That is just so obvious. I usually [speak to them] if they're rude in the manner in which they deal with people. [What do they say about that?] Oh, stuff like, "Oh, excuse me." And some are really unconscious about it, say "Excuse me," and put the change in your hand, that's happened. But I've watched other people be rude, and I've been told to mind my own business. . . . [But you still do it?] Oh, sure, because for the most part I think that people do have to learn to think for themselves, and demand respect for themselves. . . . I find my best weapon of defense is to educate them, whether it's in the store, in a line at the bank, any situation. I teach them. And you take them by surprise because you tell them and show them what they should be doing, and what they should be saying and how they should be thinking. And they look at you because they don't know how to process you. They can't process it because you've just shown them how they should be living, and the fact that they are cheating themselves, really, because the racism is from fear. The racism is from lack of education.

This excessive surveillance of blacks' shopping was reported by several respondents in our study and in recent newspaper accounts (see Jaynes and Williams 1989, 140). Several white stereotypes seem to underlie the rejection discrimination in this instance— blacks are seen as shoplifters, as unclean, as disreputable poor. The excessive policing of black shoppers and the discourtesy of clerks illustrate the extra burden of being black in public places. No matter how affluent and influential, a black person cannot escape the stigma of being black, even while relaxing or shopping. There is the recurring strain of having to craft strategies for a broad range of discriminatory situations. Tailoring her confrontation to fit the particular discrimination, this respondent interrupted the normal flow of the interaction to call the whites to intersubjective account and make a one-way experience into a two-way experience. Forced into new situations, offending whites frequently do not know how "to process" such an aggressive response. Again we see how middle-class blacks can force a reconstruction of traditional responses by whites to blacks. The intensity of her discussion suggests that the attempt to "educate" whites comes with a heavy personal cost, for it is stressful to "psych" oneself up for such incidents. . . .

Middle-class black parents often attempt to protect their children from racial hostility in public places, but they cannot always be successful. A manager at an electronics firm in the Southwest gave an account of his daughter's first encounter with a racial epithet. After describing racist graffiti on a neighborhood fence in the elite white suburb where he lives, he described an incident at a swimming pool:

> I'm talking over two hundred kids in this pool; not one black. I don't think you can go anywhere in the world during the summertime and not find some black kids in the swimming pool. . . . Now what's the worst thing that can happen to a ten-year-old girl in a swimming pool with all

white kids? What's the worst thing that could happen? It happened. This little white guy called her a "nigger." Then called her a "motherfucker" and told her to "get out of the goddamn pool." . . . And what initiated that, they had these little inner tubes, they had about fifteen of them, and the pool owns them. So you just use them if they are vacant. So there was a tube setting up on the bank, she got it, jumped in and started playing in it. . . . And this little white guy decided he wanted it. But, he's supposed to get it, right? And he meant to get it, and she wouldn't give it to him, so out came all these racial slurs. So my action was first with the little boy. "You know you're not supposed to do that. Apologize right now. Okay, good. Now, Mr. Lifeguard, I want him out of this pool, and you're going to have to do better. You're going to have to do better, but he has to leave out of this pool and let his parents know, okay?"

Taking his daughter back the next day, he observed from behind a fence to make certain the lifeguard protected her. For many decades black adults and children were excluded from public pools in the South and Southwest, and many pools were closed during the early desegregation period. These accommodations have special significance for middle-class black Americans, and this may be one reason the father's reaction was so decisive. Perhaps the major reason for his swift action was because this was the first time that his daughter had been the victim of racial slurs. She was the victim of cutting racist epithets that for this black father, as doubtless for most black Americans, connote segregated institutions and violence against blacks. Children also face hostility in public accommodations and may never shake this kind of experience. At a rather early point, many black parents find it necessary to teach their children how to handle discriminatory incidents. . . .

Careful Situation Assessments

We have seen in the previous incidents some tendency for blacks to assess discriminatory incidents before they act. Among several respondents who discussed discrimination at retail stores, the manager of a career development organization in the Southwest indicated that a clear assessment of a situation usually precedes confrontations and is part of a repertoire of concatenated responses:

If you're in a store—and let's say the person behind the counter is white—and you walk up to the counter, and a white person walks up to the counter, and you know you were there before the white customer, the person behind the counter knows you were there first, and it never fails, they always go, "Who's next." Ok. And what I've done, if they go ahead and serve the white person first, the I will immediately say, "Excuse me, I was here first, and we both know I was here first." . . . If they get away with it once, they're going to get away with it more than once, and then it's going to become something else. And you have to, you want to make sure that folks know that you're not being naive, that you really see through what's happening. Or if it's a job opportunity or something like that, too, [we should do the] same thing. You first try to get a clear assessment of what's really going on and sift through that information, and then . . . go from there.

The executive's coping process typically begins with a sifting of information before deciding on further action. She usually opts for immediate action so that whites face the reality of their actions in a decisive way. Like the account of the school board member who noted that whites would sometimes not put money directly in her hand, this account illustrates another aspect of discrimination in public accommodations: For many whites racial hostility is imbedded in everyday actions, and there is a deep, perhaps subconscious, recoil response to black color and persona.

The complex process of evaluation and response is described by a college dean, who commented generally on hotel and restaurant discrimination encountered as he travels across the United States:

> When you're in a restaurant and . . . you notice that blacks get seated near the kitchen. You notice that if it's a hotel, you room is near the elevator, or your room is always way down in a corner somewhere. You find that you are getting the undesirable rooms. And you come there early in the day and you don't see very many cars on the lot and they'll tell you that this is all we've got. Or you get the room that's got a bad television set. You know that you're being discriminated against. And of course you have to act accordingly. You have to tell them, "Okay the room is fine, [but] this television set has got to go. Bring me another television set." So in my personal experience, I simply cannot sit and let them get away with it [discrimination] and not let then know that I know that's what they are doing. . . .
>
> When I face discrimination, first I take a long look at myself and try to determine whether or not I am seeing what I think I'm seeing in 1989, and if it's something that I have an option [about]. In other words, if I'm at a store making a purchase, I'll simply walk away from it. If it's at a restaurant where I'm not getting good service, I first of all let the people know that I'm not getting good service, then I [may] walk away from it. But the thing that I have to do is to let people know that I know that I'm being singled out for a separate treatment. And then I might react in a any number of ways—depending on where I am and how badly I want whatever it is that I'm there for.

This commentary adds another dimension to our understanding of public discrimination, its cumulative aspect. Blacks confront not just isolated incidents—such as a bad room in a luxury hotel once every few years—but a lifelong series of such incidents. Here again the omnipresence of careful assessments is underscored. The dean's interview highlights a major difficulty in being black—one must be constantly prepared to assess accurately and then decide on the appropriate response. . . .

Using Middle-Class Resources for Protection

One advantage that middle-class blacks have over poorer blacks is the use of the resources of middle-class occupations. A professor at a major white university commented on the varying protection her middle-class status gives her at certain sites:

> If I'm in those areas that are fairly protected, within gatherings of my own group, other African Americans, of if I'm in the university where my status as a professor mediates against the way I might be perceived, mediates against the hostile perception, then it's fairly comfortable. . . . When I divide my life into encounters with the outside world, and of course that's ninety percent of my life, it's fairly consistently unpleasant at those sites where there's nothing that mediates between my race and what I have to do. For example, if I'm in a grocery store, if I'm in my car, which is a 1970 Chevrolet, a real old ugly car, all those things—being in a grocery store in casual clothes, or being in the car—sort of advertises something that doesn't have anything to do with my status as far as people I run into are concerned.
>
> Because I'm a large black woman, and I don't wear whatever class status I have, or whatever professional status [I have] in my appearance when I'm in the grocery store, I'm part of the mass of large black women shopping. For most whites, and even for some blacks, that translated into negative status. That means that the are free to treat me the way they treat most poor black people, because they can't tell by looking at me that I differ from that.

This professor notes the variation in discrimination in the sites through which she travels, from the most private to the most public. At home with friends, she faces no problems, and at the university her professorial status gives her some protection from discrimination. The increase in unpleasant encounters as she moves into public accommodations sites such as grocery stores is attributed to the absence of mediating factors such as clear symbols of middle-class status—displaying the middle-class symbols may provide some protection against discrimination in public places.

An east coast new anchorperson reported a common middle-class experience of good service from retailers over the phone:

> And if I was seeking out a service, like renting a car, or buying something I could get a wonderful, enthusiastic reaction to what I was doing. I would work that up to such a point that this person would probably shower me with roses once they got to see me. And then when I would show up, and they're surprised to see that I'm black, I sort of remind them in conversation how welcome my service was, to put the embarrassment on them, and I go through with my dealings. In fact, once my sister criticized me for putting [what] she calls my "white-on-white voice" on to get a rental car. But I needed a rental car and I knew that I could get it. I knew if I could get this guy to think that he was talking to some blonde, rather than, you know, so, but that's what he has to deal with. I don't have to deal with that. I want to get the car.

Being middle-class often means that you, as many blacks say, "sound white" over the phone. Over the phone middle-class blacks find they get fair treatment because the white person assumes the caller is white, while they receive poorer (or no) service in person. Race is the only added variable in such interpersonal contact situations. Moreover, some middle-class blacks intentionally use this phone-voice resource to secure their needs.

Responses to Discrimination: The Street

Reacting to White Strangers

As we move away from public accommodations settings to the usually less protected street sites, racial hostility can become more fleeting and severer, and thus black responses are often restricted. The most serious form of street discrimination is violence. Often the reasonable black response to street discrimination is withdrawal, resigned acceptance, or a quick verbal retort. The difficulty of responding to violence is seen in this report by a man working for a media surveying firm in a southern industrial city:

> I was parked in front of this guy's house . . . . This guy puts his hands on the window and says, "Get out of the car, nigger." . . . So, I got out, and I thought, "Oh, this is what's going to happen here." And I'm talking fast. And they're, "What are you doing here?" And I'm, "This is who I am. I work with these people. This is the man we want to put in the survey." And I pointed to the house. And the guy said, "Well you have an out-of-state license tag, right?" "Yeah." And he said, "If something happened to you, your people at home wouldn't know for a long time, would they?" . . . I said, "Look, I deal with a company that deals with television. [If] something happens to me, it's going to be a national thing. . . . So, they grab me by the lapel of my coat, and put me in front of my car. They put the blade on my zipper. And now I'm thinking about this guy that's in the truck [behind me], because now I'm thinking that I'm going to have to run somewhere. Where am I going to run? Go to the police? [laughs] So, after a while they, bash up my headlight. And I drove [away].

Stigmatized and physically attacked solely because of his color, this man faced verbal hostility and threats of death with courage. Cautiously drawing on his middle-class resources, he told the attackers his death would bring television crews to the town. This resource utilization is similar to that of the news director in the restaurant incident. Beyond this verbal threat his response had to be one of caution. For most whites threatened on the street, the police are a sought-after source of protection, but for black men this is often not the case. . . .

A middle-class student with dark skin reported that on her way to university classes she had stopped at a bakery in a white residential area where very few blacks live or shop. A white couple in front of the store stared intently and hatefully at her as she crossed the sidewalk and entered and left the bakery. She reported that she had experienced this hate stare many times. The incident angered her for some days thereafter, in part because she had been unable to respond more actively to it.

For young middle-class blacks street harassment can generate shock and disbelief, as in the case of this college student who recounted a street encounter near her university in the Southwest:

> I don't remember in high school being called a "nigger" before, and I can remember here being called a "nigger." [When was this?] In my freshman year, at a university student parade. There was a group of us, standing there, not knowing that this was not an event that a lot of black people went to! [laughs] You know, our dorm was going, and this was something we were going to go to because we were students too! And we were standing out there and [there were] a group of white fraternity boys — I remember the southern flag — and a group of us, five or six of us, and they went past by us, before the parade had actually gotten underway. And one of them pointed and said. "Look at that bunch of niggers!" I remember thinking, "Surely he's not talking to us!" We didn't even use the word "nigger" in my house. . . . [How did you feel?] I think I wanted to cry. And my friends—they were from a southwestern city—they were ready to curse them, and I was just standing there with my mouth open. I think I wanted to cry, I could not believe it, because you get here and you think you're in an educated environment and you're dealing with educated people. And all of this backward country stuff . . . you think that kind of stuff is not going on, but it is.

The respondent's first coping response was to think the assailants were not speaking to her and her friends. Again we see the tendency for middle-class blacks to assess situations carefully and to give whites the benefit of the doubt. Her subsequent response was tearful acquiescence, but her friends were ready to react in a more aggressive way. . . .

It seems likely that for middle-class blacks the street is the site of recurring encounters with various types of white malevolence. A vivid example of the cumulative character and impact of this discrimination was given by another black student at a white university, who recounted his experiences walking home at night from a campus job to his apartment in a predominantly white residential area:

> So, even if you wanted to, it's difficult just to live a life where you don't come into conflict with others. Because every day you walk the streets, it's not even like once a week, once a month. It's every day you walk the streets. Every day that you live as a black person you're reminded how you're perceived in society. You walk the streets at night; white people cross the streets. I've seen white couples and individuals dart in front of cars to not be on the same side of the street. Just the other day, I was walking down the street, and this white female with a child, I saw her pass a young white male about twenty yards ahead. When she saw me, she quickly dragged the child and herself across the busy street. What is so funny is that this area has had an unknown white rapist in the area for about four years. [When I pass] white men tighten their grip on their women. I've seen people turn around and seem like they're going to take blows from me. The police constantly make circles around me as a I walk home, you know, for blocks, I'll walk, and they'll turn a block. And they'll come around me just to make sure, to find out where I'm going. So, every day you realize [you're black]. Even though you're not doing anything wrong; you're just existing. You're just a person. But you're a black person perceived in an unblack world. . . .

Responses to Discrimination by White Police Officers

Most middle-class blacks do not have governmental authority as their personal protection. In fact, white police officers are a major problem. Encounters with the police can be life-threatening and thus limit the range of responses. . . .

Scattered evidence suggests that by the time they are in their twenties, most black males, regardless of socioeconomic status, have been stopped by the police because "blackness" is considered a sign of possible criminality by police officers (Moss 1990; Roddy 1990). This treatment probably marks a dramatic contrast with the experiences of young, white middle-class males. . . .

Black women can also be the targets of police harassment. A professor at a major white university in the Southwest describes her encounters with the police:

> When the cops pull me over because my car is old and ugly, they assume I've just robbed a convenience store. Or that's the excuse they give: "This car looks like a car used to rob a 7-11 [store]." And I've been pulled over six or seven times since I've been in this city—and I've been here two years now. Then I do what most black folks do. I try not to make any sudden moves so I'm not accidentally shot. Then I give them my identification. And I show them my university I.D. so they won't think that I'm someone that constitutes a threat, however they define it, so that I don't get arrested.

She adds:

> [One problem with] being black in America is that you have to spend so much time thinking about stuff that most white people just don't even have to think about. I worry when I get pulled over by a cop. I worry because the person I live with is a black male, and I have a teen-aged son. I worry what some white cop is going to think when he walks over to our car, because he's holding on to a gun. And I'm very aware of how many black folks accidentally get shot by cops. I worry when I walk into a store, that someone's going to think I'm in there shoplifting. And I have to worry about that because I'm not free to ignore it. And so, that thing that's supposed to be guaranteed to all Americans, the freedom to just be yourself is a fallacious idea. And I get resentful that I have to think about things that a lot of people, even my very close white friends whose politics are similar to mine, simply don't have to worry about.

This commentary about a number of encounters underscores the pyramiding character of discrimination. This prominent scholar has faced excessive surveillance by white police officers, who presumably view blacks as likely criminals. There is a great fear of white officers, but she draws on her middle-class resources for protection; she cautiously interposes her middle-class status by pulling out a university I.D. card. In the verbal exchange her articulateness as a professor probably helps protect her. This assertive use of middle-class credentials in dealing with police marks a difference from the old asymmetrical deference rituals, in which highlighting middle-class status would be considered arrogant by white officers and increase the danger. Note, too, the explicity theory of rights that she, like many other middle-class blacks, holds as part of her American dream.

Conclusion

I have examined the sites of discrimination, the types of discriminatory acts, and the responses of the victims and have found the color stigma still to be very important in the public lives of affluent black Americans. The sites of racial discrimination range from relatively protected home sites, to less protected workplace and educational sites, to the even less protected public places. The 1964 Civil Rights Act guarantees that black Americans are "entitled to the full and equal enjoyment of the goods, services, facilities, privileges, advantages, and accommodations" in public accommodations. Yet the interviews indicate that deprivation of full enjoyment of public facilities is not a relic of the past; deprivation and discrimination in public accommodations persist. Middle-class black Americans remain vulnerable targets in public places. Prejudice-generated aggression in public places is, of course, not limited to black men and women — gay men and white women are also targets of street harassment (Benokraitis and Feagin 1986). Nonetheless, black women and men face an unusually broad range of discrimination on the street and in public accommodations. . . .

The cumulative impact of racial discrimination accounts for the special way that blacks have of looking at and evaluating interracial incidents. One respondent, a clerical employee at an adoption agency, described the "second eye" she uses:

> I think that it causes you to have to look at things from two different perspectives. You have to decide whether things that are done or slights that are made are made because you are black or they are made because the person is just rude, or unconcerned and uncaring. So it's kind of a situation where you're always kind of looking to see with a second eye or a second antenna just what's going on.

The language of "second eye" suggests that blacks look at white-black interaction through a lens colored by personal and group experience with cross-institutional and cross-generational discrimination. This sensitivity is not new, but is a current adaptation transcending, yet reminiscent of, the black sensitivity to the etiquette of racial relations in the old South (Doyle 1937). What many whites see as black "paranoia" (e.g., Wieseltier 1989) is simply a realistic sensitivity to white-black interaction created and constantly reinforced by the two types of cumulative discrimination cited above.

Blacks must be constantly aware of the repertoire of possible responses to chronic and burdensome discrimination. One older respondent spoke of having to put on her "shield" just before she leaves the house each morning. When quizzed, she said that for more than six decades, as she leaves her home, she has tried to be prepared for insults and discrimination in public places, even if nothing happens that day. . . .

Another respondent was articulate on this point:

> . . . if you can think of the mind as having one hundred ergs of energy, and the average man uses fifty percent of his energy dealing with the everyday problems of the world—just general kinds of things—then he has fifty percent more to do creative kinds of things that he wants to do. Now that's a white person. Now a black person also has one hundred ergs; he uses fifty percent the same way a white man does, dealing with what the white man has [to deal with], so he has fifty percent left. But he uses twenty-five percent fighting being black, [with] all the problems being black and what it means. Which means he really only has twenty-five percent to do what the white man has fifty percent to do. . . . You just don't have as much energy left to do as much as you know you really could if you were free, [if] your mind were free.

The individual cost of coping with racial discrimination is great, and, as he says, you cannot accomplish as much as you could if you retained the energy wasted on discrimination. This is perhaps the most tragic cost of persisting discrimination in the United States. In spite of decades of civil rights legislation, black Americans have yet to attain the full promise of the American dream.

References

Allport, Gordon. 1958. The *Nature of Prejudice*, abridged. New York: Doubleday Anchor Books.

Benokraitis, Nijole and Joe R. Feagin. 1986. *Modern Sexism: Blatant, Subtle and Covert Discrimination.* Englewood Cliffs: Prentice-Hall.

Doyle, Betram W. 1937. *The Etiquette of Race Relations in the South.* Port Washington, N.Y.: Kennikat Press.

Gardner, Carol Brooks. 1980. "Passing By: Street Remarks, Address Rights, and the Urban Female." *Sociological Inquiry* 50, 328–56.

Jaynes, Gerald D. and Robin Williams Jr., eds. 1989. *A Common Destiny: Blacks and American Society.* Washington, D.C.: National Academy Press.

Landry, Bart. 1987. *The New Black Middle Class.* Berkeley: University of California Press.

Moss, E. Yvonne. 1990. "African Americans and the Administration of Justice." In *Assessment of the Status of African-Americans*, ed. Wornie L. Reed. Boston: University of Massachusetts, William Monroe Trotter Institute.

Roddy, Dennis B. 1990, "Perceptions Still Segregate Police, Black Community." *Pittsburgh Press*, August 26, B 1.

Wieseltier, Leon. 1989. "Scar Tissue." *New Republic*, June 5, 19–20.

11

Seeing More than Black and White

Elizabeth Martínez

When today's activists try to learn from the movements of the 1960s, one simple lesson should be remembered: liberation has similar meanings for all people of color engaged in struggle. It means an end to racist oppression, the birth of collective self-respect and genuine hope of the social justice that we sometimes call equality. That common dream requires us to build alliances among progressive people of color.

Such alliances require a knowledge and wisdom that we have yet to acquire. Today it remains painful to see how divide-and-conquer strategies succeed among people of color. It is painful to see how prejudice, resentment, petty competitiveness and sheer ignorance fester. It is positively pitiful to see how we echo Anglo stereotypes about each other.

These divisions indicate that we urgently need some fresh and fearless thinking about racism, which might begin with analyzing the strong tendency to frame U.S. racial issues in strictly Black-white terms. Such terms make little sense when a 1996 U.S. Census report says that 33 percent of our population will be Asian/Pacific Island-American, Latino, Native American/Indigenous (which includes Hawaiian) and Arab-American by the year 2050—in other words, neither white nor Black. (Steven A. Holmes, "Census Sees a Profound Ethnic Shift in U.S.," *New York Times*, March 14, 1996.) Also, we find an increasing number of mixed people who incorporate two, three or more "races."

The racial and ethnic landscape has changed too much in recent years to view it with the same eyes as before. We are looking at a multi-dimensional reality in which race, ethnicity, nationality, culture and immigrant status come together with breathtakingly new results. We are also seeing global changes that have a massive impact on our domestic situation, especially the economy and labor force. For a group of Korean restaurant entrepreneurs to hire Mexican cooks to prepare Chinese dishes for mainly African-American customers, as happened in Houston, Texas, has ceased to be unusual.

The ever-changing demographic landscape compels those struggling against racism and for a transformed, non-capitalist society to resolve several strategic questions. Among them: doesn't the exclusively Black-white framework discourage the perception of common interests among people of color and thus sustain White Supremacy? Doesn't the view that only African Americans face serious institutionalized racism isolate them from potential allies? Doesn't the Black-white model encourage people of color to spend too much energy understanding our lives in relation to whiteness, obsessing about what white society will think and do?

That tendency is inevitable in some ways: the locus of power over our lives has long been white (although big shifts have recently taken place in the color of capital, as we see in Japan, Singapore and elsewhere). The oppressed have always survived by becoming experts on the oppressor's ways. But that can become a prison of sorts, a trap of compulsive vigilance. Let us liberate ourselves, then, from the tunnel vision of whiteness and behold the many colors around us! Let us summon the courage to reject outdated ideas and stretch our imaginations into the next century. . . .

The current, exclusively Black-white framework for racism prevails throughout U.S. society, even when it is obviously inappropriate. Everywhere we can find major discussions of race and race relations that totally ignore people of color other than African Americans. President Bill Clinton led the way in the first stages of his "dialogue on race" during 1997, with a commission that included no Native Americans, Asian Americans or Latinos. East Coast-based institutions including academia and the media, our ideological mentors, are especially myopic. Books continue to be published that define U.S. race relations in exclusively Black-white terms, like Simon & Schuster's 1997 volume *America in Black and White: One Nation, Indivisible,* coauthored by Stephan Thernstrom and Abigail Thernstrom. Television programs, panel discussions and conferences on race see only in bipolar terms (does ABC's Ted Koppel ever see more than Black and white in his reports on racial issues?). Major outbreaks of Latino unrest, like the uprisings in Morningside Heights, New York City, and the Mt. Pleasant district of Washington, D.C., make little if any dent; Latinos are in the news today and invisible again tomorrow. Except in the arena of electoral politics, much of New York City appears indifferent to the fact that, as of the early 1990s, Latinos totalled 24.4 percent of its population while Asians formed 6.9 percent. New Yorkers often dismiss the need for a new, more complex model of racial issues as "a California hangup."

Not that California is so much less myopic than the East and the Midwestern states. In fact the West Coast has only recently begun to move away from its own denial. In California, this most multinational of states, where Latinos have usually been the largest population of color, it is not rare for reports on racial issues to stay strictly inside the Black-white framework. In San Francisco, whose population is almost half Latino and Asian/Pacific Island American, the media often use that afterthought phrase, "Blacks and other minorities." Millions of Americans saw massive Latino participation in the April 1992 Los Angeles uprising on their television screens. The most heavily damaged areas were 49 percent Latino; of the dead, 18 out of 50 were Latino; and the majority of people arrested were Latino, according to a 1993 report by the Tomás Rivera Center, a research institute in Claremont, California. Yet the mass media and most people continue to call that event "a Black riot."

For its annual conference held in northern California in August 1997, the American Civil Liberties Union had 18 panelists listed in the program; only one had a Spanish surname. Across the nation, educational resource projects do not include Latinos except in the category of "immigrants." In daily life, to cite several personal experiences, Anglos will admit to having made a racist remark or gesture toward an African American much more quickly than one made toward a Latino. Or they will respond to an account of police brutality toward some Latino/a with an irrelevant remark about the terrible crimes committed by Spanish *conquistadores* against indigenous people. (In other words, "your people" did the same thing, so don't complain.) Or: try to discuss racist acts against Asians, and people of any color will complain about rich Japanese businessmen supposedly taking over everything.

Innumerable statistics, reports and daily incidents should make it impossible to exclude Latinos and other non-Black populations of color when racism is discussed, but they don't. Police killings, hate crimes by racist individuals and murders with impunity by border officials should make it impossible, but they don't. With chilling regularity, ranch owners compel migrant workers, usually Mexican, to repay the cost of smuggling them into the United States by laboring the rest of their lives for free. The forty-five Latino and Thai garment workers locked up in an El Monte, California, factory—working eighteen hours a day, seven days a week for $299 a month—can also be considered slaves (and one must ask why it took three years for the Immigration and Naturalization Service to act on its own reports about this horror) (*San Francisco Examiner*, August 8, 1995). Abusive treatment of migrant workers can be found all over the United States. In Jackson Hole, Wyoming, for example, police and federal agents rounded up 150 Latino workers in 1997, inked numbers on their arms and hauled them off to jail in patrol cars and a horse trailer full of manure (*Los Angeles Times*, September 6, 1997).

These experiences cannot be attributed to xenophobia, cultural prejudice, or some other term, less repellent than *racism*. Take the case of two small Latino children in San Francisco who were found in 1997 covered from head to toe with flour. They explained they had hoped to make their skin white enough for school. There is no way to understand their action except as the result of fear in the racist climate that accompanied passage of Proposition 187, which denies schooling to the children of undocumented immigrants. Another example: Mexican and Chicana women working at a Nabisco plant in Oxnard, California, were not allowed to take bathroom breaks from the assembly line and were told to wear diapers instead. Can we really imagine white workers being treated that way? (The Nabisco women did file a suit and won, in 1997.)

No "model minority" myth protects Asians and Asian Americans from hate crimes, police brutality, immigrant-bashing, stereotyping and everyday racist prejudice. Scapegoating can even take their lives, as happened with the murder of Vincent Chin in Detroit some years ago. Two auto workers thought he was Japanese (he was Chinese) and thus responsible for all those Japanese cars that left them unemployed. Hate crimes against Asians mounted steadily in the 1990s, with a leap of 17 percent nationwide in one year alone—from 1995 to 1996 (*San Francisco Examiner*, October 26, 1997). A Chinese-American man outside a supermarket was killed in 1995 in northern California by an unemployed meat cutter who said he just felt an urge to "kill me a Chinaman" (*New York Times*, December 13, 1995). A popular Vietnamese youth, Thien Minh Ly, was stabbed twenty-three times while skating at the local high school in Tustin, California; the murderer wrote in a letter, "Oh, I killed a Jap" (*San Francisco Chronicle*, October 22, 1996). As in the Vincent Chin killing, this case exemplifies the confusion over nationality, another similarity between the experience of Latinos and Asian/Pacific Island Americans: both are homogenized.

In a particularly outrageous case, police killed a young Chinese engineer and father of three young children in Rohnert Park, California, on April 24, 1997. The man had received racist insults while at a bar celebrating a new job, and had gone home furious. Hearing his drunken shouts, neighbors called police, who shot him immediately when he waved a long stick at them that he had grabbed from the garage. Police would not let his wife convince him to go inside their home, as she thought she could, or give him cardiopulmonary resuscitation (she is a nurse) after he was shot. Instead, they handcuffed the man and left him to die in his driveway. Their explanation was a racist stereotype: the stick (which was all of one-eighth inch thick) made the officer think the man would use "martial arts" against them. When we hear about this unending list of racist horrors, it is hard to understand how Asian/Pacific Island Americans, like Latinos and other peoples of color, have been excluded from the framework of racism.

We also need to look at the often stunning commonalities of racist experience. When some 120,000 Japanese—most of them U.S. citizens—were packed off to "internment" camps during World War II, this should have rung an old, familiar bell. We have lived with the internment camp under so many other names: reservation, plantation, migrant labor camp. It is not hard to imagine Arab Americans being rounded up someday for imprisonment in "terrorist camps."

Along with African Americans, millions of other people of color have been invisibilized, terrorized, demonized and dehumanized by White Supremacy. Yet up to now, the prevailing framework for racial issues has not included them, except occasionally in books and articles (mainly by people of color). We need to ask: why?

Why the Black-White Model?

A bipolar model of racism has never been really accurate for the United States. Early in this nation's history, Benjamin Franklin perceived a triracial society based on skin color— "the lovely white" (Franklin's words), the Black, and the "tawny," as Ronald Takaki tells us in his *Iron Cages* (1979). But this concept changed as capital's need for labor intensified in the new nation and came to focus on African slave labor. The "tawny" were decimated or forcibly exiled to distant areas; Mexicans were not yet available to be the main labor force. As enslaved Africans became the crucial labor force for the primitive accumulation of capital, they also served as the foundation for the very idea of whiteness— based on the concept of blackness as inferior.

Three other reasons for the Black-white framework seem obvious: numbers, geography and history. African Americans have long been the largest population of color in the United States; only recently has this begun to change. Also, African Americans have long been found in sizable numbers in most parts of the United States, including major cities, which has not been true of Latinos until recent times. Historically, the Black-white relationship has been entrenched in the nation's collective memory for some 300 years— whereas it is only 150 years since the United States seized half of Mexico and incorporated those lands and their peoples. Slavery and the struggle to end it formed a central theme in this country's only civil war—a prolonged, momentous conflict. Above all, enslaved Africans in the United States, and subsequent African Americans, have created an unmatched heritage of massive, persistent, dramatic and infinitely courageous resistance, with individual leaders of worldwide note.

We also find sociological and psychological explanations for the Black-white model's persistence. From the days of Thomas Jefferson onward, Native Americans, Mexicans and later the Asian/Pacific Islanders did not seem as much a threat to racial purity or as capable of arousing white sexual anxieties as did Blacks. A major reason for this must have been Anglo ambiguity about who could be called white. Most of the Mexican *ranchero* elite in California had welcomed the U.S. takeover, and Mexicans were partly European—therefore "semicivilized"; this allowed Anglos to see them as white, unlike lower-class Mexicans. For years Mexicans were legally white, and even today we hear the ambiguous U.S. Census term "Non-Hispanic Whites."

Like Latinos, Asian Americans have also been officially counted as white in some historical periods. They have been defined as "colored" in others, with "Chinese" being yet another category. Like Mexicans, they were often seen as not really white but not quite Black either. Such ambiguity tended to put Asian Americans along with Latinos outside the prevailing framework of racism.

Blacks, on the other hand, were not defined as white, could rarely become upper-class and maintained an almost constant rebelliousness. Contemporary Black rebellion has been urban: right in the Man's face, scary. Mexicans, by contrast, have lived primarily in rural areas until a few decades ago and "have no Mau-Mau image," as one Black friend said, even when protesting injustice energetically. Only the nineteenth-century resistance heroes labeled "bandits" stirred white fear, and that was along the border, a limited area. Latino stereotypes are mostly silly: snoozing next to a cactus, eating greasy food, always being late and disorganized, rolling big Carmen Miranda eyes, shrugging with self-deprecation "me no speek good eengleesh." In other words, *not serious*. This view may be altered today by stereotypes of the gangbanger, criminal or dirty immigrant, but the prevailing image of Latinos remains that of a debased white, at best.

In his book *Racial Oppression in America* (1972), Robert Blauner, an Anglo and one of the few authorities on racism to have questioned the Black-white framework, looks at some psychological factors as revealed in literature:

> We buy black writers, not only because they can write and have something to say, but because the white racial mind is obsessed with blackness. . . . Mexican-Americans, on the other hand, have been unseen as individuals and as a group. . . . James Baldwin has pointed to the deep mutual involvement of black and white in America. The profound ambivalence, the love-hate relationship, which Baldwin's own work expresses and dissects, does not exist in the racism that comes down on La Raza. . . . Even the racial stereotypes that plague Mexican-Americans tend to lack those positive attributes that mark antiblack fantasies: supersexuality, inborn athletic and musical power, natural rhythm.

In short: whiteness would not exist without blackness to define its superiority, nor does whiteness exist without envy of blackness. But white envy of *mexicanidad*, "Mexicanness," has always been very limited, and even less so white envy of the so-called Oriental. Anglo attitudes toward the Native American combine romanticized envy with racist stereotypes, yet carry too little weight numerically to challenge the existing racist model.

Among other important reasons for the exclusively Black-white model, sheer ignorance leaps to mind. The oppression and exploitation of Latinos (like Asians) have historical roots unknown to most Americans. People who learn at least a little about Black slavery remain totally ignorant about how the United States seized half of Mexico or how it has colonized Puerto Rico. Robert Blauner has rightly commented on the Latino situation that

> [e]ven informed Anglos know almost nothing about La Raza, its historical experience, its present situation. . . . And the average citizen doesn't have the foggiest notion that Chicanos have been lynched in the Southwest and continue to be abused by the police, that an entire population has been exploited economically, dominated politically, and raped culturally.

One other important reason for the bipolar model of racism is the stubborn self-centeredness of U.S. political culture. It has meant that the nation lacks any global vision other than relations of domination. In particular, the United States refuses to see itself as one among some twenty countries in a hemisphere whose dominant languages are Spanish and Portuguese, not English. It has only a big yawn of contempt or at best indifference for the people, languages and issues of Latin America. It arrogantly took for itself alone the name of half the western hemisphere, America, as was its "Manifest Destiny," of course.

So Mexico may be nice for a vacation and lots of Yankees like tacos, but the political image of Latin America combines incompetence with absurdity, fat corrupt dictators with endless siestas. Similar attitudes extend to Latinos within the United States. My parents, both Spanish teachers, endured decades of being told that students were better off learning French or German. The mass media complain that "people can't relate to Hispanics (or Asians)." It takes mysterious masked rebels, a beautiful young murdered singer or salsa outselling ketchup for the Anglo world to take notice of Latinos. If there weren't a mushrooming, billion-dollar "Hispanic" market to be wooed, the Anglo world might still not know we exist. No wonder that racial paradigm sees only two poles.

The exclusively Black-white framework is also sustained by the "model minority" myth, because it distances Asian Americans from other victims of racism. Portraying Asian Americans as people who work hard, study hard, obey the established order and therefore prosper, the myth in effect admonishes Blacks and Latinos: "See, anyone can make it in this society if you try hard enough. The poverty and prejudice you face are all *your* fault."

The "model" label has been a wedge separating Asian Americans from others of color by denying their commonalities. It creates a sort of racial bourgeoisie, which White Supremacy uses to keep Asian Americans from joining forces with the poor, the homeless and criminalized youth. People then see Asian Americans as a special class of yuppie: young, single, college-educated, on the white-collar track—and they like to shop for fun. Here is a dandy minority group, ready to be used against others.

The stereotype of Asian Americans as whiz kids is also enraging because it hides so many harsh truths about the impoverishment, oppression and racist treatment they experience. Some do come from middle- or upper-class families in Asia, some do attain middle-class or higher status in the U.S., and their community must deal with the reality of class privilege where it exists. But the hidden truths include the poverty of many Asian/Pacific Islander groups, especially women, who often work under intolerable conditions, as in the sweatshops. Many youths are not students but live on the streets or in pool halls. A 1993 U.S. Census study reported that the poverty rate for peoples of Asian origin in the United States ran as high as 26 percent (Vietnamese), 35 percent (Laotian), 43 percent (Cambodian) and a monstrous 64 percent (Hmong) (*San Francisco Examiner*, October 7, 1997). Just how "model" is that? . . .

Racism Evolves

A glimpse into the next century tells us how much we need to look beyond the bipolar model of race relations. Black and white are real poles, central to the history of U.S. racism. We should not ignore them; neither should we stop there. Our effectiveness in fighting racism depends on seeing the changes taking place today and trying to perceive the contours of the future, which includes defining new poles. . . . Racism has had certain common characteristics around the world but no permanently fixed character. So it is today as well.

Racism evolves. If you thought Latinos were just "Messicans" down at the border, wake up. They are all over North Carolina, Pennsylvania and Manhattan, too, although you may not see them on *your* streets. If you thought Asians were just a few old guys chatting in Chinatown, look again at a California mall or the Atlanta, Georgia, airport or a New York state university campus. Qualitative as well as quantitative changes are taking place. With the broader geographic spread of Latinos and Asian/Pacific Island Americans, policies and attitudes that were once regional have become national. California leads the way: the West is going east and the oldest part of this country is taking on many new colors.

Racism evolves; our models must also evolve. Today's challenge is to move beyond the Black-white dualism that has served as the foundation of White Supremacy. In taking up this challenge, we have to proceed with both boldness and infinite care. Talking race in these United States is an intellectual minefield; for every observation, one can find three contradictions and four necessary qualifications from five different racial groups. Making your way through that complexity, you have to think: keep your eyes on the prize.

References

Blauner, R. (1972). *Racial Oppression in America.* New York: Harper and Row.

Takaki, R. T. (1979). *Iron Cages: Race and Culture in Nineteenth Century America.* Seattle: University of Washington Press.

12

The Heartland's Raw Deal: How Meatpacking Is Creating a New Immigrant Underclass

Marc Cooper

Storm Lake, Iowa: Thirty-year-old Lauro Ibarro left his wife and daughter behind in Reynosa, Mexico, and dodged the traps of U.S. Immigration to make a better life for them all by slaughtering pigs in the mammoth plant that defines life in this northwest Iowa town of ten thousand. Instead, a few days before Christmas, he met a horrible death. Awakened in the middle of the night by flames and smoke inside the small uninsulated trailer that he shared with his sister and her family, Lauro ran instinctively out into the foot of snow piled on the ground. Realizing that his two nieces, five-year-old Karent Luna and three-year-old Crystal Luna, were still inside, Lauro dove back into the blaze to rescue them. But neither he nor the two little girls escaped. A police report identified a malfunctioning kerosene space heater as the culprit—the same device that so many Latino working families have here as their only feeble defense against Iowa's five long months of winter.

At the wake the next evening, dusted by snow and dressed in jeans, parkas and workboots, some two hundred or more of Lauro Ibarro's neighbors—all Latinos—overflowed the Sliefert Mortuary in a rare exercise of public, collective grief. Sometimes only a tragedy of such proportions is sufficient to overcome the inertia imposed by the routine disappointments of everyday life lived out so far from what was once home.

The death of these three was a reminder of the precarious, undignified life shared not only by the mourners at the wake but by the six hundred or more Mexican and Central American workers and their families who have come to live here in Storm Lake. Alongside fifteen hundred Laotians, these immigrant workers are now the majority of the work force at the world's second-largest pork factory, operated by Iowa Beef Processors (IBP). And it's not just here in Storm Lake. In a sweeping regional arc from the Dakotas through Minnesota, Nebraska and Iowa, and down through Kansas into northern Texas and the foothills of the Missouri Ozarks, dozens of once lily-white heartland meatpacking communities have become the new homes to tens of thousands of impoverished Third World workers.

Putting the lie to the conventional wisdom undergirding our immigration policy, the arrival of these workers en masse is neither serendipitous nor the product of cunning smugglers. Rather, it is the direct result of a conscious survival strategy undertaken by a key U.S. industry, a plan developed and fully implemented only in the past few years.

Beef, pork and poultry packers have been aggressively recruiting the most vulnerable of foreign workers to relocate to the U.S. plains in exchange for $6-an-hour jobs in the country's most dangerous industry. Since permanence is hardly a requirement for these jobs, the concepts of promotion and significant salary increase have as much as disappeared. That as many as half of these new immigrants lack legal residence seems no obstacle to an industry now thriving on a docile, disempowered work force with an astronomical turnover.

Staggering illness and injury rates—thirty-six per one hundred workers in meat—and stress caused by difficult, repetitive work often means employment for just a few months before a worker quits or the company forces him/her off the job. (Government safety inspections have dropped 43 percent overall since 1994, because of budget cuts and an increasingly probusiness slant at the Occupational Safety and Health Administration.) When disabled workers and their families remain in their new homes, the social cost of their survival is then passed on by the company to the public.

Moreover, this radical restructuring of food processing could be carried out only with the acquiescence of local and state governments, which have showered the meatpacking giants with millions in tax rebates and subsidies, and only with the hypocrisy of our immigration policy–makers, who abhor illegal aliens—except when they're desperate enough to accept underpaid jobs under the most adverse conditions. "The entire debate over whether or not immigrants are of economic benefit is disingenuous," says University of Northern Iowa anthropologist Mark Grey, an expert on the restructured packing industry. "No one wants to state the truth—that food processing in America today would collapse were it not for immigrant labor."

As an added insult, these new immigrants are being left even more vulnerable by the Clinton Administration's new welfare and immigration reforms, which have a direct and devastating impact on their already fragile existence. Taken together, these economic and political factors have converged in the heartland to lay the foundations for a new rural underclass. Welcome to Mexico on the Missouri.

Bringing the War Back Home

Twenty-five years ago, when the population of this town—which bills itself as The City Beautiful—was sitting at 8,400, the government counted twenty-two minority residents, mostly students at the small Buena Vista University. Today, nearly half of Storm Lake's kindergarten class is nonwhite. With nearly everyone in town working at either IBP or at Sara Lee's Bil-Mar turkey plant, unemployment here is about 2 percent. But the prevailing low wage insured that one in four families was the recipient of some sort of public or private charity this past year. Over the past decade the county hospital has seen its unpaid costs zoom from $129,000 a year to $3 million. In 1996 three cases of full-blown tuberculosis, the classic disease of poverty, were reported, and another 380 residents were treated for TB infection.

"Living here is like living on the moon," says the Reverend Tom Lo Van, a pudgy thirty-four-year-old Laotian Lutheran with an infectious laugh. "Our people don't know the law, their rights, or where to go when they are sick. We work, we pay taxes and we have problems like everyone else. But there isn't a single person in the government who speaks our language."

Reverend Tom is about as unlikely a candidate for social agitator as you could find. He was born in the U.S. Embassy in Laos, and his father was the U.S. mission's cook after serving fifteen years with the CIA's favorite cutout, Air America. The only professional-class Laotian in town, the Reverend is his community's most forceful—some would say lone—public advocate.

In the mid-seventies, Iowa Republican politicians seeded Storm Lake with twenty-four

Laotian refugee families, most of them headed by veterans of the Royal Laotian Army, allies of the U.S. forces in Vietnam. A half-dozen years later, when IBP came to town, it hired some of the local Laotians and offered them $150 bounties to recruit relatives to come to Storm Lake. The company itself sent out headhunting teams to other Laotian settlements in the United States, causing the Laotian population to swell to fifteen hundred or more—almost all of them of the Tai Dam ethnic minority.

Reverend Tom takes me on a daylong tour of his flock, an itinerary with no geographical or community anchor. Despite their strong presence, the Lao have no newspaper or radio in town, no Lao "district" per se. On the edge of town two Lao-run convenience markets selling sticky rice and magazines imported from Thailand serve as the unofficial gathering and gossip point. "No one wants to rent to us," says the Reverend. "We get what nobody else will take." . . .

In a walk-up apartment with a surplus army cot for a bed and discarded patio lounge as a couch, one male worker, Symery, greets us with what seems to be a permanently crooked wrist. After being recruited by friends in 1992 to work at IBP, he took a job cutting the meat off backbones. In his fifth month on the job, thirty days before the company began granting its limited health care package, he slashed his palm open. He paid for the medical care himself, with the company discounting his weekly check. A second accident this past July left him disabled, he says. But IBP recognizes only the reports of its own contract doctors, and they certified Symery as fit to work. The result: he has had no income since the summer. "IBP isn't humane," he says. "No one worked like I did. No one could do boning like me." . . .

But Reverend Tom's greatest lament is reserved for the Laotian youth. He sees little evidence that the current plight of his people is just the newest chapter in the U.S. immigration story, where the first generation suffers but its children prosper. "This new generation is worse off," he says. "Our kids have no self-identity, no sense of belonging. They see no way out—only picking up at IBP when their parents leave off. No role models. Eighty percent of our kids drop out of high school."

Life Underground

At least the Storm Lake Lao have Reverend Tom. The more transient Latino community, bunkered mostly into two dilapidated trailer parks known as Little Mexico, has produced no visible community leaders. The handful of clergy and social workers who are this group's only advocates insist on remaining anonymous and low profile. This is, after all, a company town, and paranoia runs deep.

And rightfully so. Unlike the Lao, who are all legal residents, something like half the Latino workers and their families here are undocumented. Several workers tell me that valid Social Security cards—that belong to others—can be purchased for three hundred to five hundred dollars and that the company does no checking. Other workers contend that IBP management personnel moonlight in document trafficking. That's a story the company denies.

IBP openly admits that many of these Latinos—legal residents and otherwise—have come here recruited by the company, which has consistently used labor brokers to comb the border areas in south Texas and California to shuttle up new recruits at as much as three hundred dollars a head. A cursory look at a birth certificate or Social Security card was enough to satisfy the broker and the personnel department that the labor draftees were legal.

"The company loves to work with illegals," says forty-five-year-old Heriberto from inside his trailer, a few yards away from the scene of the December fire. "When you are illegal you can't talk back" he adds. Heriberto brings home three hundred dollars for a six-day, forty-eight-hour week. One paycheck goes for trailer rent. Another is sent back to relatives in Mexico. "You keep your head down and follow orders. We say you can't do nothing." Switching to Spanish, he says, *"Dices nada porque la planta es del gobierno"* (You say nothing because the plant is the government). Indeed. Though Latinos make up about a quarter of the IBP work force and have the most dangerous jobs, Latino surnames show up on less than 5 percent of the worker compensation claims filed between 1987 and 1995.

But as inhospitable as work is at Storm Lake, the average wage of about seven dollars an hour still trumps Mexico's four-dollar-a-day minimum wage. Now that a migrant trail is firmly in place, the company has been able to scale back but not eliminate its overt recruitment and rely on word of mouth. As many as 150 Mexican workers in Storm Lake, for example, come from the same small village of Santa Rita in the state of Jalisco. There's a constant commerce of workers, relatives, and friends between Storm Lake and Santa Rita. This human conveyor belt is powered by the grueling work regimen, which generates an astonishing worker turnover rate of more than 80 percent a year—a rate common to the entire industry. "Perfect for the company," says Heriberto. "Most workers leave before six months is up and the company has to start paying health insurance."

Meanwhile, in 1995 IBP stripped off a juicy $257 million in profits on sales of $12 billion. Its CEO, Robert Peterson, made $1 million in salary and $5.2 million in bonuses that year. Storm Lake shows none of the blight that metastasized through the region after the 1980s farm collapse. Its small and tidy downtown has no board-ups or vacancies. Four locally owned banks are thriving. The housing market is corset-tight. "You can't even rent," says Mayor Sandra Madsen. "We have two big payrolls, a stable downtown. Five years from now I think this town will realize we are all better off for the change we have gone through." . . .

"Your Tired, Your Poor ... "

IBP doesn't like chatting with the press. But Roberto Treviño, the twenty-nine-year-old personnel director at the Heartland Company, a turkey processing plant, gave me a gracious tour of his facility a few hours up the road in Marshall, Minnesota. Five hundred workers—70 percent of them Latinos and Asians, and some Somalis, all in white smocks and caps and under the stress of constantly clanging machinery and chilly temperatures—slaughter, carve, trim and package thirty-two thousand gobblers a day and then ship them throughout America under more than sixty different brand names, including Manor House and Janet Lee.

The college-educated son of Chicano farm workers, Treviño sees his work at least in part as philanthropic. "This is about the whole American immigrant experience. We are providing a stepping stone," he says. "We go to areas of unemployment to recruit. To South Texas: Eagle Pass, El Paso, Brownsville. If you are new in this country you are not going to be a doctor. Instead you take the jobs Americans don't want and you may not get ahead. But you do it for your kids." Yet even Treviño indirectly admits that in the restructured, low-pay workplace, there is little of the stability that we have come to associate with earlier waves of immigration. His turnover hovers at one hundred percent. One of five workers is a "re-hire."

"With our workers coming from Texas and Mexico we realize this is *not* home," he says, contradicting his earlier notion of facilitating assimilation. "This is where you work."

That's not true for the one hundred fifty or so Somalis who live and work in Marshall. They can't go back. Some were in a Kenyan refugee camp on a Friday only to find themselves by the next Monday resettled in Minnesota and slashing away at turkeys. In the early nineties other Somalis had poured into Marshall from San Diego, where work had become scarce. But that inflow has now slowed. "A few years back there was a misunderstanding in our plant over rest periods and there was a Somali strike," says Treviño with a chuckle. "The first in the U.S. We fired them all. About eighty workers. Let me tell you, the word got out on the Somali grapevine fast. And now when they come to work here they understand what American work standards are. No labor trouble since then." Treviño's hard-line attitude is emblematic of an industry that has reinvented itself over the past fifteen years. . . .

The pattern of deunionization and ruralization was regional. One after another, meatpacking plants moved from the big cities, where they were close to labor, into the countryside, where they were near the animals and could save on transportation costs. As supermarkets took on more specialty butchers, the processing plants needed more, but less-skilled, workers. Unions became anathema. The industry's hourly pay, including benefits, peaked at nineteen dollars in 1980. By 1992 it was below 1960s levels at twelve dollars an hour, and it has continued to fall. By 1995 unionization was half of what it was in 1963. . . .

And so it has been primarily over the past five to eight years that the industry has implemented a strategy of targeted recruitment and begun to employ methods of labor control that one group of researchers says "recall systems of peonage."

"The best hope these new communities have is that they become unionized someday," says Joe Amato, director of regional studies at Southwest State University in Marshall. "But how? How can transitory, invisible communities articulate what they want, let alone achieve it?"

With a Wink and a Handcuff

Since 1992 the INS has arrested more than one thousand meat-packing workers in the Midwest. This past summer, as part of a six-week regional sweep ordered by the Clinton Administration, two hundred nine undocumented workers were detained in Iowa. The average pay for those arrested was $6.02 an hour. Now the four biggest meatpackers, including IBP and Swift, have agreed to participate in an INS program that will use computers to check IDs.

Local Latino workers laugh it all off. "Everyone knows the company and the INS are in together on all this. They never make the company pay a fine, do they?" says Javier, an IBP worker in Storm Lake who works under the ID he purchased in the name of a legal resident. "Everyone knows they are never going to arrest all of us. Who would do this shitty work for them? We know that every now and then the *migra* will come in and take a few away to keep the politicians happy. And then we won't see them again for another two years. That's how it works."

For more than a century now there's been a pattern of U.S. industries—one after another—actively recruiting Mexican labor while the rest of society turned a blind eye, says Fred Krissman, anthropologist at Washington State University. "You can go back to the 1920s and find all sorts of academic research in that period referring to Mexicans who could be brought here to work and then sent back home like homing pigeons to procreate." And there's always been that cognitive dissonance between the reality and the policy. "In 1954 during what was called Operation Wetback, a million Mexicans were randomly rounded up in the United States and deported," says Krissman. "At the same time we were bringing in 300,000 Mexicans in the Bracero program. We had trains running both ways on public money!"

The solution, he argues, is to dump current immigration policy and opt for the model of the European Union. When you have a system that frees the flow of capital across borders, you should move toward a transnationalization of labor, too. If you work in the United States you should have legal papers in the United States, and all such workers should be protected by serious enforcement of health and safety regulations on the books. This doesn't mean immigrant workers would suddenly make middle-class wages, but it would be the first step toward eliminating the employer abuses rained down on people with no legal standing. Most important, it would be a radical leap toward stabilizing these now underground communities. At best, unions would have a better shot at organizing; at a minimum, individual workers would stand a better chance of raising their wages.

This is not a likely option when politicians from both parties struggle to outdo each other in cracking down on illegal aliens. . . .

That's the thought that keeps running through my mind as I sit and talk with Mark Prosser, the beefy, blond, self-described "very conservative" police chief of Storm Lake. I ask him how, if at all, he's changed since the influx of immigrants. "We are all prejudiced," he says, "but I really had to face and confront my biases. I don't think the people I used to work with in East St. Louis where I worked on the [police] force would even recognize me today." . . .

"I've come to a conclusion. The emphasis has to be on legalization, not arrests. There's just got to be a better way. We have to get these people into the system and get them legalized. You know, I really admire these people. Really. I doubt seriously I would ever invite a federal agency to come in again."

I leave Chief Prosser's office and pick up the paper on the corner. A headline says that the day before, in nearby Omaha, IN. agents raided a city-contracted garbage hauler and arrested more than seventy illegals—about half the company work force. One shot was fired at an escaping alien.

Personal Voices

13

White Men and the Denial of Racism

Cooper Thompson

"I had to work hard for what I have, but the recipients of Affirmative Action are getting something for nothing. Why should I support that? It's not democratic." You're at a party, or in a class, and some white men let loose with their anger at those "unqualified minorities" who are getting all the good jobs while white guys like themselves are getting screwed. You know that this is a serious distortion of reality, but you also know that these

I want to thank the many colleagues and friends who have helped me understand the dynamics of racism, and who have helped me conceptualize parts of this article, particularly Valerie Batts, Harry Brod, Angela Bryant, Pat Griffin, Tom Griggs, Gerald Jackson, Jim Kilpatrick, Wekesa Olatunji Madzimoyo, Horace Seldon, Althea Smith, and Mark Wise.

"angry white men" truly believe what they're saying and that they have a lot of support from millions of like-minded Americans. And so you wonder: How did these guys come to believe that race-conscious remedies like affirmative action and equal opportunity employment were so wildly successful that they are the ones who now need protection from "reverse discrimination"?

Although these white men are badly misinformed about racial progress, they probably are on one end of a continuum that includes progressive and liberal white men. The continuum is called "denial of racism." As I've thought about the comments of "angry white men," and reflected on my experiences as an antiracist white man, I've come to believe that all of us white men are, to some extent, in denial about the ways that racism continues to benefit us and hurt people of color. Understanding the mindset of "angry white men" may help the rest of us realize how our thinking about race is clouded, and, hopefully, increase our clarity about white male privilege and racism as we speak out in support of racial justice.

"Why do we have to keep talking about racism?"

A few years ago, I was checking into a hotel with a Black male colleague. When he asked the white man behind the counter for our rooms, the clerk ignored him and spoke to me. I was stunned. That evening, in talking about the incident, my colleague was surprised that I was surprised; he assumed that I knew that such treatment was routine for him. As I began to notice the different ways we were treated in ordinary situations, I realized how frequently he, and other colleagues of color, were treated as if they were invisible while I was noticed and treated with respect.

When people of color try to tell us about racism they've experienced, we often stop listening or discount their interpretation of events, as if they were crazy and we knew "the truth." Let's suppose a co-worker tells us about white men who repeatedly question her qualifications, who won't talk to or sit with her in the break room, or who constantly refuse to believe the facts she's presenting. When we hear about these incidents, we often jump to the conclusion that we are being personally attacked as bigots and angrily defend ourselves. In our defensiveness, we miss the point that she was talking about systemic issues, not accusing us of anything. If we don't take it personally, we sometimes come to the defense of the organization, blame her for being too sensitive, or problem solve about how she can avoid such treatment in the future. None of these reactions give us any new information. Unfortunately, many white men don't have daily, intimate contact with people who are experiencing discrimination and so we don't even hear about it.

In writing about the white reaction to his book *The Rage of A Privileged Class* (an account of the pain and anger of Black professionals), Ellis Cose (1993) described what could be a case study of white male denial:

> Many white readers suspect the Blacks in the book of seeing prejudice where none exists. Other whites accused those Blacks in the book of blaming their own shortcomings on racism, or of existing in some wacky, unreal universe where, as one reviewer put it, 'life is supposed to be perfect.' Many said, in effect, that they were tired of hearing about Black problems and that the 'whiners' should simply shut up (conveniently ignoring the book's point that those complaining generally kept their thoughts to themselves.)

"What privilege?"

The debate over the legitimacy of race-conscious remedies has focused almost exclusively on the extent to which "minorities" should be compensated for past discrimination. Some say that the bill is long overdue; some say that the bill is paid and "minorities" should not get further compensation; and some say that the bill has been overpaid and that white men are due some compensation. For some white men, the debate is more narrowly focused: how long will white men have to pay for the sins of slavery?

Framed in this way, the issue seems absurd to many white men. We didn't own slaves and most (but not all) of our relatives didn't own slaves. That may be true. But what's also true is that there is a long and deep history of quotas and preferences favoring white men; in fact, for most of the history of the United States, the sign outside most workplaces has been, "white men only need apply." It could easily be said that there has been "affirmative action" in education and employment for white men in this country for at least three hundred years. This includes colleges that set rigid quotas limiting or preventing the admission of Jews, women, and people of color, thereby accepting some white men who otherwise wouldn't be admitted if it weren't for the lower standards artificially created by keeping out so many applicants; children of alumni ("legacies") being admitted to prestigious schools with substantially lower qualifications than those entering students whose parents were not alumni; restrictive social clubs and sports facilities where white men "networked" for jobs, long before the term was a cliché; veterans who received additional points on civil service exams; and nepotism that got white men in the door or on the fast track, allowing them to skirt the competitive process that other applicants had to follow —assuming, of course, that the others even got in the door to apply.

Most white men don't need to look very far in their own lives to see how we have benefited from opportunities available to us and denied to all others. In 1966, while growing up in Northern New Jersey, I got my first job at the age of sixteen as a house painter through my fathers' connections at the paint store where he worked. My boss patiently instructed me, as if he were my mentor; none of the painting contractors I saw were even hiring young men of color. (In fact young African-Americans or Latinos would have entered a hostile environment, given the daily barrage of racist comments about Blacks and Puerto Ricans.) In high school, I was encouraged to do well academically and placed in the college track; the young Black men in my high school were put into the vocational classes. Upon graduation, I was expected to go to a four year college; the young Black men disappeared from my life.

"These people want something for nothing."

Some white men work very hard, giving everything they have, in stressful and dangerous jobs, to take care of their families; some white men put in a good day's work, provide for their families, and still have time to be with the guys; some white men have abandoned their families. The same can be said about men of color and female heads-of-households, regardless of race.

What is different is the amount of work it takes to reach a comparable level of success. People of color often have the sense that they have to do "twice as much to go half as far." A colleague once said to me, "I feel like I have to be twice as good to accomplish anything as a Black man, and even if I'm in a strong position, I know that some whites will not see my strengths." In addition, work is made harder simply by the daily experience of subtle and overt racism.

Even more disturbing is the historical legacy of free or underpaid labor provided by people of color; white men who are angry that the recipients of Affirmative Action are "getting something for nothing" generally forget that the United States, under capitalism, was built on the backs of slave and indentured labor, and that the economy today is built on the backs of underpaid labor. In this way, white people benefit today from both past and current patterns of racism. This point is dramatically brought home to me whenever I stay at a hotel—the service staff is largely recent immigrants, usually women of color, working for low wages and little or no benefits—or when I hear about consumer goods sold for a nice profit in the United States but produced by third world workers earning pennies a day in slave-like conditions. Seeing the comfort and success of white men as dependent on the underpaid work of people of color gives new meaning to the question of who deserves what.

"Affirmative Action is the politically correct way to say Quotas."

Affirmative Action is a very varied and complex set of policies that is often described (or lambasted) as if it were simply a system of mandatory quotas. To reduce Affirmative Action to quotas is a gross distortion; in fact, the courts have reaffirmed on numerous occasions that Affirmative Action policies are not quotas and cannot, in their implementation, discriminate against the majority. In practice, Affirmative Action varies tremendously from organization to organzation. It can mean an aggressive search for job candidates in a human service agency, "set-aside" positions for contractors, plans to reserve places in a training program, and hiring goals and timetables for certain positions in a corporation. Any of these policies can be voluntary or mandated, with a wide variety of quality and compliance.

"Is she qualified?"

Affirmative Action was never designed to be a program to hire "unqualified" people; it was designed to get women and people of color in the door to compete with us, when we found ways to lock the door on anyone but white men like ourselves. And while there are cases where poor implementation of Affirmative Action led to the hiring of an unqualified person of color, there are also plenty of situations where incompetent white men have been hired.

I believe that it is race-based prejudice that leads us to routinely question the qualifications of people of color. Why is it that we don't routinely wonder about a white guy's qualifications? Why is it that we always wonder, and comment on, the qualifications of the person of color who got a job previously held by a white man? Can it be anything other than deeply held beliefs about who is qualified? Or, as Roger Wilkins (1995, 416) suggests in "Racism Has Its Privileges," using the term "unqualified" may be simply an updated and more socially acceptable version of referring to people of color as "inferior."

A colleague of mine, Gerald Jackson, recently suggested to me that most people are, in fact, initially "unqualified" to do the jobs they are hired to do. It makes sense: generally, people are hired or promoted based on their potential to do a job they don't yet know how to do. My colleague concluded that people of color should have the same opportunity as white men to be "unqualified" when hired.

"There are no opportunities for us."

When we blame "minorities" for a lack of job opportunities, we are simply following an old pattern in which the members of oppressed groups attack each other, or members of other oppressed groups, rather than challenging the oppressor directly. When it comes to white men losing job opportunities, the "oppressor" is not undocumented workers, legal immigrants, or "Affirmative Action hire," it is the corporate mentality that downsizes, sends jobs overseas, breaks unions, outsources, and prefers technology to people, all in the interest of stock holders and top management who benefit from an improvement in the bottom line. Under capitalism, some unemployment is desirable; under capitalism, exploitation is a given. It's easier to blame "minorities" than the CEO and board; it's difficult to criticize capitalism when you've always been told that the United States is the land of opportunity for white guys like you.

"The minorities have taken my job."

For some white men, the scapegoating of people of color for the failures of capitalism is made easier by an underlying belief that white men deserve to have the good jobs. During a period of plant closures at a major U.S. corporation, I repeatedly heard comments like this one: "My father and grandfather worked here their whole lives, I've put in 25 years in this plant, and now they're taking my job and giving it to some Mexicans." For these white men, there was a clear recognition that the company was to blame; over the course of several days, I heard about all the lies they were told concerning job security. But their comments about "the Mexicans" suggest not only prejudice but also anxiety about the presence of people of color in formerly white-held occupations.

This leads to me to speculate that underneath white male anger is fear of competing with people of color. It's one thing to compete with other white men and lose; but to compete with people who you've always been told are "less than" strikes at the heart of our sense of (racial) self-worth. I have painful memories of working as an assistant to an African-American woman as she taught a class, and wondering to myself, What do the white men in the audience think of me as I sit here next to this Black woman, "beneath" her? Regardless of how she saw my role, or what the white men actually thought, I carried the prejudice inside myself. How many other white men carry this same fear?

"We're now the minority."

There are places in the United States where people of color are sometimes the numerical majority: in some urban neighborhoods (but not inside most office buildings located in or near those same neighborhoods); in some rural areas when crops are being harvested; at some religious and cultural events; and occasionally in some social and work-related settings within an organization.

But for most white men, our daily experience is one of being the majority, and in many cases, living and working in racially segregated environments where there are few, if any, people of color. If we look at all the places where white men are "in control," it seems obvious that people of color aren't even close to "taking over": white men are 82.5 percent of the wealthiest Americans, 77 percent of Congress, 92 percent of state governors, 70 percent of tenured college faculty, 90 percent of daily newspaper editors, and 77 percent of television news directors. In most workplaces, the vast majority of white men report to another white man.

This fear of non-white people taking over may be a matter of perception. Widely quoted "Workforce 2000" (1987) statistics citing the decline of white men in the U.S. workforce by the turn of the century may have been taken more seriously than the authors anticipated. According to the Bureau of Labor Statistics, the racial shifts among white collar workers from 1975 to 1994 are real but meager: the percentage of white workers dropped from 92.3 percent to 89.7 percent over twenty years, a change of less than 3 percent. And although white people will become less than 50 percent of the US population sometime in the next century, the Urban Institute estimates this will not happen until the year 2090. When this data is combined with the evidence that racial segregation in residential areas is actually higher than it was two or three decades ago, it becomes clear that most adult white men have a good chance of living out their lives in the company of other white people.

The false perception of being a racial minority may be further explained by the fact that white people typically overestimate the number of people of color present in a particular context. In a 1990 Gallup poll, the average white American estimated that 32 percent of the US population was Black and 21 percent was Hispanic; the real figures were 12 percent and 9 percent. Recently, while doing a presentation to a group of employees at a corporation, I experienced this phenomenon first-hand: glancing at the audience, I thought that white people were the minority, until I actually did a head count. Of the 42 people present, there were 17 white men, 9 white women, 12 African-American women, 3 African-American men, and 1 Asian-American man—a total of 26 white people and 16 people of color.

Speaking Out about Racism

Not all white men are in denial about the impact of racism; some white men recognize that discrimination still exists, some support Affirmative Action, some even account for the privileges they get as white men. But I'm struck by the relative absence of these voices of allies in the fight against racism. As their white brothers speak up in anger at immigrants, welfare recipients, and "inner city" youth—to name a few of the current scapegoats—these allies against racism contribute to what Dr. Martin Luther King called "the appalling silence of the good people." These white men aren't talking even though they know, through the experiences of friends and colleagues, that sexism, racism, and other forms of oppression are daily experiences for many citizens of the United States.

My wish is that more white men speak out about racism. I'd like to see more statements like this letter to the editor of the *Boston Globe* (1995):

> The opponents of Affirmative Action say the only discrimination that remains is reverse discrimination. This is absurd. . . . Affirmative Action is a sometimes clumsy attempt to remove the extra hurdle that no white male applicant would have faced. It is clumsy because on some occasion a woman or a person of color may seem to be given an unfair advantage over a white male. The fact is that the white male has an unfair advantage everyday of his life. . . . I don't want to bash white males. I'm one myself. But I do acknowledge that my life is easier because I am white and male. I wish that opponents of Affirmative Action would acknowledge the same thing and admit that they don't want to surrender the unfair advantage they possess.

When these types of comments are as frequent as those that deny the realities of racism, I'll begin to trust that, in my lifetime, there might be substantial progress on our unfullfilled commitment to racial justice in the United States. If, however, the attacks on race-conscious remedies continue, unchallenged, I'll wonder if we aren't headed for what Derrick Jackson, a columnist for the *Boston Globe* (23), has called the "racial ice age," referring to the fifty-to-one-hundred year cycles of progress and backlash for people of color. In a June 16, 1995 column, he concluded, "There is nothing in the history of this country to suggest that the glaciers of the new racial age will do anything but slice through the trees, rip up the roots, and leave behind mere moraines of racial progress—when there should have been mountains."

References

Cose, Ellis. 1993. *The Rage of the Privileged Class.* New York: HarperCollins.

Graham, John R. November 16. *USA Today.*

Jackson, Derrick. 1995, June 16. "The Racial Ice Age." *Boston Globe*, 23.

Johnston, William B., and Arnold E. Packer. 1987. *Workforce 2000: Work and Workers in the 21st Century.* Indianapolis: Hudson Institute.

Mantsios, Gregory. 1998. "Class in America: Myths and Realities." In P. S. Rothenberg, ed., *Race, Class, and Gender in the United States: An Integrated Study,* fourth ed. New York: St. Martin's Press.

Wilkins, Roger. 1995, March 27. "Racism Has Its Privileges." *The Nation* 260, no. 12, 412–16.

14

Red Clay, Blue Hills: In Honor of My Ancestors

John Brown Childs

> In every place visited among the Sakalava we found events and
> names recalled by tradition still living in memory . . . we have heard
> the Sakalava invoke these names in all important activities of their
> social life and recall with pride these events. . . .
>
> —Charles Guillain (1845), cited in Raymond K. Kent, *Early
> Kingdoms in Madagascar, 1500–1700*

I must speak about my ancestors. It is from them that I have received the desire to contribute to the best of my ability to what I hope is constructive cooperation leading to justice, equality, and peace in the world. I owe it to them to make these comments. What I say in these pages flows from two great currents, the African and the Native American, whose conflux runs through my family and infuses my spirit today. In the 1990s, when I went to visit my family in Marion, Alabama, my cousin Arthur Childs, who had served as lieutenant in World War II in Burma, and who was the family storyteller, took me immediately to the cemetery, where in the midst of red clay dust he told me the histories of those who had passed on.

The African-Malayo grandmother of my grandmother of my grandmother of my grandmother, known as The Princess to her captors, was born in Madagascar, an island peopled by populations from the Pacific and Africa. In 1749, The Princess was a member of a Madagascan delegation on board a French ship bound for France, where she apparently was to go to convent school. Their ship was captured by English privateers. All the Madagascans on board were captured and sold into slavery in the English colonies. My ancestress found herself in chains, being sold as property to a Thomas Burke, a leading figure in North Carolina government, to be given as a wedding present for his new wife at a wedding ceremony in Norfolk, Virginia (Bond 1972, 22). The story handed down within both the Burke family and my relations is that when "the 'Princess' was brought first to the Virginia plantation where she began her career as a slave, the other enslaved Africans acknowledged her royal origin and gave her the respect due to one of her background" (Bond 1972, 23).

The descendants of The Princess established their families in the red clay country of Marion, where they (as property of whites) had been transferred through the infamous network of the slave trade. Marion, in Perry County, Alabama, has for a long time been a dynamic wellspring in southern African-American life. Marion is where my father's forebears, Stephen Childs and family, created the Childs Bakers and Confectioners, Growers, and Shippers store on Main Street. This store was an economic bulwark of the African-American community there. My father, born in the heart of what had been the slave-holding region of the southern United States, was named after John Brown, the revolutionary fighter who gave his life in the battle against slavery.

Marion is where James Childs and nine other African-Americans, newly liberated from slavery after the Civil War, established the first African-American school, The Lincoln Normal School, in the late 1860's. . . .

The school's teachers were housed in a building that had been taken away from the Ku Klux Klan, whose aim was to keep people of African descent in subordination and indignity. . . .

Lincoln Normal School went on to become an influential African-American educational institution. Dr. Horace Mann Bond noted the broad community significance of the Perry County Lincoln Normal School in his study *Black American Scholars*, which analyzes the roots of southern African-Americans holding Ph.Ds after the Civil War. . . .

Among my relatives influenced by Lincoln Normal was William Hastie, a civil rights legal advocate and the first African-American federal circuit court of appeals judge, as well as an important participant in President Franklin Delano Roosevelt's "Black Cabinet." In 1943 Hastie resigned a government position as assistant to the U.S. Secretary of War in protest over racial segregation of African-Americans in the U.S. military. . . .

My Childs family relations, along with other African-Americans in Marion, worked in the midst of Ku Klux Klan country, to create Lincoln Normal School as a sustaining community in the midst of a dangerous, often lethal environment of racial oppression. They sought to use their roots in the rural and small-town Deep South as a basis for construction of a bastion of justice and dignity.

I was born in 1942, in the Roxbury ghetto of Boston, Massachusetts. As a small child I lived in a housing project called Bataan Court. My birthplace is only a few miles north of a state recreational park; there, in the Blue Hills is a body of water called by its Native American name *Punkapoag*, which means "The Place of the Fresh Water Pond." Punkapoag is where some of my mother's Native-American ancestors once lived. My relations were members of the Algonkian confederacy known as the Massachusett—or to be more precise, *Massachuseuck*, which means "The Place of The Big Hills." The Massachusett nation, like many Native-American nations, was an egalitarian confederacy comprising several communities such as the Punkapoag, the Nipmuck, the Neponset, and the Wesaguset.*

Closely related neighbors of the Wampanoag ("The People of the Dawn"), who, as with the Nipmuck ("The People of the Fresh Water Place") today are vibrant communities in Massachusetts, these ancestors of mine encountered Europeans under the command of Giovanni da Verrazano in 1524. Verrazano described the Massachusett as a "most beautiful" people who were "sweet and gentle, very like the manner of the ancients." They were, he observed, expert sailors who can, "go to sea without any danger" in boats made "with admirable skill" (Brasser, 1978: 78). Almost one hundred years later, in 1614, Captain John Smith, while "visiting" the Massachusett, described their land as "the paradise [*sic*] of all these parts" (Salwen, 1978: 170). This paradise was soon decimated by the wave of epidemics that ravaged much of New England as larger ships carrying more Europeans brought diseases such as smallpox, to which native peoples had no immunity. . . .

The Massachusett people were particularly hard hit this way. Their population plummeted from an estimated thirty thousand to a few hundred by the mid 1650s. By

---

*Such confederacies were fluid, and their composition could change over time.

that time, the surviving members of those nations that had been undermined were forcibly concentrated into small villages called "Praying Towns" where they were supposed to adapt to and adopt Christianity. One of these towns was Punkapoag, originally the main home of the Massachusett, but later turned into a mix of concentration camp/refugee center. . . .

Many of the Praying Town inhabitants, the so called Praying Indians, although they provided men to serve in colonial militias (against the French) were attacked, dispersed, and killed. For those who survived, and for their descendants, such atrocities clearly drew the final bloody message that their ancient homelands were no longer the richly textured environments of deeply rooted free-life, but had to a large degree become the places of tears. Many Narragansett, Pequod, Mohegan, Massachusett, and other natives were now exiles "in the land of the free" (Lyons 1992). As a coherent cultural entity, the Punkapoag community of the Massachusett confederacy, with its members forced into exile and finding intermarriage with other peoples the only means of survival, ceased to exist as a social whole.

Responding to long decades of cultural erosion and terrorism directed against them, a gathering of Christian Native peoples, including some of my ancestors, under the leadership of Rev. Samson Occom—a Mohegan man and a Presbyterian minister who had struggled against great odds to attain his "calling"—sought and were generously given land by the Oneida nation in what is now New York State. It was there, in a 1774 ceremony, that they were adopted as "the younger brothers and sisters" of the Oneida.

My Native-American ancestors, whose family name had become Burr, intermarried with the Oneida. Eventually, in the early 1800s, they moved back to their ancestral homeland of Massachusetts (see Doughton 1998). Eli and Saloma Burr, my great, great, great grandfather and grandmother, settled in the western part of Massachusetts near Springfield. Eli and Saloma, and their children Vianna, Fidelia, Alonzo, and Albert, are listed in the 1868 Massachusetts State "Indian" census as Oneida people, Eli's grandfather had been an "Oneida chief" according to these state records. Eli and Saloma's children married African-Americans, including Zebadee Carl Talbott, a sharpshooter and "one of the best pistol shots in the country" according to a *Springfield Republican* report. One of the grandchildren, James Burr, became well known as an African-American inventor.

A 1915 obituary in the Massachusetts *Springfield Republican* newspaper noting the death of one of their grandsons, John Burr, contains information that could have only come from the Burrs, namely, that his ancestors were originally from "Ponkapog" Massachusetts, and that they had been adopted by the Oneida in the 1700s. So, well over 100 years after their ancestors had left New England for the Oneida sanctuary of Brothertown, the Burrs still carried the memories both of their Massachusett origins and of the importance of their adoptive Oneida homeland.

From these currents of Massachusueck/Brothertown-Oneida, and Africa came my mother Dorothy Pettyjohn, who was born in Amherst, Massachusetts. She became a teacher who, as a young woman, went to "Cotton Valley" in Alabama of the 1930's to teach in a school for impoverished rural African-American children not far from Marion and its Lincoln Normal School. It was there that she met and married my father. So, the waves of oppression, crashing over many peoples, driven from their land, forged many of them into complex syntheses of memory and belonging that link Africa and Native America for me.

In 1835, Alexis de Tocqueville's soon to be famous, vast overview of the young United States, entitled *Democracy in America*, was published. Among his otherwise astute descriptions based on his travels in "America," Tocqueville inaccurately pictures what he calls "the three races of the United States." These are, he says, "the white or European, the

Negro, and the Indian" which he claims are always distinctly separate populations. Concerning "the Negro" and "the Indian" he writes that these "two unhappy races have nothing in common, neither birth, nor features, nor language, nor habits" (1954, 343; for an epic depiction of the cross-currents created by oppression in the Americas, see Galeano 1985).

If this assertion by Tocqueville were true, then I could not exist, given my African and Native American currents that have flowed together for more than two hundred years. My family relations cannot be compartmentalized into these rigid sealed-off categories such as those suggested by Tocqueville. Nor can the depths of their courage be plumbed by his superficial description of the "unhappy races," no matter how terrible their tribulations as they have flowed through so many valleys of oppression. Today I recognize that from Punkapoag in Massachusetts, and Brothertown in New York State, to Lincoln Normal School in Alabama, my relations were among those establishing roots in what they hoped would be sustaining communities that could buffer people against the forces of hatred while offering solid ground for justice and dignity. I know that my connection to my ancestors is not only genealogical, as important as that is. My connection to them is also that of the spirit. I have for many years worked alongside those trying to create places of freedom from injustice. I continue to do so today. I now understand, after years of my own internal development, with guidance from elders and friends, that this work of mine is propelled by those currents flowing from the springing hopes of my ancestors.

I do not feel like one of those "crossing border hybrids" now so much discussed by scholars who examine post-modernity. Nor does the older Latin American term "Zambo" for "half Black/half Indian, "describe how I know myself. It is not in such a divided fashion that I recognize my existence. To the contrary, in the language of my Algonkian ancestors, *Noteshem*—I am a man—who stands at *newichewannock*, "the place between two strong currents." Without these two distinct streams there can be no such "in-between place" to be named as such. But, at the same time, this place is real and complete unto itself. In the same way, I emerge a full man, not a simple bifurcated halfling, from the two strong currents of Africa and Native America. It is this *newichewannock* that marks the place of my spirit, and that propels me today.

References

Bond, Horace Mann. *Black American Scholars: A Study of Their Origins*, 1972. Detroit, Mich.: Balamp.
Brasser, T. J. "Early Indian-European Contacts." In *Handbook of North American Indians*, 1978, ed. Bruce Trigger, et. al. Washington, D.C., Smithsonian Press.
Doughton, Thomas L. "Unseen Neighbors: Native Americans of Central Massachusetts, A People Who Had 'Vanished.'" In *After King Philip's War: Presence and Persistence in Indian New England*, 1998, ed. Colin G. Calloway. Hanover, N. H.: University Presses of New England.
Galeano, Eduardo. *Memory of Fire* (3 volumes), 1985. New York: Pantheon.
Kent, Raymond K. *Early Kingdoms in Madagascar, 1500–1700*, 1970. New York, Holt, Rinehart and Winston.
Lyons, Oren. "The American Indian in the Past." In *Exiled in the Land of the Free: Democracy, Indian Nations, and the U.S. Constitution.* 1992, ed. Oren Lyons, et al. Santa Fe: Clear Light.
Salwen, Bert. "Indians of Southern New England and Long Island, Early Period." In *Handbook of North American Indians*, 1978, ed. Bruce Trigger, et al. Washington, D.C.: Smithsonian Institution.
Tocqueville, Alexis de. *Democracy in America.* 1960. New York, Vintage.

15

Complexion

Richard Rodriguez

Visiting the East Coast or the gray capitals of Europe during the long months of winter. I often meet people at deluxe hotels who comment on my complexion. (In such hotels it appears nowadays a mark of leisure and wealth to have a complexion like mine.) Have I been skiing? In the Swiss Alps? Have I just returned from a Caribbean vacation? No, I say no softly but in a firm voice that intends to explain: My complexion is dark. (My skin is brown. More exactly, terra-cotta in sunlight, tawny in shade. I do not redden in sunlight. Instead, my skin becomes progressively dark; the sun singes the flesh.)

When I was a boy the white summer sun of Sacramento would darken me so, my T-shirt would seem bleached against my slender dark arms. My mother would see me come up the front steps. She'd wait for the screen door to slam at my back. "You look like a *negrito*," she'd say, angry, sorry to be angry, frustrated almost to laughing, scorn "You know how important looks are in this country. With *los gringos* looks are all that they judge on. But you! Look at you! You're so careless!" Then she'd start in all over again. "You won't be satisfied till you end up looking like *los pobres* who work in the fields, *los braceros.*"

(*Los braceros:* Those men who work with their *brazos*, their arms: Mexican nationals who were licenced to work for American farmers in the 1950s. They worked very hard for very little money, my father would tell me. And what money they earned they sent back to Mexico to support their families, my mother would add. *Los pobres*-the poor, the pitiful, the powerless ones. But paradoxically also powerful men. They were the men with brown-muscled arms I stared at in awe on Saturday mornings when they showed up downtown like gypsies to shop at Woolworth's or Penney's. On Monday nights they would gather hours early on the steps of the Memorial Auditorium for the wrestling matches. Passing by on my bicycle in summer, I would spy them there, clustered in small groups, talking—frightening and fascinating men—some wearing Texas sombreros and T-shirts which shone fluorescent in the twilight. I would sit forward in the back seat of our family's 48 Chevy to see them, working alongside Valley highways; dark men on an even horizon, loading a truck amid rows of straight green. Powerful, powerless men. Their fascinating darkness—like mine—to be feared.)

"You'll end up looking just like them."

Regarding my family, I see faces that do not closely resemble my own. Like some other Mexican families, my family suggests Mexico's confused colonial past. Gathered around a table, we appear to be from separate continents. My father's face recalls faces I have seen in France. His complexion is white—he does not tan; he does not burn. Over the years, his dark wavy hair has grayed handsomely. But with time his face has sagged to a perpetual sigh. My mother, whose surname is inexplicably Irish—Moran—has an olive complexion. People have frequently wondered if perhaps, she is Italian or Portuguese. And, in fact, she looks as though she could be from southern Europe. My mother's face has not aged as quickly as the rest of her body; it remains smooth and glowing —a cool tan—which her gray hair cleanly accentuates. My older brother has inherited her good looks. When he was a boy people would tell him that he looked like Mario Lanza, and hearing it he would smile with dimpled assurance. He would come home from high school with girl friends who seemed to me glamorous (because they were) blondes. And during those years I envied him his skin that burned red and peeled like the skin of the *gringos*. His complexion never darkened like mine. My youngest sister is exotically pale, almost ashen. She is delicately featured. Near Eastern, people have said. Only my older sister has a complexion as dark as mine, though her facial features are much less harshly defined than my own. To many people meeting her, she seems (they say) Polynesian. I am the only one in the family whose face is severely cut to the line of ancient Indian ancestors. My face is mournfully long, in the classical Indian manner; my profile suggests one of those beak-nosed Mayan sculptures—the eaglelike face upturned, open-mouthed, against the deserted, primitive sky.

"We are Mexicans," my mother and father would say, and taught their four children to say whenever we (often) were asked about our ancestry. My mother and father scorned those "white" Mexican-Americans who tried to pass themselves off as Spanish. My parents would never have thought of denying their ancestry. I never denied it: My ancestry is Mexican. I told strangers mechanically. But I never forgot that only my older sister's complexion was as dark as mine.

My older sister never spoke to me about her complexion when she was a girl. But I guessed that she found her dark skin a burden. I knew that she suffered for being a "nigger." As she came home from grammar school, little boys came up behind her and pushed her down to the sidewalk. In high school, she struggled in the adolescent competition for boyfriends in a world of football games and proms, a world where her looks were plainly uncommon. In college, she was afraid and scornful when dark-skinned foreign students from countries like Turkey and India found her attractive. She revealed her fear of dark skin to me only in adulthood when, regarding her own three children, she quietly admitted relief that they were all light.

That is the kind of remark women in my family have often made before. As a boy, I'd stay in the kitchen (never seeming to attract any notice, listening while my aunts spoke of their pleasure at having light children. (The men, some of whom were dark-skinned from years of working out of doors, would be in another part of the house.) It was the woman's spoken concern: the fear of having a dark-skinned son or daughter. Remedies were exchanged. One aunt prescribed to her sisters the elixir of large doses of castor oil during the last weeks of pregnancy. (The remedy risked an abortion.) Children born dark grew up to have their faces treated regularly with a mixture of egg white and lemon juice concentrate. (In my case, the solution never would take) One Mexican-American friend of my mother's, who regarded it a special blessing that she had a measure of English blood, spoke disparagingly of her husband, a construction worker for being so dark. "He doesn't take care of himself," she complained. But the remark, I noticed, annoyed my mother, who sat tracing an invisible design with her finger on the tablecloth.

There was affection too and a kind of humor about these matters. With daring tenderness, one of my uncles would refer to his wife as *mi negra*. An aunt regularly called her dark child *mi feito* (my little ugly one), her smile only partially hidden as she bent down to dig her mouth under his ticklish chin. And at times relatives spoke scornfully of pale, white skin. A *gringo's* skin resembled *masa*-baker's dough-some-one remarked. Everyone laughed. Voices chuckled over the fact that the *gringos* spent so many hours in summer sunning themselves. ("They need to get sun because they look like *los muertos.*")

I heard the laughing but remembered what the women had said, with unsmiling voices, concerning dark skin. Nothing I heard outside the house, regarding my skin, was so impressive to me.

In public I occasionally heard racial slurs. Complete strangers would yell out at me. A teenager drove past, shouting, "Hey, Greaser! Hey, Pancho!" Over his shoulder I saw the giggling face of his girl friend. A boy pedaled by and announced matter-of-factly, "I pee on dirty Mexicans." Such remarks would be said so casually that I wouldn't quickly realize that they were being addressed to me. When I did, I would be paralyzed with embarrassment, unable to return the insult. (Those times I happened to be with white grammar school friends, *they* shouted back. Imbued with the mysterious kindness of children, my friends would never ask later why I hadn't yelled out in my own defense.)

In all, there could not have been more than a dozen incidents of name-calling. That there were so few suggests that I was not a primary victim of racial abuse. But that, even today, I can clearly remember particular incidents is proof of their impact. Because of such incidents, I listened when my parents remarked that Mexicans were often mistreated in California border towns. And in Texas, I listened carefully when I heard that two of my cousins had been refused admittance to an "all-white" swimming pool. And that an uncle had been told by some man to go back to Africa. I followed the progress of the southern black civil rights movement, which was gaining prominent notice in Sacramento's afternoon newspaper. But what most intrigued me was the connection between dark skin and poverty. Because I heard my mother speak so often about the relegation of dark people to menial labor, I considered the great victims of racism to be those who were poor and forced to do menial work. People like the farmworkers whose skin was dark from the sun.

After meeting a black grammar school friend of my sister's, I remember thinking that she wasn't really "black." What interested me was the fact that she wasn't poor. (Her well-dressed parents would come by after work to pick her up in a shiny green Oldsmobile.) By contrast, the garbage men who appeared every Friday morning seemed to me unmistakably black. (I didn't bother to ask my parents why Sacramento garbage men always were black. I thought I knew.) One morning I was in the backyard when a man opened the gate. He was an ugly, square-faced black man with popping red eyes, a pail slung over his shoulder. As he approached, I stood up. And in a voice that seemed to me very weak, I piped, "Hi." But the man paid me no heed. He strode past to the can by the garage. In a single broad movement, he overturned its contents into his larger pail. Our can came crashing down as he turned and left me watching, in awe.

"*Pobres negros,*" my mother remarked when she'd notice a headline in the paper about a civil rights demonstration in the South. "How the *gringos* mistreat them." In the same tone of voice she'd tell me about the mistreatment her brother endured years before. (After my grandfather's death, my grandmother had come to America with her son and five daughters.) "My sisters, we were still all just teenagers. And since *mi papa* was dead, my brother had to be the head of the family. He had to support us, to find work. But what skills did he have! Twenty years old. *Pobre.* He was tall, like your grandfather. And strong. He did construction work. 'Construction!' The *gringos* kept him digging all day, doing the dirtiest jobs. And they would pay him next to nothing. Sometimes they promised him one salary and paid him less when he finished. But what could he do? Report them? We weren't citizens then. He didn't even know English. And he was dark. What chances could he have? As soon as we sisters got older, he went right back to Mexico. He hated this country. He looked so tired when he left. Already with a hunchback. Still in his twenties. But old-looking. No life for him here. *Pobre."*

Dark skin was for my mother the most important symbol of a life of oppressive labor and poverty. But both my parents recognized other symbols as well.

My father noticed the feel of every hand he shook. (He'd smile sometimes—marvel more than scorn—remembering a man he'd met who had soft, uncalloused hands.)

My mother would grab a towel in the kitchen and rub my oily face sore when I came in from playing outside. "Clean the *graza* off your face!" *(Greaser!)*

Symbols: When my older sister, then in high school, asked my mother if she could do light housework in the afternoons for a rich lady we knew, my mother was frightened by the idea. For several weeks she troubled over it before granting conditional permission: "Just remember, you're not a maid. I don't want you wearing a uniform." My father echoed the same warning. Walking with him past a hotel, I watched as he stared at a doorman dressed like a Beefeater. "How can anyone let himself be dressed up like that? Like a clown. Don't you ever get a job where you have to put on a uniform." In summertime neighbors would ask me if I wanted to earn extra money by mowing their lawns. Again and again my mother worried: "Why did they ask *you?* Can't you find anything better?" Inevitably, she'd relent. She knew I needed the money. But I was instructed to work after dinner. ("When the sun's not so hot.") Even then, I'd have to wear a hat. *Un sombrero de* baseball.

(Sombrero. Watching gray cowboy movies. I'd brood over the meaning of the broadrimmed hat—that troubling symbol—which comically distinguished a Mexican cowboy from real cowboys.)

From my father came no warnings concerning the sun. His fear was of dark factory jobs. He remembered too well his first jobs when he came to this country, not intending to stay, just to earn money enough to sail on to Australia. (In Mexico he had heard too many stories of discrimination in *Los Estados Unidos.* So it was Australia, that distant island–continent, that loomed in his imagination as his "America.") The work my father found in San Francisco was work for the unskilled. A factory job. Then a cannery job. (He'd remember the noise and the heat.) Then a job at a warehouse. (He'd remember the dark stench of old urine.) At one place there were fistfights; at another a supervisor who hated Chinese and Mexicans. Nowhere a union.

His memory of himself in those years is held by those jobs. Never making money enough for passage to Australia; slowly giving up the plan of returning to school to resume his third grade education—to become an engineer. My memory of him in those years, however, is lifted from photographs in the family album which show him on his honeymoon with my mother—the woman who had convinced him to stay in America. I have studied their photographs often, seeking to find in those figures some clear resemblance to the man and the woman I've known as my parents. But the youthful faces in the photos remain, behind dark glasses, shadowy figures anticipating my mother and father. . . .

16

An Asian Lesbian's Struggle

C. Allyson Lee

By virtue of the shape of my eyes and the colour of my hair, I am considered by Canadian society to have membership in a "visible" minority, and am also called a "woman of colour". This means that I could never "pass" for white, even if I tried. It has long been regarded as a privilege, to be able to be thought of as white, to have no physical characteristics which could set one apart for looking different. After all, in Canada, a white person can walk down any street and not be called a "jap", "chink" or "nigger" and not be asked "where do you come from—originally?" or "where were you born?"

Aside from the obvious racism generated from external sources, many people of colour often suffer from a more concealed form of oppression: internalized racism. This could be described as fear or hatred of one's own ethnic heritage or prejudice against one's own race. For myself, it has taken decades to get to the point of claiming ownership of such feelings. For most of my life, I belonged to the "Don't Wanna Be" tribe, being ashamed and embarrassed of my Asian background, turning my back on it and rejecting it. I did not want to be associated with, let alone belong to a group which was stereotyped by whites as being noisy, slanty-eyed rice gobblers, "gooks" or chinks.

In spite of my being born and raised on the prairies, in a predominantly white neighbourhood with all white friends, my father tried his best (albeit unsuccessfully) to jam "Chineseness" down my throat. He kept telling me that I should be playing with Chinese kids—there were none in our neighbourhood. He chastised me for not being able to speak Chinese—by the time I entered Grade One public school, I was fluent in both English and Chinese, but my parents, worried that I may not develop good English skills, stopped conversing with me in Chinese. And my father warned me ominously, "You'd better marry a Chinese. If you marry a white, we'll cut you out of our will." All of this succeeded in driving me further away from my roots, leading me to believe that if I acted white enough, i.e. not chatter noisily in Chinese and not hang around in groups, I would actually not look Chinese.

Throughout my home life it was unacceptable for me to embrace my father's traditional Chinese culture and values unconditionally, because, in my mind, I would be accused by others of "sticking to my own kind" and would therefore be set apart from whites. But along with my father's wish for my awareness of cultural identity came along his expectation that I grow up to be a "nice Chinese girl." This meant that I should be a ladylike, submissive, obedient, morally impeccable puppet who would spend the rest of her life deferring to and selflessly appeasing her husband. He wanted me to become all that was against my nature, and so I rebelled with a fury, rejecting and denying everything remotely associated with Chinese culture.

When I moved away from the prairies to the West Coast, I remained somewhat colourless. Still denying any association with my ethnic background, I often voiced, along with others, utter contempt for Hong Kong immigrants who were, in our minds, nothing but repugnant, obnoxious, spoiled rich kids. And it was in this city that I first experienced being called chink and gook on the street.

The connection between my sinophobia (fear or hatred of anything or anyone Chinese) and rebellion against my father did not become obvious to me until years later. Moving into another province meant that there was no longer daily contact with my father, the object of my defiance. I was becoming a little less resistant to Chinese culture, as I busied myself with the task of forming a new life in the city. Seeing new places, meeting new people and taking in new experiences left me a little less time to practice this form of self-hate.

Becoming a lesbian challenged everything in my upbringing and confirmed the fact that I was not a nice, ladylike pamperer of men. Somehow I must have known from an early age that I would never fit into this conformation. My friendships with women had always been more satisfying and intense than those with men. I had grown up with a secret morbid fear of marriage, and I did not know why until I became involved with a woman.

By coincidence, my first lover was a woman of colour, someone who was proud of her own heritage. She became interested in mine, and through her support and love, I began to look more positively at my culture and see that it did hold a few interesting qualities. Her heritage and mine, although distinct and separate, had some notable and fascinating similarities. Both celebrated yearly festivals. And both cherished the importance of higher education and the formation of a solid family structure. She helped me see that it could be fun to explore the various aspects of my culture, but at this point I still did not claim it as my own.

Years later, white woman lovers came into my life, teasing me and calling me a "fake" Chinese because, after all, I did not even speak the language. This helped to bring back the old feelings of sinophobia again, and it did not occur to me then that certain white people would seek me out and be attracted to me because of my ethnic background. I had heard of "rice queens," white men who go after Chinese men. But there was no such term for white women who felt a strong affinity towards Chinese women. It would be much later that I would coin the phrase "Asianophile," my own description of such women.

Another woman entered my life, and by another coincidence, she was Chinese, born in Canada, and proud of her heritage. This I found to be both mystifying and affirming at the same time. She had not developed an attitude of sinophobia in her childhood, and as a result never felt contempt or derision for her background or her association with it. It felt like a bonus to be able to talk with her without having to explain little idiosyncrasies of our common culture and language. I no longer felt ashamed of it. She was starting to help me reclaim a heritage I had previously denied.

I felt certain that we were the only two Chinese lesbians in the world, until I began to meet others from different Asian backgrounds. At an Asian lesbian conference in California, I learned that there were indeed others who shared similar stories of struggles against externalized and internalized racism. Meeting Asian lesbians in my own city was like taking a course in Anti-Racism 101, which helped to raise my political awareness. These special women made me realize that it was fine to get upset over injustice and oppression, great to speak out about it, and necessary to fight against it. Gradually my awareness of my background was no longer the source of my shame, but the beginning of my empowerment.

My attempts at conquering my sinophobia continues to be an uphill struggle, as I deliberately seek out to meet other Asian lesbians and maintain friendships with them. Years ago I would have shunned them, or at best, ignored them. There is still a sense of discomfort, however, when I go out socially with a group of Asian women (and I find myself looking around the room hoping not to catch contemptuous racist stares from white patrons), or when my white friends tell me that they feel left out or uncomfortable around a large group of my Asian women friends.

As I go through this struggle, however, there are many bonuses in my life. I am enriched by the company of some very supportive and loving friends: Asian women, other women of colour, white women and men. I have reached a point of understanding about the origins of my previous self-hate and how it has pervaded my life and magnified the dysfunctional relationship with my father. And there is always that private joy in knowing that my father (who doesn't even know it) won't have to worry about my marrying a white boy.

Next Steps and Action

17

A Bill of Rights for Racially Mixed People

Maria P. P. Root

Countless number of times I have fragmented and fractionalized myself in order to make the other more comfortable in deciphering my behavior, my words, my loyalties, my choice of friends, my appearance, my parents, and so on. And given my multiethnic history, it was hard to keep track of all the fractions, to make them add up to one whole. It took me over thirty years to realize that fragmenting myself seldom served a purpose other than to preserve the delusions this country has created around race.

Reciting the fractions to the other was the ultimate act of buying into the mechanics of racism in this country. Once I realized this, I could ask myself other questions. How exactly does a person be one fourth, one eighth, or one half something? To fragment myself and others—"she is one half Chinese and one half white," or "he is one quarter Native, one quarter African American, and one half Spanish"—was to unquestioningly be deployed to operate the machinery that disenfranchised myself, my family, my friends, and others I was yet to meet. . . .

The Bill of Rights proposed was developed in the historical context of three interacting factors and the social forces that enable them:

1. a critical number of multiracial people of an age and in positions to give voice to concerns and injustices;

2. a biracial baby boom; and

3. a continued social movement to dismantle racism.

The affirmation of rights below reflects *resistance, revolution,* and ultimately *change* for the system that has weakened the social, moral, and spiritual fiber of this country. This chapter offers a set of affirmations or "rights" as reminders to break the spell of the delusion that creates race to the detriment of us all.

Resistance

Resistance is a political act. It is also a nonviolent strategy for changing a status quo that perpetuates race wars and violates civil rights. To resist means that one does not accept the belief system, the data as they are presented, or the rationalizations used to perpetuate the status quo around race relations. In fact, the final test case that overturned all remaining state laws against interracial marriage in 1967 (*Loving v. Virginia*) came about because two individuals, Mildred Jetters and Perry Loving, resisted the laws prohibiting interracial marriage. Subsequently, the Supreme Court invoked an interpretation of the Fourteenth Amendment to repeal these laws because they interfered with a basic civil liberty in this country, the pursuit of happiness.

Resistance also means refusing to fragment, marginalize, or disconnect ourselves from people and from ourselves. This is accomplished by refusal to uncritically apply to others the very concepts that have made some of us casualties of race wars. Four assertions listed following the Bill of Rights embody this resistance.

Bill of Rights for Racially Mixed People

I have the right
> not to justify my existence in this world
> not to keep the races separate within me
> not to be responsible for people's discomfort with my physical ambiguity
> not to justify my ethnic legitimacy

I have the right
> to identify myself differently than strangers expect me to identify
> to identify myself differently than how my parents identify me
> to identify myself differently than my brothers and sisters
> to identify myself differently in different situations

I have the right
> to create a vocabulary to communicate about being multiracial
> to change my identity over my lifetime—and more than once
> to have loyalties and identify with more than one group of people
> to freely choose whom I befriend and love

I Have the Right Not to Justify My Existence in This World

Multiracial people blur the boundaries between races, the "us" and "them." They do not fit neatly into the observer's schema of reality. Questions such as "What are you?" "How did your parents meet?" and "Are your parents married?" indicate the stereotypes that make up the schema by which the *other* attempts to make meaning of the multiracial person's existence.

Many people still have a limited understanding of the racially mixed person's place in society. Images abound of slave masters raping black women, U.S. military men carrying on sexually illicit relationships with Asian women during wars along the Pacific rim, and rebels and curiosity seekers having casual affairs.

The multiracial person's existence challenges the rigidity of racial lines that are a prerequisite for maintaining the delusion that race is a scientific fact. The multiracial person may learn to cope with these questions by asking questioners why they want to know or how this information will be useful, or by simply refusing to answer.

I Have the Right Not to Keep the Races Separate Within Me

The original racial system has been transformed and embedded into our country's political system by both the oppressors and the oppressed. A five-race framework adopted by the Federal Office of Management and Budget drives the categories of racial classification throughout the United States (Sanjek 1994), leaving no room to acknowledge self-identified multiracial people.

Resistance means asking yourself the questions, Do I want to fit into a system that does not accommodate my reality? What would I be fitting into? What is the price? Will I have to be less than a whole person? Change often requires the presentation of extremely different realities and strategies (Freire 1994) in order to break free from rigid realities. Multiracial people have a place and a purpose at this point in history to cross the borders built and maintained by delusion by creating emotional/psychic earthquakes in the social system. Declaring multiple racial affiliations and/or ethnic identities may have this effect on other people.

The biracial baby boom, the debate over racial classification for upcoming decennial census taking, and contemporary research on biracial children clarify the question: What about the children? This question is based on the belief that race dictates differences in human needs and problem solving, that racial differences are irreconcilable. To prove otherwise, the biracial or multiracial person challenges the delusional biases upon which racism is maintained.

I Have the Right Not to Be Responsible for People's Discomfort with My Physical Ambiguity

The physical ambiguity of many multiracial people, as well as mistaken identifications about their heritage, clearly challenges the notion of "pure race." The physical look of some racially mixed people is a catalyst for psychological change in how race is understood and employed. For example, many Eurasians are misidentified as Latino or Native Americans. Some words, such as *exotic*, referring to the physical appearance of multiracial people may be used as tools to reduce discomfort. Unfortunately, such terms declare social distance between people in the guise of something special or positive being offered (Bradshaw 1992; Root 1994a).

Jean-Paul Sartre (1976) suggests that people define self in terms of the subjective experience of the *other*. In this case, multiracial people are the inkblot test for the *other's* prejudices and fears.

I Have The Right Not to Justify My Ethnic Legitimacy

Tests of ethnic legitimacy are always power struggles, demonstrating the internalization of oppressive mechanisms. They employ social distance through the use of rationalized interpretation of behavior understood within an oppressive system of beliefs. These tests serve purposes of increasing divisiveness around ethnicity and delusions around race. These tests usually require that multiracial people exaggerate caricatures of ethnic and racial stereotypes. Those who initiate such struggles usually win, because they create the rules—or change the rules to suit themselves. Anyone who unquestioningly accepts these tests, begging for acceptance, remains a prisoner of the system (Freire 1970). Belonging remains fragile.

The existence of multiracial individuals requires that the common definition of ethnicity be revised. Specifically, race must not be synonymous with it. We must also challenge the notion that multiracial people will be the harbingers of doom to ethnic solidarity or ethnic continuity. Research shows that ethnicity to some extent is dynamic over time and that multiracial people are variable to the degree to which they are ethnically identified (Mass 1992; Stephan 1992).

Revolution

Everyone who enters into an interracial relationship or is born of racially different heritages is conscripted into a quiet revolution. People who voluntarily cross the border are often viewed in such strong terms as "race traitors," a sure sign that they have unwittingly created a emotional/psychic earthquake with emotional reverberations. They have refused to confirm the reality predicated on a belief in racial immutability and segregation at the most intimate level. Their resistance suggests that another reality exists. This suggests choice. Choice is frightening for some—often because it opens the door to the unknown in social relations and redefines self in relation to others.

The second set of four assertions further challenges the social construction of race in relationships. The individual has the right to resist this oppressive construction, as Paulo Freire (1970) observes:

> [The] marginal [person] has been expelled from and kept outside of the social system. . . . Therefore, the solution to their problem is not to become "beings inside of" but . . . [people] freeing themselves; for in reality, they are not marginal to the structure, but oppressed . . . [people] within it. (10-11)

I Have the Right to Identify Myself Differently Than Strangers Expect Me to Identify

Asserting this right meets with tremendous social resistance in the form of comments such as, "You can't be . . . " or "You don't look . . . " Such declarations of self-identity challenge the classification schema of the reactor. The declaration also exposes the rules that this person follows. More and more people took this tack in responding to the 1990 U.S. Census question about race. Almost a quarter of a million people wrote in a multiracial identifier (Waters 1994).

I Have the Right to Identify Myself Differently Than My Parents Identify Me

Parents are not usually aware of the identity tasks their multiracial children face unless they, too, are multiracial. Parents often will racially identify a child in a way that they feel will make for the most welcome reception of their child socially—this means not challenging social convention but usually acquiescing to our country's rules around race, which enforce singular racial identities.

Sometimes race is avoided as a topic because parents do not know how to talk about it without pain. Sometimes they assume their ability to transcend racial barriers affords a certain protection for their offspring. Parents can support the identity process by inviting conversations about race so that the illogical rules can be exposed and children can be explicitly taught how to take care of themselves as potential targets of racism (Greene 1990; Miller & Miller 1990). Parents' invitations for conversations in which they attempt to understand how and why their multiracial children identify themselves the way they do promote self-esteem and foster respect and psychological intimacy. These conversations in any household support revolutionary change.

I Have the Right to Identify Myself Differently Than My Brothers and My Sisters

Siblings can have different experiences and different goals and purposes that guide them and shape their experiences of themselves in the world. It is possible that gender influences how one comes to experience multiraciality, although this link is not yet clear.

I Have the Right to Identify Myself Differently in Different Situations

Many biracial and multiracial people identify themselves differently in different situations, depending on what aspects of identity are salient. This "situational ethnicity" is often misinterpreted. In the novel *The Crown of Columbus,* by Louise Erdrich and Michael Dorris (1991), one of the main characters, Vivian, a mixed-blood Native-American woman, describes this process as watering whatever set of her ethnic roots needs it most. This changing of foreground and background does not usually represent confusion, but it may confuse someone who insists that race is an imperturbable fact and synonymous with ethnicity. The essence of who one is as a person remains the same. Changeability is a familiar process for most people, if they consider the roles by which they identify themselves in different situations: child, parent, lover, employee, student, friend, and so on.

Situational ethnicity is a natural strategy in response to the social demands of a situation for multiethnically and multiracially identified people. For example, participants in Stephan's (1992) research on people of Asian European heritage in Hawaii and people of Hispanic European mixed ethnic heritage in New Mexico usually gave more than one identity in replying to questions about how they experienced their own identity in five different contexts. Only 26 percent of people with mixed Japanese heritage, 11 percent of those with several different ethnic heritages in Hawaii, and 56 percent of people of mixed Hispanic heritage gave the same identification in each of the five situations posed. Funderburg's (1994) research on black and white biracial Americans reveals some similar process and exposes the formidable resistance and reluctance of outsiders to accept multiple ethnic identification.

Change

The third set of assertions frees us further from the constrictions of racialized existences created by delusional beliefs and rationalizations. It directs change to build upon previous and current willingness to resist social convention and its implicit rules around race. It removes one of the most insidious barriers to collective power, social distance, and attempts to replace it with connection.

Connection is never accomplished through fear. Fear drives racism and other injustices. Connection is gained through the possession of respect, esteem, and love for oneself and others. Connection acknowledges that our social fates are intertwined and our present and future are dependent on how we interact with one another now. It is predicated on an appreciation for differences that is destructive to "racist unity" (C. K. Bradshaw, personal communication, January 1995). Connection, wholeness, and a sense of belonging decrease the likelihood that one can commit atrocities against another human being.

I Have the Right to Create a Vocabulary to Communicate About Being Multiracial

Society's vocabulary for race relations, the experience of being racialized, and the attempt to break free from concepts embedded in vocabulary requires some new terms. We must all take time and responsibility to reexamine vocabulary that has depicted racialized experience, the way Daniel (1992) has done with his examination of the concept of "passing."

It is important to think about the meaning and origin of the terms that we use to refer to ourselves. New terms are necessarily being created by multiracial people as a step toward empowerment. Self-labeling is empowerment (Helms 1990). It is a proclamation of existence.

I Have the Right to Change My Identity Over My Lifetime—and More Than Once

Identity is dynamic on the surface, whereas the core maintains some constancy. Identity is shaped by interpersonal, global, and spiritual experiences that are personally interpreted. This interpretation, however, is guided by cultural values. Thus it is possible to change one's identity over a lifetime as part of the process of clarifying or declaring who one is (Root 1990). This is an extended conceptualization of situational ethnicity. The process of identity change may reflect a shift from a passive acceptance of the identity that society expects one to accept to a proactive exploration and declaration of who one believes oneself to be—and this may include identifying differently in different situations (Stephan 1992). Ironically, these identities can even be the same, although the process is different (Root, 1990).

I Have the Right to Have Loyalties and Identify With More Than One Group of People

You have the right to loyalties and identification with more than one group of people. In fact, this fosters connections and bridges, broadening one's worldview, rather than perpetuating "us" versus "them" schisms and antagonisms. The allegiance to a greater number and variety of people increases the individual's sense of connection. The sense of connection makes it less likely that people will hurt one another by ignorance or malice. We are all empowered by connection. *The more connected we feel, the less threatening differences feel.*

I Have the Right to Freely Choose Whom I Befriend and Love

Who the racially mixed person chooses to befriend, and particularly love, does not necessarily declare his or her racial identity or ethnic loyalty. The social folklore that racially mixed people tend to "outmarry" is a statement of the rules of the social order including hypodescent, singular allegiances, and us versus them mentality. One has the right to judge people as individuals, to know that skin color, hair texture, or eye, nose, and mouth shapes are not what measures endurance during times of hardship in love and friendship. Connection, respect, and willingness to understand, compromise, and negotiate make relationships work.

I hope this Bill of Rights exposes how insidiously entwined the mechanics of oppression are in our everyday lives—systematic beliefs, biased data or interpretation of data, rationalization, and ultimately social distance. Oppression always fragments people, as energy and attention are diverted from the experience of wholeness. A society that creates race as a difference to contend with places inordinate importance on this difference in the most negative of ways. It obscures important facts about the essence of an individual. Subsequently, instead of being seen as a *dependent* variable, the result of conditions, race is now often manipulated in the daily news, daily conversations about the motives of individuals, and in research as an *independent* variable.

If we resist this fragmentation, if we revolutionize the way we think about identity and the self in relationship to the *other*, we begin to free ourselves from an oppressive structure. When we refuse to fragment ourselves or others, then we become capable of embracing the humanity in ourselves and in others. We become less fearful, less judgmental, and less subject to defining ourselves by other's opinions of us. Then we can approach differences with respect and wonderment rather than with fear. It is respect that gives us the courage for resistance, revolution, and change in tackling racial boundaries for changing race relations.

References

Bradshaw, C. K. (1992). Beauty and the beast: On racial ambiguity. In M. P. P. Root, ed., *Racially Mixed People in America*. Newbury Park, Calif.: Sage.

Daniel, G. R. (1992b). "Passers and Pluralists: Subverting the Racial Divide." In M. P. P. Root, ed., *Racially Mixed People in America*. Newbury Park, Calif.: Sage.

Erdrich, L., and M. Dorris. (1991). *The Crown of Columbus*. New York: HarperCollins.

Freire, P. (1970). *Pedagogy of the Oppressed*. New York: Seabury.

———. (1994). *Pedagogy of Hope*. New York: Continuum.

Funderburg, L. (1994). *Black, White, Other: Biracial Americans Talk about Race and Identity*. New York: William Morrow.

Greene, B. (1990). "What Has Gone Before: The Legacy of Racism and Sexism in the Lives of Black Mothers and Daughters." *Women and Therapy* 9, 207–30.

Helms, J. (1990). *Black and White Racial Identity: Theory, Research, and Practice*. Westport, Conn.: Greenwood.

Mass, A. (1992). "Interracial Japanese Americans: The Best of Both Worlds or the End of the Japanese American Community?" In M.P. P. Root, ed., *Racially Mixed People in America*. Newbury Park, Calif.: Sage.

Miller, R., and B. Miller. (1990). "Mothering the Biracial Child: Bridging the Gaps between African American and White Parenting Styles." *Women and Therapy* 10, nos. 1–2, 169–79.

Root, M. P. P. (1990). "Resolving 'Other' Status: Identity Development of Biracial Individuals." In L. Brown and M. P. P. Root, eds., *Complexity and diversity in feminist theory and therapy*. New York: Haworth.

———. (1994). "Mixed-Race Women." In L. Comas-Díaz and B. Greene, eds., *Women of Color: Integrating Ethnic and Gender Identities in Psychotherapy*. New York: Guilford.

Sanjek, R. (1994). "Intermarriage and the Future of Races in the United States." In S. Gregory and R. Sanjek, eds., *Race*. New Brunswick, N.J.: Rutgers University Press.

Sartre, J. (1976). *Critique of Dialectical Reasoning: Theory of Practical Ensembles*, tr. A. Sheridan-Smith. London: New Left Books.

Stephan, C. W. (1992). "Mixed-Heritage Individuals: Ethnic Identity and Trait Characteristics." In M. P. P. Root, ed., *Racially Mixed People in America*. Newbury Park, Calif.: Sage.

Waters, M. C. (1994). "The Social Construction of Race and Ethnicity: Some Examples from Demography." Paper presented at American Diversity: A Demographic Challenge for the Twenty-First Century, Center for Social and Demographic Analysis Conference, State University of New York at Albany.

18

Moving Beyond White Guilt

Amy Edgington

How We Can Defuse the Negative Aspects of Guilt

Get information: The more I learn about racism, the less I tend to see it as an individual moral problem and the fewer mistakes I make as an individual. The more I learn about racism the less work people of color have to do to explain to me how they experience the world. The more I learn about the ethic of domination the more I understand what I would gain by living in a world free of supremacist blinders, capable of respecting differences, and filled with true self-respect that does not demand submissive gestures from anyone.

Do something: The strongest antidote to guilt is action. The less I do about racism, the guiltier I feel. White supremacy is built largely on the complicity and inaction of white people. The simplest thing, such as interrupting a racist joke or writing a letter to the editor about police brutality is a significant break with the image of white solidarity that racism depends on. Racism is so huge that all my acts seem small in comparison, but it is precisely this kind of lifelong chipping-away that we must commit ourselves to doing.

Listen: When a person of color says, "That's racist," it's time to take a deep breath, close my mouth, sit down and listen, because school is in session. I'm in the first grade again and it's gonna take a lot of study to move on to the next class. I try to put my feelings on the back burner. I tell myself that if I have hurt someone, even inadvertently, she needs to be taken care of first. I try not to expect instant forgiveness or restoration of trust. I must follow through on any commitment I make to change.

I can take care of my guilt later by breaking it down into pieces. What do I feel remorse about? What am I scared of? Why do I feel resentment? What changes do I need to make? What do I need to know? Who can help me? How can I help other white people change?

Talk: Undoing racism cannot be done alone. It's important for me to find other white people who share the same goals. We must also seek converts, to try to turn the souls of other white people from the racism's cynical fear, mean-spiritedness, narrowness and indifference, to the kind of love for self and others that values diversity and feels no need to dominate. This is how white people can practice what Cornel West calls the "politics of conversion."

There are clearly many white people who are deeply committed to white supremacy; they are unlikely to be swayed. It's important to let them know that they face white resistance, to tell them, in effect, "If I cannot change your mind, I will put my body in your path." We should measure our commitment to fighting racism not by how many people of color we count as friends (or lovers), but by how many white people we are willing to speak to about racism.

Back to the Past

Finally, I cannot talk about white guilt without talking about the collective guilt our race bears for atrocities such as slavery and the genocide of Indian peoples. History threatens to crash down on us whenever we are confronted with our individual racist behavior in the here and now. Collective guilt is like a herd of elephants in the living room that white people have been trained to ignore, and we tend to get freaked out when someone calls the dung to our attention.

Slavery and genocide are part of every aspect of contemporary white racism. All white privileges have their roots in these historical outrages. Americans, particularly white Americans, are allergic to looking at the past; we glorify the endless frontier of the future. We have been taught that this is a land where people can put aside their past and become whatever they wish to be. This dream is only attainable for white people, however; people of color are never allowed to leave their ancestry behind them.

White people often protest, in anger or frustration, that there is nothing we can do to change history. But in fact, history is collective memory. . . . Our first duty to history is to know it, to look deeply and unflinchingly at the successive enslavements of Indians and Africans, at the forced labor of the Chinese who built our railroads, at the massacres, imprisonment and broken treaties Indians have suffered, at lynching and segregation (the evil step-twins of slavery), at the incarceration of Japanese Americans and the anti-Semitic immigration policies that helped condemn Jews to Hitler's gas chambers.

Finding Our Heroes and Sheroes

It's not just the racist past that's been buried. The long history of anti-racist work in this country has been buried as well. Some white people may know the names, if not the lives, of some of the Black heroes and sheroes of abolition, thanks to the efforts of African-Americans to educate us. But the abolition of slavery, the most hopeful event in the history of social justice, was due, in part, to the efforts of a significant minority of white men and women. Did we learn their names in school?

How many Americans know that the hymn, "Amazing Grace," was written by a slave trader, describing a religious conversion that led him to spend the rest of his life working to abolish the slave trade in Great Britain? It serves the interests of white supremacy for white people to forget both our frightful legacy of racism and those ancestors who opposed racism.

For me, the personal stories, fiction and poetry of those who experienced these atrocities, or whose ancestors did, are the most compelling kind of history. This is the only history not written by "winners," and it's very different from what we read in school. It has the power to open our eyes to the concrete details of oppression and to the interior lives of those we were trained not to see. This writing is full of hope and with despair and courage; it colors in the blanks in our vision of what it means to be human.

Moving On

Collective guilt might seem like an even bigger pit to fall into than individual guilt. But listening to the past is the first step in turning collective guilt into collective accountability. The next step is collective responsibility: to look carefully at exactly how we experience privilege today and yet are able for the most part to remain blissfully unaware of it in a society dominated by white people.

Most importantly, we can begin to turn collective guilt into collective action, to transform or overthrow institutions such as the racist educational system, media, courts, prisons and police that put the power behind white privilege. It's hard work and it's scary, but it feels a whole lot better than wallowing in guilt.

19

Linguicism

Nancy Schniedewind and Ellen Davidson

Language is yet another way to categorize people and reinforce their dominant or subordinate status. Tove Skutnabb-Kangas (1988) has proposed the term "linguicism" to refer to discrimination based particularly on language. Language oppression, often tied to discrimination based on race, ethnicity, and class, has become more visible to educators in recent years as varied groups of immigrant children with limited English proficiency enter school. Linguicism thwarts equality to the extent that these students are not provided an education in a language they understand and in schools that respect their linguistic and cultural backgrounds.

Linguicism often reinforces the dominant culture and prevailing power relationships. In some situations students with limited English proficiency are encouraged to give up their mother tongue, when in fact the more they improve in their native language the better they will learn English. Sometimes in the same school, English-speaking students are encouraged to learn a second language and become bilingual when Spanish-speaking children, for example, must give up their language, learn English and lose their bilingualism. Such a situation not only presents a double standard but perpetuates power imbalances among groups of people in our society.

How well does your school handle language differences? To what extent is the language and culture of students who speak English as their first language considered superior to students whose first language is not English? Is a bilingual student's first language seen as an asset to the classroom and school, or a detriment? Are bilingual students encouraged to use their language and teach it to their peers? Is there a difference in the tone of teacher interaction with those students who speak English and those who do not? Is Black English, sometimes called African American Language, appreciated as a distinct language that is legitimate for some types of writing in school?

Is the language and culture of students and parents whose first language is not English respected and included in all aspects of school life? Are signs and posters in the different languages represented in your school? Are parents involved through programs like home-school reading projects and bilingual events at school? If you have bilingual programs in your district, has the district considered two-way bilingual programs? Some schools have Ohighly effective programs which bring language majority and language minority students together in one setting where each group learns in the other's language for half of their instructional time together. Do you avoid types of instruction where students with English as a second language are constantly corrected? Instead, do you use instruction that encourages their speaking and writing in expressive ways to make meaning of their experiences and to generate knowledge? Are parents given a choice about the kind of program they want for their children?

Linguicism has an impact both on students whose second language is English and on language-dominant students. Academic achievement of limited-English-proficiency students is negatively affected when their language and culture isn't used for some instruction or represented in school. They can experience isolation, alienation, and inferiority when their language and culture are not validated in the school. High drop-out rates ultimately result. Students can come to devalue their own language and stop using it, even in situations where it would be appropriate.

Language-majority students can come to believe that their language and culture are superior if they experience it as the norm. They miss out on opportunities to learn other languages through experience with their peers. They miss out on friendships with students whose first language isn't English. In our increasingly global community they will pay a price for ethnocentric ideas about the primacy of English and for limited understanding of different languages and cultures.

Reference

Skutnabb-Kongas, J. and J. Cummings, eds. (1998). *Minority Education: From Shame to Struggle.* Clevedon, U.K.: Multicultural Matters.

20

Develop Cross-Cultural Communication Skills

Clyde W. Ford

We ordinarily assume that most people are "just like us." While this is true for many aspects of being human, culture and ethnicity demonstrate human uniqueness and difference. When we expect others to be "just like us," and they aren't, we can get caught in a cultural gap: something is said that offends us; someone acts in a way that shocks or angers us; another response causes us fear. One reaction is to pull back and withdraw into what is familiar and acceptable. This reaction, however, does not further communication; instead, it often gives rise to racist attitudes, actions, and beliefs. Discovering that others are "not just like us" can create a boundary between "them" and "us." Across this boundary, stereotypical labeling is substituted for real communication; honest human interchange is replaced by reactions based on anger, fear, and unresolved emotions.

There are other options when we come upon unexpected cultural interchanges. We can simply become aware of our reaction, whatever that reaction is: fear, anger, frustration, being offended. Without withdrawing we can observe our reaction and its source—

our preconditioned expectations and beliefs. This awareness can lead us to change how we interact with others; and we can develop more realistic expectations about communicating with people from different cultural backgrounds.

But awareness does not come without work. Since it runs against what we have been taught throughout our life, we have to cultivate the art of being aware in the process of communicating with others. In other words, awareness of our reactions to others is something we need to practice. Through this awareness we can readjust how we interact with others. We can accept others because we can accept ourselves. We can honor human differences through our awareness, and through our ability to change how we interact with people from other cultures and ethnic groups.

Did You Know

In one study a group of African Americans identified seven major determinants of satisfying communication with whites:

- The degree of *negative stereotyping* involved in conversations. This included forms of "indirect stereotyping" like talking about "black topics" (such as music or sports) or assuming that any African American represented the views of all African Americans. Minimal negative stereotyping was more satisfying.

- How much *acceptance* they felt for their expressed feelings and opinions.

- The amount of *emotional expressiveness.* Greater emotional expressiveness was linked to more satisfying interethnic communication.

- *Authenticity,* or the degree to which these African Americans could "be themselves" in conversation with whites. Satisfying communication went along with higher degrees of authenticity.

- *Understanding.* When respondents felt understood, good communication was reported.

- *Goal attainment.* Satisfactory communication frequently resulted in problem solving, information exchange, or the completion of a project.

- *Powerlessness.* When respondents felt controlled, trapped, or manipulated, poor communication was described. Some examples: when the conversation was "hogged" by the other person; when someone attempted to persuade them through aggressive or subtle tactics; when they were repeatedly interrupted.

Steps to Communicating Cross-Culturally

- *Build mutual understanding* rather than trying to understand where another is "coming from." No one is really able to "walk in another person's shoes." When we try to understand where someone is "coming from," we end up superimposing our life experience on theirs.

- *Be open-minded.* Accept your views as just one of many possible filters on reality, while accepting someone else's views as just another filter on reality.

- *Bridge differences* rather than insist on similarity of views.

- *Seek agreement through synthesis* rather than taking sides. Instead of giving up your views, or asking others to give up theirs, find a third position that offers common ground between differing views. This results in a cocreated, or shared, reality.

- *Focus on the relationship* rather than the individual parties to the relationship. Instead of being concerned with "what I said" and "what was said to me," be aware of the quality of the communication that takes place. In other words, move beyond "self" and "other" and focus on the interaction that takes place while communicating.

- Learn to hold the parties you communicate with in the *highest positive regard.* You may not agree with or fully understand the other person, but you can allow him or her to be with whatever feeling or thought is present in the moment—confusion; resentment, anger, courage, or love. This is holding someone in the highest positive regard. You accept and respect whatever he or she communicates without trying to change, control, or alter that communication.

Antisemitism

Introduction by Maurianne Adams

Antisemitism has been called "the longest hatred" (Wistrich 1991) to describe the conditions under which for three thousand years the Jews as a people in diaspora (from the Greek for "dispersion") successfully maintained their collective identity—first, as the only monotheistic people in pagan states whose rulers were often closely identified with polytheistic deities, and later as separate social and religious communities in Christian or Islamic countries. The early and brief period of national independence of the Hebrew monarchy in Palestine (1200 to 900 BCE) ended with Assyria's conquest of the northern kingdom of Israel (800 BCE) and Babylonia's deportation of Jews from the southern kingdom of Judah (600 to 500 BCE). Thus, Jewish identity, religion, law, and custom were all forged in diaspora, and established Jewish communities throughout European, Arab and African countries experienced cycles of relative acceptance, assimilation, and prosperity interacting cyclically with periods of enslavement, expulsion, massacre, organized pogroms, and state-organized genocide.

The biblical account of Joseph in Egypt is emblematic of this cyclical experience. Joseph, who was descended from the Hebrew patriarch Abraham (also called Israel), was sold into slavery in Egypt by his brothers but became the pharaoh's second in command and governor. For several generations his family and his people flourished in Egypt. But under a later pharaoh, the threatened massacre of the "children of Israel" resulted in the Exodus, in which Moses led his people out of bondage from Egypt to the promised land of Canaan (also called Palestine or Israel). This pattern of slavery followed by prosperity, and oppression followed by deliverance (recounted every year at Passover) captures the experience of Jewish communities in diaspora. In the centuries following 700 BCE (when Jerusalem was destroyed), Jews settled in areas now known as Spain, France, Germany, Poland, Turkey, Iraq, Iran, Yemen, Ethiopia, and Morocco, to name only a few of the historical Jewish communities. The Bene Israel community developed in India; the Jews of Cochin were in China. Yet as Christianity became the state religion throughout the countries of Europe, Jews were stripped of citizenship, reduced to dependent status as church or state property, restricted to ghettos, barred from membership in professions or craft guilds, forbidden to own land or intermarry with Christians, and made to wear special clothes or symbols that identified them as Jews. Iris Marion Young's "Five Faces of Oppression" (see chapter 5 in this volume) is useful in establishing these dimensions of Jewish oppression under categories such as social *marginalization,* economic *exploitation,* political *powerlessness,* and the cultural *imperialism* imposed in some cases by the Christian (and in other cases Islamic) majorities in European, Arab, or African countries.

Young's fifth face of oppression is *violence,* which Jewish communities experienced regularly in Christian Europe in the massacres of the late eleventh century along the route of the First Crusade from Europe to the Holy Land, in the massacres that preceded the expulsion of Jews from England in 1290, the massacres preceding expulsion from Spain in 1492, as well as the Inquisition directed against those who converted and remained as "New Christians," and in the pogroms that destroyed Jewish communities in Poland, Ukraine, and Russia from the 1880s through the early 1900s. The selections in this section that are written by Leonard Dinnerstein, Martin Gilbert, David S. Wyman, and Cornel West convey something of this long and brutal pattern in which social, political, and legal institutions were manipulated by governments to scapegoat, disenfranchise, and oppress Jews. This historical experience provides an important background for understanding antisemitism in the United States, because most American Jews immigrated to the Americas from Spain or Portugal as Sephardic Jews (in the fifteenth and sixteenth centuries), and from Central and eastern Europe (1840s onward and 1880s onward, respectively) as Ashkenazi Jews, with both the hopes and the anxieties born out of centuries of repeated oppression. Jews from the older and more established communities of Ethiopia, Egypt, Morocco or Iran, for example, have immigrated to the United States more recently, but also in smaller numbers.

The fact that most American Jews are ethnically Ashkenazi or Sephardic has led to racial stereotypes of Jews as "white," a designation that makes obvious sense in a United States racial context (see the introduction to section 2, and the selections from Ronald Takaki and Michael Omi), but that does not make sense for Jews who immigrate to the United States from Jewish communities in Africa or Asia, their descendants in the United States, American Jews of racially mixed parentage, or blacks who are members of black Hebrew congregations (for an overview, see Adams and Bracey 2000).

Thus, the question "Who (or what) is a Jew?" is a perplexing one that defies or questions established social group categories in the United States. If Jews constitute a *religious* category only, then how does one account for nonbelieving or nonpracticing Jews, or the range of religious beliefs and practices that differentiate Hasidic or Orthodox Jews from those who are Reform or Reconstructionist? If Jews in the United States are understood to belong to an *ethnic* group (parallel to Irish or Italian Americans), then how might one account for the ethnic differences among Sephardic and Ashkenazi Jews? If Jews are seen in relation to *national origins,* then what of Jews from Cuba or Morocco; or those from France, Russia, or Germany; or American Jews as distinct from Israeli Jews? And if Jews are identified as a *race,* then how can one square the assumption that today Jews are "white" in the United States, but one and two generations ago they were officially designated non-Aryan in Germany and throughout Nazi-occupied Europe? Jews immigrating from European countries (where they had been legally subordinated as an inferior a racial group) to the United States (where racial designations separate whites from peoples of color—the "one drop" rule), experienced a confusing transformation of racial categories. Thus, social group designations that reflect either/or categories of ethnicity, religion or culture in the United States do not appear to be especially helpful in understanding the Jews as a diaspora people who have crossed national, ethnic, and racial boundaries; who have maintained separate or affiliated community identities across thousands of years and in many lands; and who have intermarried among Europeans, Africans, Arabs to produce offspring who look like other Europeans, Africans or Arabs but who are nonetheless known to themselves and to others as Jews. One scholar says inclusively that Jews constitute "a religious community, a nation, an ethnic group, a cultural group, a race" (Petersen 1997, 241), which is a way of saying all or none of the above. The opening chapter in this section, by Melanie Kaye/Kantrowitz raises and personalizes some of these identity and definitional questions.

Michael Lerner (1992) has defined *antisemitism* as the systematic discrimination against Jews and against Jewish cultural, intellectual, and religious heritage. He also sees hatred of Jews as "the oldest and most continuous form of racism in the Western and Islamic worlds." These two statements taken together convey something of the complexity of antisemitism. First, as noted above, we understand antisemitism as long-standing oppression directed against Jews both historically and globally (in ancient Egypt, classical Rome, Christian Europe, North Africa, and the Middle East) and also contemporaneously and locally within the United States (from the colonial period to the present day), although obviously varying in its visibility or virulence. This variability is illustrated in this section by a local community's response to antisemitism ("Menorah light banishes hate") and by Varian Fry's 1942 "you are there" eyewitness account of the emerging Holocaust in Europe, "The Massacre of the Jews."

Second, antisemitism can also be understood as a persistent form of racism, especially as it evolved in Europe from the fifteenth-century Spanish doctrine of *limpieze de sangre* (or pure Spanish blood) as defined by descent (designed to separate Jewish converts from "old" Christians), to the twentieth-century Nazi ideology of Aryan racial superiority and Jewish racial inferiority (Mosse 1985). The term *antisemitism* was itself coined in the 1870s by the Austrian anti-Jewish journalist Wilhelm Marr to describe a hatred of Jews and Judaism that was based upon social, economic, political, and racial stereotypes rather than on the earlier religious grounds. It appropriates a linguistic term (Semitic, derived from the biblical Shem who was one of Noah's three sons) originally used to describe a group of cognate languages (Hebrew, Arabic, Aramaic) as distinct from Aryan or Indo-European language groupings (Wistrich 1991). The pseudoscientific racial thinking that became associated with this equally discredited linguistic grouping was widespread in Europe and the United States during the nineteenth and early-to-middle twentieth centuries (Mosse 1985). Because Jews were the peoples speaking so-called Semitic languages (e.g., Hebrew) toward whom this specific form of racism was directed, we continue to use the term *antisemitism* to refer explicitly to this oppression directed against the Jewish people and their culture, language, heritage, and religion.

Of course, the prejudices against Jews as a group, often reflecting self-contradictory social and economic stereotypes (Jews as misers *and* as philanthropists, Jews as capitalists *and* as communists, Jews as clannish *and* as plotting world control) had been prepared for by centuries of religious antisemitism (Jews as Christ-killers, Jews in a world conspiracy against Christians), and are described in several chapters in this section. A noted historian has demonstrated that virtually every policy, decree, or exclusion used against Jews in Nazi Germany had parallel practices in early Christian Europe (Hilberg 1961). An understanding of the history and dynamics of antisemitism gives us a window onto the nature and dynamics of this specific form of racism, albeit a racism that evolved in Europe rather than in the United States where Jews of European descent have been "whitened," even if "not quite white" (Weinberg 1986; Brodkin 1998).

Readings in This Section

This section presents various "snapshots" from the long history of antisemitism. The chapter by Kaye/Kantrowitz asks provocative and difficult questions about the racial and religious meanings usually associated with the terms *Jew* and *Jewish*, especially given racial dichotomies of Black and White that dominate racial discourse in the United States. The selection by Leonard Dinnerstein describes early virulent phases of European antisemitism within Europe that precede and contextualize the Nazi Holocaust. The maps in the chapter by Martin Gilbert, together with the essay by David S. Wyman, convey a vivid sense of the destruction of European Jewry during the Holocaust as well as the formidable barriers in America against rescue or immigration. Similarly, Varian Fry conveys the urgency and horror felt by an American bystander and witness writing about the Holocause as it was happening in 1942, and in terms strikingly reminiscent of the breaking news of "ethnic cleansing" in newspaper accounts in the 1990s.

Although these are the only selections in this chapter to deal explicitly with the Holocaust, this enormous crisis of antisemitism in Europe casts a shadow across much else in this chapter that focus upon the United States. For example, Cornel West's account of black-Jewish relations in the United States places black-Jewish coalitions and conflicts within the histories of oppression experienced by both groups while also noting their differences of degree, scope, and time frame. Jennifer Krebs reflects back upon her family's direct experience of the Holocaust, interweaving themes and nuances of gender and sexual orientation into her personal reflection. Peter F. Langman discusses some of the ways that contemporary American antisemitism is both visible and invisible, as well as the personal damage that results when American Jews internalize antisemitic stereotypes. Bernice Mennis provides a personal testimonial of the ways in which internalized antisemitism and internalized classism intersect for someone who is both working-class and Jewish.

The 1996 newspaper article on Newtown, Pennsylvania (chapter 30), illustrates a community's action against antisemitism, an action initiated by the earlier "Not in Our Town" joint action in Billings, Montana (see the videotape *Not in Our Town* in the Further Resources section) and repeated in responses to antisemitism and racism in communities across the country. In closing, Reena Bernards talks about Arab-Jewish dialogue as a way to forge new relationships, to resolve intergroup conflict, to form new coalitions, and to take social action. Teachers and students can use the Further Resources section to learn more about the complex situation in the Middle East, where two historically oppressed and stateless peoples, the Jews and the Palestinians, have been in violent and often bitter contention but also engaged in efforts toward conflict-resolution and peace (Falbel et al. 1990; Fernea and Hocking 1992; Lerner 1992). The videotape listings also present the courage of rescuers of Jews during the Holocaust (see *Courage to Care,* and *Weapons of the Spirit*) and of allies of Jews during other periods of oppression. Additional references in the Further Resources section concern the organized efforts by Jews as individuals and as Jewish organizations to effect social change—efforts that represent both a response to oppression but also an affirmation of group empowerment and ethical as well as religious identity (Shepherd 1993; Svonkin 1997; Adams and Bracey 2000).

References

Adams, M., and J. Bracey, eds. (2000). *Strangers and Neighbors: Relations between Blacks and Jews in the United States.* Amherst, Mass.: University of Massachusetts Press.

Brodkin, K. (1998). *How Jews Became White Folks and What That Says about Race in America.* New Brunswick, N.J.: Rutgers University Press.

Dinnerstein, L. (1994). *Antisemitism in America.* New York: Oxford University Press.

Falbel, R., I. Klepfisz, and D. Nevel, eds. (1990). *Jewish Women's Call for Peace: A Handbook for Women on the Israeli/Palestinian Conflict.* Ithaca, N.Y.: Firebrand Books.

Fernea, E. W., and M. W. Hocking, eds. (1992). *The Struggle for Peace: Israelis and Palestinians.* Austin: University of Texas Press.

Hilberg, Raul (1961). *The Destruction of the European Jews.* New York: Harper.

Lerner, M. (1992). *The Socialism of Fools: Anti-Semitism on the Left.* Oakland, Calif.: Tikkun Books.

Mosse, G. L. (1985). *Toward the Final Solution: A History of European Racism.* Madison: University of Wisconsin Press.

Pedersen, W. (1997). "Who Is a Jew?" In *Ethnicity Counts.* New Brunswick, N.J.: Transaction Publishers.

Sachar, H. M. (1992). *A History of the Jews in America.* New York: Vintage.

Shepherd, N. (1993). *A Price below Rubies: Jewish Women as Rebels and Radicals.* Cambridge, Mass.: Harvard University Press.

Svonkin, S. (1997). *Jews against Prejudice: American Jews and the Fight for Civil Liberties.* New York: Columbia University Press.

Weinberg, M. (1986). *Because They Were Jews: A History of Antisemitism.* Westport, Conn.: Greenwood Press.

Weinstein, G. and D. Mellen. (1997). "Antisemitism Curriculum Design." In Adams, M., L. A. Bell, and P. Griffin, eds. *Teaching for Diversity and Social Justice: A Sourcebook.* New York: Routledge.

Wistrich, R. S. (1991). *Antisemitism: The Longest Hatred.* New York: Pantheon Books.

Contexts

21

Jews in the U.S.: The Rising Costs of Whiteness

Melanie Kaye/Kantrowitz

Before America No One Was White

In 1990 I had returned to New York City to do antiracist work with other Jews, when a friend sent me an essay by James Baldwin. "No one was white before he/she came to America," Baldwin had written:

> It took generations, and a vast amount of coercion, before this became a white country. . . . It is probable that it is the Jewish community—or more accurately, perhaps, its remnants—that in America has paid the highest and most extraordinary price for becoming white. For the Jews came here from countries where they were not white, and they came here in part because they were not white, and incontestably—in the eyes of the Black American (and not only in those eyes) American Jews have opted to become white. . . .[1]

Everything I think about Jews, whiteness, racism, and contemporary U.S. society begins with this passage. What does it mean: *Jews opted to become white*. Did we opt? Did it work? Was it an illusion? Could we have opted otherwise? Can we still?

Rachel Rubin, a college student who's been interning at Jews for Racial and Economic Justice, where I'm the director, casually mentions: when she was eight, a cross was burned on her lawn in Athens, Georgia. I remember the house I moved into Down East Maine in 1979. On the bedroom door someone had painted a swastika in what looked like blood. I think about any cross-country drive I've ever taken, radio droning hymn after Christian hymn, 2000 miles of heartland.

On the other hand, I remember the last time I was stopped by cops. It was in San Francisco. I was getting a ride home after a conference on Jews and multiculturalism. In the car with me were two other white Jews. My heart flew into my throat, as always, but they took a quick look at the three of us and waved us on—*We're looking for a car like this, sorry*. I remember all the stories I've heard from friends, people of color, in which a quick look is not followed by a friendly wave and an apology. Some of these stories are about life and death.

Liberals and even progressives kneejerk to simplistic racial—black/white—terms, evade the continuing significance of race, and confound it with class.[2] Race becomes an increasingly complex muddle.[3] Growing numbers of bi- and multiracial children. *Hispanic*—not a racial identity, but a cultural/linguistic category conflating Spain with its former colonies. No one was *Asian* before they came to America, either; the term masks cultures diverse and polychromatic as anything Europe has to offer; yet *Asian American* has emerged as a critical and powerful identity. In the academy, obligatory nods to issues of race/class/gender result in language so specialized it's incomprehensible to most people, including those most pressured by these biases, and students tell me, "When Jews are mentioned in class, there's an awkward silence."[4]

Where is *Jewish* in the race/class/gender grid? Does it belong? Is it irrelevant? Where do those crosses and swastikas fit in?

Race or Religion?

"Race or religion?" is how the question is usually posed, as though this doublet exhausts the possibilities. Christians—religiously observant or not—usually operate from the common self-definition of Christianity, a religion any individual can embrace through belief, detached from race, peoplehood, and culture.[5]

But I have come to understand this detachment as false. Do white Christians feel kinship with African-American Christians? White slaveowners, for example, with their slaves? White Klansmen with their black neighbors? Do white Christians feel akin to Christians converted by colonialists all over the globe? Doesn't Christianity really, for most white Christians, imply *white*? And for those white Christians, does *white* really include *Jewish*? Think of the massive Christian evasion of a simple fact: Jesus Christ was not, was never, a Christian. He was a Jew. What did he look like, Jesus of Nazareth, 2000 years ago? Blond, blue-eyed?

Of course Jewish is not a race, for Jews come in all races.[6] Though white-identified Jews may skirt the issue, Jews are a multiracial people. There are Ethiopian, Indian, Chinese Jews. And there are people of every race who choose Judaism, or were adopted or born into it from mixed parents. The dominant conception of Jewish—European, Yiddish-speaking—is in fact a subset, Ashkenazi. Estimated at 85–97 percent of Jews in the U.S. today, Ashkenazi Jews are those whose religious practice and diaspora path can be traced through Germany.[7] The huge wave of Jewish immigration from Eastern Europe was Ashkenazi (as was the earlier, much smaller, highly assimilated community of German Jews, who looked with dread upon the arrival of—from their perspective—an impoverished, Yiddish-babbling, superstitious horde). Ashkenazi Jews also migrated to the far points of the globe—to South America, Australia, Africa, Asia. They may be very fair or very dark.

Sephardic Jews are those whose mother tongue is/was Ladino (Judeo-Español) and whose religious practice and diaspora path can be traced at some point through the Iberian Peninsula (Spain and Portugal), where they flourished, unghettoized, contributing along with Muslims to Spanish culture, until the Inquisition (read: *torture*) forced conversion or expulsion from Spain of all non-Christians. Sephardim migrated to—and lived for generations and even centuries—in Holland, Germany, Italy, France, Greece, the Middle East, and the Americas. The first Jews in the New World were Sephardim: 1492 marks not only Columbus's voyage but also the expulsion of the Jews from Spain. Some Sephardim consider themselves the aristocrats of the Jews, and look with contempt upon the Ashkenazi history of ghettoization and persecution. They may also be quite fair or quite dark.

Mizrachi Jews are those who lived in the Arab world and Turkey (basically, what was once the Ottoman Empire), as minorities in Muslim rather than Christian culture. Their mother tongue often is/was Judeo-Arabic. *Mizrachi* means "Eastern," commonly translated as "Oriental," and is used by and about Israelis, often interchangeably with *Sephardim*. The Spanish Sephardim sometimes resent the blurring of distinctions between themselves and the Mizrachim, reacting with pride in their history and with Eurocentric bias against non-Europeans, referring to themselves as "true" or "pure" Sephardim.[8] The confusion between the categories is only partly due to Ashkenazi ignorance/arrogance, lumping all non-Ashkenazi together. Partly, it's the result of Jewish history: some Jews never left the Middle East, and some returned after expulsion from Spain, including to Palestine. Some kept Ladino, some did not. I imagine there was intermarriage. Mizrachim, though they may also range from fair to dark, are usually defined as "people of color."

The point is, categories of white and color don't correspond neatly to Jewish reality. (What does correspond is Ashkenazi cultural hegemony—in the U.S., where they are dominant by numbers, and in Israel, where Sephardi/Mizrachi Jews make up about two-thirds of the Jewish population and strongly contest this hegemony.) Jewish wanderings have created a people whose experience eludes conventional categories of race, nationality, ethnicity, geography, language—even religion. Cataclysm and assimilation have depleted our store of common knowledge.

No, Jews are not a single race. Yet there is confusion here, and subtext. Confusion because we have so often been racialized, hated *as if* we were a race. Ethnic studies scholars have labored to document the process of racialization, the fact that race is not biological, but a sociohistorically specific phenomenon. Observing Jewish history, Nancy Ordover has noted, offers an opportunity to break down this process of racialization, because by leaving Europe, Jews changed our "race," even as our skin pigment remained the same.[9]

> For the Jews came here from countries where they were not white, and they came here in part because they were not white. . . .

Confusion, too, because to say someone *looks Jewish* is to say something both absurd (Jews look a million different ways) and commonsense communicative.

When I was growing up in Flatbush, Brooklyn, every girl with a certain kind of nose—sometimes named explicitly as a Jewish nose, sometimes only as "too big"—wanted a nose job, and if her parents could pay for it, often she got one. I want to be graphic about the euphemism *nose job.* A nose job breaks the nose, bruises the face and eye area like a grotesque beating. It hurts. It takes weeks to heal.

What was wrong with the original nose, the Jewish one? Noses were discussed ardently in Flatbush, this or that friend looking forward to her day of transformation.[10] My aunts lavished on me the following exquisite praise: *Look at her—a nose like a shiksa* (gentile woman). This hurt my feelings. Before I knew what a *shiksa* was, I knew I wasn't it, and, with that fabulous integrity of children, I wanted to look like who I was. But later I learned my nose's value, and would tell gentiles this story so they'd notice my nose.

A Jewish nose, I conclude, identifies its owner as a Jew. Nose jobs are performed so that a Jewish woman does not look like a Jew.

Tell me again Jewish is just a religion.

Yet Nazi racial definitions have an "only a religion" response. Even earlier, the lure of emancipation (in Europe) and assimilation (in the U.S.) led Jews to define Judaism as narrowly as possible, as religion only: "a Jew at home, a man in the streets,"[11] a private matter, taken care of behind closed doors, like bathing.

Judaism, the religion, does provide continuity and connection to Jews around the globe. There is something powerful even for atheists about entering a synagogue across the continent or the ocean, and hearing the familiar service. [12]

But to be a Jew one need not follow religious practice; one need not believe in god—not even to become a rabbi (an element of Judaism of which I am especially fond).[13] Religion is only one strand of being Jewish. It is ironic that it is precisely this century's depletion of Jews and of Jewish identity, with profound linguistic and cultural losses—continuing as Yiddish and Ladino speakers age and die[14]—that makes imaginable a Jewishness that is *only a religion*—only now, when so much else has been lost. But to reduce *Jewishness* to *Judaism* is to forget the complex indivisible swirl of religion, culture, language, history that *was* Jewishness until, in the eighteenth century, Emancipation began to offer some Jews the possibility of escaping from a linguistically/culturally/economically isolated ghetto into the European "Enlightenment." To equate Jewishness with religion is to forget how even the contemporary, often attenuated version of this Jewish cultural swirl is passed down *in the family*, almost like genetic code.

Confusion and subtext. *Jewish* is often trivialized as something you choose, a preference, like tea over coffee. In contrast with visible racial identity, presumptions of choice—as with gayness—are seen as minimizing one's claim to attention, sympathy, and remedy. As a counter to bigotry, *I was born like this* strategically asserts a kind of victim-status, modeled on race, gender, and disability: If you can't help yourself, maybe you're entitled to some help from others. . . .

What happens if, instead, I assert my right to choose and not suffer for it. To say, *I choose*—my lesbianism and my Jewishness.[15] Choose to come out, be visible, embrace both. I could live loveless or sexless or in the closet. I could have kept the name *Kaye*, and never once at Christmas—in response to the interminable "What are you doing for . . . ? Have you finished your shopping?"— answer, "I don't celebrate Christmas. I'm a Jew." I could lie about my lover's gender. I could wear skirts uncomfortably. I could bleach my hair again, as I did when I was fifteen. I could monitor my speech, weeding out the offensive accent, as I was taught at City College, along with all the other first and second generation immigrants' children in the four speech classes required for graduation, to teach us not to sound like ourselves. I could remain silent when queer or anti-Semitic jokes are told, or when someone says, "You know how *they* are." I could endure the pain in the gut, the hot shame. I could scrunch up much, much smaller.

In the U.S., *Christian*, like *white*, is an unmarked category in need of marking.[16] Christianness, a majority, dominant culture, is not about religious practice and belief, any more than Jewishness is. As *racism* names the system that normalizes, honors, and rewards whiteness, we need a word for what normalizes, honors and rewards Christianity. Jews designate the assumption of Christianity-as-norm, the erasure of Jews, as *anti-Semitic*. In fact, the erasure and marginalization of non-Christians is not just denigrating to Jews. We need a catchier term than *Christian begemony* to help make visible the cultural war against all non-Christians.

Christianism? Awkward, stark, and kind of crude—maybe a sign that something's being pushed; *sexism* once sounded stark and kind of crude. Such a term would help contextualize Jewish experience as an experience of marginality shared with other non-Christians. Especially in this time of rising Christian fundamentalism, as school prayer attracts support from "moderates," this contextualization is critical for progressive Jews, compelling us to seek allies among Muslims and other religious minorities.

I also want to contextualize Jews in a theoretical framework outside the usual bipolar frame of black/white—to go beyond dualism; to distinguish race from class, and both from culture; to understand whiteness as the gleaming conferral of normality, success, even survival; to acknowledge who owns what, and in whose neighborhood; to witness how money does and does not "whiten."

> For in the eyes of the Black American (and not only in those eyes) American Jews have opted to become white. . . .

To begin to break out of a polarity that has no place for Jews, I survey the range of color in the United States. People of color, a unity sought and sometimes forged, include a vast diversity of culture and history, forms of oppression and persecution. Contemporary white supremacists hate them all, but define some as shrewd, evil, inscrutable, sexually exotic, and perverse, and others as intellectually inferior, immoral, bestial, violent, and sexually rapacious. If it is possible to generalize, we can say that the peoples defined as shrewd and evil tend to be better off economically—or at least *perceived* as better off economically—than those defined as inferior and violent, who tend to remain in large numbers stuck at the bottom of the economic ladder (and are assumed by the dominant culture to be stuck there), denied access to decent jobs and opportunities, systematically disadvantaged and excluded by the educational system.

In other words, among the creeping fearsome dark ones are, on the one hand, those who exploit, cheat, and hoard money they don't deserve, and, on the other, those (usually darker) who, not having money, threaten to rob and pillage hard-working tax-paying white Christians. In this construct, welfare fits as a form of robbery, the women's form; the men are busy mugging. Immigrant bashing—whether street violence or political movements like "English-only" and California's overwhelming passage of Proposition 187—becomes a "natural" response to "robbery."

It is easier now to see where Jews fit: we are so good with money. Our "darkness" may not show, and this ability to pass confers protection and a host of privileges. But we are the model money-grubbing money-hoarding scapegoats for an increasingly punitive economic system. Jews, Japanese, Koreans, Arabs, Indians, and Pakistanis—let's face it: *interlopers*—are blamed for economic disaster; for controlling the economy or making money on the backs of the poor; for raising the price of oil; for stealing or eliminating jobs by importing goods or exporting production.

At the same time, those defined as inferior and violent are blamed for urban crime and chaos, for drugs, for the skyrocketing costs and failures of social programs. This blame then justifies the oppression and impoverishment of those brought here in chains and the peoples indigenous to this continent. Add in the darker, poorer immigrants from Latin America and the Caribbean, and recent immigrants from China and Southeast Asia. Media codes like "inner-city crime" and "teen gangs" distort and condense a vast canvas of poverty, vulnerability, and exploitation into an echoing story of some young men's violent response to these conditions. Thus those who are significantly endangered come to be defined as inherently dangerous.

That is, one group is blamed for capitalism's crimes; the other for capitalism's fallout. Do I need to point out who escapes all blame?

When a community is scapegoated, members of that community are most conscious of how they feel humiliated, alienated, and endangered. But the other function of scapegoating is at least as pernicious. It is to protect the problem which scapegoats are drafted to conceal: the vicious system of profit and exploitation, of plenty and scarcity existing side by side.

The Cost of Whiteness

Aryan ideology aside, Jews are often defined as white, though this wipes out the many Jews who are by anyone's definition people of color, and neglects the role of context: many Jews who look white in New York City look quite the opposite in the South and Midwest. Radicals often exclude the category *Jewish* from discussion, or subsume us into *white*, unless we are by *their* definition also people of color, in which case they subsume us as *people of color.*

The truth is, Jews complicate things. *Jewish* is both a distinct category and an overlapping one. Just as homophobia is distinct from sexism yet has everything to do with sexism, anti-Semitism in this country is distinct from racism yet has everything to do with racism. It's not that a Jew like myself should "count" as a person of color, though I think sometimes Jews do argue this because the alternative seems to be erasure. But that means we need another alternative. The problem is a polarization of white and color that excludes us. We need a more complex vision of the structure of racism, one that attends to the sick logic of white supremacists. We need a more complex understanding of the process of "whitening."

Notes

I thank Esther Kaplan, Roni Natov, and Nancy Ordover for substantial critical feedback. Sections of this essay are drawn from earlier writings: "To Be a Radical Jew in the Late 20th Century"; "Class, Feminism, and the Black-Jewish Question"; and "Jews, Class, Color and the Cost of Whiteness," all published in *The Issue Is Power: Essays on Women, Jews, Violence and Resistance* (San Francisco: Aunt Lute, 1992).

1. James Baldwin, "On Being 'White' . . . and Other Lies," *Essence*, April, 1984. Sharon Jaffe, activist extraordinaire, is the friend who sent me this.
2. "Closing Pandora's Box—Race and the 'New Democrats'," in Michael Omi and Howard Winant, *Racial Formation in the United States*, 2nd ed. (New York: Routledge, 1994), 145ff. Omi and Winant point out Lani Guinier's fatal flaw, from the Clinton neoliberal downplay-race perspective, as "her willingness, indeed her eagerness, to discuss the changing dimensions of race in contemporary U.S. politics" (156).
3. Steven Holmes, "Federal Government Is Rethinking Its System of Racial Classification," *New York Times*, July 8, 1994, explores the confusion from a bureaucratic perspective.
4. Students tell me, on one hand, that they learn in their women's studies classes not to make a hierarchy of oppression, but, on the other hand, that these classes rarely contain anything Jewish.
5. Christians usually see this as a generous feature of their religion—after all, anyone can become one (forgetting that not all of us wish to do so).
6. On the other hand, Karen Sacks, "How Did Jews Become White Folks?" in *Race*, ed. Steven Gregory and Roger Sanjek (New Brunswick: Rutgers University Press, 1994), points to "a 1987 Supreme Court ruling that Jews and Arabs could use civil rights laws to gain redress for discrimination against them . . . on the grounds that they are not racial whites."
7. *Ashkenazim* comes from the word for Germany; *Sephardi*, from Spain.
8. For Sephardi in the former Ottoman Empire, see "Interview with Chaya Shalom," in *The Tribe of Dina: A Jewish Women's Anthology*, ed. Melanie Kaye/Kantrowitz and Irena Klepfisz (Boston: Beacon Press, 1989: 1st published by Sinister Wisdom, 1986). Shalom, a fourth- or fifth-generation Jerusalemite and a political radical, was raised in a traditional Ladino-speaking family to identify as *samakbet*—pure Sephardim. She describes Ashkenazi racism against Sephardi, *samakbet* racism against Arab Jews, and the complexities of passing and assimilation in Israel. See, also Ella Shohat's analysis of Israeli Eurocentrism, *Israeli Cinema: East/West and the Politics of Representation* (Austin: University of Texas Press, 1989).
9. Nancy Ordover, oral critique, December, 1994. For an excellent discussion, see Michael Omi and Howard Winant, *Racial Formation in the United States* (New York: Routledge, 1986).
10. See Aisha Berger's poem, "Nose is a country . . . I am the second generation," in Kaye/Kantrowitz and Klepfisz, eds., *The Tribe of Dina*. One of Berger's many illuminating images: "this unruly semitic landmass on my face." The era of Jewish nose jobs is not over, though Barbra Streisand broke the spell that mirrored Jewish noses as inherently ugly.
11. This was first expressed by Moses Mendelssohn (1729–1786), the central figure in the German Jewish *Haskalah* (Enlightenment), as the ideal of Jewish assimilation.
12. At least partly familiar; Sephardic and Ashkenazi practices often use different cantillation (chanting the prayers), and there are also variations between Reform, Conservative, Orthodox, and Reconstructionist Judaism.
13. One is, however, hard put to be a Jew without Jewish community. Even in religious practice, the unit of prayer is not the individual but the *minyan*, at least ten adult Jews, the Jewish quorum—in Orthodox Judaism, ten men.
14. There is painful irony in the fact that Yiddish, the beloved *mame-losbn* of Jewish socialists, is dwindling to a living language only for the ultra-orthodox Hasidim. For information about

the Bund (Jewish socialists, for whom Yiddish culture was an important aspect of political life), see Irena Klepfisz, "Secular Jewish Identity: Yidishkayt in America," in Kaye/Kantrowitz and Klepfisz, eds., *The Tribe of Dina*, and in *Dreams of an Insomniac* (Portland: Eighth Mountain Press, 1990); Klepfisz, "*Di mames, dos losbn*/The mothers, the language: Feminism, *Yidishkayt*, and the Politics of Memory," *Bridges* 4, no. 1 (Winter/Spring 1994), 5754; and Jack Jacobs, *On Socialists and "the Jewish Question" after Marx* (New York: New York University Press, 1992).

15. In this discussion I am indebted to Nancy Ordover, "Visibility, Alliance, and the Practice of Memory," unpublished paper (Berkeley: University of California, 1993).

16. Ruth Frankenberg's *White Women/Race Matters* (Minneapolis: University of Minnesota, 1993) offers useful insight on whiteness as an unmarked racial category, but Frankenberg misses opportunities to note the significance of *Jewish* as a category, even though she and a disproportionate number of the white antiracist activists she interviewed are Jews.

22

The Christian Heritage

Leonard Dinnerstein

Antisemitism is a real and ignoble part of America's cultural heritage. It was brought to the New World by the first settlers, instilled by Christian teachings, and continually reinforced by successive waves of Protestants and Catholics who populated American shores. Like a genetic disease, it has been transmitted from one generation to the next but, like a folktale, it has been added to, transformed, and adapted to particular times, places, and circumstances. It has been present in Christian societies for almost two millennia but its manifestations have varied according to historic circumstances. One or more of the following symptoms, however, is used as an excuse whenever the disease occurs: the Jew is the Christ-killer, the economic exploiter, the eternal alien, the subversive element within Christian civilization, or the embodiment of evil.

Although hostility toward Jews predates the Christian era, it is the Christian image of the Jew that has dominated the consciousness of the western world. That image took over a thousand years to draw, and another three or four centuries to complete the most extraordinary details. By the middle of the fourteenth century the perception of the "perfidious" Jew had been so thoroughly embedded in the mind of Christian Europe that seven hundred years later its essential ingredients still remain in place. And across two millennia, animosity toward Jews was not only encouraged but also lauded as a religious virtue. Indeed, the "alien race's" continuing resistance to Christian missionary activity was a major factor fanning the hatred of Jews. Their refusal to acknowledge that Judaism had been "fulfilled" in the person of Christ, and hence made obsolete, stood as a constant rebuke to Christians everywhere.[1]

Conflicts between Christians and Jews evolved in the first century between those who believed Christ and those who did not. In the Acts of Apostles, Jews are portrayed as vicious murderers and on numerous occasions in the New Testament Jews are mentioned as continually plotting the deaths of Christians. While writings by Jews about Christians showed marked indifference to the new cultists, Christian writers were full of malice toward Jews for their alleged persecution of Christians. Accusations of mistreatment of Christians by Jews had no basis in fact but the opposite is not true.[2] Nonetheless, Christian writers continually attacked the Jews.

The fourth century proved crucial in determining the fate of Jews. In 337, Emperor Constantine converted to Christianity on his deathbed, thereby opening the door for the eventual establishment of that faith as the religion of the empire. Christianity spread throughout Europe during the next several hundred years. England became Christian in the seventh century, Saxony and Bohemia in the ninth, Scandinavia and Poland in the tenth, and by the eleventh century the Christianization of Western Europe was largely complete. As Christianity successfully spread and allegedly indicated the will of God, the antisemitic tone of tracts and sermons increased. The question most frequently posed was why Jews were so reluctant to admit the verdict of history and accept the truthfulness of Christian teaching. A Christian approach developed that branded Jews as stubborn enemies of the human race whose only hope for salvation lay in conversion. In the meantime, God would punish them for their obstinacy, force them to wander the earth, and make them bear witness to the triumph of Christianity.[3] . . .

It was also universally assumed in the Christian world that Jewish contemporaries of Jesus had murdered Him and that for all time thereafter their descendants would be held collectively responsible for His death.[4] This idea may have come directly from Matthew, who wrote about how Pilate had given them the choice of releasing Jesus or the notorious criminal Barab'bas from prison, and the Jews had demanded freedom for the latter. "Then what shall I do with Jesus who is called Christ?" Pilate asked. "Let him be crucified," Jews allegedly responded. Then, according to Matthew, Pilate replied, "I am innocent of this man's blood; see to it yourselves," And all the people answered, "His blood be on us and on our children!"[5]

No idea in Christian teaching has been more solidly implanted among adherents of the faith, and more devastating to Christian-Jewish relations, than the accusation that the Jews had killed their Savior.[6] For this alleged crime the Jews have supposedly been rejected by God and doomed to eternal punishment. Characterized in church teachings as a "demonic" and "accursed" people, only by embracing Jesus would there be any chance for acceptance and forgiveness.[7]

Thus, by the sixth century, the basis for Christian hatred of Jews had been firmly implanted. Nonetheless, Pope Gregory I, who reigned from 590 through 604, forbade persecution of the Jews and during the next five hundred or so years life for European Jews was not particularly uncomfortable except in Visigothic Spain, where royal edict mandated forced conversion of Jews in 613.[8] After taking the reins of power in England in 1066, William the Conqueror imported Jews to the realm to serve, along with others, in setting up a new regime.[9] Despite numerous humiliations, restrictions, and second-class citizenship, they remained there until King Edward I banished them from the kingdom in 1290. The expulsion of Jews from medieval England reflected the triumph of the antisemitism that was always latent in the Christian world.

The almost three-hundred-year era of savaging Jews began at the end of November 1095 in Clermont, France, when Pope Urban II called for a Christian crusade to recover the Holy Land from the "infidels." The first crusaders embarked in the summer of 1096, as Christian soldiers headed for the Holy Land. Along the way they zealously vented their wrath on the Jews in Europe. During the eleventh century the Jews had become increasingly unpopular as larger numbers of people borrowed money from them and found difficulty repaying the loans. The Crusades added to this resentment. It was costly for knights to outfit themselves for the march to Jerusalem and they again had to borrow from Jews. Therefore, there was little opposition to slaughtering those who not only aroused resentment because of their failure to embrace Christianity but who were also seen as the cause for trying economic circumstances. The first massacre of Jews by the crusaders occurred in Rouen, France, and as the Christian armies proceeded through Europe they decimated Jewish communities in their path. Massacres of nonbelievers would be the rule rather than the exception, so long as Christ's soldiers strove to implant Christianity on the known world.[10]

One of the most bizarre accusations against Jews that took hold during the years of the Crusades was that they sacrificed Christian children for religious purposes. This belief had its historic origins in fifth-century tales that a group of Jews had tortured and murdered a Christian child to mock Christ.[11] Not until the twelfth century, however, did that story reappear. Then, in 1144, William of Norwich died of a cataleptic fit. Theobald of Canterbury, a Jew who had converted to Christianity, spread the word that Jews must have been responsible for the deed since the Jewish faith required the sacrifice of a Christian child annually "in scorn and contempt of Christ, so that they might avenge their sufferings on Him."[12] At the time of William's death few people accepted this ludicrous and inaccurate explanation. Nonetheless, the libel circulated and as the decades passed more credence was given to it. In England, ritual murder accusations were aimed at the Jews of Gloucester in 1168, of Bury St. Edmunds in 1181, and of Bristol in 1183. The same accusations were hurled at French Jews in Blois in 1171, at Jews in Erfurt, Saxony, in 1191, and later on in Paris, Weissenburg, Salzburg, Bern, and Seville. All told, there were at least six such accusations in the twelfth century, fifteen in the thirteenth, ten in the fourteenth, sixteen in the fifteenth, thirteen in the sixteenth, eight in the seventeenth, fifteen in the eighteenth, and thirty-nine in the nineteenth century. Similar charges erupted in both Europe and the United States in the twentieth century.[13]

The most notorious of all ritual murder allegations occurred in England following the death of Hugh of Lincoln in 1255.[14] After a woman found the body of her eight-year-old child in a well, a Jew who lived nearby was arrested and tortured into confessing his culpability. On the basis of this "confession," he and ninety-two other Jews were imprisoned and had their possessions confiscated. Eighteen of them were hanged. Throughout the village of Lincoln people first whispered that Hugh had been tortured and crucified but as the story passed from one lip to another it was further embellished. The boy had supposedly been stolen away, his body fattened on white bread and milk for ten days, and then slaughtered so that his blood could by used by Jews for ritual purposes. The alleged crime had occurred near Passover and Easter, and over the years rumor had it either that during Passover week the Jews crucified Christian children to reenact the execution of Jesus, or that the child was killed so that Jews might use his blood in the food for their Passover service. . . .

Another seemingly ineradicable image dating back to medieval times is that of the Jew as economic exploiter. As part of the economic growth that made the Crusades possible, money became an essential ingredient in the new European economy. Full-time bankers were necessary to lend and provide funds to kings and princes, merchants and peasants, yet the Church forbade Christians to engage in that "accursed" business; it was left to Jews to fill the need. Those already accursed for the rejection of Christ became even more despicable for being engaged in a sinful and disreputable occupation.[15] Although the vocation of banking was necessary, and many Christians practiced it, the activity aroused the ire of almost the entire populace. Borrowers saw lenders not as valued members of society but as usurers who charged too much interest.[16] Since usurers charged rates that borrowers often found difficult to repay, lenders incurred the rancor of both debt-ridden peasants and impoverished noblemen. The image of the Jew as usurer, therefore, combined with the metaphor of "bloodsucking" and coalesced with the blood-libel parable to complete the picture of Jews as parasites on society, performing no useful function but draining the blood out of the hardworking Christian peasantry.[17] . . .

Also during the Middle Ages, a strengthened Papacy institutionalized what would later be considered appropriate behavior toward those who lived among them. Pope Innocent III, the most power of the medieval popes, presided over the fourth Lateran Council in 1215 and had the bishops decree that non-Christians must wear distinctive garments. Jews specifically were prohibited from appearing in public during Holy Week because their usual dress was interpreted as mocking the Christians clad in mourning. Decrees of the Council reemphasized the separateness of the Jews; their lower status in society allowed humiliating regulations to be imposed on them. Jews possessed some rights, albeit of a subordinate nature, but Innocent III stated that they were only for those "who have not presumed to plot against the Christian faith."[18] Innocent III opposed the killing of Jews "against whom the blood of Jesus Christ calls out," and, echoing St. Augustine, stated that "as wanderers must they remain upon the earth, until their countenance be filled with shame and they seek the name of Jesus Christ, the Lord."[19] In 1239, Pope Gregory IX concluded that following Talmudic forms was the chief cause of the Jews' "perfidiousness," and within three years Parisians began burning Talmuds.[20] The cumulative effect of these allegations was that Europeans increasingly saw Jews as subversive elements in their midst, as agents of Satan intent on destroying Christian civilization.

The onset of that catastrophic European event in 1347, the plague, or "Black Death" as it was known, sealed the fate of the Jews in Christian minds. Within three years the "Black Death" combined with widespread famine and ultimately killed about one-third of western Europe's population, unhinged people's minds, aroused expectations of the apocalypse, and fostered popular obsessions with the devil and his alleged servants, the Jews. Obviously some rationale had to be found to comprehend this horrible and apparently unending punishment from God. No phenomenon of such magnitude could be explained away without someone being responsible and Jews, believed to have rejected God and acting for the Devil, were the answer. Stories circulated that a Jewish conspiracy aimed at Christians existed and that Jews, either alone or in connivance with lepers, poisoned the wells in an effort to exterminate Christians. Ignoring the numbers of Jews who fell victim to the plague, peasants asked why else Jews would live and Christians die. Having answered their own question, Christians embarked on pogroms that led to the arrest, torture, and killing of Jews throughout Europe. In 1348, virtually every European Jewish community, save those in Vienna and Regensburg, was attacked. Every Jew in one French town was burned at the stake, and over two hundred Jewish communities in Europe were totally destroyed.[21]

Despite the belligerence that Jews encountered everywhere in medieval Europe, they always found a place to dwell because after the "Black Plague" one town or another needed the economic skills that many Jews allegedly possessed, and rulers recalled them. Never much liked, they remained under the protection of the sovereigns until, having served their purpose, they were expelled and forced to find residence elsewhere. In the German parts of the old Holy Roman Empire ghettos were established for Jews. The gates were locked at night but the residents were permitted to walk on Christian streets during the daytime.[22] On the other hand, as the mercantile age in Europe unfolded, especially between 1570 and 1713, the fortunes of many Jews in western Europe improved. During the Puritan interlude in England, from 1649 to 1661, Oliver Cromwell invited Jews to return to that country; the seventeenth century also found them in Holland. The perceived commercial skills of Jews made them valuable residents during the years of European expansion.[23]

The Protestant Reformation of the sixteenth century revolutionized religious practice in northern and western Europe but did little to alter popular attitudes toward Jews. Martin Luther at first tried to befriend Jews, but after they spurned his offer of love and conversion he, like both predecessors and successors, savagely turned against them. His venom then knew no bounds. Jews, he alleged, are foreigners, they do not work, yet they keep our money and have become our masters. [24] "Know my dear Christians," he wrote in 1542, "and do not doubt that next to the devil you have no enemy more cruel, more venomous and virulent, than a true Jew." Luther's heartless words have been studied continually since the sixteenth century and, as historian Heiko Oberman has pointed out, it is important to note that they were similar in tone and content to the writings of his contemporaries.[25] Calvin also thought Judaism a creed riddled with errors, but acknowledged that this faith prepared the world for Christianity.[26] In both Catholic and Protestant Europe, Jews found few friends—they remained always the alien, the other.

Many of the most destructive modern images of, and visceral reactions to, Jews developed between the eleventh and fourteenth centuries. Virtually every affliction of those troubled centuries was attributed to Jews. During that period no crime was too fanciful to ascribe to them as they were accused of witchcraft, devil worship, and magic. They allegedly used sorcery, poisoned wells, tortured Christian children, and sacrificed unbaptized infants to Satan. In tapestries, drawings, and other forms of art Jews were pictured as having horns and sometimes a tail; Jewish males sported the beard of a goat, a particularly lecherous beast. They were made to seem inhuman because that is how many Christians viewed them.[27] Peter the Venerable of Cluny, who lived in the early decades of the eleventh century, doubted "whether a Jew can be human, for he will neither yield to human reasoning, nor find satisfaction in authoritative utterances, alike divine and Jewish."[28] People in the medieval world also believed that if the Jews were allowed to do so they would destroy Christian civilization. This theme was never far from the surface in subsequent centuries, and in the twentieth, *The Protocols of the Elders of Zion* spelled out and exaggerated the fears that millions of people in both the Christian and Moslem worlds had always harbored.[29]

Notes

1. Jacob Katz, *From Prejudice to Destruction* (Cambridge, Mass.: Harvard University Press, 1980), 322; Jacob R. Marcus, *The Colonial American Jew, 1492–1776* vol. 3 (Detroit: Wayne State University Press, 1970), 1114; M. Ginsberg, "Anti-Semitism," *The Sociological Review* 35 (January–April, 1943), 4; Joshua Trachtenberg, *The Devil and the Jews* (New Haven: Yale University Press, 1943), 6; Glenn T. Miller, *Religious Liberty in America* (Philadelphia: Westminster Press, 1976), 92.

2. James Parkes, *The Conflict of the Church and the Synagogue* (New York: Hermon Press, 1934), 373; Hyam Maccoby, *The Sacred Executioner* (New York: Thames and Hudson, 1982), 147, 151.

3. Rosemary Radford Ruether, "Anti-Semitism and Christian Theology," in Eva Fleischner, ed., *Auschwitz: Beginning of a New Era? Reflections on the Holocaust* (New York: KTAV Publishing, 1977), 79, 85; Marcus, *Colonial American Jew* vol. 3, 1114–15; Trachtenberg, *The Devil*, 159; Esther Yolles Feldblum, *The American Catholic Press and the Jewish State, 1917–1959* (New York: KTAV Publishing., 1977), 12; Katz, *From Prejudice*, 323; Sergio I. Minerbi, *The Vatican and Zionism* (New York: Oxford University Press, 1990), 93; "Spiritually, We Are All Semites," *America* 152 (March 9, 1985), 185; Cecil Roth, "The Feast of Purim and the Origins of the Blood Accusation," in Alan Dundes, ed., *The Blood Libel Legend: A Casebook in Anti-Semitic Folklore* (Madison: University of Wisconsin Press, 1991), 270.

4. Joseph L. Lichten, "Polish Americans and American Jews: Some Issues Which Unite and Divide," *The Polish Review* 18 (1973), 57; Edward H. Flannery, 1985. *The Anguish of the Jews: Twenty-Three Centuries of Antisemitism,* rev. and updated ed. (New York: Paulist Press), 47.

5. Matthew 27:15, 24, 27.

6. Jules Isaac, *The Teaching of Contempt: Christian Roots of Anti-Semitism* (New York: Holt, Rinehart and Winston, 1964), 109; Wall, James M. "The Virulent Disease of Anti-Semitism," *Christian Century* 91 (April 24, 1974), 443; Claire Huchet Bishop, "Learning Bigotry," *Commonweal* 80 (May 22, 1964), 264ff.; Bruno Lasker, *Race Attitudes in Children* (New York: Greenwood, 1968; originally published in 1929), 179, 181–82, 252, 279; John B. Sheerin, "Catholic Anti-Semites," *Catholic World* 203 (July, 1966), 201; James Brown, "Christian Teaching and Anti-Semitism," *Commentary* 24 (December, 1957), 495; Feldblum, *The American Catholic Press,* 14; Parkes, *The Conflict,* 376; Rodney Stark, Bruce D. Foster, Charles Y. Glock, and Harold E. Quinley, *Wayward Shepherds: Prejudice and the Protestant Clergy* (New York: Harper and Row, 1976), 39; John T. Pawlikowski, *Cathechetics and Prejudice: How Catholic Teaching Materials View Jews, Protestants and Racial Minorities* (New York: Paulist Press, 1973), 8; Flannery, *The Anguish,* 62; Hannah Adams, *The History of the Jews from the Destruction of Jerusalem to the Present Times* (London: n. p., 1818), 53.

7. Isaac, *The Teaching,* 43; Adams, *The History,* 53; Minerbi, *The Vatican,* 93; Katz, *From Prejudice,* 323; Maccoby, *The Sacred,* 175; Bishop, Claire Huchet. 1974. *How Catholics Look at Jews.* (New York: Paulist Press), 53.

8. Thomas F. Gossett, *Race: The History of an Idea in America* (New York: Schocken Books, 1965), 10; Flannery, *The Anguish,* 67, 73; Trachtenbereg, *The Devil,* 159; Sidney Ahlstrom, *A Religious History of the American People* (New Haven: Yale University Press, 1972), 574; Marc Saperstein, *Moments of Crisis in Jewish-Christian Relations,* (London: SCM Press, 1989), 16.

9. Ellen Schiff, *From Stereotype to Metaphor: The Jew in Contemporary Drama* (Albany: State University of New York Press, 1982), 5; J. Von Dollinger, "The Jews in Europe," *Popular Science* 21 (July, 1882), 301.

10. Leon Poliakov, *The History of Antisemitism,* vol. 1 (New York: The Vanguard Press, 1965), 41; Gavin I. Langmuir, *From Ambrose of Milan to Emicho of Leningen: The Transformation of Hostility against Jews in Northern Christendom* (Spoleto: n.p., 1980), 21; Flannery, *The Anguish,* 91.

11. "Jews and Christians in the Middle Ages," *Saturday Review* (London) 56 (July 14, 1883), 41; Florence H. Ridley, "A Tale Told Too Often," *Western Folklore* 26 (1967), 153.

12. Roth, "Feast of Purim," 155.

13. Maccoby, *The Sacred,* 155; Gavin I. Langmuir, "The Knight's Tale of Young Hugh of Lincoln," *Speculum* 47 (July, 1972), 462; Ridley, "A Tale," 155; Flannery, *The Anguish,* 99; Edward J. Bristow, *Prostitution and Prejudice: The Jewish Fight Against White Slavery, 1870–1939* (New York: Schocken Books, 1983), 46; Paul Coates, "An Ugly Lie, Once Nailed Here, Spreads Eastward to Maryland," *Los Angeles Times,* April 20, 1965, part 2, p. 6.

14. See Langmuir, "The Knight's Tale."

15. Bishop, *How Catholics,* 53; Flannery, *The Anguish,* 96; Maccoby, *The Sacred,* 166.

16. My colleague, Alan Bernstein, has pointed out to me that in the Middle Ages the word "usury" was a synonym for "interest." In our own day, however, "usury" means *excessive* interest.

17. Maccoby, *The Sacred,* 166.

18. Quoted in Jeremy Cohen, *The Friars and the Jews* (Ithaca, N.Y.: Cornell University Press, 1982), 243; Poliakov, *History* vol. 1, 64.

19. Quoted in Flannery, *The Anguish,* 102.

20. Cohen, *The Friars,* 242.

21. Cohen, *The Friars,* 244; Ruether, "Anti-Semitism," 88; Poliakov, *History* vol. 1, 104, 109–10, 113; Paul E. Grosser and Edwin G. Halperin, *Anti-Semitism: Causes and Effects* (New York: Philosophical Library, 1983), 132; Jacobson, *The Affairs of Dame Rumor* (New York: Rinehart, 1948), 159; Trachtenberg, *The Devil,* 100–101; "The Inquisition, the Reformation, and the Jews," *Christian Century* 44 (June 9, 1927), 715; Flannery, *The Anguish,* 108, 109.

22. Flannery, *The Anguish,* 111; Poliakov, *History* vol. 1, 165; Arthur A. Goren, *The American Jews* (Cambridge, Mass.: The Belknap Press of Harvard University Press, 1982), 7–8.

23. Egal Feldman, *Dual Destinies: The Jewish Encounter with Protestant America* (Urbana: University of Illinois Press, 1990), 4; Marcus, *Colonial American Jew* vol. 3, 1116; "The Modern Jews,"

North American Review 60 (1845), 348; Jonathan I. Israel, *European Jewry in the Age of Mercantilism, 1550–1750* (Oxford: Clarendon Press, 1985), 1.

24. Poliakov, *History* vol. 1, 216–17, 222–23.
25. Franklin H. Littell, "American Protestantism and Antisemitism," in Naomi Cohen, ed., *Essential Papers on Jewish-Christian Relations in the United States* (New York: New York University Press, 1990), 176; Heiko Oberman, *Roots of Antisemitism in the Age of Renaissance and Reformation* (Philadelphia: Fortress Press, 1984), 84ff., 140.
26. Feldman, *Dual Destinies*, 4.
27. Lucy S. Dawidowicz, "Can Anti-Semitism Be Measured?" *Commentary* 50 (July, 1970), 36–43; Ginsberg, "Anti-Semitism," 5, 8, 11; Jean-Paul Sartre, *Anti-Semite and Jew* (New York: Schocken Books, 1948), 7; Jacobson, *The Affairs*, 312; Katz, *From Prejudice*, 320; Otto Fenichel, "Psychoanalysis of Antisemitism," *The American Imago* 2 (March, 1940), 35; Gossett, *Race*, 10; Trachtenberg, *The Devil*, 50–51, 101, 210; Maccoby, *The Sacred*, 163; "The Inquisition, the Reformation, and the Jews," 715; Poliakov, *History* vol. 1, 142; Ruether, "Anti-Semitism," 88.
28. Quoted in Gossett, *Race*, 11.
29. Trachtenberg, *The Devil*, 12, 13, 155.

23

The Holocaust: Maps

Martin Gilbert

In these maps, I have tried to tell something of the story of those whose lives were destroyed. . . . The terrible story outlined in these maps took place within the last fifty years. It has recently become the subject of efforts to deny that it ever took place. These denials are a cruel travesty of the truth. They are an insult to the memory of the dead, and a danger for the future. . . .

Each map is intended to show what actually happened: the scale of the slaughter—six million Jews murdered—the extraordinarily courageous acts of Jewish resistance, the fate of many millions of non-Jews who were also murdered, the often inadequate response of the world outside Europe, and the rescue of Jews by exceptionally courageous individuals who were themselves under Nazi rule. None of this can be denied without falsifying history.

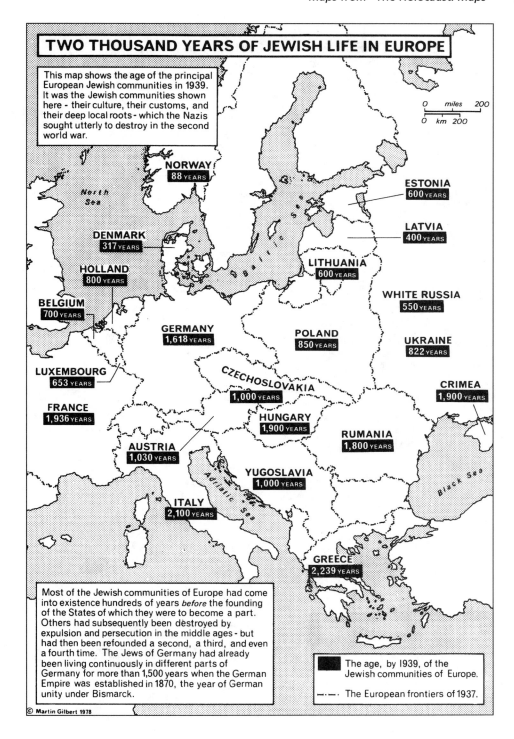

TWO THOUSAND YEARS OF JEWISH LIFE IN EUROPE

This map shows the age of the principal European Jewish communities in 1939. It was the Jewish communities shown here - their culture, their customs, and their deep local roots - which the Nazis sought utterly to destroy in the second world war.

NORWAY
88 YEARS

ESTONIA
600 YEARS

LATVIA
400 YEARS

DENMARK
317 YEARS

LITHUANIA
600 YEARS

HOLLAND
800 YEARS

WHITE RUSSIA
550 YEARS

BELGIUM
700 YEARS

GERMANY
1,618 YEARS

POLAND
850 YEARS

UKRAINE
822 YEARS

LUXEMBOURG
653 YEARS

CZECHOSLOVAKIA
1,000 YEARS

CRIMEA
1,900 YEARS

FRANCE
1,936 YEARS

HUNGARY
1,900 YEARS

RUMANIA
1,800 YEARS

AUSTRIA
1,030 YEARS

YUGOSLAVIA
1,000 YEARS

ITALY
2,100 YEARS

GREECE
2,239 YEARS

Most of the Jewish communities of Europe had come into existence hundreds of years *before* the founding of the States of which they were to become a part. Others had subsequently been destroyed by expulsion and persecution in the middle ages - but had then been refounded a second, a third, and even a fourth time. The Jews of Germany had already been living continuously in different parts of Germany for more than 1,500 years when the German Empire was established in 1870, the year of German unity under Bismarck.

The age, by 1939, of the Jewish communities of Europe.

—·—·— The European frontiers of 1937.

© Martin Gilbert 1978

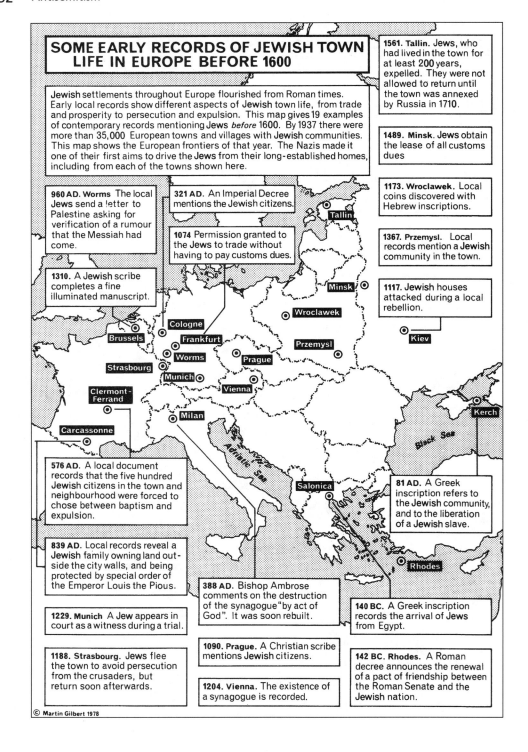

SOME EARLY RECORDS OF JEWISH TOWN LIFE IN EUROPE BEFORE 1600

Jewish settlements throughout Europe flourished from Roman times. Early local records show different aspects of Jewish town life, from trade and prosperity to persecution and expulsion. This map gives 19 examples of contemporary records mentioning Jews *before* 1600. By 1937 there were more than 35,000 European towns and villages with Jewish communities. This map shows the European frontiers of that year. The Nazis made it one of their first aims to drive the Jews from their long-established homes, including from each of the towns shown here.

1561. Tallin. Jews, who had lived in the town for at least 200 years, expelled. They were not allowed to return until the town was annexed by Russia in 1710.

1489. Minsk. Jews obtain the lease of all customs dues

1173. Wroclawek. Local coins discovered with Hebrew inscriptions.

1367. Przemysl. Local records mention a Jewish community in the town.

1117. Jewish houses attacked during a local rebellion.

960 AD. Worms The local Jews send a letter to Palestine asking for verification of a rumour that the Messiah had come.

321 AD. An Imperial Decree mentions the Jewish citizens.

1074 Permission granted to the Jews to trade without having to pay customs dues.

1310. A Jewish scribe completes a fine illuminated manuscript.

576 AD. A local document records that the five hundred Jewish citizens in the town and neighbourhood were forced to chose between baptism and expulsion.

839 AD. Local records reveal a Jewish family owning land outside the city walls, and being protected by special order of the Emperor Louis the Pious.

1229. Munich A Jew appears in court as a witness during a trial.

1188. Strasbourg. Jews flee the town to avoid persecution from the crusaders, but return soon afterwards.

1090. Prague. A Christian scribe mentions Jewish citizens.

1204. Vienna. The existence of a synagogue is recorded.

388 AD. Bishop Ambrose comments on the destruction of the synagogue "by act of God". It was soon rebuilt.

81 AD. A Greek inscription refers to the Jewish community, and to the liberation of a Jewish slave.

140 BC. A Greek inscription records the arrival of Jews from Egypt.

142 BC. Rhodes. A Roman decree announces the renewal of a pact of friendship between the Roman Senate and the Jewish nation.

Tallin
Minsk
Wroclawek
Przemysl
Kiev
Cologne
Brussels
Frankfurt
Worms
Prague
Strasbourg
Munich
Vienna
Clermont-Ferrand
Milan
Carcassonne
Kerch
Black Sea
Adriatic Sea
Salonica
Rhodes

© Martin Gilbert 1978

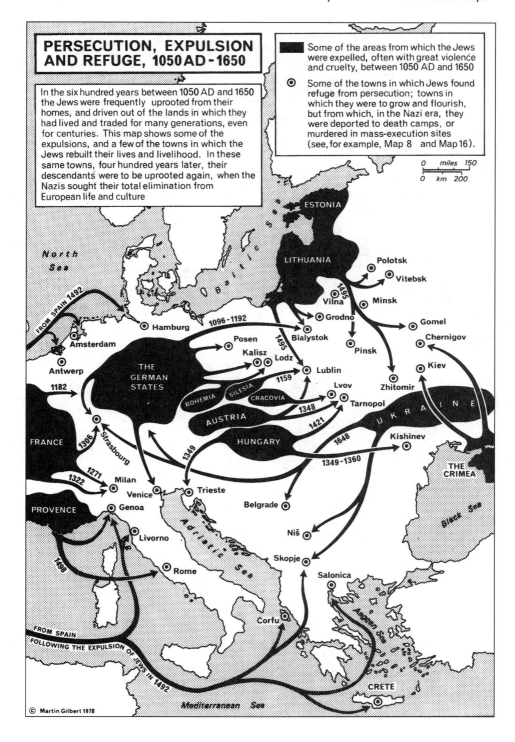

PERSECUTION, EXPULSION AND REFUGE, 1050 AD - 1650

In the six hundred years between 1050 AD and 1650 the Jews were frequently uprooted from their homes, and driven out of the lands in which they had lived and traded for many generations, even for centuries. This map shows some of the expulsions, and a few of the towns in which the Jews rebuilt their lives and livelihood. In these same towns, four hundred years later, their descendants were to be uprooted again, when the Nazis sought their total elimination from European life and culture

■ Some of the areas from which the Jews were expelled, often with great violence and cruelty, between 1050 AD and 1650

◉ Some of the towns in which Jews found refuge from persecution; towns in which they were to grow and flourish, but from which, in the Nazi era, they were deported to death camps, or murdered in mass-execution sites (see, for example, Map 8 and Map 16).

© Martin Gilbert 1978

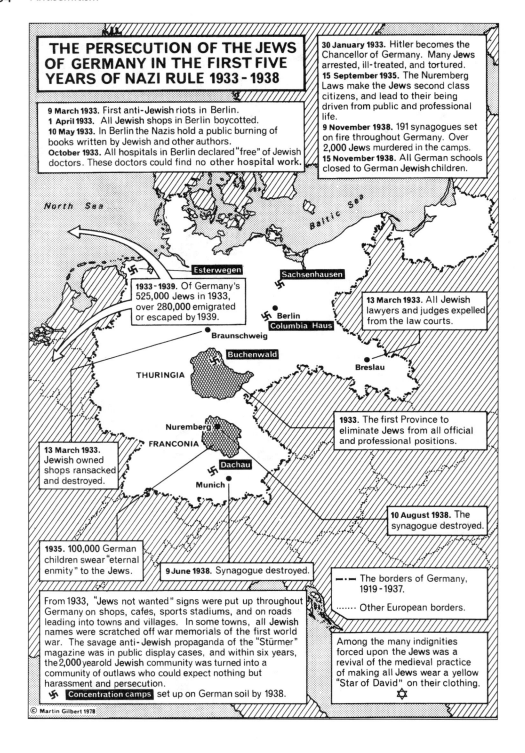

THE PERSECUTION OF THE JEWS OF GERMANY IN THE FIRST FIVE YEARS OF NAZI RULE 1933-1938

9 March 1933. First anti-Jewish riots in Berlin.
1 April 1933. All Jewish shops in Berlin boycotted.
10 May 1933. In Berlin the Nazis hold a public burning of books written by Jewish and other authors.
October 1933. All hospitals in Berlin declared "free" of Jewish doctors. These doctors could find no other hospital work.

30 January 1933. Hitler becomes the Chancellor of Germany. Many Jews arrested, ill-treated, and tortured.
15 September 1935. The Nuremberg Laws make the Jews second class citizens, and lead to their being driven from public and professional life.
9 November 1938. 191 synagogues set on fire throughout Germany. Over 2,000 Jews murdered in the camps.
15 November 1938. All German schools closed to German Jewish children.

North Sea

Baltic Sea

Esterwegen

Sachsenhausen

1933-1939. Of Germany's 525,000 Jews in 1933, over 280,000 emigrated or escaped by 1939.

13 March 1933. All Jewish lawyers and judges expelled from the law courts.

Berlin
Columbia Haus

Braunschweig

Buchenwald

THURINGIA

Breslau

1933. The first Province to eliminate Jews from all official and professional positions.

Nuremberg

FRANCONIA

13 March 1933. Jewish owned shops ransacked and destroyed.

Dachau

Munich

10 August 1938. The synagogue destroyed.

1935. 100,000 German children swear "eternal enmity" to the Jews.

9 June 1938. Synagogue destroyed.

—·— The borders of Germany, 1919-1937.

······· Other European borders.

From 1933, "Jews not wanted" signs were put up throughout Germany on shops, cafes, sports stadiums, and on roads leading into towns and villages. In some towns, all Jewish names were scratched off war memorials of the first world war. The savage anti-Jewish propaganda of the "Stürmer" magazine was in public display cases, and within six years, the 2,000 year old Jewish community was turned into a community of outlaws who could expect nothing but harassment and persecution.

Concentration camps set up on German soil by 1938.

Among the many indignities forced upon the Jews was a revival of the medieval practice of making all Jews wear a yellow "Star of David" on their clothing.

© Martin Gilbert 1978

GERMAN OFFICIAL PLANS FOR THE "FINAL SOLUTION", 20 JANUARY 1942

The number of Jews mentioned at the **Wannsee Conference**, country by country and area by area, for eventual deportation, and subsequent death. More than 14 million people were thus marked out for death.

One of the macabre features of the numerical list of the Jews submitted to the Wannsee Conference was the fact that no figure was given for the Jews of Estonia, merely a brief note that Estonia was 'Free of Jews'. This was true; the 1,000 Estonian Jews who had come under German rule in October 1941 had all been murdered during the three months before the Wannsee Conference.

ESTONIA "Free of Jews"

USSR 5 million

NORWAY 1,300

LATVIA 3,500

DENMARK 5,600

HOLLAND 160,800

BIALYSTOK DISTRICT 400,000

LITHUANIA 34,000

BELGIUM 43,000

WHITE RUSSIA 446,484

Wannsee
GERMANY 131,800 ●Berlin   Chelmno

FRANCE OCCUPIED ZONE 165,000

BOHEMIA AND MORAVIA 74,200

GENERAL GOVERNM. 2,284,000

EASTERN TERRITORIES 420,000

88,000

UKRAINE 2,994,684

SLOVAKIA

AUSTRIA 43,700

HUNGARY 742,800

FRANCE UNOCCUPIED ZONE 700,000

CROATIA 40,000

SERBIA 10,000

RUMANIA 342,000

ITALY 58,000

BULGARIA

ALBANIA 200

48,000

0   miles   200
0   km   300

GREECE 69,600

In December 1941, a month *before* the Wannsee Conference, the first Nazi extermination camp had already come into operation, at Chelmno, responsible for the mass-murder of Jews, Gypsies, and Soviet prisoners-of-war. After passing through corridors marked 'To the showers' and 'To the doctor', the victims were forced into a large truck which was in fact a gas-chamber, where they were killed within a few minutes. By the end of 1944 more than 360,000 Jews had been murdered in Chelmno alone.

The Wannsee Conference also specified the number of Jews in *unconquered* countries for eventual destruction, including 330,000 from Britain, 18,000 from Switzerland, 6,000 from Spain and 4,000 from Ireland.

© Martin Gilbert 1978

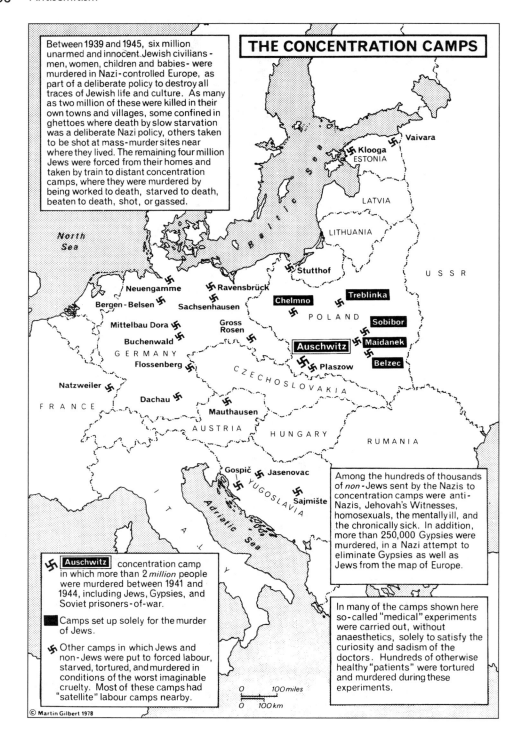

THE CONCENTRATION CAMPS

Between 1939 and 1945, six million unarmed and innocent Jewish civilians - men, women, children and babies - were murdered in Nazi-controlled Europe, as part of a deliberate policy to destroy all traces of Jewish life and culture. As many as two million of these were killed in their own towns and villages, some confined in ghettoes where death by slow starvation was a deliberate Nazi policy, others taken to be shot at mass-murder sites near where they lived. The remaining four million Jews were forced from their homes and taken by train to distant concentration camps, where they were murdered by being worked to death, starved to death, beaten to death, shot, or gassed.

North Sea

Baltic Sea

Vaivara

Klooga
ESTONIA

LATVIA

LITHUANIA

U S S R

Stutthof

Neuengamme   Ravensbrück

Bergen-Belsen   Sachsenhausen

Chelmno   Treblinka

POLAND

Mittelbau Dora   Gross Rosen

Sobibor

Buchenwald   Auschwitz   Maidanek

GERMANY   Flossenberg   Plaszow   Belzec

C Z E C H O S L O V A K I A

Natzweiler

FRANCE   Dachau

Mauthausen

AUSTRIA   HUNGARY

RUMANIA

Gospič   Jasenovac

Y U G O S L A V I A   Sajmište

Adriatic Sea

I T A L Y

Among the hundreds of thousands of *non*-Jews sent by the Nazis to concentration camps were anti-Nazis, Jehovah's Witnesses, homosexuals, the mentally ill, and the chronically sick. In addition, more than 250,000 Gypsies were murdered, in a Nazi attempt to eliminate Gypsies as well as Jews from the map of Europe.

In many of the camps shown here so-called "medical" experiments were carried out, without anaesthetics, solely to satisfy the curiosity and sadism of the doctors. Hundreds of otherwise healthy "patients" were tortured and murdered during these experiments.

Auschwitz concentration camp in which more than 2 *million* people were murdered between 1941 and 1944, including Jews, Gypsies, and Soviet prisoners-of-war.

Camps set up solely for the murder of Jews.

Other camps in which Jews and non-Jews were put to forced labour, starved, tortured, and murdered in conditions of the worst imaginable cruelty. Most of these camps had "satellite" labour camps nearby.

0   100 miles

0   100 km

© Martin Gilbert 1978

NON-JEWISH VICTIMS OF NAZI RULE

In all occupied lands, the Nazis carried out large-scale reprisals against completely innocent and unarmed civilians, whenever a single German soldier was killed by partisans, or even when German property was attacked. In mass-murder actions against non-Jews, they also massacred 4 *million* unarmed Soviet prisoners-of-war, 1 *million* Soviet civilians, more than 1 *million* Polish civilians, and 1½ *million* Yugoslav civilians. In May 1940, at two villages near Dunkirk, a total of 170 *disarmed* British prisoners-of-war were murdered in cold blood. In June 1944, at three villages near Caen, 70 *disarmed* Canadian prisoners-of-war were likewise murdered, by German S.S. troops.

Twenty-six of many thousands of Nazi reprisal and murder actions against unarmed *non*-Jews, with the approximate number murdered in each massacre.

Countries in each of which more than a *million* non-Jewish civilians died as a result of deliberate Nazi brutality.

Burashevo 350
U.S.S.R.
Jeglava 700
Mikulino 275
Baranowicze 1,000
North Sea
Holland 7 March 1945 400
Prague 860
Zinyany 484
Gorodets 434
POLAND
Ala 1,758
English Channel
GERMANY
Borow 300
Studenets 402
Dunkirk 170
Zamosc 200
Caen 70
Lidice 250
CZECHOSLOVAKIA
Brno 395
FRANCE
AUSTRIA
HUNGARY
Oradour-sur-Glane 642
RUMANIA
Belgrade 4,750
Kragujevac 7,253
YUGOSLAVIA
Black Sea
Kraljevo 1,700
BULGARIA
Mediterranean Sea
Rome 335
I T A L Y
Adriatic Sea
GREECE
Distomon 270
Kalvrithia 50
Athens 200
miles 200
km 150
Klissura 233
Kastelli 200
CRETE

In each of the actions shown here, unarmed men, women and children, almost all non-Jews, were chosen as the victims of Nazi hatred and vengeance. Many of those killed were beaten to death by blows of rifle butts, burned to death after petrol had been poured over them and ignited *while they were still alive*, or stripped naked and then shot. Those murdered at Klissura included 50 children under ten years of age. At Mikulino, all those killed were women patients in a mental hospital. In the Ardeatine caves in Rome, 253 Catholics and 70 Jews were murdered, among them many shopkeepers, students, lawyers and peddlers.

An estimated 32,000 German civilians were executed between 1933 and 1945 for so-called "political" offences. Those killed included Conservatives, Socialists, Communists, Catholics, Protestants, writers, journalists and teachers. All over Europe, non-Jews who were discovered sheltering Jews were also shot.

© Martin Gilbert 1978

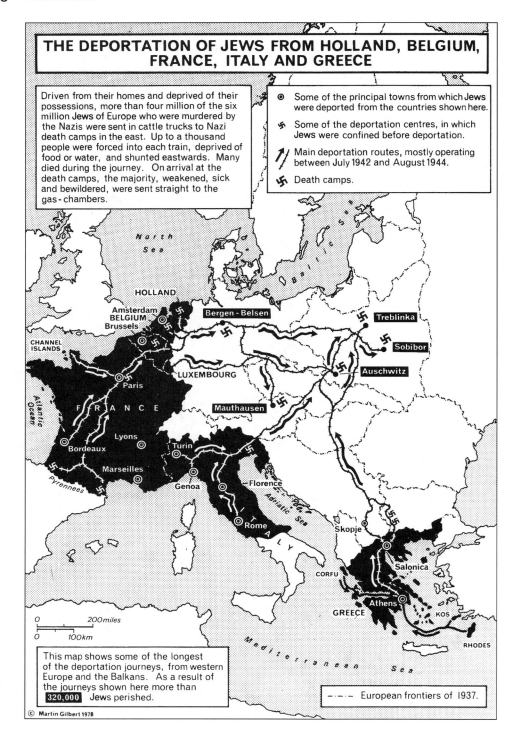

THE DEPORTATION OF JEWS FROM HOLLAND, BELGIUM, FRANCE, ITALY AND GREECE

Driven from their homes and deprived of their possessions, more than four million of the six million Jews of Europe who were murdered by the Nazis were sent in cattle trucks to Nazi death camps in the east. Up to a thousand people were forced into each train, deprived of food or water, and shunted eastwards. Many died during the journey. On arrival at the death camps, the majority, weakened, sick and bewildered, were sent straight to the gas-chambers.

◎   Some of the principal towns from which Jews were deported from the countries shown here.

卐   Some of the deportation centres, in which Jews were confined before deportation.

↗↗   Main deportation routes, mostly operating between July 1942 and August 1944.

卐   Death camps.

This map shows some of the longest of the deportation journeys, from western Europe and the Balkans. As a result of the journeys shown here more than **320,000** Jews perished.

—·—·—   European frontiers of 1937.

© Martin Gilbert 1978

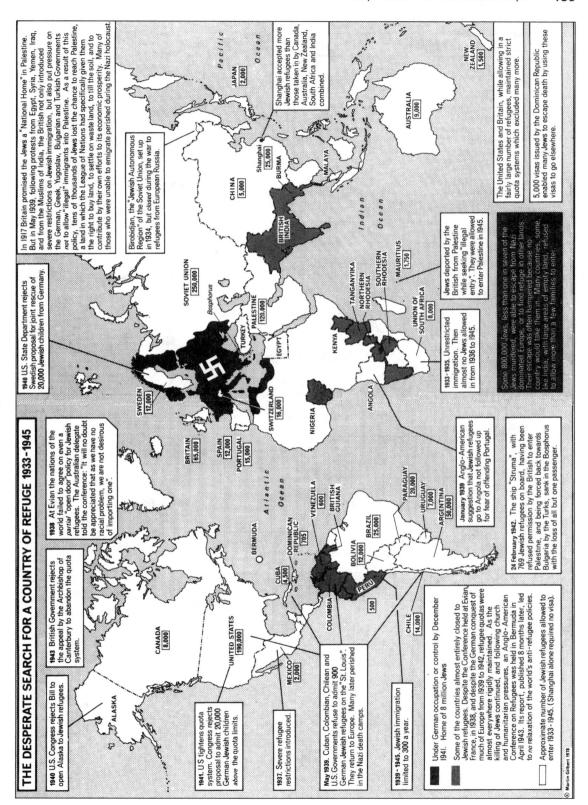

THE DESPERATE SEARCH FOR A COUNTRY OF REFUGE 1933-1945

© Martin Gilbert 1978

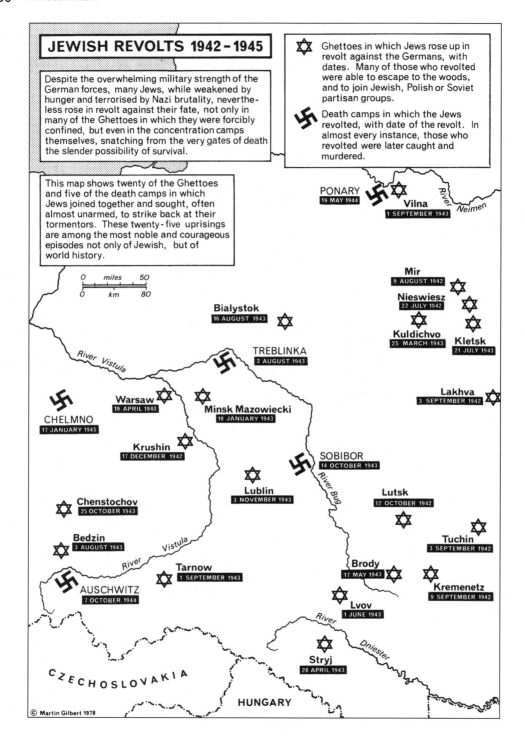

JEWISH REVOLTS 1942-1945

Despite the overwhelming military strength of the German forces, many Jews, while weakened by hunger and terrorised by Nazi brutality, nevertheless rose in revolt against their fate, not only in many of the Ghettoes in which they were forcibly confined, but even in the concentration camps themselves, snatching from the very gates of death the slender possibility of survival.

This map shows twenty of the Ghettoes and five of the death camps in which Jews joined together and sought, often almost unarmed, to strike back at their tormentors. These twenty-five uprisings are among the most noble and courageous episodes not only of Jewish, but of world history.

✡ Ghettoes in which Jews rose up in revolt against the Germans, with dates. Many of those who revolted were able to escape to the woods, and to join Jewish, Polish or Soviet partisan groups.

卐 Death camps in which the Jews revolted, with date of the revolt. In almost every instance, those who revolted were later caught and murdered.

PONARY
19 MAY 1944

Vilna
1 SEPTEMBER 1943

River Neimen

Mir
9 AUGUST 1942

Nieswiesz
22 JULY 1942

Kuldichvo
25 MARCH 1943

Kletsk
21 JULY 1943

0   miles   50
0   km   80

Bialystok
16 AUGUST 1943

River Vistula

TREBLINKA
2 AUGUST 1943

Lakhva
3 SEPTEMBER 1942

Warsaw
19 APRIL 1943

Minsk Mazowiecki
10 JANUARY 1943

CHELMNO
17 JANUARY 1945

Krushin
17 DECEMBER 1942

SOBIBOR
14 OCTOBER 1943

River Bug

Lutsk
12 OCTOBER 1942

Lublin
3 NOVEMBER 1943

Chenstochov
25 OCTOBER 1943

Tuchin
3 SEPTEMBER 1942

Bedzin
3 AUGUST 1943

River Vistula

Brody
17 MAY 1943

Tarnow
1 SEPTEMBER 1943

Kremenetz
9 SEPTEMBER 1942

AUSCHWITZ
7 OCTOBER 1944

Lvov
1 JUNE 1943

River Dniester

Stryj
28 APRIL 1943

C Z E C H O S L O V A K I A

HUNGARY

© Martin Gilbert 1978

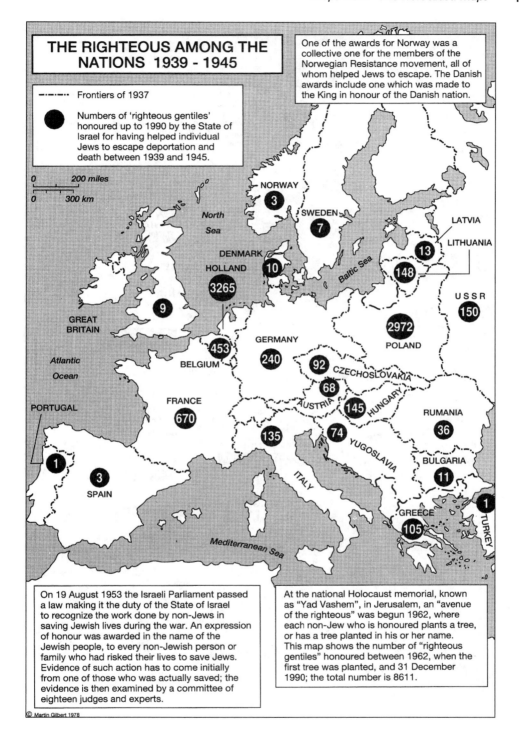

THE RIGHTEOUS AMONG THE NATIONS 1939 - 1945

One of the awards for Norway was a collective one for the members of the Norwegian Resistance movement, all of whom helped Jews to escape. The Danish awards include one which was made to the King in honour of the Danish nation.

—·—·—· Frontiers of 1937

● Numbers of 'righteous gentiles' honoured up to 1990 by the State of Israel for having helped individual Jews to escape deportation and death between 1939 and 1945.

0 — 200 miles
0 — 300 km

NORWAY 3
SWEDEN 7
LATVIA
LITHUANIA 13
DENMARK
HOLLAND 10
148
North Sea
Baltic Sea
USSR 150
GREAT BRITAIN 9
2972 POLAND
GERMANY
453 240 92 CZECHOSLOVAKIA
BELGIUM 68
AUSTRIA 145 HUNGARY
Atlantic Ocean
FRANCE 670
135 74 YUGOSLAVIA
RUMANIA 36
PORTUGAL
ITALY
BULGARIA 11
1
3 SPAIN
GREECE 1 TURKEY
105
Mediterranean Sea

On 19 August 1953 the Israeli Parliament passed a law making it the duty of the State of Israel to recognize the work done by non-Jews in saving Jewish lives during the war. An expression of honour was awarded in the name of the Jewish people, to every non-Jewish person or family who had risked their lives to save Jews. Evidence of such action has to come initially from one of those who was actually saved; the evidence is then examined by a committee of eighteen judges and experts.

At the national Holocaust memorial, known as "Yad Vashem", in Jerusalem, an "avenue of the righteous" was begun 1962, where each non-Jew who is honoured plants a tree, or has a tree planted in his or her name. This map shows the number of "righteous gentiles" honoured between 1962, when the first tree was planted, and 31 December 1990; the total number is 8611.

© Martin Gilbert 1978

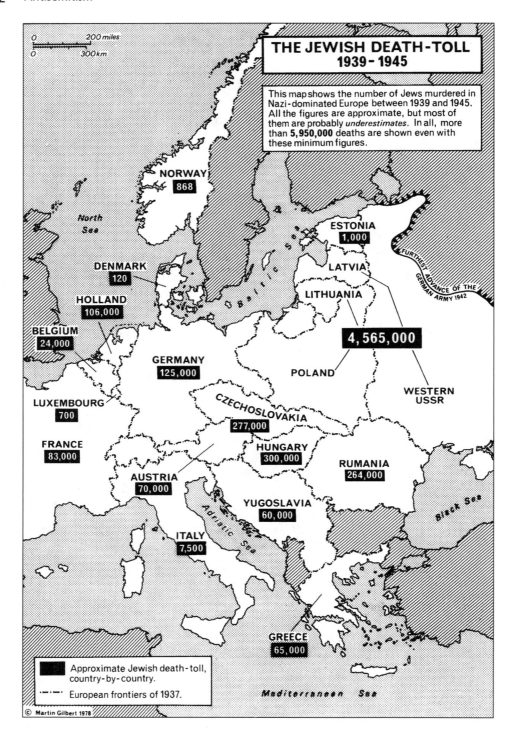

THE JEWISH DEATH-TOLL
1939-1945

This map shows the number of Jews murdered in Nazi-dominated Europe between 1939 and 1945. All the figures are approximate, but most of them are probably *underestimates*. In all, more than **5,950,000** deaths are shown even with these minimum figures.

NORWAY
868

ESTONIA
1,000

North Sea

DENMARK
120

LATVIA

LITHUANIA

HOLLAND
106,000

BELGIUM
24,000

4,565,000

GERMANY
125,000

POLAND

WESTERN USSR

LUXEMBOURG
700

CZECHOSLOVAKIA
277,000

FRANCE
83,000

HUNGARY
300,000

RUMANIA
264,000

AUSTRIA
70,000

YUGOSLAVIA
60,000

Black Sea

ITALY
7,500

GREECE
65,000

Approximate Jewish death-toll, country-by-country.

European frontiers of 1937.

Mediterranean Sea

FURTHEST ADVANCE OF THE GERMAN ARMY 1942

Baltic Sea

Adriatic Sea

© Martin Gilbert 1978

24

The Setting: Europe and America

David S. Wyman

In Europe: The "Final Solution"

During the spring of 1941, while planning the invasion of Russia, the Nazis made the decision to annihilate the Jews in the territories to be taken from the USSR. On June 22, before dawn, the German army opened its drive against the Soviet forces. Following directly behind the frontline troops were special mobile units (*Einsatzgruppen*) that rounded up Jews and killed them in mass shootings. Typical of these scenes of horror is an eyewitness report by a German construction engineer:

> I saw one family of about six, all already stripped naked and waiting for the order to get down into the grave. Next to the father was a boy of ten or twelve years old. He placed a hand on the boy's head and pointed the other towards heaven and said something to the boy, who, I could see, was trying to keep back his tears. The man's wife was standing near an old woman with snow-white hair, either her mother or the mother of her husband, who held a baby in her arms, singing softly to it and stroking it. Then came the order, "Next ten!" and the family started moving round the mound of earth to climb into the grave. . . .
>
> Then the next were called out to make themselves ready, that is, to take off their clothes. And then I heard shooting and believed that everything was over. . . . I then walked round the grave and saw a few people still moving. Not all the shots had killed. An S.S. man sat on the edge of the grave, with one leg crossed over the other. . . . I called out to the S.S. man, "Look, they're not all dead!" to which he replied, "Ach! Tonight the grave will be filled up with rubbish and so it'll all be finished!"[1]

Between June and December 1941, the *Einsatzgruppen* and associated support units murdered some 500,000 Jews in what had been eastern Poland and Russia. A second sweep through the occupied territory, lasting from fall 1941 through 1942, annihilated close to 900,000 more.[2]

Meanwhile, Hitler had ordered the systematic extermination of all Jews in the Nazi grip. The directive, issued on July 31, 1941, by Reich Marshal Hermann Goering, instructed Reinhard Heydrich, chief of the Reich Security Main Office, to organize "a complete solution of the Jewish question in the German sphere of influence in Europe." Heydrich, who was already in charge of the mobile killing operations in Russia, began preparations for collecting the Jews in the rest of the Nazi domain and deporting them to eastern Europe. The organization of the deportations was assigned to Adolf Eichmann.[3]

Advanced planning for the extermination of the Jews took place in Berlin on January 20, 1942, at the Wannsee Conference. There Heydrich outlined the basic program to a group of German officials whose agencies would collaborate in carrying out what the conference minutes called "the final solution of the Jewish question." In the interval between Goering's directive to Heydrich and the Wannsee Conference, the Nazis had acted to hem in their victims. From October 1941 on, Jews were forbidden exit from German-held territory.[4]

Most of the slaughter of Jews by the *Einsatzgruppen* in the East in 1941 and 1942 involved mass shooting at large grave sites. For the rest of Europe's Jews, the Germans established six extermination centers in Poland. The first of these, at Chelmno, began its work in late 1941, with gassing vans as the instrument of murder. The victims, packed into the enclosed trucks, were suffocated by carbon monoxide from the vehicles' exhaust systems. Mass annihilation at most of the other locations (Belzec, Majdanek, Treblinka, Sobibor, Auschwitz) was well under way by the spring and summer of 1942. There, gas-chamber buildings and crematoriums were constructed. Gassing was by carbon monoxide fumes produced by stationary engines, except at Auschwitz, where the crystalline Zyklon B (hydrogen cyanide, or prussic acid) was used. Country by country, Jews from most parts of Europe were crowded into freight cars and carried to these assembly lines of death throughout 1942, 1943, and 1944. Nearly three million were murdered in the six killing centers.[5] Of the approximately 5.5 million Jews killed by the Nazis, close to 3 million were slaughtered in the six extermination centers and almost 1.5 million were massacred in the mobile killing actions. Most of the rest died in other mass shootings, or on the deportation trains, or from the lethal conditions that prevailed in the ghettos (starvation, cold, disease, and crowding).[6]

The Nazis assigned very high priority to the annihilation of European Jewry. Locked in a world conflict in which the very existence of their nation was at stake, Germany's leaders diverted significant amounts of war potential into the genocide program. *Einsatzgruppen* activities absorbed ammunition and able manpower. At several points in the march of murder, gasoline was used to burn the bodies of victims. The extermination process strained the overburdened German administrative machinery, but the heaviest costs were paid in transportation and labor.[7]

Moving millions of Jews across Europe to the death factories in Poland overloaded a railroad system that was hard put to meet essential transportation of troops and war material. Most important, despite a constant labor shortage, one that reached four million by 1944, the Nazis wiped out a capable work force of two to three million Jews. Even skilled Jews employed in war-related industries were deported to the gas chambers. And this occurred despite the recognition that Jewish labor productivity was frequently well above the norm, because Jews saw their best hope for survival in making themselves economically valuable.[8]

To kill the Jews, the Nazis were willing to weaken their capacity to fight the war. The United States and its allies, however, were willing to attempt almost nothing to save them.

In America: Barriers to Rescue

Until the Nazis blocked the exits in the fall of 1941, the oppressed Jews of Europe might have fled to safety. But relatively few got out, mainly because the rest of the world would not take them in. The United States, which had lowered its barriers a little in early 1938, began raising them again in autumn 1939. Two years later, immigration was even more tightly restricted than before 1938. In fact, starting in July 1941, America's gates were nearly shut. The best chance to save the European Jews had passed.[9] After 1941, with the Holocaust under way, the need for help became acute. By then, though, saving Jews was much more difficult, for open doors in the outside world, while essential, would not be enough. Determined rescue efforts would also be needed to salvage even a segment of European Jewry. But the United States did not take rescue action until January 1944, and even then the attempt was limited. Nor were America's nearly closed doors open: immigration was held to about 10 percent of the already small quota limits. (The quotas, established in the 1920s, set specific limits on the number who could immigrate to the United State in any given year from any given foreign country. Eligibility was based on country of birth. There was, for example, a German quota, a British quota, and so on. The total of all quotas was 154,000. Almost 84,000 of this was assigned to the British and Irish, peoples who had no need to flee.) Thus the second—and last—chance to help the Jews of Europe came and went.[10]

In the years before the Pearl Harbor bombing, the United States had reacted to the European Jewish crisis with concern but had refused to permit any sizable immigration of refugees. Although Congress and the Roosevelt administration had shaped this policy, it grew out of three important aspects of American society in the 1930s: unemployment, nativistic restrictionism, and anti-Semitism.

After Pearl Harbor, the war itself narrowed the possibilities for saving Jews. In addition, the mass media's failure to draw attention to Holocaust developments undercut efforts to create public pressure for government rescue action. But the deeper causes for the lateness and weakness of America's attempts at rescue, and for its unwillingness to take in more than a tiny trickle of fleeing Jews, were essentially the same ones that had determined the nation's reaction to the refugee crisis before Pearl Harbor.

American Restrictionism

From 1933 to 1941, opponents of refugee immigration had built their case around the high unemployment of the Great Depression. Restrictionists persistently asserted that refugees who came to the United States usurped jobs that rightfully belonged to unemployed American workers. Their viewpoint was widely accepted. The counterargument, that refugees were consumers as well as workers and thus provided as many jobs as they took, made little headway.

Economic pressures against immigration had been reinforced by strong currents of nativism of "one hundred percent Americanism." These xenophobic feelings, which had run very high in the aftermath of World War I, had combined with economic forces during the 1920s to install the quota system, the nation's first broad restriction of immigration. Then, during the 1930s, anti-alien attitudes had played a major part in keeping refugee immigration at low levels. American nativism continued strong throughout World War II.

Wartime prosperity did not dissolve the economic argument against immigration. Fear was widespread that the Depression would return with the end of hostilities. Millions believed that demobilization of the armed forces and reconversion to a peacetime economy would bring, at the very least, an extended period of large unemployment.

Veterans' organizations were especially forceful in insisting on the protection of employment rights for returning servicemen. In their view, every foreigner allowed into the country meant unwarranted job competition. Accordingly, throughout the war, the American Legion called for a virtual ban on immigration, to last well into the postwar period. The Veterans of Foreign Wars demanded similarly tough restrictions. By August 1944, the VFW was urging a stop to all immigration for the next ten years. In the early 1940s, American Legion membership exceeded 1.2 million and included 28 senators and 150 congressmen. Enrollment in the VFW stood at nearly one million. In addition, a large array of patriotic groups actively backed the veterans' organizations in the drive to cut off immigration. At the forefront were the influential Daughters of the American Revolution and the American Coalition of Patriotic Societies, a body that represented the legislative interests of 115 different organizations with combined memberships of some 2.5 million.[11]

The anti-immigration forces wielded substantial political power. Moreover, a large number of congressmen were staunchly restrictionist, a reflection of their own views as well as of attitudes that were popular in their home districts. Many of them, typified by Senator Robert Reynolds (Dem., N.C.), Senator Rufus Holman (Rep., Oreg.), and Representative William Elmer (Rep., Mo.), embraced an intense anti-alienism that shaded into anti-Semitism.[12]

Holman, who introduced a bill in 1942 to end all immigration (except for temporary visits), constantly kept an eye open for attempts to weaken the barriers that kept aliens out. He once blocked legislation in the Senate simply because it aroused his suspicion "that it relaxes the immigration laws," though he openly admitted, "I know nothing about this bill." (It did not concern immigration.) Elmer, equally distrustful, warned the House of Representatives in October 1943 of "a determined and well-financed movement . . . to admit all the oppressed, Hitler-persecuted people of Germany and other European countries into our country."[13]

Even lawmakers as far removed from Reynolds, Holman, and Elmer as Senator Harold Burton (Rep., Ohio) lined up on the restrictionist side. Burton, a committed internationalist and a liberal-minded Unitarian, believed the United States should channel refugees "toward areas other than our own." He maintained that "there are many other places in the world where there is much more room for their reception than there is here."[14]

During the war, hundreds of bills were introduced in Congress to decrease immigration. Among the most important—and the most typical—were three put forward in the House. Leonard Allen (Dem., La.) initiated two of them. One would have suspended all immigration until the end of hostilities; the other called for terminating immigration when the war was over. Edward Rees (Rep., Kan.) sponsored a more moderate proposal: to cut the quotas in half for a ten-year period.[15]

The tendency in Congress was clear, and it frightened the leadership of several refugee aid and social service organizations. On the basis of their own information sources throughout the country, they were convinced by the fall of 1943 that a rising tide of public opinion, along with the anti-refugee mood in Congress, endangered the entire quota system. In response, these organizations began to plan an educational and lobbying effort to head off legislation for a "drastic curtailment of immigration." Their campaign probably helped preserve the quota system and avoid a complete stoppage of immigration; none of the many restrictionist bills were enacted. But it did not succeed in widening America's virtually closed doors during the war, even to the extent of increasing the tiny percentage of the quotas that was being made available.[16]

America's limited willingness to share the refugee burden showed clearly in national opinion polls. In 1938, a year when the Nazis had sharply stepped up their persecution of Jews, four separate polls indicated that from 71 to 85 percent of the American public opposed increasing the quotas to help refugees; 67 percent wanted refugees kept out altogether. In a survey taken in early 1939, 66 percent even objected to a one-time exception to allow ten thousand refugee children to enter outside the quota limits.[17]

Five years later, in the middle of the war, attitudes were no different. Asked in January of 1943 whether "it would be a good idea or a bad idea to let more immigrants come into this country after the war," 78 percent of those polled thought it would be a bad idea. At the end of 1945, when the terrible conditions facing European displaced persons were widely known, only 5 percent of the respondents thought the United States should "permit more persons from Europe to come to this country each year than we did before the war." (Thirty-two percent believed the same number should be allowed in as before, 37 percent wanted fewer to enter, and 14 percent called for closing the doors entirely.)[18]

American Anti-Semitism

While it is obvious that many who opposed refugee immigration felt no antipathy toward Jews, much restrictionist and anti-refugee sentiment was closely linked to anti-

Semitism. The plain truth is that many Americans were prejudiced against Jews and were unlikely to support measures to help Jewish refugees. Anti-Semitism had been a significant determinant of American ungenerous response to the refugee plight before Pearl Harbor. During the war years, it became an important factor in the nation's reaction to the Holocaust.[19]

American anti-Semitism, which had climbed to very high levels in the late 1930s, continued to rise in the first part of the 1940s. It reached its historic peak in 1944. By the spring of 1942, sociologist David Riesman described it as "slightly below the boiling point." Three years later, public-opinion expert Elmo Roper warned that "anti-Semitism has spread all over the nation and is particularly virulent in urban centers."[20]

During the decade before Pearl Harbor, more than a hundred anti-Semitic organizations had pumped hate propaganda throughout American society. At the head of the band were Father Charles E. Coughlin and his Social Justice movement, William Dudley Pelley's Silver Shirts, the German-American Bund, and the Reverend Gerald B. Winrod's Protestant fundamentalist Defenders of the Christian Faith. Within a few months of America's entry into the war, these four forces were effectively silenced, along with many of the lesser anti-Semitic leaders and their followings. Coughlin, stilled by his archbishop, also saw his *Social Justice* tabloid banned from the mails. Pelley received a fifteen-year prison sentence for sedition. The German-American Bund disintegrated; some members were jailed and several others were interned as dangerous enemy aliens. Winrod, under indictment for sedition during much of the war, continued to publish his *Defender* magazine, but its contents moderated noticeably.[21]

Organized anti-Semitism had been set back, but by no means did it go under. During the war, several of the minor demagogues remained vocal and new ones came forward. Father Edward Lodge Curran, president of the International Catholic Truth Society, worked to maintain the momentum of the Christian Front, a militant Coughlinite group. And in 1942 the fundamentalist preacher Gerald L. K. Smith came into his own as a front-ranking anti-Semitic agitator. That was the year Smith launched his magazine, *The Cross and the Flag*, inaugurated the Committee of One Million, and achieved a reasonably strong showing in the Republican primary for election, running for the U.S. Senate from Michigan. The next year, he formed the America First Party, an isolationist, anti–New Deal venture. From his various platforms, Smith spread anti-refugee and anti-Semitic propaganda, along with attacks on internationalism, Communism, and the New Deal.[22]

It was during the war, too, that anti-Jewish hatreds that had been sown and nurtured for years ripened into some extremely bitter fruits. Epidemics of serious anti-Semitic actions erupted in several parts of the United States, especially the urban Northeast. Most often, youth gangs were the perpetrators. Jewish cemeteries were vandalized, synagogues were damaged as well as defaced with swastikas and anti-Semitic slogans, anti-Jewish markings were scrawled on sidewalks and Jewish stores, and anti-Semitic literature was widely distributed. Most upsetting of all, in scores of instances bands of teenagers beat Jewish schoolchildren—sometimes severely, as when three Jewish boys in Boston were attacked by twenty of their classmates. In another incident, in a Midwestern city, young hoodlums stripped a twelve-year-old Jewish boy to the waist and painted a Star of David and the word *Jude* on his chest.[23]

The worst outbreaks occurred in New York City and Boston. In New York, the incidents began in 1941 and continued at least through 1944. They spread throughout the metropolis but hit hardest in Washington Heights, where almost every synagogue was desecrated and where attacks on Jewish youngsters were the most widespread. In the fall of 1942, the city's commissioner of investigation, William B. Herlands, started a formal inquiry into the situation. His comprehensive report, released to the press in January 1944, analyzed thirty-one of the cases of anti-Semitic violence and vandalism and examined the backgrounds of fifty-four of the offenders. The Herlands Report criticized the city police for laxity and inaction in 70 percent of the cases. As for the perpetrators, the investigation found them to be typically in their middle to late teens, from poor and troubled home situations, and with records of low achievement in school. All had been influenced by anti-Semitic propaganda and indoctrination, received mostly at home, at school, and through pamphlets.[24]

Notes

1. Hilberg (1961), ch 7, esp 177, 182–3, 261; quotation is from *Yad Vashem Studies* (YVS), v 6, 301.
2. Hilberg (1961), 196, 225, 242, 256, 767.
3. Ibid. 257, 262; Raul Hilberg, ed., *Documents of Destruction: Germany and Jewry, 1933–1945* (1971), 88.
4. Hilberg (1961), 264–5; Wyman, 205; Leavitt to Aufbau, 2/27/42, American Joint Distribution Committee Archives, General & Emergency File, Germany-Emig Gen.
5. Hilberg (1961), 209, 265, 309–11, 555, 561–6, 572, 767; Lucy Dawidowicz, *The War Against the Jews, 1933–1945* (1975), 181.
6. Hilberg (1961), 767.
7. Ibid, 643.
8. Ibid, 247, 284–7, 298, 311, 333–7, 377, 645–6.
9. Wyman, vii, 35–9, 168–83, 191–205, 209.
10. *National Legionnaire (Natl Legionnaire)*, 10/42, 2; *American Legion Magazine (Am Legion Magazine)*, 11/43, 37; *Foreign Service (VFW)*, 7/43, 30, 10/44, 13; *New York Times (NYT)*, 4/19/44, 11; *Interpreter Releases (IR)*, 7/18/44, 233–4; *Rescue (HIAS)*, 2/45, 6; *Reader's Digest (RD)*, 3/43, 44.
11. Sources in preceding note. Also Clarence E. Pickett's Journal (CEP Jour), June 18, 1943, American Friends Service Committee Archives, Philadelphia; *Monthly Review (MR)*. 12/43, 12; *Rescue (HIAS)*, 2/45, 6; NYT, 9/21/42, 1, 9/23/43, 13, 4/19/44, 11, 10/13/44, 8, 10/21/45, 40; *New York Herald Tribune (NYHT)*, 9/26/44, 2; *Am Legion Magazine*, 4/43, 2; *Foreign Service*, 12/45, 11; *New York Post (NYP)*, 4/18/44, 4; Wyman, 79.
12. Travers to Foster, 4/6/45, SD150.01 Bills/3–3045, State Department Decimal Files (SD), National Archives, Washington, DC; IR, 6/21/43, 169–85; CEP Jour, 1/26/44; MR, 12/43, 11–13; NYT 8/22/44,32; *American Vindicator (Am Vindicator)*, 4/42, 1, 5/42, 7, 11/42, 3; *National Record (Natl Record)*, 4/43, 1, 12/44, 6.
13. *NYT*, 9/22/42, 16; *Congressional Record (CR)*, v 89, 7107–8, 8594.
14. Burton to Joy, 5/7/44, Unitarian Universalist Committee Papers (USC), Tufts University, Medford, MA, Sen Burton.
15. AF Minutes, Foreign Service Staff, American Friends Service Committee Archives (AF), Philadelphia, 5/14/45; NYT, 3/6/44, 9; IR, 10/9/42, 342, 11/9/43, 364, 12/14/43, 391, 8/8/44, 250–8; MR, 12/43, 12–13; *Jewish Telegraphic Agency Daily News Bulletin (JTA)*, 1/9/44; Hull to Dickstein, 12/15/43, 12/13/43, SD 150.01 Bills/507 & 509; HR 3487, 10/18/43, copy in Breckinridge Long Papers, Library of Congress, Washington, DC, B 198, Legislation.
16. AF Minutes, Joint Foreign Service Executive Committee, 3/6/44, 4/17/44, 8/21/44 (AF); Pickett to Vail and Rogers, 10/21/43, Report on Recommendations, 10/15/43 (with Minutes of Executive Committee of National Refugee SErvice, 10/20/43), AF, Refugee Service Files, National Refugee Service Papers; US House of Representatives, 1976. *Problems of World War II and Its Aftermath: Part 2, The Palestine Question*.
17. Wyman, 47, 95, 210; Stember, 145, 149.
18. Cantril, 307.
19. Wyman, 14–26, 85–6, 94–5, 103, 111, 128, 163–5.
20. Ibid, 14–23; Stember, 67, 84–5, 130–3, 208–10, 214; *Public Opinion Quarterly*, spr 1942, 56; *NYT*, 4/11/45, 21.
21. Wyman, 14–22; *American Jewish Year Book (AJYB)*, v 44, 157–60, v46, 137–8; Charles Tull,

Father Coughlin and the New Deal (1965), 234–7; Sander Diamond, *The Nazi Movement in the United States, 1924–1941* (1974), 345–8; *NYT*, 12/16/41, 31, 4/4/42, 11, 4/15/42, 1, 4/19/42, IV, 7, 7/24/42, 1, 8, 8/13/42, 6, 3/24/43, 16, 6/19/43, 1, 28.

22. *AJYB*, v 44, 159–60, v46, 133–142, v47, 268–79; *Jewish Veteran (JV)*, 10/42, 3, 5/44, 8, 21, 8/44, 9; *National Jewish Monthly (NJM)*, 5/42, 296–7; *Congress Weekly (CW)*, 4/30/43, 9–10, 10/29/43, 2; *Atlantic Montly (AtM)*, 7/44, 49–50; *Cross and the Flag*, 4/42, 2, 5/42, 2,3, 3/43, 17, 9/43, 268–9, 12/43, 315, 3/44, 363, 10/44, 455, 3/45, 530.

23. *AJYB*, v 46, 141; *Contemporary Jewish Record (CJR)*, 2/44, 65, 4/44, 179; *CW*, 1/2/42, 3, 11/19/43, 20; *NJM*, 12/43, 114, 2/44, 178; *JV*, 6/42, 15, 12/42, 7; *Tomorrow*, 9/44, 55.

24. *NYT*, 11/16/42, 21, 12/30/43, 19, 1/11/44, 1, 24; *CW*, 1/2/42, 3, 10/23/42, 2, 4/2/43, 2, 11/5/43, 20; *JV*, 12/42, 7–8; *NJM*, 2/44, 178; *PM (New York City)*; 8/10/44, 13.

References

Cantril, Hadley, ed. 1951. *Public Opinion: 1935–1946*. Princeton: Princeton University Press.

Dawidowicz, Lucy. 1975. *The War Against the Jews, 1933–1945*. New York: Holt, Rinehart & Winston.

Diamond, Sander. 1974. *The Nazi Movement in the United States, 1924–1941*. Ithaca: Cornell University Press.

Hilberg, Raul. 1961. *The Destruction of the European Jews*. Chicago: Quadrangle Books.

Hilberg, Raul, ed. 1971. *Documents of Destruction: Germany and Jewry, 1933–1945*. Chicago: Quadrangle Books.

Stember, Charles, ed. 1966. *Jews in the Mind of America*. New York: Basic Books.

Tull, Charles. 1965. *Father Couglin and the New Deal*. Syracuse, N.Y.: Syracuse University Press.

Wyman, David. 1968. *Paper Walls: America and the Refugee Crisis, 1938–1941*. Amherst: University of Massachusetts Press.

25

Including Jews in Multiculturalism

Peter F. Langman

This article is an attempt to answer two questions. First, why have non-Jews not included Jews in multiculturalism? Responses consider the level of assimilation of American Jews; their classification as White; the idea that Jews are members of a religion, not a culture; their economic success; and the exclusion of anti-Semitism as an issue worth addressing.

The second question is, Why have Jews not included themselves in multiculturalism? The issues discussed here are the divorce between Jews' public and private identities, the lack of validation of their experience as members of a minority, their fear or anxiety surrounding being publicly Jewish, and the self-hatred that can occur when Jews internalize anti-Semitism.

These speculations are based on personal experience and observations, discussions with Jews and non-Jews, and texts from a variety of disciplines, including history, sociology, psychology, and Judaica. Of course, any attempt to speak for large groups of people runs the risk of stereotyping, but that is not the intent of this article. . . .

Why Non-Jews Have Not Included Jews

Jews Seen as an Assimilated Nonminority

Perhaps American Jews are considered to be so well integrated into American society that they no longer constitute a separate culture. If Jews are simply mainstream Americans, there is no need to include them in discussions of multiculturalism. This view is understandable; Jews often become so American that it is hard to see that any Jewishness remains. This is why the issues of assimilation and intermarriage are of such great concern in many Jewish communities. Yet many assimilated, nonobservant Jews still carry a strong sense of being outside mainstream American culture. This has been expressed to me at times with surprising vehemence, even from people who are unconnected to any Jewish community. Thus, despite appearances, Jews experience themselves as members of a minority culture.

The fact that Jews are a minority is not widely acknowledged. Or, if they are acknowledged as a numerical minority, they are relegated to a status of somehow "not counting" as a minority. Perhaps the extent to which Jews are a minority is not widely appreciated. If the world were reduced to 1,000 people, with the same population proportions that currently exist, there would be 331 Christians and only 3 Jews. Whereas Christians are approximately 33 percent of the world's population, Jews are approximately one third of 1 percent of the world's people (World Almanac, 1994). Even in America, Jews are less than 2.5 percent of the population (U.S. Bureau of the Census 1994, 70).

Jews tend to be acutely aware of their minority status and have referred to themselves as being "endangered" (Siegel 1986). Jewish existence has historically been precarious and subject to whatever winds of bigotry happen to be blowing at the time. To be a Jew in a predominantly Christian population is not always comfortable. Although the word *minority* typically refers to race, it applies to religion as well, and although the United States is 83 percent White, it is approximately 95 percent Christian (based on figures from World Almanac 1994, 375, 729). To be non-Christian in America is more uncommon than to be nonwhite.

The sense of being a minority, combined with a knowledge of the history of Jewish persecution, makes it difficult for Jews to take their safety for granted. Outwardly it may look as if Jews are perfectly at home in America, but this is misleading. As one account notes,

> There is one thing that every Jew knows: Jewish history has been a succession of rises and falls. So you wait for the other shoe to drop. We are now on an upswing, but all of Jewish history guarantees that there will be a downswing. Look how great the German Jews once had it. (Stallsworth 1987, 74)

To non-Jews this may seem paranoid. To Jews, however, who are more familiar with the history of anti-Semitism, this "paranoia" has, all too often, been justified:

> What is the first lesson a Jew learns? That people want to kill Jews. . . . To be a Jew in America, or anywhere, today is to carry with you the consciousness of limitless savagery. It is to carry that consciousness with you not as an abstraction, but as a reality; not, God help us all, only as memory, but also as possibility. (Fein, 1988, 59–60)

Thus, Jews experience themselves not only as a minority, but as one whose very existence is perennially in question.

Jews Seen as Economically Privileged

Another view is that although Jews are a numerical minority, they do not "need" the same attention that other groups do. Jews have been referred to as a "model minority" because of their success in adapting to American culture. As previously mentioned, however, this "success" raises its own issues, those of assimilation and intermarriage. Also, although Jews as a group may be better off materially than other minorities, this does not negate the intensity and prevalence of anti-Semitism: if anything, it may add to it by "proving" the stereotype of the "rich Jew."

The truth, of course, is that not all Jews have "made it." A recent study found that nearly 22 percent of Jewish households in Brooklyn are below the poverty line (Metropolitan New York Coordinating Council on Jewish Poverty 1993). If that many are below, there must be many more who are not far above it. Also, it has been estimated that there are three thousand homeless Jews in New York City (Pollock 1993). The extent to which people do not believe that there are poor Jews and even homeless Jews in America is the extent to which the stereotype has triumphed.

Also, it is limiting to think of oppression strictly in terms of economics. Even if all Jews were wealthy, they could still be victims of oppression. Blacks who achieve financial success are not magically delivered from the impact of racism. Neither are women immune to sexism simply because of economic status. Anti-Semitism victimizes Jews, rich or poor. The noneconomic oppression of Jews is discussed later in terms of anti-Semitism, Jewish fear, and Jewish self-hatred. . . .

Jews Seen as Part of the White Majority

In today's racial divisions of Black, White, and Asian, Jews fall into the category of White. This is a problematic conception, however, and a recent historical development. In discussing Jews and race, it is first necessary to state that Jews do not constitute a race. There are Black Jews, White Jews, Asian Jews, Hispanic Jews, and Native-American Jews. Although Jews have been called a race, this is incorrect. A race cannot be joined voluntarily, whereas people can voluntarily become Jews.

For centuries in Europe, Jews were considered non-White (Gilman 1991). More than this, it was thought that they had intermarried with Africans and were thereby considered Black. Although it seems strange today, this idea was well entrenched. In the 1780s a writer described Jews thus: "There is no category of supposed human beings which comes closer to the Orang-Utan than does a Polish Jew. . . . Covered from foot to head in filth, dirt and rags . . . the color of a Black" (Gilman 1991, 172). A nineteenth-century writer referred to "the African character of the Jew, his muzzle-shaped mouth and face removing him from certain other races" (Gilman 1991, 174). As a result, "Being black, being Jewish, being diseased, and being 'ugly' come to be inexorably linked" (Gilman 1991, 173).

The Nazis continued this tradition of classifying Jews as a darker race, and the Holocaust was based on the idea that Jews were non-Aryan (i.e., non-White). Even today, White supremacists in America see Jews as being something other than White.

In America, Jews historically have not been viewed as African, but rather as Asian (Singerman 1986). In the late nineteenth and early twentieth centuries, there was much opposition to the immigration of Jews into America. It was feared that because they were an alien race either they would not assimilate, or would intermarry and thus pollute the racial purity of America. Jews were called Asiatic and Mongoloid, as well as "primitive, tribal, Oriental." Immigration laws were changed in 1924 in response to the influx of these undesirable "Asiatic elements" (Gilman 1991, 116, 117).

Thus, the idea that Jews are White is relatively new and provides the irony that Jews, who have a long history of being oppressed by Whites as a non-White "other," are now grouped with the same Whites who have been their oppressors. Putting Jews and neo-Nazis in the same racial category is probably offensive to both.

Obviously, many American Jews can pass as being White and thereby reap the benefits of White privilege. Based on interviews with American Jews, however, they do not think of themselves as Whites, but as Jews. This distinction was noted by Ralph Ellison: "Many Negroes, like myself, make a positive distinction between Whites and Jews. Not to do so could be either offensive, embarrassing, unjust or even dangerous" (Gould 1991, 561). In a more pointed passage, Michael Lerner (1992) has written, "The linguistic move of substituting 'people of color' for 'oppressed minorities,' coupled with the decision to refer to Jews as 'whites,' becomes an anti-Semitic denial of Jewish history" (123).

Jews Seen as Members of a Religion, Not a Culture

To some non-Jews, Jews are members of a religion, and because Christians are not a major focus in multiculturalism, there is no reason to study Jews. Being Jewish, however, means more than belonging to a religion. Jews have been called a religious group, a people, an ethnicity, a culture, and a civilization. Some Jews are primarily religious and center their lives around Judaism. Others are primarily ethnic, maintaining the traditional foods, customs, songs, and so forth, that constitute a culture. There are "political Jews" whose main sense of Jewishness comes from the support of Israel or fighting anti-Semitism. As one scholar has noted, "All attempts to categorize or identify Jews as an ethnic, religious, or national group are simply inadequate and incomplete. . . . Perhaps the closest any identification can come is to view the Jews holistically as a culture" (Lemish 1981, 28).

Lack of Knowledge of Jewish Oppression

A final reason that non-Jews may not include Jews in multiculturalism is that they are not aware of the history of Jewish oppression or of the extent of current anti-Semitism. In addition to lack of awareness, there may also be reluctance or outright resistance to recognizing that anti-Semitism is worth addressing. When Melanie Kaye/Kantrowitz (1986) raised the issue among colleagues who fought racism and sexism, she was met with "an inability to grasp what was being said about antisemitism . . . an incapacity to recognize why it mattered" (269). Irena Klepfisz (1982) has stated that the "issue of anti-Semitism has been ignored, has been treated as either non-existent or unimportant" (47). Anti-Semitism often is not included with racism, sexism, homophobia, and other forms of bigotry. For a discussion as to why there have been large-scale public campaigns against racism and sexism, but not against anti-Semitism, see "The Denial of Anti-Semitism in the Contemporary World" (in Lerner 1992).

Why Jews Have Not Included Themselves

Jewishness Separate from Professional Identity

Some Jews who identify as Jews at home and synagogue do not carry that identity into the workplace. At work they experience themselves as "Americans"; elsewhere, they experience themselves as Jews. Unlike other minorities, Jewish Americans are often not recognizable on sight. Thus, they are probably less aware of their ethnicity throughout the day than members of other minorities are. This can create a difference in public and private experiences of identity.

A professor I once had was active in her synagogue; she also taught courses in multiculturalism. She did not include Jews as a topic in her courses, not because she had dismissed the idea, but because the idea had simply never occurred to her. Confronted with this anomaly, she began questioning the place of Jewishness in her life and the forces that had influenced her so profoundly. Some of these forces are discussed in the following sections.

The Invalidation of Jewish Experience

Even if it does occur to someone to raise the issues of Jewishness or anti-Semitism in a professional context, this is not easy. Although Jews experience themselves as a minority, this experience receives little validation from non-Jews. Because Jews are not given a place in the common list of minorities, it is easy for them to doubt the validity of their experiences as members of a minority. Klein (1976) mentions "a Jewish English teacher who led the fight for an ethnic studies department on her campus, but did not know if it was appropriate for the department to teach a course on Jewish American literature" (27).

This behavior is well known among Jews in the form of supporting the causes of other groups but not supporting Jewish causes (Lerner 1992). Although many Jews have been involved in the battles against racism and sexism, these same Jews often made no effort to fight anti-Semitism. The other causes were recognized as legitimate struggles and had the stamp of approval as politically correct; Jewish issues typically have not been perceived in this light.

A related phenomenon is that because of the lack of recognition accorded to Jews as a minority, some Jews think that raising their voices as Jews is not appropriate and would be greeted with disdain. One woman, who confronted an anti-Semitic speaker, reported that she received no support from those around her: "I felt, instead, like a 'typical' pushy, whining, arrogant, self-pitying Jew" (DeLynn 1989, 63). This feeling was echoed by Henry Stern (see "Now for the Really Hard Part," 1993 1, 4), who has expressed the sense among Jews that, as perceived by non-Jews, "the Jew who complains about oppression is not a martyr but a kvetch [complainer]" (1993, 1, 4).To speak up as a Jew runs the risk of being perceived as a stereotypically unpleasant Jew. Reluctance among Jews to speak out on anti-semitism or other Jewish issues has been discussed by Irena Klepfisz (1982).

Fear of Visibility as Jews

Fear leads many Jews to keep a low profile and not call attention to themselves as Jews. Historically, being Jewish has been dangerous, and that legacy is deeply imbedded in the consciousness of Jews. As stated, Jews can essentially be invisible as Jews in America, and because conditions are relatively good in America, why risk trouble by demanding attention as Jews?

A few quotes will suggest the pervasiveness of this fear: "Our goal was to fade into the crowd" (Silberman 1985, 29); "The old fear of making ourselves too visible, drawing too much attention to Jewish things in a world that will never be anything but anti-Semitic" (Lopate 1989, 296), the desire to "become invisible. . . . This may well account for the self-imposed invisibility of Jews as Jews in certain social and political contexts. For visibility brings with it true risk" (Gilman 1991, 236); the need for "keeping a low profile, not making waves—prudence at the expense of self-respect" (Himmelfarb 1987, 6); "This need to deny our particular cultural heritage in order to protect ourselves is another manifestation of the way Jews are oppressed in America" (Lerner 1992, 82).

One psychologist referred to "what, for Jews, is the most feared question: 'Are you Jewish?'"(Weinrach 1990, 548). This question is feared because Jews never know what will happen if they answer it truthfully, and there are Jews who simply lie and say, "No, I'm not Jewish." As previously quoted (Himmelfarb), it is a matter of prudence at the expense of self-respect. Too many Jews have been killed simply for being Jews to take any unnecessary risk.

Jewish Self-Hatred

Jewish self-hatred can be compared with the feelings that other minorities experience. Black identity-stage theories, for example, typically involve an early stage in which Blacks "disidentify" from the Black community, denigrate Black culture, deny the existence or impact of racism, and adopt aspects of White culture (Helms, 1990). This phenomenon is comparable with that of Jews who are embarrassed by their Jewishness or who reject their culture and do not identify as Jews. Obviously, these Jews would have no interest in studying Jewish issues and may be in denial that Jewish issues even exist or have any relevance.

Ironically, Jewish self-hatred developed as the oppression of Jews was lifted by some nations, and Jews had the option of joining the mainstream culture. When Jews were limited to ghetto life, assimilation was not an option and Jews were immersed in Jewish life. Once assimilation became an option, Jewishness became a stigma. For those who sought to assimilate, any vestige of Jewish culture was a blemish to be hidden. Jews became embarrassed or ashamed of being Jewish and tried to eliminate any sign of their minority status. Merkin (1989) stated:

> There was no direct route to unambivalent ethnic pride because there was something I imbibed very early on about the possibility—even in my highly identified family—of seeming too Jewish. . . . Floating always unseen among us was an awareness of the importance of avoiding, if one could help it, too "Jewish" an appearance, the dreaded stigma of too "Jewish" a voice. (Merkin 1989, 16)

The lesson that Merkin learned is a common one for Jewish children, who often grow up being the victim of anti-Semitic comments, jokes, or even violent or intimidating incidents. Many Jews attempt to erase all signs of their Jewishness, even if it means changing their names, their hair, their accents, or their noses (Gilman 1991). Many others look with disdain on Judaism, Yiddish, or any manifestation of Jewish culture.

One writer reported that after being called "Christ-killer" and being rejected by a group of peers, "I suddenly became aware that I was one of a group that was hated in a very intense fashion" (Lax and Richards 1981, 302). This awareness profoundly affects Jewish identity development (Ostow 1977). Diller (1980) has studied the rejection of Jewish identity, Kaufman and Raphael (1987) have written about shame as a central component of Jewish identity, and Lax and Richards have concluded from their research that "Being Jewish has a slightly 'torturous' quality" (1981, 306).

Knowledge of Jewish Culture

Knowledge of Jewish culture is difficult to achieve because there is no single Jewish culture; there are many clusters of Jewish cultures. This is no different from the categories of *Asian, Latino,* or *Native American.* Each label includes a multitude of nationalities and ethnicities.

Although this is not the forum for a course in Jewish cultures, some basic divisions can be mentioned. One way of studying Jewish culture is based on geography. The major geographical grouping is into Ashkenazic or Sephardic Jews. Ashkenazic Jews are those who are from or are descendants from Jews in central and eastern Europe. Sephardic Jews originally were Spanish Jews, but with their expulsion from Spain in 1492 were forced to settle elsewhere; many settled around the Mediterranean Sea. Thus, Sephardic Jews include those from Morocco, Syria, Turkey, Yemen, and so on. Ashkenazic and Sephardic Jews developed different traditions in terms of customs, food, clothing, language, and, to some extent, religious practice.

Although Ashkenazic and Sephardic are the major categories, Jews live and have lived throughout the world. It is important to obtain some knowledge and understanding of Jewish cultural backgrounds; whether a Jew is from Russia, Israel, France, Scotland, India, China, Ethiopia, or Argentina makes a difference.

Most Jews in America today, however, are of Ashkenazic ancestry. This group can be further divided into various religious denominations. Although Jewish denominations are often said to consist of Reform, Conservative, and Orthodox, this is a bit simplistic. In my view, it makes sense to first divide the groups into Orthodox and non-Orthodox. Broadly speaking, Orthodox Jews accept the Torah (Genesis, Exodus, Leviticus, Numbers, and Deuteronomy) as the word of God. This means that the commandments contained in the Torah (and interpreted in the Talmud) cannot be changed or ignored. Thus, Orthodox Jews strive to follow the commandments. The three main areas of observance that define Orthodoxy are keeping kosher (observing dietary restrictions), observing the sabbath, and following the laws of family purity (which regulate sexual behavior and ritual cleanliness).

Orthodox Jews can be divided into Hasidic and non-Hasidic groups. Hasidism is a movement that began in the 1700s. Hasidic men can be distinguished by their black clothing (pants, coats, hats), as well as their beards and "sidelocks," known as *peyos*. There are perhaps one hundred Hasidic sects in Brooklyn alone, and although they have many commonalities, they also have their differences. Non-Hasidic orthodoxy also includes a variety of groups: Orthodox, Modern Orthodox. Centrist Orthodox. Once again, although these groups share many customs and beliefs, there are significant differences among them.

The non-Orthodox denominations, which have the greater number of members in the United States, are Reform, Conservative, and Reconstructionist. The denominations vary in their attitudes toward traditional Judaism, with Conservative being more traditional than Reform and Reconstructionist. In addition to religious denominations, there are other movements including Humanistic Judaism and Jewish Renewal, which involves Jews belonging to a number of denominations. Knowing a person's denomination, however, only reveals his or her formal religious affiliation. Do not assume that this is the same as knowing his or her culture.

It is essential to keep in mind not only the incredible diversity among Jewish groups, but also that each group consists of individuals who differ from each other. References are often made to Jews or "the Jews" as if this were a monolithic group. This is no more valid than referring to Christians as if they constituted a single entity.

In addition to knowing what the denominations are, it is essential to understand the antagonisms that exist among the different groups. The main antagonism seems to exist between the Orthodox and non-Orthodox groups (although fierce differences can occur within either side of this boundary). A non-Orthodox family may react with horror if a son or daughter decides to become Orthodox or Hasidic: this may be seen as equivalent to joining a cult. An Orthodox family may react with horror if a son or daughter decides to leave orthodoxy; this may be seen as spiritual death.

Conclusion

This article has attempted to account for the lack of attention to Jews and to Jewish issues in discussions of multiculturalism and has divided this phenomenon into two subtopics. The neglect of Jewish issues by non-Jews has resulted in the idea that Jews have a religion, not a culture, in the view of Jews by non-Jews as assimilated, successful, White Americans, and in the ignorance of Jewish oppression. The neglect of Jewish issues by Jews is viewed as being a result of the bicultural split in Jewish identity, the invalidation of the Jewish experience, the fear of being visible as Jews, and Jewish self-hatred. . . .

For multiculturalism to fulfill its promise of inclusiveness, it needs to recognize Jews as an ethnic minority and to realize that knowledge of Jewish culture, Jewish history, and anti-Semitism are important in working with Jews. In addition, anti-Semitism needs to be addressed alongside racism, sexism, homophobia, and other forms of oppression. Finally, Jews are encouraged to raise Jewish issues in a professional context, whether in the form of teaching about the Jewish experience, discussions or research on Jewish identity, improving Jewish-Christian understanding, or combating anti-Semitism. Multiculturalism is the ideal vehicle for promoting positive Jewish development and enhanced intergroup relationships.

References

DeLynn, J. (1989). "Hitler's World." In D. Rosenberg, ed., *Testimony: Contemporary Writers Make the Holocaust Personal.* New York: Random House.

Diller, J. (1980). "Identity Rejection and Reawakening in the Jewish Context." *Journal of Psychology and Judaism,* 5, 38–47.

Fein, L. (1988). *Where Are We? The Inner Life of America's Jews.* New York: Harper ans Row.

Gilman, S. (1991). *The Jew's Body.* New York: Routledge, Chapman, Hall.

Gould, A. (1991). *What Did They Think of the Jews?* Northvale, N.J.: Aronson.

Helms, J. (Ed.). (1990). *Black and White Racial Identity: Theory, Research, and Practice.* New York: Greenwood.

Himmelfarb, M. (1987). "Jewish Perceptions of the New Assertiveness of Religion in American Life." In R. J. Neuhaus, ed., *Jews in Unsecular America.* Grand Rapids. Mich.: Eerdmans.

Kaufman, G., and L. Raphael. (1987). "Shame: A Perspective on Jewish Identity." *Journal of Psychology and Judaism,* 11, 30–40.

Kaye/Kantrowitz, M. (1986). "To Be a Radical Jew in the Late 20th Century." In M. Kaye/Kantrowitz and I. Klepfisz, eds., *The Tribe of Dina: A Jewish Women's Anthology.* Montpelier, Vt: Sinister Wisdom.

Klein, J. (1976). "Ethnotherapy with Jews." *International Journal of Mental Health,* 5, 26–38.

Klepfisz, I. (1982). "Anti-Semitism in the Lesbian/Feminist Movement." In E. T. Beck, ed., *Nice Jewish Girls: A Lesbian Anthology.* Watertown, Mass.: Persephone.

Lax, R., and A. Richards. (1981). "Observations on the Formation of Jewish Identity in Adolescents." *The Israel Journal of Psychiatry and Related Sciences,* 18, 299–310.

Lemish, P. (1981). "Hanukah Bush: The Jewish Experience in America." *Theory into Practice,* 20, 26–34.

Lerner, M. (1992). *The Socialism of Fools: Anti-Semitism on the Left.* Oakland, Calif.: Tikkun Books.

Lopate, P. (1989). Resistance to the Holocaust. In D. Rosenberg, ed., *Testimony: Contemporary Writers Make the Holocaust Personal.* New York: Random House.

Merkin, D. (1989). "Dreaming of Hitler: A Memoir of Self-Hatred." In D. Rosenberg, ed., *Testimony: Contemporary Writers Make the Holocaust Personal.* New York: Random House.

Metropolitan New York Coordinating Council on Jewish Poverty. (1993). *Jewish Poverty in New York City in the 1990's.* Preliminary Report: April, 1993, New York.

Nicholls, W. (1993). *Christian Antisemitism: A History of Hate.* Northvale, N.J.: Aronson.

"Now for the Really Hard Part." (1993). *Forward,* October 8, 1, 4.

Ostow, M. (1977). "The Psychologic Determinants of Jewish Identity." *The Israel Annals of Psychiatry* and *Related Disciplines.* 5, 313–35.

Pollock, B. (1993). "For Homeless Jews, the Days of Awe Feel Awfully Lonely." *Forward,* September 24, 1, 4.

Siegel, R. (1986). "Antisemitism and Sexism in Stereotypes of Jewish Women." *Women and Therapy* 5, 249–57.

Silberman, C. E. (1985). *A Certain People: American Jews and Their Lives Today.* New York: Summit Books.

Singerman, R. (1986). "The Jew as Racial Alien: The Genetic Component of American Anti-Semitism." In D. Gerber, ed., *Anti-Semitism in American History.* Urbana, Ill.: University of Illinois Press.

Stallsworth, P. (1987). "The Story of an Encounter." In R. Neuhaus, ed., *Jews in Unsecular America*. Grand Rapids, Mich: Eerdmans.

U.S. Bureau of the Census. (1994). *Statistical Abstract of the United States: 1994.* Washington, D.C.: U.S. Government Printing Office.

Weinrach, S. (1990). "A Psychosocial Look at the Jewish Dilemma." *Journal of Counseling and Development.* 68, 548–49.

The World Almanac and Book of Facts, 1995. (1994). New York: Funk and Wagnalls.

26

On Black–Jewish Relations

Cornel West

Black anti-Semitism and Jewish antiblack racism are real, and both are as profoundly American as cherry pie. There was no *golden age* in which blacks and Jews were free of tension and friction. Yet there was a *better* age when the common histories of oppression and degradation of both groups served as a springboard for genuine empathy and principled alliances. Since the late sixties, black-Jewish relations have reached a nadir. Why is this so?

In order to account for this sad state of affairs we must begin to unearth the truth behind each group's perceptions of the other (and of itself). For example, few blacks recognize and acknowledge one fundamental fact of Jewish history: a profound hatred of Jews sits at the center of medieval and modern European cultures. Jewish persecutions under the Byzantines; Jewish massacres during the Crusades; Jewish expulsions in England (1290), France (1306), Spain (1492), Portugal (1497), Frankfurt (1614), and Vienna (1670); and Jewish pogroms in the Ukraine (1648, 1768), Odessa (1871), and throughout Russia—especially after 1881, culminating in Kishinev (1903)—constitute the vast historical backdrop to current Jewish preoccupations with self-reliance and the Jewish anxiety of group death. Needless to say, the Nazi attempt at Judeocide in the 1930s and 1940s reinforced this preoccupation and anxiety.

The European hatred of Jews rests on religious and social grounds—Christian myths of Jews as Christ killers and resentment over the disproportionate presence of Jews in certain commercial occupations. The religious bigotry feeds on stereotypes of Jews as villainous transgressors of the sacred; the social bigotry, on alleged Jewish conspiratorial schemes for power and control. Ironically, the founding of the state of Israel—the triumph of the quest for modern Jewish self-determination—came about less from Jewish power and more from the consensus of the two superpowers, the United States and the USSR, to secure a homeland for a despised and degraded people after Hitler's genocidal attempt.

The history of Jews in America for the most part flies in the face of this tragic Jewish past. The majority of Jewish immigrants arrived in America around the turn of the century (1881–1924). They brought a strong heritage that put a premium on what had ensured their survival and identity—institutional autonomy, rabbinical learning, and business zeal. Like other European immigrants, Jews for the most part became complicitous with the American racial caste system. Even in "Christian" America with its formidable anti-Semitic barriers, and despite a rich progressive tradition that made Jews more likely than other immigrants to feel compassion for oppressed blacks, large numbers of Jews tried to procure a foothold in America by falling in step with the widespread perpetuation of antiblack stereotypes and the garnering of white-skin privilege benefits available to nonblack Americans. It goes without saying that a profound hatred of African people (as seen in slavery, lynching, segregation, and second-class citizenship) sits at the center of American civilization.

The period of genuine empathy and principled alliances between Jews and blacks (1910–1967) constitutes a major pillar of American progressive politics in this century. These supportive links begin with W. E. B. Du Bois's *The Crisis* and Abraham Cahan's *Jewish Daily Forward,* and are seen clearly between Jewish leftists and A. Philip Randolph's numerous organizations, between Elliot Cohen's *Commentary* and the early career of James Baldwin, between prophets like Abraham Joshua Heschel and Martin Luther King, Jr., or between the disproportionately Jewish Students for a Democratic Society (SDS) and the Student Non-Violent Coordinating Committee (SNCC). Presently, this inspiring period of black-Jewish cooperation is often downplayed by blacks and romanticized by Jews. It is downplayed by blacks because they focus on the astonishingly rapid entrée of most Jews into the middle and upper middle classes during this brief period—an entrée that has spawned both an intense conflict with the more slowly growing black middle class and a social resentment from a quickly growing black impoverished class. Jews, on the other hand, tend to romanticize this period because their present status as "upper middle dogs" and some "top dogs" in American society unsettles their historic self-image as progressives with a compassion for the underdog.

In the present era, blacks and Jews are in contention over two major issues. The first is the question of what constitutes the most effective means for black progress in America. With over half of all black professionals and managers being employed in the public sphere, and those in the private sphere often gaining entry owing to regulatory checks by the Equal Employment Opportunity Commission, or EEOC, attacks by some Jews on affirmative action are perceived as assaults on black livelihood. And since a disproportionate percentage of poor blacks depend on government support to survive, attempts to dismantle public programs are viewed by blacks as opposition to black survival. Visible Jewish resistance to affirmative action and government spending on social programs pits some Jews against black progress. This opposition, though not as strong as that of other groups in the country, is all the more visible to black people because of past Jewish support for black progress. It also seems to reek of naked group interest, as well as a willingness to abandon compassion for the underdogs of American society.

The second major area of contention concerns the meaning and practice of Zionism as embodied in the state of Israel. Without a sympathetic understanding of the deep historic sources of Jewish fears and anxieties about group survival, blacks will not grasp the visceral attachment of most Jews to Israel. Similarly, without a candid acknowledgment of blacks' status as permanent underdogs in American society, Jews will not comprehend what the symbolic predicament and literal plight of Palestinians in Israel means to blacks. Jews rightly point out that the atrocities of African elites on oppressed Africans in Kenya, Uganda, and Ethiopia are just as bad or worse than those perpetrated on Palestinians by Israeli elites. Some also point out—rightly—that deals and treaties between Israel and South Africa are not so radically different from those between some black African, Latin American, and Asian countries and South Africa. Still, these and other Jewish charges of black double standards with regard to Israel do not take us to the heart of the matter. Blacks often perceive the Jewish defense of the state of Israel as a second instance of naked group interest, and, again, an abandonment of substantive moral deliberation. At the same time, Jews tend to view black critiques of Israel as black rejection of the Jewish right to group survival, and hence as a betrayal of the precondition for a black-Jewish alliance. What is at stake here is not simply black-Jewish relations, but, more important, the *moral content* of Jewish and black identities and of their political consequences. . . .

The present impasse in black-Jewish relations will be overcome only when self-critical exchanges take place within and across black and Jewish communities not simply about their own group interest but also, and, more importantly, about what being black or Jewish means in *ethical terms*. This kind of reflection should not be so naive as to ignore group interest, but it should take us to a higher moral ground where serious discussions about democracy and justice determine how we define ourselves and our politics and help us formulate strategies and tactics to sidestep the traps of tribalism and chauvinism.

The vicious murder of Yankel Rosenbaum in Crown Heights in the summer of 1991 bore chilling testimony to a growing black anti-Semitism in this country. Although this particular form of xenophobia from below does not have the same institutional power of those racisms that afflict their victims from above, it certainly deserves the same moral condemnation. Furthermore, the very *ethical* character of the black freedom struggle largely depends on the open condemnation by its spokespersons of *any* racist attitude or action. . . .

Black people have searched desperately for allies in the struggle against racism—and have found Jews to be disproportionately represented in the ranks of that struggle. The desperation that sometimes informs the antiracist struggle arises out of two conflicting historical forces: America's historically weak will to racial justice *and* an all-inclusive moral vision of freedom and justice for all. Escalating black anti-Semitism is a symptom of this desperation gone sour; it is the bitter fruit of a profound self-destructive impulse, nurtured on the vines of hopelessness and concealed by empty gestures of black unity. The images of black activists yelling "Where is Hitler when we need him?" and "Heil Hitler," juxtaposed with those of David Duke celebrating Hitler's birthday, seem to feed a single line of intolerance, burning on both ends of the American candle, that threatens to consume us all.

Black anti-Semitism rests on three basic pillars. First, it is a species of "anti-whitism." Jewish complicity in American racism—even though less extensive than the complicity of other white Americans—reinforces black perceptions that Jews are identical to any other group benefitting from the white-skin privileges in racist America. This view denies the actual history and treatment of Jews. And the particular interactions of Jews and black people in the hierarchies of business and education cast Jews as the public face of oppression for the black community, and thus lend evidence to this mistaken view of Jews as any other white folk.

Second, black anti-Semitism is a result of higher expectations some black folk have of Jews. This perspective holds Jews to a moral standard different from that extended to other white ethnic groups, principally owing to the ugly history of anti-Semitism in the world, especially in Europe and the Middle East. Such double standards assume that Jews and blacks are "natural" allies, since both groups have suffered chronic degradation and oppression at the hands of racial and ethnic majorities. So when Jewish neoconservatism gains a high public profile at a time when black people are more and more vulnerable, the charge of "betrayal" surfaces among black folk who feel let down. Such utterances resonate strongly in a black Protestant culture that has inherited many stock Christian anti-Semitic narratives of Jews as Christ-killers. These infamous narratives historically have had less weight in the black community, in stark contrast to the more obdurate white Christian varieties of anti-Semitism. Yet in moments of desperation in the black community, they tend to reemerge, charged with the rhetoric of Jewish betrayal.

Third, black anti-Semitism is a form of underdog resentment and envy, directed at another underdog who has "made it" in American society. The remarkable upward mobility of American Jews—rooted chiefly in a history and culture that places a premium on higher education and self-organization—easily lends itself to myths of Jewish unity and homogeneity that have gained currency among other groups, especially among relatively unorganized groups like black Americans. The high visibility of Jews in the upper reaches of the academy, journalism, the entertainment industry, and the professions—though less so percentage-wise in corporate America and national political office—is viewed less as a result of hard work and success fairly won, and more as a matter of favoritism and nepotism among Jews. Ironically, calls for black solidarity and achievement are often modeled on myths of Jewish unity—as both groups respond to American xenophobia and racism. But in times such as these, some blacks view Jews as obstacles rather than allies in the struggle for racial justice.

These three elements of black anti-Semitism—which also characterize the outlooks of some other ethnic groups in America—have a long history among black people. Yet the recent upsurge of black anti-Semitism exploits two other prominent features of the political landscape identified with the American Jewish establishment: the military status of Israel in the Middle East (especially in its enforcement of the occupation of the West Bank and Gaza); and the visible *conservative* Jewish opposition to what is perceived to be a major means of black progress, namely, affirmative action. Of course, principled critique of U.S. foreign policy in the Middle East, of Israeli denigration of Palestinians, or attacks on affirmative action *transcend* anti-Semitic sensibilities. Yet vulgar critiques do not—and often are shot through with such sensibilities, in white and black America alike. These vulgar critiques—usually based on sheer ignorance and a misinformed thirst for vengeance—add an aggressive edge to black anti-Semitism. And in the rhetoric of a Louis Farrakhan or a Leonard Jeffries, whose audiences rightly hunger for black self-respect and oppose black degradation, these critiques misdirect progressive black energies arrayed against unaccountable corporate power and antiblack racism, steering them instead *toward* Jewish elites and antiblack conspiracies in Jewish America. This displacement is disturbing not only because it is analytically and morally wrong; it also discourages any effective alliances across races.

The rhetoric of Farrakhan and Jeffries feeds on an undeniable history of black denigration at the hands of Americans of every ethnic and religious group. The delicate issues of black self-love and black self-contempt are then viewed in terms of white put-down and Jewish conspiracy. The precious quest for black self-esteem is reduced to immature and cathartic gestures that bespeak an excessive obsession with whites and Jews. There can be no healthy conception of black humanity based on such obsessions. The best of black culture, as manifested, for example, in jazz or the prophetic black church, refuses to put whites or Jews on a pedestal or in the gutter. Rather, black humanity is affirmed alongside that of others, even when those others have at times dehumanized blacks. To put it bluntly, when black humanity is taken for granted and not made to prove itself in white culture, whites, Jews, and others are not that important; they are simply human beings, just like black people. If the best of black cultures wanes in the face of black anti-Semitism, black people will become even more isolated as a community and the black freedom struggle will be tarred with the brush of immorality.

My fundamental premise is that the black freedom struggle is the major buffer between the David Dukes of America and the hope for a future in which we can begin to take justice and freedom for all seriously. Black anti-Semitism—along with its concomitant xenophobias, such as patriarchal and homophobic prejudices—weakens this buffer. In the process, it plays into the hands of the old-style racists, who appeal to the worst of our fellow citizens amid the silent depression that plagues the majority of Americans. Without some redistribution of wealth and power, downward mobility and debilitating poverty will continue to drive people into desperate channels. And without principled opposition to xenophobias from above *and* below, these desperate channels will produce a cold-hearted and mean-spirited America no longer worth fighting for or living in.

Personal Voices

27

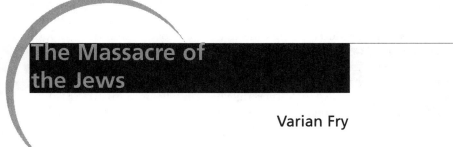

The Massacre of the Jews

Varian Fry

There are some things so horrible that decent men and women find them impossible to believe, so monstrous that the civilized world recoils incredulous before them. The recent reports of the systematic extermination of the Jews in Nazi Europe are of this order. . . .

I remember how skeptical I was myself the first time a Nazi official told me that Hitler and Goebbels were bent on the physical annihilation of the Jews. On July 15, 1935, the S.A. staged its first pogrom in Berlin. I was in Berlin at the time and witnessed the whole thing. I saw the S.A. men, unmistakable despite their mufti, throwing chairs and tables through the plate-glass windows of Jewish-owned cafés, dragging Jewish men and women out of buses and chasing them up the streets, or knocking them down and kicking them in the face and belly as they lay prostrate on the sidewalk. And I heard them chanting their terrible song:

Wenn Judenblut vom Messer spritzt,
Dann geht es nochmal so gut!*

The next day, in a state of high indignation, I went to see "Putzi" Hanfstaengl, then chief of the Foreign Press Division of the Propaganda Ministry. On my way to his office, I learned that one of the victims of the previous night's bestiality had already died of his injuries. Yet, when Hanfstaengl told me, in his cultured Harvard accent, that the "radicals" among the Nazi Party leaders intended to "solve" the "Jewish problem" by the physical extermination of the Jews, I only half believed him. It was not much more than a

---

*When Jewish blood spurts from the knife,
Then everything will be fine again.

year after the Blood Bath of June 30, 1934; yet even then I could not believe that there were men in positions of power and authority in Western Europe in the twentieth century who could seriously entertain such a monstrous idea.

I learned better in November, 1938, when the Nazi leaders openly encouraged the burning of synagogues, the pillage of Jewish homes and the murder of their inhabitants. . . .

The program is already far advanced. According to a report to the President by leaders of American Jewish groups, nearly 2,000,000 European Jews have already been slain since the war began, and the remaining 5,000,000 now living under Nazi control are scheduled to be destroyed as soon as Hitler's blond butchers can get around to them. Of the 275,000 Jews who were living in Germany and Austria at the outbreak of the war, only 52,000 to 55,000 remain. The 170,000 Jews in Czecho-Slovakia have been reduced to 35,000. The figures for Poland, where the Nazi program has been pushed very rapidly, are uncertain. There were 3,300,000 Jews in Poland at the beginning of the war, but some 500,000 fled to Russia, leaving approximately 2,800,000 behind. By the beginning of the summer of 1942, this number had already been reduced to 2,200,000, and deportations and massacres since that time have been on an ever increasing scale. In the ghetto of Warsaw, in which 550,000 Jews once dwelt, there are today fewer than 50,000. In the city of Riga, Latvia, 8,000 Jews were killed in a single night. A week later 16,000 more were led into a woods, stripped and machine-gunned.

It is not merely central and eastern Europe that are being "purged," or rendered "Judenrein," as the Nazis like to say. The Netherlands has already given up 60,000 of its 180,000 Jews. Of the 85,000 who once lived in Belgium only 8,000 remain today, while of the 340,000 Jews of France, more than 65,000 have been deported. Even Norway has begun to ship her Jewish citizens eastward to the Nazi slaughter houses and starvation pens.

The methods employed by the Nazis are many. There is starvation: Jews all over Europe are kept on rations often only one-third or one-fourth what is allowed to non-Jews. Slow death is the inevitable consequence. There is deportation: Jews by the hundreds of thousands have been packed into cattle cars, without food, water or sanitary conveniences of any sort, and shipped the whole breadth of Europe. When the cars arrive at their destination, about a third of the passengers are already dead. There are the extermination centers, where Jews are destroyed by poison gas or electricity. There are specially constructed trucks, in which Jews are asphyxiated by carbon monoxide from the exhausts, on their way to burial trenches. There are the mines, in which they are worked to death, or poisoned by fumes of metals. There is burning alive, in crematoria, or buildings deliberately set on fire. There is the method of injecting air-bubbles into the blood stream: it is cheap, clean and efficient, producing clots, embolisms, and death within a few hours. And there is the good old-fashioned system of standing the victims up, very often naked, and machine-gunning them, preferrably beside the graves they themselves have been forced to dig. It saves time, labor, and transportation.

A few weeks ago a letter reached me from Paris. It had been smuggled over the demarcation line and two international borders and mailed in Lisbon. It told of the deportation of the Jews of Paris, which occurred in July. All Polish, Czech, German, Austrian, and Russian Jews between the ages of two and fifty-five were arrested. The women and children, to the number of 15,000, were herded into the notorious Vélodrome d'Hiver, where they were kept for a week, without any bedding but straw, with very inadequate food, and with virtually no sanitary facilities. Then they were packed into cattle cars and shipped to an unknown destination in eastern Europe. My informant, a member of the trade-union underground, tells me that some days later a French railway worker picked up a scrap of paper on the tracks. On it was written this message: "There are more than fifty women in this cattle car, some of them ill, and for days we have been refused even the most elementary conveniences."

Another letter, from a French Red Cross nurse who worked in the Vélodrome, tells exactly the same story, describing it as "something horrible, fiendish, something that takes hold of your throat and prevents you from crying out."

A German Social Democrat whom I know well sent me a long report on the deportations, written at the beginning of September. "I am an incorrigible optimist," he concluded, "but this time I see dark things ahead. . . . I am afraid not many of us will live to see the end of this war."

And a Frenchman, not himself a Jew, wrote a long report on the deportations and had it brought to me in a toothpaste tube. "We were at the Camp des Milles [near Marseilles] the day the last train left," he says,

> The spectacle was indescribably painful to behold. All the internees had been lined up with their pitifully battered valises tied together with bits of string. Most of them were in rags, pale, thin, worn out with the strain, which had dragged out for more than a week. Many of them were quietly weeping. . . . There was no sign of revolt: these people were broken. Their faces showed only hopeless despair and a passive acceptance of their fate.

Later, when Jews not already in concentration camps were being rounded up, he wrote,

> A large number of these desperate people, in just about all sections, tried to end their lives. In Marseilles, in the Cours Belsunce [the heart of the city], a refugee couple jumped out of the window at the very moment the police arrived to arrest them. . . . Many, realizing the danger they were in . . . disappeared from their homes and hid.

These are all letters I myself have received from persons I know, or know to be reliable. They concern only France. But the evidence for the other countries is of a similar, direct sort. . . .

The New York office of the General Jewish Workers' Union of Poland has received from a Polish Socialist underground worker known to it an account of gas executions the details of which are as revolting as they are convincing.

In the office of the World Jewish Congress in Geneva there is an affidavit, attested copies of which have been received here, recounting the extraordinary odyssey of a Polish Jew who was living in Brussels. On August 12 he was arrested and deported to Rumania. There were seventy men in his cattle car, packed in like crowds in the subway during rush hour. After two and a half days, their train stopped in Upper Silesia, and they were allowed to get out of the car, have a short rest, and eat a little soup. Those too exhausted to continue the journey were carried away, as were all boys between fourteen and twenty (to work, it was said, in the coal mines and the iron mills). The others were then loaded back into the cars and shipped on to the Ukraine. There they were asked whether they felt able to work or not. About half said that they were not able to work. These were led away. The others were given the uniforms of the Todt Organization and set to work building fortifications. From where they were working they could hear the rumble of big guns to the east, and once they saw a sign reading "Stalingrad—50 km."

The Jew from Brussels made friends with a young Bavarian officer, not a Nazi, and learned from him that the men who had not been able to work had all been immediately shot. Anyone who was sick for more than two days was shot also, the officer said. In the end the officer helped the Jew to hide himself in a train that was returning to the West. After many days the Jew found himself on a siding at the Gare de l'Est in Paris. From there he made his way to Switzerland, where he told his story.

This is the nature of the evidence. Letters, reports, cables all fit together. They add up to the most appalling *picture* of mass murder in *all human history*. . . .

Meanwhile, there are some things which can be done now, slight as the chances are that they will have much effect in deterring Hitler and his followers from their homicidal mania. President Roosevelt could and should speak out again against these monstrous events. A stern warning from him will have no effect on Hitler, but it may impress some Germans like the officer who helped the Jew from Brussels to escape. A similar warning from Churchill might help, too. A joint declaration, couched in the most solemn terms, by the Allied governments, of the retribution to come might be of some avail. Tribunals should be set up now to begin to amass the facts. Diplomatic warnings, conveyed through neutral channels, to the governments of Hungary, Bulgaria and Rumania might save at least some of the 700,000 to 900,000 Jews still within their borders. The Christian churches might also help, at least in countries like France, Holland, Belgium, and Norway, the Pope by threatening with excommunication all Catholics who in any way participate in these frightful crimes, the Protestant leaders by exhorting their fellow communicants to resist to the utmost the Nazis' fiendish designs. We and our allies should perhaps reconsider our policy of total blockade of the European continent and examine the possibilities of extending the feeding of Greece to other occupied countries, under neutral supervision. Since one of the excuses the Nazis now offer for destroying the Jews and Poles is that there is not enough food to go around, we might at least remove the grounds for the excuse by offering to feed the populations of the occupied countries, given proper guarantees that the food will not fall into the hands of the enemy.

If we do any or all of these things, we should broadcast the news of them day and night to every country of Europe, in every European language. There is a report, which I have not been able to verify, that the OWI [Office of War Information] has banned mention of the massacres in its shortwave broadcasts. If this is true, it is a sadly mistaken policy. We have nothing to gain by "appeasing" the anti-Semites and the murderers. We have much to gain by using the facts to create resistance and eventually rebellion. The fact that the Nazis do not commit their massacres in Western Europe, but transport their victims to the East before destroying them, is certain proof that they fear the effect on the local populations of the news of their crimes.

Finally, and it is a little thing, but at the same time a big thing, we can offer asylum now, without delay or red tape, to those few fortunate enough to escape from the Aryan paradise. We can do this without any risk to ourselves, because we can intern the refugees on arrival, and examine them at leisure before releasing them. If there is the slightest doubt about any of them, we can keep them interned for the duration of the war. Despite the fact that the urgency of the situation has never been greater, immigration into the United States in the year 1942 will have been less than ten percent of what it has been in "normal" years before Hitler, when some of the largest quotas were not filled. There have been bureaucratic delays in visa procedure which have literally condemned to death many stalwart democrats. These delays have caused an understandable bitterness among Jews and non-Jews in Europe, who have looked to us for help which did not come.

My Marseilles correspondent, who is neither a Jew nor a candidate for a visa, writes that, "in spite of the Nazi pressure, which she feels more than any other neutral, and in spite too of the reactionary tendencies of her middle class, the little country of Switzerland will [by accepting 9,000 refugees from Nazi terror since July] have contributed more to the cause of humanity than the great and wealthy United States, its loud declamations about the rights of the people and the defense of liberty notwithstanding."

This is a challenge that we cannot, must not, ignore.

28

Short Black Hair

Jennifer Krebs

My short black hair. My sister studying to be a hairdresser cuts it shorter still. Much to my parents' horror. My mother mumbles: you look like a man. You look like your great aunt Adele, my father tells me.

Wasn't she the poet? Aunt Adele.

No. She was a bookkeeper. Although she might have written a poem or two. Bad poems. Pure emotion. Rhymes without meter, rhythm.

Aunt Adele. Foremother I never met. Aunt Adele. I probably don't look a thing like her.

On my father's side of the family there were two unmarried women.

Grandma's sister Paula, the tailor. I met her twice. She sewed me a brown corduroy dog with floppy ears and a black button nose. I named her Cleo. I still have Cleo somewhere in my bedroom in my parents' house.

Grandpa's sister Adele. The poet.

My grandma kneads bread dough. Tells me about the world. Before. In Germany. Waltzes and polkas and farms and trips to Frankfurt. My father as a baby. Grandma's eleven sisters and brothers. Mainly sisters. Grandpa getting drafted in World War I. Grandma lost two brothers in that war. She met and married Grandpa after he came back.

All my grandpa's brothers and sisters married after the war. Except Adele.

Why?

A cousin tells me Adele fell in love with a Gentile poet or teacher. They wrote poems to each other. Her father Levi forbade her to intermarry.

My grandma doesn't understand the question. She just didn't marry.

My grandpa died before I had time to ask.

My father says my cousin is wrong. There was no poet. Where did she/I get such ideas? My father thinks the inquiry is pointless.

But I'm not getting married. I'm getting my hair cut. Short. These questions are vital. My aunt's life is vital. Her life is denied.

Germany killed her.

Except a poem. She wrote in Theresienstadt. A poem, I am told, about the winds. A poem. A prayer for the messiah.

My father wants to know why I want to be a writer. To contribute to magazines? *Time, Commentary, National Geographic?* Write about politics—after all I studied International Affairs.

No.

They shaved Adele's hair off to do brain surgery. Incised a cross in her skull to find out why she stopped walking. A cross in her skull right above her spine.

They opened her up. Saw her grey brain matter. Same as anyone's grey brain matter. Sewed her back up. Still didn't know why she couldn't walk anymore.

She couldn't walk. She couldn't go.

My cousin says I should be fair to the doctors at Marburg. It was a university hospital. Not a Nazi hospital. They were scholars, surgeons. Not Nazi quacks. But it was Nazi Germany. They cut a cross in her head. She wore a cross of scar tissue for the rest of her life.

She couldn't walk.

She stopped walking because they took her job away. They took her job away because she was a Jewish woman. And because it was 1933.

She couldn't go.

She went to the town school through the eighth grade. Then she went to a business high school. A bookkeeper. An accountant. She became the merchandise manager of the local chain of grocery stores. She was efficient. She was competition for any man.

They fired her. On the way home from work she collapsed in the street. She never walked again.

Or maybe she did. My father can't remember. Maybe she did walk a little bit now and again. Maybe.

The family got her a wheelchair.

I took care of a woman in a wheelchair for three years. Twice a week. I was a college student. I needed money. She asked me: Can you push a wheelchair? I said I'd try. She had multiple sclerosis.

I spent two Christmases with her. Her family was far away. She spent Christmases with Jews. I got her up in the morning. Dressed her in her newest wraparound skirt. Took her to the toilet. Opened her Christmas presents. Spoonfed her turkey and cranberry sauce and pearl onions.

Tried to help. Aunt Adele. Help. Felt sick. Adele. Screamed. When I left.

In 1941, my grandpa secured visas for himself, his father, his wife, his children to the U.S. In 1941, they didn't let Adele out. Or they didn't want Adele in.

She couldn't walk. She couldn't go.

My grandpa, grandma, father, aunts, great-grandfather left. Adele.

Stayed behind in Germany. Short black hair. Wheelchair.

My father says she screamed. Short black hair. Alone. Screamed. Alone. When they left. They left.

They moved the rest of the Jews in town into her house. Her father Levi's house. My family's house. A woman came every day to take care of Adele.

A Gentile woman. Came every day for a year. She got Adele up in the morning. Cooked. Fed. Got Adele ready to celebrate Jewish Holidays. They didn't celebrate Jewish Holidays in 1941.

I fed her turkey and cranberry sauce and pearl onions.

My grandpa worked as a painter in New York City nine years before he and his brothers made enough money to buy a farm in upstate New York like the farm they had in Germany.

My grandma bakes bread. Feeds the cats. Sleeps under German quilts. Eats on linen tablecloths her mother embroidered.

My father is a mechanical engineer turned farmer. Returned to farmer. Like his father. I write.

Aunt Adele wrote poetry.

They put her on a train to Theresienstadt with her wheelchair and the rest of the Jews. She wrote a letter to the woman who took care of her after my family left.

I got a letter last week from the woman with multiple sclerosis. She's got a new college student working for her. Who writes. Who wrote the letter for her. She's well. Except the bed sores. Except she can't move by herself.

I sent her a letter yesterday. I'm writing. I'll send her a story or a poem. Soon. Next letter.

Adele sent a poem to the woman who took care of her. She was a writer. Even in the concentration camp. She wrote. She wrote about the winds. She prayed for the messiah.

They tossed her body in an unmarked grave.

She had short black hair.

I'm getting my hair cut. Short.

29

Jewish and Working Class

Bernice Mennis

When I was called to speak about working-class experience, my immediate reaction was: "No, get someone else." One voice said: "I have nothing worthwhile to say." A second voice said: "I was not born poor. I always ate well. I never felt deprived. I have not suffered enough to be on this panel." Both voices silenced me. The first came from my class background—A diminished sense of competence, ability, control, power. ("Who are you anyway? You have nothing to say. No one cares or will listen.") The second, the guilt voice, comes from a strange combination of my Jewishness, my fear of anti-Semitism, my own psychological reaction to my own deprivations: a denial of my own pain if someone else seems to suffer more.

Economic class has been a matter of both shame and pride for me, depending on the value judgments of the community with which I identified. The economic class reality has always remained the same: My father had a very small outdoor tomato and banana stand and a small cellar for ripening the fruit. Until he was 68, he worked twelve hours a day, six days a week, with one week vacation. Although he worked hard and supported our family well, my father did not feel proud of his work, did not affirm his strength. Instead, he was ashamed to have me visit his fruit stand; he saw his work as dirty, himself as an "ignorant greenhorn." The legacy of class.

And I accepted and echoed back his shame. In elementary school, when we had to go around and say what work our parents did, I repeated my father's euphemistic words: "My father sells wholesale and retail fruits and vegetables." It's interesting that later, when I was involved in political actions, my shame turned to pride of that same class background. The poorer one was born the better, the more credit. . . .

What becomes difficult immediately in trying to understand class background is how it becomes hopelessly entangled with other issues: the fact that my father was an immigrant who spoke with a strong accent, never felt competent to write in English, always felt a great sense of self-shame that he projected onto his children; that my father had witnessed pogroms and daily anti-Semitism in his tiny *shtetl* in Russia, that we were Jewish, that the Holocaust occurred; that neither of my parents went to school beyond junior high school; that I was the younger daughter, the "good" child who accepted almost everything without complaining or acknowledging pain; that my sister and I experienced our worlds very differently and responded in almost opposite ways. It's difficult to sort out class, to see clearly. . . .

Feelings of poverty or wealth are based on one's experiences and where one falls on the economic spectrum. The economic class and the conditions we grow up under are very real, objective, but how we label and see those circumstances is relative, shaped by what we see outside ourselves. Growing up in the Pelham Parkway-Lydig Avenue area of the Bronx, I heard my circumstances echoed everywhere: Everyone's parents spoke Yiddish and had accents; they all spoke loudly and with their hands; few were educated beyond junior high school; no one dressed stylishly or went to restaurants (except for special occasions) or had fancy cars or dishwashers or clothes washers. (Our apartment building had, and still has, only one washing machine for forty-eight apartments. The lineup of baskets began early in the morning. My mother and I hung the clothes on the roof.) We ate good kosher food and fresh fruits and vegetables (from my [father's] stand). My mother sewed our clothes or we would shop in Alexander's and look for bargains (clothes with the manufacturers' tags removed). Clothes were passed between sisters, cousins, neighbors. I never felt poor or deprived. I had no other perspective, no other reality from which to judge our life. . . .

Class background reveals itself in little ways. Around food, for example. My family would sip their soup loudly, putting mouth close to bowl. We would put containers directly on the table and never use a butter dish. We would suck bone marrow with gusto, pick up chicken bones with our hands, crunch them with our teeth, and leave little slivers on our otherwise empty plates. We would talk loudly and argue politics over supper. Only later did I become conscious of the judgment of others about certain behavior, ways of eating, talking, walking, dressing, being. Polite etiquette struck me as a bit absurd, as if hunger were uncivilized: the delicate portions, the morsels left on the plate, the proper use of knife and fork, the spoon seeming to go in the opposite direction of the mouth. The more remote one was from basic needs, the higher one's class status. I usually was unconscious of the "proper behavior": I did not notice. But if I ever felt the eye of judgment, my first tendency would be to exaggerate my "grossness" in order to show the absurdity of others' snobbish judgments. I would deny that that judgment had any effect other than anger. But I now realize that all judgment has effect. Some of my negative self-image as *klutz, nebbish,* ugly, or unsophisticated is a direct result of the reflection I saw in the judging, sophisticated eye of the upper class.

Lack of education and lack of money made for an insecurity and fear of doing almost anything, a fear tremendously compounded by anti-Semitism and World War II. My parents were afraid to take any risks—from both a conviction of their own incompetence and a fear that doing anything big, having any visibility, would place them in danger. From them I inherited a fear that if I touched something, did anything, I would make matters worse. There was an incredible nervousness in my home around fixing anything, buying anything big, filling out any forms. My mother still calls me to complete forms for her. When my father was sick, my parents needed me to translate everything the doctor said, not because they did not understand him, but because their fear stopped them from listening when anyone very educated or in authority spoke.

That feeling of lack of control over one's environment, of no right to one's own space, was psychologically intensified by my parents' experiences of anti-Semitism and by the Holocaust. These fostered a deep sense of powerlessness and vulnerability and, on an even more basic level, a doubt whether we really had a right to exist on this earth. . . .

What happens when one feels self-conscious and small and is seen as large, wealthy, powerful, controlling? At a young age, I knew the anti-Semitic portrait of the wealthy, exploitative Jew. I also knew that I did not feel powerful or controlling. My parents and I felt powerless, fearful, vulnerable. We owned nothing. All my parents saved, after working fifty years, would not equal the cost of one year of college today. What does it mean to have others' definition of one's reality so vastly different from one's experience of it? The effects are confusion, anger, entrapment. I lost touch with what was real, what my own experiences really were.

As a political person I felt particularly vulnerable to the hated image of "the Jew." I knew it was a stereotype and not my experience or the experience of the Jews I grew up with—but it still made me feel guilt, not pride, for any success I did have, for any rise in status. If the stereotype said "Jews have everything," the only way I could avoid that stereotype would be to have nothing. If you are poor, you are not a Jew. If you are successful, you are a bad Jew. The trap.

The economic and professional success of many second-generation Jews became tinged for me, as if we had done something wrong. To feel bad about achievement, to hold back one's power, is very destructive. My aunts and uncles, my parents, my friends' parents all had little education and little money. Yet we—my cousins, my sister, my friends—not only went to college, but even to graduate school and law school. I was speaking the other day with my aunt, who was saying what a miracle it was that her four children were all professionals and she was poor and uneducated. But the miracle was not really a miracle at all. It was the result of parents who saw education as very, very important—as a way out of the entrapment of class and prejudice. It was the result of parents who worked desperately hard so that their children could have that way out. It was a City College system in New York City that provided completely free education while we worked and lived at home.

In one generation we created an incredible economic, class, professional, and educational distance between ourselves and our parents. The danger of this success is that we forget the material soil that nourished us, the hard work that propped us up; that we lose our consciousness of the harm and evil of condescension, exploitation, oppression, the pain of being made to feel inferior and invisible. Anzia Yezierska, a Jewish immigrant writer, says "Education without a heart is a curse." But to keep that consciousness and that heart and to be able to step onto the dance floor of life and say "I am here," reflecting back to our parents the beauty and strength we inherited from them, that would be a very real "miracle" indeed.

Next Steps and Action

30

Menorah Light Banishes Hate

The Associated Press

Newtown, Pa.—Chanukah candles are flickering alongside Santa's reindeer, wreaths and Nativity scenes in some windows of this Philadelphia suburb, in what neighbors call a show of force against hate.

Early Sunday, after the third night of Chanukah, someone threw a rock through the Markovitz family's front window, grabbed the electric menorah that had blazed from within, and smashed it to the ground, breaking all nine bulbs.

"Have you ever seen real fear and devastation?" asked Margie Alexander, 36, a Christian neighbor who saw Judy Markovitz in the hours after the vandalism. "It was real pain. You don't see something like that and not do something."

So Alexander did something. And so did her neighbors. And their neighbors. Yesterday, the final night of the eight-day Jewish Festival of Lights, 25 Christian homes had menorahs burning in their windows.

And the vandals never returned.

"It just blossomed," said Lisa Keeling, 35, a former police officer who raced from store to store in search of scarce menorahs for neighbors to display before candle lighting time arrived at sundown.

Markovitz, a 42-year-old mother of two, emigrated to the United States from the Ukraine as a child to escape persecution. Her mother is a Holocaust survivor, and her father, a dentist, was unable to practice because he was a Jew.

She did not know of the neighborhood menorah effort until she returned home Sunday night and saw the orange bulbs burning.

"It actually brought tears to my eyes," Markovitz said. She immediately replaced the broken bulbs in her own menorah and put it back up in the window.

Keeling said the experience has been so profound that she will put a menorah up again next year and for years to come.

A Jewish neighbor, Andrew Lasner, said he hopes that with all the attention, "someone will talk" and the vandals will be found.

As for Markovitz, she said she is no longer afraid and feels only sadness for her attackers: "To . . . do such a thing, they must have had a lot of hatred."

"This is what the holiday is about," Markovitz said. "I feel that we beat the evil, and the Chanukah lights are glowing even more."

31

Pioneers in Dialogue: Jews Building Bridges

Reena Bernards

At every family seder when I was young, along with my grandmother who made the gefilte fish and horseradish with her own hands, and my father at the head of the table in a big chair fluffed with pillows, there were always some Gentiles. I remember being surprised that a Lutheran minister could sing along in Hebrew, which he was required to learn in seminary. And I remember the five-year-old daughter of one minister who enthusiastically took a big bite out of a fresh piece of horseradish, only to turn beet red and gag when she learned what this bitter herb was all about. These were not ordinary Christians. They were ministers, priests, nuns, educators, and theologians who had dedicated themselves to understanding Jews. They came to our seder year after year because my father was one of the pioneers in Christian–Jewish dialogue.

In the 1960s *dialogue* meant Jews and Christians studying together to understand the differences and similarities of their beliefs. It meant explaining to Christians that, in the eyes of Jews, Christianity did not supersede Judaism and that the religion of the Jews remains a unique and philosophically distinct monotheistic faith. It meant exploring with Christians the religious roots of anti-Semitism, helping them reexamine their contemporary texts to remove references to Jews as killers of Jesus or doomed souls because of a lack of belief in Christ. For Jews such as my father, dialogue was a natural response to living as a minority in a Christian-dominated society. It was a way to make oneself understood, and to help create a safer environment for other Jews.

The historic course of Jewish involvement in cross-cultural dialogue changed dramatically after the Six-Day War in 1967. The day after the war began my father frantically tried to gather signatures from his Gentile friends for a newspaper ad in support of Israel, to no avail. He was particularly pained by the lack of support from Black leaders. Along with other rabbis he had marched in Selma, Alabama, during the civil rights battles and assumed that the Black-Jewish alliance was strong and in the interest of both communities.

By the late 1960s that alliance could no longer be taken for granted. The painful rift brought yet another phase of dialogue into Jewish life during the 1970s and 1980s, this time between Blacks and Jews seeking to establish an alliance based on a more in-depth understanding of each other. No longer could issues such as Israel, the Palestinians, South Africa, and, most important, the economic disparity between Jews and Blacks be avoided. Many Black-Jewish groups also moved to the personal level, as participants told and compared their stories of growing up as members of a minority community.

My own work in dialogue began well into this stage in the history of Jewish engagement in cross-cultural communication. I founded the Dialogue Project between American Jewish and Palestinian Women in 1989, after the outbreak of the Palestinian intifada. My goal was to build an understanding between mainstream women leaders from both communities. Although it now seems obvious, it wasn't until years later that I realized the connection between my work and my father's. Both come from a commitment to breaking Jews' historic isolation from other peoples. This isolation is certainly a result of anti-Semitism, and it serves to reinforce it.[1]

My father and I came to the process of dialogue from very different directions. He was a leader in the Jewish community (as National Director of Inter-religious Cooperation for the Anti-Defamation League); I was a community organizer active in grassroots efforts to bring together low-income Whites and Blacks on issues of housing, neighborhood development, and community empowerment. I left community organizing to work for Middle East peace because it was an issue that deeply affected me personally. Before I knew it I was promoting dialogue as a means of bridging the tremendous ideological and political gaps between American Jews and Arabs, as earlier Jewish leaders in the United States had used dialogue to bridge gaps between American Jews and Christians.

The Role of Dialogue

This work in Arab-Jewish relations led me to consider the role of dialogue in our increasingly multiethnic society, and I began to teach the practice of cross-cultural dialogue to diverse groups of community leaders in the United States. Other communities, such as African Americans and Asian Americans, are using dialogue as a method of bridging understanding between communities that are often pitted against one another. One such group, the Afro-Asian Relations Counsel, was founded in Washington, D.C., after Korean grocery store owners came in conflict with their Black customers. They discovered that through intensive discussions they were able to separate the cultural issues from the political ones. Whereas they had previously seen the other community as committed to their downfall and in collusion with the racism they faced in the broader society, through the process of dialogue they were able to stop seeing the other as their enemy. Blacks came to understand that immigrant Koreans were able to succeed in opening businesses because they pool capital and help one another overcome economic obstacles. Koreans came to understand that their ways of showing respect to a stranger are seen as distancing and actually disrespectful in the more outwardly expressive African American community.

Such lessons are important, but they do not go far enough in their impact. In order for dialogue to affect significantly the nature of race relations in our country, it must lead to deeper alliances and actions. For example, one potential project that came out of an African-Asian dialogue suggested that Black and Korean college students do internships in the businesses in each other's community, leading to an exchange of skills and knowledge as well as a sense of joint purpose. A Black-Jewish dialogue group in Washington, D.C., decided to focus on the issue of gun control, holding weekly vigils outside the headquarters of the National Rifle Association as well as lobbying for local legislation.

The ultimate purpose of dialogue is to create new relationships that work to change society. While the process may seem slow to many activists, the underlying thrust is radical. By forging alliances among minority groups where differences have kept them apart, the dialogue process breaks down the ability of the ruling establishment to divide and conquer. If members of minority communities do not allow themselves to be polarized, stronger movements for change can emerge. The point is not to recreate the civil rights alliance as it was, but to come together with a new understanding and create new movements that are stronger and have a heightened awareness of the richness of diversity.

Dialogue can also be used to bridge groups that are ideologically opposed to each other. Over the past few years there have been attempts to bring together members of the pro-choice and the pro-life communities.[2] Some of these groups have found common ground on issues such as the need to improve adoption practices, the need for better access to sex education, and the need to better support economically vulnerable families.

The purpose of dialogue is not to obliterate legitimate conflict between groups. Dialogue participants are often aware that the people to whom they are talking are their opponents in a political battle. Each side maintains its right to continue to wage the political fight at every level; participation in a dialogue is not a truce. Yet dialogue enables groups to search for new options and possibilities and to create win-win solutions that were not considered before.

Jewish Participation in Dialogue

In many ways dialogue comes naturally to Jews. Several years ago I attended a workshop for Jews, Christians, and Muslims in Louisiana, led by the renowned Rev. Scott Peck. The purpose was ambitious: to build community with each other. Each group responded differently to the task. The Christians spoke in soft, conciliatory tones. The Muslims were guarded as they rationally explained Islam to the group. The Jews jumped in and bared our chests. We spoke about our own personal dilemmas, argued with fellow Jews, revealed our psychological pain, and challenged the other groups on basic assumptions—all without stopping to catch our breath.

We were at home in that process: this is the water we swim in. Dialogue fits Jewish notions of how you make change in the world: you talk, you study, you discuss, you argue. The Talmud itself is the record of an internal dialogue between rabbis as they tried to figure out the controversial issues of their day. Perhaps, it is no surprise that Sigmond Freud, the father of psychotherapy, was a Jew. What could be more Jewish than having a dialogue with the different parts of yourself?

As members of a minority cultural and religious group in an increasingly multicultural society, Jews have important talents to bring to the table. Jewish community efforts at dialogue with Christians, Blacks, and Arabs give us a body of experience that provides lessons to others embarking on this road. We are not afraid to talk to our adversaries and venture into areas that others fear, believing in the healing power of building relationships.[3]

Yet I have also noticed that the comfort Jews have with dialogue can lead to some serious problems between ourselves and the other groups we wish to engage. First, we sometimes have a need to control the agenda and are often fearful of giving up this control to the will of the group. Perhaps this comes from our fear of being used, which we have in common with other oppressed groups. Our history makes us mistrustful of those who have not already shown their allegiances to us. But because we Jews are often the initiators of dialogue, we need to remember that for the effort to be successful we have to overcome our fears and allow the power and control to be shared.

Second, Jews are often more willing to talk than to take concrete political action. To many Jews sitting and talking until agreements are hammered out is a natural part of the dialogue process. We believe that our very survival depends on being understood. Our yardstick of success is often whether we think learning is taking place on both sides. In addition, while early Christian-Jewish dialogue was often motivated by Jewish concerns for our own safety, dialogue with African American or American Arab partners requires a commitment to their security needs as well. At this point in history they often feel more urgent about their political and economic situation than we do as Jews. We therefore need to note that, to others, "just talking" is often seen as useless and a dialogue is successful only if it leads to concrete political action.

Because of these different expectations and tendencies, it is important to carefully craft the dialogue experience. Every group should pay attention to the steps involved in creating a dialogue, and should build the experience according to the particular needs of their group. What follows are some suggestions.

Setting Up a Dialogue

One important principle applies to all successful dialogues: *all sides must feel empowered by the process.* This means that they should feel that their needs are being considered in the development of the dialogue group. This principle needs to be followed in making decisions on such issues as sponsorship, leadership, place, participant list, development of the agenda, and funding.

There are many other issues to consider over the life of a dialogue group that relate to this sense of empowerment. Should the group be public or confidential, short-term or long-term, discussion-only or action-oriented? Answers to these questions often reveal the important differences between participating communities. Resolving them collectively could be the most important test of the success of a dialogue experience.

I like to talk of a *leadership partnership* as an important ingredient in dialogue. When I started the dialogue between American Jewish and Palestinian women, I put a great deal of energy into building a relationship with my counterpart in the Palestinian community, Najat Arafat Khelil, president of the Arab Women's Council. Najat and I have spent many hours together, building both our friendship and our work relationship. We have lived through political crises together, including the intifada and the Gulf War, working to understand each other's perspective. It hasn't always been easy, and there were times when we shouted at each other or went for days without talking. We always knew, however, that we would work through it because we have a deep commitment to each other and to the success of our group. I believe that this was the glue that held our project together. Najat and I modeled that it is possible to work through issues and to bridge the ideological, religious, and political gaps.

Due to the sensitive nature of the dialogue experience, it is important to use a consultatory leadership style in order to involve other people in the decision-making process. I recommend that early on leaders set up a steering committee with an equal number of members from the different communities.[4] This committee can help decide all structural issues for the group, setting up the agenda for meetings and deciding on joint projects. . . .

All parties in the dialogue need to be involved in the fundraising efforts, even if the dollar amounts they are able to raise are different. Some groups make the mistake of allowing one community to raise the funds, with the understanding that the other community will take on other pieces of the work. This can lead to a power imbalance and a difference in the sense of ownership of the project. A more equitable solution is to engage each community in raising what it can in the manner that it is most accustomed. In addition, the two communities can meet together with foundation boards or donors, helping expand and share access to funding sources.

Agreeing on Goals and Expectations

There are five potential goals for a dialogue group:

1. *Building community and celebrating differences.* Members of an organization or community come together to learn about each other's culture. The sharing of music, dance, food, and life stories is used as a means of building a sense of camaraderie.

2. *Healing pain and building understanding.* Participants are given an opportunity to voice their unique feelings and perspectives on a given problem or experience. This kind of open dialogue can be used after a traumatic event occurs in a community, or as a means of hearing from diverse people within a common institution.

3. *Problem solving about areas of conflict.* A more in-depth discussion occurs to find new solutions to intercommunal conflicts. Participants move from seeing the problem as a conflict between them, to seeing it as a common dilemma, engaging in joint problem solving.

4. *Modeling a different relationship.* Community leaders make a conscious commitment to demonstrate to the broader community that a more positive type of relationship is possible between members of their groups. They show by example that a relationship of mutual respect can lead to alternative ways of interacting.

5. *Action toward political change.* Dialogue participants embark on a joint political campaign, organizing their communities to change the conditions that lead to separation between groups. Groups sign a joint statement, hold press conferences, organize rallies, support candidates, and engage in other visible activities designed to build coalitions on issues where there is common ground.

The most important criterion for a successful dialogue is that the goals and expectations be clear from the beginning. It is legitimate to say that you just want to celebrate differences, and to accomplish those goals you organize a potluck dinner or a cultural event. It is also all right to build a dialogue around problem solving without going to the next stage of action, *as long as this is clear from the beginning.* But most leaders and community activists will want to be engaged in dialogue for the purpose of ultimately taking action. Be aware of differences in expectations that need to be acknowledged and managed along the way.

In addition, dialogue organizers need to be persistent and at the same time pay close attention to timing. Does your group want to attract publicity or remain confidential? Sometimes agreeing on stages of public exposure is helpful. For example, members may choose to first write or speak about a dialogue only within their own communities. As the project proceeds, the group can then decide to more fully go public. . . .

Using an experienced facilitation team will often enable a group to handle difficult conflicts more successfully. This special team can include members of each community (such as the organizers), who can understand what the participants are going through and detect any unexpressed emotions. You may also want to add a third member of the team from outside both communities who is able to provide support to both groups. In addition, the facilitation team can help the group reexamine its guidelines for dialogue. These guidelines should be periodically reviewed by the group, so that any necessary changes can be made. For example, a group may decide to add to its original guidelines that certain words not be used if they are found to be inflammatory to one of the parties. These suggestions help ensure safety even when the issues feel scary.

Another important ingredient for safety is to allow for separate caucuses. Caucusing means that there are times when the members of each community will go into separate meetings to check in with members of their own group. For example, if you as a Jewish participant have a strong reaction to what a member of the other group has said, before getting angry you can discuss your feelings with your fellow Jews, ask for their advice, and hear their perspectives. Then, if you decide to confront the issue in the dialogue, you will feel on stronger footing and will have had a chance to work out some of your own emotions first. . . .

Expecting Crisis

Every dialogue group can expect to go through at least one major crisis. In fact, every dialogue meeting will have its own "mini-crisis"; that is the time when the group is experiencing some chaos as it faces unresolved issues. This is the nature of group interaction, but it is also endemic to the dialogue process. If you expect a crisis then you will not be overwhelmed when it happens, nor will you experience the crisis as a failure. Instead, the crisis becomes an opportunity for each group to go deeper and to further understand the nature of its relationship to others.

When the Dialogue Project was on its joint trip to the Middle East, our major crisis involved visiting Yad Vashem, the Holocaust memorial museum. We had agreed ahead of time that each community could show the other community its homeland in any way it chose. The Jewish women decided a visit to the museum should be on the agenda. Palestinians, however, were reluctant to go. They already knew about the Holocaust and felt that its memory had been used politically against their community despite the fact that they were not responsible for its occurrence. The tensions this caused the group were resolved only after a visit to a refugee camp in Gaza. The Palestinian women could see that the Jews were deeply affected by the visit, and they were moved by the Jewish women's recognition of their pain. They then told the Jewish women that they would go to Yad Vashem, because they understood the need to witness each community's pain together. In this case, the group came through this crisis stronger and more assured of everyone's commitment to peace.

The Limits of Dialogue

The process of dialogue has its critics. Jonathan Kuttab, a West Bank human rights lawyer who was one of the first Palestinians to meet with Israeli Jews after the 1967 war, speaks of the pitfalls of a "false dialogue."[5] A false dialogue is one in which participants are more interested in getting along than in delving into the depths of the conflict. Kuttab warns that dialogue groups may abandon moral positions in the name of compromise. Because of the desire to succeed there may be a tendency to underplay political differences and to focus on more comfortable issues such as mutual stereotypes, which downplay the nature of the oppressive situation. Dialogue participants can be tempted to ignore the realities in their own societies as they attempt to build a bridge to the other side.

Kuttab claims that a key pitfall in dialogue is the assumption of a false symmetry between groups where there is actually a large power imbalance. The basic condition of oppressor and oppressed is ignored, and members of the group are subtly pressured into an acceptance of the status quo. In this sense participants in dialogue can be coopted or misused. Finally, Kuttab charges that dialogue should never be a substitute for action.

Yet Kuttab himself speaks of a dialogue in service of "peace, justice, and reconciliation." By setting up a process that empowers both sides, an honest and open exchange can occur. Potentially through the process of exploring the dynamics of conflict, each community and individual will find new sources of power to effect political change.

Conclusion

When Israeli Prime Minister Yitzhak Rabin and Palestine Liberation Organization (PLO) Chairman Yassir Arafat shook hands on an initial agreement, it was perhaps the most powerful example yet of the value and special contribution of dialogue. The agreement would not have been signed if it were not for the Norwegians, who brought Israeli academics together with members of the PLO for nonstop meetings in mansions and apartments throughout their country. Their walks together in the woods, meals together, and late-night laughs were crucial to the process. These encounters followed hundreds of dialogue meetings, conferences, and informal living room discussions between thousands of Jews and Palestinians over the course of the past twenty-five years. What official diplomats could not accomplish in suits and ties in formal negotiations, others made happen away from the camera's eye. The lessons they learned "filtered up" to the governmental level and saw their way into a historic agreement. This type of citizen dialogue, known as "track two diplomacy,"[6] augments governmental efforts and can keep the reconciliation process moving forward when "track one diplomacy"—official diplomacy—stagnates.

In a world where interethnic, interreligious, and intercommunal conflicts threaten global security, conflict resolution methods are needed more than ever. Here in the United States, as our country becomes more multicultural, building an understanding among groups is essential for our cohesion as a nation. The experience that Jews bring is a vital resource. The more we as Jews can hone our skills, improve in problem areas, and become conscious about what makes dialogue work, the more we will be able to make a valuable contribution to a multicultural society. Dialogue is the wave of the future.

Notes

1. The connection between breaking down Jewish isolation and safety for Jews may not have been fully understood at the time, but Eva Fogelman, in her study of Christian rescuers of Jews during the Holocaust, found that 28 percent were people who had a close connection to Jews or a strong, positive feeling about the Jewish people. See Eva Fogelman, *Conscience and Courage* (New York: Anchor Books/Doubleday, 1994).
2. Carol Becker, Laura Chasin, Richard Chasin, Margaret Herzing, and Sallyann Roth, "The Public Conversation Project Focuses Dialogue on Abortion," *Family Therapy News*, June 1992.

3. There is even a dialogue taking place between children of survivors of the Holocaust and children of the Third Reich. These brave souls, led by two Boston women, one Jewish and one German, have traveled with their group People Helping People: Face to Face, to Germany to bring their message of reconciliation to high school students. The students were so moved by their joint presentation that some of them insisted on going with the American group to Buchenwald, where they prayed together.

4. Contrary to common belief, a dialogue does not necessarily imply a discussion between only two groups. The word *dialogue* can be traced from the Greek words *dia*, which means "through," and *logos*, which means "words or reason" (William Morris, ed., *The American Heritage Dictionary of the English Language* [Boston: Houghton Mifflin, 1969]). In our multicultural society we may need to engage with a variety of groups at any one time, further enriching but also complicating the process.

5. Jonathan Kuttab and Edy Kaufman," An Exchange on Dialogue," *Journal of Palestine Studies* 17, no. 2 (Winter 1988).

6. The phrase "track two diplomacy" was coined by former U.S. ambassador Joseph V. Montville. See his, "The Arrow and the Olive Branch: A Case for Track Two Diplomacy," in *The Psychodynamics of International Relationships*, vol. 2, *Unofficial Diplomacy at Work*, ed. V. Volkan, J. Montville, and D. Julius (Lexington, Mass.: Lexington Books, 1990).

Sexism

Introduction by Heather W. Hackman

Our ideas of ourselves, our roles in the world, the comments we hear throughout our day, the reactions of family and friends to us, and even the way we dress, speak volumes about the pervasiveness of sexism in the culture that surrounds us. Sexism goes beyond obvious examples such as sexual harassment, rape, and "the glass ceiling" to include notions of sex and gender divisions that are so deeply rooted in our national psyche that, as Shulamith Firestone (1970) suggests, they are practically invisible.

In broad brush strokes, this section presents a range of perspectives to illustrate what sexism is, its impact on all of our lives, and some concrete next steps that women and men can take to change our environments and our lives. My approach grows out of three perspectives: an overarching theory of the dynamics of social oppression, a historical view of the emergence of women's consciousness, and the connection of sexism to other issues. The first perspective is drawn from discussions of oppression presented in section 1 (see Harro, Young, and Wildman). The second perspective underscores the role of women's history in understanding the contexts and conditions under which women and men have fought for social change, in the United States. The third perspective acknowledges the interconnectedness of sexism to other issues in this book and the importance of women and men working in coalition across "isms."

First, in considering oppression theory, the question "What is sexism?" is addressed through a definition that combines prejudicial attitudes or beliefs with social power. Suzanne Pharr defines sexism as "an enforced belief in male dominance and control" held in place by systems of power and control that ultimately keep women subordinate to men (1988, 8). These systems of power and control take place at institutional, cultural, and individual levels. Examples of sexism range from denigrating jokes, to objectifying females in the media, to job discrimination, to acts of violence against women. Sexism can be directed at a girl or woman individually or, on a larger scale, can encompass cultural views, social attitudes, or institutional policies. The severity of these examples may differ, but they all serve to undermine the power, safety, and personal freedom of women.

Understanding the systemic manifestations of sexism is only the first step. Students in my classes offer numerous examples to argue that "men are just as oppressed as women" or that men are "victims of reverse sexism." But an understanding of the larger, systemic perspective encourages students to consider who occupies the most powerful seats in government, business, the judiciary, law enforcement, and the media—in short, who controls the *systems* of power and control in this country. This point is summarized well in the following quote taken from Marilyn Frye's famous essay on women's oppression:

> The experience of oppressed people is that the living of one's life is confined and shaped by forces and barriers which are not accidental or occasional and hence avoidable, but are systematically related to each other in such a way as to catch one between and among them and restrict . . . motion in any direction. It is the experience of being caged in. . . .
>
>   Consider a birdcage. If you look very closely at just one wire in the cage, you cannot see the other wires . . . you could look at that one wire . . . and be unable to see why a bird would not just fly around the wire anytime it wanted to go somewhere. . . . It is only when you step back . . . and take a macroscopic view of the whole cage, that you can see why the bird does not go anywhere. (1983, 4)

History presents a second perspective toward exploring the question, "What is sexism?" This history has been described by some feminists as consisting of three "waves" of women's movements in the United States, the first an outgrowth of the abolitionist movement in the mid-1800s, the second an outgrowth of the civil rights movement in the 1950s and 1960s, and the third the contemporary effort to build a comprehensive and inclusive movement today. The essay by Sojourner Truth in this chapter states the perspective of women who were excluded by class and race in the first wave. It highlights how race and class divided and weakened the first wave's success. The first wave's ambitious agenda of changing women's position in society regarding women's roles (family roles and marriage rights) and access to resources (education, voting rights, labor, and property, to name a few) was steadily whittled down by the racism, class divisions, and backlash at the turn of the century. By 1920, women's rights had narrowed to suffrage and the broader agenda was lost. Decades later, the second wave had crowds of women marching for women's reproductive freedom and bringing to the forefront issues of economic injustice, racism, heterosexism, and violence against women, even protesting the 1968 Miss America pageant. The women of this wave carried a message via the media, schools, and the streets that demanded equality.

Despite the gains made by these two women's movements, each of these first two "waves" was met with a cultural, political, and social backlash that undermined or eroded a number of the advances they obtained. The most recent backlash period arose in the 1980s with the emergence of federal policies and media images that undermined earlier advances leading to women's independence. It is worth noting that most of us have learned only brief excerpts from this long and powerful history of women addressing sexism. Despite its relative absence from the "mainstream" historical record, a full understanding of the complexity of women's on-going struggles highlights the tension points, the advances, and the backlash that hold in bold relief the patterns of sexism in U.S. culture.

One of the key oversights of the first two waves of the women's movement was the failure to see how the fate of one woman is tied to the fate of all women. Race and class divisions undermined the first wave just as race, class, and homophobia undermined the second. Today, there is what some observers view as a third wave women's movement that is attempting to take into account the mistakes of these previous movements, working to build coalitions among women, and addressing a broader range of women's issues.

This most recent wave also emphasizes a third, key perspective on sexism—namely its interconnectedness with other issues. Over the last decade there has been a reinvigoration of women's activism, primarily by young women, in an effort establish broad-based coalitions that will dismantle the larger systems of sexism and oppression as a whole. An awareness of the need for coalitions is reflected in Patricia Hill Collins's essay "Toward a New Vision: Race, Class and Gender as Categories of Analysis and Connection," included in chapter 87 of this volume, where she clearly states that if women do not begin to build coalitions among themselves, all women will remain targets of sexism.

Readings in This Section

To return to Frye's analogy of the birdcage: the articles in this section describe the wires of the cage (contexts), their impact on women and men (personal voices), and how we can bend or break those wires to create change regarding sexism in our society (next steps and action). We begin the chapter with the issue of gender construction and socialization. *Gender,* in the words of Judith Lorber (chapter 32), refers to the socially constructed ideas of what it means to be "man" or "woman" in this society. As Lorber explains, "Most people find it hard to believe that gender is constantly created and re-created out of human interaction, out of social life, and is the texture and order of that social life" (p. 203). The "Cycle of Socialization," presented in the selection by Roberta L. Harro in section 1, helps to explain this creation and recreation of gender by analyzing our socialization as women and men, and the ways in which socialization embeds sexist notions in us on conscious and unconscious levels. The belief that gender is socially con-structed in this way is evidenced by the constantly evolving and changing roles of women and men throughout the short history of the United States. (How gender differs from "sex" and "sexual orientation" will be discussed in section 5.) For the purposes of the present section we will be using both the Judith Lorber and the Sandra Lipsitz Bem articles to examine how gender roles are constructed, who benefits and who loses by this construction, and how these roles have served and continue to serve to keep women subordinate. When reading these articles, I encourage students in my classes to consider their own gender socialization while also critically thinking about the connections of gender roles to the larger systems of power and privilege that maintain sexism in this society. As Lorber mentions, gender is such an assumed aspect of our culture that it takes a deliberate examina-tion to understand how it is constructed and maintained.

The selection by Michael S. Kimmel describes how male gender is constructed in this culture, the weapons used to keep boys and men in certain roles, and the price that boys and men pay when they attempt to step out of those roles. Kate

Bornstein's examination of gender roles and transgender issues is both personal and analytical, and questions the issues of gender production and reproduction. Transgender issues are included in this section as well as in section 5 in order to clearly demonstrate the intimate links among sexism; gender role production; and the oppression of gay, lesbian, bisexual and transgendered people.

Much has changed for women in the last three decades, and many students find it desirable to consider only these changes and deny the existence of sexism in today's culture. As a result, our understanding of sexism becomes ambiguous and is laden with debilitating notions of "male bashing" and of "feminism" being equated with "man-hating." The selection by bell hooks examines feminism and the backlash against it. She helps us understand the language used to obscure the issue of sexism and mire our understanding down in a sea of "political correctness," political backlash, and social conservatism, and she offers hope and positive direction. "Fresh Lipstick: Rethinking Images of Women in Advertising," by Linda M. Scott, challenges and updates our understanding of how media affects and transforms women's notions of beauty.

These theoretical pieces are followed by a number of "Personal Voices" readings that help to explore the personal dimensions, complexity, and impact of sexism on women and men today. Sojourner Truth's classic question, "Ain't I a Woman?" holds as true today as in 1851. Her statement challenges us to consider the double standards that are handed to women and to acknowledge the interaction of race and class in the construction of gender.

The personal essays by Christy Haubegger, Abra Chernick, Jackson Katz, and the anonymous article "The Rape of Mr. Smith" all express ways in which socially constructed images of women and women's objectification create a culture of violence against women. Haubegger highlights the cultural differences that accompany our images of female beauty and demonstrates the link between sexism and racism in the United States. Chernick describes her struggle with eating disorders and the ways in which our culture's construction of ideal female beauty made her an object to herself, denying her agency, voice, and a sense of social power. Katz further describes the objectification of women by discussing how the representation of women through pornography supports a culture in which women are viewed as objects for men's pleasure and ultimately men's dominance. "The Rape of Mr. Smith" exposes the absurdity of our culture's response to rape and what some have called a "rape culture" (Buchwald et al. 1993). Further, this piece shows us that rape is not about sex, a common cultural myth, but rather about power and control individually expressed but deeply connected to the domination of women through institutional structures.

The "Next Steps and Action" readings consider why women and men need to mobilize and take action in our lives and the larger society around us. Whitney Walker's personal and compelling story of her own consciousness-raising and movement toward action provides inspiration and direction for women wanting to create change in their lives and on larger societal levels. Ian Law's remarks concerning men and feminism provides a starting point for those men who are looking for ways to be part of the solution rather than part of the problem. Law's perspective challenges men who declare they are not sexist and yet stay silent when instances of sexism arise, behavior he sees as complicity. He outlines how silence is no longer an option for men who are concerned about these issues and explains that men must begin to take action. The chapter concludes with an essay in which Gloria Steinem outlines a concrete plan of action for all of us to follow if we hope to live in a world where women (and men) can be free.

I hope these selections help readers better understand sexism in our culture. I encourage readers to continue to examine who we are as male and female in this society, how we are socialized into gender roles, and how these roles maintain the oppression of women. I also invite readers to identify and to think critically about the larger systems that keep sexism in place. Seeing the connections among issues such as welfare, reproductive rights, the labor movement, health care, domestic violence, and women's body image, to name a few examples, opens the door for broader and more lasting change. It is only through questioning, analysis, and action that we can create a society free of sexism.

References

Buchwald, E., P. R. Fletcher, and M. Roth, eds. (1993).*Transforming a Rape Culture*. Minneapolis, Minn.: Milkweed Editions.

Firestone, S. (1970). *The Dialectic of Sex: The Case for Feminist Revolution*. New York: William Morrow.

Frye, M. (1983). *The Politics of Reality*. New York: Crossing Press.

Pharr, S. (1988). *Homophobia as a Weapon of Sexism*. Little Rock, Ark.: Chardon Press.

Contexts

32

"Night to His Day": The Social Construction of Gender

Judith Lorber

Talking about gender for most people is the equivalent of fish talking about water. Gender is so much the routine ground of everyday activities that questioning its taken-for-granted assumptions and presuppositions is like wondering about whether the sun will come up.[1] Gender is so pervasive that in our society we assume it is bred into our genes. Most people find it hard to believe that gender is constantly created and re-created out of human interaction, out of social life, and is the texture and order of that social life. Yet gender, like culture, is a human production that depends on everyone constantly "doing gender" (West and Zimmerman 1987).

And everyone "does gender" without thinking about it. Today, on the subway, I saw a well-dressed man with a year-old child in a stroller. Yesterday, on a bus, I saw a man with a tiny baby in a carrier on his chest. Seeing men taking care of small children in public is increasingly common—at least in New York City. But both men were quite obviously stared at—and smiled at, approvingly. Everyone was doing gender—the men who were changing the role of fathers and the other passengers, who were applauding them silently. But there was more gendering going on that probably fewer people noticed. The baby was wearing a white crocheted cap and white clothes. You couldn't tell if it was a boy or a girl. The child in the stroller was wearing a dark blue T-shirt and dark print pants. As they started to leave the train, the father put a Yankee baseball cap on the child's head. Ah, a boy, I thought. Then I noticed the gleam of tiny earrings in the child's ears, and as they got off, I saw the little flowered sneakers and lace-trimmed socks. Not a boy after all. Gender done.

Gender is such a familiar part of daily life that it usually takes a deliberate disruption of our expectations of how women and men are supposed to act to pay attention to how it is produced. Gender signs and signals are so ubiquitous that we usually fail to note them—unless they are missing or ambiguous. Then we are uncomfortable until we have successfully placed the other person in a gender status; otherwise, we feel socially dislocated. In our society, in addition to man and woman, the status can be *transvestite* (a person who dresses in opposite-gender clothes) and *transsexual* (a person who has had sex-change surgery). Transvestites and transsexuals carefully construct their gender status by dressing, speaking, walking, gesturing in the ways prescribed for women or men—whichever they want to be taken for—and so does any "normal" person.

For the individual, gender construction starts with assignment to a sex category on the basis of what the genitalia look like at birth.[2] Then babies are dressed or adorned in a way that displays the category because parents don't want to be constantly asked whether their baby is a girl or a boy. A sex category becomes a gender status through naming, dress, and the use of other gender markers. Once a child's gender is evident, others treat those in one gender differently from those in the other, and the children respond to the different treatment by feeling different and behaving differently. As soon as they can talk, they start to refer to themselves as members of their gender. Sex doesn't come into play again until puberty, but by that time, sexual feelings and desires and practices have been shaped by gendered norms and expectations. Adolescent boys and girls approach and avoid each other in an elaborately scripted and gendered mating dance. Parenting is gendered, with different expectations for mothers and for fathers, and people of different genders work at different kinds of jobs. The work adults do as mothers and fathers and as low-level workers and high-level bosses, shapes women's and men's life experiences, and these experiences produce different feelings, consciousness, relationships, skills—ways of being that we call feminine or masculine.[3] All of these processes constitute the social construction of gender.

Gendered roles change—today fathers are taking care of little children, girls and boys are wearing unisex clothing and getting the same education, women and men are working at the same jobs. Although many traditional social groups are quite strict about maintaining gender differences, in other social groups they seem to be blurring. Then why the one-year-old's earrings? Why is it still so important to mark a child as a girl or a boy, to make sure she is not taken for a boy or he for a girl? What would happen if they were? They would, quite literally, have changed places in their social world.

To explain why gendering is done from birth, constantly and by everyone, we have to look not only at the way individuals experience gender but at gender as a social institution. As a social institution, gender is one of the major ways that human beings organize their lives. Human society depends on a predictable division of labor, a designated allocation of scarce goods, assigned responsibility for children and others who cannot care for themselves, common values and their systematic transmission to new members, legitimate leadership, music, art, stories, games, and other symbolic productions. One way of choosing people for the different tasks of society is on the basis of their talents, motivations, and competence—their demonstrated achievements. The other way is on the basis of gender, race, ethnicity—ascribed membership in a category of people. Although societies vary in the extent to which they use one or the other of these ways of allocating people to work and to carry out other responsibilities, every society uses gender and age grades. Every society classifies people as "girl and boy children," "girls and boys ready to be married," and "fully adult women and men," constructs similarities among them and differences between them, and assigns them to different roles and responsibilities. Personality characteristics, feelings, motivations, and ambitions flow from these different life experiences so that the members of these different groups become different kinds of people. The process of gendering and its outcome are legitimated by religion, law, science, and the society's entire set of values. . . .

Western society's values legitimate gendering by claiming that it all comes from physiology—female and male procreative differences. But gender and sex are not equivalent, and gender as a social construction does not flow automatically from genitalia and reproductive organs, the main physiological differences of females and males. In the construction of ascribed social statuses, physiological differences such as sex, stage of development, color of skin, and size are crude markers. They are not the source of the social statuses of gender, age grade, and race. Social statuses are carefully constructed through prescribed processes of teaching, learning, emulation, and enforcement. Whatever genes, hormones, and biological evolution contribute to human social institutions is materially as well as qualitatively transformed by social practices. Every social institution has a material base, but culture and social practices transform that base into something with qualitatively different patterns and constraints. The economy is much more than producing food and goods and distributing them to eaters and users; family and kinship are not the equivalent of having sex and procreating; morals and religions cannot be equated with the fears and ecstasies of the brain; language goes far beyond the sounds produced by tongue and larynx. No one eats "money" or "credit"; the concepts of "god" and "angels" are the subjects of theological disquisitions; not only words but objects, such as their flag, "speak" to the citizens of a country.

Similarly, gender cannot be equated with biological and physiological differences between human females and males. The building blocks of gender are *socially constructed statuses*. Western societies have only two genders, "man" and "woman." Some societies have three genders—men, women, and *berdaches* or *hijras* or *xaniths*. Berdaches, hijras, and xaniths are biological males who behave, dress, work, and are treated in most respects as social women; they are therefore not men, nor are they female women; they are, in our language, "male women."[4] There are African and American Indian societies that have a gender status called *manly hearted women*—biological females who work, marry, and parent as men; their social status is "female men" (Amadiume 1987; Blackwood 1984). They do not have to behave or dress as men to have the social responsibilities and prerogatives of husbands and fathers; what makes them men is enough wealth to buy a wife.

Modern Western societies' *transsexuals* and *transvestites* are the nearest equivalent of these crossover genders, but they are not institutionalized as third genders (Bolin 1987). Transsexuals are biological males and females who have sex-change operations to alter their genitalia. They do so in order to bring their physical anatomy in congruence with the way they want to live and with their own sense of gender identity. They do not become a third gender; they change genders. Transvestites are males who live as women and females who live as men but do not intend to have sex-change surgery. Their dress, appearance, and mannerisms fall within the range of what is expected from members of the opposite gender, so that they "pass." They also change genders, sometimes temporarily, some for most of their lives. Transvestite women have fought in wars as men soldiers as recently as the nineteenth century; some married women, and others went back to being women and married men once the war was over.[5] Some were discovered when their wounds were treated; others not until they died. In order to work as a jazz musician, a man's occupation, Billy Tipton, a woman, lived most of her life as a man. She died recently at seventy-four, leaving a wife and three adopted sons for whom she was husband and father, and musicians with whom she had played and traveled, for whom she was "one of the boys" (*New York Times* 1989).[6] There have been many other such occurrences of women passing as men to do more prestigious or lucrative men's work (Matthaei 1982, 192–93).[7]

Genders, therefore, are not attached to a biological substratum. Gender boundaries are breachable, and individual and socially organized shifts from one gender to another call attention to "cultural, social, or aesthetic dissonances" (Garber 1992, 16). These odd or deviant or third genders show us what we ordinarily take for granted—that people have to learn to be women and men. Men who cross-dress for performances or for pleasure often learn from women's magazines how to "do" femininity convincingly (Garber 1992, 41–51). Because transvestism is direct evidence of how gender is constructed, Marjorie Garber claims it has "extraordinary power . . . to disrupt, expose, and challenge, putting in question the very notion of the 'original' and of stable identity" (1992, 16). . . .

For Individuals, Gender Means Sameness

Although the possible combinations of genitalia, body shapes, clothing, mannerisms, sexuality, and roles could produce infinite varieties in human beings, the social institution of gender depends on the production and maintenance of a limited number of gender statuses and of making the members of these statuses similar to each other. Individuals are born sexed but not gendered, and they have to be taught to be masculine or feminine.[8] As Simone de Beauvoir said: "One is not born, but rather becomes, a woman . . . ; it is civilization as a whole that produces this creature . . . which is described as feminine" (1952, 267). . . .

Many cultures go beyond clothing, gestures, and demeanor in gendering children. They inscribe gender directly into bodies. In traditional Chinese society, mothers once bound their daughters' feet into three-inch stumps to enhance their sexual attractiveness. Jewish fathers circumcise their infant sons to show their covenant with God. Women in African societies remove the clitoris of prepubescent girls, scrape their labia, and make the lips grow together to preserve their chastity and ensure their marriageability. In Western societies, women augment their breast size with silicone and reconstruct their faces with cosmetic surgery to conform to cultural ideals of feminine beauty. Hanna Papanek (1990) notes that these practices reinforce the sense of superiority or inferiority in the adults who carry them out as well as in the children on whom they are done: The genitals of Jewish fathers and sons are physical and psychological evidence of their common dominant religious and familial status; the genitals of African mothers and daughters are physical and psychological evidence of their joint subordination.[9]

Sandra Bem (1981, 1983) argues that because gender is a powerful "schema" that orders the cognitive world, one must wage a constant, active battle for a child not to fall into typical gendered attitudes and behavior. In 1972, *Ms. Magazine* published Lois Gould's fantasy of how to raise a child free of gender-typing. The experiment calls for hiding the child's anatomy from all eyes except the parents' and treating the child as neither a girl nor a boy. The child, called X, gets to do all the things boys *and* girls do. The experiment is so successful that all the children in X's class at school want to look and behave like X. At the end of the story, the creators of the experiment are asked what will happen when X grows up. The scientists' answer is that by then it will be quite clear what X is, implying that its hormones will kick in and it will be revealed as a female or male. That ambiguous, and somewhat contradictory, ending lets Gould off the hook; neither she nor we have any idea what someone brought up in a totally androgynous manner would be like sexually or socially as an adult. The hormonal input will not create gender or sexuality but will only establish secondary sex characteristics; breasts, beards, and menstruation alone do not produce social manhood or womanhood. Indeed, it is at puberty, when sex characteristics become evident, that most societies put pubescent children through their most important rites of passage, the rituals that officially mark them as fully gendered—that is, ready to marry and become adults.

Most parents create a gendered world for their newborn by naming, birth announcements, and dress. Children's relationships with same-gendered and different-gendered caretakers structure their self-identifications and personalities. Through cognitive development, children extract and apply to their own actions the appropriate behavior for those who belong in their own gender, as well as race, religion, ethnic group, and social class, rejecting what is not appropriate. If their social categories are highly valued, they value themselves highly; if their social categories are of low status, they lose self-esteem (Chodorow 1974). Many feminist parents who want to raise androgynous children soon lose their children to the pull of gendered norms (Gordon 1990, 87–90). My son attended a carefully nonsexist elementary school, which didn't even have girls' and boys' bathrooms. When he was seven or eight years old, I attended a class play about "squares" and "circles" and their need for each other and noticed that all the girl squares and circles wore makeup, but none of the boy squares and circles did. I asked the teacher about it after the play, and she said, "Bobby said he was not going to wear makeup, and he is a powerful child, so none of the boys would either." In a long discussion about conformity, my son confronted me with the question of who the conformists were, the boys who followed their leader or the girls who listened to the woman teacher. In actuality, they both were, because they both followed same-gender leaders and acted in gender-appropriate ways. (Actors may wear makeup, but real boys don't.)

For human beings there is no essential femaleness or maleness, femininity or masculinity, womanhood or manhood, but once gender is ascribed, the social order constructs and holds individuals to strongly gendered norms and expectations. Individuals may vary on many of the components of gender and may shift genders temporarily or permanently, but they must fit into the limited number of gender statuses their society recognizes. In the process, they re-create their society's version of women and men: "If we do gender appropriately, we simultaneously sustain, reproduce, and render legitimate the institutional arrangements. . . . If we fail to do gender appropriately, we as individuals—not the institutional arrangements—may be called to account (for our character, motives, and predispositions)" (West and Zimmerman 1987, 146).

The gendered practices of everyday life reproduce a society's view of how women and men should act. Gendered social arrangements are justified by religion and cultural productions and backed by law, but the most powerful means of sustaining the moral hegemony of the dominant gender ideology is that the process is made invisible; any possible alternatives are virtually unthinkable (Foucault 1972; Gramsci 1971).[10]

For Society, Gender Means Difference

The pervasiveness of gender as a way of structuring social life demands that gender statuses be clearly differentiated. Varied talents, sexual preferences, identities, personalities, interests, and ways of interacting fragment the individual's bodily and social experiences. Nonetheless, these are organized in Western cultures into two and only two socially and legally recognized gender statuses, "man" and "woman."[11] In the social construction of gender, it does not matter what men and women actually do; it does not even matter if they do exactly the same thing. The social institution of gender insists only that what they do is *perceived* as different.

If men and women are doing the same tasks, they are usually spatially segregated to maintain gender separation, and often the tasks are given different job titles as well, such as executive secretary and administrative assistant (Reskin 1988). If the differences between women and men begin to blur, society's "sameness taboo" goes into action (Rubin 1975, 178). At a rock and roll dance at West Point in 1976, the year women were admitted to the prestigious military academy for the first time, the school's administrators "were reportedly perturbed by the sight of mirror-image couples dancing in short hair and dress gray trousers," and a rule was established that women cadets could dance at these events only if they wore skirts (Barkalow and Raab 1990, 53).[12] Women recruits in the U.S. Marine Corps are required to wear makeup—at a minimum, lipstick and eye shadow—and they have to take classes in makeup, hair care, poise, and etiquette. This feminization is part of a deliberate policy of making them clearly distinguishable from men Marines. Christine Williams quotes a twenty-five-year-old woman drill instructor as saying, "A lot of the recruits who come here don't wear makeup; they're tomboyish or athletic. A lot of them have the preconceived idea that going into the military means they can still be a tomboy. They don't realize that you are a *Woman* Marine" (1989, 76–77).[13]

If gender differences were genetic, physiological, or hormonal, gender bending and gender ambiguity would occur only in hermaphrodites, who are born with chromosomes and genitalia that are not clearly female or male. Since gender differences are socially constructed, all men and all women can enact the behavior of the other, because they know the other's social script: "'Man' and 'woman' are at once empty and overflowing categories. Empty because they have no ultimate, transcendental meaning. Overflowing because even when they appear to be fixed, they still contain within them alternative, denied, or suppressed definitions" (Scott 1988a, 49). Nonetheless, though individuals may be able to shift gender statuses, the gender boundaries have to hold, or the whole gendered social order will come crashing down. . . .

Gender as Process, Stratification, and Structure

As a social institution, gender is a process of creating distinguishable social statuses for the assignment of rights and responsibilities. As part of a stratification system that ranks these statuses unequally, gender is a major building block in the social structures built on these unequal statuses.

As a *process*, gender creates the social differences that define "woman" and "man." In social interaction throughout their lives, individuals learn what is expected, see what is expected, act and react in expected ways, and thus simultaneously construct and maintain the gender order: "The very injunction to be a given gender takes place through discursive routes: to be a good mother, to be a heterosexually desirable object, to be a fit worker, in sum, to signify a multiplicity of guarantees in response to a variety of different demands all at once" (Butler 1990, 145). Members of a social group neither make up gender as they go along nor exactly replicate in rote fashion what was done before. In almost every encounter, human beings produce gender, behaving in the ways they learned were appropriate for their gender status, or resisting or rebelling against these norms. Resistance and rebellion have altered gender norms, but so far they have rarely eroded the statuses.

Gendered patterns of interaction acquire additional layers of gendered sexuality, parenting, and work behaviors in childhood, adolescence, and adulthood. Gendered norms and expectations are enforced through informal sanctions of gender-inappropriate behavior by peers and by formal punishment or threat of punishment by those in authority should behavior deviate too far from socially imposed standards for women and men.

Everyday gendered interactions build gender into the family, the work process, and other organizations and institutions, which in turn reinforce gender expectations for individuals.[14] Because gender is a process, there is room not only for modification and variation by individuals and small groups but also for institutionalized change (Scott 1988, 7).

As part of a *stratification* system, gender ranks men above women of the same race and class. Women and men could be different but equal. In practice, the process of creating difference depends to a great extent on differential evaluation. As Nancy Jay (1981) says: "That which is defined, separated out, isolated from all else is A and pure. Not-A is necessarily impure, a random catchall, to which nothing is external except A and the principle of order that separates it from Not-A" (45). From the individual's point of view, whichever gender is A, the other is Not-A; gender boundaries tell the individual who is like him or her, and all the rest are unlike. From society's point of view, however, one gender is usually the touchstone, the normal, the dominant, and the other is different, deviant, and subordinate. In Western society, "man" is A, "wo-man" is Not-A. (Consider what a society would be like where woman was A and man Not-A.)

The further dichotomization by race and class constructs the gradations of a heterogeneous society's stratification scheme. Thus, in the United States, white is A, African American is Not-A; middle class is A, working class is Not-A, and "African-American women occupy a position whereby the inferior half of a series of these dichotomies converge" (Collins 1990, 70). The dominant categories are the hegemonic ideals, taken so for granted as the way things should be that white is not ordinarily thought of as a race, middle class as a class, or men as a gender. The characteristics of these categories define the Other as that which lacks the valuable qualities the dominants exhibit.

Societies vary in the extent of the inequality in social status of their women and men members, but where there is inequality, the status "woman" (and its attendant behavior and role allocations) is usually held in lesser esteem than the status "man." Since gender is also intertwined with a society's other constructed statuses of differential evaluation—race, religion, occupation, class, country of origin, and so on—men and women members of the favored groups command more power, more prestige, and more property than the members of the disfavored groups. Within many social groups, however, men are advantaged over women. The more economic resources, such as education and job opportunities, are available to a group, the more they tend to be monopolized by men. In poorer groups that have few resources (such as working-class African Americans in the United States), women and men are more nearly equal, and the women may even outstrip the men in education and occupational status (Almquist 1987).

As a *structure*, gender divides work in the home and in economic production, legitimates those in authority, and organizes sexuality and emotional life (Connell 1987, 91–142). As primary parents, women significantly influence children's psychological development and emotional attachments, in the process reproducing gender. Emergent sexuality is shaped by heterosexual, homosexual, bisexual, and sadomasochistic patterns that are gendered—different for girls and boys, and for women and men—so that sexual statuses reflect gender statuses.

When gender is a major component of structured inequality, the devalued genders have less power, prestige, and economic rewards than the valued genders. In countries that discourage gender discrimination, many major roles are still gendered; women still do most of the domestic labor and child rearing, even while doing full-time paid work; women and men are segregated on the job and each does work considered "appropriate"; women's work is usually paid less than men's work. Men dominate the positions of authority and leadership in government, the military, and the law; cultural productions, religions, and sports reflect men's interests. . . .

Gender inequality—the devaluation of "women" and the social domination of "men"—has social functions and a social history. It is not the result of sex, procreation, physiology, anatomy, hormones, or genetic predispositions. It is produced and maintained by identifiable social processes and built into the general social structure and individual identities deliberately and purposefully. The social order as we know it in Western societies is organized around racial ethnic, class, and gender inequality. I contend, therefore, that the continuing purpose of gender as a modern social institution is to construct women as a group to be the subordinates of men as a group. The life of everyone placed in the status "woman" is "night to his day—that has forever been the fantasy. Black to his white. Shut out of his system's space, she is the repressed that ensures the system's functioning" (Cixous and Clément [1975] 1986, 67). . . .

There is no core or bedrock human nature below these endlessly looping processes of the social production of sex and gender, self and other identity and psyche, each of which is a "complex cultural construction" (Butler 1990, 36). *For humans, the social is the natural.* Therefore, "in its feminist senses, gender cannot mean simply the cultural appropriation of biological sexual difference. Sexual difference is itself a fundamental—an scientifically contested—construction. Both 'sex' and 'gender' are woven of multiple, asymmetrical strands of difference, charged with multifaceted dramatic narratives of domination and struggle" (Haraway 1990, 140).

Notes

1. Gender is, in Erving Goffman's words, an aspect of *Felicity's Condition*, "any arrangement which leads us to judge an individual's . . . acts not to be a manifestation of strangeness. Behind Felicity's Condition is our sense of what it is to be sane" (1983, 27). Also see Bem 1993; Frye 1983, 17-40; Goffman 1977.
2. In cases of ambiguity in countries with modern medicine, surgery is usually performed to make the genitalia more clearly male or female.
3. See Butler 1990 for an analysis of how doing gender *is* gender identity.
4. On the hijras of India, see Nanda 1990; on the xaniths of Oman, see Wikan 1982, 168–86; on the American Indian berdaches, see Williams 1986. Other societies that have similar institutionalized third-gender men are the Koniag of Alaska, the Tanala of Madagascar, the Mesakin of Nuba, and the Chukchee of Siberia (Wikan 1982, 170).
5. Durova 1989; Freeman and Bond 1992; Wheelwright 1989.
6. Gender segregation of work in popular music still has not changed very much, according to Groce and Cooper 1989, despite considerable androgyny in some very popular figures. See Garber 1992 on the androgyny. She discusses Tipton on pp. 67-70.
7. In the nineteenth century, not only did these women get men's wages, but they also "had male privileges and could do all manner of things other women could not: open a bank account, write checks, own property, go anywhere unaccompanied, vote in elections" (Faderman 1991, 44).
8. For an account of how a potential man-to-woman transsexual learned to be feminine, see Garfinkel 1967, 116–85, 285–88.
9. Paige and Paige (1981, 147–49) argue that circumcision ceremonies indicate a father's loyalty to his lineage elders—"visible public evidence that the head of a family unit of their lineage

is willing to trust others with his and his family's most valuable political asset, his son's penis" (147). On female circumcision, see El Dareer 1982; Lightfoot-Klein 1987; van der Kwaak 1992; Walker 1992. There is a form of female circumcision that removes only the prepuce of the clitoris and is similar to male circumcision, but most forms of female circumcision are far more extensive, mutilating, and spiritually and psychologically shocking than the usual form of male circumcision. However, among the Australian aborigines, boys' penises are slit and kept open, so that they urinate and bleed the way women do (Bettelheim 1962, 165–206).

10. The concepts of moral hegemony, the effects of everyday activities (praxis) on thought and personality, and the necessity of consciousness of these processes before political change can occur are all based on Marx's analysis of class relations.

11. Other societies recognize more than two categories, but usually no more than three or four (Jacobs and Roberts 1989).

12. Carol Barkalow's book has a photograph of eleven first-year West Pointers in a math class, who are dressed in regulation pants, shirts, and sweaters, with short haircuts. The caption challenges the reader to locate the only woman in the room.

13. The taboo on males and females looking alike reflects the U.S. military's homophobia (Bérubé 1989). If you can't tell those with a penis from those with a vagina, how are you going to determine whether their sexual interest is heterosexual or homosexual unless you watch them having sexual relations?

14. On the "logic of practice," or how the experience of gender is embedded in the norms of everyday interaction and the structure of formal organizations, see Acker 1990; Connell 1987; Smith 1987.

References

Acker, Joan. 1990. "Hierarchies, Jobs, and Bodies: A Theory of Gendered Organizations." *Gender and Society* 4, 139–58.

Almquist, Elizabeth M. 1987. "Labor Market Gendered Inequality in Minority Groups." *Gender and Society* 1, 400–414.

Amadiume, Ifi. 1987. *Male Daughters, Female Husbands: Gender and Sex in an African Society.* London: Zed Books.

Barkalow, Carol, with Andrea Raab. 1990. *In the Men's House.* New York: Poseidon Press.

Beauvoir, Simone de. 1953. *The Second Sex,* translated by H. M. Parshley. New York: Knopf.

Bem, Sandra Lipsitz. 1981. "Gender Schema Theory: A Cognitive Account of Sex Typing." *Psychological Review* 88, 354–64.

——.1983. "Gender Schema Theory and Its Implications for Child Development: Raising Gender-Aschematic Children in a Gender-Schematic Society." *Signs: Journal of Women in Culture and Society* 8, 598–616.

——.1993. *The Lenses of Gender: Transforming the Debate on Sexual Inequality.* New Haven: Yale University Press.

Bérubé, Allan. 1989. "Marching to a Different Drummer: Gay and Lesbian GIs in World War II." In Duberman, Vicinus, and Chauncey, eds., *Hidden from History: Reclaiming the Gay and Lesbian Past.* New York: New American Library.

Bettelheim, Bruno. 1962. *Symbolic Wounds: Puberty Rites and the Envious Male.* London: Thames and Hudson.

Blackwood, Evelyn. 1984. "Sexuality and Gender in Certain Native American Tribes: The Case of Cross-Gender Females." *Signs: Journal of Women in Culture and Society* 10, 27–42.

Bolin, Anne. 1987. "Transsexualism and the Limits of Traditional Analysis." *American Behavioral Scientist* 31, 41–65.

Butler, Judith. 1990. *Gender Trouble: Feminism and the Subversion of Identity.* New York: Routledge.

Chodorow, Nancy. 1974. "Family Structure and Feminine Personality." In Rosaldo and Lamphere, eds., *Women, Culture and Society.* Stanford, Calif.: Stanford University Press.

Cixous, Hélenè, and Catherine Clément. [1975] 1986. *The Newly Born Woman,* translated by Betsy Wing. Minneapolis: University of Minnesota Press.

Collins, Patricia Hill. 1990. *Black Feminist Thought: Knowledge, Consciousness, and the Politics of Empowerment*. Boston: Unwin Hyman.

Connell, R[obert] W. 1987. *Gender and Power: Society, the Person, and Sexual Politics*. Stanford, Calif.: Stanford University Press.

Duberman, Martin Bauml, Martha Vicinus, and George Chauncey Jr., eds. 1989. *Hidden from History: Reclaiming the Gay and Lesbian Past*. New York: New American Library.

Durova, Nadezhda. 1989. *The Cavalry Maiden: Journals of a Russian Officer in the Napoleonic Wars*, translated by Mary Fleming Zirin. Bloomington: Indiana University Press.

El Dareer, Asma. 1982. *Woman, Why Do You Weep? Circumcision and Its Consequences*. London: Zed Books.

Faderman, Lillian. 1991. *Odd Girls and Twilight Lovers: A History of Lesbian Life in Twentieth-Century America*. New York: Columbia University Press.

Foucault, Michel. 1972. *The Archeology of Knowledge and the Discourse on Language*, translated by A. M. Sheridan Smith. New York: Pantheon.

Freeman, Lucy, and Alma Halbert Bond. 1992. *America's First Woman Warrior: The Courage of Deborah Sampson*. New York: Paragon.

Frye, Marilyn. 1983. *The Politics of Reality: Essays in Feminist Theory*. Trumansburg, N.Y.: Crossing Press.

Garber, Marjorie. 1992. *Vested Interests: Cross-Dressing and Cultural Anxiety*. New York and London: Routledge.

Garfinkel, Harold. 1967. *Studies in Ethnomethodology*. Englewood Cliffs, N.J.: Prentice-Hall.

Goffman, Erving. 1977. "The Arrangement between the Sexes." *Theory and Society* 4, 301–33.

1983. "Felicity's Condition." *American Journal of Sociology* 89, 1–53.

Gordon, Tuula. 1990. *Feminist Mothers*. New York: New York University Press.

Gould, Lois. 1972. "X: A Fabulous Child's Story." *Ms.*, December, 74–76, 105–106.

Gramsci, Antonio. 1971. *Selections from the Prison Notebooks*, translated and edited by Quintin Hoare and Geoffrey Nowell Smith. New York: International Publishers.

Groce, Stephen B., and Margaret Cooper. 1990. "Just Me and the Boys? Women in Local-Level Rock and Roll." *Gender and Society* 4, 220–29.

Haraway, Donna. 1990. "Investment Strategies for the Evolving Portfolio of Primate Females." In Jacobus, Keller, and Shuttleworth, eds., *Body/Politics: Women and the Discourses of Science*. New York: Routledge.

Jacobs, Sue-Ellen, and Christine Roberts. 1989. "Sex, Sexuality, Gender, and Gender Variance." In *Gender and Anthropology*, ed. Sandra Morgen. Washington, D.C.: American Anthropological Association.

Jacobus, Mary, Evelyn Fox Keller, and Sally Shuttleworth, eds. 1990. *Body/Politics: Women and the Discourses of Science*. New York and London: Routledge.

Jay, Nancy. 1981. "Gender and Dichotomy." *Feminist Studies* 7, 38–56.

Lightfoot-Klein, Hanny. 1989. *Prisoners of Ritual: An Odyssey into Female Circumcision in Africa*. New York: Harrington Park Press.

Matthaei, Julie A. 1982. *An Economic History of Women's Work in America*. New York: Schocken.

Nanda, Serena. 1990. *Neither Man nor Woman: The Hijiras of India*. Belmont, Calif.: Wadsworth.

New York Times. 1989. "Musician's Death at 74 Reveals He Was a Woman." February 2.

Paige, Karen Ericksen, and Jeffrey M. Paige. 1981. *The Politics of Reproductive Ritual*. Berkeley and Los Angeles: University of California Press.

Papanek, Hanna. 1990. "To Each Less Than She Needs, From Each More Than She Can Do: Allocations, Entitlements, and Value." In Tinker, ed., *Persistent Inequalities: Women and World Development*. New York: Oxford University Press.

Reskin, Barbara J. 1988. "Bringing the Men Back In: Sex Differentiation and the Devaluation of Women's Work." *Gender and Society* 7, 58–81.

Rosaldo, Michelle Zimbalist, and Louise Lamphere, eds. 1974. *Woman, Culture and Society*. Stanford, Calif.: Stanford University Press.

Rubin, Gayle. 1975. "The Traffic in Women: Notes on the Political Economy of Sex." In *Toward an Anthropology of Women*, edited by Rayna R[app] Reiter. New York: Monthly Review Press.

Scott, Joan Wallach. 1988 *Gender and the Politics of History*. New York: Columbia University Press.

Smith, Dorothy E. 1987. *The Everyday World as Problematic: A Feminist Sociology.* Toronto: University of Toronto Press.

Tinker, Irene, ed. 1990. *Persistent Inequalities: Women and World Development.* New York: Oxford University Press.

van der Kwaak, Anke. 1992. "Female Circumcision and Gender Identity: A Questionable Alliance?" *Social Science and Medicine* 35, 777–87.

Walker, Alice. 1992. *Possessing the Secret of Joy.* New York: Harcourt Brace Jovanovich.

West, Candace, and Don Zimmerman. 1987. "Doing Gender." *Gender and Society* 1, 125–51.

Wheelwright, Julie. 1989. *Amazons and Military Maids: Women Who Cross-Dressed in Pursuit of Life, Liberty and Happiness.* London: Pandora Press.

Wikan, Unni. 1982. *Behind the Veil in Arabia: Women in Oman.* Baltimore, Md.: Johns Hopkins University Press.

Williams, Christine L. 1989. *Gender Differences at Work: Women and Men in Nontraditional Occupations.* Berkeley: University of California Press.

Williams, Walter L. 1986. *The Spirit and the Flesh: Sexual Diversity in American Indian Culture.* Boston: Beacon Press.

33

Masculinity as Homophobia: Fear, Shame, and Silence in the Construction of Gender Identity

Michael S. Kimmel

We think of manhood as eternal, a timeless essence that resides deep in the heart of every man. We think of manhood as a thing, a quality that one either has or doesn't have. We think of manhood as innate, residing in the particular biological composition of the human male, the result of androgens or the possession of a penis. We think of manhood as a transcendent tangible property that each man must manifest in the world; the reward presented with great ceremony to a young novice by his elder for having successfully completed an arduous initiation ritual. In the words of poet Robert Bly (1990), "the structure at the bottom of the male psyche is still as firm as it was twenty thousand years ago" (230). . . .

This idea that manhood is socially constructed and historically shifting should not be understood as a loss, that something is being taken away from men. In fact, it gives us something extraordinarily valuable—agency, the capacity to act. It gives us a sense of historical possibilities to replace the despondent resignation that invariably attends timeless, ahistorical essentialisms. Our behaviors are not simply "just human nature," because "boys will be boys." From the materials we find around us in our culture—other people, ideas, objects—we actively create our worlds, our identities. Men, both individually and collectively, can change. . . .

Masculinity as a Homosocial Enactment

Other men: We are under the constant careful scrutiny of other men. Other men watch us, rank us, grant our acceptance into the realm of manhood. Manhood is demonstrated for other men's approval. It is other men who evaluate the performance. Literary critic David Leverenz (1991) argues that "ideologies of manhood have functioned primarily in relation to the gaze of male peers and male authority" (769). Think of how men boast to one another of their accomplishments—from their latest sexual conquest to the size of the fish they caught—and how we constantly parade the markers of manhood—wealth, power, status, sexy women—in front of other men, desperate for their approval.

That men prove their manhood in the eyes of other men is both a consequence of sexism and one of its chief props. "Women have, in men's minds, such a low place on the social ladder of this country that it's useless to define yourself in terms of a woman," noted playwright David Mamet.

"What men need is men's approval." Women become a kind of currency that men use to improve their ranking on the masculine social scale. (Even those moments of heroic conquest of women carry, I believe, a current of homosocial evaluation.) Masculinity is a *homosocial* enactment. We test ourselves, perform heroic feats, take enormous risks, all because we want other men to grant us our manhood.

Masculinity as a homosocial enactment is fraught with danger, with the risk of failure, and with intense relentless competition. "Every man you meet has a rating or an estimate of himself which he never loses or forgets," wrote Kenneth Wayne (1912) in his popular turn-of-the-century advice book. "A man has his own rating, and instantly he lays it alongside of the other man" (18). Almost a century later, another man remarked to psychologist Sam Osherson (1992) that "[b]y the time you're an adult, it's easy to think you're always in competition with men, for the attention of women, in sports, at work" (291). . . .

Homophobia is a central organizing principle of our cultural definition of manhood. Homophobia is more than the irrational fear of gay men, more than the fear that we might be perceived as gay. "The word 'faggot' has nothing to do with homosexual experience or even with fears of homosexuals," writes David Leverenz. "It comes out of the depths of manhood: a label of ultimate contempt for anyone who seems sissy, untough, uncool" (1986, 455). Homophobia is the fear that other men will unmask us, emasculate us, reveal to us and the world that we do not measure up, that we are not real men. We are afraid to let other men see that fear. Fear makes us ashamed, because the recognition of fear in ourselves is proof to ourselves that we are not as manly as we pretend, that we are, like the young man in a poem by Yeats, "one that ruffles in a manly pose for all his timid heart." Our fear is the fear of humiliation. We are ashamed to be afraid.

Shame leads to silence—the silence that keeps other people believing that we actually approve of the things that are done to women, to minorities, to gays and lesbians in our culture. The frightened silence as we scurry past a woman being hassled by men on the street. That furtive silence when men make sexist or racist jokes in a bar. That clammy-handed silence when guys in the office make gay-bashing jokes. Our fears are the sources of our silences, and men's silence is what keeps the system running. This might help to explain why women often complain that their male friends or partners are often so understanding when they are alone and yet laugh at sexist jokes or even make those jokes themselves when they are out with a group.

The fear of being seen as a sissy dominates the cultural definitions of manhood. It starts so early. "Boys among boys are ashamed to be unmanly," wrote one educator in 1871 (cited in Rotundo 1993, 264). I have a standing bet with a friend that I can walk onto any playground in America where 6-year-old boys are happily playing and by asking one question, I can provoke a fight. That question is simple: "Who's a sissy around here?" Once posed, the challenge is made. One of two things is likely to happen. One boy will accuse another of being a sissy, to which that boy will respond that he is not a sissy, that the first boy is. They may have to fight it out to see who's lying. Or a whole group of boys will surround one boy and all shout, "He is! He is!" That boy will either burst into tears and run home crying, disgraced, or he will have to take on several boys at once, to prove that he's not a sissy. (And what will his father or older brothers tell him if he chooses to run home crying?) It will be some time before he regains any sense of self-respect.

Violence is often the single most evident marker of manhood. Rather it is the willingness to fight, the desire to fight. The origin of our expression that one "has a chip on one's shoulder" lies in the practice of an adolescent boy in the country or small town at the turn of the century, who would literally walk around with a chip of wood balanced on his shoulder—a signal of his readiness to fight with anyone who would take the initiative of knocking the chip off (see Gorer 1964, 38; Mead 1965).

As adolescents, we learn that our peers are a kind of gender police, constantly threatening to unmask us as feminine, as sissies. One of the favorite tricks when I was an adolescent was to ask a boy to look at his fingernails. If he held his palm toward his face and curled his fingers back to see them, he passed the test. He'd looked at his nails "like a man." But if he held the back of his hand away from his face, and looked at his fingernails with arm outstretched, he was immediately ridiculed as a sissy.

As young men we are constantly riding those gender boundaries, checking the fences we have constructed on the perimeter, making sure that nothing even remotely feminine might show through. The possibilities of being unmasked are everywhere. Even the most seemingly insignificant thing can pose a threat or activate that haunting terror. On the day the students in my course "Sociology of Men and Masculinities" were scheduled to discuss homophobia and male-male friendships, one student provided a touching illustration. Noting that it was a beautiful day, the first day of spring after a brutal northeast winter, he decided to wear shorts to class. "I had this really nice pair of new Madras shorts," he commented. "But then I thought to myself, these shorts have lavender and pink in them. Today's class topic is homophobia. Maybe today is not the best day to wear these shorts."

Our efforts to maintain a manly front cover everything we do. What we wear. How we talk. How we walk. What we eat. Every mannerism, every movement contains a coded gender language. Think, for example, of how you would answer the question: How do you "know" if a man is homosexual? When I ask this question in classes or workshops, respondents invariably provide a pretty standard list of stereotypically effeminate behaviors. He walks a certain way, talks a certain way, acts a certain way. He's very emotional; he shows his feelings. One woman commented that she "knows" a man is gay if he really cares about her; another said she knows he's gay if he shows no interest in her, if he leaves her alone.

Now alter the question and imagine what heterosexual men do to make sure no one could possibly get the "wrong idea" about them. Responses typically refer to the original stereotypes, this time as a set of negative rules about behavior. Never dress that way. Never talk or walk that way. Never show your feelings or get emotional. Always be prepared to demonstrate sexual interest in women that you meet, so it is impossible for any woman to get the wrong idea about you. In this sense, homophobia, the fear of being perceived as gay, as not a real man, keeps men exaggerating all the traditional rules of masculinity, including sexual predation with women. Homophobia and sexism go hand in hand.

The stakes of perceived sissydom are enormous—sometimes matters of life and death. We take enormous risks to prove our manhood, exposing ourselves disproportionately to health risks, workplace hazards, and stress-related illnesses. Men commit suicide three times as often as women. . . . In one survey, women and men were asked what they were most afraid of. Women responded that they were most afraid of being raped and murdered. Men responded that they were most afraid of being laughed at (Noble 1992, 105–6).

Homophobia as a Cause of Sexism, Heterosexism, and Racism

Homophobia is intimately interwoven with both sexism and racism. The fear—sometimes conscious, sometimes not—that others might perceive us as homosexual propels men to enact all manner of exaggerated masculine behaviors and attitudes to make sure that no one could possibly get the wrong idea about us. One of the centerpieces of that exaggerated masculinity is putting women down, both by excluding them from the public sphere and by the quotidian put-downs in speech and behaviors that organize the daily life of the American man. Women and gay men become the "other" against which heterosexual men project their identities, against whom they stack the decks so as to compete in a situation in which they will always win, so that by suppressing them, men can stake a claim for their own manhood. Women threaten emasculation by representing the home, workplace, and familial responsibility, the negation of fun. Gay men have historically played the role of the consummate sissy in the American popular mind because homosexuality is seen as an inversion of normal gender development. There have been other "others." Through American history, various groups have represented the sissy, the non-men against whom American men played out their definitions of manhood, often with vicious results. In fact, these changing groups provide an interesting lesson in American historical development.

At the turn of the 19th century, it was Europeans and children who provided the contrast for American men. The "true American was vigorous, manly, and direct, not effete and corrupt like the supposed Europeans," writes Rupert Wilkinson (1986). "He was plain rather than ornamented, rugged rather than luxury seeking, a liberty loving common man or natural gentleman rather than an aristocratic oppressor or servile minion" (96). The "real man" of the early nineteenth century was neither noble nor serf. By the middle of the century, black slaves had replaced the effete nobleman. Slaves were seen as dependent, helpless men, incapable of defending their women and children, and therefore less than manly. Native Americans were cast as foolish and naive children, so they could be infantilized as the "Red Children of the Great White Father" and therefore excluded from full manhood.

By the end of the century, new European immigrants were also added to the list of the unreal men, especially the Irish and Italians, who were seen as too passionate and emotionally volatile to remain controlled sturdy oaks, and Jews, who were seen as too bookishly effete and too physically puny to truly measure up. In the mid-twentieth century, it was also Asians—first the Japanese during the Second World War, and more recently, the Vietnamese during the Vietnam War—who have served as unmanly templates against which American men have hurled their gendered rage. Asian men were seen as small, soft, and effeminate—hardly men at all.

Such a list of "hyphenated" Americans—Italian-, Jewish-, Irish-, African-, Native-, Asian-, gay—composes the majority of American men. So manhood is only possible for a distinct minority, and the definition has been constructed to prevent the others from achieving it. Interestingly, this emasculation of one's enemies has a flip side—and one that is equally gendered. These very groups that have historically been cast as less than manly were also, often simultaneously, cast as hypermasculine, as sexually aggressive, violent rapacious beasts, against whom "civilized" men must take a decisive stand and thereby rescue civilization. Thus black men were depicted as rampaging sexual beasts, women as carnivorously carnal, gay men as sexually insatiable, southern European men as sexually predatory and voracious, and Asian men as vicious and cruel torturers who were immorally disinterested in life itself, willing to sacrifice their entire people for their whims. But whether one saw these groups as effeminate sissies or as brutal uncivilized savages, the terms with which they were perceived were gendered. These groups become the "others," the screens against which traditional conceptions of manhood were developed.

Being seen as unmanly is a fear that propels American men to deny manhood to others, as a way of proving the unprovable—that one is fully manly. Masculinity becomes a defense against the perceived threat of humiliation in the eyes of other men, enacted through a "sequence of postures"—things we might say, or do, or even think, that, if we thought carefully about them, would make us ashamed of ourselves (Savran 1992, 16). After all, how many of us have made homophobic or sexist remarks, or told racist jokes, or made lewd comments to women on the street? How many of us have translated those ideas and those words into actions, by physically attacking gay men, or forcing or cajoling a woman to have sex even though she didn't really want to because it was important to score?

Power and Powerlessness in the Lives of Men

I have argued that homophobia, men's fear of other men, is the animating condition of the dominant definition of masculinity in America, that the reigning definition of masculinity is a defensive effort to prevent being emasculated. In our efforts to suppress or overcome those fears, the dominant culture exacts a tremendous price from those deemed less than fully manly: women, gay men, nonnative-born men, men of color. This perspective may help clarify a paradox in men's lives, a paradox in which men have virtually all the power and yet do not feel powerful (see Kaufman 1993).

Manhood is equated with power—over women, over other men. Everywhere we look, we see the institutional expression of that power—in state and national legislatures, on the boards of directors of every major U.S. corporation or law firm, and in every school and hospital administration. Women have long understood this, and feminist women have spent the past three decades challenging both the public and the private expressions of men's power and acknowledging their fear of men. Feminism as a set of theories both explains women's fear of men and empowers women to confront it both publicly and privately. Feminist women have theorized that masculinity is about the drive for domination, the drive for power, for conquest.

This feminist definition of masculinity as the drive for power is theorized from women's point of view. It is how women experience masculinity. But it assumes a symmetry between the public and the private that does not conform to men's experiences. Feminists observe that women, as a group, do not hold power in our society. They also observe that individually, they, as women, do not feel powerful. They feel afraid, vulnerable. Their observation of the social reality and their individual experiences are therefore symmetrical. Feminism also observes that men, as a group, are in power. Thus, with the same symmetry, feminism has tended to assume that individually men must feel powerful.

This is why the feminist critique of masculinity often falls on deaf ears with men. When confronted with the analysis that men have all the power, many men react incredulously. "What do you mean, men have all the power?" they ask. "What are you talking about? My wife bosses me around. My kids boss me around. My boss bosses me around. I have no power at all! I'm completely powerless!"

Men's feelings are not the feelings of the powerful, but of those who see themselves as powerless. These are the feelings that come inevitably from the discontinuity between the social and the psychological, between the aggregate analysis that reveals how men are in power as a group and the pyschological fact that they do not feel powerful as individuals. They are the feelings of men who were raised to believe themselves entitled to feel that power, but do not feel it. No wonder many men are frustrated and angry. This may explain the recent popularity of those workshops and retreats designed to help men to claim their "inner" power, their "deep manhood," or their "warrior within." . . .

The dimension of power is now reinserted into men's experience not only as the product of individual experience but also as the product of relations with other men. In this sense, men's experience of powerlessness is *real*—the men actually feel it and certainly act on it—but it is not *true*, that is, it does not accurately describe their condition. In contrast to women's lives, men's lives are structured around relationships of power and men's differential access to power, as well as the differential access to that power of men as a group. Our imperfect analysis of our own situation leads us to believe that we men need more power, rather than leading us to support feminists' efforts to rearrange power relationships along more equitable lines.

Philosopher Hannah Arendt (1970) fully understood this contradictory experience of social and individual power:

> Power corresponds to the human ability not just to act but to act in concert. Power is never the property of an individual; it belongs to a group and remains in existence only so long as the group keeps together. When we say of somebody that he is "in power" we actually refer to his being empowered by a certain number of people to act in their name. The moment the group, from which the power originated to begin with . . . disappears, "his power" also vanishes. (44)

Why, then, do American men feel so powerless? Part of the answer is because we've constructed the rules of manhood so that only the tiniest fraction of men come to believe that they are the biggest of wheels, the sturdiest of oaks, the most virulent repudiators of femininity, the most daring and aggressive. We've managed to disempower the overwhelming majority of American men by other means—such as discriminating on the basis of race, class, ethnicity, age, or sexual preference.

Masculinist retreats to retrieve deep, wounded, masculinity are but one of the ways in which American men currently struggle with their fears and their shame. Unfortunately, at the very moment that they work to break down the isolation that governs men's lives, as they enable men to express those fears and that shame, they ignore the social power that men continue to exert over women and the privileges from which they (as the middle-aged, middle-class white men who largely make up these retreats) continue to benefit—regardless of their experiences as wounded victims of oppressive male socialization.

Others still rehearse the politics of exclusion, as if by clearing away the playing field of secure gender identity of any that we deem less than manly—women, gay men, nonnative-born men, men of color—middle-class, straight, white men can reground their sense of themselves without those haunting fears and that deep shame that they are unmanly and will be exposed by other men. This is the manhood of racism, of sexism, of homophobia. It is the manhood that is so chronically insecure that it trembles at the idea of lifting the ban on gays in the military, that is so threatened by women in the workplace that women become the targets of sexual harassment, that is so deeply frightened of equality that it must ensure that the playing field of male competition remains stacked against all newcomers to the game.

Exclusion and escape have been the dominant methods American men have used to keep their fears of humiliation at bay. The fear of emasculation by other men, of being humiliated, of being seen as a sissy, is the leitmotif in my reading of the history of American manhood. Masculinity has become a relentless test by which we prove to other men, to women, and ultimately to ourselves, that we have successfully mastered the part. The restlessness that men feel today is nothing new in American history; we have been anxious and restless for almost two centuries. Neither exclusion nor escape has ever brought us the relief we've sought, and there is no reason to think that either will solve our problems now. Peace of mind, relief from gender struggle, will come only from a politics of inclusion, not exclusion, from standing up for equality and justice, and not by running away.

References

Arendt, H. (1970). *On Revolution.* New York:Viking.

Bly, R. (1990). *Iron John: A Book about Men.* Reading, Mass.: Addison-Wesley.

Gorer, G. (1964). *The American People: A Study in National Character.* New York: Norton.

Kaufman, M. (1993). *Cracking the Armour: Power and Pain in the Lives of Men.* Toronto: Viking Canada.

Leverenz, D. (1986). "Manhood, Humiliation and Public Life: Some Stories." *Southwest Review* 71, Fall.

Leverenz, D. (1991). "The Last Real Man in America: From Natty Bumppo to Batman." *American Literary Review* 3.

Mead, M. (1965). *And Keep Your Powder Dry.* New York: William Morrow.

Noble, V. (1992). "A Helping Hand from the Guys." In K. L. Hagan, ed., *Women Respond to the Men's Movement.* San Francisco: HarperCollins.

Osherson, S. (1992). *Wrestling with Love: How Men Struggle with Intimacy, with Women, Children, Parents, and Each Other.* New York: Fawcett.

Rotundo, E. A. (1993). *American Manhood: Transformations in Masculinity from the Revolution to the Modern Era.* New York: Basic Books.

Savran, D. (1992). *Communists, Cowboys and Queers: The Politics of Masculinity in the Work of Arthur Miller and Tennessee Williams.* Minneapolis: University of Minnesota Press.

Wayne, K. (1912). *Building the Young Man.* Chicago: A. C. McClurg.

Wilkinson, R. (1986). *American Tough: The Tough-Guy Tradition and American Character.* New York: Harper and Row.

34

Which Outlaws? Or, "Who Was That Masked Man?"

Kate Bornstein

On the day of my birth, my grandparents gave me a television set. In 1948, this was a new and wonderful thing. It had a nine-inch screen embedded in a cherrywood case the size of my mother's large oven.

My parents gave over an entire room to the television set. It was "the television room."

I've tried to figure out which questions get to the core of transgender issues—the answer to the riddle of my oddly-gendered life would probably be found in the area we question the least, and there are many areas of gender we do not question. We talk casually, for example, about *trans*-gender without ever clearly stating, and rarely if ever asking, what one gender or the other really is. We're so sure of our ability to categorize people as either men or women that we neglect to ask ourselves some very basic questions: What is a man? What is a woman? And why do we need to be one or the other?

If we ask by what criteria a person might classify someone as being either male or female, the answers appear to be so self-evident as to make the question trivial. But consider a list of items that differentiate females from males. There are none that always and without exception are true of only one gender.
—Kessler and McKenna, *Gender: An Ethnomethodological Approach, 1976*

Touching All the Basis

Most folks would define a man by the presence of a penis or some form of a penis. Some would define a woman by the presence of a vagina or some form of a vagina. It's not that simple, though. I know several women in San Francisco who have penises. Many wonderful men in my life have vaginas. And there are quite a few people whose genitals fall somewhere between penises and vaginas. What are *they*?

Are you a man because you have an *XY* chromosome? A woman because you have *XX*? Unless you're an athlete who's been challenged in the area of gender representation, you probably haven't had a chromosome test to determine your gender. If you haven't had that test, then how do you know what gender you are, and how do you know what gender your romantic or sexual partner is? There are, in addition to the *XX* and *XY* pairs, some other commonly occurring sets of gender chromosomes, including *XXY*, *XXX*, *YYY*, *XYY*, and *XO*. Does this mean there are more than two genders?

Let's keep looking. What makes a man—testosterone? What makes a woman—estrogen? If so, you could buy your gender over the counter at any pharmacy. But we're taught that there are these things called "male" and "female" hormones; and that testosterone dominates the gender hormone balance in the males of any species. Not really—female hyenas, for example, have naturally more testosterone than the males; the female clitoris resembles a very long penis—the females mount the males from the rear, and proceed to hump. While some female humans I know behave in much the same manner as the female hyena, the example demonstrates that the universal key to gender is not hormones.

Are you a woman because you can bear children? Because you bleed every month? Many women are born without this potential, and every woman ceases to possess that capability after menopause—do these women cease being women? Does a necessary hysterectomy equal a gender change?

Are you a man because you can father children? What if your sperm count is too low? What if you were exposed to nuclear radiation and were rendered sterile? Are you then a woman?

Are you a woman because your birth certificate says female? A man because your birth certificate says male? If so, how did *that* happen? A doctor looked down at your crotch at birth. A doctor decided, based on what was showing of your external genitals, that you would be one gender or another. You never had a say in that most irreversible of all pronouncements—and according to this culture as it stands today, you never *will* have a say. What if you had been born a hermaphrodite, with some combination of both genitals? A surgeon would have "fixed" you—without your consent, and possibly without the consent or even knowledge of your parents, depending on your race and economic status. You would have been fixed—fixed into a gender. It's a fairly common experience being born with different or anomalous genitals, but we don't allow hermaphrodites in modern Western medicine. We "fix" them.

But let's get back to that birth certificate. Are you female or male because of what the law says? Is law immutable? Aren't we legislating every day in order to change the laws of our state, our nation, our culture? Isn't that the name of the game when it comes to political progress? What about other laws—religious laws, for example? Religions may dictate right and proper behavior for men and women, but no religion actually lays out what is a man and what is a woman. They assume we know, that's how deep this cultural assumption runs.

I've been searching all my life for a rock-bottom definition of woman, an unquestionable sense of what is a man. I've found nothing except the fickle definitions of gender held up by groups and individuals for their own purposes.

> Every day I watched it, that television told me what was a man and what was a woman.
>
> And every day I watched it, that television told me what to buy in order to be a woman.
>
> And everything I bought, I said to myself I am a real woman, and I never once admitted that I was transsexual. You could say I'm one inevitability of a post-modern anti-spiritualist acquisitive culture.

A Question of Priorities

I haven't found any answers. I ask every day of my life what is a man and what is a woman, and those questions beg the next: why? Why do we have to be one or the other? Why do we have to be gendered creatures at all? What keeps the bi-polar gender system in place?

I started out thinking that a theory of gender would bridge the longstanding gap between the two major genders, male and female. I'm no longer trying to do that. Some people think I want a world without gender, something bland and colorless: that's so far from how I live! I love playing with genders, and I love watching other people play with all the shades and flavors that gender can come in. I just want to question what we've been holding on to for such an awfully long time. I want to question the existence of gender, and I want to enter that question firmly into the fabric of this culture.

> I used to watch **The Lone Ranger** on television. I loved that show. This masked guy rides into town on a white horse, does all these great and heroic deeds, everyone falls in love with him and then he leaves. He never takes off his mask, no one ever sees his face. He leaves behind a silver bullet and the memory of someone who can do no wrong. No bad rumors, no feet of clay, no cellulite. What a life! There's a self-help book in there somewhere: **Who Was That Masked Man? Learning to Overcome the Lone Ranger Syndrome.**

As I moved through the '50s and '60s, I bought into the fear and hatred that marks this culture's attitude toward the genderless and the nontraditionally gendered. People are genuinely afraid of being without a gender. I've been chewing on that fear nearly all my life like it was some old bone, and now I want to take that fear apart to see what makes it tick. Nothing in the culture has encouraged me to stay and confront that fear. Instead, the culture has kept pointing me toward one door or the other:

Girls or Boys
Men or Women
Ladies or Gentlemen
Cats or Chicks
Faggots or Dykes

I knew from age four on, that something was wrong with me being a guy, and I spent most of my life avoiding the issue of my transsexuality. I hid out in textbooks, pulp fiction, and drugs and alcohol. I numbed my mind with everything from peyote to Scientology. I buried my head in the sands of television, college, a lot of lovers, and three marriages. Because I was being raised as a male, I never got to experience what it meant to be raised female in this culture. All I had were my observations, and all I could observe and assimilate as a child were differences in clothing and manners. I remember building a catalogue of gestures, phrases, body language, and outfits in my head. I would practice all of these at night when my parents had gone to sleep. I'd wear a blanket as a dress, and I'd stand in front of my mirror being my latest crush at school—I was so ashamed of myself for that.

> I was obsessed, and like most obsessed people, I was
> the last one to know it. The culture itself is obsessed
> with gender—and true to form, the culture as a
> whole will be the last to find out how obsessed it
> really has been.

Why We Haven't Asked Questions

I know there must have been other kids—boys and girls—going through the same remorse-filled hell that held me prisoner in front of my bedroom mirror, but we had no way of knowing that: there was no language for what we were doing. Instead, cardboard cut-out versions of us were creeping into the arts and media: in poetry, drama, dance, music, sculpture, paintings, television, cinema—in just about any art form you can think of there have been portrayals of people who are ambiguously or differently-gendered, all drawn by people who were not us, all spoken in voices that were not ours.

> Dominant cultures tend to colonize and control
> minorities through stereotyping—it's no different
> with the transgender minority. Make us a joke and
> there's no risk of our anger, no fear we'll raise some
> unified voice in protest, because we're not organ-
> ized. But that's changing.

We never did fit into the cultural binary of male/female, man/woman, boy/girl. No, we are the clowns, the sex objects, or the mysteriously unattainable in any number of novels. We are the psychotics, the murderers, or the criminal geniuses who populate the movies. Audiences have rarely seen the real faces of the transgendered. They don't hear our voices, rarely read our words. For too many years, we transgendered people have been playing a hiding game, appearing in town one day, wearing a mask, and leaving when discovery was imminent. We would never tell anyone who we were, and so we were never really able to find one another. That's just now beginning to change.

> See, when we walk into a restaurant and we see
> another transsexual person, we look the other way,
> we pretend we don't exist. There's no sly smile, no
> secret wink, signal, or handshake. Not yet. We still
> quake in solitude at the prospect of recognition,
> even if that solitude is in the company of our own
> kind.

Silence=Death
> —ACT UP slogan

Silence of the Meek-as-Lambs

Simply saying "Come out, come out, wherever you are," is not going to bring the multitudes of transgendered people out into the open. Before saying that coming out is an option (and I believe it's an inevitable step, one we're all going to have to take at some time), it's necessary to get transgendered people talking with one another. The first step in coming out in the world is to come out to our own kind.

Before I dealt with my gender change, I had gold card membership in the dominant culture. To all appearances, I was a straight, white, able-bodied, middle-class male. I fought so hard against being transsexual because I heard all the teasing and jokes in the locker rooms. I saw people shudder or giggle when they'd talk about Renee Richards or Christine Jorgensen. I was all too aware of the disgust people were going through when *Playboy* published its interview with Wendy Carlos. I watched Caroline Cossey (Tula) get dragged through the mud of the press on two continents. The lesson was there time after time. Of course we were silent.

In the summer of 1969, I drove across Canada and the United States, living out of my Volkswagen station wagon that I'd named Mad John after my acting teacher. I was a hippie boy, hair down past my shoulders and dressed very colorfully: beads, headband, bellbottoms. I pulled into a state park in South Dakota to camp for the night. Some good ol' boys came up to my campsite and began the usual "Hey, girl" comments. I ignored them, and they eventually went away. Later that night, I woke up in my sleeping bag with a hand on my chest and a knife in front of my face. "Maybe we wanna fuck you, girl," is what this guy said. He brought the knife down to my face—I could feel how cold and sharp it was. "Maybe you oughta get outa here before we fuck you and beat the shit outa you." Then I was alone in the dark with only the sound of the wind in the trees. I packed up camp and left.

The following summer, I traveled across country again, this time in a VW mini-bus, but I stuck to more populated areas: I'd learned. Too many transgendered people don't get off that easy.

What a Tangled Web We Weave ...

A less visible reason for the silence of the transgendered hinges on the fact that transsexuality in this culture is considered an illness, and an illness that can only be cured by silence.

Here's how this one works: we're taught that we are literally sick, that we have an illness that can be diagnosed and maybe cured. As a result of the medicalization of our condition, transsexuals must see therapists in order to receive the medical seal of approval required to proceed with any gender reassignment surgery. Now, once we get to the doctor, we're told we'll be cured if we become members of one gender or another. We're told not to divulge our transsexual status, except in select cases requiring intimacy. Isn't that amazing? Transsexuals presenting themselves for therapy in this culture are channeled through a system which labels them as having a disease (transsexuality) for which the therapy is to lie, hide, or otherwise remain silent.

> I was told by several counselors and a number of
> transgendered peers that I would need to invent a
> past for myself as a little girl, that I'd have to make
> up incidents of my girl childhood; that I'd have to
> say things like "When I was a little girl ... " I never
> was a little girl; I'd lied all my life trying to be the
> boy, the man that I'd known myself **not** to be. Here I
> was, taking a giant step toward personal integrity by
> entering therapy with the truth and self-acknowl-
> edgment that I was a transsexual, and I was told,
> "Don't **tell** anyone you're transsexual."

Transsexuality is the only condition for which the therapy is to lie. This therapeutic lie
is one reason we haven't been saying too much about ourselves and our lives and
our experience of gender; we're not allowed, in therapy, the right to think of ourselves
as transsexual.

This was where a different kind of therapy might
have helped me. Perhaps if I hadn't spent so much
time thinking and talking about being a woman,
and perhaps if the psychiatrist who examined me
had spent less time focusing on those aspects of my
life which could never be changed by surgery, I
would have had more opportunity to think about
myself as a transsexual. It was exposure to the press
that forced me to talk about my transsexuality, and
it was a painful way to have to learn to do so.
—Caroline Cossey, *My Story, 1992*

Another reason for the silence of transsexuals is the mythology of the transgender subculture. Two or more transsexuals together, goes the myth, can be read more easily *as*
transsexual—so they don't pass. I don't think that's it.

> I think transsexuals keep away from each other
> because we threaten the hell out of one another.

Each of us, transsexual and non–transsexual, develop a view of the world as we grow
up—a view that validates our existence, gives us a reason for being, a justification for the
nuttinesses that each of us might have. Most non-transsexuals have cultural norms on
which to pin their world view, broadcast by magazines, television, cinema, electronic bulletin boards, and the continually growing list of communications environments.

Since transsexuals in this culture are neither fairly nor accurately represented in
the media, nor championed by a community, we develop our world views in solitude.
Alone, we figure out why we're in the world the way we are. The literature to date on
the transgender experience does not help us to establish a truly transgender world view
in concert with other transgender people, because virtually all the books and theories
about gender and transsexuality to date have been written by non-transsexuals who,
no matter how well-intentioned, are each trying to figure out how to make us fit
into *their* world view. Transgendered people learn to explain gender to themselves from a
very early age.

> When I was ten or eleven years old, I used to play alone in the basement, way back in the corner where no one would come along to disturb me. There was an old chair there to which I attached all manner of wires and boxes and dials: it was my gen-der-change machine. I would sit in that chair and twist the dials, and—presto—I was off on an adventure in my mind as a little girl, usually some budding dykelet like Nancy Drew or Pippi Longstocking.

Most transsexuals opt for the theory that there are men and women and no in-between ground: the agreed-upon gender system. That's what I did—I just knew I had to be one or the other—so, in my world view, I saw myself as a mistake: some*thing* that needed to be fixed and then placed neatly into one of the categories.

> There are some wonderfully subtle differences in the world views developed by individual transsexuals. Talk to a few transgendered people and see how beautifully textured the normally drab concept of gender can become.

We bring our very personal explanations for our existence into contact with other trans-sexuals who have been spending *their* lives constructing their *own* reasons for existence. If, when we meet, our world views differ radically enough, we wind up threatening each other's basic understanding of the world—we threaten each other. So we'd rather not meet, we'd rather not talk. At this writing, that's starting to change. Transsexuals and other transgendered people are finally sitting down, taking stock, comparing notes—and it's the dominant culture that's coming up short. Some of us are beginning to actually like ourselves and each other for the blend we are. Many of us are beginning to express our discontent with a culture that wants us silent.

> This Western culture of ours tends to sacrifice the full range of experience to a lower common denominator that's acceptable to more people; we end up with McDonald's instead of real food, Holiday Inns instead of homes, and **USA Today** instead of news and cultur-al analysis. And we do that with the rest of our lives.
> Our spirits are full of possibilities, yet we tie our-selves down to socially-prescribed names and cate-gories so we're acceptable to more people. We take on identities that no one has to think about, and that's probably how we become and why we remain men and women.

The first step in liberating ourselves from this meek-as-lambs culturally-imposed silence is for transgendered people to begin talking with each other, asking each other sincere questions, and listening intently.

Myths And Myth-Conceptions

A transgender subculture is at this writing developing, and it's subsequently giving rise to new folk tales and traditions of gender fluidity and ambiguity. . . .

>> *We are normal men and women.*

> Is there such a thing as a normal man or woman? I have this idea that there are only people who are fluidly-gendered, and that the norm is that most of these people continually struggle to maintain the illusion that they are one gender or another. So if someone goes through a gender change and then struggles to maintain a (new) rigid gender, I guess that does make them normal. That's the only way I can see the grounding to this myth.

>> *We are better men or women than men born men or women born women, because we had to work at it.*

> I don't know about this one—I think everyone has to work at being a man or a woman. Transgendered people are probably more aware of doing the work, that's all. The concept of some nebulously "better" class of people is not an idea of love and inclusion, but an idea of oppression.

>> *We have an incurable disease.*

> No, we don't.

>> *We are trapped in the wrong body.*

> I understand that many people may explain their pre-operative transgendered lives in this way, but I'll bet that it's more likely an unfortunate metaphor that conveniently conforms to cultural expectations, rather than an honest reflection of our transgendered feelings. As a people, we're short on metaphors, any metaphors, and when we find one that people understand, we stop looking. It's time for transgendered people to look for new metaphors—new ways of communicating our lives to people who are traditionally gendered....

>> *There is a transgender community.*

*Someone asked me if the transgendered community is like the lesbian/gay communities. I said no, because the lesbian/gay communities are based on who one relates to, whereas the transgendered experience is different: it's about identity—relating to oneself. It's more an inward thing. When you have people together with **those** issues, the group dynamic is inherently very different.*
> —David Harrison, in conversation
> with the author, 1993

We're at the beginning stages of a transgender community, but, at this writing, there are still only small groups of people who live out different aspects of gender. I'm extremely interested in seeing what develops, taking into account Harrison's analogy of personal and group dynamics. Just now, pockets of resistance to social oppression are forming, most often in conjunction with various gay and lesbian communities. . . . I really *would* like to be a member of a community, but until there's one that's based on the principle of constant change, the membership would involve more rules, and the rules that exist around the subject of gender are not rules I want to obey.

35

The Conundrum of Difference

Sandra Lipsitz Bem

Stated in its most dichotomous form, the question that has plagued the debate on female inequality for 150 years is whether women and men are fundamentally the same or fundamentally different. This recurring question of sexual difference has prevented even feminists from achieving consensus of social policy because besides being inherently irresolvable itself, it has generated yet another set of apparently irresolvable dichotomies. These second-order dichotomies are revealed in answers to the following three questions: (1) What is the cause of female inequality? (2) What is the best strategy for ending female inequality? and (3) What is the meaning, or definition, of female equality?

In the current cultural debate, female inequality is typically attributed to one or the other of two causal factors, which need not be treated as mutually exclusive but usually are. Either women are being denied access to economic and political resources by policies and practices that intentionally discriminate against even those women "whose situation is most similar to men's," in which case the consensus is that the government must step in to remedy the situation; or, alternatively, women's biological, psychological, and historical differences from men—especially their psychological conflict between career and family—lead them to make choices that are inconsistent with building the kind of career that would enable them to attain those economic and political resources, in which case there is no one to blame for female inequality and hence no consensus about any need for remediation.[1]

Surprising as it may seem at first glance, recent economic studies have demonstrated that women as a group are as economically disadvantaged in U.S. society today as they were in 1960, with only the subgroup of young, white, unmarried, and well-educated women showing any substantial economic progress and with everyone else so segregated into the lowest-paid occupations and part-time work that overall, women as a group still earn a mere 65 percent or so of what men earn.[2] Although this persistent female inequality after thirty years of antidiscrimination law is frequently taken as evidence that discrimination against women is not nearly so important a cause of female inequality as female choice, I think this persistent female inequality is instead a testimony to the inadequacy of the understanding of how discrimination against women actually works.

Ever since the Supreme Court ruled in *Muller v. Oregon* (1908) that protective legislation could be used to compensate women for their "disadvantage in the struggle for subsistence," two opposing strategies for ending female inequality have been at the center of the debate on gender policy. Gender neutrality, also known as gender blindness, mandates that no distinctions of any sort ever be made on the basis of sex; and special protection for women, also known as sensitivity to sexual difference, mandates that special provision be made in the workplace to compensate women for their biological and historical role as the caregivers for children.

The gender-neutral approach to sexual equality was popular during the 1960s and early 1970s, as indicated not only by the Supreme Court's willingness in *Reed v. Reed* to finally declare explicit discrimination against women to be unconstitutional but also by the willingness of almost all feminists of the day to enthusiastically support the passage of that most gender-blind of all feminist proposals, the equal rights amendment. The gender-neutral approach was so popular because it was consistent with three important facts that feminists were just then managing to bring to the attention of the general public: (1) discrimination on the basis of sex had long denied women the equal protection under the law that should have been guaranteed to all citizens by the Fourteenth Amendment to the U.S. Constitution; (2) protective legislation designed over the years to benefit women in the workplace had done more to hurt them economically than to help them; and (3) women are as inherently intelligent, responsible, and capable of supporting themselves, if given the opportunity to do so, as men—not inherently inferior, as legislators and judges traditionally represented them to be.

By the late 1970s and 1980s, however, champions of equal rights increasingly realized that gender neutrality so deemphasized the differences in the life situations of women and men that as a strategy, it was helping only those few women who were similarly situated to men while doing little, if anything, to help those many women who were locked into low-paying jobs by their gendered life situations as wives and mothers. Not only that, but when applied mindlessly and formulaically in divorce settlements, gender neutrality was actually harming differently situated women by falsely presupposing them to have as much earning potential—and hence as little need for alimony—as their husbands (Weitzman 1985). Concentrating on this very large group of differently situated women highlighted the shortcomings of gender neutrality and thereby brought special protection back to center stage.

This time around, the advocates of special protection supported, not the kind of special limits for women that were at issue in *Muller v. Oregon*, but instead, special benefits for women. Specifically, they proposed work-related policies designed to make it possible for women to be both highly paid workers and responsible primary parents, policies such as mandatory insurance coverage for pregnancy leave and a guaranteed return to one's job at the end of such a leave, paid days off for mothers of sick children, and even subsidized childcare. Although demands for these kinds of sex-specific arrangements in the workplace would have been beyond imagining in the difference-blind heyday of the equal rights amendment, they were not all that exceptional in an era when virtually all minority groups were vigorously asserting the values of pluralism and sensitivity to difference—including even physically disabled people, who were at last beginning to get the special access to the mainstream of American life that they need.

In the 1990s, a great deal of support for these kinds of special benefits remains, as does a great deal of resistance to them. The support comes primarily from those feminists who see gender neutrality as having failed and, worse, as having required women to virtually become men to make it in the world of paid employment. The resistance comes from other feminists and from nonfeminists.

The feminist resisters think special protection homogenizes women too much and reinforces the old sexist stereotype that women as a group are inherently incapable of competing successfully with men until and unless special provisions compensate them for their special needs. The nonfeminist resisters, on the other hand, see no justification for making special arrangements to help a group whose economic and political disadvantages derive not from discrimination but from their own decision to invest time and energy in their children, rather than in their careers. As these nonfeminist resisters see it, to prevent employers from doing harm to women through outright discrimination makes sense, but to mandate that employers make special arrangements to help women in a marketplace that is not discriminatory does not.

But as controversial as special protection for a woman's biological and historical role as mother has been since the Supreme Court first upheld it in 1908, yet another form of special protection has become equally controversial since the 1960s. I refer here to the special protection against subtle and indirect discrimination that is embodied in the twin policies of comparable worth and preferential hiring. Comparable worth would move beyond the mandate that women and men doing the same work be paid equal wages to mandate equal wages for women and men doing different work that is of comparable value. Preferential hiring would move beyond simply prohibiting discrimination against women to mandate that an individual woman be hired over an individual man with similar qualifications and that goals and timetables be set for the hiring of a certain percentage of women by a certain time. Setting goals could, in turn, foster the use of quotas to reserve positions exclusively for women.

From the point of view of proponents, comparable worth and preferential hiring are necessary because discrimination against women often targets not women per se but anyone and everyone with the kinds of jobs or job histories that women as a group are much more likely to have than men as a group. From the point of view of opponents of these policies, preferential hiring unfairly deprives innocent males of equal opportunity by violating the almost sacred principle of gender neutrality, and comparable worth violates yet another sacred American principle—the right of employers to set wages in accordance with the free market.[3]

Just as those who emphasize discrimination as the cause of women's inequality, and gender neutrality as the cure, presuppose male-female similarity, then, so those who emphasize female choice as the cause of women's inequality, and special benefits as the cure, presuppose male-female difference. This dichotomy between similarity and difference shows up again in the two opposing definitions of female equality; with one group envisioning that women and men will come to play exactly the same roles both at home and at work and the other group envisioning that women will come to have exactly the same level of economic well-being, or equity, as men, despite continuing to play their traditionally different roles as homemakers and mothers.

Not surprisingly, the sameness conception of female equality was popular during the era when discrimination, gender neutrality, and the equal rights amendment dominated the feminist discourse and the concept of psychological androgyny was being celebrated as well. As feminists then saw it, the only effective way to end the sexist stereotyping of women and the discrimination against women that stereotyping inevitably produces was to abolish gender distinctions once and for all—that is, to move at last toward an androgynous future, where women and men would have not only the same level of economic and political power but the same rights, the same responsibilities, and even the same roles.

Although initially only antifeminists like Phyllis Schlafly opposed this definition of equality as sameness (on the grounds that it demeaned and destroyed the woman's role within the home), in time a great many feminists came to have that view as well. Defining female equality as sameness to men, they argued, was tantamount to saying that a woman's historical role and the values that it represents are of no intrinsic value.

So yes, the argument continued, women are inherently as competent as men are—there is no disagreement about that—but women are also inherently different from men in a special way having to do with their biological capacity for childbearing; and because of that difference, any worthwhile definition of equality must preserve the woman's biological and historical role as mother and give that role as much cultural value as has traditionally been given to male roles. In other words, the feminist goal should not be to facilitate women's acting exactly like men in order to earn what men earn; rather, women should be able to earn what men earn while still preserving their distinctive concern with the welfare of their own, and other, children.

After more than a century of dichotomies that relate to the single question of whether women are basically the same as men or basically different from men, feminists have recently begun to concentrate on yet another dichotomy. It is best captured by the following question: Are women of different races, classes, religions, sexual preferences, ethnicities, and perhaps even nationalities sufficiently similar to one another in their needs, goals, and experiences to constitute the kind of a political interest group that could possibly be served by any single program of social change, or are women of different groups so inherently different from one another that there can be little or no common cause among them and hence no possibility of a common feminist solution to their female inequality?[4]

These female-female differences notwithstanding, the historian Estelle Freedman eloquently defends the continuing validity of the feminist struggle,

> In a historical moment when the category 'woman' continues to predict limited access to material resources, greater vulnerability to physical and psychological abuse, and underrepresentation in politics, . . . we must avoid the tendency to assume both a false unity across genders and a greater disunity within our gender than in fact exists." (1990, 261)

Put somewhat differently, if feminists are to keep from getting mired in yet another set of impasse-producing dichotomies, they must not allow their newfound appreciation for the differences among women to undermine the longstanding feminist project of creating a social world in which the category of woman is no longer synonymous with the category of inequality.[5]

With that said, however, the question remains: How can feminists construct the kind of discussion about gender policy that would enable a male-dominated society like the United States to finally create such a social world? How, in other words, can Americans transcend all the irresolvable dichotomies that have plagued even feminist discussions of female inequality for 150 years? My answer is that those dichotomies can be transcended—and a consensus on gender policy can be forged—if a certain level of male-female difference is accepted as axiomatic, and the starting point for the discussion is thereby shifted from difference per se to the society's situating of women in a social structure so androcentric that it not only transforms male-female difference into female disadvantage; it also disguises a male standard as gender neutrality.[6]

Notes

1. For a relatively benign example of this "Feminist Choice" reasoning, see Kirp et al. (1986).
2. The most concise and convincing presentation of these data is in Fuchs (1988).
3. For other discussions of the overall conflict between gender neutrality and special protection, see Baer (1978), Kaminer (1990), and Kirp et al. (1986). For an excellent introduction to the comparable-worth debate, see Gold (1983). For a radical proposal related to the preferential hiring of women, see Hawkesworth (1990).

4. This recent feminist concern with female-female difference grew out of the legitimate accusation made by women of color in the 1970s that feminists, and feminism, were guilty of falsely universalizing what were really just the interests of white, middle-class women; feminists were also accused of denying their own complicity in the racist and classist oppression of people of color, both male and female. For more on the perspectives of feminists from different races and classes, see Davis (1981), hooks (1984), Hull, Scott and Smith (1982), and Joseph and Lewis (1981).

5. Freedman's remarks about the continuing validity of the feminist project were made in 1987 at a Stanford University conference on feminist approaches to sexual difference. Although the conference was much more oriented to theory than to social policy, the collection that grew out of it (Rhode 1990) nevertheless provides an excellent example of the debate over difference that I have characterized here.

6. This argument that androcentrism turns difference into disadvantage has many features in common with arguments put forth elsewhere by MacKinnon (1987), Okin (1989), and Rhode (1989).

References

Baer, J. A. (1978). *The Chains of Protection: The Judicial Response to Women's Labor Legislation.* Westport, Conn.: Greenwood.

Davis, A. Y. (1981). *Women, Race and Class.* New York: Random House.

Freedman, E. B. (1990). "Theoretical Perspectives on Sexual Difference: An Overview." In Rhode 1990, 257–61.

Fuchs, V. F. (1988). *Women's Quest for Economic Equality.* Cambridge, Mass.: Harvard University Press.

Gold, M. E., ed. (1983). *A Dialogue on Comparable Worth.* Ithaca, N.Y.: Industrial and Labor Relations Press.

Hawkesworth, M. E. (1990). *Beyond Oppression: Feminist Theory and Political Strategy.* New York: Continuum.

hooks, b. (1984). *Feminist Theory: From Margin to Center.* Boston: South End Press.

Hull, G. T., P. B. Scott, and E. Smith, eds. (1982). *All the Women Are White, All the Blacks are Men, but Some of Us Are Brave: Black Women's Studies.* New York: Feminist Press.

Joseph, G. I., and J. Lewis. (1981). *Common Differences: Conflicts in Black and White Feminist Perspectives.* Boston: South End Press.

Kaminer, W. (1990). *A Fearful Freedom: Women's Flight from Equality.* Reading, Mass.: Addison-Wesley.

Kirp, D. L., M. G. Yudof, and M. S. Franks. (1986). *Gender Justice.* Chicago: University of Chicago Press.

MacKinnon, C. A. (1987). "Difference and Dominance: On Sex Discrimination." In C. A. MacKinnon, ed., *Feminism Unmodified: Discourses on Life and Law.* Cambridge, Mass.: Harvard University Press.

Okin, S. M. (1989). *Justice, Gender, and the Family.* New York: Basic Books.

Rhode, D. L. (1989). *Justice and Gender: Sex Discrimination and the Law.* Cambridge, Mass.: Harvard University Press.

———, ed. (1990). *Theoretical Perspectives on Sexual Difference.* New Haven, Conn.: Yale University Press.

Weitzman, L. J. (1985). *The Divorce Revolution: The Unexpected Social and Economic Consequences for Women and Children in America.* New York: Free Press.

36

Fresh Lipstick: Rethinking Images of Women in Advertising

Linda M. Scott

For more than one hundred years, American feminist thought has held that the pursuit of a fashionably beautiful appearance is a sign of low self-esteem and a symptom of political oppression. One of the longest-standing gestures of defiance among feminist activists, therefore, has been a refusal to conform to the grooming practices that fashion deemed "beautiful" or "feminine."

Yet feminism's political imperative to reject the pursuit of "beauty" has presented an insuperable obstacle to some women, becoming a barrier that often marks a schism in the movement. "An unadorned face became the honorable new look of feminism in the early 1970s, and no one was happier with the freedom not to wear makeup than I," wrote Susan Brownmiller in *Femininity* (1984), musing on the depth of divisiveness that could be caused by so seemingly trivial an issue. "Yet it could hardly escape my attention that more women supported the Equal Rights Amendment and legal abortion than would walk out of the house without their eye shadow."

> "Did I think of them as somewhat pitiable?" Brownmiller asked. "Yes, I did. Did they bitterly resent the righteous pressure put on them to look, in their terms, less attractive? Yes, they did. A more complete breakdown and confusion of aims, goals and values could not have occurred, and of all the movement rifts I have witnessed, this one remains for me the most poignant and the most difficult to resolve." . . .

Let's begin by looking at a recent advertisement, a Nike ad that ran in many American fashion magazines during 1992. The image is a photograph of Marilyn Monroe, but it is not the simpering starlet, the sex symbol playing to the male gaze. Instead, this is one of those pictures of Marilyn Monroe that experience and convention tell us to read as "the real Marilyn," an innocent destroyed by the beauty myth. So when we look at this ad, we do not topple over in our desire to look like Marilyn Monroe, though she is beautiful and blonde. On the contrary, we know to read this image as a poignant combination of beauty and tragedy. That is, we look at this image critically. In fact, the sense of the ad *depends* on viewing the image critically, as is clear from the copy.

"A woman is often measured by the things she cannot control," the copy begins. We know this feeling of being "measured," so we let the ad talk to us some more. The voice goes on about the way a body curves or doesn't, and how the "inches and ages and numbers . . . don't ever add up to who she is on the inside." This, we know, is the moral of

Marilyn. We share this inside/outside paradox with her, whether our bodies curve voluptuously or not. The voice takes on the edge of indignation: "If a woman is to be measured, let her be measured by the things she can control, by who she is and who she is trying to become." We are "with" this voice; it is our own manifesto. The call builds to its climax: "Measurements are only statistics and statistics lie." We laugh, perhaps ruefully.

From the logo of the well-known maker of athletic shoes displayed unconventionally in the upper right corner, we infer that the voice wants us to buy tennis shoes and start some athletic activity. We are now dealing with another ideal, the one that prefers beauty "from within," the one that advocates exercise rather than creams and lipsticks and the over-obvious eyeliner poor Marilyn is wearing. So the ad itself is discursive, representing an argument between one politics of beauty and another. If we have any historical awareness at all (and we must have *some* in order to get the Marilyn reference in the first place), then we know that the "beauty through health and exercise" position is the one long advocated by feminism.

Perhaps we are pleased that an advertiser is on the "right" side, for once. Or, perhaps we are bothered, as some readers of this ad were, that this voice is advocating a path to beauty that many women are already following to destruction. The fight for "control" here has the intonation of the anorexic, who, in a desperate effort to have control over *something*, works with a vengeance to control her body. In this alternative politics of beauty lies the potential to emerge taut, toned and totally twisted. Now shamelessly curvy Marilyn looks downright healthy, her eyeliner notwithstanding. We have arrived at one of the paradoxes that the beauty controversy produces: the ultimately deceptive idea that one way of being beautiful will be, for all times and all places, more healthy, more natural, and less harmful than all others. . . .

But just this once, I'm going to ask you to do something that is seldom done: knock down the screen and take a look at the wizard behind it. In this case, we do not find a snarling group of male capitalists, but two young women with counterculture loyalties. Charlotte Moore, an art director, and Janet Champ, a copywriter, work in a team, as is the tradition in advertising. Also according to tradition, they have been segregated as a "girls' team" and been given responsibility for Nike's "women's campaign."

Moore and Champ's first ads for Nike opened with long lists that evoked futility and harmfulness: "Face lifts, body tucks, liposuction, electrolysis, collagen implants, breast lifts, wrinkle creams, face masks, mud baths, chemical peels, wrinkle fills, liquid diets, cellulite reduction, tweezing, plucking, straightening, waxing, waving, herbal heat wraps." Then you turned the page and saw a young woman in athletic gear sprinting up some stairs, and the headline, "The 60-minute makeover from Nike. Just do it." Champ contends their campaign strategy was to attack the other speakers in the beauty discourse, both commercial and editorial. "I mean, every one of them is how to be beautiful and how to get your man and how to be skinny and how to be—you know—cosmetic surgery and everything else," she told an oral-history interviewer from the Smithsonian's Center for Advertising History. "We wanted to show real women, talk to women one on one, and start debunking all these myths that we have to live with every day." The Marilyn ad was another attempt to go after the same myths.

"We'd always been very, very interested in this whole idea of being held up to be the icon of perfection, of beauty, and what happens to a woman when she starts to believe that, what happens to other women when they're forced to try to *be* that," Champ says. "So we started talking about what kind of ad we could do that talked about being a statistic and being accepted as a false image of yourself, and how, once you present that image to the world, you are never accepted for who you really are."

Instead of being motivated by a desire to manipulate or by a feeling of condescension toward their readers, Champ and Moore felt able to communicate their message to other women because they had "been there" themselves. This experience increased Champ's political awareness and renewed a sense of activism she thought she had lost. That a feminist would be reclaimed by writing ads may seem an unlikely turn of events; on the contrary, however, the history of the beauty controversy is full of paradoxical characters, contradictory polemics and the struggle of competing interests in surprising places. . . .

Current feminist theorizing generally treats modern corporate capitalism as a uniquely white male phenomenon, but cosmetics companies are an exception that produces a curious contradiction. Lois Banner bemoans the dearth of entrepreneurial women in the history of the garment industry, which resulted in female seamstresses going to work for male-dominated factories. In contrast, with the important exceptions of Charles Revson and Richard Hudnut, nearly all the founders of major cosmetics companies in America were women: Elizabeth Arden, Helena Rubinstein, Estée Lauder, Dorothy Gray and others. Banner criticizes these women precisely *because* they were entrepreneurial and commercial. She, like many other feminists writing today, seems unwilling to let *any* commercial enterprise be acceptable to feminism. While such a view may satisfy doctrinaire Marxism, it seems a crude way to deal with a situation that is hardly absolute. The commercial beauty culture has seen upstart challengers, working-class enterprises and avant-garde expressions. A cultural philosophy that cannot distinguish between The Body Shop and Revlon, or between Benetton and Sears, is insufficiently calibrated.

Ignoring or dismissing the women of industry allows critics to claim that cosmetics ads are the patriarchy's directives of "how women should look." Here arises another puzzle, though, because cosmetics advertisements have traditionally been written by women. Historically, advertising has employed more women than other industries, and at higher levels and salaries. But women were usually segregated into their own groups and given a carefully circumscribed list of products to work on, usually the ones men were embarrassed about, including cosmetics if the agency had any.

Models are a third group of women involved in the production of the beauty culture's texts. In the 1900s, artists' models were considered one tiny step up from prostitutes. As mass production of images grew, the beautiful woman who could pose for brush or camera was an increasingly valued player. The anti-beauty faction of feminism still tends to treat models as non-persons, referring to them as "flat images" or "mannikins." This characterization is snobbish, demeaning, inaccurate, and unfair. The relationship between a model and a photographer, artist or designer is not passive, but dialogic and creative, much like that between an actress and a director.

The model's social ascent was indicative of a new ethic of beauty emerging. Arthur Marwick, in his *Beauty in History*, argues that in the "modern" concept of beauty, good looks may be exploited for their own sake to the economic benefit of the bearer, without necessarily being tied to the granting of sexual favors. Beautiful persons, male or female, may use their beauty to please audiences, win contests, advertise products, gain employment in various capacities or, as traditionally, make a good marriage. Physical beauty became another attribute, like intelligence, talent, or wealth, that could be used toward the achievement of material and emotional success. Naomi Wolf's *The Beauty Myth* (1991) discusses the unconscionable discrimination that has resulted from the "Professional Beauty Qualification." However, her assertion that the "beauty myth" arose in the 1980s as part of a backlash against feminism is quite inaccurate and obscures the economic benefits and social mobility offered by this historical shift.

Over the course of this period, advertisements tell much about the ups and downs, the back and forth of the discourse on beauty. Several notions of "the beautiful" can be seen to compete in any particular period and, over time, the ideals of feminism – athleticism, health, and natural products – make themselves felt in the popular discourse over and over again. Many graphic ideals of beauty followed the Gibson Girl: Maxfield Parrish's girl on a rock, John Held's flappers, the pinups of World War II, and so on. In each, the themes of "modern" versus "traditional," "proper" versus "unconventional," can be discerned, weaving through various strains of the discourse on what it meant to be "modern," "feminine," and even, "feminist." One must interpret these images in context or, as with the Gibson Girl, risk being tricked by contemporary perceptions. Furthermore, understanding one image often requires knowing how it speaks to other images, other ideals, other speakers.

A famous example is the dialogue between Revlon and Cover Girl. Introduced in the early 1950s, Revlon's "Fire and Ice Girl" had several characteristics of the "modern" woman: she dresses as if she were a little "loose" ("Have you ever wanted to wear an ankle bracelet?"), embraces the controversial ("Do you secretly hope the next man you meet will be a psychiatrist?"), is the object of jealousy ("Do you sometimes feel that other women resent you?"), is independent ("Would you streak your hair with platinum without consulting your husband?") and she is frankly interested in sex ("Do you close your eyes when you're kissed?"). Behind the Revlon girl is the fusion of two opposing class standards of beauty: Charles Revson himself referred to her as a "Park Avenue whore." No matter how endearing her lusty unconventionality may be, though, her life's work seems to be presenting the picture of an oversexed "piece of fluff" to men and engaging in a mutually destructive competition with other women. She is the side of Marilyn Monroe we don't like, gripped by the neurosis of narcissism that Simone de Beauvoir was writing about at this time—always playing to the imagined male gaze. She is Betty Friedan's feminine mystique out for the evening.

When Cover Girl cosmetics were introduced in the late 1950s, the new brand was a nuisance upstart and Revlon was a giant. Cover Girl's chemical base was Noxema with a new postwar wonder added, "hexachlorophene," which allowed the ads to make many truthful health claims: using antiseptic, Cover Girl was actually better for your skin than using no makeup at all. In the ad campaign, a beautiful but unknown young woman told how "natural" and "good for you" Cover Girl was, then her face was framed by a famous magazine masthead—and the viewer "discovered" her as that month's "cover girl." After the removal of hexachlorophene from the market (it had started going into nearly everything, and if a little hexachlorophene was a good thing, too much was not), Cover Girl continued to emphasize its "natural, clean" look and began to show the models sailing, swimming, and riding. Thus, the campaign came to have the desirable attributes of a "feminist" approach to makeup: it looked "natural," it was "good for you" and it was associated with a healthy and athletic lifestyle. Cover Girl was tremendously popular among younger women, stepping in line with the growing idealization of athletic women that begins with the Gibson Girl, produces the cult of the cheerleader, and probably reaches its peak in the fitness craze of the 1980s. Cover Girl's arch rival and alter ego was the sexy, night-clubbing Revlon girl, and all the ads were written with that distinction in mind.

Today, Cover Girl is still the biggest seller among women under forty, an honor it owes in no small part to the new aesthetic of beauty espoused by the second wave of feminism. Lynn Giordano was an undergraduate in journalism at the University of Wisconsin during the late 1960s, but by the late 1980s, she was creative director for Cover Girl makeup. Giordano recalls that, with the rise in feminist activity on college campuses, Cover Girl became the makeup you could wear and still hold on to your politics. "No woman, no matter how radical her politics—this is the real truth, I mean, you'll never get women to admit this, but no matter how left of center they stood, they wanted to look good when they were standing there," she told the Smithsonian's advertising historians. "And they would claim they weren't wearing makeup but you'd sneak some stuff in. And one of the reasons Cover Girl went through the roof was that they were selling a no-makeup look right when it was great to be a no-makeup look."

This is the same moment described by Susan Brownmiller, the ultimate irony: choosing a brand of makeup that will help you look like "a good feminist" when feminism did not allow makeup. It is, again, the complex politics of appearance. Much of the argument against the beauty culture is based on the assumption that the sole purpose for aspiring to beauty is to attract men, despite substantial documentation that cultivating one's appearance has both economic and psychic benefits that may be unrelated to sexual allure. Reducing "beauty" to "sex" ignores other roles played by grooming and fashion, such as the communication of character, the acknowledgment of setting or occasion, the display of rank, the challenge to authority and so forth. In this light, categorically denouncing cosmetics and other beauty tools is an overly simplistic, insensitive response to a complex human practice.

The Cover Girl campaign continued to evolve toward a blonde, blue-eyed ideal of beauty, an athletic, ostensibly "natural" perfection that was airbrushed and retouched into unattainability. By the 1980s, however, other aesthetics began to emerge as challengers: the "Dress for Success" look of new female professionals, the "punk" look of Deborah Harry, Madonna, and Cyndi Lauper, as well as the athletic look epitomized by the aerobics fad. Each of these could make a claim to be more "feminist" than the other. Each had its commercial counterparts in advertising. Each was subject to controversy. Early in the 1980s, for example, feminist students of pop culture buzzed over whether Cyndi Lauper was a better role model for women than Madonna, though both were highly theatrical in their self-presentation. The issue then, as now, was whether Madonna is simply too pretty and too sexy to be a good feminist. We seem to have forgotten (or are now too young to remember) that the same things were once said about Gloria Steinem.

Though feminism has tended to treat beauty as a symbol of oppression, what lurks not far beneath the surface is the reality of beauty as power. In a world in which women have had few legal rights, and even fewer economic ones, beauty has sometimes provided women with some relief and some control over their circumstances. From histories like Lois Banner's *American Beauty* (1983) to contemporary studies like Robin Lakoff and Raquel Scherr's *Face Value: The Politics of Beauty* (1984), we can see that the power of beautiful women is not only over men, but also over other women. "Women cannot join with women in thinking about—much less talking about—looks, without great anguish," Lakoff and Scherr write.

Beauty is extraordinarily difficult for women to talk about with each other, but once they started in interviews with Lakoff and Scherr, the authors felt as if a floodgate had opened. The responses were passionate, poignant, sometimes tearful. Lakoff and Scherr concluded that the intractable position of "official" feminism had made beauty a taboo topic. We are not supposed to care about it, so we don't talk about it (except in so far as the problem can be demonized and externalized). Attempts to rethink the issue are quickly silenced with charges of "antifeminism" or "backlash." As a consequence, what masquerades for criticism on the topic is often closer to superstition than analysis, more dogma than insight, demagoguery rather than revolution.

References

Brownmiller, S. (1984). *Femininity* (New York: Linden Press).

Lakoff, R. and R. Scherr. (1984). *Face Value: The Politics of Beauty* (New York: Routledge).

Marwick, A. (1988). *Beauty in History* (London: Thames and Hudson).

Wolf, N. (1991). *The Beauty Myth: How Images of Beauty Are Used against Women* (New York: William Morrow).

37

Feminism: A Movement to End Sexist Oppression

bell hooks

A central problem within feminist discourse has been our inability to either arrive at a consensus of opinion about what feminism is or accept definition(s) that could serve as points of unification. Without agreed upon definition(s), we lack a sound foundation on which to construct theory or engage in overall meaningful praxis. Expressing her frustrations with the absence of clear definitions in the essay "Towards A Revolutionary Ethics," Carmen Vasquez comments:

> We can't even agree on what a "Feminist" is, never mind what she would believe in and how she defines the principles that constitute honor among us. In key with the American capitalist obsession for individualism and anything goes so long as it gets you what you want. Feminism in American has come to mean anything you like, honey. There are as many definitions of Feminism as there are feminists, some of my sisters say, with a chuckle. I don't think it's funny.[1]

It is not funny. It indicates a growing disinterest in feminism as a radical political movement. It is a despairing gesture expressive of the belief that solidarity between women is not possible. It is a sign that the political naïveté which has traditionally characterized woman's lot in male-dominated culture abounds.

Most people in the United States think of feminism, or the more commonly used term "women's lib," as a movement that aims to make women the social equals of men. This broad definition, popularized by the media and mainstream segments of the movement, raises problematic questions. Since men are not equals in white supremacist, capitalist, patriarchal class structure, which men do women want to be equal to? Do women share a common vision of what equality means? Implicit in this simplistic definition of women's liberation is a dismissal of race and class as factors that, in conjunction with sexism, determine the extent to which an individual will be discriminated against, exploited, or oppressed. Bourgeois white women interested in women's rights issues have been satisfied with simple definitions for obvious reasons. Rhetorically placing themselves in the same social category as oppressed women, they were not anxious to call attention to race and class privilege.

Women in lower-class and poor groups, particularly those who are non-white, would not have defined women's liberation as women gaining social equality with men since they are continually reminded in their everyday lives that all women do not share a common social status. Concurrently, they know that many males in their social groups are exploited and oppressed. Knowing that men in their groups do not have social, political, and economic power, they would not deem it liberatory to share their social status. While they are aware that sexism enables men in their respective groups to have privileges denied them, they are more likely to see exaggerated expressions of male chauvinism among their peers as stemming from the male's sense of himself as powerless and ineffectual in relation to ruling male groups, rather than an expression of an overall privileged social status. From the very onset of the women's liberation movement, these women were suspicious of feminism precisely because they recognized the limitations inherent in its definition. They recognized the possibility that feminism defined as social equality with men might easily become a movement that would primarily affect the social standing of white women in middle and upper class groups while affecting only in a very marginal way the social status of working class and poor women. . . .

In a recent article in a San Francisco newspaper, "Sisters—Under the Skin," columnist Bob Greene commented on the aversion many women apparently have to the term feminism. Greene finds it curious that many women "who obviously believe in everything that proud feminists believe in dismiss the term 'feminist' as something unpleasant; something with which they do not wish to be associated." Even though such women often acknowledge that they have benefited from feminist-generated reform measures which have improved the social status of specific groups of women, they do not wish to be seen as participants in feminist movement:

> There is no getting around it. After all this time, the term "feminist" makes many bright, ambitious, intelligent women embarrassed and uncomfortable. They simply don't want to be associated with it.
>
> It's as if it has an unpleasant connotation that they want no connection with. Chances are if you were to present them with every mainstream feminist belief, they would go along with the beliefs to the letter—and even if they consider themselves feminists, they hasten to say no.[2]

Many women are reluctant to advocate feminism because they are uncertain about the meaning of the term. Other women from exploited and oppressed ethnic groups dismiss the term because they do not wish to be perceived as supporting a racist movement; feminism is often equated with white women's rights effort. Large numbers of women see feminism as synonymous with lesbianism; their homophobia leads them to reject association with any group identified as pro-lesbian. Some women fear the word "feminism" because they shun identification with any political movement, especially one perceived as radical. Of course there are women who do not wish to be associated with women's rights movement in any form so they reject and oppose feminist movement. Most women are more familiar with negative perspectives on "women's lib" than the positive significations of feminism. It is this term's positive political significance and power that we must now struggle to recover and maintain.

Currently feminism seems to be a term without any clear significance. The "anything goes" approach to the definition of the word has rendered it practically meaningless. What is meant by "anything goes" is usually that any woman who wants social equality with men regardless of her political perspective (she can be a conservative right-winger or a nationalist communist) can label herself feminist. Most attempts at defining feminism reflect the class nature of the movement. Definitions are usually liberal in origin and focus on the individual woman's right to freedom and self-determination. . . .

This definition of feminism is almost apolitical in tone; yet it is the type of definition many liberal women find appealing. It evokes a very romantic notion of personal freedom which is more acceptable than a definition that emphasizes radical political action. . . . Feminism defined in political terms that stress collective as well as individual experience challenges women to enter a new domain—to leave behind the apolitical stance sexism decrees is our lot and develop political consciousness. . . . By repudiating the popular notion that the focus of feminist movement should be social equality of the sexes and emphasizing eradicating the cultural basis of group oppression, our own analysis would require an exploration of all aspects of women's political reality. This would mean that race and class oppression would be recognized as feminist issues with as much relevance as sexism.

When feminism is defined in such a way that it calls attention to the diversity of women's social and political reality, it centralizes the experiences of all women, especially the women whose social conditions have been least written about, studied, or changed by political movements. When we cease to focus on the simplistic stance "men are the enemy," we are compelled to examine systems of domination and our role in their maintenance and perpetuation. . . .

Feminism is the struggle to end sexist oppression. Its aim is not to benefit solely any specific group of women, any particular race or class of women. It does not privilege women over men. It has the power to transform in a meaningful way all our lives. . . . Feminism as a movement to end sexist oppression directs our attention to systems of domination and the inter-relatedness of sex, race, and class oppression. Therefore, it compels us to centralize the experiences and the social predicaments of women who bear the brunt of sexist oppression as a way to understand the collective social status of women in the United States. Defining feminism as a movement to end sexist oppression is crucial for the development of theory because it is a starting point indicating the direction of exploration and analysis.

The foundation of future feminist struggle must be solidly based on a recognition of the need to eradicate the underlying cultural basis and causes of sexism and other forms of group oppression. Without challenging and changing these philosophical structures, no feminist reforms will have a long range impact. Consequently, it is now necessary for advocates of feminism to collectively acknowledge that our struggle cannot be defined as a movement to gain social equality with men; that terms like "liberal feminist" and "bourgeois feminist" represent contradictions that must be resolved so that feminism will not be continually co-opted to serve the opportunistic ends of special interest groups.

Notes

1. Carmen Vasquez, "Towards a Revolutionary Ethics," *Coming Up*, January 1983, 11.
2. Bob Greene, "Sisters Under The Skin," *San Francisco Examiner*, May 15, 1983.

Personal Voices

38

Ain't I a
Woman?

Sojourner Truth
(1797–1883)

Well, children, where there is so much racket there must be something out of kilter. I think that 'twixt the negroes of the South and the women at the North, all talking about rights, the white men will be in a fix pretty soon. But what's all this here talking about?

That man over there says that women need to be helped into carriages, and lifted over ditches, and to have the best place everywhere. Nobody ever helps me into carriages, or over mud-puddles, or gives me any best place! And ain't I a woman? Look at me! Look at my arm! I have ploughed and planted, and gathered into barns, and no man could head me! And ain't I a woman? I could work as much and eat as much as a man—when I could get it—and bear the lash as well! And ain't I a woman? I have borne thirteen children, and seen them most all sold off to slavery, and when I cried out with my mother's grief, none but Jesus heard me! And ain't I a woman?

Then they talk about this thing in the head: what's this they call it? [Intellect, someone whispers.] That's it, honey. What's that got to do with women's rights or negro's rights? If my cup won't hold but a pint, and yours holds a quart, wouldn't you be mean not to let me have my little half-measure full?

Then that little man in black there, he says women can't have as much rights as men, 'cause Christ wasn't a woman! Where did your Christ come from? Where did your Christ come from? From God and a woman! Man had nothing to do with Him.

If the first woman God ever made was strong enough to turn the world upside down all alone, these women together ought to be able to turn it back, and get it right side up again! And now they is asking to do it, the men better let them.

Obliged to you for hearing me, and now old Sojourner ain't got nothing more to say.

39

I'm Not Fat, I'm Latina

Christy Haubegger

I recently read a newspaper article that reported that nearly 40 percent of Hispanic and African-American women are overweight. At least I'm in good company. Because according to even the most generous height and weight charts at the doctor's office, I'm a good twenty-five pounds overweight. And I'm still looking for the panty-hose chart that has me on it (according to Hanes, I don't exist). But I'm happy to report that in the Latino community, my community, I fit right in.

Latinas in this country live in two worlds. People who don't know us may think we're fat. At home, we're called *bien cuidadas* (well cared for).

I love to go dancing at Cesar's Latin Palace here in the Mission District of San Francisco. At this hot all-night salsa club, it's the curvier bodies like mine that turn heads. I'm the one on the dance floor all night while some of my thinner friends spend more time waiting along the walls. Come to think of it, I wouldn't trade my body for any of theirs.

But I didn't always feel this way. I remember being in high school and noticing that none of the magazines showed models in bathing suits with bodies like mine. Handsome movie heroes were never hoping to find a chubby damsel in distress. The fact that I had plenty of attention from Latino boys wasn't enough. Real self-esteem cannot come from male attention alone.

My turning point came a few years later. When I was in college, I made a trip to Mexico, and I brought back much more than sterling-silver bargains and colorful blankets.

I remember hiking through the awesome ruins of the Maya and the Aztecs, civilizations that created pyramids as large as the ones in Egypt. I loved walking through temple doorways whose clearance was only two inches above my head, and I realized that I must be a direct descendant of those ancient priestesses for whom those doorways had originally been built.

For the first time in my life, I was in a place where people like me were the beautiful ones. And I began to accept, and even like, the body that I have.

I know that medical experts say that Latinas are twice as likely as the rest of the population to be overweight. And yes, I know about the health problems that often accompany severe weight problems. But most of us are not in the danger zone; we're just *bien cuidadas*. Even the researchers who found that nearly 40 percent of us are overweight noted that there is a greater "cultural acceptance" of being overweight within Hispanic communities. But the article also commented on the cultural-acceptance factor as if it were something unfortunate, because it keeps Hispanic women from becoming healthier. I'm not so convinced that we're the ones with the problem.

If the medical experts were to try and get to the root of this so-called problem, they would probably find that it's part genetics, part enchiladas. Whether we're Cuban-American, Mexican-American, Puerto Rican or Dominican, food is a central part of Hispanic culture. While our food varies from fried plaintains to tamales, what doesn't change is its role in our lives. You feed people you care for, and so if you're well cared for, *bien cuidada*, you have been fed well.

I remember when I used to be envious of a Latina friend of mine who had always been on the skinny side. When I confided this to her a while ago, she laughed. It turns out that when she was growing up, she had always wanted to look more like me. She had trouble getting dates with Latinos in high school, the same boys that I dated. When she was little, the other kids in the neighborhood had even given her a cruel nickname: *la seca*, "the dry one." I'm glad I never had any of those problems.

Our community has always been accepting of us well-cared-for women. So why don't we feel beautiful? You only have to flip through a magazine or watch a movie to realize that beautiful for most of this country still means tall, blond and underfed. But now we know it's the magazines that are wrong. I, for one, am going to do what I can to make sure that *mis hijas*, my daughters, won't feel the way I did.

40

The Body Politic

Abra Fortune Chernik

My body possesses solidness and curve, like the ocean. My weight mingles with Earth's pull, drawing me onto the sand. I have not always sent waves into the world. I flew off once, for five years, and swirled madly like a cracking brown leaf in the salty autumn wind. I wafted, dried out, apathetic.

I had no weight in the world during my years of anorexia. Curled up inside my thinness, a refugee in a cocoon of hunger, I lost the capacity to care about myself or others. I starved my body and twitched in place as those around me danced in the energy of shared existence and progressed in their lives. When I graduated from college crowned with academic honors, professors praised my potential. I wanted only to vanish.

It took three months of hospitalization and two years of outpatient psychotherapy for me to learn to nourish myself and to live in a body that expresses strength and honesty in its shape. I accepted my right and my obligation to take up room with my figure, voice and spirit. I remembered how to tumble forward and touch the world that holds me. I chose the ocean as my guide.

Who disputes the ocean's fullness?

Growing up in New York City, I did not care about the feminist movement. Although I attended an all-girls high school, we read mostly male authors and studied the history of men. Embracing mainstream culture without question, I learned about womanhood from fashion magazines, Madison Avenue and Hollywood. I dismissed feminist alternatives as foreign and offensive, swathed as they were in stereotypes that threatened my adolescent need for conformity.

Puberty hit late; I did not complain. I enjoyed living in the lanky body of a tall child and insisted on the title of "girl." If anyone referred to me as a "young woman," I would cry out, horrified, "Do not call me the *W* word!" But at sixteen years old, I could no longer deny my fate. My stomach and breasts rounded. Curly black hair sprouted in the most embarrassing places. Hips swelled from a once-flat plane. Interpreting maturation as an unacceptable lapse into fleshiness, I resolved to eradicate the physical symptoms of my impending womanhood.

Magazine articles, television commercials, lunchroom conversation, gymnastics coaches, and write-ups on models had saturated me with diet savvy. Once I decided to lose weight, I quickly turned expert. I dropped hot chocolate from my regular breakfast order at the Skyline Diner. I replaced lunches of peanut butter and Marshmallow Fluff sandwiches with small platters of cottage cheese and cantaloupe. I eliminated dinner altogether and blunted my appetite with Tab, Camel Lights, and Carefree bubble gum. When furious craving overwhelmed my resolve and I swallowed an extra something, I would flee to the nearest bathroom to purge my mistake.

Within three months, I had returned my body to its preadolescent proportions and had manipulated my monthly period into drying up. Over the next five years, I devoted my life to losing my weight. I came to resent the body in which I lived, the body that threatened to develop, the body whose hunger I despised but could not extinguish. If I neglected a workout or added a pound or ate a bite too many, I would stare in the mirror and drown myself in a tidal wave of criticism. Hatred of my body generalized to hatred of myself as a person, and self-referential labels such as "pig," "failure" and "glutton" allowed me to believe that I deserved punishment. My self-hatred became fuel for the self-mutilating behaviors of the eating disorder.

As my body shrank, so did my world. I starved away my power and vision, my energy and inclinations. Obsessed with dieting, I allowed relationships, passions and identity to wither. I pulled back from the world, off of the beach, out of the sand. The waves of my existence ceased to roll beyond the inside of my skin.

And society applauded my shrinking. Pound after pound the applause continued, like the pounding ocean outside the door of my beach house. . . .

By the time I entered the hospital, a mess of protruding bones defined my body, and the bones of my emaciated life rattled me crazy. I carried a pillow around because it hurt to sit down, and I shivered with cold in sultry July. Clumps of brittle hair clogged the drain when I showered, and blackened eyes appeared to sink into my head. My vision of reality wrinkled and my disposition turned mercurial as I slipped into starvation psychosis, a condition associated with severe malnutrition. People told me that I resembled a concentration camp prisoner, a chemotherapy patient, a famine victim or a fashion model.

In the hospital, I examined my eating disorder under the lenses of various therapies. I dissected my childhood, my family structure, my intimate relationships, my belief systems. I participated in experiential therapies of movement, art and psychodrama. I learned to use words instead of eating patterns to communicate my feelings. And still I refused to gain more than a minimal amount of weight.

I felt powerful as an anorexic. Controlling my body yielded an illusion of control over my life; I received incessant praise for my figure despite my sickly mien, and my frailty manipulated family and friends into protecting me from conflict. I had reduced my world to a plate of steamed carrots, and over this tiny kingdom I proudly crowned myself queen. . . .

I spent my remaining month in the hospital supplementing psychotherapy with an independent examination of eating disorders from a social and political point of view. I needed to understand why society would reward my starvation and encourage my vanishing. In the bathroom, a mirror on the open door behind me reflected my backside in a mirror over the sink. Vertebrae poked at my skin, ribs hung like wings over chiseled hip bones, the two sides of my buttocks did not touch. I had not seen this view of myself before.

In writing, I recorded instances in which my eating disorder had tangled the progress of my life and thwarted my relationships. I filled three and a half Mead marble notebooks. Five years' worth of *I wouldn't sit with Daddy when he was alone in the hospital because I needed to go jogging; I told Derek not to visit me because I couldn't throw up when he was there; I almost failed my comprehensive exams because I was so hungry; I spent my year at Oxford with my head in the toilet bowl; I wouldn't eat the dinner my friends cooked me for my nineteenth birthday because I knew they had used oil in the recipe; I told my family not to come to my college graduation because I didn't want to miss a day at the gym or have to eat a restaurant meal.* And on and on for hundreds of pages. ·

This honest account of my life dissolved the illusion of anorexic power. I saw myself naked in the truth of my pain, my loneliness, my obsessions, my craziness, my selfishness, my defeat. I also recognized the social and political implications of consuming myself with the trivialities of calories and weight. At college, I had watched as classmates involved themselves in extracurricular clubs, volunteer work, politics and applications for jobs and graduate schools. Obsessed with exercising and exhausted by starvation, I did not even consider joining in such pursuits. Despite my love of writing and painting and literature, despite ranking at the top of my class, I wanted only to teach aerobics. Despite my adolescent days as a loud-mouthed, rambunctious class leader, I had grown into a silent, hungry young woman.

And society preferred me this way: hungry, fragile, crazy. *Winner! Healthy! Fantastic!* I began reading feminist literature to further understand the disempowerment of women in our culture. I digested the connection between a nation of starving, self-obsessed women and the continued success of the patriarchy. I also cultivated an awareness of alternative models of womanhood. In the stillness of the hospital library, new voices in my life rose from printed pages to echo my rage and provide the conception of my feminist consciousness.

I had been willing to accept self-sabotage, but now I refused to sacrifice myself to a society that profited from my pain. I finally understood that my eating disorder symbolized more than "personal psychodynamic trauma." Gazing in the mirror at my emaciated body, I observed a woman held up by her culture as the physical ideal because she was starving, self-obsessed and powerless, a woman called beautiful because she threatened no one except herself. Despite my intelligence, my education, and my supposed Manhattan sophistication, I had believed all of the lies; I had almost given my life in order to achieve the sickly impotence that this culture aggressively links with female happiness, love and success. And everything I had to offer to the world, every tumbling wave, every thought and every passion, nearly died inside me.

As long as society resists female power, fashion will call healthy women physically flawed. As long as society accepts the physical, sexual and economic abuse of women, popular culture will prefer women who resemble little girls. Sitting in the hospital the summer after my college graduation, I grasped the absurdity of a nation of adult women dying to grow small.

Armed with this insight, I loosened the grip of the starvation disease on my body. I determined to recreate myself based on an image of a woman warrior. I remembered my ocean, and I took my first bite.

Gaining weight and getting my head out of the toilet bowl was the most political act I have ever committed. . . . Eating disorders affect us all on both a personal and a political level. The majority of my peers—including my feminist peers—still measure their beauty against anorexic ideals. Even among feminists, body hatred and chronic dieting continue to consume lives. Friends of anorexics beg them to please start eating; then these friends go home and continue their own diets. Who can deny that the millions of young women caught in the net of disordered eating will frustrate the potential of the next wave of feminism? . . .

As young feminists, we must place unconditional acceptance of our bodies at the top of our political agenda. We must claim our bodies as our own to love and honor in their infinite shapes and sizes. Fat, thin, soft, hard, puckered, smooth, our bodies are our homes. By nourishing our bodies, we care for and love ourselves on the most basic level. When we deny ourselves physical food, we go hungry emotionally, psychologically, spiritually and politically. We must challenge ourselves to eat and digest, and allow society to call us too big. We will understand their message to mean too powerful.

Time goes by quickly. One day we will blink and open our eyes as old women. If we spend all our energy keeping our bodies small, what will we have to show for our lives when we reach the end? I hope we have more than a group of fashionably skinny figures.

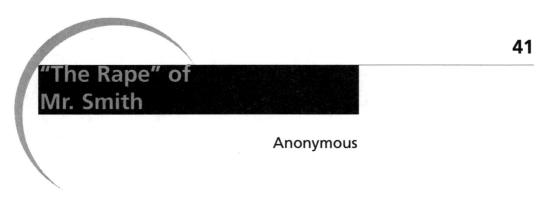

41

"The Rape" of Mr. Smith

Anonymous

The law discriminates against rape victims in a manner which would not be tolerated by victims of any other crime. In the following example, a holdup victim is asked questions similar in form to those usually asked a victim of rape.

"Mr. Smith, you were held up at gunpoint on the corner of 16th & Locust?"
"Yes."
"Did you struggle with the robber?"
"No."
"Why not?"
"He was armed."
"Then you made a conscious decision to comply with his demands rather than to resist?"
"Yes."
"Did you scream? Cry out?"
"No. I was afraid."
"I see. Have you ever been held up before?"
"No."
"Have you ever given money away?"
"Yes, of course—"
"And did you do so willingly?"

"What are you getting at?"

"Well, let's put it like this, Mr. Smith. You've given away money in the past—in fact, you have quite a reputation for philanthropy. How can we be sure that you weren't *contriving* to have your money taken from you by force?"

"Listen, if I wanted—"

"Never mind. What time did this holdup take place, Mr. Smith?"

"About 11 p.m."

"You were out on the streets at 11 p.m.? Doing what?"

"Just walking."

"Just walking? You know that it's dangerous being out on the street that late at night. Weren't you aware that you could have been held up?"

"I hadn't thought about it."

"What were you wearing at the time, Mr. Smith?"

"Let's see. A suit. Yes, a suit."

"An *expensive* suit?"

"Well—yes."

"In other words, Mr. Smith, you were walking around the streets late at night in a suit that practically *advertised* the fact that you might be a good target for some easy money, isn't that so? I mean, if we didn't know better, Mr. Smith, we might even think you were *asking* for this to happen, mightn't we?"

"Look, can't we talk about the past history of the guy who *did* this to me?"

"I'm afraid not, Mr. Smith. I don't think you would want to violate his rights, now, would you?"

Naturally, the line of questioning, the innuendo, is ludicrous—as well as inadmissible as any sort of cross-examination—unless we are talking about parallel questions in a rape case. The time of night, the victim's previous history of "giving away" that which was taken by force, the clothing—all of these are held against the victim. Society's posture on rape, and the manifestation of that posture in the courts, help account for the fact that so few rapes are reported.

42

Pornography and Men's Consciousness

Jackson Katz

I'd rather talk about pornography than the First Amendment. The former has been an important influence in my life and the lives of most of the men I know.

Unfortunately, we rarely discuss that influence. Too often, when I've been involved in discussions about pornography with groups of men, usually in a college or high school setting, the talk quickly goes to a debate about free speech and the Constitution.

Sometimes that focus, while evading the more difficult personal issues, can be enlightening and productive. But most of the time such debates are dominated by knee-jerk invocations of the Bill of Rights and the need to combat "censorship." The subject is framed as one of "individual rights" versus "government control," and the entire exercise is then dominated by men (and less frequently, women) who compete with each other to see who has the most compelling grasp of constitutional principles.

And no one talks about pornography.

For many of us who grew up with magazines like *Playboy* and *Penthouse*, this comes as a relief. It's a lot easier to talk politics and legal issues than it is to discuss masturbation, fantasy, and the sexual objectification of the women we work with, sleep with, and love. That stuff is . . . private. For many of us, it's shrouded in shame. And let's face it, it's embarrassing.

Conversational avoidance is one of the ways that men, myself included, have managed to dodge the kind of introspection that feminists have been engaged in for decades. Only in the past decade or so have a number of men begun to apply some of the feminist ideas linked to the insight that the personal-is-political and started talking about our own experiences and attitudes in an honest and self-revelatory way.

When the subject is pornography, this sort of critical male self-disclosure can lead to new insights both about sexism and men's violence against women, and about the sexual and emotional problems of many men.

But before I get to some of these, I have to acknowledge that my focus here is the effects on men of heterosexual pornography aimed at straight men. The consumption of pornography by gay males has its own dynamics, as does the consumption by lesbians of lesbian porn. There are common issues of sexual objectification, the commodification of people's bodies, domination and submission, and so forth. But the overwhelming percentage of pornography consumed in our culture today is heterosexually oriented, and that is the sphere with which I'm best acquainted.

So what kinds of things can we learn when men talk about our use of pornography and not the First Amendment? I realized when I first read seriously and considered the ideas of anti–pornography feminists that it is naive and facile to equate pornography to media representations of "sex" and not deconstruct further its function within the system of gender relations. This insight seems obvious in retrospect, but I never thought about that when I was growing up in the 1970s. Even today, despite more than a quarter century of feminist anti-porn writing, teaching, and political activism, most young men I talk with think that the only people with a reason to oppose it are uptight and prudish religious fanatics and man-hating radical lesbians.

This ignorance is partially based in a defensive form of denial. It is unsettling to learn that what we experienced as so pleasurable, masturbating to images and videos of nude women, has harmful effects. If it really is harmful to women, and to our relationships with them, we'd rather not think about it.

How is our private pleasure harmful to women? One way to conceptualize this is to consider pornography as an industry. It is a huge industry, taking in an estimated $10 billion in annual revenues. (According to the *Los Angeles Times*, nearly 10,000 new porn videos were released in 1999 alone.) And who are the workers in this industry? They are, contrary to our convenient stereotype of high class models, largely poor or working-class women, many of color, who are often treated with outright contempt and coercion by the men who control the business. Further, the vast majority of women who pose for magazines or act in porn movies have been sexually abused as children and may have been raped or abused as adolescents. So we need to be aware that by purchasing and using pornography, whatever our motives, we are perpetuating the exploitation of women and girls who have already been victimized by male domination and violence.

But apart from these exploited women, does pornography "cause" violence against women? Some people argue that, after all, most of the 90-odd percent of men who have consumed pornography at some point in their lives do not rape and sexually assault women. While technically accurate, this misses one of the central points that feminists make: pornographic representations of women affect the way that all men see and relate to women. Visual imagery is powerful. It's not harmless fun. There is a vast amount of information contained in a picture or a video.

Most white people I know accept the concept that blatantly demeaning and degrading media representations of African-Americans are unacceptable. We see them for what they are: racist. We understand that the problem is not simply the injury done to the individual actors. Rather, we recognize that all African-Americans suffer, because our feelings about the entire race are influenced by those images. Most Gentiles I know accept the same reasoning when it involves popular caricatures of Jews in Germany in the 1930s.

But when many men consider demeaning and degrading images of women, they quickly discard logic and the consensus breaks down. "That's not sexism," they'll say. "It's sex. Can't you understand that I like looking at nude women's bodies?" In the debate about pornography and men's violence against women, many men simply refuse to ascribe the exact same causal connection between objectification and violence that they make when the subject is race.

Furthermore, arguing that the pornography industry is not sexist requires a willful ignorance about the deep misogyny that pervades porn culture. It's not just the images. One representative e-mail solicitation I received through my regular account with a leading internet service provider aimed this message at young men: "Summer vacation is here and we have the college sluts to prove it! Their idea of a 'summer job' is spreading their legs and taking it live on camera. . . . It's so easy to get those hot little bikinis off the sluts. It's what they want."

Men who are not troubled by this type of blatant anti-woman aggression, including those who consume some of the really outrageous pornography available today, probably know at some level that they are "getting off" on a celebration of their power over women (i.e., *sexism*).

But for some men, including the majority who have not been exposed to overtly violent pornography, the reasoning process is more complicated. I know. I went through it myself. Initially I found it difficult to understand how pornography that is not explicitly violent can be harmful. The standard arguments were sufficient to soothe my conscience: I'm not going to rape anyone; these women are consenting adults.

When I began listening to some of my women friends' feelings about pornography I was forced to reassess my thoughts. These were intelligent, urbane women, far from prudish, for whom pornography was saddening and degrading. Because I respected them, I had no choice but to take this seriously.

Some of my friends' discomfort with pornography was linked to their level of consciousness about the subjugation of women. But it was more than that. Women with a feminist political consciousness, like all women, carry with them the personal scars and baggage of living in a male-dominated world. Some of the most painful of these involve issues of body image and sexuality. Women inevitably internalize the culture's misogyny, which then contributes to all sorts of problems in their relationships with men.

One woman I was close to was deeply disturbed by the sexual exploitation of women in the media. This included media far more mainstream than hard- or soft-core pornography. Whenever we'd see a particularly "sexploitative" beer commercial or MTV music video, she'd feel personally violated, then morose. As a man I could empathize to some degree, but I rarely had the same visceral response. This inevitably affected the way we related to each other, including the way we related sexually: how safe she'd allow herself to feel, how vulnerable.

But it's not fair to say that pornography worked only on her psyche. It touched mine as well. The reduction of women to body parts for men's consumption can significantly damage women's self-respect. But repeated exposure to pornography also can reduce men's ability to form intimate relationships with women. Such exposure conditions us to relate sexually not to unique, complex women, but to interchangeable bodies who are "fuckable" to the degree that we like looking at their breasts, vaginas, and buttocks. I'm sure that few men who use pornography ever pause to consider how their long-term consumption of it contributes to the impoverishment of their relationships with real women.

For many men, the short-term pleasure provided by pornography overshadows any harm it might cause. As the saying goes, if it feels nice, don't think twice. How bad can it be if it gets you off?

If a consumer of child pornography made that argument, we would have a ready rebuttal: we don't care if you get off to it, it's wrong (and you have serious problems). There are more important matters here to consider beyond your immediate sexual gratification. And though the arguments can get tricky when considering the case of consenting adults, the moral, if not the legal, principle holds: your right to get off sexually has to be balanced against women's rights to live free and dignified lives.

How does pornography perpetuate the subordination of women? The level of male violence against women in this society is out of control. Despite decades of feminist activism, boys and men are still sexually abusing, battering, raping, and murdering girls and women at an alarming rate. While this violence has no single cause, the dehumanization and objectification of women in the media is surely one of the contributing factors. Consider the pervasiveness of sexual harassment that women suffer from men in school, the workplace, on the street. Men aren't born biologically programmed to sexually harass women. We learn it. We learn it through continuous exposure to a media culture that is profoundly influenced by the ideological and stylistic conventions of pornography. It is impossible to discuss the way American boys have been socialized into manhood over the past three decades without talking about the effects of pornography.

I know that many of my thoughts and feelings about women, men, and sexuality were shaped by some of the dominant themes of the genre. For example, one of the more popular themes is that while they might like "sensitive" guys for friends, most women are sexually attracted to rough, aggressive men.

This didn't cause me to become a jerk, but it did cause undo self-doubt and insecurity. For other young men, this same media message is taken as a license to be sexually callous if not abusive toward women. This isn't to say, simplistically, that men see women in movies and magazines enjoying rape and sexual harassment, and are thereby encouraged to go out and assault them. That happens, but the long term effects of media messages are even more troubling. The blatant sexism and misogyny of the pornography industry has pervaded all other forms of media, inevitably permeating our consciousness.

But we're not passive agents. We can't reverse the entire process overnight, but we can choose to stop supporting the degradation of women and the dehumanization of our own sexuality by refusing to purchase or rent porn magazines and videos, or subscribe to porn sites on the World Wide Web. There's no getting around it: the personal is political.

At the same time, personal change on the part of a handful of sensitized men is insufficient. We need also to express publicly our unhappiness and outrage at the way the pornography industry fuels sexism and violence against the girls and women we claim to love. This can help stimulate discussions among men about our sexual and gender identities, utilizing some of the growing body of pro-feminist men's research and literature. Just like women, men go through a process of consciousness-raising as the first step toward politicization.

This isn't going to be easy. The question of motivation is especially problematic. People wonder: what do men have to gain by making these changes? What's in it for them?

It's really pretty simple. If we want to be able to look the women we care about in the eye and say that we respect them and support their struggle for dignity and equality, then we really have no other choice.

Next Steps and Action

43

Why I Fight Back

Whitney Walker

"Take a look," he said.

My fingers stopped on my combination lock as I looked to my right to see a man, naked from the waist down, standing a foot away from my locker.

For years I'd heard about girls getting flashed near my suburban California high school. When it had happened to my sister a few years earlier, it had been broad daylight and she and her girlfriends laughed until the man ran away. It was not like that tonight. It was dark and we were alone.

All I could do for a moment was follow his orders and look at him. He carried his pants over his left arm, and his right hand was shoved into the pocket of his grey-and-blue running jacket. Was he holding a weapon beneath his jacket? Was he going to rape me? Did he move closer? Did I hear someone else?

"What do you want?" I finally managed.

"Just take a long look."

I stood frozen in front of him for a long time. I thought about running or yelling for help, but told myself it wouldn't work: He would be too fast, no one would hear. I was feeling desperate. My car keys were cutting into my hand. Were they a weapon?

"I could stab you," I warned him, gripping my keys.

"I'd like to see you try."

I recoiled, shaking with both fear and anger. He was right, I wasn't going to try. "All right, I saw you, just leave."

"Close your locker."

I did, and was relieved when the next order was to walk away slowly and not look back.

When I began to run, he disappeared into a dark hallway and did not follow me. I went home and told my mother what had happened, and we called the police. To my knowledge, he was never caught.

It would be several years before I'd take my first self-defense class and stop seeing myself as a failure that night. I wanted to stab him, stop him, scare him the way he scared me. I wanted to be unafraid of him. But he overpowered me, ordered my obedience and received it. "I'd like to see you try." His words followed me long after I stopped hearing his voice. It was typical teenage insecurity that made me freeze up during tests, get tongue-tied during arguments, fumble the winning shot during soccer games. But I'm sure those words contributed. They taunted me, pushed me down, reminded me: He won.

As a kid with an equal-rights, athletic mom and a dad who wanted daughters rather than sons, I was raised on feminist children's books like *Free to Be . . . You and Me*, and I knew boys weren't better than girls. I also refused to believe they were stronger. When bullies picked on me or my friends, I hit them in the knees with my Holly Hobby lunch pail and that was that. But as with most girls, my self-confidence decreased as I grew. I continued to believe in equal rights, but—since I didn't excel on the playground and wasn't allowed to hit boys—I gave up on being athletic or tough. . . .

That all changed my junior year, when I took my first self-defense class with Karla Grant. A fifth-degree black belt in karate who has taught self-defense for fifteen years, Karla explained to me how tradition and the media warned me not to fight back against men. She told me how I could fight back, where and when to strike and with what. She told me why I must fight back, both to save myself and to help stop the growing number of attacks on women every day. Then she taught me how to punch and kick; how to block a blow from a fist, a club, a knife or a gun; how to fight two attackers, or three, or five, or a gang. At the end of eight weeks, I broke a two-inch-thick wooden board with my fist, and Karla told me, "If you can break a board, you can break his nose."

I've carried that message with me ever since, through three years of martial arts and self-defense training. When I hear the words of my attacker attempting to push me down, the voices of my three feminist teachers—Karla, Kathy and Roberta—tell me to push back. I see that night in high school differently now: I was not a failure, I was brave. I did not risk my life. I got away. . . .

I feel more independent because of my self-defense training, not less so, and I am grateful for the female senseis who encourage questions and focus on women's strengths. Women's bodies are perfect for karate: We have more lower-body strength and tend to be more agile than men. Most important, our attackers do not expect us to fight back, so women have the element of surprise.

I've been a pacifist all my life, and yet I relish the knowledge that my front kick can reach someone's head, my punch can knock someone to the floor. These are not completely incompatible notions. Passivity does not mean submission—it means de-escalation. Fighting back does not mean warfare—it means handing over the money if I'm mugged, but going for the testicles if he grabs me. Equal rights means women should be equal to (not the same as, but equal to) men in all ways—including equal fighters. . . .

Women who study martial arts say they are calm in the world and that they wear their training like an extra layer of protection, a warning: I can take care of myself. Women have long been striving to say that with confidence on an economic level. Self-defense provides the strength to reinforce it on a physical level. Living with the fundamental knowledge that I can protect myself against a man has changed my life completely, inside the dojo and out. I no longer question my instincts. I know them to be good when my arms block a punch before my eyes see it. I don't apologize for being in the way; I have seen the usefulness of my body. Knowing that I am strong, I refuse to be weak.

It's self-confidence that doesn't come from a gun or a can of Mace, and it won't leave you fumbling through your purse in a dark alley. It's not surprising that women have responded to the marketing tactics of gun manufacturers and deterrent-spray dealers. Cultural "wisdom" has always held that women's bodies were not made to fight, and that we are constantly vulnerable to sexual violence. With that kind of setup, movies supply the ending: She beats his chest and hysterically pleads for mercy; he doesn't grant it. She runs away but trips; he walks slowly and still catches up. Even if she's a strong female character and lands a swift knee to the groin, he's the Terminator; he stumbles for a millisecond, smiles, and then keeps coming.

These are ridiculous scenarios, but they've made their way into the consciousness of every woman and still succeed in scaring us and preventing us from fighting back. So does this warning: Don't fight back, you'll only get him angry. Everyone's heard it from the most well-meaning of sources, like the high school sex education teacher or the cops who speak to first-year female students in the dorms. The idea is that if you submit to brutal rape and torture, you may get away with your life. *May.* But as Karla explained to my first self-defense class, an attacker is already angry and not very trustworthy as a bargainer. He may say, "Don't scream and you won't get hurt," but he's already breaking the law; why should he keep his promise? The best time to fight back is when he's least expecting it—when he puts down the gun or the knife to assault you, when he gets the rope to tie you up. After that point, you don't know what he's going to do. And then there's the double standard that comes from the same sources that advise against self-defense. If you get raped, the first question is, "Did you fight back?" "No." The response then is usually, "You must have wanted it."

When I began seeing the hypocrisy of these messages from male authority figures, I also began to see the hypocrisy in all of patriarchal society. My self-defense training became connected to my awakening as a feminist. The questions began to sound the same and have similar answers. Why is a woman's right to control her body constantly threatened? Whether referring to reproductive rights or sexual violence, the answer is to take control back. With self-defense, I am in control.

Karla also told my class that the one-in-four statistic left something out—the possibility that women can successfully take down their attackers and get away. It should read: One in four women between eighteen and twenty-four will be targeted for rape in her lifetime. And every time a woman isn't attacked because she defends herself this statistic is whittled down even further. The National Women's Martial Arts Federation estimates that women make up 30 percent of all martial artists in the United States. To me, that's not enough, but it's up from 10 percent ten years ago and one percent twenty years ago. When rapists are thwarted because women fight back, attackers will stop assuming their victims will be intimidated into obedience.

I was flashed again recently, on the subway in Manhattan. An older man stood next to me, his coat draped over his arm to hide his fly, which was open to expose his penis. He was trying to show only me, but I didn't notice for a while. When I finally saw what he was doing, I immediately thought about all I could do to take him out. His knee was in a perfect position for me to break it with a kick. I could smash his elbow with a punch, or karate chop his neck. And I could certainly knee him in the groin. We were in a crowded, well-lit car, and he was no threat to me. Instead I looked to his face and showed him that he had not succeeded in frightening or arousing me, whichever his purpose might have been. At the next stop, he covered himself up with his coat and exited the car. I laughed to myself.

44

Adopting the Principle of Pro-Feminism

Ian Law

When I was first asked to speak at a seminar on the issue of "pro-feminism," I was hesitant. I was unsure if I, as a man, should be talking about what it might mean to be pro-feminist. I discussed it first with a number of people close to me, particularly women, to get their advice on the matter before making the decision.

When I reflect on this, it struck me how different my response would have been in the not-too-distant past. I would have confidently accepted, sure in the knowledge that the right to make that decision in isolation was mine, confident that I, as a man, could assert what being pro-feminist was and was not. I had, after all, been claiming my support of feminism as an ideology since my early adolescence. I would engage in political debate and action in support of feminist causes.

Yet, when I look back on that time, I am ashamed to recognize my own sexism and perpetuation of male dominance through my lifestyle, in relationships, and in how I conducted myself in my daily life. In retrospect, the contradiction between what I did and what I said I supported seems embarrassingly clear. However, at the time I was completely blind to it.

Gradually, over time, I have had pointed out to me the way in which I have been caught out by the ways of thinking and acting of dominant male culture, and have come to recognise some of these ways and challenge them in myself.

Some of the ways of thinking and acting that I, like so many other men, have challenged, involve:

- dominating airspace, making sure it is my voice and views that get heard;

- feeling a responsibility to come up with a solution, to problem-solve rather than listen and understand;

- keeping control of decision-making, seeing co-operation as a loss of control;

- not being able to accept responsibility for perpetuating injustice, either deliberately or unwittingly;

- not being able to apologise, to say that I was sorry;

- assuming that another person's or group's silence meant that they had forgotten about my wrongdoing and that I could carry on my relationship with them without doing anything to redress the injustice;

- searching for a woman's opinion that supported my own opinion, rather than listening to women's opinions which were different;

- dividing women from each other by quoting or representing a woman's view that supported my own, to other women who had a different view;

- undermining or silencing women's challenges of my behaviours by labeling them "hard-line" or over-critical;

- dismissing issues raised by women because they were not raised in what I believed to be the right manner or context.

Now, I have not said much so far about how I can act in a pro-feminist way, but I think it can be suggested that acting in the ways I have just outlined would fit more with acting in a sexist way than in a pro-feminist way. . . .

So when I look back in my life I can see that, although I believed that I was acting in a pro-feminist way, I was at the same time blind to my own sexism. It is clear that I was a poor judge of whether I was acting in a pro-feminist way or not.

I could clearly not rely on myself to hold myself accountable. I could not rely on other men to hold me accountable for my sexism when they were blind to these practices, not only in me but also in themselves. It is clear that it was women, those persons who experienced the effects of my sexism, who were in the best position to judge whether I was acting in a pro-feminist way or in a sexist way. I have to say, of course, that when I look back on this current period in my life, from some future point, there will be aspects of my perpetuation of sexist practices that I am at present blind to that will become embarrassingly clear through the ongoing efforts of women to challenge me.

However, if I as a man leave it to women to take on the responsibility to educate me in my sexism, is that not shirking my responsibility to take action against the abuses of power perpetuated by my gender?

Yet, if I take on this responsibility as a man, or with my gender in isolation, how can I know I am challenging and not perpetuating our abuse of male privilege? . . .

To return to the beginning, I spoke of how I consulted women on their views of my speaking on the issue of pro-feminism and their views of what needed to be said. A better process might have been to apply a partnership accountability process. Such a process could have been:

- gathering a group of men to discuss what it might mean to adopt a principle of pro-feminism;

- having a group of women observe this discussion and, following this, have a discussion among themselves about their responses to what the men said;

- the men would be an audience to their responses and would, in turn, discuss among themselves their responses to the women's experience of their initial discussion;

- finally, observers who had witnessed the entire proceedings could be called upon to reflect upon the whole process.

Such a process of partnership accountability with men and women, in a context of respect, trust, partnership, and openness to critical analysis, can lead to men taking the responsibility for taking action against the abuse of male culture while gaining access to the knowledge and partnership of women. . . . The best judges of whether these practices are occurring are not men, but the women who experience the effects of these practices; and the knowledge, wisdom, and partnership of women can be achieved through structured prcocesses of accountability.

45

Revving Up for the Next Twenty-Five Years

Gloria Steinem

> We who like the children of Israel have been wandering in the wilderness of prejudice and ridicule . . . feel a peculiar tenderness for the young women on whose shoulders we are about to leave our burdens . . . they will have more courage to take the rights which belong to them.
>
> —Elizabeth Cady Stanton

Feminism isn't called the longest revolution for nothing. I hope this more realistic perspective is something the second wave has gained in the last twenty-five years, because we certainly didn't begin with it. We had come out of various movement stages that were focused on immediate goals: the anti–Vietnam war movement to stop the body bags arriving home every day; the reenergized and more militant civil rights movement's efforts to desegregate and fight for voting rights; and a male-led intellectual Left that sometimes practiced what Robin Morgan humorously called "ejaculatory politics"—*revolution tomorrow, or I'm going home to my father's business.*

We also lacked women's studies, black studies—all the courses that might better be called remedial studies—to teach us that suffragists and abolitionists had struggled for more than a century to gain a legal *identity* for women of all races and men of color, so we had better be prepared for at least a century of struggle to gain a legal and social *equality*. (Not to mention the newly demanded human right of reproductive freedom, which attacks the very foundation of patriarchy.)

I don't regret one moment of those early firecracker days when explosions of consciousness lit up the sky. Somewhere, women go through them again every day when they discover how much of female experience is political, not inevitable. Even we golden oldies reexperience this excitement when new perceptions and issues arise. But bursts of light tend to flatten out the subtlety of differences between and among women, and a movement fueled only by adrenaline burns out its members—as many of us can testify.

On the other hand, younger women and newer activists checked into a world that already has a degree of feminist consciousness. They have higher expectations and an acute awareness of the backlash to the growing power of the women's movement. They generate a steadier light that exposes the tangled patterns of race, class, sexuality, and physical ability in women's lives. Where my generation externalized almost everything and used this energy to confront injustice, younger and later activists admit how much of that injustice has been internalized, and use this energy to dig deeper into individual psyches and family patterns. Where we risked repeating the same behavior because we hadn't dug out its personal and family roots, they risk re-creating a social pattern because they neglected its politics.

Thanks to feminist parents as well as to women's studies and a popular culture that occasionally pays tribute to a feminist worldview, this new generation has a better idea of the complexity involved in making lasting change. But now that's countered by a sound-bite culture, and the resistance to equality that is ever ready with terms like "postfeminism," which makes no more sense than "postdemocracy."

Without the excitement and mutual support of early, small-group feminism, I fear this and future generations won't have the personal rewards and fireworks that hooked us for a lifetime. On the other hand, without large organizations to turn out the vote and raise money to keep generations of struggle going, suffragists and abolitionists couldn't have won—and we can't either.

That's why old or young, experienced or brand-new, we have to achieve balance in the next quarter-century: between present and future, external and internal, spontaneity and long-term planning. We have to get beyond *either/or* to *and;* beyond ranking to linking; beyond such artificial labels as "equality feminists" versus "difference feminists," and into a full circle of tactics that surround the goal instead of approaching it from one direction. We need *both* excitement and steadiness, small feminist support groups and national organizations, bursts of new consciousness that are rewards in themselves, and the satisfaction of repeating what has been planned and perfected.

To accomplish this, we're going to need crazy women marching in the street who make women working inside seem reasonable *and* inside negotiators who turn street demands into practical alternatives; radical feminists who confront the roots of injustice *and* liberal feminists who build bridges for reforms that are radical in the long term; feminists who focus on the shared origins of sexism, racism, and homophobia *and* feminists who work in intimate depth within their own communities; feminist economists who take on the System of National Accounts plus the structural readjustment of poorer nations' debt *and* women who expose their own childhood sexual abuse in order to end abusive cycles that have made generations of women believe "I'm good for nothing else."

Your part in this next quarter-century depends on the groups, issues, and styles that make you feel supported, angry, inspired, or energized. I'll briefly list some new or neglected ideas here—each one of which demands balance and deserves a bibliography of its own. My hope is that one or more might incite, invite, enrage, and tantalize you into becoming a long-distance runner. So here's to the year 2022:

Making Men Equal

In the last twenty-five years, we've convinced ourselves and a majority of the country that women can do what men can do. Now we have to convince the majority of the country—and ourselves—that men can do what women can do. If we don't, the double burden of working inside and outside the home—always a reality for poor women, and now one for middle-class women, too—will continue to be the problem most shared by American women nationwide. Let's face it: until men are fully equal inside the home, women will never be really equal outside it.

This journey has even more importance in the long term. Children who grow up seeing nurturing men (and women) and achieving women (and men) will no longer have to divide their human qualities into "masculine" or "feminine." Gender will no longer be the dominant/passive model for race and class.

It's a journey that can start with women who make the presence of nurturing men a condition for bearing children—whether the men are biological fathers, friends and relatives, or workers in child care centers. It can start with boys who are raised to raise children, and with young men who ask the same question that young women do: "How can I combine career and family?" It's a journey we have begun by the demands for parental leave, shorter workdays or workweeks, and other structural changes needed to make both work and parenthood possible—for both men and women.

We'll know we're getting there when an article like this tries to convince readers that women were once more responsible for child care and family than men were, and younger readers say, "Give me a break."

Daughter of "The Personal Is Political"

In the last twenty-five years, we've learned that patriarchy and racism politicize almost every facet of life, from who does the dishes to the definition of a war crime. Now we need to begin rescuing whole areas of human experience from being devalued by association with women—to the detriment of everyone. The personal/private sphere has been divided from the political/public sphere; the "feminine" from the "masculine." As a result, the importance of the first has been lost, and its impact on the second has been ignored.

Nowhere is this more disastrous than in the failure to link child-rearing methods to political structures; to connect democracy (or the lack of it) in the family to democracy (or the lack of it) in the nation. Except for works like Alice Miller's *For Your Own Good: Hidden Cruelty in Child-Rearing and the Roots of Violence*, or Philip Greven's *Spare the Child: The Religious Roots of Punishment and the Psychological Impact of Physical Abuse*, there have been few studies of, say, German child-rearing methods as a source of Germany's political history, or the link between child abuse in the U.S. and the apocalyptic thinking now found in fundamentalism and the militias.

We need political science courses that include child-rearing changes in the study of the decline of totalitarianism in the former Soviet Union, plus the absence of abusive child-rearing methods in many of the indigenous cultures that govern through reciprocity and consensus. So far, we rarely even have psychology courses that routinely explore the link between the abusive intertwining of pain and love in child-rearing and traditions of sado-masochism in sex. We need the personal is political—but writ much larger.

Beyond Reproductive Freedom

Opposition to women's control of reproduction isn't going to end in the next quarter-century. Patriarchal, racist, classbound, and other birth-based hierarchies must exert some control over women's bodies as the most basic means of production—the means of reproduction—if they are to perpetuate themselves. That's the deepest reason for women's oppression.

But while we fight for reproductive freedom, we can expand this demand into the larger right of bodily integrity, a principle that includes freedom from involuntary testing, unwanted medical treatments, unchosen life-prolonging methods, capital punishment, pressures to provide organs, eggs, sperm, blood, other body products, and more. Not only will we gain new allies for reproductive freedom, but we will eventually benefit from a new legal principle: the power of the state stops at our skin.

How We Use Our Money

For the last twenty-five years, we've fought for equal pay, pensions, and benefits—to equalize the amount of money we earn—all of which must continue. For the next twenty-five years, however, we need to add a focus on how we spend.

Think about other liberation movements, from Gandhi's refusal to buy British-made products to African American efforts to support black-owned businesses. There has been some of that in the women's movement—boycotting states that failed to ratify the ERA, the Nestlé boycott, and more—but in general, we've assumed that earning more was progress in itself.

In fact, the question should not only be "How much do we spend?" but "How do we spend it?" Are we spending more on our outsides (clothing and appearance) than our insides (health and learning)? More on Hollywood movies than feminist political candidates? More on instant satisfaction than long-term security? Are we tithing to patriarchal religions but not to feminist groups? Supporting women-owned businesses? Seeking out companies with fair hiring and environmental policies? Saving for our own independence? In other words, are we using our dollars as consciously as we would our votes?

Welfare That Deserves the Name

I'm proud of the women's movement for opposing two welfare reform bills that were even more punishing than the current one. I'm proud of the National Organization for Women for staging a hunger strike outside the White House in a vain attempt to elicit a third veto from President Clinton. But many people on welfare don't support the original national system or the punishing state-based one that has succeeded it. You can't beat something with nothing. We need a positive alternative.

How about legislation that attaches a minimum income to every child? It would declare the minimum necessary for a child's shelter, nutrition, and health care—and then provide it. We know that investment in childhood saves money later. We also know that a floor income for every child would end the cruel and crazy inequities that now exist: foster care payments that are higher than welfare payments—thus punishing kids who remain with their biological parents—and welfare that provides health care that employed single mothers can rarely afford.

Yes, such a bill would require a broad coalition to design, but similar models in Europe could keep us from reinventing the wheel. Yes, it would require a national mobilization and years to pass, but the political climate is probably more open to aiding kids than single mothers—and definitely more open to providing health care for children than for adults. At a minimum, we would have a positive goal to support instead of only a danger to oppose. At a maximum, we would have a New Deal for children.

Economics—With Values Added

Once we understand the secret that economics is only a system of values, we begin to question: Why don't we attribute value to the roughly 50 percent of productive labor in this country that is done in the home? Some economists predict that the gross national product would go up by about 26 percent if homemakers' labor were included at only its replacement cost. There are also many kinds of economic planning that are rendered impossible by keeping this huge segment of the economy invisible.

Why don't we attribute value to the environment? If a tree has no value when it's standing there giving us oxygen—not to mention serving as a home for many species—and only acquires a value when it is cut down, then the entire force of economic motive is on the side of environmental destruction.

From the work of Vandana Shiva in India to Marilyn Waring in New Zealand and Hazel Henderson in the U.S., feminist scientists and economists are asking these questions, demystifying national and international finance, and attacking such pillars of the current system as the Census (which decides what is visible) and the System of National Accounts (which decides what is valuable). We've been learning how to play the game. Now we have to change the rules.

There are so many more magnets to draw you into the future. I hope to be with you—dreaming, fighting, planning, laughing, and transforming all the way. But as Elizabeth Cady Stanton understood at 72, with no chance of living to see victory: If any of us make it, we all will.

Heterosexism

Introduction by Warren J. Blumenfeld

> If we are to achieve a richer culture, rich in contrasting values, and we must recognize the whole gamut of human potentialities, and so we weave a less arbitrary social fabric, one in which each diverse human gift will find a fitting place.
>
> —Margaret Mead, *Sex and Temperament in Three Primitive Societies* (1935, 322)

Throughout the world, on university and grade school campuses, in communities and homes, and in the media, issues of homosexuality, bisexuality, and transgenderism are increasingly "coming out of the closet." We see young people developing positive identities at earlier ages than ever before. Activists are gaining selective electoral and legislative victories. Primarily in academic circles, greater emphasis and discussion is centering on what has come to be called "queer theory," where writers, educators, and students are analyzing and challenging current notions and categories of sexuality and gender. With this increased visibility, however, has come increased backlash.

Hate-motivated violence against lesbian, gay, bisexual, and transgender (LGBT) people is on the rise. Almost every week we hear of brutal and senseless attacks known as "gay bashings." In our schools and on our streets, groups of males wielding baseball bats and guns target anyone who acts or looks "different." For example, in Alabama, two men bludgeoned to death Billy Jack Gaither—a thirty-nine-year-old gay man—with an ax handle and tossed his limp body onto a pyre of burning tires. Brandon Teena, a female-to-male transgender person, was gang raped in Nebraska when the men found out he had a vagina. Teena reported the incident to local police officials who basically discounted his story. Soon thereafter, the perpetrators entered Teena's home and murdered him along with two of his nontransgendered friends.

There is a tradition in the western United States of ranchers killing a coyote and tying it to a fence to scare off other coyotes, and to keep them from coming out of their hiding places. On October 6, 1998, two young men lured twenty-one-year-old Matthew Shepard—a gay college student at the University of Wyoming in Laramie—into their truck and drove him to a remote spot on the Wyoming prairie, pistol whipped him, and shattered his skull. They then tied him, still alive, to a wooden fence as if he were a lifeless coyote, where he was bound for over eighteen hours in near freezing temperature. The message from his attackers seemed quite clear: to all LGBT people, stay locked away in your suffocating closets of denial and fear and don't ever come out into the light of day.

Matthew Shepard had hoped to dedicate his life to advancing the cause of human rights for all people. His uncle, R. W. Eaton, said that Matt was "a small person with a big heart, mind, and soul that someone tried to beat out of him." Matthew never regained consciousness, and died six days later. And even following his death, the hatred continued. Within days of the attack, some students at Colorado State University spray painted a scarecrow at their homecoming parade with vicious epithets in reference to Matthew Shepard, and the Reverend Fred Phelps and his followers picketed and protested Matt's funeral, claiming that God had punished him for being gay.

And these are only the more high-profile examples of hate-related violence directed against LGBT people, for the perpetrators of these injustices live in a society that promotes intolerance against people who do not conform to mainstream norms. A survey of over two thousand gay and lesbian people found that 90 percent have experienced some form of victimization on account of their perceived or actual sexual orientation, and more than one-third have been threatened directly with violence. Nineteen percent of all assaults have occurred on college and university campuses (NGLTF 1984).

In a Massachusetts study, 97 percent of high school students said they heard homophobic remarks from other students at school, and 53 percent reported hearing these remarks from school staff (Governors Commission 1993). LGBT youth are more than four times more likely to have been threatened with a weapon at school, and they are five times more likely to miss school because of safety concerns (*Pediatrics* 1998). Twenty-eight percent of LGBT students drop out of high school, and 26 percent are forced to leave home because of conflicts over their sexual orientation (Gibson 1989).

Because they often live in a society that teaches them to hide and to hate themselves, LGBT youth are two to three times more likely to attempt suicide than their heterosexual counterparts, and they comprise 30 percent of all completed youth suicides (Gibson 1989; Remafedi, Farrow, and Deisher 1991; Garofalo 1999).

Oppression based on sexual, affectional, and gender orientation or identity goes by many names, and has a number of subdivisions and definitions. *Heterosexism* in this section I define as the overarching system of advantages bestowed on heterosexuals. *Heterosexism,* which has its roots in *sexism,* is the institutionalization of a heterosexual norm or standard, which establishes and perpetuates the notion that all people are or should be heterosexual, thereby privileging heterosexuals and heterosexuality, and excluding the needs, concerns, cultures, and life experiences of LGBT people. At times subtle, heterosexism is oppression by neglect, omission, erasure, and distortion.

Heterosexism's more active and at times visible component, *homophobia,* is oppression by intent, purpose, and design. Derived from the Greek terms *homos,* meaning "same," and *phobikos,* meaning "having a fear of and/or an aversion to," the word *homophobia* was coined by George Weinberg in his 1972 book *Society and the Healthy Homosexual.* Other terms include: *homosexphobia, homonegativism,* lesbian-hatred (or -hating), gay-hatred (or -hating), and others. I define *homophobia* as the fear and hatred of those who love and sexually desire those of the same sex. Homophobia includes prejudice, discrimination, harassment, and acts of violence brought on by that fear and hatred. (Note: Some people choose not to use the word *homophobia,* preferring to use *heterosexism* as a more inclusive term by expanding its traditional definition to include that of *homophobia.*)

A closely-related concept is *biphobia,* which is oppression directed against people who love and sexually desire both males and females. *Transphobia* (or *transgenderphobia*) is oppression directed against those who challenge or do not conform to standard conceptualizations of gender expression.

Because heterosexism involves oppression directed against people on the basis of certain actual or perceived social identities, I find it helpful first to clarify the working definitions of these continually changing categories of sexuality and gender.

Sexual orientation is generally determined by those to whom we are sexually (or erotically) attracted, meaning our sexual/erotic drives, desires, fantasies. Current (Western) categories of sexual orientation include *homosexuals*—gay males and lesbians—attracted to some members of the same sex; *bisexuals,* attracted to some members of two sexes to varying degrees; *heterosexuals,* attracted to some members of the other sex; and *asexuals,* attracted to no other sex.

Regarding issues around sexual orientation, students in my classes often ask such questions as: "What causes sexual orientation?" and "Can our sexual orientation ever change?" The origins of sexual orientation are not completely understood. It is believed to be influenced by a variety of factors including genetics and hormones, as well as unknown environmental factors. Though we are not certain what determines a person's primary sexual attractions, our culture heavily influences peoples' actions and sexual behaviors. For example, one may be attracted to people of the same sex, but due to overriding condemnations against same-sex sexual expression, may attempt to "pass" as heterosexual by having sex only with people of the other sex.

Sexuality researcher Alfred C. Kinsey and his colleagues devised a seven-point scale to chart the full spectrum of human sexual *behavior,* with "0" representing those whose histories are exclusively heterosexual, and "6" for those who are exclusively homosexual in behavior. Others were placed along the scale (1–5) depending on the percentage of heterosexual (other sex) or homosexual (same sex) sexual behavior. Kinsey's and other studies suggest that sexuality is indeed more fluid and complex than once believed.

In addition to the two categories of sexual orientation and sexual behavior, our *sexual identity* is what we call ourselves. Such labels include *lesbian, gay, bisexual, bi, queer, pomosexual* (postmodern sexual), *questioning, undecided, undetermined, heterosexual, straight, asexual,* and others. Though some people assume that our sexual identity is static, actually it evolves through a multistage dynamic process.

Though another concept—*gender identity*—is closely related to sexual identity, it is, in fact, also distinct. *Gender identity* is an individual's innermost concept of self as "male" or "female"—what we perceive and call ourselves. Most people develop a gender identity aligning with their anatomical sex. For some, however, their gender identity is different from their anatomical sex. Sometimes these folks call themselves "transsexuals," some of whom hormonally and/or surgically change their anatomical sex to more fully match their gender identity.

A related concept is *gender role*. This is the set of *socially defined* roles and behaviors assigned to females and males. These roles can vary from culture to culture. Our society recognizes basically two distinct gender roles: one is the *masculine,* having qualities or characteristics attributed to males; the other is the *feminine,* having qualities or characteristics attributed to females. A third gender role, increasingly accepted in our society, is *androgyny,* combining assumed male (*andro*) and female (*gyne*) cultural qualities. Some people (of *all* sexual orientations) step out of their socially assigned gender roles or "cross-dress" (wear the clothing traditionally reserved for the other sex). Though *transgender* has increasingly become an umbrella term referring to people who cross gender and/or anatomical sex barriers, many people find *any* umbrella term problematic because it combines and confuses many different categories into one oversimplified category.

There are those who have told me that by including transgender people (many of whom may actually define themselves as "heterosexual") in a section on heterosexism/homophobia, I am confusing gender identity and/or gender role with sexual orientation and sexual identity.

I believe, however, that transgender persons, who have for so long been hidden from mainstream cultural diversity, are among those who are targeted by multiple forms of oppression. I believe they illustrate the clear and stunning connections between sexism (discussed in the previous chapter) and heterosexism/homophobia. As I stated earlier, heterosexism has its roots in sexism, and heterosexism (as well as homophobia, biphobia, and transphobia) is actually an extension or even subdivision of sexism. Simply by feeling desire for people of the same or both sexes, lesbian, gay, and bisexual people challenge current constructions of gender-based roles (one of the foundations on which sexism is based). Likewise, transgender people, who often more visibly challenge these constructions of gender expression, are often accused of being "gender traitors," and are targeted with *homophobic* epithets (for example, "faggot," "sissy," "dyke," "lezzie"), often assumed by others to be homosexual, and, therefore, face harassment and extreme forms of violence. Subsequently, we address transgender issues in both the sexism and heterosexism sections of this reader.

The histories of homosexuality, bisexuality, and transgenderism are filled with incredible pain and enormous pride, of overwhelming repression and victorious rejoicing, of stifling invisibility and dazzling illumination. Throughout the ages, homosexuality, bisexuality, and transgenderism have been called many things: from "sins," "sicknesses," and "crimes" to "orientations," "identities," and even "gifts from God."

Many historians believe that, although same-sex behavior has probably always existed, the concepts of sexual orientation and gender identity in general and the construction of an identity and sense of community based on these is a relatively modern Western invention. A historic shift occurred in the early to mid-nineteenth century, brought about by the growth of industrialization, competitive capitalism, and the rise of modern science, which provided people with more social and personal options outside the home. It is only within the last 150 or so years that there has been an organized and sustained political effort to protect the rights of people with same-sex or both-sex attractions, and those who cross traditional constructions of gender expression. However, oppression against perceived sexual and gender nonconformists has existed throughout the ages in varying degrees and locations.

In modern times, it is important to note that people experience heterosexism in different ways, and we cannot lump all people into one unified category. Subcultures and regional cultures within countries exert varying degrees of pressure to conform to a mainstream norm; individuals appear at differing points on the sexuality and gender continuum and on the path toward a definition of their identity(ies); and individuals come from disparate racial, sexual, gender, class, ethnic, religious, age, and regional backgrounds as well as physical and mental abilities. Therefore, the weight of oppression does not fall on them uniformly. Lesbians and bisexual women, for example, struggle against both homophobia/biphobia *and* sexism. LGBT people of color must also contend with the effects of racism. LGBT people with disabilities struggle against ableism. Issues of class most detrimentally affect those with the least access to economic resources. Challenging standard conceptions of gender often place transgender people at high risk for discrimination. Lesbians, gays, and bisexuals who can "pass" as heterosexual seem at times to experience less verbal harassment and acts of discrimination and violence than those who are more visible or "out." Bisexual people, potential bridge builders between the heterosexual and the gay and lesbian communities, are often distrusted by members of all these communities.

I cannot help thinking, however, about something Frederick Douglass, the escaped slave and abolitionist, once said when he described the dehumanizing effects of slavery not on slaves alone, but also on white slave owners whose position to slavery corrupted their humanity. While the social conditions of the nineteenth century were very different from today, nonetheless, I believe Douglass's words hold meaning by analogy: "No [person] can put a chain about the ankle of another [person] without at last finding the other end fastened about his [or her] own neck" (Douglass 1883). In this connection, I believe that heterosexism/homophobia/biphobia/transphobia *oppress* LGBT people, and on many levels also *hurt* people identified as heterosexual.

Readings in this Section

The section begins with a number of essays conveying key historical and social contexts for this form of oppression. My essay, "How Homophobia Hurts Everyone," provides a conceptual framework for the section by discussing what homophobia is and how it affects everyone regardless of their actual or perceived sexual orientation or identity. Marcia Deihl and Robyn Ochs, in their essay "Biphobia," define the concept of biphobia and investigate myths about bisexual people. Gregory Herek, in "Internalized Homophobia among Gay Men and Lesbians," introduces the concept and manifestations of "internalized homophobia." bell hooks provides a personal and social analysis in her essay "Homophobia in Black Communities." Neil Miller, in "Stonewall and the Birth of Gay and Lesbian Liberation," summarizes an important point in LGBT history, the 1969 rebellion in New York City at a small bar in Greenwich Village. "What Does the Bible Say about Homosexuality?" by F. Jay Deacon, discusses biblical references of same-sex expression. And in her essay "Murder Will Out—But It's Still Open Season on Gays," Donna Minkowitz examines incidents of "gay bashing" and inequalities in the U.S. system of "justice."

In "Personal Voices," Sharon Lim-Hing connects issues of racism and homophobia in her essay "Dragon Ladies, Snow Queens, and Asian-American Dykes: Reflections on Race and Sexuality"; Joshua Clark Meiner talks about his experiences with homophobia in "Memoirs of a Gay Fraternity Brother"; and Richard Plant gives a personal reflection on the Nazi persecution of gays in "The Men with the Pink Triangles." And Lisa J. Lees explains "The Transgender Spectrum" from the viewpoint of a transsexual woman.

In the concluding "Next Steps and Action," William David Burns shares his journey as a heterosexual college administrator in becoming a true ally to lesbians, gays, and bisexuals in his ironically titled "Why Don't Gay People Just Keep Quiet?"; the "International Bill of Gender Rights" adopted in Houston, Texas, at the International Conference on Transgender Law and Employment Policy suggests next steps in public policy; and Jamie Washington and Nancy J. Evans, in "Becoming An Ally," provide both a theoretical and practical foundation on the ways in which heterosexual people can become allies to lesbian, gay, bisexual, and transgender people.

This section represents heteterosexism from multiple perspectives, while emphasizing primarily overt forms of this oppression as seen from the perspective of targets in different historical and social contexts. Other selections that convey the joyful and day-to-day lived experiences, and illustrate the diverse and multifaceted historical and cultural aspects of LGBT people in Western as well as non-Western (primarily non-U.S. centered) perspectives, are included in the Further Resources section at the back of this volume.

References

Douglass, F. (1883). Speech at Civil Rights Mass Meeting. Washington, D.C. October 22.

Garofalo, R. (1999). "Youth Suicide." *Archives of Pediatric and Adolescent Medicine*, May, 487–93.

Gibson, J. P. (1989). "Gay Male and Lesbian Youth Suicide." In *U. S. Department of Health and Human Services. Report to the Secretary's Task Force on Youth Suicide*. Washington, D.C.: U.S. Government Printing Office.

Governor's Commission on Gay and Lesbian Youth. (1993). "Lincoln-Sudbury High School Study: Education Report." In *Making Schools Safe for Gay and Lesbian Youth*. Boston: Governor's Commission on Gay and Lesbian Youth.

Mead, M. (1935). *Sex and Temperament in Three Primitive Societies*. New York: William Morrow/Quill

NGLTF/National Gay and Lesbian Task Force (1984). *National Anti-Gay/Lesbian Victimization Report*. New York: NGLTF.

Remafedi, G., J. Farrow, and R. Deisher. (1991). "Risk Factors for Attempted Suicide in Gay and Bisexual Youth." In *Pediatrics* 87, no. 6: 869–76.

Weinberg, G. (1972). *Society and the Healthy Homosexual*. New York: St. Martin's Press.

Contexts

46

How Homophobia Hurts Everyone

Warren J. Blumenfeld

It is often said that, in the midst of misfortune, something unexpectedly valuable arises, and this has indeed been my experience. While traveling alone through Scandinavia one summer, I began to lose the vision in both my eyes. When I reached Denmark, I went to a hospital for an evaluation, and, after a number of tests, a physician notified me that my retinas had detached, probably because of a congenital defect. She advised immediate surgery to prevent further deterioration, and I was admitted to the Community Hospital in Copenhagen.

The next day, my sister, Susan, flew to Copenhagen to be with me for what turned out to be nearly two months.

That summer in this distant northern land, fearing the permanent loss of my vision, I lay in a narrow hospital bed longing for friends and relatives back home. But as Susan sat with me day after day, giving her love, her courage, her humor (and spectacular Danish pastries), something remarkable happened. Amid the bells of a distant church tolling away the passing hours, Susan and I genuinely got to know one another for the first time.

Although we inhabited the same house for over seventeen years, there was always some unspoken tension between us, some wall keeping us apart. Having only eighteen months separating us in age, we attended the same schools and had similar peer groups. For the first few years of our lives, we seemed to get along fine. We had a few friends in common, and we usually found time to play together most days. Our closeness, however, was soon to come to an end.

By the time I reached the age of seven or eight, I was increasingly becoming the target of harassment and attack by my peers, who perceived me as someone who was different. Names like *queer, sissy, little girl,* and *fag* were thrown at me like the large red ball the children hurled on the school yard in dodge ball games. During subsequent years, the situation only got worse. I tried to avoid other children and increasingly kept to myself. Susan and I grew apart. Only when we were both in our early twenties, about the time I went to Denmark, were we beginning to rediscover one another and to share the details of our lives.

While in college, I began to sort out how I had suffered as a gay male under the force of homophobia, but until my hospitalization I had very little idea how it had also affected Susan growing up as my heterosexually oriented younger sister. Smart, attractive, outgoing, she appeared to have, at least from my vantage point, plenty of friends and seemed to fit in. In Denmark, however, she confided to me that, throughout our school years, she was continually teased for having a "faggot" brother. On one occasion, she recalled some of the older boys laughing at her, asking if she were "like her brother." When she witnessed other students harassing me, peer pressure, coupled with her own fear of becoming a target, compelled her to distance herself from me by adding her voice to the chorus of insults. I felt betrayed, and at the time despised her for it.

Our time together in my hospital room permitted us the needed chance to define the basis of our past estrangement. Through the tears, the apologies, the rage at having been raised in an oppressive environment, and the regrets over losing so much precious time, we began the process of healing our relationship. As it turned out, my vision was not the only thing restored to me that summer.

This essay represents the growth of a seed planted in my mind back in Denmark. It centers around one primary premise: within each of the numerous forms of oppression, members of the target group (sometimes called "minority") are oppressed while on some level members of the dominant or agent group are hurt. Although the effects of oppression differ qualitatively for specific target and agent groups, in the end everyone loses.

Most of us hold simultaneous membership in a number of groups based, for example, on our personal and physical characteristics, on our abilities and class backgrounds, and on our cultural, racial, or religious identifications. We may find ourselves both in groups targeted for oppression and in those dominant groups granted relatively higher degrees of power and prestige. By examining how we are disadvantaged as well as looking at the privileges we have, we can develop empathy for individuals different from ourselves and create a basis for alliances.

This essay, therefore, is really about alliances: support for the maintenance and strengthening of alliances where they currently exist and assistance in forging new ones where none has existed before—specifically, alliances between and among lesbians, gay males, bisexuals, transgender people, and heterosexuals.

How Are LGBT People Oppressed by Homophobia?

Lesbians, gay males, bisexuals, and transgender (LGBT) people—are among the most despised groups in the United States today. Perhaps paradoxically, for many in our society, love of sameness (i.e., *homo*-sexuality) makes people different, whereas love of difference (i.e., *hetero*-sexuality) makes people the same.

Much has been written about the ways homophobia in many Western cultures targets LGBT people, ranging from negative beliefs about these groups (which may or may not be expressed), to exclusion, denial of civil and legal protections, and, in, some cases, overt acts of violence. Negative attitudes internalized by members of these groups often damage the spirit and stifle emotional growth.

Homophobia operates on four distinct but interrelated levels; the *personal,* the *interpersonal,* the *institutional,* and the *cultural* (also called the collective or societal) (Thompson and Zoloth 1989).

Personal homophobia refers to a personal belief system (a prejudice) that LGBT people either deserve to be pitied as unfortunate beings who are powerless to control their desires or should be hated, that they are psychologically disturbed, genetically defective, unfortunate misfits, that their existence contradicts the "laws" of nature, that they are spiritually immoral, infected pariahs, disgusting—to put it quite simply, that they are generally inferior to heterosexuals.

Interpersonal homophobia is manifest when a personal bias or prejudice affects relations among individuals, transforming prejudice into its active component—discrimination. Examples of interpersonal homophobia are name calling or "joke" telling intended to insult or defame individuals or groups; verbal and physical harassment and intimidation as well as more extreme forms of violence; the withholding of support, rejection, or abandonment by friends and other peers, coworkers, and family members; refusal of landlords to rent apartments, shop owners to provide services, insurance companies to extend coverage, and employers to hire on the basis of actual or perceived sexual identity. And the list goes on.

A study by the National Gay and Lesbian Task Force (NGLTF) found that more than 90 percent of the respondents had experienced some form of victimization based on their sexual identity and that over 33 percent had been threatened directly with violence: "More than one in five males, and nearly one in ten females, say they were 'punched, hit, kicked, or beaten,' and approximately the same ratios suffered some form of police abuse. Assaults with weapons are reported by one in ten males and one in twenty females. Many of those who report having been harassed or assaulted further state that incidents occurred multiple times" (1984, 4). Approximately one-third of the respondents were assaulted verbally, while more than one in fifteen were physically abused by members of their own families.

Reports of violence directed against lesbians, gay males, bisexuals, and transgender people have increased each year since the NGLTF has been keeping records, and such incidents are only the tip of the iceberg. By no means are they isolated to certain locales; rather, they are widespread, occurring throughout the country.

Institutional homophobia refers to the ways in which governments, businesses, and educational, religious, and professional organizations systematically discriminate on the basis of sexual orientation or identity. Sometimes laws, codes, or policies actually enforce such discrimination. Few institutions have policies supportive of LGBT people, and many actively work against not only those minorities but also heterosexuals who support them.

Consider, for example, the "Briggs" Initiative in the late 1970s: had it passed, it would have required the dismissal of California teachers who support gay, lesbian, and bisexual rights regardless of those teachers' actual sexual identification. The U.S. military has a long-standing policy excluding lesbians, gays, and bisexuals from service. In most instances, rights gained through marriage, including spousal benefits and child custody considerations, do not extend to LGBT people. Homosexual acts are outlawed in a number of states. And although a number of municipalities and some states have extended equal protection in the areas of employment, housing, insurance, credit, and public accommodations, no such statute exists on the national level.

Although agreement concerning same-sex relationships and sexuality does not exist across the various religious communities, and while some denominations are rethinking their negative stands on homosexuality and bisexuality, others preach against such behaviors, and as a matter of policy exclude people from many aspects of religious life simply on the basis of sexual identity.

Until 1973, established psychiatric associations considered homosexuality a disordered condition. People were often institutionalized against their will, made to undergo dangerous and humiliating "aversion therapy," and even, at times, lobotomized to alter their sexual desires. Same-sex lovers and friends are often still denied access to loved ones in hospital intensive-care units because of hospital policy allowing only blood relatives or a legal spouse visitation rights.

Today, although a number of practitioners within both the psychiatric and the medical professions hold genuinely enlightened attitudes regarding the realities of homosexuality, bisexuality, and transgendering, some, unfortunately, remain entrenched in their negative perceptions of same-sex attractions and gender expression, and these perceptions often affect the manner in which they respond to their clients.

Cultural homophobia (sometimes called *collective* or *societal* homophobia) refers to the social norms or codes of behavior that, although not expressly written into law or policy, nonetheless work within a society to legitimize oppression. It results in attempts either to exclude images of lesbians, gays, bisexuals, and transgender people from the media or from history or to represent these groups in negative stereotypical terms. The theologian James S. Tinney (1983) suggests seven overlapping categories by which cultural homophobia is manifested.

1, 2.   *Conspiracy to silence* and *denial of culture*. These first two categories are closely aligned. Although not expressly written into law, societies informally attempt to prevent large numbers of individuals of a particular minority (or target) group from congregating in any one place (e.g., in bars and other social centers), deny them space to hold social or political functions, deny them access to materials, attempt to restrict representation in any given educational institution or employment in any business, and inhibit frank, open, and honest discussion of topics of interest to or concerning these groups.

3.   *Denial of popular strength*. Many studies have found that a significant percentage of the population experiences same-sex desires, and that these individuals often define their identity in terms of these desires. The cultural assumption exists, however, that one is heterosexual until "proven guilty." According to Tinney, "Society refuses to believe how many blacks there are in this country 'passing' for white and how many lesbians and gays [and bisexuals] there are out there passing as heterosexuals" (Tinney 1983, 5).

4.   *Fear of overvisibility*. A form of homophobia is manifested each time LGBT people are told that they should not define themselves in terms of their sexuality or gender identity or when they are accused of being "blatant" by expressing signs of affection in public, behaviors that heterosexual couples routinely take for granted. They are given the message that there is something inherently wrong with same-sex desire and that individuals so inclined should keep such desire well hidden and to themselves.

5.   *Creation of defined public spaces*. Society tends to force disenfranchised individuals and groups into ghettos, where there is little possibility of integration into the general life of the community. Neighborhoods, business establishments, and even professions are thus set aside for LGBT people as they are for other target groups. Individuals enter these areas hoping to find temporary respite from the outside world's homophobia.

6.   *Denial of self-labeling*. Epithets and other derogatory labels are directed at every target group. LGBT people have chosen terms of self-definition (e.g., gay, lesbian, bisexual, transgender, for example) to portray the positive aspects of their lives and loves more adequately. Recently, increasing numbers of lesbians, gays, bisexuals, and transgender people have reappropriated such terms as *queer, faggot,* and *dyke* in order to transform these venomous symbols of hurt and bigotry into tools of empowerment.

7.   *Negative symbolism* (stereotyping). Stereotyping groups of people is used as a means of control and a further hindrance to understanding and to meaningful social change. Stereotypes about LGBT people abound, ranging from their alleged predatory appetites, to their physical appearance, to the possible "causes" of their desires.

In addition to Tinney's categories of cultural homophobia, psychologist Dorothy Riddle (1985) suggests that the concepts of *tolerance* and *acceptance* should also be included: tolerance because it can, in actuality, be a mask for an underlying fear or even hatred (one is tolerant, e.g., of a baby crying on an airplane while simultaneously wishing it would stop or go away), and acceptance because it assumes that there is indeed something to accept.

How Homophobia Hurts Everyone

It cannot be denied that homophobia, like other forms of oppression, serves the dominant group by establishing and maintaining power and mastery over those who are marginalized or disenfranchised. Individuals maintain oppressive behaviors to gain certain rewards or to avoid punishment, to protect their self-esteem against psychological doubts or conflicts, to enhance their value systems, or to categorize others in an attempt to comprehend a complex world. By excluding entire groups of people, those in positions of power obtain economic, political, ideological, and other privileges. In many ways, through, oppression, in this instance homophobia, ultimately limits heterosexuals.

Homophobia inhibits the ability of heterosexuals to form close, intimate relationships with members of their own sex.

Young people often form close same-sex attachments during their childhood years. But once they reach a certain age (usually around the time of puberty), their elders encourage them to distance themselves from these friends, with the implication that if they do not, their sexuality will be called into question. This means—especially for males—no more sleeping over at each other's houses, no more sharing intimate secrets, no more spending as much time together. Ultimately, this situation tends to hinder the ability of heretosexual adults to get as close to a same-sex friend as they once did when they were very young.

Homophobia locks all people into rigid gender-based roles that inhibit creativity and self-expression.

Much has been written about gender roles and how they constrain both females and males. In Western culture, concepts of masculinity and feminity promote the domination of males over females and reinforce the identification of maleness with power. Males are encouraged to be independent, competitive, goal oriented, and unemotional, to value physical courage and toughness. Females, on the other hand, are taught to be nurturing, emotional, sensitive, expressive, to be caretakers of others while disregarding their own needs.

Gender roles maintain the sexist structure of society, and homophobia reinforces those roles—for example, by casting such epithets as *faggot*, *dyke*, and *homo* at people who step outside designated gender roles. This pervasive social conditioning based on anatomical sex effectively generates great disparities between males and females. For evidence of this inequality one need only look at the preponderance of men over women in upper management positions and other positions of prestige, or at the fact that women still do not earn equal pay for equal work. There is also evidence, in a classic 1935 anthropological study of three cultures by Margaret Mead, that there is an increased incidence of violence against women in male-dominated societies.

Homophobic conditioning (and indeed all forms of oppression) compromises the integrity of heterosexual people by pressuring them into treating others badly, actions contrary to their basic humanity.

By way of analogy, Frederick Douglass, the famous nineteenthth-century escaped slave and abolitionist, described what he called "the dehumanizing effects" of slavery not on slaves alone, but also on white slave owners, whose position to slavery corrupted their humanity. Describing his experiences with Mrs. Sophia Auld, mistress of the Baltimore household in which Douglass lived and worked during the 1820s, Douglass wrote,

> My new mistress proved to be a woman of the kindest heart and finest feelings. But, alas, this kind heart had but a short time to remain such. The fatal poison of irresponsible power was already in her hands, and soon commenced its infernal work. Slavery soon proved its ability to divest her of (her) heavenly qualities. Under its influence, the tender heart became stone, and the lamblike disposition gave way to one of tigerlike fierceness. (Douglass 1845, 77–78)

Homophobia can be used to stigmatize, silence, and, on occasion, target people who are perceived or defined by others as gay, lesbian, or bisexual but who are in actuality heterosexual.

For more than two millennia in the West, antihomosexual laws and decrees have been enacted by religious denominations and governments carrying punishments ranging from ridicule to death of the "accused." These decrees have been used to justify harsh treatment of those discovered or believed to have engaged in same-sex activity. But what is often forgotten or overlooked is the fact that these same laws have, on occasion, been used by individuals and governments to silence opponents, regardless of whether they have engaged in same-sex activity.

In our own century, Paragraph 175 of the German Penal Code, which banned homosexuality, was used by the Nazi regime to incarcerate and ultimately to send great numbers of men suspected of being homosexual to their death, and was also at times employed to incarcerate Catholic clergy, many of whom were heterosexual, as well as non-Catholic heterosexuals who opposed state authority. In addition, "sodomy" laws remain on the books in many states. Although designed chiefly to harass persons engaging in same-sex activity, they have also been used to prosecute heterosexuals.

The Lambda Legal Defense and Education Fund—a New York–based gay, lesbian, bisexual, and transgender-oriented legal organization—defended a twenty-six-year-old heterosexual man who was denied health insurance because he was unmarried, living in New York City with a male roommate, and therefore presumed to be gay and stereotypically assumed to be at increased risk for HIV/AIDS. Heterosexual male hairdressers and female gym teachers and other heterosexuals working in professions widely perceived to be "gay," along with single people living in red-lined "gay" zip codes, are also vulnerable to victimization by similar homophobia-based discrimination.

Violent "queer-bashing" is not infrequently directed against heterosexuals who are also perceived to be gay or lesbian. The clear implication here is that all people are at risk for attack, irrespective of their actual sexual identity, so long as any group remains the target of violent hate-motivated assaults.

Homophobia generally restricts communication with a significant portion of the population and, more specifically, limits family relationships.

No matter how they are constituted, families will continue to produce lesbian, gay, bisexual, and transgender offspring. The political and theocratic Right argues loudly that homosexuality poses a direct threat to "traditional family values." In actuality, however, it is homophobia that strains family relationships by restricting communication among family members, loosening the very ties that bind. Children, fearing negative reactions from parents, hold back important information about their lives. Parents, often not wanting to hear about their child's sexual or gender identity, never truly get to know their children. Even when parents and children reside in the same house, secret upon secret adds up to polite estrangement and sometimes to a total break.

When LGBT people finally do "come out" to their relatives and friends, the heterosexual relatives and friends sometimes go into a "closet" as their homophobia and/or that of those around them leads them to withhold the truth from friends and neighbors. Indeed, family members sometimes become targets of stigmatization when the truth about an LGBT relative becomes known. In any case, the emotional toll can be great.

Homophobia ultimately undermines the process of parenting in all families. It harms not only those in the more obvious cases where there are LGBT children, or LGBT parents, but that it also imposes great impediments to "mainstream" heterosexual families with heterosexual children.

Societal homophobia prevents some lesbian, gay, bisexual, and transgender people from developing an authentic self identity, and adds to the pressure to marry, which in turn places undue stress and oftentimes trauma on themselves as well as their heterosexual spouses and their children.

The suppression of information about the gay, lesbian, bisexual, and transgender experience reinforces the heterosexist assumption that everyone is or should be heterosexual and should conform to standard conceptualizations of gender expression. This assumption, coupled with the frequently very real penalties for not conforming to heterosexual norms, has pressured many people either to hide their true sexual and/or gender identity or has restricted their self realization. Some have married in an attempt to "fit in" or "pass," or in hopes of "being cured" of their same-sex attractions and/or their gender expressions.

Homophobia is one cause of premature sexual involvement that increases the chances of teen pregnancy and the spread of sexually transmitted diseases (STDs).

Young people, of all sexual identities, are often pressured to become *heterosexually* active to prove to themselves and others that they are "normal." If homophobia were reduced in the schools and society at large, in all likelihood, fewer young people would act out *heterosexually* during adolescence.

Homophobia combined with sexphobia (fear and revulsion of sex) results in the elimination of any discussion of the lives and sexuality of sexual minorities as part of school-based sex education, keeping vital information from all students. Such a lack of information can kill people in the age of AIDS.

Some religious and community leaders, educators, and parents actively work to prevent honest and nonjudgmental information concerning homosexuality, bisexuality, and transgenderism—indeed, sexuality and gender in general—from reaching young people. Students of all sexual and gender identities need this information to make informed decisions about their sexual activity. Without it, they are placed at greater risk for unwanted pregnancy, STDs, and HIV infection.

Homophobia (along with racism, sexism, classism, sexphobia, and others) inhibits a unified and effective governmental and societal response to AIDS.

It can be reasonably argued that if the majority of people with AIDS had initially been middle-class, white, suburban heterosexual males, rather than gay and bisexual men, people of color, working-class people, sex workers (prostitutes), and drug users, then governmental and societal institutions would have mobilized immediately to defeat the epidemic.

Because of the lack of wide-scale early attention, AIDS has spread to pandemic proportions. The government and society, at least initially, did not make a true commitment to education, research, and treatment. Funding remained insufficient for as many years as AIDS retained its erroneous reputation of a disease of outcast sexual and social minorities. The result was, and in some sectors continues to be, that many heterosexuals have a false sense that they will not be affected, and take no precautions.

Homophobia prevents heterosexuals from accepting the benefits and gifts offered by the lesbian, gay, bisexual, and transgendered communities: theoretical insights, spiritual visions and options, contributions in the arts and culture, to religion, to family life, indeed to all facets of society.

In cultures where homophobia is present, there have been active attempts to falsify historical accounts of same-sex love—through censorship, deletion, half-truths, and altering pronouns signifying gender—making accurate reconstruction extremely difficult. This effectively distorts society's collective memory (i.e. history), clouding our sense of identity as individuals and as social beings. Everyone loses from this suppression of the truth.

John Boswell cites an example of this censorship in a manuscript of *The Art of Love* by the Roman author Ovid. A phrase that originally read, "A boy's love appealed to me less" (*Hoc est quod pueri tanger amore minus*) was altered by a Medieval moralist to read, "A boy's love appealed to me not at all" (*Hoc est quod pueri tanger amore nihil*), and an editor's note that appeared in the margin informed the reader, "Thus you may be sure that Ovid was not a sodomite" (*Ex hoc nota quod Ovidius nonfrerit Sodomita*) (Boswell 1980, 18).

Boswell also cites a Renaissance example of homophobic censorship in which Michelangelo's grand-nephew changed the sex of the subject of his uncle's sonnets to make them more acceptable to the public.

Closer to our time, government-sponsored censorship of art deemed "homoerotic" by the National Endowment for the Arts ultimately restricts creativity and freedom of expression of the entire artistic community.

In addition, traditional religious teachings on homosexuality keep lesbians, gays, bisexuals, and transgender people from entering religious life or from being true to themselves. These teachings also inhibit the ability of many congregations to value and celebrate human diversity and, most importantly, impedes spiritual growth.

Homophobia saps energy from more constructive endeavors.

Like all forms of oppression, homophobia inhibits our ability to understanding the nature and scope of truly serious and far-reaching social problems (e.g. poverty, illiteracy, war, disease, environmental decay, crime, and drug addiction). Oppression results in the scapegoating and distancing of people from one another, diminishing our capacity to address these problems and thereby degrading the quality of life for all of us. By reducing the various forms of oppression, we quite literally make our society more socially efficient, increasing our ability to find solutions to the social and ecological challenges that threaten our collective future.

Homophobia inhibits appreciation of other types of diversity, making it unsafe for everyone because each person has unique traits not considered mainstream or dominant. Therefore, we are all diminished when any one of us is demeaned.

As Reverend Martin Niemoeller, wrote during World War II,

In Germany they came first for the Communists, and I didn't speak up because I wasn't a Communist. Then they came for the Jews, and I didn't speak up because I wasn't a Jew. Then they came for the trade unionists, and I didn't speak up because I wasn't a trade unionist. Then they came for the Catholics, and I didn't speak up because I was a Protestant. Then they came for me, and by that time no one was left to speak up.

The meaning is quite clear. When any particular group of people is scapegoated, it is ultimately everyone's concern. For today, gay, lesbian, bisexual, and transgender people are targeted. Tomorrow, they may come for you. Therefore, it is in everyone's self-interest to work actively to dismantle all the many forms of oppression, including homophobia.

Conclusion

In truth, homophobia is pervasive throughout the society and each of us, irrespective of sexual or gender identity, is at risk of its harmful effects. Within the schools, homophobia compromises the entire educational environment. Though homophobia did not originate with us and we are not to blame, we are all responsible for its elimination and, therefore, all can gain by a closer examination of the issues.

Lesbians, bisexuals, gay males, and transgender people have been, and continue to be, on the front lines in fighting against homophobia, and standing by our sides are supportive heterosexual allies—people who have worked and continue to work through their own homophobic conditioning, who are secure with their own sexual identities, who have joined us and have not cared when others called their sexuality into question.

We are *all* born into a great pollution called homophobia (one among many forms of oppression) that falls upon us like acid rain. For some people, spirits are tarnished to the core; others are marred on the surface, but no one is completely protected. Yet neither are we to blame. We had no control over the formulation of this pollution, nor did we direct it to pour down upon us. On the other hand, we all have a responsibility, indeed an opportunity, to join together to construct protective shelters from the corrosive effect of oppression while working to clean up the homophobic environment in which we live. Once sufficient steps are taken to reduce this pollution, we will all breathe a lot easier.

References

Blumenfeld, W. J., ed. (1992). *Homophobia: How We All Pay the Price.* Boston: Beacon Press.

Boswell, J. (1980). *Christianity, Social Tolerance, and Homosexuality: Gay People in Western Europe from the Beginning of the Christian Era to the Fourteenth Century.* Chicago: University of Chicago Press.

Thompson C., and B. Zoloth. (1989). "Homophobia." A pamphlet . Cambridge, Mass.: Campaign to End Homophobia.

Douglass, F. (1982 [1845]). *Narrative of the Life of Frederick Douglass, an American Slave, Written by Himself.* ed. H. A. Baker, Jr. New York: Penguin.

Mead, M. (1935). *Sex and Temperament in Three Primitive Societies.* New York: William Morrow/Quill.

National Gay and Lesbian Task Force. (1984). *National Anti-Gay/Lesbian Victimization Report.* Washington, D.C.: NGLTF

Riddle, D. (1985). "Homophobia Scale." In *Opening Doors to Understanding and Acceptance.* ed. K. Obear and A. Reynolds. Boston: Unpublished essay.

Tinney, J. S. (1983). "Interconnections." In *Interracial Books for Children Bulletin* 14, nos. 3–4. New York: Council on Interracial Books for Children.

47

Biphobia

Marcia Deihl and Robyn Ochs

I was in a feminist bookstore. As the woman rang up my purchase, she asked me if a "lesbian discount" was appropriate. I was somewhat taken aback, but I said (half in jest), "Well, I'm bisexual, so how about half?" She didn't smile and I didn't get a discount.

— Marcia

I came out to my brother several years ago and he seems on many levels to accept my bisexual identity. However, about a year ago I was visiting him and he took special care to request that I not discuss being bisexual in front of his roommates.

— Robyn

A friend of ours had been active in her lesbian community for several years. Then she fell in love with a man. When her lesbian "friends" found out, they ostracized her and held a "funeral" for her.

— Robyn and Marcia

I told a heterosexual male friend that I was bisexual. His response was to make repeated attempts to sexualize our relationship. He made the false assumption that since I was bi-SEX-ual, I was attracted to everybody.

— Robyn

Stories and Stereotypes

These are all stories that happen to bisexuals. Some of these mirror homophobia, others heterophobia, and still others are specifically "biphobic." All of them oppress bisexuals.

Biphobia: What is it? It is fear of the other and fear of the space between categories. Our sexual categories have long been founded on the illusion that there are two separate and mutually exclusive sexual identities: homosexual and heterosexual. The assumption is that you are either one or the other; those who are not like you are very different, and you needn't worry about becoming like them. Biphobia, like homophobia, is prejudice based on negative stereotypes. It is often born of ignorance, but sometimes it is simply bigotry:

Everybody knows about bisexuals—they're *confused* ("just a stage you're going through . . . you'll eventually choose . . . you're not secure in your mature heterosexuality yet . . . you're afraid of the other sex and the same sex is less threatening . . . "); they're *'sex maniacs'* ("They will do it with anyone, anytime") they're *shallow* ("They can't commit themselves to any one person or even any one sex for a long-term relationship. . . . They're typical swingers . . . they're fickle. . . ."). (Deihl in Blumenfeld and Raymond 1988, 81)

In April of 1983, an "April Fools" cartoon appeared in Boston's *Gay Community News*. It showed a jilted lesbian who had been left by her bisexual lover for a man. The next time, she was prepared with "bisexuality insurance." The BiVocals, a new bisexual support group, angrily responded, "Sometimes we do leave women for men. We also leave men for women, women for women, and men for men. But we don't leave our lovers any more cruelly or frequently than any other group. . . . And sometimes we are assholes, just like some lesbians." (BiVocals, 1983, 4)

Fear from Heterosexual People

Homophobic heterosexual men and women alike react to bisexuality as they react to homosexuality. But with bisexuality, there is the added dimension of identification with the "straight half" of a bisexual person. They may be even more threatened, because they see that the "other" is not quite so different as they had believed. It could be a case of fantasy turning into a very real possibility.

Sigmund Freud and Alfred Kinsey agree that there is a spectrum of sexuality from "purely" gay to "purely" straight. (Freud 1938; Kinsey et al. 1948). Scholars working in other disciplines have made similar observations. Margaret Mead, for example, said "I think extreme heterosexuality is a perversion"; W. Somerset Maugham stated, "I tried to persuade myself that I was three-quarters normal and that only a quarter of me was queer . . . whereas it was the other way round" and Richard Aldington, biographer and friend of D. H. Lawrence, wrote, "I should say Lawrence was about eighty-five percent hetero and fifteen percent homo" (all quoted in Rutledge 1988: 20, 46, 142).

If internalized homophobia is keeping some heterosexual people from acting on their gay fantasies, they will probably be biphobic. If they are living a heterosexual life out of negative reasons (e.g., "I don't deserve what I really want"; "It's sick and perverse and sinful to act on these feelings"), then they will probably be threatened by others' bisexuality. If they are truly choosing to respond heterosexually for positive, clear, inner-directed reasons, their chances of being threatened are lessened.

We can't "convert" anyone. We don't have the right to come out for anyone else or to say that someone is "really bisexual." We don't have the right to judge another's reasons for avoiding intimacy with a given sex. We simply want it to be known that there is a third option, encompassing a wide range of variations. Some of our best allies are secure heterosexual people.

Heterosexual men and women will react slightly differently to bisexual men and bisexual women than they might react to gay men and lesbians. A homophobic straight man may respond similarly to a bisexual man as he does to a gay man (e.g., "Sissy!"). This sentiment may mask the outrage that men feel about other men renouncing their patriarchal prerogative of superiority to women. (Matteson 1989, 6). We have seen documentaries in which the Marines refer to recruits in basic training as "ladies" and "girls" in a derogatory sense. These names are considered the worst possible put-down for men who aren't being "masculine" enough. Similarly, taunting gay men with feminine names is a thinly veiled disrespect for all women. Another typical homo-phobic reaction is, "I just know he's going to make a pass at me." For the first time, a heterosexual man is in the position of potential "prey." Terrified and outraged, he may not be able to say "No!" safely.

Heterosexual women cannot write off bisexual men as "just friends" with no sexual undercurrents the way they might gay men. But, they cannot assume that these men are attracted to them either. Heterosexual women may see bisexual women as better "initiation" experiences than lesbians, or they may assume that bisexual women are after them.

Bisexuality defies old categories and evokes new responses. Bisexuals are relegated to a netherworld by heterosexuals and homosexuals alike. Our sexual minority status is simply one of nonexistence. What fears are expressed about us are largely based on ignorance rooted in our invisibility. (In the mainstream media, gay men and lesbians are becoming more visible.)

Bisexual women who are not middle class or rich, traditionally "beautiful," able-bodied, or white are invisible. Thus, it is hardly surprising that when *Newsweek* finally got around to publishing a feature story on bisexuality in 1995, the principal focus was on the secretive married bisexual men who are passing AIDS along to their wives. The gay community fares little better. We hear in conversation that bisexuals are "really lesbians who want access to heterosexual privilege" and that bisexuals were "really heterosexuals who want access to the support and excitement of the lesbian community."

Fear from Gay and Lesbian People

The early homophile (1950s and 1960s) and later (1970s) gay liberation movements have fought for the right of gay men and lesbians to exist, to love, and to be treated with dignity. Therefore, any perceived "regression" by gay people "converting" back to heterosexuality is considered a threat. This feeling is understandable. The gay and lesbian communities are under siege, especially in this age of AIDS; people under constant siege band together to form a united front. Thus formerly gay and lesbian people who "turn bi" are often met with feelings of betrayal and anger, but these reactions do not do justice to the truth of the situation.

Why are bisexuals perceived as such a threat to so many gay men and lesbians? We see a combination of society's homophobia and internalized biphobia at work here. A recurring theme in my [Robyn] lesbian relationships is the voiced fear on the part of my lover that I would choose to leave her for a man. After all, so much of our society is structured to encourage and support heterosexual relationships—families, the media, institutions such as marriage and corporations providing health insurance "family plans" are all based on the configuration of the heterosexual couple. Therefore, how could she possibly "compete" with the odds so stacked against us? There is no denying that the encouragement of heterosexuality and the discouragement of homosexuality is a very real fact. However, I also felt that there was a certain amount of internalized homophobia at work here, too: the feeling that whatever she had to offer me and whatever we had together couldn't possibly outweigh the external benefits of being in a heterosexual relationship. There's an underlying assumption there that anyone who has the choice will ultimately choose heterosexuality, that lesbians and gay men choose homosexual relationships because they are unable to be heterosexual. The number of bisexuals who have chosen homosexual relationships shows that this isn't necessarily so.

Some say that bisexuals are only half-oppressed. Yet we are not put on half-time when we are fired by a homophobic boss; we do not lose only half our children when we lose a custody battle; we cannot say to the gay-basher, "Oh! Please only beat me up on one side of my body."

We hear others stating that bisexual women dilute the power of the lesbian community. According to this reasoning, bisexual women should be banned from attending lesbian events despite the fact that bisexual women have greatly contributed to women's music and culture. Ironically, many lesbian organizers and performers downplay the lesbian energy in their own lives and in the history of feminism. For example, many performers who are or have been lesbians never use the "L-word" on stage. The brave ones acknowledge this problem, and address questions of privacy, expectations, and the right to change. Holly Near recently said at a concert, "I know that some of you are uncomfortable because you think I might be a lesbian. And there are others who are upset because I might not be one." Though not explicitly stated, Near seems to be referring to the ongoing and often angry controversy in the women's community over rumors of her involvement with a man.

After I [Marcia] was asked if I warranted the "lesbian discount," I thought seriously about it. I respected the woman's right to run her store the way she wanted. I loved the idea that there was such a thing as a lesbian discount—a rare opportunity for lesbians to be rewarded, not made invisible or degraded. But, then I thought of my ten years of gay marches and my six years of playing in a feminist band that performed 25 to 50 percent lesbian material. I think I *did* deserve at least half of the discount!

Bisexuals should not automatically be categorized along with heterosexuals; bisexuals should not be excluded from the lesbian and gay community. Yet, it is generally only famous bisexual persons—reclassified as "gay" or "lesbian"—(e.g., Virginia Woolf, Sappho, Christopher Isherwood, James Baldwin, Vita Sackville-West, Colette, Kate Millet) who are embraced by lesbians and gay men; modern-day bisexuals working common jobs and bearing ordinary names are not. For example, if we want to put our name into an organization, we are often called "intruders."

We won't accept it both ways; the lesbian and gay community cannot have it both ways; either bisexuals are in or we're out. The feminist bookstore offering a lesbian discount was a store for *all* women, but, lesbians got a discount; heterosexual and bisexual women did not. It seemed in this instance we were *out* of the lesbian-gay community. We want to be in, but we are called "divisive" when we name ourselves as a third category. Such attitudes often keep us away and only reinforce the impression that we have "deserted the ranks."

Like heterosexual people who may be ignoring their homosexual inner signals, some gay men and lesbians may be repressing their bisexuality. They may fear the loss of their gay identity and their closest friends if they act on these desires. Others are happy. They have chosen positively to be gay or lesbian. These persons tend to be supportive of bisexuality in others; those who are threatened or unsure of themselves are less so.

A clear example of biphobia is the ostracism of some bisexuals from the lesbian and gay community. When women and men come out as bisexuals, their gay and lesbian friends often tell them that they can't really be bisexuals—that they are confused, or that they are waiting to reap the benefits of heterosexism. This is ironic where one considers that the lesbian and gay liberation movement in the United States is united around the right to love whomever we please, and to have our relationships validated and recognized, even when they do not conform to society's norms. Bisexuals are often pushed into a closet *within* a closet.

Our Vision: The Bisexual Artist/Citizen Today

Can you spot a bisexual when you meet one? Is there any hidden meaning to someone who is wearing one long earring and one short one, very short bangs with long hair in the back, dresses with hightops, or heels with pants (even the women!)? Perhaps. We come in every conceivable outer package—just like all other groups. What is important is what is inside. Our psyches are not split down the middle. We do not get up everyday and think, "Should I be straight or gay today?" We are, every day, in all situations, bisexual. We are like the mint breath freshener, Certs: "TWO . . . TWO . . . TWO sexualities in one." We are like the yin and yang symbol, perhaps emphasizing one aspect but with the seed of the other always present. We are simply a third option.

In sum, we are not defined by our behavior, but by our essence. If we walk down the street holding hands with a woman, people will assume we are lesbians. If we walk down the street holding hands with a man, people will assume we are heterosexual. We aren't shifting; others' perceptions are.

As public television's Mr. Rogers tells very young children, each of us is unique. We are all completely different from anyone else, with our own gifts and limitations. We are all artists; we are all queers; we are all "oddists." And lesbian, gay, bisexual, and transgender people have practically been forced to be creative. We experience a conflict between inner signals and outer demands that requires that we invent ourselves and think on our feet at every moment. Perhaps this is why we have contributed more than our share to the arts. As Fran Lebowitz quipped, "If you removed all of the homosexuals and homosexual influence from what is generally regarded as American culture, you would be pretty much left with *Let's Make a Deal* (quoted in Rutledge 1988, 93). We would do well to join some old Native American Indian cultures in considering differences in sexuality and gender expression as special, honored gifts, not as threatening deviations (Williams 1986).

Being bisexual and naming ourselves makes us special. Yet, we have our cultural work cut out for us. We must invent and create our own lives, music, theater, writing, and art, just as some of us did with women's culture. We need art that reflects, analyzes, reinvents, and inspires our daily lives. We must not simply react to biphobia, we must come together with others like ourselves to name and love ourselves.

Though we are unique, we are also like everyone else: we are citizens of this planet. We need to work in coalitions because we want to help clear up the many problems that face us and our children and grandchildren today. Problems of poverty, pollution, and violence are obvious to us all—female and male, gay, lesbian, bisexual, and straight. In order to solve these problems, action must be taken against heterosexism, sexism, racism, and class privilege. And since we are all minorities, we must work together on common projects in order to be effective. Bisexuals are natural leaders for uniting progressive men and women, and also gays and straights.

Bisexuals are not fence-sitters; there is no fence. Sexuality is a giant field in which mostly lesbian- and gay-identified people are clustered on one side and mostly heterosexual-identified people on the other. We are the middle; sometimes we travel toward one end or the other in a day, in a lifetime. We hereby declare a field day!

References

Blumenfeld, W. J. and D. Raymond. (1988/1993). *Looking at Gay and Lesbian Life*. New York: Beacon Press.

BiVocals (1983, April 23). "Gay-Identified Bisexuals" [letter to the editor]. *Gay Community News*, 4.

Freud, S. (1938). "Infantile Sexuality." In *The Basic Writings of Sigmund Freud*, trans. A. Brel. New York: Modern Library.

Kinsey, A., W. Pomeroy, C. Martin, and R. Gebhard. (1948). *Sexual Behavior in the Human Male*. Philadelphia: Saunders.

Matteson, D. (1989). "Racism, Sexism, and Homophobia." *Empathy* 1: 6.

Rutledge, L. (1988). *Unnatural Quotations*. Boston: Alyson Publications.

Williams, W. (1986). *The Spirit and the Flesh*. Boston: Beacon Press.

48

Internalized Homophobia among Gay Men, Lesbians, and Bisexuals

Gregory M. Herek

Like members of other stigmatized groups, lesbian, gay and bisexual (LGB) people face numerous psychological challenges as a result of society's hostility toward them. One challenge results from the consequences of hiding one's sexual orientation. LGB people must traverse a sequence of events, through which they recognize their homosexual or bisexual orientation, develop an identity based on it, and disclose their orientation to others, a process usually termed "coming out" (a shortened form of "coming out of the closet"). Conversely, being "in the closet" or "closeted" refers to "passing" as heterosexual. Because of cultural heterosexism, people generally are presumed to be heterosexual. Coming out, therefore, is an ongoing process; lesbians, gay males, and bisexuals continually must come out as they encounter new people. Different people are out of the closet to varying degrees.

Most children internalize society's ideology of sex and gender at an early age. As a result, lesbians, gay males, and bisexuals usually experience some degree of negative feeling toward themselves when they first recognize their homosexuality or bisexuality in adolescence or adulthood. This sense of what is usually called "internalized homophobia" often makes the process of identity formation more difficult (Malyon 1982). In the course of coming out, most lesbians, gay males, and bisexuals successfully overcome the threats to psychological well-being posed by heterosexism. They manage to reclaim disowned or devalued parts of themselves, developing an identity into which their sexuality is well integrated. Psychological adjustment appears to be highest among men and women who are committed to a gay, lesbian, or bisexual identity and who do not attempt to hide their homosexuality or bisexuality from others. Conversely, people with a homosexual or bisexual orientation who have not yet "come out," who wish that they could become heterosexual, or who are isolated from the LGB community may experience greater psychological distress (Bell and Weinberg 1978; Hammersmith and Weinberg 1973; Malyon 1982; Weinberg and Williams 1974).

As a result of heterosexism, many individuals feel compelled to hide their homosexuality or bisexuality or "pass" as heterosexual. Respondents to the *San Francisco Examiner*'s 1989 national survey of lesbians and gay men, for example, waited an average of 4.6 years after knowing they were gay until they came out (which presumably involved disclosing their homosexual orientation to another person). Depending on the area of the country, between 23 percent and 40 percent had not told their family that they were gay, and between 37 percent and 59 percent had not disclosed their sexual orientation to coworkers (*San Francisco Examiner* 1989).

Hiding one's sexual orientation can create a painful discrepancy between public and private identities. Because they face lack of acceptance by prejudiced heterosexuals, LGB people who are "passing" may feel inauthentic, that they are living a lie, and that others would not accept them if they knew the truth. The need to "pass" is likely to disrupt long-standing family relationships and friendships if lesbians, gay males, and bisexuals feel they must distance themselves from others to avoid revealing their sexual orientation. When contact with heterosexuals cannot be avoided, they may keep their interactions at a superficial level as a self-protective strategy.

Passing also creates considerable strain for LGB partnerships. As already noted, even openly LGB people are generally deprived of the many tangible supports afforded to married heterosexuals (e.g., insurance benefits and inheritance rights). In addition, those who are "passing" must actively hide or deny their same-sex relationship to family and friends. Consequently, the problems and stresses common to any relationship must be faced without the social supports typically available to heterosexual lovers or spouses.

When heterosexism is expressed through overt hostility and attacks, it creates additional psychological challenges for LGB people. Once they come out, they risk rejection by others, discrimination, and even violence, all of which can have psychological consequences that endure long after their immediate physical effects have dissipated. Being the target of discrimination, for example, often leads to prolonged feelings of sadness and anxiety; it also can lead to an increased sense that life is difficult and unfair and to dissatisfaction with one's larger community (Garnets et al. 1990).

LGB victims of hate crimes may face special psychological challenges. Because hate crimes represent an attack on the victim's identity and community, they may affect a victim's feelings about self-worth as a lesbian, gay, or bisexual individual, as well as feelings toward the LGB community. The victim's homosexuality or bisexuality may become directly linked to the heightened sense of vulnerability that normally follows victimization. One's homosexual or bisexual orientation consequently may be experienced as a source of danger, pain, and punishment rather than intimacy, love, and community. After an attack, internalized homophobia may reemerge or may be intensified. Attempts to make sense of the attack, coupled with the common need to perceive the world as a just place, may lead to feelings that one has been justifiably punished for being LGB. Such characterological self-blame can lead to feelings of depression and helplessness, even in individuals who are otherwise comfortable with their sexual orientation (Garnets et al. 1990).

Furthermore, an LGB hate-crime survivor may experience increased discrimination or stigma when others learn about her or his sexual orientation as a consequence of the victimization. Such *secondary victimization* (Berrill and Herek 1992), which can further intensify the negative psychological consequences of victimization, is often expressed explicitly by representatives of the criminal justice system, including police officers and judges. Yet the consequences can also extend outside the criminal justice system. If someone's sexual orientation becomes publicly known as the result of a crime, for example, some LGB people risk losing employment or child custody. Even in jurisdictions where statutory protection is available, many LGB people fear that disclosure of their sexual orientation consequent to victimization will result in hostility, harassment, and rejection from others. Secondary victimization may be experienced as an additional assault on one's identity and community, and thus become an additional stress. The threat of secondary victimization often acts as a barrier to reporting a crime or seeking medical, psychological, or social services.

A third consequence of heterosexism is its effects on heterosexuals. Because of the stigma attached to homosexuality, many heterosexuals monitor and restrict their own behavior to avoid being labeled as "gay"; this pattern appears to be especially strong among American males. For example, many men avoid clothing, hobbies, and mannerisms that might be labeled "effeminate." Antigay prejudice also interferes with same-sex friendships. Males with strongly antigay attitudes appear to have fewer intimate nonsexual friendships with other men than do males with tolerant attitudes (Devlin and Cowan 1985).

References

Bell, A. P. and M. S. Weinberg. (1978). *Homosexualities: A Study of Diversity among Men and Women.* New York: Simon and Schuster.

Berrill, K. T. and G. M. Herek. (1992). "Primary and Secondary Victimization in Anti-Gay Hate Crimes: Official Response and Public Policy," in *Hate Crimes: Confronting Violence Against Lesbians and Gay Men,* ed. G. M. Herek and K. T. Berrill. Newbury Park, Calif.: Sage.

Devlin, P. K. and G. A. Cowan. (1985). "Homophobia, Perceived Fathering, and Male Intimate Relationships." *Journal of Personal Assessment* 49, 467–73.

Garnets, L., G. M. Herek, and B. Levy. (1990). "Violence and Victimization of Lesbians and Gay Men: Mental Health Consequences." *Journal of Interpersonal* Violence 5, 366–83.

Hammersmith, S. K. and M. S. Weinberg. (1973). "Homosexual Identity: Commitment, Adjustment, and Significant Others." *Sociometry* 36, 56–79.

Malyon, A. K. (1982). "Psychotherapeutic Implications of Internalized Homophobia in Gay Men." *Journal of Homosexuality* 7, 59–69.

San Francisco Examiner. (1989). Results of poll. June 6, A19.

Weinberg, M. S. and C. J. Williams. (1974). *Male Homosexuals: Their Problems and Adaptations.* New York, Oxford University Press.

49

Homophobia in Black Communities

bell hooks

Recently I was at my parents' home and heard teenage nieces and nephews expressing their hatred for homosexuals, saying that they could never like anybody who was homosexual. In response I told them, "There are already people who you love and care about who are gay, so just come off it!" They wanted to know who. I said, "The who is not important. If they wanted you to know, they would tell you. But you need to think about the shit you've been saying and ask yourself where it's coming from."

Their vehement expression of hatred startled and frightened me, even more so when I contemplated the hurt that would have been experienced had our loved ones who are gay heard their words. When we were growing up, we would not have had the nerve to make such comments. We were not allowed to say negative, hateful comments about the people we knew who were gay. We knew their names, their sexual orientation. They were our neighbors, our friends, our family. They were *us*—a part of our black community.

The gay people we knew then did not live in separate subcultures, not in the small, segregated black community where work was difficult to find, where many of us were poor. Poverty was important; it created a social context in which structures of dependence were important for everyday survival. Sheer economic necessity and fierce white racism, as well as the joy of being there with the black folks known and loved, compelled many gay blacks to live close to home and family. That meant however that gay people created a way to live out sexual orientations within the boundaries of circumstances that were rarely ideal, no matter how affirming. In some cases, this meant a closeted sexual life. In other families, an individual could be openly expressive, quite "out."

The homophobia expressed by my nieces and nephews coupled with the assumption in many feminist circles that black communities are somehow more homophobic than other communities in the United States—more opposed to gay rights—provided the stimulus for me to write this piece. Initially, I considered calling it "homophobia in the black community." Yet it is precisely the notion that there is a *monolithic* black community that must be challenged. Black *communities* vary—urban and rural experiences create diversity of culture and lifestyle.

I have talked with black folks who were raised in southern communities where gay people were openly expressive of their sexual orientation and participated fully in the life of the community. I have also spoken with folks who say just the opposite.

In the particular black community where I was raised there was a real double standard. Black male homosexuals were often known, were talked about, were seen positively, and played important roles in community life, whereas lesbians were talked about solely in negative terms, and the women identified as lesbians were usually married. Often, acceptance of male homosexuality was mediated by material privilege—that is to say that homosexual men with money were part of the materially privileged ruling black group and were accorded the regard and respect given that group. They were influential people in the community. This was not the case with any women.

In those days homophobia directed at lesbians was rooted in deep religious and moral belief that women defined their womanness through bearing children. The prevailing assumption was that to be a lesbian was "unnatural" because one would not be participating in child-bearing. There were no identified lesbian "parents" even though there were gay men known to be caretakers of other folks' children. I have talked with black folks who recall similar circumstances in their communities. Overall, a majority of older black people I spoke with, raised in small, tightly knit southern black communities, suggested there was tolerance and acceptance of different sexual practices and orientations. One black gay male I spoke with felt that it was more important for him to live within a supportive black community, where his sexual orientations were known but not acted out in an overt, public way, than to live away from a community in a gay subculture where this aspect of his identity could be openly expressed.

Recently, I talked with a black lesbian from New Orleans who boasted that the black community has never had any "orange person like Anita Bryant running around trying to attack gay people." Her experience coming out to a black male roommate was positive and caring. But for every positive story one might hear about gay life in black communities, there are also negative ones. Yet these positive accounts call into question the assumption that black people and black communities are necessarily more homophobic than other groups of people in this society. They also compel us to recognize that there are diversities of black experience. Unfortunately, there are very few oral histories and autobiographies that explore the lives of black gay people in diverse black communities. This is a research project that must be carried out if we are to fully understand the complex experience of being black and gay in this white-supremacist, patriarchal, capitalist society. Often we hear more from black gay people who have chosen to live in predominantly white communities, whose choices may have been affected by undue harassment in black communities. We hear hardly anything from black gay people who live content-edly in black communities.

Black communities may be perceived as more homophobic than other communities because there is a tendency for individuals in black communities to verbally express in an outspoken way antigay sentiments. I talked with a straight black male in a California community who acknowledged that though he has often made jokes poking fun at gays or expressing contempt as a means of bonding in group settings, in his private life he was a central support person for a gay sister. Such contradictory behavior seems pervasive in black communities. It speaks to ambivalence about sexuality in general, about sex as a subject of conversation, and to ambivalent feelings and attitudes toward homosexuality, various structures of emotional and economic dependence create gaps between attitudes and actions. Yet a distinction must be made between black people overtly expressing prej-udice toward homosexuals and homophobic white people who never make homophobic comments but who have the power to actively exploit and oppress gay people in areas of housing, employment, etc. While both groups perpetuate and reinforce each other, and this cannot be denied or downplayed, the truth is that the greatest threat to gay rights does not reside in black communities.

It is far more likely that homophobic attitudes can be altered or changed in environ-ments where they have not become rigidly institutionalized. Rather than suggesting that black communities are more homophobic than other communities, and thus dismissing them, it is important for feminist activists (especially black folks) to examine the nature of that homophobia, to challenge it in constructive ways that lead to change. Clearly, religious beliefs and practices in many black communities promote and encourage homo-phobia. Many Christian black folks (like other Christians in this society) are taught in churches that it is a sin to be gay, ironically sometimes by ministers who are themselves gay or bisexual.

In the past year I talked with a black woman Baptist minister, who, although con-cerned about feminist issues, expressed very negative attitudes about homosexuality, because, she explained, the Bible teaches that it is wrong. Yet in her daily life she is tremendously supportive and caring of gay friends. When I asked her to explain this con-tradiction, she argued that it was not a contradiction, that the Bible also teaches her to identify with those who are exploited and oppressed, and to demand that they be treated justly. To her way of thinking, committing a sin did not mean that one should be exploited or oppressed.

The contradictions, the homophobic attitudes that underlie her attitudes, indicate that there is a great need for progressive black theologians to examine the role black churches play in encouraging persecution of gay people. Individual members of certain churches in black communities should protest when worship services become a platform for teaching antigay sentiments. Often individuals sit and listen to preachers raging against gay people and think the views expressed are amusing and outmoded, and dis-miss them without challenge. But if homophobia is to be eradicated in black communi-ties, such attitudes must be challenged.

Recently, especially as black people all over the United States discussed the film version of Alice Walker's novel *The Color Purple,* as well as the book itself (which includes a posi-tive portrayal of two black women being sexual with each other), the notion that homo-sexuality threatens the continuation of black families seems to have gained new momentum. In some cases, black males in prominent positions, especially those in media, have helped to perpetuate this notion. Tony Brown stated in one editorial, "No lesbian relationship can take the place of a positive love relationship between black women and black men." It is both a misreading of Walker's novel and an expression of homophobia for any reader to project into this work the idea that lesbian relationships exist as a competitive response to heterosexual encounters. Walker suggests quite the contrary.

Just a few weeks ago I sat with two black women friends eating bagels as one of us expressed her intense belief that white people were encouraging black people to be homosexuals so as to further divide black folks. She was attributing the difficulties many professional heterosexual black women have finding lovers, companions, and husbands, to homosexuality. We listened to her, and then the other woman said, "Now, you know we are not going to sit here and listen to this homophobic bull without challenging it!"

We pointed to the reality that many black gay people are parents, hence their sexual orientation does not threaten the continuation of black families. We stressed that many black gay people have white lovers and that there is no guarantee that were they heterosexual they would be partnered with other black people. We argued that people should be able to choose and claim the sexual identity that best expresses their being, suggesting that while it is probably true that positive portrayals of gay people encourage people to see this as a viable sexual orientation, it is equally true that compulsory heterosexuality is promoted to a far greater extent. We suggested that we should all be struggling to create a climate where there is freedom of sexual expression.

She was not immediately persuaded by our arguments, but at least she had different perspectives to consider. Supporters of gay rights in black communities must recognize that education for critical consciousness that explains and critiques prevailing stereotypes is necessary for us to eradicate homophobia. A central myth that must be explored and addressed is the notion that homosexuality means genocide for black families. . . .

To strengthen solidarity between black folks irrespective of sexual orientation, allegiance must be discussed. This is especially critical as more and more black gay people live outside black communities. Just as black women are often compelled to answer certain questions—Which is more important, feminist movement or black liberation struggle? Women's rights or civil rights? Which are you first: black or female?—gay people face similar questions. Are you more identified with the political struggle of your race and ethnic group, or the gay rights struggle? This question is not a simple one. For some people it is raised in such a way that they are compelled to choose one identity over another.

In one case, when a black family learned of their daughter's lesbianism, they did not question her sexual orientation (saying they weren't stupid, they had known she was gay), but the racial identity of her lovers: Why white women and not black women? Her gayness, expressed exclusively in relationships with white women, was deemed threatening because it was perceived as estrangment from blackness.

Little is written about this struggle. Often black families who can acknowledge and accept gayness find interracial coupling harder to accept. Certainly among black lesbians, the issue of black women preferring solely white lovers is discussed, but usually in private conversation. These relationships, like all cross-racial intimate relationships, are informed by the dynamics of racism and white supremacy. Black lesbians have spoken about absence of acknowledgment of one another at social gatherings where the majority of black women present are with white women lovers. Unfortunately, such incidents reinforce the notion that one must choose between solidarity with one's ethnic group and solidarity with those with whom one shares sexual orientation, irrespective of class and ethnic difference or differences in political perspective.

Black liberation struggle and gay liberation struggle are both undermined when these divisions are promoted and encouraged. Both gay and straight black people must work to resist the politics of domination as expressed in sexism and racism that lead people to think that supporting one liberation struggle diminishes one's support for another or stands one in opposition to another. As part of education for critical consciousness in black communities, it must be continually stressed that our struggle against racism, our struggle to recover from oppression and exploitation, are inextricably linked to all struggles to resist domination—including gay liberation struggle.

Often black people, especially nongay folks, become enraged when they hear a white person who is gay suggest that homosexuality is synonymous with the suffering people experience as a consequence of racial exploitation and oppression. The need to make gay experience and black experience of oppression synonymous seems to be one that surfaces much more in the minds of white people. Too often, it is seen as a way of minimizing or diminishing the particular problems people of color face in a white-supremacist society, especially the problems encountered because one does not have white skin. Many of us have been in discussions where a nonwhite person—a black person—struggles to explain to white folks that while we can acknowledge that gay people of all colors are harassed and suffer exploitation and domination, we also recognize that there is a significant difference that arises because of the visibility of dark skin. Often homophobic attacks on gay people occur in situations where knowledge of sexual identity is indicated or established—outside of gay bars, for example. While it in no way lessens the severity of such suffering for gay people, or the fear that it causes, it does mean that in a given situation the apparatus of protection and survival may be simply not identifying as gay.

In contrast, most people of color have no choice. No one can hide, change, or mask dark skin color. White people, gay and straight, could show greater understanding of the impact of racial oppression on people of color by not attempting to make these oppressions synonymous, but rather by showing the ways they are linked and yet also differ. Concurrently, the attempt by white people to make synonymous experience of homophobic aggression with racial oppression deflects attention away from the particular dual dilemma that nonwhite gay people face, as individuals who confront both racism and homophobia.

Often black gay folk feel extremely isolated because there are tensions in their relationships with the larger, predominately white gay community created by racism, and tensions within black communities around issues of homophobia. Sometimes it is easier to respond to such tensions by simply withdrawing from both groups, by refusing to participate or identify oneself politically with any struggle to end domination. By affirming and supporting black people who are gay within our communities, as well as outside our communities, we can help reduce and change the pain of such isolation.

Significantly, attitudes toward sexuality and sexual identity are changing. There is greater acknowledgement that people have different sexual orientations and diverse sexual practices. Given this reality, it is a waste of energy for anyone to assume that their condemnation will ensure that people do not express varied sexual orientations. Many gay people of all races, raised within this homophobic society, struggle to confront and accept themselves, to recover or gain the core of self-love and well-being that is constantly threatened and attacked both from within and without. This is particularly true for people of color who are gay. It is essential that nongay black people recognize and respect the hardships, the difficulties gay black people experience, extending the love and understanding that is essential for the making of authentic black community. One way we show our care is by vigilant protest of homophobia. By acknowledging the union between black liberation struggle and gay liberation struggle, we strengthen our solidarity, enhance the scope and power of our allegiances, and further our resistance.

50

Stonewall and the Birth of Gay and Lesbian Liberation

Neil Miller

At 1:20 A.M. on June 28, 1969, eight officers from the Public Morals Section of the First Division of the New York City Police Department raided the Stonewall Inn, a gay bar located on Christopher Street, just off Seventh Avenue, in Greenwich Village. . . .

The raid on the Stonewall that morning followed the usual pattern of police harassment of gay bars in New York. The manager was served with a warrant for selling liquor without a license. Police ordered patrons to leave the bar; those who had no identification or who were wearing clothes of the other sex were to be taken to police headquarters. Usually, in such raids (four Village gay bars had been raided in the preceding few weeks), those given permission to leave would file out docilely to avoid further tempting arrest or exposure. However, this evening, instead of going home, the patrons began to congregate outside the bar. The mood was festive. As those "released" emerged one by one from the Stonewall—often striking poses and making campy comments—the crowd greeted them with cheers. *Village Voice* reporter Lucian Truscott IV (1969), who described the events in a front-page article headlined "Gay Power Comes to Sheridan Square," takes up the story:

> Suddenly, the [police]wagon arrived and the mood of the crowd changed. Three of the more blatant queens—in full drag—were loaded inside, along with the bartender and doorman, to a chorus of catcalls and boos from the crowd. A cry went up to push the [police]wagon over, but it drove away before anything could happen. . . . The next person to come out was a dyke, and she put up a struggle—from car to door to car again. It was at that moment that the scene became explosive. Limp wrists were forgotten. Beer cans and bottles were heaved at the windows, and a rain of coins descended on the cops. . . . (1)

The police took refuge within the bar. Outside, someone uprooted a parking meter and tried to break down the Stonewall's front door. Someone else squirted lighter fluid through the window, followed by a few matches. From inside the bar, the police—clearly rattled—turned a fire hose on the crowd. A few minutes later several carloads of police reinforcements arrived and attempted to clear the street, but just when they thought they had succeeded in dispersing the crowd, people would regroup behind them, yelling, throwing bricks and bottles, and setting fire to trash cans. According to Martin Duberman's (1993) account (although the *Voice*'s Truscott claims this took place the following evening), the police found themselves face to face with a chorus line of mocking queens, kicking their heels in the air and singing:

We are the Stonewall girls
We wear our hair in curls
We wear no underwear
We show our pubic hair . . .
We wear our dungarees
Above our nelly knees!
(quoted in Duberman 1993, 201)

By the time order was restored, thirteen people had been arrested.

The next night, Saturday, the police were back, but so were the crowds, and the events were already beginning to take on a more political character. Signs had been scrawled on the boarded-up front window of the bar: THEY INVADED OUR RIGHTS; LEGALIZE GAY BARS; SUPPORT GAY POWER. As the crowds faced off against the police, there were shouts of "Gay Power" and "Christopher Street belongs to the queens." Like the night before, the rioters threw bottles and bricks; the police charged into the crowd on two occasions, attacking the rioters with nightsticks. On Sunday night, things had calmed down somewhat. The Stonewall was open again; employees had managed to clear away the debris. Among the patrons was Allen Ginsberg, who was making his first visit to the Stonewall. That night, Ginsberg uttered his oft-quoted remark, "You know the guys there were so beautiful—they've lost that wounded look that fags all had ten years ago" (quoted in Teal 1971, 22).

It was the "Boston Tea Party of the gay movement," as the writer Dennis Altman (1973, 117) put it. It was "the hairpin drop heard around the world," as a Mattachine Society leaflet described it (quoted in Marotta 1981, 77). In just three nights, something had changed. And Judy Garland was dead. It was uncannily symbolic that the Friday the riots began was also the day of the funeral of the most beloved icon of the *Boys in the Band* gay culture that worshiped the tenacity of female entertainers like Garland but mirrored their helplessness as well. Twenty thousand people had stood in line to view Garland's body at an uptown funeral parlor. On the streets outside the Stonewall that weekend and in the days and months that followed, the "old" gay culture and the homosexual male that sustained it was (mostly) laid to rest as well. From now on, everything would be described as "pre-Stonewall" or "post-Stonewall." . . .

The gay and lesbian revolution was the stepchild of all the radical social and political movements of the decade—the student movement and the New Left, the anti–Vietnam War movement, radical feminism, the Black Panthers, hippies and yippies. It began in New York but became international in scope. Soon London and Paris and Rome, Sydney and Melbourne, even Buenos Aires, would follow.

References

Altman, D. (1973). *Homosexual Oppression and Liberation.* New York: Avon.
Duberman, M. (1993). *Stonewall.* New York: Penguin.
Marotta, T. (1981). *The Politics of Homosexuality.* Boston: Houghton Mifflin.
Teal, D. (1971). *The Gay Militants.* New York: Stein and Day.
Truscott, L. (1969). "Gay Power Comes to Sheridan Square." *Village Voice,* July 3.

51

What Does the Bible Say about Homosexuality?

Rev. Dr. F. Jay Deacon

Do the Hebrew and Christian scriptures tell us homosexuality is immoral or unnatural?

It all depends on how you understand the Bible. It depends on whether your faith is a living, dynamic one, or whether it's just a lot of rules and formulas. There have always been those who, despite their sincerity, misunderstand faith as a set of legalistic moralisms. Remember, such folks demanded the death of Jesus on the grounds that he took the legalisms of their common religious tradition too lightly.

In recent times there have appeared those who want to read the Bible literally and legalistically, like a technical manual. Read literally, certain sections of the Bible support slavery, the property status of women, racial segregation, and genocide on religious grounds. And sure enough, several American church denominations were split not long ago when Christians used the Bible to support slavery and racial segregation. Some Christians have earned a reputation for being on the least human side of every issue!

Jesus was quite different. To him, the living God was always greater than even the words of the Bible, which his opponents used to attack him.

The fact is, those who now go around condemning gay people base their arguments on about six "proof texts" of Scripture, while missing the main point of Scripture as a whole. And they've even misunderstood their "proof texts!"

The Bible and Gay People

It is unfortunate that a society that considers itself tolerant of all religious beliefs should attempt to base its civil legislation on the Bible or on any other arbitrarily selected holy book of scriptures. But because this is so, it's important to realize exactly what the Bible does and does not say about sexual and emotional relations between individuals of the same sex.

It is sometimes said that the Bible will justify nearly anything. When isolated verses are pulled out of context, anything can happen. But when considered in the literary and historical contexts, these passages do not mean what many people think they mean. Have a look.

Leviticus 18:22 and 20:13

No section of the Bible has made more trouble for gay people than these frequently mentioned verses in Leviticus. They were probably composed during a late period of Israel's history while under Persian domination. These texts call for the death penalty for sexual acts between men. But then, the same book of Leviticus prohibits eating rabbit, oysters, clams, shrimp, and pork (Leviticus 21). And much, much more. Why should two verses in Leviticus be considered still valid when so much else in the same book is not?

Genesis 19:4–11 and Judges 19:22

The Sodom story (Genesis 19:4–11) is one of a mob's violation of the ancient value of hospitality toward two angelic visitors to their city, in the form of an attempted homosexual rape. The Gibeah story (Judges 19:22) is strikingly similar, but the rape is heterosexual. In Ezekiel 16:49, Isaiah 1:9–17 and 3:9–15, and Jeremiah 23:14, the sins of Sodom are described as arrogance, adultery, lies, insincere religious practices, political corruption, oppression of the poor, and neglect of the fatherless and widows. Homosexuality is not mentioned. When Jesus refers in Luke 10:10–13 to Sodom's sin, he's speaking about inhospitality. So much inhospitality has been practiced against homosexuals!

Romans 1:26-32

Saint Paul believed homosexual acts to be unnatural. In fact, he viewed all sexuality with fear and disapproval, urging those who could to abstain. But today's psychological, sociological, and scientific knowledge indicates that it is unnatural for a gay man or lesbian to defy his/her own "nature" and personality structure by attempting heterosexual relationships and sexual activity. And the language about "giving up" heterosexual relations does not describe a homosexual person, who did not deliberately choose to be homosexual just to defy God!

One could also argue that much of Paul's writing on social issues has little bearing on modern society. No one today would argue for the restoration of slavery in the United States based on Paul, although he very clearly condones slavery. Paul also commands women to be silent and not to teach men.

I Corinthians 6:9-10 and I Timothy 1:5-10

Problems of mistranslation arise in these epistles, one by Saint Paul and the other by an unknown author. The word *homosexuals* is not justified by the Greek text, which reads *malakoi* and *arsenokoitai*. Scholars do not know what these words mean (they have something to do with prostitution), so some translations have arbitrarily inserted the word *homosexual*. Earlier editions of the Revised Standard Version of the Bible read *homosexual* here, but the later (1977 and on) editions of the same fine translation have dropped the word.

Of course, many zealously self-righteous folks would rather go on reading certain select passages of Scripture literally and even inaccurately to use as ammunition against people they hate or fear. Such literalism is always selective, though! No one— repeat, *no one*—should actually take the *whole* Bible literally. If that were the case, they would not allow women to speak in church or ever teach men, demanding instead that women wear veils (1 Corinthians 14:34–35, 11:1–16); we would demand the death penalty for lending money with interest (Ezekiel 18:5–18, Deuteronomy 23:19–20). Should bankers be ordained? Should they be protected by civil rights statutes? Should they *live*?

Those who use the Bible like ammunition, singling out homosexual people for special abuse, miss the main point of the Bible as a whole. What follows are some of the themes they miss.

The Gospels

Jesus, who had a great deal to say about the impossibility of the rich attaining salvation, had nothing to say about homosexuality.

Jesus is hardly a "role model" for heterosexual family life. Jesus' lifestyle represented a dramatic break with the way almost all people, especially religious people, were expected to live. Instead of marrying, he associated intimately with twelve men. One loved him so much he was called "The Beloved Disciple," or "The disciple whom Jesus loved." One of the last times Jesus was seen alive by the twelve, this disciple was lying with his head on Jesus. He wrote a deep, emotional book about Jesus, called the Book of John. Jesus seems to define an alternative style of family in Mark 3:19–35.

The Bible is essentially a history of love—divine love, reaching out to ever broadening circles of humanity as one category of prejudice and exclusion after another is overcome by love, the cohesive force that draws all God's creation together into one whole. Jesus preached and practiced an inclusive, universal Gospel that set aside cheap moralisms in favor of love.

About Jonathan and David

Here's Scripture the opponents of homosexual people won't quote. It's the moving story of love between Jonathan and David (I Samuel 16–20, 1:19–27). Jonathan's father, King Saul, is clearly disturbed by the relationship: "You son of a perverse, rebellious woman, do I not know that you have chosen David the son of Jesse to your own shame?" But Israel has celebrated David as its greatest hero. In this passage, we read, "Your love to me was wonderful, passing the love of women." (Incidentally, the story of Ruth and Naomi, in the book of Ruth, portrays a woman's love passing—for a woman—the love of men.) For many of these reasons, many progressive theologians, Catholic, Protestant, and Jewish, now believe the real message of the Bible is not in conflict with gay and lesbian orientation.

52

Murder Will Out—But It's Still Open Season on Gays

Donna Minkowitz

On January 10, 1992, Erik Brown, twenty-one, and Esat Bici, nineteen, were sentenced to twenty-five years to life for the July 2, 1990, murder of Julio Rivera, a gay man from the South Bronx. The two youths had bragged to friends about killing the twenty-nine-year-old bartender "because he was gay," but nobody, gay and lesbian activists included, really expected them to go to jail for it. Most antigay murders are never prosecuted, and those that are, typically result in acquittals or light sentences. No wonder Brown's and Bici's families, friends, and attorneys were outraged. Suddenly, a district attorney and a judge had diverged from the criminal justice system's time-honored view of gay-bashing as an offense on a par with jaywalking.

Bici's aunt, Aferdita Suljovic, shouted homophobic execrations for twenty minutes outside the courtroom as Rivera's friends and the media filed out: "It's about time we started picking on them! They have special privileges, but we're *real people*—people that didn't lose any chromosomes! Because [Queens D.A. Richard] Brown wants to keep his job, you know who's gonna be voting for him—pretty in pink!" Brown's and Bici's friends taunted, "Put your lipstick on, honey!" as Rivera's lover walked by in tears. (During the trial, they had baited gay spectators with whispers of "faggot.") Like Brown's and Bici's defense lawyers, they didn't seem to grasp that open expressions of disdain for gay people might hurt the defendants' case.

At the sentencing hearing, Bici's lawyer, Barry Rhodes, acknowledged for the first time that the defendants "went out to commit an assault, to beat someone up," but asked for leniency on the grounds that they hadn't planned for the victim to actually *die*. Rhodes, who'd earlier informed a reporter that "Bici is normal—he likes girls," laid ultimate blame for the tragedy at the feet of gay and lesbian activists, whom—in a gorgeous example of doublespeak—he termed a "lynch mob." Hearing the phrase, I could only think of the way Rivera died, butchered by Bici, Brown, and codefendant Daniel Doyle with a hammer, knife, and plumber's wrench after the three had gone out looking for a "homo" to "tune up"—as Doyle put it—after a skinhead party. Combing a popular gay cruising area in Jackson Heights, Queens, for a likely victim, they lured Rivera into a secluded alcove in a schoolyard and then beat him viciously.

Harold Harrison, Erik Brown's attorney, also made gay people out to be the real criminals in the case. The jury, he declared, "ended up carrying out the desires of the gay rights activists" pressing for "the furtherance of the 'No Gay-Bashing' doctrine they espoused." Harrison actually argued that the trial had been unfair because defense attorneys were not allowed to exclude gays and lesbians from the jury.

During the trial itself, both defense lawyers relied heavily on homophobic arguments.

Harrison and Rhodes frequently alluded to Rivera's active sex life, implying that, as a promiscuous gay man, he deserved what he got. Rhodes asked Alan Sack, Rivera's lover, what precautions he had taken while holding Rivera's blood-covered body, so that the attorney could elicit the term "AIDS" in response. An eyewitness who saw Brown and Bici fleeing the scene of the crime was asked, "Weren't you cruising that night?" Even in jury selection, Harrison and Rhodes had appealed to potential jurors' homophobia by asking if they'd ever heard of Dykes on Bikes, a lesbian social group completely unconnected to the case.

It's customary for defense lawyers in gay-bashing cases to use homophobia as their main trial strategy. But what was unusual about the Rivera trial was that the judge, jury, and prosecutors declined to aid them in this effort. In a 1983 case in Washington, D.C., two college students were found guilty of torturing a gay man (taking a knife to his testicles and nearly killing him) in a public park. Yet the judge sentenced them to four hundred hours of community service on the ground that they had acted in response to a sexual proposition from the victim. In a 1988 trial of an antigay murder in Broward County, Florida, the judge chucklingly asked the prosecutor, "That's a crime now, to beat up a homosexual?" It's not uncommon for antigay killers to brag about the deed—as Brown and Bici did—and get acquitted anyway. In a 1986 Kalamazoo, Michigan, case, seventeen-year-old Terry Kerr had boasted to friends about killing a "fag." Prosecutors said he'd kicked Harry Wayne Watson "until blood sprayed from his face" and then gone home and returned with a sledgehammer to administer the fatal blows. But a jury acquitted Kerr because he claimed he was reacting to a sexual advance from Watson. The presiding judge in the case, Robert Borsos, later said, "I would have found first degree murder if it had been a bench trial."

Defense attorneys who use homophobia as a tactic have good reason to believe they will find friends on the bench or in the jurors' box. At a 1988 sentencing hearing for the convicted killer of two gay men, Dallas judge Jack Hampton referred to the victims as "queers" and said he was handing down a light sentence because "I put prostitutes and queers at the same level. . . . And I'd be hard put to give somebody life for killing a prostitute." The prostitute comparison is telling: to authorities like Hampton, both women and gay people deserve a beating if they're sexually active. Victims of gay-bashing often receive the same judicial treatment as rape victims; both sets of complainants are said to be "asking for it."

Even prosecutors are often reluctant to ask for harsh sentences in gay-bashings and frequently decline to argue that antigay bias was the motive. Even more disturbing, some have made egregiously homophobic statements to the press. In a January 6, 1992, letter to the editor of the New York *Daily News*, Nassau County D.A. Denis Dillon described gays and lesbians as engaging in "deviant disordered sexual practices which contravene Catholic moral teaching," and he applauded the organizers of the St. Patrick's Day parade for keeping out "militant homosexuals." Dillon was at the time supervising the prosecution of Angelo Esposito, accused in the December 28, 1991, antigay slaying of twenty-six-year-old Henry Marquez near a gay bar in Bellmore, Long Island. How could Dillon be expected to deliver a strong prosecution if he says gay people are immoral? Similarly, the district attorney of Niagara County, New York, Peter Broderick, declared in a 1989 radio interview that lesbians and gay men are "sick people" and "queers." If prosecutors think that such statements are appropriate, no wonder gay-bashers do.

But the biggest obstacle to prosecuting antigay murders is often the police. Even in New York City, one of the few cities where cops deign to keep records on antigay crimes, police consistently undercount homophobic attacks, refusing in many instances to label them as bias crimes. A bias label brings heightened scrutiny that often gives police and other officials greater incentive to pursue the case. In 1990 the NYPD classified 102 cases as antigay, but at least three times that number had been reported to them, according to data compiled by the New York City Gay and Lesbian Anti-Violence Project. In more than two-thirds of the cases, police disputed victims' belief that the attacks were bias-motivated. In the Rivera case, it took nine months to classify the murder as a bias crime, and they never assigned a full-time detective to the murder. They let valuable early leads slip out of their hands because, among other reasons, they were reluctant to give credence to the statements of a gay prostitute who linked the three skinheads to the crime. The Anti-Violence Project and Queer Nation had to demonstrate for four months and heckle Mayor David Dinkins at a fund-raiser before any arrests were made.

Police in other cities are often worse. In Dallas, recruit Mica England was told she could not be hired as a police officer because she is a lesbian. (A Texas state court recently ruled that the department could no longer use such criteria in hiring.) Thomas Woodard, a bisexual deputy sheriff in Orange County, Florida, was fired when supervisors heard of his relationship with a man. And do we even have to mention the callousness of the Milwaukee police, who nonchalantly returned a bleeding fourteen-year-old boy to the clutches of serial killer Jeffrey Dahmer because they apparently assumed violence between "gay lovers" was natural? When police are openly homophobic, how can they be relied on to solve antigay hate crimes? In a 1989 study, 73 percent of gay-bashing survivors surveyed had declined to report the attack to police; most said their reason was fear of encountering antigay treatment from police officers. In fact, police homophobia nationwide is the main reason there are no meaningful national statistics on antigay murders. The Hate Crimes Statistics Act, passed by Congress, mandates that the FBI keep records on crimes motivated by homophobia (among other biases), but the FBI receives all its data on nonfederal crimes from local police departments. Since most departments still refuse to keep records on antigay offenses, the only homophobic crimes the FBI can be expected to chart with any accuracy are federal ones—a category into which very few gay-bashings fit. And only a few cities have gay and lesbian antiviolence organizations with sufficient resources to tally the crimes themselves. . . .

Unlike the vast majority of homophobic killings, however, the murder of Julio Rivera resulted in arrests, convictions, and substantial jail time for the killers. The reason can be expressed in one word: *activism.* Led by Matt Foreman of the Anti-Violence Project, by Queer Nation, and by Alan Sack, activists bit onto this case and would not let go, harrying police, prosecutors, and the mayor for more than a year and a half to treat this crime with the seriousness it deserved. Finally in January 1992, they saw the fruits of their labor: Judge Ralph Sherman stated from the bench that "courts of this state should send out a message that our society cannot, will not, and must not tolerate these crimes of senseless intolerance—by imposing the maximum sentence." What does it say about the current situation of gay people in America that we must count it as a mammoth victory when someone actually serves time in jail for killing one of us? Ending gay-bashing itself—the most common kind of bias attack, according to the U.S. Justice Department—is still another matter.

Personal Voices

53

Dragon Ladies, Snow Queens, and Asian-American Dykes: Reflections on Race and Sexuality

Sharon Lim-Hing

I'd like to approach the subject of race and sexuality two ways: first, how my race has influenced my understanding of my sexuality, and second, how my sexuality has influenced my understanding of my race. . . .

I'm Chinese. I was born in Kingston, Jamaica. My parents moved to Miami when I was eleven, and I grew up in Florida. I came to Boston about six years ago for graduate school.

Racial Understanding Informing Sexual Understanding

One day when I was about five years old, I was masturbating in the front yard. My mother came out, saw me, and quite sternly told me not to do that. Instead of explaining to me not to play with myself in public places, she simply told me to desist — for the rest of my life, presumably.

That was the extent of the sexual education I received from both my parents until the advent of my first period. I had been kept so ignorant that I thought I was sick, or that I had internal injuries from racing on my ten-speed bike. My mom then squeamishly completed my education by telling me the function of menstruation, and how to prevent blood from getting all over my clothes.

I've talked to other Asians, and I don't think the extreme prudishness of my childhood is characteristically Asian. However, health professionals who work with Boston Chinatown residents describe Chinese attitudes toward sex as "puritanical," citing patients' avoiding the discussion of sexual matters unless they relate directly to some malady. This cultural penchant, the silencing of sex and often of subjective, private feelings, was compounded in my parents' case by the Roman Catholic Church.

If run-of-the-mill sexuality is taboo for conversations in such a family, how would other forms of sexuality be treated? Well, quite simply, it wasn't treated at all. My family looked the other way; one of my sisters knew I was a lesbian and she was very supportive. There was some tacit acceptance of my proclivities. I remember giggling and holding my first lover's hand in the back seat of the family car while my mother was driving. She was dropping us off at a theater, because we were too young to drive. My mother never so much as glanced in the rearview mirror, although she took an undue dislike to Karen. Whenever stray, unidentified panties showed up in the family wash, presumably discarded by a guest who found the raiment too encumbering, the cleaned object would mysteriously appear on my dresser, as if I knew who left them. To this day I still wonder which one of my siblings knew the owner of those small, black lace panties.

The implicit message my family gave me was not so much a condemnation as an embarrassed tolerance inextricably tied to a plea for secrecy. I complied with this request, waiting until I had moved fifteen-hundred miles away from the family homestead to begin coming out. When I did come out to my mother, she was staying with me and my lover, and could easily see only one bedroom with a single large futon.

"Mom," I said hesitantly, "you know I'm gay, don't you?" I couldn't say the word "lesbian" to my mother. She began with a remark on how as a child I didn't play with dolls—which is untrue. I had a couple of favorite G.I. Joes, but I didn't argue the point.

"I never talk about things you children don't talk about first," she then said, letting me know that she already knew. Then she said that she would always love me, and that if I was happy it was alright with her. I don't know if she told my father. Like my mother, he seems to have been able to figure things out on his own. In any case, I've never felt the need to do an official coming out with him. During a recent visit home, I sensed my father fidgeting uneasily as the news broadcast a story about "outing" closeted figures. At the end of my stay, he asked me if "they" would pick me up at Logan airport, although he knows Jacquelyn's name. My father's inability to accept my being a lesbian is related to his more traditional values: family first; make money and buy land; don't stand out.

Now that I'm more or less out to my immediate family and to some of my relatives, they've all stopped sending me invitations to weddings, on the presumption that I wouldn't want to get all dressed up—in a dress—to celebrate some heterosexual union. Of course they're right, but by not inviting me, they are trying to keep me a skeleton in their closet, in keeping with the same plea made years ago: don't tell anyone we know ("we" would include the loose network of Jamaican-Chinese spread over the Americas). This tolerance, curiously ambivalent, tells me that I'm still part of the family, but that being gay or having a gay person in the family is shameful.

What about the Asian pressure to procreate? Some Asians feel as if their parents push them to get married, so they can have lots of kids—at least one male child—to feed lots of white rice to, so they in turn can grow up to get married and have lots of kids. I never felt this pressure, but maybe that's because I'm the youngest of four children, and by the time my true tendencies had fully unfurled, my siblings were well on the way to marriage (with the appropriate sex) and procreation.

Up until the exodus of many Jamaican-Chinese in the 1970s (due to fear of the island becoming communist), there was a sizable Chinese community. If we had not left Jamaica, I would have been expected to find a husband from among the Chinese men there. Throughout my childhood I remember hearing the racist Chinese term for Black people, *black ghost*. It was sometimes preceded by *damn*, which used to convey much more venom than it does today. Much later I was surprised to find that an equivalent term exists for those of a paler shade (*white ghost*, strangely enough), though it was hardly ever used. When my mother explained this term, she said that Chinese people are arrogant, believing they are superior to others. Even though my siblings have married white individuals my parents seem quite happy—though I remember the time I came home with a black male friend, my father threw a fit.

Sexual Understanding Informing Racial Understanding

How has my sexuality affected my race? Here I feel comfortable using the amorphous term *race* because non-Asian people perceive me as belonging to this huge varied group, "Asian." In fact, the first thing many of you would think if you walked into a room and saw me is "Asian woman." Not young, old, badly or well-dressed, intellectual, punk, jock, diesel dyke, girlie girl—just "Asian." Whites get to play all the roles, while Asians are invisible or are stuck in a few stereotypes. So pervasive is the mindset that holds white as the norm that when describing a white individual to a third party, we usually don't state that person's race, but if the person being described is not white, we do specify the race. Female Asian characters make rare appearances throughout Hollywood film history as the personable Suzy Wong prostitute, the throwaway Vietnam War prostitute, the Dragon Lady, and the Submissive Lotus Flower; male Asian characters are portrayed as asexual, arch-villans, or aberrant detectives, all fantastically inhuman.

Luckily, in real life we have more choices; we have the "model minority" stereotype. This covers those typical Asian characteristics—such as introverted, dorky, hardworking, smart like computers, especially good at math and sciences, passive, and apolitical.

About two years ago I became involved with a group called the Alliance for Massachusetts Asian Lesbians and Gay Men (AMALGM), a loosely organized group with social and political aims. We have different events, some open to everyone, some for Asians only; we publish a newsletter. Through experiences and talks with AMALGM members, I've become more aware of not only racism in the gay community but also tokenism and the lack of sufficient dialogue about race. At AMALGM we talk about Asian invisibility in what is called the "gay community."

As Asians, we go into bars, and we fell less attractive or simply undesirable. This is because we have been inculcated to appreciate and emulate white standards and types of beauty, like anyone who has ever seen a billboard, TV, magazine, or film. And how well trained we are; we even have slang to describe gay Asians who lust chiefly after white people: *snow queen* or *potato queen*. One corollary of the supremacy of white beauty is the ugliness of all those who are not white.

I'd like to underscore the paradox of Asian Americans. Not all Asians were born in Asia. Some like myself don't speak any Asian language and haven't been closer to the Pacific Rim than San Francisco. We grow up in a white culture—a culture that believes it is, and prides itself on being, primarily white. Some of us grow up thinking we are white: we believe we can get a job, make good, buy a home, and somehow avoid the war raging silently in this country. Some of us know better. Then we enter a subculture of the gay community—a community of "pariahs" and "radicals." Even there we discover that we are perceived as alien entities.

Last summer I was in a Boston gay bar. I was ordering drinks. I heard a voice behind me say, "Go back to your oriental country." I turned around and I saw two white men.

"You talkin' to me?" I asked, quickly pulling myself up to my full five feet, four inches.

"No, I'm just talking to my friend here," one man replied.

I should have said, "Oh, I thought you just made a racist, asshole comment. But what I thought I heard was so ludicrously ignorant that no one would dare say such a stupid thing. Don't you agree?" Of course, I thought of that later. At the time, all I said was, "Oh."

I was stunned. It was easier for me to think I was having a hallucination than to recognize that a gay man was making a blatantly racist remark to me in a gay bar. Only later did I realize that I was operating on the assumption that a member of an oppressed group will try to understand your oppression rather than try to oppress you.

During a recent conversation on race, a white woman who is aware of many types of oppression said to me, "I would never think of having a relationship with an Asian, but I don't think I'm racist." She reminded me of the old liberal cliché, "Some of my best friends are . . . ," a strange bundle of guilt and self-deception. I wasn't mad at her because at least she had the guts to say that. Many people go around thinking unconsciously, yet not saying, "I would never have a romantic or erotic relationship with an Asian, or with a Black person, or with a Latino/a person, but I don't think I'm racist." These people might wish to reflect on their personal definition of racism.

The private realm of desire is where the little racist in each one of us will make its last stand. I am not suggesting the policing of desire, but I bring up this aspect of racism because it is this very intangible—sexual orientation—that has driven bisexuals, lesbians, and gay men to question most givens of the dominant culture. Why not put the *sex* back into *homosexuality?*

I have no solutions to the racism we carry in our hearts, except the slow process of self-questioning and self-education.

An analogy is frequently made between racism and homophobia. Well, there is at least one fundamental difference. Most of us (not all) if we really had to could pass as straight. Yet, to walk through the Somerville, Massachusetts hinterland, I can't change my clothes, my buttons, the way I walk, to avoid being thought of or harassed as a "Chink."

I'm not saying that racism is somehow worse that homophobia. In some ways, the fact that gayness has not yet been linked to biologically determined factors makes choosing our own sexuality harder to justify to our foes, who would like us to just change our behavior and conform to their standards.

Racism and homophobia are two different forms of oppression that have similar and different sources, that function differently, and that have different effects. They need to be discussed in more than a superficial way. What makes it hard to discuss is the fact that if we are gay, lesbian, or bisexual, we are supposed to be "politically correct," making it harder to admit having racist thoughts. In spite of this, I hope we will all continue to talk about the convergence of race and sexuality, and that members of the gay community will look more closely at their own racism.

54

Memoirs of a Gay Fraternity Brother

Joshua Clark Meiner

It is 7:30 in the morning on a Friday. I don't want to get up, but if I want to have hot water, I must get up early. Not many brothers living in Sigma Phi Epsilon ever get up this early. Drake University offers early morning classes, but I seem to be the only one who takes them. I get out of bed, get my shower stuff, and shuffle into the hall to the bathroom. The air is still a little thick with cigarette smoke from last night's second-semester senior drinkfest. Once in the bathroom, I quickly check the mirror to see if "FAG" has been scrawled in red lipstick across it by fraternity brothers. But the mirror is clear. All I see looking back at me is a college sophomore, tired from studying too much organic chemistry. I came to Drake to get an education; I never dreamed I'd be fighting for gay rights.

I clear the empty beer bottles off the sink, turn on the shower, and lather up to shave. I try to get the smoothest and closest shave possible, but I always nick myself. Some days I look like my father with a half roll of toilet paper stuck to my face to stop the bleeding. Mom and Dad are so proud of me, and brag about me often to the neighbors back on the North Side of Chicago. Finally, I hop into the shower. The hot water feels good on my sore muscles from yesterday's workout. I take a quick shower, get dressed, and stop at Olmsted Dining Hall for breakfast, and off to history class to listen to a professor drone on about the rise of neocolonialism in Latin America. It's a nice spring day, and the wind is slightly blowing, but I don't need a jacket. Things are just beginning to "awake" from their winter sleep, so my allergies are not bothering me yet. Now, off to work. A full-filled three hours of work-study making acids, bases, and cleaning up mercury spills. It seems that since I "came-out" to my coworkers I get all the shit jobs. People say they have no problem with my so-called "lifestyle," but I think it affects them more then they are willing to admit.

Finally, it's lunch time . . . time to relax. I meet Bob, a guy in my education class; Rick, a gay friend from the Bisexual, Gay, and Lesbian Alliance at Drake (BGLAD); and Sara, a lesbian in my history class, and we drive down to Java Joe's for lunch. Since my auto accident, the ride on the expressway always makes me nervous, but we arrive in one piece. We reach Java Joe's, and I can already smell the coffee and fresh desserts, which makes me feel fat. We get our food, sit down to eat, and gossip: who's doing whom, who's doing what to whom, who's available, and who's a jerk. I jokingly tell Sara that she can't be a lesbian because she isn't wearing a leather jacket. She retorts by telling me that I can't be gay because my socks don't match my shirt. Rick jokingly suggests that Bob must be gay, as a cute guy like him should have a girlfriend. It's nice to get out with my good friends now and then. There's no pressure to be someone I'm not, and I feel as if I have a few allies out in the world. We finish lunch, and they drop me off at my house. They promise to stop by for tonight's late night. . . Hell, I need someone to dance with. Most fraternity brothers use the late night as an excuse to bring drink and seduce women. It's basically like something in any dance club with a younger, more intoxicated crowd.

I pick up my mail, and head to my room. I throw out the bills not stamped "LAST NOTICE," as fraternal life and "the Drake experience" are expensive, and get my one phone message. It's from my mother. I'll call her and see what she wants. "Yes, Mom, I'm practicing safe sex. . . . No, mom, I don't think Brian Boitano is cute, and yes, I'm getting another AIDS test in April when I get my physical for the research internship at Iowa State dealing with polymers. . . . Yes, Mom, I'll see you at Easter . . . bye-bye." My mother says she will be supportive of my "lifestyle," but all she does is send me "cute" articles on gay issues that she cuts out of the newspaper. I think she's very concerned that I'm going to contract AIDS and "leave" her. I also think that most mothers want to see their sons (a) graduate college and (b) see them get married at a huge straight wedding, and I'll be depriving my mother of "b."

It's now time for dinner, and some of the "brothers" are grilling Polish sausage and hot dogs on the front porch. I'm invited to join them. I wonder how life will change when they all find out I'm gay, and sleeping with another member. I wonder how safe I actually am. They pass me the beer and hot dogs. It's amazing to me how quickly I am accepted since, to them, I don't "look gay" or "act gay."

The night dwindles away, and suddenly there is music blaring from every corner of the house, which is usual on Fridays. Rick shows up and explains the others had to cancel because of "other plans." How typical. I ask him if he wants to dance, but he'd prefer to sit in my room and drink. We're alone in my room. My ceiling is rumbling from the weight of all the dancers. At this point in the night, I'm not sure if they are dancing or just jumping around.

Our conversation turns from "How are classes going?" to "What's the kinkiest thing you've ever done?" The conversation abruptly stops, and we're caught in an eye lock. He walks over, and puts his hands between my legs. He leans over to kiss me. I turn away. "Not tonight, hon," I say, "I'm out of condoms, and you're drunk." I'm quite sure a few fraternity brothers would take advantage of this same situation if they were with a woman. He curses under his breath, and backs off. I get him his coat, and offer to walk him home. He reluctantly agrees. We walk out of the house, and pass two drunken fraternity brothers crashed out on a couch. One viciously mumbles "faggots" at us, and I push Rick out the door. It's amazing to me that this fraternity brother, whom I was earlier grilling dinner with, after a few drinks, is suddenly a bigot.

After successfully getting Rick back into his dorm room, putting him in bed, putting the garbage can next to his bed, I begin my trek home. It's now about 3:00. I'm beginning to realize that my fraternity won't be my home much longer. Once they all find out I'm gay, I'm positive the comments will get worse. A few members are so conservative, and so militant, that I fear for my personal safety. It's amazing to me that these brothers I've eaten with, studied with, and shared good and bad times with suddenly won't want me around. A garbage truck rumbles by, and I'm snapped back to reality. Walking alone in the streets of Des Moines at this hour, even near campus, is scary, and I'm even more cautious since I got mugged. A red sports car slows as it approaches me, and the person on the passenger side rolls down his window. "Homo!" the young male voice yells. The car speeds off, all the occupants laughing. I think I've seen that car parked in another fraternity lot. I soon get home, and finally crawl into bed, alone.

Days and months later, I become more comfortable with my gayness, and get more involved with BGLAD. "Brothers" notice the pink triangles on my door, and wonder why I never go to any of the date parties. Rumors soon spread that I am gay, and alumni begin to withhold funding from the fraternity. Someone caught me and another "brother" in an act of passion. Members and alumni begin to fear that the Iowa Delta Chapter of Sigma Phi Epsilon will be labeled as the "gay house." They fear they will lose potential new members to other houses. To them, the only "logical" choice, instead of acceptance and support, is to make the faggot's life miserable, and they find a loophole in the bylaws to deactivate me. They hurl slurs and verbally harass me, my friends, and my parents. Threats of physical violence become frequent. Due to my circumstances, I am deactivated, but of course a repeal process is never explained to me. I decide, however, to pursue this matter with legal representation, and I am very happy with the results.

Sometimes in bed at night, I look back at this series of events and I wonder if I'll be alone my entire life. I decide that's too depressing to think about, and I roll over and fall asleep. Maybe I'll wake up tomorrow in a world where there is no homophobia, where people understand the difference between friend and lover, where people accept sexuality as a basic human right, and, most important, where there are no boring history professors.

55

The Men with the Pink Triangles

Richard Plant

Over the last few years enough evidence has been accumulated to prove that the Third Reich exterminated countless gays throughout Europe. Numerous documents have finally come to light proving that many gays, arrested and indicted, but without a trial, were put into concentration camps and forced to wear a pink triangle (the homosexual equivalent to the Jews' yellow star) on shirt sleeves and pants; within the camps, gays were often beaten, tortured, or killed. The persecution started around 1935, and in many ways ran parallel to that of the Jews. . . .

I was a witness to the happenings in Germany, though fortunately from a privileged position at the border of the Third Reich. In February, 1933, while a freshman at Frankfurt University, I realized I had to get out if I wanted to stay alive. My father, a liberal, a Jew, and the cofounder of the League of Socialist Physicians, had been arrested when Adolf Hitler took power. Some time later the authorities released him—he had served as a front physician in World War I. They set him free but he did not survive the "Crystal Night" (November 9, 1938), when the Nazis destroyed over two hundred synagogues and burned down the houses of Jews, socialists, and other "treacherous elements." I immediately registered at the University of Basel (Switzerland), a city ten minutes away from the German border. There I began to collect everything available about the antiminorities' campaigns undertaken by the Nazis. Several of the trends that later surfaced in Germany I had experienced myself as a member of the Wandervögel (Birds of Passage), one of the many youth movements in Germany similar to the Boy Scouts, whose leaders were elected without adult supervision. . . . The Wandervögel, with the other youth groups, most of them religious, such as the Evangelical and Catholic youth groups, were slowly coerced by the Nazis into surrendering their independence: they were channeled into the Hitler Youth.

One of my earliest playmates, Ferdi, left the Wandervögel when I did, though for different reasons. A bit older than I, blond, stocky, sexually experienced, very much an extrovert, he worked at the pharmacy that supplied my father's office. He didn't hold it against me that he had to scrounge for a living—his father, a drunkard, hated him and gave him no help—while I was "The Red Doctor's Boy" who would go on to the University. Ferdi joined the SA—the Nazi "Brown Shirt" paramilitary organization—which soon got him a better job. When he showed up in his dull-brown uniform, I cursed him. But Ferdi continued to be friendly with me, even though things got tougher. When my father was taken to jail, it was Ferdi who persuaded me to leave Frankfurt right away. He discovered my passport was not valid, and managed to get me to the passport office, at the top floor of police headquarters, before it officially opened. He bribed another gay man working there, and I got on the train to Basel with a passport valid for five years. Without it, I wouldn't have been able to survive in Switzerland and migrate to the United States some years later. . . .

In Germany, the famous Paragraph 175 concerning sexual acts between males was changed to 175A. While the old 175 had not included mutual masturbation but only acts of penetration, now any contact between males of any age that could be construed as sexual would be severely punished. Even having your name listed in a suspect's address book could lead to incarceration. This new law was made public on June 28, 1935, as a directive for "the ruthless persecution of sexual vagrants."

If sufficient pretexts to prosecute a political enemy could not be found, he could always be accused of having proposed "unnatural acts," and the Gestapo regularly provided some youngster, released from jail and well rehearsed, to swear to that. In October, 1936, Heinrich Himmler—Gestapo chief and architect of the Nazi antigay campaign—demanded the "elimination of all degenerates." He proceeded without legal procedure to move those already arrested—numbering thousands by now—into the camps. By November 1941, Himmler, now in total command of all internal security operations, proposed castration for minor offenses, death for major ones. . . .

The Schutzstaffeln, or SS, was Himmler's creation, an outgrowth not only of his anti-Semitism but also of his aversion to all "contragenics." I have coined this expression to characterize any group that doesn't fit into the framework of society—here anything non-Germanic, anything nonstandard: Jews, gays, Romani (gypsies), the disabled, Jehovah's Witnesses. Strangely enough, Himmler showed no interest in lesbianism. When lesbian incidents were reported in Camp Ravensbrück, a camp reserved for women that supplied prostitutes to the all-male camps, he reacted with indifference although a number of lesbians were incarcerated as political prisoners or for being so-called "vagrants."

By 1941, Himmler ruled over twelve separate SS fiefdoms, keeping a tight rein on each, playing one against the other, his agents infiltrating every level of society. The SS established its own courts of justice; the regular judiciary had caved in shortly after 1935. By then Himmler had organized the first concentration camps, though the extermination camps—most of them in Eastern Europe—did not start their activities before 1942. Himmler could order the "definitive resettlement" of thousands without a moment's hesitation, but he collapsed when witnessing an execution. He was totally removed from reality—the only sentiments he mustered while speeding the annihilation of contragenics was pity for the "brave SS elite" troops who had to carry out these orders.

While in Basel from 1933 to 1934, I learned that almost all the members of my liberal student group had either been arrested or fled to a foreign country—most to Czechoslovakia or France—where they were later caught. Then after June, 1935, I received an unsigned note postmarked Frankfurt/Main. It was from Ferdi, my early companion, and it hinted that he would try to get out to Holland. He also mentioned a few other gay men we knew had disappeared—and I noticed even then what could be called a "conspiracy of silence." Neither the Swiss nor the French papers I read mentioned the arrest or disappearance of any gay men in the Third Reich. Of course in those days we didn't hear much about concentration camps. Only in the forties, mostly through the efforts of Jewish organizations, did we learn what had been happening there. Furthermore, the gays who managed to escape always declared themselves to be political refugees; if they were Jewish, they didn't need to furnish any explanations.

We also learned much later that at the height of the extermination campaign, around 1943 to 1944, Himmler added something new for men who wore pink triangles. Those who agreed to castration would be discharged from the camps. A few really believed this; they were castrated, but not freed. Instead the authorities transferred them to the feared Dirlewanger Penal Division, which consisted of former criminals. Oskar Dirlewanger, one of the most hated leaders of World War II, specialized in liquidating partisans, but also had his own men shot from the back if he didn't trust them. It is no wonder that almost none of the castrated soldiers survived. . . .

Dr. L. D. von Classen-Neudegg, a physician from Sachsenhausen concentration camp, published several accounts in a small magazine during the 1950s.

> Forced to drag along twenty corpses, the rest of us encrusted with blood, we entered the Klinker works. . . . We had been there for almost two months but it seemed like endless years to us. At the time of our "transfer" here, we had numbered around three hundred men. Whips were used more frequently each morning when we were forced down into the clay pits under the wailing of the camp sirens. "Only fifty are still alive," whispered the man next to me. . . .

The witness gives three to four more pages of the deadly work in the clay pits. Among the victims: an elderly reverend who committed suicide, several youngsters, a gay Jew. He had to wear both the pink triangle and the yellow star. . . .

Another survivor witnessed several of the sadistic games the SS organized when ordered to "liquidate vigorously the 'derailed deviants'" to make room for the newly arrested gays from the occupied territories. One game: The prisoners worked in a quarry surrounded by a high voltage fence. If they stepped within five feet of the fence, they were shot. The SS would throw a prisoner's cap against the fence and order him to retrieve it. He would be electrocuted if he touched the cap, or he was shot for disobedience if he refused to go after the cap.

Later on, as the situation worsened, as the cities were bombed and food was getting scarce, as more prisoners crowded the camps, the SS invented other methods. They picked an inmate they didn't like, either one with a pink triangle or one with a yellow star—by now more and more Jews were brought in. Two guards threw him on the floor, a third put a metal bucket over his head. The first two men then started drumming on the bucket. After a while the victim began to lose control, to thrash around, to shout in terror. When the bucket was suddenly removed, they pushed him in the direction of the high voltage fence. Half unconscious, he would stumble against it and be electrocuted; if he didn't touch it, then they would shoot him for disobeying orders. . . .

I returned to Germany for the first time after the war in 1954 to search for a few missing friends. In Frankfurt/Main, my hometown, I found severed gay groups, among which was one nicknamed the "Farinellis," after a famous eighteenth-century operatic castrato. Why these castrated men frequented the gay bars, though they could only be partially interested in sexual contacts, later became clear to me: like members of any minority in an alien territory, they liked to be with their own people.

Aftermath

In 1969, a compromise law was pushed through in West Germany that abolished all of Hitler's Paragraph 175A and most of 175. But while those who had worn the yellow star, or the red triangle (political) were often granted some form of restitution, the courts ruled that gays imprisoned and/or tortured were not to be considered political, but criminal inmates. West Germany, like the former East Germany before it, has abolished the worst features of the antigay legislation, but it apparently still considers the killings of the men with the pink triangles legally justified.

56

The Transgender Spectrum

Lisa J. Lees

Sex and gender. At birth a quick look between your legs determines whether an "F" or an "M" appears on your birth certificate. What they see between your legs is your "sex," what they put on your birth certificate is your "gender."

The first question anyone asks about a baby is, "Is it a girl or a boy?" They don't ask if it has a vagina or a penis. No one is going to care about that for well over a decade. They want to know whether to give it a pink or a blue blanket, whether to call it pretty or handsome, whether it will play with dolls or trucks, be a cheerleader or a football star. They want to know the baby's *gender*, not its sex.

Based on the answer to "Is it a girl or a boy?" people have preconceptions about the entire life of this little person. If it conforms to those expectations, the ones predicated on being a girl or a boy, fine. Otherwise it is transgendered, and it is in for some rough times.

Many people are transgendered to some extent. Some girls are tomboys and some boys are sissies. (You'll notice that at all ages, females are given much more leeway with gender expression.) Women in professions traditionally dominated by men are pressured to act like men. Men in jobs traditionally dominated by women (women don't have *professions*) are assumed to have some feminine streak, or be gay (which is considered an effeminate trait by most of those who aren't gay).

At the extreme are the classic transsexuals who totally disagree with their initial gender label and seek to change their public presentation of gender and even their sex to match what they believe their true gender to be. (If our culture did not claim such a rigid correlation between sex and gender, and such rigid definitions of gender, would there be any transsexuals? Excellent question. I don't know.)

There seems to be a whole range between being totally happy with one's initial gender label and being a "classic" transsexual. Sorting that out looks to me to be an impossible task. Why bother?

If your assigned gender and your felt gender conflict to the point that you are having trouble living a happy, functional life, then you must do something about it. What you must and can do varies, and is at least partially determined by how accepting our culture is of gender variation.

It's sad to think of all the permutations and combinations of talent and ability that have been lost because their expression hasn't conformed to one of the two standard genders. It's worse than sad to think of all the people who have had their hopes and dreams crushed because "boys don't do that" or "girls don't do this." Many of us have been beaten, raped, tortured, or murdered because we are not just exactly like some ideal to which almost no one, in truth, conforms.

I think one of the things about me that most upsets people is that I am living proof of just how tenuous is the distinction between female and male. I can tell that some people (men, generally) are really upset knowing that a little purple pill can do this to a supposedly male body. It shakes their foundations. If I catch their eyes looking at the usual places men look, I can almost see their minds churning, wrestling with their reaction to me. I suspect that the inability to cope with these feelings is behind some of the hatred of transsexuals.

What's it feel like inside to "change sex"? As I've said other places, this does not seem like much of a change to me. I have not changed gender. I have always known that I was a woman. What I'm doing is a little more dramatic than losing weight, but it's kind of the same thing. I look in a mirror and I think, "I look pretty nice." But I still see me, I see the transsexual woman I've always been.

What is very much different is that now I am happy. I no longer hold back from social events and activity. I no longer sit or stand silently in a group, hoping no one will notice me. I'm learning to use personal pronouns and first names again, now that I have ones that fit me. It is easier for me to live as a known transsexual woman than it ever was when people assumed I was a man.

So what does it mean to be transgendered? I guess, bottom line, it means to be different. If you really, truly support diversity and individuality, you are supporting transgendered people. You don't have to label us; we'll do that ourselves if we feel it is needed. You don't have to understand us. You certainly don't have to approve of us. I never did or will ask anyone if it is okay for me to be a transsexual woman. I am. That's a given. I accept it. All I ask is that you, also, accept what I am.

Once you accept me, then you can move on to decide where and if I fit into your life. Just like anyone else. And—who knows—maybe I have something unique and important to contribute to our culture and our future, something that I would never have been able to do if I had spent my energy and my life pretending to be something I never was.

Next Steps and Action

57

Why Don't Gay People Just Keep Quiet? Listening to the Voices of the Oppressed

William David Burns

We achieve one ideal of a university education when we learn from each other.

Last year I learned a great deal from many colleagues and students. But especially I learned from Susan, Eli, Ron, and Dan—all students and members and leaders of the

Rutgers University Lesbian/Gay Alliance (RULGA). Like most learning, this was not without some discomfort. Yet these students from RULGA helped me see something important about the complaints, suggestions, claims, and protests coming from organized lesbian and gay people. This "random walk" will describe what I learned.

Rutgers has a long-standing policy of barring discrimination on the basis of "sexual orientation," and we have, according to RULGA's brochure, the "second-oldest active lesbian and gay student group in the United States."

Before getting to know the RULGA students, I had what I thought was a "liberal" view of homosexuality—liberal in the sense of generous, tolerant, open to new ideas and human difference. I certainly had no wish to see government control the essentially private areas of another person's life.

As an administrator, I had done what I could to be sure that the staffs in my departments were prepared to do their work with a sensitivity to "difference" and different needs. Reports of attacks on people who were thought to be, or who actually—as the phrase goes—"admitted to being" homosexual disturbed me deeply. So did the fact that one of the few bigotries that many colleges openly permit themselves is a persistent and unremitting homophobia. This homophobia ranges from subtle insinuations, to blatant accusations, to acts of violence.

I had given no credence to the argument that to talk about homosexuality is to "promote" homosexuality. I had disagreed with the notion that to love someone of the same sex is unnatural and, therefore, to be condemned. Those were essentially my beliefs, save one that I will describe in a moment. Thus, I did not think I had joined in any way in the hostile chorus—the incantation, one might say—directed against this human difference. But I was mistaken.

In spite of the above, I still sometimes found myself annoyed by those gay and lesbian members of our community who made so much ado about their sexual orientation. Why did they have to tell me they were lesbian or gay, as if in prelude to anything else?

After all, I valued privacy. Don't we all keep our sex lives private? I don't tell everyone about my sexuality, so why do some gay men and lesbians make such a big deal about theirs? I wondered—and I was not alone in wondering—why we had to have all these gay dances, gay pride week, "wear blue jeans if you are gay" days. I remarked to myself about the "stridency" of this form of politics. I guess I would have preferred silence.

I learned a lot this past year.

Eli—a transfer student to Rutgers—helped me learn when he asked how we could reconcile the university's mission of searching for the truth and its complementary ethic of intellectual honesty with a position that essentially asks some people to engage in a lifetime of deception about some of the most basic of human feelings. Did the university want to change its mission as it applied to Eli?

And Susan—a political science major—helped me see how, if she had chosen to "pass" as a heterosexual, she could never openly express spontaneous sentiment or openly hug the person she loved. What some of us find so appealing about college students is their spontaneity and exuberance, their openness and honesty. Wouldn't we like to think that this is Susan's university too?

Then Dan—who is studying art and design—painstakingly and patiently explained to me that a student he knows would not report to our university police that someone had vandalized his car by scrawling "FAG" on it. Why? Because, first, he didn't entirely trust the police to take him seriously, and, second, he was afraid that the insurance/police report might reach his parents, who could then learn something they don't know about their son. Without being "out," this student felt afraid to avail himself of the help of our police department. A crime went unreported.

And Ron—a graduate student in political theory—helped me see that to stay silent is never to ask about yourself, never to have an opportunity to share in learning about the history and culture of those like yourself, as other students do in the process of becoming educated. Ron's arguments force us to ask ourselves what we mean by equal opportunity and equal treatment.

These students helped me see why it is necessary for some students to be open, even emphatically vocal, about who they are.

Two other examples brought the point home poignantly. I agreed to write a letter of recommendation for a gay student who, in showing me his résumé, included a letter of reference that said what a splendid young man he was, how excellent his work record had been, and then volunteered the sentiment that the letter writer would be proud to have this young man marry one of his daughters someday! Another student told me that his mother had asked him to leave home because she was afraid that his father would literally kill him if his suspicions of their son's homosexuality were confirmed.

I came to see that my notion of sexuality as a private matter is essentially a conceit. To be sure, the specific details of my sexual life are private, but the broad outlines of heterosexuality are not. Heterosexuality screams at us in this culture—in the way we talk, the jokes we tell, the expectations we have, the assumptions we make. Heterosexual love imagery drives large parts of our culture—from product advertisements and success symbols to what we learn in school. Anything else is exotic, and any attention it gets is given only to its most exotic detail.

But this heterosexuality is so "normal" that it becomes invisible to those who stay within its traces. Heterosexual activity as such may be only a small part of such a life—in fact, one can be heterosexual without ever actually engaging in a sexual act.

By contrast, homosexuality conjures up (for some at least) specific sexual visions—not of a range of attractions, affections, desires, or expressions of love. Absent from this view of homosexuality is any appreciation for the common, daily experiences of work and worship, in community and at home, and all the other dimensions of living that homosexuals and heterosexuals share. The narrow but vivid—sometimes lurid, and usually uninformed—construction of homosexuality in the minds of heterosexuals explains why some would prefer that gay people remain in the closet, or at least be quiet about it. It is as if to say, "If we don't talk about it, we can all be 'normal.'"

Especially where young people are concerned, not talking about homosexuality seems a strong tendency, because many of us would prefer not to think of our children as being sexually active at all. Homosexuality implies a *fait accompli*.

Being silent or openly asserting a difference are choices we all make about a range of issues all the time. What I learned from RULGA students is that, for some, breaking silence and asserting one's gayness is akin to talking out loud when you are in a dark place. There are good reasons to do so: you hear a voice that reassures you and helps you feel a little less afraid; it might also help someone else to find you.

Now, in a hostile situation, talking aloud in a dark place means you could be discovered. Breaking the silence is a risk. It is a risk some never take, because the consequence can be grave, indeed—especially in a society where basic rights to employment, housing, and health care are not secured to all regardless of sexual orientation.

On campus this semester, we see stickers on lampposts and students wearing buttons bearing a pink triangle and the statement Silence = Death. The pink triangle is a symbol homosexuals were forced to wear in Adolf Hitler's death camps. Today, breaking silence is an affirmation of self, a form of resistance, an emblem of liberation. It is talking aloud in the dark.

Breaking silence is a choice I have come to respect. Some might say it is easy for me to have an opinion on just how explicit others ought to be—I have so little to lose by being complicit, even in small and subtle ways, with any cultural force that threatens our fellow humans.

That these students who are no longer silent, are brave, is the thing I admire most. They are being brave by being honest. Their bravery exposes them to risk, but it can be a source of strength to themselves, their friends, and families. We cannot expect everyone else to take the risks involved in breaking silence; some believe they can't afford to place themselves in a hostile environment. Others have adapted in their own way. But there is much to be learned from the pioneers who have taken this courageous step. We can all benefit from trying to listen.

58

International Bill of Gender Rights

(As adopted July 4th, 1996, Houston, Texas, U.S.A.)

History of the International Bill of Gender Rights

The restatement of the International Bill of Gender Rights (IBGR) was first drafted in committee and adopted by the International Conference on Transgender Law and Employment Policy, Inc. (ICTLEP) at that organization's second annual meeting held in Houston, Texas, August 26-29, 1993. The IBGR has been reviewed and amended at subsequent annual meetings of ICTLEP in 1994, 1995, and 1996.

The Purpose and Effect of the International Bill of Gender Rights

The IBGR strives to express fundamental human and civil rights from a gender perspective. However, the ten rights enunciated below should not be viewed as special rights applicable only to transgendered people. Nor should these rights be limited in application to persons for whom gender identity and gender role issues are of paramount concern. All ten sections of the IBGR are universal rights that can be claimed and exercised by every human being regardless of sex or gender.

The IBGR is a theoretical expression that has no force of law absent its adoption by legislative bodies or recognition of its principles by courts of law, or by administrative agencies and international structures such as the United Nations.

In recent years, the IBGR's principles have been embodied in various legislative acts and constitutional provisions designed to protect the rights of transgendered people. Several such laws have been adopted by municipalities, and in the state of Minnesota. Meanwhile, the rights of transgendered people are gaining increased recognition and protection in such countries as Canada, South Africa, Australia, Great Britain, and the countries of Western Europe and Scandinavia.

Apart from legislative and constitutional reform, individuals in many countries are free to adopt the universal truths expressed in the IBGR, and to lead their lives accordingly. In this fashion, the truths recited in the IBGR will liberate and empower humankind in ways that transcend the powers of legislators, judges, government officials, and diplomats.

As the principles of the IBGR are understood, embraced, and given expression by humankind, the acts of legislatures and the pronouncements of courts and administrative bureaucracies will necessarily follow. Thus, the path of free expression trodden by millions of human beings seeking to define and express their own identities and give meaning to their lives will ultimately determine the course of the culture and civilization.

The IBGR is a transformative and revolutionary document. It is grounded, however, in the bedrock of individual liberty and free expression. As our lives unfold, these kernels of truth are here for all who would claim and exercise them.

The International Bill of Gender Rights

The Right to Define Gender Identity

All human beings carry within themselves an ever-unfolding idea of who they are and what they are capable of achieving. The individual's sense of self is not determined by chromosomal sex, genitalia, assigned birth sex, or initial gender role. Thus, the individual's identity and capabilities cannot be circumscribed by what society deems to be masculine or feminine behavior. It is fundamental that individuals have the right to define, and to redefine as their lives unfold, their own gender identities, without regard to chromosomal sex, genitalia, assigned birth sex, or initial gender role.

Therefore, all human beings have the right to define their own gender identity regardless of chromosomal sex, genitalia, assigned birth sex, or initial gender role, and further, no individual shall be denied Human or Civil Rights by virtue of a self-defined gender identity which is not in accord with chromosomal sex, genitalia, assigned birth sex, or initial gender role.

The Right to Free Expression of Gender Identity

Given the right to define one's own gender identity, all human beings have the corresponding right to free expression of their self-defined gender identity.

Therefore, all human beings have the right to free expression of their self-defined gender identity, and further, no individual shall be denied Human or Civil Rights by virtue of the expression of a self-defined gender identity.

The Right to Secure and Retain Employment And to Receive Just Compensation

Given the economic structure of modern society, all human beings have a right to train for and to pursue an occupation or profession as a means of providing shelter, sustenance, and the necessities and bounty of life, for themselves and for those dependent upon them, to secure and retain employment, and to receive just compensation for their labor regardless of gender identity, chromosomal sex, genitalia, assigned birth sex, or initial gender role.

Therefore, individuals shall not be denied the right to train for and to pursue an occupation or profession, nor be denied the right to secure and retain employment, nor be denied just compensation for their labor, by virtue of their chromosomal sex, genitalia, assigned birth sex, or initial gender role, or on the basis of a self-defined gender identity or the expression thereof.

The Right Of Access To Gendered Space And Participation In Gendered Activity

Given the right to define one's own gender identity and the corresponding right to free expression of a self-defined gender identity, no individual should be denied access to a space or denied participation in an activity by virtue of a self-defined gender identity which is not in accord with chromosomal sex, genitalia, assigned birth sex, or initial gender role.

Therefore, no individual shall be denied access to a space or denied participation in an activity by virtue of a self-defined gender identity which is not in accord with chromosomal sex, genitalia, assigned birth sex, or initial gender role.

The Right To Control And Change One's Own Body

All human beings have the right to control their bodies, which includes the right to change their bodies cosmetically, chemically, or surgically, so as to express a self-defined gender identity.

Therefore, individuals shall not be denied the right to change their bodies as a means of expressing a self-defined gender identity, and further, individuals shall not be denied Human or Civil Rights on the basis that they have changed their bodies cosmetically, chemically, or surgically, or desire to do so as a means of expressing a self-defined gender identity.

The Right To Competent Medical And Professional Care

Given the individual's right to define one's own gender identity, and the right to change one's own body as a means of expressing a self-defined gender identity, no individual should be denied access to competent medical or other professional care on the basis of the individual's chromosomal sex, genitalia, assigned birth sex, or initial gender role.

Therefore, individuals shall not be denied the right to competent medical or other professional care on the basis of chromosomal sex, genitalia, assigned birth sex, or initial gender role, when changing their bodies cosmetically, chemically, or surgically.

The Right To Freedom From Involuntary Psychiatric Diagnosis And Treatment

Given the right to define one's own gender identity, individuals should not be subject to involuntary psychiatric diagnosis or treatment.

Therefore, individuals shall not be subject to involuntary psychiatric diagnosis or treatment as mentally disordered, dysphoric, or diseased on the basis of a self-defined gender identity or the expression thereof.

The Right To Sexual Expression

Given the right to a self-defined gender identity, every consenting adult has a corresponding right of free sexual expression.

Therefore, no individual's Human or Civil Rights shall be denied on the basis of sexual orientation, and further, no individual shall be denied Human or Civil Rights for expression of a self-defined gender identity through private sexual acts between consenting adults.

The Right To Form Committed, Loving Relationships And Enter Into Marital Contracts

Given that all human beings have the right to free expression of self-defined gender identities, and the right to sexual expression as a form of gender expression, all human beings have a corresponding right to form committed, loving relationships with one another, and to enter into marital contracts, regardless of their own or their partner's chromosomal sex, genitalia, assigned birth sex, or initial gender role.

Therefore, individuals shall not be denied the right to form committed, loving relationships with one another or to enter into marital contracts by virtue of their own or their partner's chromosomal sex, genitalia, assigned birth sex, or initial gender role, or on the basis of their expression of a self-defined gender identity.

The Right To Conceive, Bear, Or Adopt Children; The Right To Nurture And Have Custody Of Children, And To Exercise Parental Capacity

Given the right to form a committed, loving relationship with another person, and to enter into marital contracts, together with the right to express a self-defined gender identity and the right to sexual expression, individuals have a corresponding right to conceive and bear children, to adopt children, to nurture children, to have custody of children, and to exercise parental capacity with respect to children, natural or adopted, without regard to chromosomal sex, genitalia, assigned birth sex, or initial gender role, or by virtue of a self-defined gender identity or the expression thereof.

Therefore individuals shall not be denied the right to conceive, bear, or adopt children, nor to nurture and have custody of children, nor to exercise parental capacity with respect to children, natural or adopted, on the basis of their own, their partner's, or their children's chromosomal sex, genitalia, assigned birth sex, initial gender role, or by virtue of a self-defined gender identity or the expression thereof.

59

Becoming an Ally

Jamie Washington
Nancy J. Evans

As most writers and scholars in the area of oppression and multicultural education will concur (Freire 1970; Katz 1982), our language is imperfect and inherently "ism"-laden or oppressive. Therefore, clarifying terms is important. For the purpose of this essay, the term most important to define is *ally*. According to *Websters New World Dictionary of the*

American Language (1966), an ally is "someone joined with another for a common purpose" (41). This definition serves as a starting point for developing a working definition of *ally* as this term relates to issues of oppression. In this essay, we will define *ally* as "a person who is a member of the 'dominant' or 'majority' group who works to end oppression in his or her personal and professional life through support of, and as an advocate with and for, the oppressed population."

The rationale behind this definition is that although an oppressed person can certainly be a supporter and advocate for his or her own group, the impact and effect of such activity are different on the dominant group, and are often more powerful when the supporter is not a member of the oppressed population. Understanding this notion is an important first step toward becoming an ally for any "targeted" or oppressed group. Given our definition, only heterosexual individuals can serve as allies of lesbian, gay, bisexual, and transgender (LGBT) people.

This chapter explores factors associated with becoming an ally of LGBT individuals, including the importance of recognizing heterosexual privilege, motivations for becoming an ally, the practice of advocacy, what an ally should know, and positive and negative consequences of advocacy.

Heterosexual Privilege

The individual who decides to undertake the ally role must recognize and understand the power and privileges that one receives, accepts, and experiences as a heterosexual person. Developing this awareness is often the most painful part of the process of becoming an ally. Janet Helms (1984) wrote about this stage of identity development for majority groups as it relates to racism, labeling it the *disintegration* stage. Although this theory is based on the development of whites or European Americans as "dominants," there are some similarities with other dominant positions in this country. Some of these similarities exist around feelings of anger and guilt.

When heterosexual persons first learn that their lesbian, gay, bisexual, or transgender friends are truly mistreated on the basis of sexual or gender identity, they often feel anger toward heterosexuals and guilt toward themselves for being members of the same group. This process can only happen, however, when persons have an understanding of sexual and gender identity and do not see it as grounds for discrimination, violence, or abuse. These feelings do not occur when the person still believes that a lesbian, gay, bisexual, or transgender person is sick sinners who either needs to have a good sexual relationship with a person of the other sex or see a psychologist or a spiritual leader so that they can be cured. Such persons, who might be classified as being at the lowest level of development according to Helms's majority-group identity model, are not yet ready to start down the ally road.

Some of the powers and privileges heterosexuals generally have that gay and lesbian, and in some cases bisexual persons do *not* have include:

■ Family memberships to health clubs, pools, and other recreational facilities

■ Legalized marriage

■ The purchase of property as an acknowledged same-sex couple

■ Filing joint income tax returns

■ The ability to adopt children

■ Health insurance for one's life partner

- Decisions on health-related issues as they relate to one's life partner
- The assumption that one is psychologically healthy

In addition to such tangible privileges of the heterosexual population, there are a great many other, not so tangible, privileges. One important intangible privilege is living one's life without the fear that people will find out that who one falls in love with, dreams about, or makes love to is someone of the same sex. This fear affects the lives of gay, lesbian, and bisexual persons from the day they first begin to have "those funny feelings" until the day they die. Although many LGBT persons overcome that fear and turn the fear into a positive component of their lives, they have still been affected, and those wounds, even after healed, can easily be reopened.

Coming to terms with the very fact that "as a heterosexual I do not experience the world in the same way as LGBT people do" is an important step in becoming an ally. This awareness begins to move the heterosexual from being a caring, liberal person who feels that we are all created equal and should be treated as such, toward being an ally who begins to realize that although equality and equity are goals that have not yet been achieved, they can have a role in helping to make these goals realities.

Motivations for Becoming an Advocate

What motivates heterosexuals to become LGBT rights advocates? There are certainly more popular and less controversial causes with which one can become involved. Since involvement in LGBT rights advocacy is often deemed a moral issue, moral development theory suggests some possible underlying reasons for such activity. Lawrence Kohlberg (1984) has hypothesized that moral reasoning develops through three levels: preconventional, conventional, and postconventional. At the preconventional level, moral decisions are based on what is good for the individual. Persons functioning at this level may choose to be involved in gay rights issues to protect their own interests or to get something out of such involvement (e.g., if this issue is particularly important to a supervisor whose approval is sought).

At the conventional level, Kohlberg indicated that decisions are made that conform to the norms of one's group or society. Individuals at this level may work for gay rights if they wish to support friends who are gay, lesbian, or bisexual, or to uphold an existing institutional policy of nondiscrimination.

Kohlberg's third level of reasoning involves decision making based on principles of justice. At this level the individual takes an active role to create policies that assure that all people are treated fairly and becomes involved in gay rights advocacy because it is the right thing to do.

Although Kohlberg focused on justice as the basis of moral decision making, Carol Gilligan (1982) used the principle of care as the basis of her model of moral reasoning. Her three levels of reasoning are (1) taking care of oneself, (2) taking care of others, and (3) supporting positions that take into consideration the impact on *both* oneself and others. Using this model, individuals at the first level become advocates to make themselves look good to others or to protect themselves from criticism for not getting involved. At the second level, individuals reason that they should "take care of" LGBT people. The final perspective leads individuals to believe that equality and respect for differences create a better world for everyone, and that these are worthwhile goals.

One could argue that the latter position in Kohlberg's and Gilligan's scheme is the enlightened perspective that any advocate needs to espouse. We should, however, be aware that not every person is functioning at a postconventional level of moral reasoning, and that arguments designed to encourage people to commit themselves to gay rights advocacy need to be targeted to the level that the individual can understand and accept. Kohlberg (1972) indicated that active involvement in addressing moral issues is an important factor in facilitating moral development along his stages. We can, therefore, expect that as people become involved in LGBT rights issues, their levels of reasoning may move toward postconventional levels.

Advocacy in Action

Advocacy can take a number of different forms and target various audiences. Heterosexual supporters may focus some of their energy toward LGBT individuals themselves. At other times the target may be other heterosexuals, and often strategies developed for college and university campuses are focused on the campus community as a whole.

Advocacy with LGBT people involves acceptance, support, and inclusiveness. Examples of acceptance include listening in a nonjudgmental way and valuing the unique qualities of each individual. Support includes such behaviors as championing the hiring of LGBT staff; providing an atmosphere in which LGBT issues can be discussed in training or programming; or attending events sponsored by LGBT student organizations. Inclusiveness involves activities such as the use of nonexclusionary language; publications, fliers, and handbooks that take into account sexual and gender identity differences; and sensitivity to the possibility that not everyone in a student organization or work setting is heterosexual.

Being an advocate among other heterosexuals is often challenging. Such a position involves modeling advocacy, support, and confronting inappropriate behavior. In this context, heterosexual supporters model nonheterosexist behaviors such as being equally physical with men and women, avoiding joking or teasing someone for nontraditional gender behaviors, and avoiding making a point of being heterosexual. Allies are spokespersons for addressing LGBT issues proactively in program and policy development. Confronting such things as heterosexist joke telling; the exclusion of LGBT people either intentionally or by using language that assumes heterosexuality; discriminatory hiring practices; or the evaluation of staff based on factors related to their sexual or gender identities is also part of the role of the advocate.

Advocacy in the institution involves making sure that issues facing LGBT students and staff are acknowledged and addressed. This goal is accomplished by developing and promoting educational efforts that raise the awareness level and increase the sensitivity of heterosexual students, staff, and faculty on campus. Such activities include inviting speakers to address topics relevant to the LGBT community; developing panel discussions on issues related to sexual and gender identities; including LGBT issues as a topic in dormitory resident advisor training programs; and promoting plays and movies featuring LGBT themes.

Encouraging LGBT student and staff organizations is also part of institutional advocacy. Such groups need to have access to the same campus resources, funding, and sponsorship as other student and staff organizations. Developing and supporting progay, prolesbian, probisexual, protransgender policies are also a necessary aspect of advocacy. Antiharassment policies, antidiscriminatory hiring policies, and provisions for nonheterosexual couples to live together in campus housing are arenas that deserve attention.

Things You Should Know as an Ally

When dealing with issues of oppression, there are four basic levels of becoming an ally. The following examples relate specifically to being an ally to LGBT persons.

- *Awareness* is the first level. It is important to become more aware of who you are and how you are different from and similar to LGBT people. Such awareness can be gained through conversations with LGBT individuals, attending awareness-building workshops, reading about LGBT life, and self-examination.

- *Knowledge/education* is the second level. You must begin to acquire knowledge about sexual and gender identities and the experiences of LGBT people. This step includes learning about laws, policies, and practices and how they affect LGBT people, in addition to educating yourself about LGBT culture and the norms of this community. Contacting local and national LGBT organizations for information can be very helpful.

- *Skills* make up the third level. This area is the one in which people often fall short because of fear, or lack of resources or supports. You must develop skills in communicating the knowledge that you have learned. These skills can be acquired by attending workshops, role-playing certain situations with friends, developing support connections, or practicing interventions or awareness raising in safe settings—for example, a restaurant or hotel out of your hometown.

- *Action* is the last, but most important, level and is the most frightening step. There are many challenges and liabilities for heterosexuals in taking actions to end the oppression of LGBT people, and some are addressed in this chapter's discussion of factors that discourage advocacy. Nonetheless, action is, without a doubt, the only way that we can effect change in the society as a whole; for if we keep our awareness, knowledge, and skills to ourselves, we deprive the rest of the world of what we have learned, thus keeping them from having the fullest possible life.

In addition to the four levels in ally development, there are five additional points to keep in mind:

1. Have a good understanding of sexual and gender identities and be aware of and comfortable with your own. If you are a person who chooses not to identify with a particular sexual or gender identity, be comfortable with that decision, but recognize that others, particularly LGBT people, may see your stance as a cop-out.

2. Talk with LGBT people and read about the coming-out process. This is a process and experience that is unique to this oppressed group. No other population of oppressed persons needs to disclose so much to family and close friends in the same way. Because of its uniqueness, this process brings challenges that are often not understood.

3. As any other oppressed group, the LGBT population gets the same messages about homosexuality, bisexuality, and gender expression as everyone else. As such, there is a great deal of internalized heterosexism, homophobia, and transphobia. There are LGBT people who believe that what they do in bed is nobody´s business, and that being an "out" lesbian, gay, bisexual, or transgender person to them would mean forcing their sexual practices on the general society, something they feel should not be done. It is, therefore, very important not only to be supportive, recognizing that you do not share the same level of personal risk as the lesbian, gay, bisexual, or transgender person, but also to challenge some of the internalized oppressive notions, thus helping to develop a different, more positive, perspective.

4. As with most oppressed groups, there is diversity within the LGBT community. Heterosexism is an area of oppression that cuts across, but is not limited to, race, ethnicity, gender, class, religion, culture, age, and level of physical or mental ability.

For all of these categories, there are different challenges. Certainly, LGBT individuals as members of these diverse populations share some common joys and concerns; however, issues often manifest themselves in very different ways in different groups, thus calling for different strategies and interventions.

5. It is difficult to enter into a discussion about heterosexism and homophobia without the topic of AIDS/HIV infection arising. Knowing at least basic information about the illness is necessary for two reasons: (1) to address myths and misinformation related to AIDS and the LGBT community, and (2) to be supportive of the members of the community affected by this disease. Although we recognize that AIDS is a health issue that has and will continue to affect our entire world, the persons who live in the most fear and have lost the most members of their community are LGBT individuals. Accepting that reality helps an ally to understand the intense emotions that surround this issue within the community.

These five points and the previous four levels of awareness provide some guidelines for becoming an effective ally. And although we recognize that these concepts seem fairly reasonable, there are some real challenges or factors that can discourage an ally from taking these steps.

Factors That Discourage Advocacy

Involvement in LGBT rights advocacy can be a scary and unpopular activity. Individuals who wish to take on such a role must be aware of and reconcile themselves to several potentially unpleasant outcomes. Some of these problems involve reactions from other heterosexuals, and some come from members of the LGBT community.

An assumption often is automatically made within the heterosexual community that anyone supporting gay rights is automatically gay, lesbian, bisexual, or transgender. Although such an identity is not negative, such labeling can create problems, especially for unmarried heterosexuals who might wish to become involved in a heterosexual romantic relationship. Heterosexuals also often experience derisive comments from other heterosexuals concerning involvement in a cause that is viewed as unimportant, unacceptable, or unpopular. Friends and colleagues who are uncomfortable with the topic may become alienated from the heterosexual supporter of LGBT rights, or may noticeably distance themselves from the individual. Difficulty may arise in social situations if the heterosexual ally is seen in the company of LGBT individuals. Discrimination, either overt or subtle, may also result from getting involved in controversial causes. Such discrimination may take the form of poor evaluations, failure to be appointed to important committees, or encouragement to seek a position at a school "more supportive of your ideas."

The LGBT community may also have trouble accepting the heterosexual ally. Often an assumption is made that such persons are really gay, lesbian, bisexual, or transgender but not yet accepting of their identity. Subtle or not-so-subtle pressure is placed on such people to come out or at least to consider the possibility of a nonheterosexual identity.

The LGBT community is one that has its own language and culture. Heterosexual supporters can feel out of place and awkward in settings populated exclusively or mainly by gay males, lesbians, bisexuals, and transgender people. LGBT people may be exclusionary in their conversations and activities, leaving the heterosexual ally out of the picture. Since most LGBT people have had mainly negative experiences with heterosexuals in the past, the motives of heterosexuals involved in LGBT rights activities are often questioned. These experiences make it difficult for LGBT people to accept that individuals will involve themselves in a controversial and unpopular cause just because it is "right."

The Benefits of Being an Ally

Although the factors that discourage individuals from being an ally are very real, there are many benefits of being an ally. What are these benefits?

1. You open yourself up to the possibility of close relationships with an additional percentage of the world.

2. You become less locked into sex-role stereotypes.

3. You increase your ability to have close and loving relationships with same-sex friends.

4. You have opportunities to learn from, teach, and have an impact on a population with whom you might not otherwise interact.

5. You may be the reason a family member, coworker, or community member finally decides that life is worth something and that dependence on chemicals or other substances might not be the answer.

6. You may make the difference in the lives of adolescents who hear you confront anti-LGBT epithets that make them feel as if they want to drop out of junior high, high school, or college. As a result of your action, they know they have a friend to turn to.

7. Lastly, you can get invited to some of the most fun parties, have some of the best foods, play some of the best sports, have some of the best intellectual discussions, and experience some of the best music in the world, because everyone knows that LGBT people are good at all these things.

Although the last factor (7) is meant as a joke, there is a great deal of truth concerning the positive experiences to which persons open themselves when they allow themselves to be a part of and include another segment of the population in their world. Imagine what it could be like to have had such close friends as Tennessee Williams, Cole Porter, Bessie Smith, Walt Whitman, Gertrude Stein, Alice Walker, James Baldwin, or Virginia Woolf. Imagine the world without their contributions. It is possible for gay, lesbian, bisexual, and transgender people, as well as heterosexuals, to make a difference in the way the world is, but we must start by realizing the equity in our humanness and life experiences.

References

Freire, P. (1970). *Pedagogy of the Oppressed*. New York: Continuum.

Gilligan, C. (1982). *In a Different Voice*. Cambridge, Mass.: Harvard University Press.

Helms, J. (1984). "Toward a Theoretical Explanation of the Effects of Race on Counseling: A Black and White Model." *Counseling Psychologist* 12, no. 4, 153–64.

Katz, J. (1982). *White Awareness: Handbook for Antiracism Training*. Norman, Ok.: University of Oklahoma Press.

Kohlberg, L. (1972). A Cognitive Developmental Approach to Moral Education. *Humanist* 6, 13–16.

Kohlberg, L. (1984). *Essays on Moral Development*, vol 2. *Psychology of Moral Development: The Nature and Validity of Moral Stages*. New York: Harper and Row.

Webster's New World Dictionary of the American Language. (1966). Cleveland: World Press.

Ableism

Introduction by Rosie Castañeda
and Madeline L. Peters

Currently more than 500 million people in the world have disabilities, including over 40 million Americans (Blaska 1997). For these individuals, gaining access to services, opportunities, employment, and independent living has been an ongoing struggle. With the passage of the <u>Americans with Disabilities Act of 1990 (ADA),</u> the difficulties for individuals with disabilities in navigating a society traditionally tailored to the needs of able-bodied persons were substantially recognized.

In this chapter we use the definition established by the ADA, which interprets disability with respect to the individual, in the following manner:

(1) a physical or mental impairment that substantially limits one or more of the major life activities of such individual;

(2) a record of such an impairment; or

(3) being regarded as having such impairment (U. S. Dept. of Justice 1999).

According to the ADA, major life activities limited by disability may include "caring for oneself, performing manual tasks, walking, seeing, hearing, speaking, breathing, learning, working, [and reproducing]" (U.S. Dept. of Justice 1999). In order to be protected by the ADA, individuals must satisfy one or more of the criteria of its definition of disability.

Before the 1990s, many Americans with disabilities were unsure whether or not they qualified for federal services. In question was how to incorporate those disabled citizens who did not qualify under earlier legislation that was not fully inclusive. The dilemma created by the range of conditions, injuries, and illnesses that fall under the umbrella of *disability* demanded action. The passage of the ADA provided a definition of who is considered disabled based upon the disruption of major life activities and daily life functions.

The ADA is an effort to provide "a clear and comprehensive national mandate for the elimination of discrimination" and "clear, strong, consistent, enforceable standards" with regard to establishing and protecting the civil rights of individuals with disabilities (U. S. Dept. of Justice 1999). As such, the ADA acknowledges that a pervasive form of disability oppression, known as ableism, exists. *Ableism* is the term used to describe the discrimination against and the exclusion of individuals with physical and mental disabilities from full participation and opportunity within society's systems and activities.

While adhering to the ADA's guidelines and simultaneously endeavoring to be as inclusive as possible, we can divide disabilities into two major types. *Physical disabilities* affect the body's participation in its environment and include physiological disorders, chronic disease, and disfigurements or anatomical losses; *mental disabilities* affect psychological, emotional, or developmental experiences (U.S. Dept. of Justice 1999). Significantly, individuals who share a disability may not necessarily encounter the same effects or the same societal barriers, nor will they all necessarily describe themselves as "disabled." The experience of disability is individualized, so that generalized responses and assistance are inadequate for providing greater opportunity for people with disabilities.

Our approach to this chapter is based upon an emerging body of theory called disability oppression theory. We identify two different systems encompassed by this theory. First, disability oppression theory describes the pervasive and systemic nature of discrimination toward people with disabilities referred to as *ableism.* Second, this theory identifies the process by which people with disabilities journey toward empowerment and liberation through the establishment of equitable access to and accommodation within society's systems, and through the creation of an interdependent social structure in which all persons are connected and depend on each other to perform equally important community roles.

Disability oppression theory advocates on the behalf of people with disabilities based on their individual needs, as opposed to ableistic oppressive ideologies, which advocate "fixing" or "correcting" people with disabilities, in order to "fit" the designs of inflexible systems and standards. The disability oppression theory model seeks to combat the stereotypes, misconceptions, and restrictive attitudes that are often internalized by individuals with disabilities and can lead to unnecessarily abrogating conceptions of disability and self-worth. The model suggests that having a disability is not inherently negative, but rather that the experience includes both losses and gains. Further, disability oppression theory insists on the culpability of society's inhibiting structures, which overvalue economic productivity, undervalue alternative social contributions, and attach positive and negative associations to the relative terms of independence and dependence.

Like other forms of oppression, ableism operates on individual, cultural, and institutional levels. Ableism affects those with disabilities by inhibiting their access to and power within institutional structures that fulfill basic needs, like health care, housing, government, education, religion, the media, and the legal system. Ableism derives from a set of rigid cultural norms that promote specific and narrow standards of beauty, rules of logic, and conceptions of value (McClintock and Raucher 1997). We believe that we all live within and share responsibility for a system that fosters ableism and allows its debilitating mechanisms to flourish. On conscious and unconscious levels our attitudes and behaviors are influenced by the society in which we live, and we bear these influences out in our personal and interpersonal relationships. Thus, ableism has functioned throughout history to "create an environment that is often hostile to those whose physical, emotional, cognitive, or sensory abilities fall outside the scope of what is currently defined as socially accept-able" (McClintock and Raucher 1997, 198).

Society's earliest conceptions categorized individuals with disabilities as having either spiritual deficits or medical problems that could then be punished, segregated, or cured; for centuries, society's solutions were abandonment or institutionalization. Beginning in the 1800s, social responsibility increased, individuals were deinstitutionalized and introduced into mainstream society, and the response to those with disabilities focused on education and rehabilitation. This emphasis on getting people with disabilities "back to work" extended into the twentieth century—due in part to the increasing numbers of people returning from World Wars I and II with disabilities. Finally, beginning in the 1970s, the disability rights movement emerged, lobbying to obtain civil liberties for those with disabilities, and initiating a progression toward independent living and eventually toward an interdependent society (Channing L. Bete 1997).

The disability rights movement has led to several liberating changes in the ways individuals with disabilities perceive themselves, and further, to alterations in the ways individuals with disabilities and able-bodied persons conceive of and reconstruct institutional, cultural and social systems. The passage of the Rehabilitation Act of 1973 replaced the vocational objectives of previous rehabilitation legislation. It prohibited discrimination against individuals with disabilities in programs and activities receiving federal aid. With this act, individuals with disabilities achieved class status and began to regard themselves as a culture with shared values and goals. They also began to see themselves as a minority group deprived of basic human and civil rights through disenfranchisement and oppression. This view led not only to political coalitions with other minority groups, like women and people of color, but also to an understanding of disability as a civil rights issue instead of a medical issue—recognition that instead of being cured and cared for, individuals with disabilities merited education and empowerment in order to achieve independence and self-sufficiency (Bryan 1996).

Further, individuals with disabilities realized that American culture wrongly equated disability with dependence, which is antithetical to a culture stressing independence and placing high value on work, productivity, and progress. Thus, the early 1970s witnessed the rise of the independent living movement in the United States, initiated by individuals with disabilities who sought to take back and maintain control over their own lives. Independent living meant having the freedom to make one's own choices among multiple options; to live, work, and raise families; to have responsibilities within communities; to minimize reliance on others; and to assert that those with disabilities know more comprehensively how to meet their own individualized needs. The independent living movement began to alter the American perception of independence and productive work, toward valuing the societal contributions of all individuals; eventually, the goal of individuals with disabilities progressed from independent communities to interdependency in a more inclusive society (Bryan 1996).

Although emerging after the formative years of the women's rights movement and the civil rights movement, the disability rights movement was incorporated into their already existing frameworks. The disability rights movement similarly addressed the concerns of a disenfranchised group, and also made use of protest and activism in order to gain recognition and equality. Although women, people of color, and those with disabilities have made great strides in attaining their constitutional rights, the process and progress has been slow and remains ongoing. Public awareness of individuals with disabilities has increased, yet a persistent lack of extensive coverage continues to threaten the visibility of the issue of disability in our culture. For example, the disabilities rights movement is unique among these other movements in the fact that the majority of the literature in the field of disabilities is not written from the experiences of individuals with disabilities, but instead from the perspectives of able-bodied persons.

Readings in this Section

We approached the editing of this chapter from the perspective of persons encountering oppression—as two women who are also people of color and individuals with learning disabilities—and the effects of multiple jeopardy in American culture. We would like to emphasize the fact that there are many people belonging simultaneously to different classes, races, religions, sexual orientations, genders, and ages who have disabilities as part of their lives. The reality of people experiencing multiple jeopardy is often underrepresented, and the characteristics and stereotypes linked to cultural group membership are further used to promote discrimination, as illustrated by the reading in this section by Joseph P. Shapiro.

We have selected and organized articles that, in combination, embody our concept of disability as a journey or learning process toward individual empowerment and societal liberation. We chose several articles for their articulation of the underlying sociohistorical foundations of the experience of disability in our culture, deeming it essential to contextualize our discussion regarding disability in order to understand contemporary issues and to advocate future progress with regard to people with disabilities. Willie V. Bryan's article is useful for its in-depth historical perspective on the independent living movement led by persons with disabilities. The article by Michelle Fine and Adrienne Asch sets forth and dispels commonly held societal stigmas and assumptions regarding people with disabilities. Carol Padden's work discusses specific aspects of the deaf community, and is integral to combating the notion that people with disabilities exist in isolation, without their own cultures. Finally, Joseph P. Shapiro's article provides historical information about the separate and unequal experiences of minority students with learning disabilities in the American educational system, and recognizes and depicts the intersection of racism with disability.

We also include articles addressing the experiences of injustice encountered by people with disabilities, in an endeavor to identify and debunk mechanisms of societal oppression. Shapiro demonstrates the ways in which people of color with disabilities experience *double jeopardy*, or the compounded effects of oppression on two fronts, in society. Anne McCormick and Faith Leonard outline the academic and social difficulties that students with attention deficit and hyperactivity disorder (ADHD) may experience in school. Sally L. Smith's article details the characteristics of a learning disability, and more specifically, describes what an organizational learning disability entails with regard to managing time and space.

It was important to us to emphasize the value of listening to and gaining knowledge from the personal experiences of people with disabilities, and thus we include several testimonials. Elizabeth Atkins Bowman and Michelle Burford's article relays the experiences of a woman who became paralyzed and now uses a wheelchair, and describes the positive experiences that having a disability has brought to her life. Patricia Deegan's piece is also a personal testimonial, about the experience of having a mental illness, specifically schizophrenia, and provides information regarding this disability and the oppression she encounters in society. Sally French's writing is a personal account of the experiences of a woman with vision impairment navigating academics and employment.

Included here are also a series of articles that discuss moving toward the next steps of empowerment and liberation. Laura Epstein Rosen and Xavier Francisco Amador direct their attention to those of us who may have friends who experience situational or chronic depression. Anne McCormick and Faith Leonard's article specifies appropriate educational accommodations for students who have ADHD. Mark and Adam Nagler address those of us with disabilities who may find that gaining information and support via the computer is itself a step toward personal empowerment. The article by Susan E. Browne, Debra Connors, and Nanci Stern is important as a testimonial by women with disabilities, and sends a powerful message about continuing to face the obstacles erected by an oppressive society.

This collection of texts attempts to illustrate the multifarious dimensions of disability as it exists in our culture and to address the ways in which society may become more aware and inclusive of the individual identities of its members. Our reading selections are intended to reflect our commitment to accurately identifying, portraying, and responding to the various experiences and concerns of individuals with disabilities, and to working toward liberation for all oppressed individuals in our society. From institutional and cultural perspectives, controversies and complexities continue to arise in relation to the issue of disability today: these include debates over the right to die and quality of life, abortion rights, genetics and biotechnology, and special education. It is our hope that, through education and increased awareness, individual perspectives and institutional and cultural systems will continue to be amended in order to address and support the diverse needs of all individuals in our society.

In this chapter, we have attempted to be as inclusive as possible, presenting a broad and diverse collection of authors and articles and giving consideration to disabilities that lack mainstream attention, such as psychological and medical disabilities, schizophrenia, ADHD, and learning disabilities. The field of disability is new, and as such the literature is relatively incomplete; we look forward to an increased availability of writing from a variety of social groups, including members of multiple underrepresented groups, such as women, people of color, and/or gay, lesbian, bi-sexual, and transgendered people with disabilities.

References

Blaska, J. (1997). "The Power of Language: Speak and Write Using 'Person First.'" In M. Nagler, ed., *Perspectives on Disability*. Palo Alto, Calif.: Health Markets Research.

Bryan, W. (1996). "Disability Rights Movement." In *In Search of Freedom: How Persons with Disabilities Have Been Disenfranchised from the Mainstream of American Society*. Springfield, Ill.: Charles C. Thomas.

Channing L. Bete Co., Inc. (1997). *Americans with Disabilities: Gaining Respect and Rights* [pamphlet]. South Deerfield, MA.

McClintock, M., and L Rauscher. (1997). "Ableism Curriculum Design." In Adams, M., L. A. Bell, and P. Griffin, eds. *Teaching for Diversity and Social Justice*. New York: Routledge.

United States Department of Justice. (1999). ADA legal documents: Public law 101-336. U.S. Department of Justice home page. Directory: usdoj.gov/crt/ada/pubs/ada.txt

Historical Perspective

Contexts

60

The Disability Rights Movement

Willie V. Bryan

Lack of Concern

Since World War II, there has been an increasing emphasis on human and civil rights in the United States. Minorities and women have spoken out on their own behalf attempting to gain the privileges, freedoms, and rights guaranteed for all Americans by the Constitution. While legal and social ground has been won and lost throughout the years, many minorities and women now enjoy a somewhat more equal existence in the United States than some forty years ago. Still, the battle for equality is far from victorious. While other groups continue their struggle, individuals with disabilities have joined forces to end discrimination in their lives and claim a life of equality in the United States.

The Civil Rights movement of the 1960s resulted in legislation designed to bar discrimination based on sex, race, and national origin; however, prohibition of discrimination based on physical and/or mental disabilities was not included (Burns 1990). As Thomas D. Schneid (1992) reminds us, a bill introduced in Congress in 1971 to amend Title VI of the Civil Rights Act of 1964 to prohibit discrimination based on physical or mental disability died in committee. Similarly, in 1972, another bill introduced in Congress, this time to amend Title VII of the Civil Rights Act to bar discrimination in employment based upon physical or mental disabilities, also died in committee. This may be seen as somewhat of a barometer of the level of concern lawmakers and many other nondisabled Americans had with regard to the civil rights of persons with disabilities.

Misconceptions regarding those with disabilities

Perhaps the lack of concern demonstrated by these actions of Congress is more of a reflection of ignorance of the needs and capabilities of persons with disabilities rather than a blatant desire to deny the civil rights of a group of people. At the time, the thought was that employers should not be forced to hire persons who could not adequately perform the required tasks. Persons with disabilities and their friends certainly were not advocating employment of nonqualified persons, they were simply asking that employers be required to look beyond a person's limitation to see his abilities and attempt to match them with the required job. Employers also had a number of misconceptions with regard to employing persons with disabilities, such as they would not be able to secure insurance for the person and the company's insurance premiums would increase. Another major misconception was the belief that persons with disabilities were unsafe employees. This erroneous belief was held despite safety records indicating that persons with disabilities had fewer accidents than nondisabled employees (Henderson and Bryan 1984). Many employers were aware that by making modifications to the work site and/ or its environment, a significant number of jobs could be made accessible to persons with disabilities; however, these same employers harbored the belief that making these accommodations would be too expensive. Again, this belief was held even though the DuPont Company had demonstrated that many changes to a work site could be done inexpensively.

These and other misconceptions were firmly held by employers because persons with disabilities and their advocates did not vigorously dispute them. The lack of opposition to discrimination against persons with disabilities with respect to employment allowed long-held stereotypes and prejudices to continue unchallenged. Activism would be necessary to dramatize the extent of the lack of concern for the rights of persons with disabilities and cause action to be taken to correct the neglect that had become an accepted method of treatment of persons with disabilities.

Minority Status

The political wheels of American progress appear to turn best when pressure is applied. For example, protests by minorities, particularly African Americans, led to the Civil Rights Act of 1964. Similarly, women's organizations engaged in various activities that placed pressure on state and federal government leaders to enact legislation that required equality of rights for women. One may assume that in a free and open democracy which most of us enjoy in America, there would be available on an equal basis to all citizens, the right to vote, to live wherever one can afford, the right to eat wherever one desires, and the right to be educated at the maximum level of one's abilities. However, it was precisely the denial of these basic rights, rights upon which this country was founded, rights for which thousands of Americans have paid the supreme price, that led multitudes of Americans into the streets to practice civil disobedience, until these and other basic rights were granted.

In the process of securing these rights, the minority groups learned that their minority status was not shameful. In fact, they learned that they were a very important cog in the wheel of American life and by withholding their labor and being selective as to how and where they spent their hard earned money, they could considerably slow down the democratic wheel of progress. These groups also learned that by networking they added strength to their demands.

Until recently, persons with disabilities were not widely considered a minority group. In fact, it was not until the Rehabilitation Act of 1973 that they were considered a "class" of people. Persons with disabilities are members of other groups of people, they are male or female, and they have an ethnic identity; their rights and privileges are associated with whatever cultural and/or gender group they belong. It is ironic that with regard to human rights their disabilities were secondary to their cultural and/or gender identity, but with regard to their rights as citizens, their disabilities were primary, overshadowing gender and/or cultural identity. Since disability groups were not considered a culture at the time, the person with a disability was viewed as a "disabled member of another class." To be more specific, they were considered to be a disabled female or a disabled American Indian female, and/or an economically disadvantaged disabled American Indian female. Hopefully, the point has been made. It is in part because of this dual and sometimes triple classification that the *disability* label was not considered a class unto itself.

Another reason for the lack of class status is that there are large numbers of disabilities and each one is considered a separate condition within its own group identity. For example, there are persons who have disabilities resulting from polio, arthritis, visual impairments, hearing impairments, lupus, mental illness, mental retardation, amputations, and paralysis, to mention only a few. In most cases, there was and continues to be associations or foundations which are considered the official representative for all who have a particular condition. This has the effect of segregating disabilities into distinct disease groups, thus causing each disabling condition to stand alone and not be part of a larger whole. This internal segregation, combined with society's segregation of persons with disabilities, has been devastating to efforts of persons with disabilities to unite and demand their constitutional rights.

Although it would not be until the passage of the Rehabilitation Act of 1973 that persons with disabilities would obtain the classification of minority status and be officially viewed as a class of people, several years before the passage of the act they began to think of themselves as a minority. And more importantly, they began to view their life conditions as having been deprived of their basic human rights similar to other minority groups. They also began to think of themselves as being oppressed and disenfranchised. With this realization, they began to unite and to speak openly about the manner in which they were being excluded from full participation in society's activities. Thinking of themselves as oppressed minorities, they also thought of the manner in which other minority groups had placed their agenda before the American people; thus a "grassroots disability rights movement" began, which resulted in the passage of the Americans with Disabilities Act, or ADA, in 1990.

The Grassroots Movement

Despite the concern exhibited by charitable organizations and Congress, the one aspect often missing was the involvement of persons with disabilities. For example, much of the legislation prior to the Rehabilitation Act of 1973 had been developed with little, if any, input from persons with disabilities. Charitable organizations established telethons to raise funds for research and/or provide services without giving much thought to the negative images being projected. This was "business as usual" or stated another way, it was the continuation of the paternalistic attitude that has existed in America for many decades. Perhaps without meaning harm to persons with disabilities, nondisabled persons have treated them as though they are incapable of determining and expressing how they would like to live their lives. Regardless of how well-intended the motivation of a nonoppressed person there are some things he/she will either overlook or not understand with regard to the effects of being oppressed. Therefore it is imperative that those affected must be involved in determining the best methods for eliminating the problems created by oppression.

There are undoubtedly many reasons why it took persons with disabilities approximately two centuries before they organized and began to speak out on their own behalf. With "sit-ins," marches, and attempts to integrate previously segregated southern schools, the 1950s served as the "staging" years of the civil rights movement; then in the 1960s the final "assault" years were launched which culminated in victory with the passage of the Civil Rights Act of 1964. Similarly for the disability rights movement, the 1960s served as the "staging" years with emphasis on consumerism, self-help, and demedication demands as well as demands for self-care rights and deinstitutionalism. Perhaps then the 1970s can be considered the "watershed" years for that movement. The 1960s was the decade when persons with disabilities began to view themselves as oppressed minorities and demanded their constitutional rights. Similar to the civil rights movement which culminated in the Civil Rights Act of 1964, the disability rights movement led to what has been called the Civil Rights Act for persons with disabilities: the Americans with Disabilities Act of 1990. . . .

Activism

Most early rehabilitation legislation's primary focus was "vocational" rehabilitation of persons with disabilities. In the early 1970s, rehabilitation leaders backed by disability rights groups began to push for changes in the legislation to advocate a broader nonvocational role for rehabilitation programs. In 1972, such legislation was passed by Congress, and Verville (1979) informs us that President Nixon vetoed the legislation because it "strayed too far from the essential vocational objective of the program."

This Act had provisions for Independent Living Centers. It would take six more years before this important concept would become a reality. The veto of the 1972 Rehabilitation Act is a classic example of not involving those most affected. Perhaps the veto served a useful purpose in that it became an issue around which the grassroots movement could unite. While attempting to get the Independent Living Centers provisions included in future legislation, the disability rights organizations gained considerable experience in politics, coalition building, and lobbying, as well as the act of compromising, thus gaining the respect of lawmakers and the admiration of millions of persons both with and without disabilities.

In the interim, additional legislation was passed with provisions to issue directives that persons with disabilities were not to be discriminated against nor treated as second-class citizens. One such piece of legislation was the Rehabilitation Act of 1973. Included in this legislation was Section 504 which forbade any United States institution that received federal financial assistance from discriminating against persons with disabilities in employment. . . .

Independent Living Movement

The quest for independence by most Americans does not occur by accident, but is a quality that is taught and reinforced to every American youth, both by formal teaching and by example. American history is replete with both fictional and factual persons accomplishing or attempting to accomplish extraordinary deeds to establish or maintain their independence.

Independence is therefore highly valued in American society; it is considered an essential building block in constructing and maintaining a democracy. Freedom, to an extent, is reliant upon its citizens having the independence to build better lives for themselves and in the process of accomplishing their dreams, they lift freedom and democracy to new levels. Conversely, being dependent is devalued in American society and those that are considered so are often assigned lower positions on the social totem pole. To many, the word "dependent" denotes lack of initiative, laziness, and a burden upon society. Although public and private social welfare agencies and organizations including hospitals, clinics, and rehabilitation centers, to mention a few, have been developed to assist persons who by virtue of illness, accident, or birth defects must rely upon assistive services, the recipients are often viewed in a negative light and at best given sympathy instead of empathy and understanding.

Illness or disability often places the individual, and sometimes the family, in a state of dependency. For some it is a permanent situation, but for the majority it is temporary. The degree to which a person becomes dependent is obviously affected by several things, not the least of which are attitudes. Attitudes of family, friends, medical and rehabilitation personnel as well as employers have an impact on the level of dependency of the person with a disability.

Given the value placed on independence by American society, no one should be amazed that persons with disabilities began to recognize and resent the limited role society drafted for them. They correctly perceived that society equated disability with dependency. They also recognized that this perception created a very low ceiling and an almost insurmountable wall around their abilities to function and achieve. . . .

In the early 1970s, persons with disabilities began to realize that to be truly free they must take and maintain control of their lives. This train of thought resulted in the development of Independent Living Centers (ILCs). Dejong (1982) provides a brief history of the genesis of Independent Living Centers as he reveals that a small group of persons with disabilities at the University of Illinois and at the University of California at Berkeley moved out of their residential hospital setting into the community and organized their own system for delivery of survival services. The centers established by these students became the blueprint by which future centers would be established. . . .

When one considers that the independent living movement was initiated by persons with disabilities, many of whom were persons with severe disabilities such as spinal cord injuries, it became quite apparent that these individuals exhibited courage of the highest magnitude. Although prior to the movement they lived in conditions that made them almost totally dependent upon others, it was however a safe environment; therefore, moving from this safe environment to face the many uncertainties created by a society with many barriers and obstacles certainly qualifies the founding members as pioneers. . . .

Laurie (1982) contributes to our understanding of the goal of independent living centers with these comments:

> Independent living is freedom of choice, to live where and how one chooses and can afford. It is living alone or with a roommate of one's choice. It is deciding one's own pattern of life: scheduling food, entertaining, vices, virtues, leisure and friends. It is freedom to take risks and freedom to make mistakes.

Frieden and Cole (1985) define the independent living concept as control over one's life based on the choice of acceptable options that minimize reliance on others in making decisions and in performing everyday activities. This may include managing one's affairs, participating in day-to-day life in the community, fulfilling a range of social roles, and making decisions that lead to self-determination and the minimizing of physical or psychological dependence upon others. . . .

While it is very important to note that the independent living movement was begun and defined by persons with disabilities, it must also be noted that to strengthen and stabilize independent living centers and their concept, federal legislation was needed, especially in the area of funding. Funding was needed to expand and improve upon the delivery of services as well as expand the centers throughout the United States. The 1972 Rehabilitation Act had provisions which would have accomplished this, but unfortunately the Act was vetoed by President Nixon. Despite this temporary setback, the seed had been sewn and Congress had demonstrated by the passage of the Act its support for this type of center. Fortunately, the Rehabilitation Act of 1973 was amended in 1978 to add Title VII, Comprehensive Services for Independent Living. With this amendment, Congress authorized support for community-based independent living centers, which had the effect of establishing a major change in federal disability policy. . . .

More Than Work

Work is so much a central part of most Americans' lives that it, in part, defines who we are. It is common for Americans to describe someone by identifying their occupation. For example we may identify someone as Mary Smith the attorney, or John Smith the teacher. Work has been the defining feature in American lives for many years. The Puritan work ethic is a standard by which Americans often judge each other. While we no longer subscribe to the theory of hard work for all, we most certainly subscribe to the idea of work for all. Work provides us with economic power to purchase goods and services which in part by virtue of the amount and types of goods we accumulate determines our social standing in America. Social condemnation is the reward for those that are able to work but do not. Work not only is a means by which we develop, maintain, or improve our societal standing in American society; it also is patriotic. In a capitalist society, it is through the production of products that our nation develops its standing in the world as compared to other nations.

Obviously, work has many important meanings to Americans and American society. Considering the position work holds in American life, it is easy to understand why virtually all rehabilitation legislation prior to the 1972 Rehabilitation Act emphasized "vocational rehabilitation." In fact, when we speak of rehabilitating a person with a disability we think the ultimate goal of the rehabilitation process is to make the person ready for a job. There is one thing wrong with this approach: what about the person who is unable to work because of the severity or perhaps type of disability? Unless they and/or their families have sufficient financial resources, they have to rely upon sympathy and charity of others as well as some social welfare assistance from the federal government. Because of the social stigma of not working and receiving charity, these persons' independence, self-dignity, and ability to participate as full American citizens are in jeopardy.

Perhaps these reasons, as well as others, caused the disability rights movement leaders to lobby Congress to deemphasize *vocational* in the Rehabilitation Act of 1972. . . . In part, what they were saying, and perhaps today we are just beginning to hear, is that a person's worth, self-respect, and dignity should not be measured by employment and moreover measured by whether employed in a job, especially if that person is unable to work. The leaders were wise to note that no person with a disability would be totally free until all persons with disabilities had opportunities to more fully participate in American life. Again it was this type of thinking that led them to push for independent living centers, and the abolishment of the segregation of persons with disabilities so they could not only become more involved in American society but also make decisions that would effect the quality of their lives. In short, they recognized that life for a person with a disability meant more than being able to work. . . .

References

Burns, B. (1990). *Americans with Disabilities Act of 1990: A Summary.* Unpublished paper. University of Oklahoma Health Sciences Center, Oklahoma City.

DeJong, G. (1982). "Independent Living." In M. G. Eisenberg, C. Giggins, and R. J. Duval, eds. *Disabled People as Second-Class Citizens.* New York: Springer.

Frieden, L. and J .A. Cole. (1985). "Independence: The Ultimate Goal of Rehabilitation for Spinal Cord–Injured Persons." *American Journal of Occupational Therapy* 39, no. 11, 734–39.

Henderson, G. and W. V. Bryan. (1984). *Psychosocial Aspects of Disability.* Springfield, Ill.: Charles C. Thomas.

Laurie, G. (1982). "Independent Living Programs." In M. G. Eisenberg, C. Giggins, and R. J. Duval, eds. *Disabled People as Second-Class Citizens.* New York: Springer.

Schneid, T. (1992). *The Americans with Disabilities Act.* New York: Van Nostrand Reinhold.

Verville, R. E. (1979). "Federal Legislative History of Independent Living Programs," cited in J. C. Spencer. (1990). "An Ethnographic Study of Independent Living Alternatives." *American Journal of Occupational Therapy* 45, no. 3, 243–51.

Common Held Societal Stigmas + Assumptions

61

Disability beyond Stigma:
Social Interaction,
Discrimination, and Activism

Michelle Fine
Adrienne Asch

Introduction

Between 1981 and 1984, the Eastern Paralyzed Veterans Association, Disabled in Action of New York City, and other organizations of people with disabilities fought a court battle with the New York City Metropolitan Transit Authority (MTA) to gain architectural access to the city's mass transit system. The MTA opposed modifying the system, claiming that the expense would never be made up by rider fares of those mobility-impaired people then denied transit access. The *New York Times* ("Editorial" 1983; "The $2,000 Subway Token" 1984), along with most other sectors of the community, generally favoring progressive social change, supported the Transit Authority in the fight it eventually lost (Katzmann 1986).

In 1982 and 1983, the national media described two cases where the parents and doctors of infants with disabilities denied the infants medical treatment based on their impairments. In the first case, an infant with Down's syndrome died of starvation six days after birth; in the second case, the parents finally consented to the surgery. The impairments of the infants were used as the basis for denying them treatment that could have alleviated certain of their medical problems but left them with permanent disabilities that no treatment would cure. Virtually the only supports of the infants' right to treatment over parental objections were those commonly associated with the right-wing and right-to-life sectors of society, and perhaps also people with disabilities themselves *(Disability Rag* 1984). . . .

In 1983 and 1984, and again in 1986, Elizabeth Bouvia, a young woman whose cerebral palsy made it impossible for her to control any of her limbs save some functions of one hand, sought to get California hospitals to allow her to die by starvation. The American Civil Liberties Union (ACLU), generally regarded as championing the progress of many social causes, wrote a brief in her behalf describing her disability as causing her "pitiful existence," referring to her "affliction" as "incurable and . . . intolerable", and commenting on the "indignity and humiliation of requiring someone to attend to her every bodily need" (ACLU Foundation of Southern California 1983, 14, 17, 35). The entire tone of the brief implied that it was not at all surprising that someone with her level of disability would wish to end her life. The ACLU was not dissuaded from its line of argument by testimony of the Disability Rights Coordinating Council (DRCC), including a psychologist who was also quadriplegic, suggesting that Ms. Bouvia's situation was complicated by a host of stresses apart from her disability: "death of a sibling, marriage, pregnancy, multiple changes in residence, financial hardship, miscarriage, increased physical pain, terminal illness of a parent, and dissolution of marriage" (DRCC 1983, 3). The DRCC did not dispute that people had the right to take their own lives. It disputed the unquestioned assumption that disability was a reason to end life.

The Superior Court of California, unmoved by those who sought to disentangle Ms. Bouvia's request from the situation of people with disabilities generally, endorsed her request, saying among other things: "She, as the patient, lying helplessly in bed, unable to care for herself, may consider her existence meaningless. She cannot be faulted for so concluding." Later, in describing her, it stated: "Her mind and spirit may be free to take great flights, but she herself is imprisoned, and must lie physically helpless, subject to the ignominy, embarrassment, humiliation, and dehumanizing aspects created by her help-lessness" (*Bouvia v. Superior Court of California* 1986, 19, 21).

Defining the Population of Interest

In 1980 Bowe estimated the total population of people with disabilities in the United States to be 36 million or perhaps 15 percent of the nation's people. In 1986, the *New York Times* reported some 37 million people over 15 years of age with disabling conditions ("Census Study" 1986). As Asch (1984) has discussed elsewhere, the mere attempt to define and enumerate the population shows that disability is a social construct. The Rehabilitation Act of 1973, as amended in 1978, defines a handicapped individual as "any person who (i) has a physical or mental impairment which substantially limits one or more of such person's major life activities, (ii) has a record of such an impairment, or (iii) is regarded as having such an impairment."

We can say the following with assurance: The nation's population includes some 10 percent of school-aged children classified as handicapped for the purposes of receipt of special educational services somewhere between 9 percent and 17 percent of those between sixteen and sixty-four years of age report disabilities that influence their employment situation (Haber and McNeil 1983); nearly half of those over sixty-five indicate having one or more disabilities that interfere with their life activities or are regarded by others as doing so (DeJong and Lifchez 1983).

Laws governing the provision of educational and rehabilitation services, and prohibiting discrimination in education, employment, and access to public programs all stress the similarities in needs and in problems of people with a wide variety of physical, psychological, and intellectual impairments. In this space, however, it is important to acknowledge the *differences* among disabling conditions and their varied impact on the lives of people in this group.

First, different conditions cause different types of functional impairment. Deafness, mental retardation, paralysis, blindness, congenital limb deficiencies, and epilepsy may pose common social problems of stigma, marginality, and discrimination, but they also produce quite different functional difficulties. Several of these disabilities obviously interfere with functions of daily life, but the last, epilepsy, may not. Some persons with epilepsy have no inherent limitations whatever. Nevertheless, they are likely to be regarded as having an impairment.

Furthermore, people with disabilities have different degrees of impairment: Amounts of hearing and visual loss differ; some people with impairment of mobility can walk in some situations while others cannot. Mental retardation ranges from profound to mild—so mild that many out of school never get the label. In addition, some disabilities are static, while others are progressive. Multiple sclerosis, muscular dystrophy, cystic fibrosis, some vision and hearing impairments, some types of cancer and heart conditions present progressive disabilities that cause ever-changing health and life situations. Some conditions are congenital, others are acquired. All of these factors that distinguish the origin, experience, and effects of disability must be kept in mind in social science research on disability.

Researchers (Davis 1961; Goffman 1963; Ladieu, Adler, and Dembo 1948) have long been aware that the degree of visibility of impairment or the age at which it was acquired (Barker 1948) may influence the psychological consequences and the social situation of people with disabilities. More recently, scholars have addressed the impact of ethnicity, class, and gender upon the experience of disability (Fine and Asch 1981). . . .

Assumptions about Disability

Considered below are a set of common assumptions about what disability means. For each, there have been important methodological and theoretical consequences:

1. *It is often assumed that disability is located solely in biology, and thus disability is accepted uncritically as an independent variable.* The disability and the person are assumed synonymous, and the cause of others' behaviors and attitudes. Several experimental social psychologists (Katz 1981; Kleck, Ono, and Hastorf 1966) have simulated disability in the laboratory to verify Goffman's reports that handicapped people arouse anxiety and discomfort in others and are socially stigmatized. In these experiments, researchers have simulated disability by using a confederate who in one experimental condition appeared disabled and in another appeared nondisabled. The experiments did support the hypothesis that nondisabled people react differently to people with disabilities than they do to people without them. Nevertheless, it should be remembered that the confederate, whose only experience of having disability may have been simulating it by sitting in a wheelchair, employed none of the strategies commonly used by disabled people to ease the discomfort of strangers in first meetings (Davis 1961; Goffman 1963). By focusing on initial encounters with strangers and by using a confederate whose only experience with disability might be simulating it, these experiments tell us nothing about how disabled people *actually* negotiate meaningful social interactions. Reports by Davis (1961) and Goffman (1963) acknowledge that obvious disability is generally prominent in initial social encounters. However, the extent to which an experimental confederate's naïveté about living with a disability can contribute to the prominence and the awkwardness of disability has not been recognized as an intervening variable. In these experiments, disability is viewed as an independent variable, much as gender had been considered prior to the early 1970s (Unger and Denmark 1975). Disability is portrayed as the variable that predicts the outcome of social interaction when, in fact, social contexts shape the meaning of a disability in a person's life.

Most social-psychological work using disability to examine the concept of stigma takes the experience as equivalent, regardless of such factors as the disabled person's race, culture, class and gender. Becker and Arnold (1986) provide valuable correctives by viewing the situation of disabled people through the disciplines of anthropology and history.

2. *When a disabled person faces problems, it is assumed that the impairment causes them.* In a very thoughtful expansion of Goffman's notion of stigma, Jones and colleagues (1984) elaborate on the consequences for the "marked" person of being singled out by others. Throughout their discussion of marking and its social-psychological consequences for disabled and nondisabled alike, however, these authors never question the extent to which disability per se poses difficulties in social participation, as contrasted with difficulties caused by the environment—architectural, social, economic, legal, and cultural. For example, in their discussion of changes in the life situations of people who

became disabled, the authors never question that *the disability* keeps the person from continuing the employment or from going to restaurants or other recreational facilities. The entire discussion of stigma and marked relationships assumes as "natural" what Hahn aptly terms as *disabling environment;* it views obstacles as being solely the person's biological limitations rather than the human-made barriers of architecture or discriminatory work practices.

Even Barker's (1948) early work went only part way to indicting the environment as an obstacle to the disabled person's participation. Far ahead of his time, he called for antidiscrimination laws in education and employment, although he failed to challenge the architecture, the transportation, and the communication methods that confronted people with disabilities and hampered full participation. Barker's concluding comments took social arrangements as given, urging counseling and psychotherapy for people with disabilities so that they could come to accept "the fact that the world in which [they live] presents serious restrictions and frustrations." He went on to say that education and antidiscrimination laws cannot "remove all restrictions on the physically deviant in a world constructed for the physically normal. The ultimate adjustment must involve changes in the values of the physically normal. The ultimate adjustment must involve changes in the values of the physically disabled person" (37).

Barker's (1948) view is understandable twenty-five years before the passage of federal legislation to modify public-sector physical environments. Jones and his colleagues' (1984) obliviousness to environmental issues is not. Their otherwise valuable work on the social-psychological consequences of disability and stigma suffers seriously from such omissions. We can contrast these omissions of attention to environmental effects with Sampson's (1983) work on justice. Sampson urges students of justice and of resource allocation to attend to and be critical of current systems rather than merely to accept them and their consequences. We urge the same for students of disability.

3. *It is assumed that the disabled person is a "victim."* In a great deal of social-psychological research on attribution, the disabled person is seen as a victim who copes with suffering by self-blame (Bulman and Wortman 1977), by reinterpreting the suffering to find positive meaning, or by denying that he or she is really suffering (Taylor, Wood, and Lichtman 1983). Bulman and Wortman studied 29 people paralyzed in accidents. Lerner (1980) describes these people as "young people who had been recently condemned to spend the rest of their lives crippled" (161). In order for Lerner to make sense of why Bulman and Wortman's respondents were not displaying a sense of victimization, he posits their belief in a just world and suggests that their interpretations of the disabling events are constructed so as to retain a strong belief that the world is a just place and that bad things only happen to people for reasons. The psychological experiences of the persons with disabilities are thus examined not on their own terms, but instead as a form of denial. Disability is used as a synonym for victimization in this theoretical analysis.

Taylor and colleagues' (1983) "It Could Be Worse" also illustrated the unchecked presumption of disabled-person-as-victim. The researchers examined the responses of people with cancer shortly after the onset of their condition and discovered that the interviewees consistently maintained that their situations "could be worse." To explain this finding, five "strategies" used by these "victims" to make sense of their situations were described. It is disturbing to us that these authors, who were interested in the rich qualitative ways that people describe their coping experiences, minimized informants' consistently expressed view that the trauma was not as severe as it could have been.

As Taylor and colleagues argued, people diagnosed as having cancer are surely traumatized, and they actively generate coping strategies. However, our concerns arise with respect to the authors' a priori assumptions. First, it should be noted that Bulman and Wortman, and Taylor and colleagues, studied people quite shortly after the onset of disability, before they had a chance to discover what would or would not be problematic about their lives. Their findings that self-blame (Bulman and Wortman, 1977) and making downward comparisons (Taylor, Wood, and Lichtman 1983) occurred within the first months or years after disability differ dramatically from those of Schultz and Decker (1985) in their study of people with spinal cord injuries five to twenty years after disability. The former authors can be read as suggesting, if inadvertently, that the experience of disability is static in a person's life and that "coping" is the same at any point in time or in one's life situation. The work of Schulz and Decker (1985) correct this prevailing assumption and enrich our understanding of disability by demonstrating that responses at a specific time may not be the ones people retain after living with a disability for several years.

There are two more problems with the interpretations of disabled-person-as-victim put forward by Bulman and Wortman (1977), Janoff-Bulman and Frieze (1983), Lerner (1980), and Taylor, Wood, and Lichtman (1983). First, in contrast to Ladieu and colleagues' (1948) report on the reactions of disabled veterans after World War II, these later researchers seem to discount the experiences described by the people they interviewed. Taylor and colleagues, for example, view their respondents as having strategies for managing or camouflaging what must be truly tragic. To the "outsider," the researcher, the "objective situation" is that a diagnosis of cancer is primarily a tragedy. That "insiders", those with cancer, overwhelmingly state that they had fared better than they would have expected is not used self-reflectively by the researchers to reframe their notions about how people think about traumatic life events. Rather, the statement is interpreted to illustrate psychological defenses that disabled people mobilize in order to manage what researchers feel is not really manageable. What needs to be stated is that disability—while never wished for—may simply not be as wholly disastrous as imagined.

Second, these authors presume that the disability itself constitutes the victimizing experience. None of them emphasize the subsequent reactions or deprivations that people experience because of social responses to their disability or environmentally imposed constraints. While Janoff-Bulman and Frieze (1983) recognize discrimination based on sex or gender to be a societal injustice, disability is assumed a biological injustice and the injustices that lie in its social treatment are ignored.

4. *It is assumed that disability is central to the disabled person's self-concept, self-definition, social comparison, and reference groups.* Taylor and her colleagues (1983) describe their respondents as having to make downward social comparisons, lest they come face to face with how bad their situations really are. Jones and colleagues (1984), in their discussion of stigma, assume that the recently disabled paraplegic compares herself to others who are also paralyzed. She may, but perhaps only when it comes to assessing her capacity to perform certain activities from a wheelchair. Gibbons (1986) claims that while such severely stigmatized people as those labeled retarded must make only downward social comparison to preserve self-esteem, more "mildly stigmatized" people such as those using wheelchairs seek out similarly disabled people with whom to compare themselves, and avoid social interactions and social comparisons with nondisabled people. Because disability is clearly salient for the nondisabled, it is assumed that the marked person incorporates the mark as central to self-definition.

The above authors forget that the woman who is paralyzed may be as likely to compare herself with other women her age, others of her occupation, others of her family, class, race, or a host of other people and groups who function as reference groups and social comparison groups for her. Disability may be more salient to the researchers studying it than to the people being studied, who may define themselves as "similar to" or worthy of comparison with people without disabilities. Gurin (1984) reminds researchers in social comparison and relative deprivation to pay more attention to the conditions under which people choose particular groups with whom to compare themselves, and she stresses that social comparison may have nothing to do with gender, race, or disability.

5.   *It is assumed that having a disability is synonymous with needing help and social support.* People with disabilities are perceived to be examples of those ever in need of help and social support (Brickman et al. 1982; Deutsch 1985; Dunkel-Schetter 1984; Jones et al. 1984; Katz 1981; Krebs 1970; Sarason 1986). Such an assumption is sustained both by what researchers study and write about those with disabilities and by their omission of disabled people in their discussions as providers of support.

The assumption that disability is synonymous with helplessness is not surprising when we remember that "the handicapped role" in the United States has been seen as one of helplessness, dependence, and passivity (Gliedman and Roth 1980; Goffman 1963). Brickman and colleagues (1982), in their excellent discussion of different models of helping and coping, review the essence of the medical model: the person is responsible for neither the problem encountered nor the solution required. The handicapped role, like the sick role of which it is an extension, compels the occupant to suspend other activities until recovered, to concentrate on getting expert therapy, to follow instructions, to get well, and only then to resume normal life. The nonhandicapped person equates having a disability with a *bad and eternal flu*, toothache, or broken leg. When such conditions are temporary, it may be acceptable to entrust oneself to helpers and to forego decision making briefly; but when forced to confront a moment of weakness, unsteadiness, or limitations in the capacity to see, hear, or move, people experience grave difficulty in adjusting. However, it is erroneous to conclude that their difficulties mirror those of the person who has a long-term disability and who has learned to use alternative methods to accomplish tasks of daily living and working.

The disability is assumed tantamount to incompetence and helplessness has been investigated, and supported in laboratory research. Unfortunately, the writing that has been generated *accepts* rather than *challenges* this stereotype. Katz (1981), who found that whites gave more help to "competent" blacks than to ones they perceived to be less competent and enterprising, expected that the same help-giving pattern would be true for nondisabled subjects when confronting a person with a disability. Contrary to his hypothesis, however, he found that nondisabled people gave *less* help to disabled persons perceived as competent and friendly than to those perceived as incompetent and unfriendly. They also gave less help to the "disabled person" (simulated) than to the nondisabled persons. To explain this, Katz relied on Goffman (1963) and Gliedman and Roth (1980) in asserting that nondisabled persons are relatively offended or uncomfortable when confronting a person with an impairment who manages life competently. As Jones and his colleagues (1984) remind us, the able-bodied deny the reality of successful adaptation by the disabled person. They perceive it as the disabled person "making the best of a bad job," and this view supports their conviction that their own health and capacities are as important, and infallible, as they think (87).

Even while we wonder whether Katz would have gotten the same finding had he used a person who actually had a disability rather than one who had simulated an impairment, it is valuable to have this experimental support for what Goffman, Gliedman and Roth, and untold numbers of people with disabilities have described. Unfortunately, Jones and colleagues (1984) fall prey to their own unchallenged assumptions in thinking about ongoing relationships between people with and without disabilities: Throughout their book, and especially in the chapter by French (1984), it is assumed that the person with the disability is in constant need of help and support, rather than being a victim of nondisabled persons' projections or fantasies. Thereby, three problems arise: first, that the person with a disability may need assistance with certain acts is generalized to all aspects of the relationship between a person with a disability and one without. Second, if the person does need assistance, it is assumed that a previous reciprocal relationship will change, rather than that new methods or relationships will develop to provide it. Concurrently, it is assumed that the biological condition rather than the environment and social context makes one-way assistance inevitable. Third, it perpetuates the idea that the impaired person is forever the recipient, rather than ever the provider, of help and support. If disabled people are mentioned, they are mentioned as only on the receiving end of a helping transaction.

In French's (1984) chapter on marriages between disabled and nondisabled people, the assumptions are never challenged that the disability causes marital roles to change fundamentally, that blindness or quadriplegia per se will make resuming a work role difficult or impossible, that recreation will have to be curtailed. The spouse who performs certain amounts of physical caretaking is seen not only as a physical caretaker but as a generous intellectual and emotional caretaker as well. Physical incapacities are perceived as leading inevitably to incapacities in other spheres of life. Wright's (1983) notion that disability "spreads" throughout a relationship is embedded unchallenged in this entire discussion.

Moreover, it is the disability, not the institutional, physical, or attitudinal environment, that is blamed for role changes that may occur. The person with a disability may (initially, or always) need physical caretaking, such as help in dressing, household chores, or reading. It must be asked, however, whether such assistance would be necessary if environments were adapted to the needs of people with disabilities—if, for example, more homes were built to accommodate those who used wheelchairs, if technological aids could be developed to assist in performing manual tasks, if existing technology to convert the printed word into speech or Braille were affordable to all who needed it. Thus, again, the physical environment as an obstruction remains an unchallenged given. In addition, the author is assuming that the role of human assistant for all these tasks will automatically fall to the "significant other" rather than considering whether such activities could be performed by others, including public sector employees, thus permitting the primary relationship to function in its primary spheres of intimacy, sharing, and emotional nurturance for both participants. If the partners reorganize their roles after the impairment of one member, such reorganizations may result from a variety of factors: the way they think about disability, their relational obligations, the way that health care professionals inform them about the implications of disability, or the difficulties faced in affording appropriate assistance in the United States. These are consequences of how people think about disability and of current national disability policy, not of disability per se. As with all too much of this literature, as Wright (1983) points out, researchers who are outsiders make attributions to persons and thus neglect the powerful role of the environment.

The third problem mentioned above—that disabled people are always seen as recipients—may stem not only from distortions about people with disabilities but also from using disability as a metaphor to illustrate theory rather than to reveal more about the lives of people with impairments. Deutsch (1985) may be correct in speculating that, at least temporarily, resources would or should go to a sick child rather than to a well one; Dunkel-Schetter (1984) may plausibly learn about the mechanisms of social support by studying what people with cancer find valuable and supportive from others after such a diagnosis; Krebs (1970) makes an important point in discussing how assumptions of legitimacy of others' dependency influence the helping process. Nonetheless, by staying with questions about theories of distributive systems (Deutsch 1985,) social support (Dunkel-Schetter 1984), or altruism (Krebs 1970) and by not focusing on ongoing reciprocal transactions, the person with a disability is never imagined or shown to be a provider of support. . . . It is regrettable that people with disabilities, when studied or considered at all in most social-psychological literature, are examined only in ways that reinforce and perpetuate existing stereotypes rather than in ways that question and challenge them. In this manner, the literature fails to enrich our understanding of the lives of people with handicapping conditions.

Particularly disturbing, as an illustration of disability-as-metaphor, is Sarason's (1986) discussion of the Baby Jane Doe case. Unfortunately, his laudable effort to call for a renewed commitment to the "public interest" and a lessening of individualism is flawed by uncritically accepting the assumption that the infant with a disability can never be expected to make a valuable contribution to family or society. He consistently refers to the existence of the severely disabled child as a problem to both family and society. Sarason's examination of the public interest and of the search for community continues in this "disabled-as-helpless" vein. He refers only to "afflicted children"; finds that families who adopt disabled children were "managing their situations in surprisingly adaptive, stable, and inspiring ways" (903); and describes the child only as a "problem," without any consideration of the possible contributions, benefits, or pleasures the infant born with a disability might bring to its family and society.

The Role of These Assumptions for Society and for Social Science

It is worth speculating on how these assumptions get made, why they persist, and what functions they serve for researchers and society. It remains a task for future research to discover the plausibility of these speculations.

Jones and his colleagues (1984) contend that the thought or awareness of disability evokes feelings of vulnerability and death. They suggest that the nondisabled person almost wants the one with the disability to suffer so as to confirm that the "normal" state is as good and as important as the "normal" thinks it is. Because disability can be equated with vulnerability to the controllable, observing someone with a disability forces all of us to wonder about the consequences of what one cannot control. In a society seeking to control ever more of life, is there a leap to the assumption that one cannot live with the consequences of what one cannot control? Social researchers are in the business of expanding knowledge of the world and trying to optimize prediction and control. As researchers, we highly prize knowledge and the control it can provide. Does such a commitment to control suggest that social scientists may view disability as fearful, unacceptable, and different because the person with the disability is a reminder that we cannot control all life events?

As discussed earlier, perceptions of disability have been the repository and projection of human needs. How much do the social and psychological problems that many people associate with disability actually pervade all of human life? If one can think of a person with a disability as needy, in contrast, one can view those without impairments as strong and as not having needs. By thinking of the disabled person as dependent in a given situation, and the one without disabilities as independent and autonomous, one can avoid considering how extensively people without disabilities too are dependent and sometimes not. Rather than the world being divided into givers and receivers of help, we are all actually interdependent. Attributing neediness and lack of control to people with disabilities permits those who are not disabled to view themselves as having more control and more strength in their lives than may be the case.

Last, perceiving a person with a disability as a suffering victim, as a stimulus object, as in need, or as different and strange, all reinforce what Goffman (1963) describes as perception of the stigmatized as "not quite human" (6). In discussing the scope of justice, Deutsch (1985) comments, "Justice is not involved in relations with others. . . . The narrower one's concept of community, the narrower will be the scope of situations in which one's actions will be governed by considerations of justice" (36–37). Deutsch goes on to contend that it has been

> [a] too-common assumption of victimizers, even those of good will, as well as of many social scientists, that the social pathology has been in the ghetto rather than in those who have built the walls to surround it, that the disadvantaged are the ones who need to be changed rather than the people and institutions who have kept the disadvantaged in a submerged position. . . . It is more important to change educational institutions and economic and political systems so that they will permit those groups who are now largely excluded from important positions of decision-making to share power than to try to inculcate new attitudes and skills in those who are excluded. (61)

These words apply as much to the situation of people with disabilities as to that of people with economic disadvantages whom Deutsch considered. By concentrating on cure or on psychological and physical restoration of the impaired person, society and the discipline of psychology have avoided the need to focus on essential changes in the environmental side of the "person-in-environment" situation. If the person with a disability is "not quite human," then that person can remain outside the community of those who must receive just distributions of rewards and resources (Deutsch, 1985). In contrast, if people with disabilities were perceived as having the same rights to mobility and life's opportunities as people without impairments, we would inevitably be compelled to rethink the view that transportation for people with mobility impairments, or access to treatment for infants or adults with disabilities, are gifts or charities that can be withdrawn when times are tight. Once people with disabilities are admitted inside the human and moral community, the task becomes one of creating an environment where all humans—including those with impairments—can truly flourish.

References

ACLU Foundation of Southern California. (1983). *Elizabeth Bouvia v. County of Riverside* (Memorandum of points and authorities in support of application for temporary restraining order and permanent injunction). Los Angeles: ACLU Foundation of Southern California.

Asch, A. (1984). "The Experience of Disability: A Challenge for Psychology." *American Psychologist* 39, 529–36.

Asch, A. and H. Rousso. (1985). "Therapists with Disabilities: Theoretical and Clinical Issues." *Psychiatry* 48, 1–12.

Barker, R. B. (1948). "The Social Psychology of Physical Disability." *Journal of Social Issues* 4, no. 4, 28–37.

Becker, G., and R. Arnold. (1986). "Stigma as a Social and Cultural Construct." In S. Ainlay, G. Becker, and L. Coleman. eds., *The Dilemma of Difference: A Multi-Disciplinary View of Stigma*. New York: Plenum.

Bouvia v. Superior Court of the State of California. (1986). Court of Appeals of the State of California. Second Appelate District, Division Two, 2nd Cir. No. B019134.

Bowe, F. (1980) *Rehabilitating America*. New York: Harper and Row.

Brickman P., V. C. Rabinowitz, J. Karuza, D. Coats, E. Cohn, E., and L. Kidder. (1982). "Models of Helping and Coping." *American Psychologist* 37, 368–84.

Bulman, R., and C. Wortman. (1977). Attributions of Blame and Coping with the 'Real World': Severe Accident Victims React to Their Lot." *Journal of Personality and Social Psychology* 35, 351–63.

Cain, L. F. (1948). "The Disabled Child in School." *Journal of Social Issues* 4, no. 4, 90–93.

"Census Study Reports One in Five Adults Suffers from Disability. "(1986, December 23). *New York Times*, 67.

Davis, F. (1961). "Deviance Disavowal: The Management of Strained Interaction by the Visibly Handicapped." *Social Problems* 9, 120–32.

DeJong, G. and R. Lifchez. (1983). Physical Disability and Public Policy." *Scientific American* 48, 240–49.

Deutsch, M. (1985). *Distributive Justice.* New Haven, Conn.: Yale University Press.

Disability Rag. (1984, February–March). Entire issue.

Disability Rights Coordinating Council (DRCC). (1983). *Elizabeth Bouvia v. County of Riverside.* Declaration of Carol Gill. Los Angeles: DRCC.

Dunkel-Schetter, C. (1984). "Social Support and Cancer: Findings Based on Patient Interviews and Their Implications." *Journal of Social Issues* 40, no. 4, 77–98.

Editorial, *New York Times.* (1983, June 17).

Fine, M. and A. Asch, eds. (1981). *Women with Disabilities: Essays in Psychology. Culture and Politics.* Phildelphia: Temple University Press.

French, R. de S. (1984). "The Long-Term Relationships of Marked People." In E. E. Jones et al., *Social Stigma: The Psychology of Marked Relationships.* New York: Freeman.

Gibbons, F. X. 1986. "Stigma and Interpersonal Relations." In S. Ainlay, G. Becker, and L. Coleman, eds. *The Dilemma of Difference: A Multi-Disciplinary View of Stigma.* New York: Plenum.

Gliedman, J. and W. Roth. (1980). *The Unexpected Minority: Handicapped Children in America.* New York: Harcourt, Brace, Jovanovich.

Goffman, E. (1963). *Stigma: Notes on the Management of Spoiled Identity.* Englewood Cliffs, N.J.: Prentice-Hall.

Gurin, P. (1984). Review of *Relative Deprivation and Working Men. Contemporary Psychology* 29, 209–10.

Haber, L. and J. McNeil. (1983) *Methodological Questions in the Estimation of Disability Prevalence.* Washington, D.C.: Population Division, U.S. Bureau of the Census.

Janoff-Bulman, R., and L. H. Frieze. (1983). "A Theoretical Perspective for Understanding Reactions to Victimization." *Journal of Social Issues* 39, no. 2, 1–17.

Jones, E .E., A. Farina, A. H. Hastorf, H. Markus, D. T. Miller, R. A. Scott, and R. de S. French. (1984) *Social Stigma: The Psychology of Marked Relationships.* New York: Freeman.

Katz, I. (1981). *Stigma: A Social-Psychological Analysis.* Hillsdale, N.J.: Erlbaum.

Katzmann, R. A. (1986). *Institutional Disability: The Saga of Transportation Policy for the Disabled.* Washington, D.C.: Brookings Institute.

Kleck, R., H. Ono, and A. Hastorf. (1966). "The Effects of Physical Deviance upon Face-to-Face Interaction." *Human Relations* 19, 425–36.

Krebs, D. L. (1970) "Altruism: An Examination of the Concept and Review of the Literature." *Psychological Bulletin* 73, 258–302.

Ladieu, G., D. L. Adler, and T. Dembo. (1948). "Studies in Adjustment to Visible Injuries: Social Acceptance of the Injured." *Journal of Social Issues* 4, no. 4, 55–61.

Lerner, M. J. (1980). *The Belief in a Just World: A Fundamental Delusion.* New York: Plenum.

Sampson, E. (1983). *Justice and the Critique of Pure Psychology.* New York: Plenum.

Sarason, S. B. (1986). "And What is the Public Interest?" *American Psychologist* 41, 899–906.

Schultz, R., and S. Decker. (1985). "Long-Term Adjustment to Physical Disability: The Role of Social Support, Perceived Control, and Self-Blame." *Journal of Personality and Social Psychology* 48, 1162–72.

Taylor, S. E., J. V. Wood, and R. R. Lichtman. (1983). "'It Could Be Worse': Selective Evaluation as a Response to Victimization." *Journal of Social Issues* 39, no. 2, 19–40.

"The $2,000 Subway Token." (1984, June 23). *New York Times.*

Unger, R. K. and F. L. Denmark. (1975). *Woman: Dependent or Independent Variable?* New York: Psychological Dimensions.

Wright, B. A. (1983). *Physical Disability: A Psycho-Social Approach.* New York: Harper and Row.

62

A Separate and Unequal Education for Minorities with Learning Disabilities

Joseph P. Shapiro

As Americans, we have marked the fortieth anniversary of *Brown v. Board of Education* (1954). As you know, it took another twenty-one years after the Brown decision before students with disabilities were guaranteed the right to any education at all. Students with disabilities, of all colors, did not even have a separate and unequal education. Many had to fight to get through the schoolhouse door at all. By the time Public Law 94-142 (the Education for All Handicapped Children Act of 1975) was passed, there were some one million children with disabilities outside the schoolhouse door.

Separate and Unequal Education

In the 1990s, the Individuals with Disabilities Education Act (IDEA) of 1990 (PL 101-476) protects the rights of children with disabilities in school, and the Americans with Disabilities Act (ADA) of 1990 (PL 101-336) protects their rights when they leave school. Yet I think it must be noted that for many students, particularly students from minority groups, special education has been a ticket to resegregation and isolation. It has been a track to dropping out without the skills necessary to work and live independently. For too many students, special education has become what *U.S. News and World Report* termed "a separate and unequal system of education" (Shapiro et al., 1993). This analysis found that African-American students are twice as likely as Caucasian students to be placed in special education. Students from minority groups are also more likely to get stigmatizing labels. They are more likely to be labeled mentally retarded or emotionally disturbed. Once in special education, a student from a minority group is more likely to be segregated. At a time when the trend is toward integrating special education students into general education schools and classrooms, it is Caucasian students who are the first to benefit from inclusion. Students from minority groups are more likely to remain in separate classes or separate schools where academics are sometimes not stressed and academic failure becomes predictable.

Who Gets Labeled?

The trends described in the preceding section are clear in a study based on the records of more than 65,000 students in special education in Connecticut (Nerney 1993). In Stamford, Connecticut, for example, 57 percent of Caucasian males in special education have a learning disability classification, but only 40 percent of African American males do. Males from minority groups, meanwhile, are more than twice as likely to be labeled as having a serious emotional disturbance (Nerney 1993).

Even when students from minority groups are diagnosed as having learning disabilities, they are more than twice as likely in Connecticut to remain in separate classes. Only 15 percent of Caucasian students with learning disabilities spend their days in separate classes. For males with learning disabilities from minority groups, 36 percent are educated in segregated classes; for females from minority groups, the number is 34 percent (Nerney 1993). So, African-American students in Connecticut are half as likely as Caucasian students to be labeled as having a learning disability, and, when they are, they are twice as likely to be separated from other students.

Who is diagnosed as having a learning disability can differ from state to state and from school district to school district. One study of students with learning disabilities found that in New York City they had an average IQ of 81, but in Westchester County, a largely white suburb, students who were classified as having a learning disability had an average IQ of 103 (Gottlieb, et al. 1994). In fact, according to the same study, 85 percent of inner-city students classified as having learning disabilities did not have any identifiable learning disability at all (Gottlieb et al. 1994). Rather, the study contends, these were students who not long ago would have been called "disadvantaged." They are the children of poor families. They come to school far behind. They are unprepared to learn; some come not knowing how to spell their own names. The deficits of these students are greater than ever and speak to the importance of prevention and early intervention.

This study (Gottlieb et al. 1994) found that 90 percent of special education students in New York City come from families who receive some form of public assistance. Most live with a single parent, almost always their mother. Many are immigrants, too. Of the students labeled as having learning disabilities, 44 percent come from households where English is not the first language, and 19 percent of these students were born outside the United States. These are the children who need individual attention the most, and they are referred to special education because their teachers realize they need one-to-one help or to be in a small group and not in a classroom with thirty-five or more students. Classes are so big that many teachers do not have time to spend with individual students. Some teachers simply do not want children with special needs in their classes. They simply do not or cannot take the time necessary to reach students who are harder to teach. Most of these students could succeed in general education classes if the classes were small enough (Gottlieb et al. 1994). But special education is not set up to reach these children. For most students in New York City, special education is a road to failure (Gottlieb et al. 1994).

One solution may be smaller classes, but it is a difficult solution for schools in a time of tight resources. Smaller classes could be achieved by hiring more teachers or by putting competent aides in each classroom to reduce student-teacher ratios. Integrating these students into general classrooms could also be achieved with better teacher preparation and by preparing *all* teachers (special and general education teachers) to teach children who learn differently. We know from the NCLD [National Center for Learning Disabilities] study that the teachers want this preparation.

There is a successful school in East Harlem, New York City, where teachers, aides, and guidance counselors are taught how to teach reading. Instead of five teachers teaching reading to all the third graders, there are eight teachers. The class size is smaller, the children receive more attention, and reading scores have improved.

Another important issue is the backlash to students and adults with disabilities. ADA and IDEA have led to a profound change in the way Americans look at disability. We see disability as an issue of rights, not as a medical problem. But any time a group gains rights, there is inevitably a backlash. It is the process of taking a few steps forward and then one back. Despite the ADA, the Department of Justice had to force the Educational Testing Service to offer equal access to SATs to students with learning and other disabilities. The Department of Justice had to force a state board of examiners to give a woman with a learning disability extra time to complete the test for licensure as a clinical social worker. These accommodations should have been automatic under the ADA. When we talk about the importance of lifetime learning for people with learning disabilities, these types of actions by the Justice Department are important.

Yesterday's poster children are not asking for pity today, they are asking for rights. In South Carolina, a young woman and her family asked to be reimbursed for the cost of sending her to a private school for students with learning disabilities. Her local school did not diagnose her learning disability until she was in high school, and then it failed to provide an adequate program to compensate. She was criticized for being so bold, but last year the U.S. Supreme Court ruled in favor of her and her family. In Virginia, a private school returned all the federal funding it received during the past seventeen years rather than enroll and include a first grader with a learning disability. The school has returned thousands of dollars it used for a school lunch program and has stripped its library shelves of reference books paid for with federal dollars.

Conclusions

Part of the backlash against people with learning disabilities is tied to the belief that special education is too expensive. Part of it is tied to a belief that people with disabilities are asking for too much, that they are asking for special rights. Part of it is tied to the general lack of sympathy in the 1990s for civil rights movements. But I think there is a real danger in this new trend, in this new readiness to scapegoat children and adults with disabilities. The backlash is dangerous because it undermines choices, and these are what people with disabilities and their parents want. Choices are what they need. They need choices about education. They need educational environments where they are challenged, where children are believed to be able to learn, and where they are not doomed by the low expectations of others.

References

Americans with Disabilities Act of 1990 (ADA), PL 101-336. (July 26, 1990). Title 42, U.S.C. §§ 12101 et seq.: *U.S. Statutes at Large, 104*, 327–78.

Brown v. Board of Education, 347 US 483 (1954).

Gottlieb, J., M. Alter, B. Gottlieb, and J. Wishner. (1994). "Special Education in Urban America: It's Not Justifiable for Many." *Journal of Special Education 27*, no. 4, 453–65.

Individuals with Disabilities Education Act of 1990 (IDEA), PL 101–476. (October 30, 1990). Title 20, U.S.C. §§ 1400 et seq.: *U.S. Statutes at Large, 104*, 1103–51.

Nerney, T. (1993). *Special Education in Connecticut: A Fiscal and Policy Analysis.* Danbury, Conn.: Western Connecticut Association for Human Rights.

Shapiro, J. P., P. Loeb, D. Bowermaster, A. Wright, S. Headden, and T. Toch. (1993, December 13). "Separate and Unequal." *U.S. News and World Report*, 46–60.

63

The Deaf Community and the Culture of Deaf People

Carol Padden

The *Dictionary of American Sign Language*, published in 1965 by William Stokoe, Carl Croneberg, and Dorothy Casterline, was unique for at least two reasons. First, it offered a new description of Sign Language based on linguistic principles. Second, it devoted a section to the description of the "social" and "cultural" characteristics of Deaf people who use American Sign Language.[1]

It was indeed unique to describe Deaf people as constituting a "cultural group." Professionals in the physical sciences and education of deaf people typically describe deaf people in terms of their pathological condition: hearing loss. There are numerous studies which list statistics about the types, ranges, and etiologies of hearing loss and how these physical deficiencies may subsequently affect the behavior of deaf people. But rarely had these professionals seriously attended to other equally important aspects of Deaf people: the fact that Deaf people form groups in which the members do not experience "deficiencies" and in which the basic needs of the individual members are met, as in any other culture of human beings.

Deaf people have long recognized that their groups are different from those of hearing people; in the "Deaf world", certain behaviors are accepted while others are discouraged. The discussion of the "linguistic community" of Deaf people in the *Dictionary of ASL* represented a break from a long tradition of "pathologizing" Deaf people. In a sense, the book brought official and public recognition of a deeper aspect of Deaf people's lives: their culture.

When I re-read the book, as I do from time to time, I am always appreciative of the many insights that I find about the structure of American Sign Language and the culture of Deaf people.

The Deaf Community

We commonly hear references to the *deaf community*.[2] The term has demographic, linguistic, political and social implications. There is a national "community" of deaf people

---

1. I will use here a convention adopted by a number of researchers where the capitalized "Deaf" is used when referring to cultural aspects, as in the culture of Deaf people. The lower-case "deaf," on the other hand, refers to noncultural aspects such as the audiological condition of deafness.
2. As will be explained in a later section, the "deaf community" as described here is not a cultural entity; thus, the capitalized Deaf adjective will not be used to describe it. This differs from earlier treatments of the deaf community such as those found in Markowicz and Woodward (1975), Padden and Markowicz (1976), and Baker and Padden (1978).

who share certain characteristics and react to events around them as a group. In addition to a national community of deaf people, in almost every city or town in the U.S. there are smaller deaf communities. But what is a "deaf community?" More precisely, who are the members of a deaf community and what are the identifying characteristics of such a community?

To answer these questions, we need first to look at a definition of community. Unfortunately, there is much disagreement among anthropologists and sociologists about what constitutes a "community."

George Hillery (1974), a sociologist, evaluated ninety-four different definitions of "community" proposed by various researchers who have studied communities of people. In search of a definition, he singled out common features from the majority of the ninety-four definitions of local communities. Other sociologists such as Allan Edwards (1976) and Dennis Poplin (1972) have come to the same definition that Hillery proposes. Hillery's definition of "community" is as follows:

1. A community is a group of people who *share common goals* and cooperate in achieving these goals. Each community has its own goals. A goal may be equal employment opportunities, greater political participation, or better community services.

2. A community occupies a *particular geographic location.*The geography of a community determines the ways in which the community functions.

3. A community has some degree of *freedom to organize the social life and responsibilities of its members.* Institutions such as prisons and mental hospitals bring together groups of people in one locality, but the people have no power to make decisions about their daily lives and routines. Thus, we cannot call these types of groups "communities."

Communities may be small and closed, such as those we find in villages and tribes; but in large, industrialized societies, communities tend to be more mixed and are composed of several smaller groups of people. Consequently, while members of a community may cooperate with each other to carry out the goals of the community, there may also be conflicts and antagonism between various groups of people within the community. The conflicts are greater when any group within a community has low status or lacks power because it is a minority group. A good case is a borough of New York City that has Black, Puerto Rican, Jewish, and Protestant residents. The members of this community may unite over common concerns such as housing, but at the same time, they may conflict over other concerns that may benefit one group, but not another.

But how do we distinguish between *community* and *culture?*

A *culture* is a set of learned behaviors of a group of people who have their own language, values, rules for behavior, and traditions. A person may be born into a culture; he is brought up according to the values of the culture and his personality and behavior are shaped by his cultural values. Or, a person may grow up in one culture and later learn the language, values, and practices of a different culture and become "enculturated" into that culture.

A *community*, on the other hand, is a general social system in which a group of people live together, share common goals, and carry out certain responsibilities to each other. For example, the culture of a community of people living in a small New England town is the same as that of the larger society in which they participate. And my example of a New York borough is one where a community may be composed of a number of different cultural groups. A Puerto Rican person has the beliefs and the behaviors of his cultural group, but he lives in a larger community of people where he works and, to some degree, socializes with other people who are not Puerto Rican. Thus, a person's beliefs and actions are mainly influenced by his *culture*, but his work and many social activities are carried out within his *community*.

With this background, we cannot begin to define "deaf community." The term has been used in two restricted ways—either meaning only those persons who are audiologically deaf, or those persons who are a part of the culture of Deaf people. But it is clear that Deaf people work with and interact with other people who are not Deaf, and who share the goals of Deaf people and work with them in various social and political activities. Earlier definitions of "deaf community," such as Schein's study of the Washington, D.C. deaf community in 1968, included only those persons who are audiologically hearing impaired. I propose a definition that differs from earlier ones:

> A deaf community is a group of people who live in a particular location, share the common goals of its members, and in various ways, work toward achieving these goals. A deaf community may include persons who are not themselves Deaf, but who actively support the goals of the community and work with Deaf people to achieve them.

The definition I have proposed here fits well with the way Hillery (1974) defined "community." A community in New York City may be composed of different cultural groups; likewise, a deaf community has not only Deaf members, but also hearing and deaf people who are not culturally Deaf, and who interact on a daily basis with Deaf people and see themselves as working with Deaf people in various common concerns.

The culture of Deaf people, however, is more closed than the deaf community. Members of the Deaf culture behave as Deaf people do, use the language of Deaf people, and share the beliefs of Deaf people toward themselves and other people who are not Deaf.

I will now discuss some characteristics of the deaf community and then turn to describing certain aspects of the American Deaf culture.

Characteristics of Deaf Communities

Location

Each deaf community in the United States is uniquely affected by its location. For example, the identity of the Washington, D.C. community is undeniably influenced by the political and educational institutions in Washington, D.C. The Los Angeles deaf community is shaped by the fact that it is located in one of the largest urban areas in the United States. A great number of deaf people are employed in this area, and thus they make up a very large and powerful community.

Other deaf communities, smaller in size than the Washington, D.C., or Los Angeles communities, may be more closed, and some have less participation of non-Deaf people in their affairs.

Deaf people can move from one geographical location to another and enter into a new community with relative ease. They carry with them the knowledge of their culture to help them establish new community ties and learn the specific issues and operations of the new community. Thus, there are many different deaf communities across the United States, but there is a single American Deaf culture with members who live in different communities.

Language Use

Since a deaf community is composed of people from different cultural groups, language use within the community is different from language use within the particular cultural group. As will be discussed in more detail in a later section, the language of the *culture* of Deaf people is American Sign Language (ASL). The use of ASL by Deaf people in *community* affairs is tolerated to some degree by community members. For example, some Deaf people prefer to use ASL in public speaking situations, and sign-to-voice interpreting is provided for them. At the same time, when Deaf people are involved in community activities which include hearing people who use English, they may choose to use a variety of Sign English. Language use at the community level is rather flexible, but within the cultural group, language is more restricted.

The distinction between *community* and *culture* allows us to explain how some Deaf people may accept, respect, and in community activities, even use the language of the majority group—English—but at the same time, they can prefer the language of their cultural group. Deaf people feel a strong identification with ASL since it is a part of their cultural background, but when they are involved in community activities, the use of another language allows them to interact with other persons who are not Deaf.

Goals

A community is a group of people in a certain geographical location who share common goals. What are the goals of deaf communities?

A primary goal of the national deaf community is to achieve public acceptance of deaf people as equals—equals in employment, in political representation, and in the control of institutions that involve deaf people, such as schools and service organizations. An equally important goal is the acceptance and recognition of their history and their use of signing as a means of communication. As an example, the National Association of the Deaf prints on its envelopes the message, Hire the Deaf—They're Good Workers! The message is a public exhortation of an important goal of the community: to convince the public that deaf workers are not a liability, and should be given equal employment opportunities. Many deaf communities have been pushing for media exposure of Sign Language in television programs and newspaper articles as a means of accomplishing another important goal: public recognition and acceptance of the use of signs to communicate.

The goals of deaf communities are derived primarily from the values of Deaf and hearing people in America. The values of a cultural group are represented in those attitudes and behaviors that the group considers most respected and important. Values can be positive: they can show what a group admires and respects. But values can also be negative: members of a cultural group may reject or be suspicious of certain attitudes and behaviors which they consider to be in conflict with their beliefs.

The Culture of American Deaf People

I will turn now to a discussion of some identifying characteristics of the American Deaf culture. My descriptions here are based first on intuition—my own understanding of how I grew up as a child of Deaf parents and how I interact with other Deaf people. I also consulted a number of books and articles written by Deaf people and have found several ideas and concerns repeated throughout these writings. I have picked out some of the more frequently occurring comments Deaf people make about themselves or their lives and have placed them in a framework of culture and cultural values. Some of the books I found helpful in explaining concerns of Deaf people are: Leo Jacobs's *A Deaf Adult Speaks Out* (1969) and W. H. Woods' *The Forgotten People* (1973). The *Deaf American* magazine is another good source of information about issues that concern Deaf people.

Deaf People

What does it mean to be Deaf? Who are Deaf people?

Deaf people can be born into the culture, as in the case of children of Deaf parents. They begin learning the language of their parents from birth and thus acquire native competence in that language. They also learn the beliefs and behaviors of their parents' cultural group. When they enter schools, they serve as cultural and linguistic models for the larger number of deaf children who do not have Deaf parents and who become a part of the culture later in life.

Being Deaf usually means the person has some degree of hearing loss. However, the type of degree of hearing loss is not a criterion for being Deaf. Rather, the criterion is whether a person identifies with other Deaf people, and behaves as a Deaf person. Deaf people are often unaware of the details of their Deaf friends' hearing loss, and for example, may be surprised to learn that some of their friends can hear well enough to use the telephone.

But the most striking characteristic of the culture of Deaf people is their cultural values—these values shape how Deaf people behave and what they believe in.

Cultural Values

What are some examples of values held by Deaf people?

Language

Certainly an all-important value of the culture is respect for one of its major identifying features: American Sign Language. Not all Deaf individuals have native competence in ASL; that is, not all Deaf individuals have learned ASL from their parents as a first language. There are many individuals who become enculturated as Deaf persons and who bring with them a knowledge of some other language, usually English. While not all Deaf people are equally competent in ASL, many of them respect and accept ASL, and more now than before, Deaf people are beginning to promote its use. For Deaf people who prefer to use ASL, the language serves as a visible means of displaying one of their unique characteristics. While use of ASL sets the Deaf person apart from the majority English-speaking culture, it also belongs to Deaf people and allows them to take advantage of their capabilities as normal language-using human beings.

Because Sign Language uses the hands, there is a "sacredness" attached to how the hands can be used to communicate. Hands are used for daily manual activities, gestures, and Sign Language, but not for other forms of communication that are *not* Sign Language. Deaf people believe firmly that hand gestures must convey some kind of visual meaning and have strongly resisted what appear to be "nonsense" use of hands—one such example is "cued speech."

Deaf people frequently explain signs in terms of the "pictures" they depict. While some signs visually represent the object in some way—for example, the sign for *house* outlines the shape of a typical house—other signs have a less clear pantomimic origin. The sign for *white* supposedly refers to the white ruffles on shirts that men used to wear. Whether the sign actually had that origin is not the point, but that the signer believes strongly that there must be "reason and rhyme" behind a sign.

Speaking

There is a general disassociation from speech in the Deaf culture. Some Deaf people may choose to use speech in community activities that involve non-Deaf people, such as mixed parties, parent education programs, or while representing the community in some larger public function. But on the cultural level, speaking is not considered appropriate behavior. Children who are brought up in Deaf culture are often trained to limit their mouth movement to only those movements that are part of their language. Exaggerated speaking behavior is thought of as "undignified" and sometimes can be interpreted as making fun of other Deaf people.

Before the 1960s and the advent of "total communication" and "simultaneous communication," many Deaf people preferred to sign with the mouth completely closed. This type of signing was considered "proper" and aesthetically pleasing. Now, usually only older Deaf people continue to sign this way. Although more mouth movement is permitted now, exaggerated mouth movement while signing is still not acceptable to Deaf people.

Mouthing and the use of speech represent things to Deaf people. Since speech has traditionally been forced on Deaf people as a substitute for their language, it has come to represent confinement and denial of the most fundamental need of Deaf people: to communicate deeply and comfortably in their own language. Deaf people often distrust speech communication for this reason. In speaking, the Deaf person feels she will always be at a disadvantage and can never become fully equal to hearing people who, from the viewpoint of the Deaf person, are always the more accurate models of speaking.

Social Relations

As with any minority group, there is strong emphasis on social and family ties when family members are of the same culture or community. Carl Croneberg commented on this fact in the *Dictionary of American Sign Language*. Deaf people consider social activities an important way of maintaining contact with other Deaf people. It has frequently been observed that Deaf people often remain in groups talking late, long after the party has ended, or after the restaurant has emptied of people. One reason is certainly that Deaf people enjoy the company of other like-minded Deaf people. They feel they gain support and trusting companionship from other Deaf people who share the same cultural beliefs and attitudes.

Additionally, in some cases, access to other culture members may be limited to parties, club meetings, or other social activities. This is often the case with Deaf people who work in a place that has no other Deaf employees. Thus, because the time that Deaf people spend together in a comfortable social atmosphere may be limited, they like to take advantage of social occasions where they are likely to meet their friends.

Stories and Literature of the Culture

The cultural values described in this paper are never explicitly stated; there are no books that Deaf children read to learn these values. Deaf children learn them through the process of training in which other Deaf people either reinforce or discourage their comments and actions. And these values are found among the symbols used in the literature of the culture. The play *Sign Me Alice* by Gil Eastman (1974) is a good example, or the poetry of Dot Miles in *Gestures: Poetry in Sign Language* (1976), and many other unrecorded stories or games. Among the stories that Deaf people tell are the famous "success stories." A typical story may go like this: a deaf person grows up in an oral environment, never having met or talked with Deaf people. Later in life, the deaf person meets a Deaf person who brings him to parties, teaches him Sign Language and instructs him in the way of Deaf people's lives. This person becomes more and more involved, and leaves behind his past as he joins other Deaf people.

In much the same way that Americans support and propagate the "American Dream," these success stories reinforce the strong belief and pride Deaf people have in their way of life: that it is good and right to be Deaf.

Entering into the Culture of Deaf People

An interesting perspective on being Deaf comes from deaf people who are going through a process of becoming Deaf and are beginning to assimilate the values of Deaf people. In a study that Harry Markowicz and I (1976) did several years ago, we described the conflicts that these people experience. For many people who grow up as part of the culture of Hearing people, they think of themselves as hearing people with a hearing loss. But when they encounter the new and different culture of Deaf people, they find that not all of their beliefs and values will be accepted. They experience a conflict between what they have always believed and what they must accept when they are with other Deaf people. Their success in becoming full members of the culture of Deaf people depends on how they are able to resolve the conflicts they experience.

An example of a conflict, a deaf person may value her speaking ability and may have always spoken when communicating with other people. But now she learns that speaking does not have the same positive value with Deaf people that it has with hearing people. Even though some Deaf people can hear some speech, and some speak well themselves, speaking is not considered usual or acceptable behavior within the cultural group. The deaf person finds that she must change the behavior that she has always considered normal, acceptable, and positive.

Another example of conflict between old and new behavior concerns how the eyes are used. In the American hearing culture, people are taught that staring is inappropriate, and many deaf people have learned to watch hearing people's faces for short periods of time, then look away quickly in order to avoid being thought as "stupid" or "making improper advances." But in ASL conversations, the listener is expected to watch the face of the signer throughout the conversation. Breaking eye contact between signer and "listener" too soon may be interpreted by Deaf people as "rude," "disinterested," or "trying to act hearing." There is a full range of rules about how to use the eyes in ASL conversations: Charlotte Baker discusses this in more detail in her 1977 article.

In learning the language of Deaf people, the deaf person needs to overcome her own cultural training in how the face is used. Facial expression among hearing people is typically quite restrained when compared with Deaf signers. However, movements of the eyes, face and head are an important part of ASL—they are used as a part of its grammar, and used to convey information necessary to control conversations between signers as well as to convey information about the emotion of the signer. Thus, the deaf person may experience a conflict between her upbringing, in which she is taught to limit the movements of her body and face, and her attempt to learn a new language in which she must "exaggerate" these behaviors.

Possibly the very first indication that another person is not a member of Deaf culture occurs during the ritual of introduction and exchanging names. Hearing people often introduce themselves by their first name only, and deaf people may do the same. However, Deaf people normally introduce themselves by their full names, and it is not unusual to also add which city or state they are from. This information is important to Deaf people because the cultural group is small, and maintaining ties with all members is a means of preserving group cohesiveness. In the same way that children long ago received names such as "John's son" or "Johnson," giving last names allows Deaf people to check the family background of the person being introduced and have additional information about that person. And when the deaf person is asked where he is "from," he may mistakenly give the city or state where he is currently living: a Deaf person would state where she went to school, or spent most of her childhood. It is important to Deaf people to ask for and give each other information about where they were raised and which schools—usually residential schools—they attended. This information allows Deaf people to identify themselves to other Deaf people in their cultural group.

Finally, an important behavior to learn is what to call yourself. In hearing culture, it is desirable to distinguish between degrees of hearing loss. "Hard-of-hearing" is more valued and indicates that the person is closer to being hearing and is more capable of interacting on an equal basis with other hearing people. However, "deaf" is viewed more negatively and usually carries the implication that the person is difficult to communicate with, or may not speak at all. Thus, a deaf person is more likely to be avoided if he calls himself "deaf." But, among Deaf people, the distinctions between hearing loss are not considered important for group relations. "Deaf" is not a label of deafness as much as a label of identity with other Deaf people. A person learning to interact with other Deaf people will quickly learn that there is one name for all members of the cultural group, regardless of the degree of hearing loss: Deaf. In fact, the sign DEAF can be used in an ASL sentence to mean "my friends," which conveys the cultural meaning of "Deaf." Although Deaf people recognize and accept members that are audiologically hard-of-hearing, calling oneself "hard-of-hearing" rather than by the group name is interpreted by some Deaf people as "putting on airs," because it appears to draw undue attention to hearing loss.

The existence of conflict brings out those aspects of the culture of Deaf people that are unique and separate from other cultural groups. It also shows that the group of Deaf people is not merely a group of like-minded people, as with a bridge club, but a group of people who share a code of behaviors and values that are learned and passed on from one generation of Deaf people to the next. Entering into Deaf culture and becoming Deaf means learning all the appropriate ways to behave like a Deaf person.

Hearing Children of Deaf Parents

As mentioned earlier, being Deaf usually means the person has a hearing loss. But there are hearing children of Deaf parents who have grown up with their parents' culture and feel a strong personal affiliation with other Deaf people. They are like other Deaf people in that they actively participate in various cultural affairs and consider themselves a part of the cultural group. However, the fact that they have an "extra sense," like the "sighted man in a country of the blind," is often a source of conflict for these hearing children of Deaf parents.

They may find themselves cast in the demanding role of being "links" between their families and the majority culture. At a very young age, they may learn to interpret for their families and make contact with other hearing people on behalf of the family. Even after they have left the family, they may still maintain the role of a "go-between," perhaps as professional interpreters, or as part of a Deaf organization that makes contact with hearing people.

Hearing children of Deaf parents are usually given greater access to the culture of Deaf people than other hearing children who do not have Deaf parents. Since they often have been brought up to share the cherished values of Deaf people, Deaf people perceive them as less likely to threaten or try to change the structure of the cultural group, and thus, will allow them to interact more fully with Deaf people. An equally important factor in their being able to become members of the cultural group is their knowledge of the group's language. Hearing children of Deaf parents may acquire native competence in ASL to the point where Deaf people will say, "he signs like Deaf people."

Some hearing children of Deaf parents are acutely aware that the behaviors they must use when they interact with a group of Deaf people are different from the behaviors they must use with a group of hearing people. When they are with Deaf people, they find that they must change many aspects of their behavior; the language they use, the kind of jokes they tell, or how they use their eyes. On the other hand, there are other hearing children of Deaf parents who do not seem to be as aware of conflicts between hearing and Deaf cultures. These children say that when interacting with Deaf people, they behave a certain way, but when with hearing people, they find that they switch behaviors unconsciously.

We need to study more deeply and carefully the experiences of hearing children of Deaf parents. Their varied experiences raise many questions about the characteristics of the culture of Deaf people. For one thing, their experiences will help us understand the role hearing loss plays in shaping the culture of Deaf people.

Summary

The term *deaf community* is used in many different ways. The fact that the word *community* has had different definitions has probably contributed to the variety of definitions that have been used for *deaf community*. I follow the definition of *community* proposed by Hillery (1974), and the term *deaf community* is used here in a more general sense than has been used before: to describe the group of people who interact and contribute to the goals of the community. These people can be members of different cultural groups, and are joined together to the extent that they share in the goals of the community as a whole.

While there is general consensus on the goals of the community, there may also be conflicts over various issues that arise in the community, resulting from the different values of each cultural group.

The culture of Deaf people has not yet been studied in much depth. One reason is that, until recently, it was rare to describe Deaf people as having a *culture*, although it has often been remarked that deaf people tend to seek out other deaf people for companionship. Descriptions of Deaf people have often focused on details of their deficiency, and not on the normal aspects of their lives: that they, like other human beings, are members of communities and cultural groups.

Values of Deaf people reflect the beliefs and ways in which Deaf people react to their social environment. These values are often different from those of the majority culture and need to be learned by incoming deaf people; this is reflected in the problems experienced by deaf people who first grow up as hearing people.

William Stokoe's perspective (1971) on the language and culture of Deaf people shows his attempt to describe Deaf people not as abnormal, pathological cases, but as individuals who have a cultural and linguistic identity. His work hopefully has begun an age in which facts about Deaf people are not hidden or ignored, but are brought out to help us reach a new stage of awareness and acceptance of Deaf people. It is only then that Deaf people can achieve the kind of equality they have long sought.

References

Baker, Charlotte (1977). "Regulators and Turn-taking in ASL Discourse." In L. Friedman, ed. *On the Other Hand: New Perspectives on American Sign Language.* New York: Academic Press.

Baker, Charlotte, and Carol Padden (1978). *ASL: A Look at Its History, Structure, and Community.* Silver Spring, Md.: TJ Publishers, Inc.

Eastman, Gilbert (1974). *Sign Me Alice: A Play in Sign Language.* Washington, D.C.: Gallaudet College.

Edwards, Allan, and D. Jones (1976). *Community and Community Development.* The Hague, Netherlands: Mouton and Co.

Hillery, George (1974). *Communal Organizations.* Chicago: University of Chicago Press

Jacobs, Leo (1969). *A Deaf Adult Speaks Out.* Washington, D.C.: Gallaudet College.

Markowicz, Harry, and James Woodward (1975, March 13–15). *Language and the Maintenance of Ethnic Boundaries in the Deaf Community.* Paper presented at the Conference on Culture and Communication held at Temple University.

Miles, Dot (1976). *Gestures: Poetry in Sign Language.* Northridge, Calif.: Joyce Publishers, Inc.

Padden, Carol, and Harry Markowicz (1976). "Cultural Conflicts between Hearing and Deaf Communities." In *Proceedings of the Seventh World Congress of the World Federation of the Deaf.* Silver Spring, Md.: National Association of the Deaf.

Poplin, Dennis (1972). *Communities: A Survey of Theories and Methods of Research.* New York: Macmillan.

Schein, Jerome. (1968). *The Deaf Community.* Washington, D.C.: Gallaudet College.

Stokoe, William C., Jr. (1971). *The Study of Sign Language.* Silver Spring, Md.: National Association of the Deaf.

Stokoe, William C., Jr., C. Croneberg, and D. Casterline. (1965). *Dictionary of American Sign Language.* Washington, D.C.: Gallaudet College Press; (1976, second edition, Silver Spring, Md.: Linstok Press).

Woods, W. H. (1973). *The Forgotten People.* St. Petersburg, Fla.: Dixie Press.

64

The Hidden Dimension of Learning: Time and Space

Sally L. Smith

Maria is a gifted graduate student studying toward a degree in social work. Her insight and her mastery of complex issues are superior. However, she is unable to complete papers for her coursework on time. Her professors claim that she is lazy, undisciplined, and even manipulative. When her cognitive abilities were tested, Maria's scores were in the gifted range. But her scores on The Test of Written Language place her planning, organizing, and sequencing abilities on a low seventh grade level.

Donald, a high school student, is late to all his classes. He has trouble going to bed on time at night and waking up in the morning, even with two alarm clocks. Donald has difficulty pacing himself and keeping track of time. His teachers think he is behaving this way on purpose to flout authority.

Annie's junior high school teachers call her "careless" and "scatterbrained" because she is always losing her homework, misplacing her backpack, and forgetting her gym clothes. They say she "needs to have her head reattached to her body" in order to get herself organized. They are very impatient with her and are now using a "demerit system" in an effort to impose order on her.

Max, a third grader, has been described as having a "faulty radar" because he always seems to end up in the wrong place at the wrong time, making his life and the lives of those around him very difficult. Max doesn't mean to, but he bumps into everyone, knocks things over, spills his milk and juice, and can't keep track of when it is his turn in games.

The problem that these individuals share is something that:

■ parents confront every morning when they try to help a child with learning disabilities get dressed and out the door for school;

■ teachers face when their students with learning disabilities cannot find their way to their next classroom, even after a month of school;

- employers encounter when their intelligent employees with learning disabilities arrive late to work, and take too long to complete required tasks or eat lunch;

- friends deal with when their friends with learning disabilities don't show up as promised and forget to call.

Individuals who struggle with issues of time and space often complain that their inner clocks are not working, their timing is off, they can't seem to pace themselves or self regulate during even familiar tasks, and they are "hopelessly lost" when tasks demand careful timing or call for a sense of space.

Most individuals acquire concepts of time and space naturally as they mature. But for those with learning disabilities, these skills don't always develop automatically and so they have to be learned. Learning disabilities can result in disorganization which can be life-long and pervasive, starting in the preschool years and, often, continuing on through adulthood. By four years of age, most children have a good understanding of spatial words and know the meaning of terms such as "beneath" and "above, " "near" and "far," "under" and "over," and "above" and "below." Confusing these terms can impede learning in such areas as reading, writing, math, geography, and even history. *use a doll house*

Two organizing systems of our society are space and time. Many people with learning disabilities have difficulties with spatial organization. They have trouble distinguishing left from right. They have a poor sense of direction, misread maps, and have trouble following printed directions. They tend to get lost even in their own neighborhoods. These individuals lack the "internal maps" that most of us use to guide how we move our bodies through space and how we travel from one place to another. "When I get lost, which is frequently, I use my portable car phone," says a doctor who has both learning disabilities and Attention Deficit/Hyperactivity Disorder (ADHD). "I always try to park in the same parking lot and use the same two rows; otherwise I never can find my car when I come back. And I'm apt to lose my parking lot ticket, too! " Feelings of helplessness and frustration frequently overtake persons with learning disabilities who stand at crossroads, bewildered about which road might lead to a chosen destination.

The person with learning disabilities who gets lost in time has life disrupted even more severely than does a person who gets lost in space. Time regulates our waking hours with tyrannical force. The alarm clock wakes us at a precise time, so that we can get to work on time. We schedule meetings and appointments throughout the day and calculate how long they will last so that we can make it to them all and still find time for lunch. We must leave work at a given time to catch a ride home, or pick up the kids, or run evening errands.

Problems for Families

The child with learning disabilities who experiences problems with space often:

- has trouble finding belongings (school books, homework, keys, toys);

- is prone to getting lost in public places (supermarkets, department stores, libraries);

- has difficulty knowing how to adjust their behavior in ways that demonstrate an appreciation of others' personal space.

This child will frequently have a room which everyone calls "the pit," with stuff piled on top of other things and little sense of organization. However, the child will claim, "I know where everything is."

The child with learning disabilities who experiences problems with time often:

- can't seem to regulate his or her daily schedule;
- is late getting to and from places;
- has difficulty with the verbal timing of remarks that is important for effective communication and is essential to others' appreciation of a sense of humor;
- has trouble picking up the rhythm of conversations.

Problems in School

Two areas where teachers must provide structure in order for children to succeed in the classroom are space (a place for all things) and time (a time for each activity). Establishing order in these two areas will create the setting for productive learning to occur.

Creating Order in Space

Organizing desk space is often a problem for those with learning disabilities—where to put the work, where to work on it, and where to put it upon completion. They need help with:

- organizing a notebook;
- organizing a backpack;
- organizing space on paper;
- following directions about spatial organization.

Creating Structure in Time

Students may have difficulty:

- with the organization of the school day;
- with rhyming, syllabification, and breaking down sounds in words;
- handing in work on time or completing assignments in an allotted timeframe;
- planning free time;
- with timed tests;
- with long-term assignments (research or book reports; science projects).

Poor time management can cause great difficulties in the school, work, home, and social environments. One young man, Andrew, said, "You know my reading and spelling didn't cause me half the trouble my stupid left-right mix up and my getting lost and being late did. It was the night before the due date on the exam when I got to work. I never thought about time. I lost a lot of jobs because I was late and I couldn't figure out how long it would take me to do various jobs." Disorganization in time and space causes problems for friends, roommates, or life-partners (meeting people in the right place at the right time, paying bills on time, keeping an orderly home).

Disorganization in Time and Space Can Make a Person Feel Rotten!

Lacking an accurate internal sense of time and space, a person with learning disabilities may race through the day, feeling out of control and rebounding from one activity to the next. It's as if time and space *happen* to this person! These individuals find themselves missing appointments, quitting classes and jobs, changing rooming arrangements, and being lost. Having an internal clock that isn't working right can make one feel like he or she is on the fringes of society. "I always feel out of it," says Clara, "because I come after they have started class, I don't catch up to them even when they leave, and what I am left with is a dismal sense of failure."

Working Toward Solutions

We have to present children with activities that help with categorization and classification (sorting objects and pictures, then symbols) in ways that correspond with their chronological ages, developing abilities, personal interests and increasing maturity. By working on their skills in grouping things together, and by expanding their understanding of relationships between items, we help them build strong mental "filing systems," so that well-organized information can be retrieved easily.

Kinesthetic Learning

Children with learning disabilities tend to learn best by doing, touching, seeing, hearing, feeling; in other words, they need to learn through experience. An often overlooked means of helping children to grow in these areas is through movement and activities that involve perceptual motor skills. Learning to use their bodies in a more organized way will help them to use their minds in a more organized manner. For example:

- music helps build rhythm and timing. A drum-beat can help reinforce syllabication in reading;

- floor maps walked on or hopped over can help teach geography;

- time lines that can be walked on can help children gain a better understanding of history by placing events in an understandable time-frame;

- elastic or rope can help children understand angles and geometric forms.

People with learning disabilities and ADHD who have difficulties with their sense of time and space can be helped to overcome their difficulties and to lead productive and fulfilling lives.

65

Understanding Disability Issues

Association on Higher Education and Disability

When people with disabilities are asked, "How do you want to be treated?" their typical response is, "Just like everybody else!" People with disabilities are human beings with feelings, hopes, dreams, and goals, "just like everybody else!" The approximately fifty million people who make up "the disabled" population in this country are as diverse and unique as any other minority group. Many of the non-disabled population continue to be uncomfortable, fearful, and confused about how to speak, treat, and interact with people who have disabilities. . . .

Individuals with disabilities progress through developmental stages similar to those who are not disabled. Individuals with disabilities, for the most part, progress through three stages: dependence, independence, and interdependence. A description of each stage follows.

- **Dependence.** The individual has just become disabled, or aware of the disability, is unaware of abilities, relies on others to make choices/decisions regarding all aspects of his or her life.

- **Independence.** The individual has accepted the disability, is aware of abilities, and has control over the disability-related aspects of his or her life. An individual in this stage may be resistant to any type of help perceived as making him or her dependent again. Breaking out of this part of the independent stage brings the person to the stage of interdependence.

- **Interdependence.** The individual accepts the fact that these may be limitations that are posed by the disability. He or she accepts these limitations and is willing to accept assistance in overcoming these situational limitations (for example, the use of a note taker by someone who has a manual dexterity limitation).

Personal Voices

66

Wheel Power

Elizabeth Atkins Bowman
with Michelle Burford

Eight years ago, this sister prayed for a little change in her life. What did she get? A whole new life.

It's a March morning in 1990, and Shelia Starks—late for her secretarial job—rushes to the front door of her Detroit apartment. Since winter, Starks has been begging God to send her a change: She'll be thirty-one in three weeks and wants a better job, a new start—a different life. On this Friday just after eight, that different life awaits outside her door:

Starks pushes the door, but it slams at her chest. She sees the arm of her ex-lover—the man she dumped two months ago because he wouldn't stop beating her. He barrels in.

"What's wrong? What are you doing here?" she says.

Starks runs for her bedroom, screaming "Get out!" as she leaps for the phone. He rips the cord from the wall. "Please leave!" she pleads, but he is zombielike. His eyes are glazed as if he's on crack.

He rips away her skirt and slams her to the bed. *He just wants sex—be calm. Let him have it, then run.* But when he can't get an erection, he stomps to the bathroom. Starks bolts for the door, but her ex-boyfriend hears her. His right hand clutches a gun.

"Help me!" she sobs. Then a gunshot. The bullet hits her spine. Silence.

He aims at her head. *Please, God, let him think I'm dead.* Another shot, this time grazing the base of her head. Then a third bullet—to his own head. Her ex-lover's body crumples over her thighs, blood gushing from his temples. It's 8:35 a.m.

Now, eight years later, from a wheelchair in her Detroit kitchen, Starks explains that the bullet to her spine left her a quadriplegic, paralyzed from the neck down. In plain talk, that means she can't use the restroom or comb her hair without help. She may regain feeling in parts of her body, but doctors say she'll never walk again.

Yet if you spent an hour with Starks, you'd feel anything but pity for her. She'd tell you the shooting was a wake-up call that led to her life's meaning: she'd explain that her dead boyfriend had abused her because she let him. Then she'd send you off with some sister-to-sister advice: "You always got to love yourself, girl." And she should know: Before the shooting, self-love is exactly what had eluded her:

Whose Face Is That?

"I don't like it, but I can't change that I'm in a chair," Starks tells ten men and women, some in wheelchairs, some with such diseases, as cerebral palsy. They're in a church rec room where Starks leads classes for the Great Lakes Center for Independent Living, a counseling agency that helps disabled people regroup. Slogans such as *"Can't! That's a bad word!"* and "Refuse to criticize yourself!" fill her talk.

"We have to learn to love ourselves and be content in our situations," she tells the group, which she calls her family. "Then you can do anything you set your mind to. For real."

Everyone sits captivated by Starks's speech. Her smile reaches across the table and gives each person a hug, and her red jogging suit adds to her glow.

"After my injury, I didn't look at myself for a long time," she says. Before shooting her, her ex-lover bit her cheek and left a gash; a black ring beneath her eye shows where he punched her: "I did not want to see my face."

Or face her future. After the shooting, Starks sank into depression about her wheelchair-bound life. Every week she replayed that Friday morning in her mind. She imagined all the ways it could have ended differently. And she wished she had left her ex-boyfriend the first time he backhanded her.

"The signs that he would one day attack me were everywhere, but I ignored them," she says. "I didn't love myself enough to end it. I accepted his 'I'm sorry's,' his tears, his candy, and I went back into the lion's den every time."

Starks's road back began two months after the shooting, with four-hour sessions of weight lifting and typing exercises. Many days she lay in bed and wept, longing to quit. But the work paid off: She eventually regained some use of her arms and a few fingers.

Emotional healing was harder to come by. First, she returned to Tabernacle Missionary;

the Baptist church of her youth, surrounding herself with supportive people and establishing a daily dialogue with God. Then she went to Detroit's Great Lakes Center for Independent Living. There, Starks learned to drive a specially equipped van—and to love herself again.

A counselor at the center told her to stare at her reflection every day and recite self-affirmations like "I am special. There's no one in the world like me." At first she didn't believe the positive words, but repeating the phrases proved magical for her self-esteem: "Finally I could look at myself and say 'You look marvelous. Shelia! I love you!'"

And that's the self-respect Starks wants to nurture in other physically challenged people, which she does by teaching classes twice a week at the center. Her mantra: Be as happy as you can in your circumstances. This message helped save fifty-two-year-old Don Williams, a nursing-home patient whose three strokes had left him immobile and despairing.

"I'll never forget meeting Shelia," Williams recalls of last year. "First you see her eyes. They're like headlights glowing from her face. Then she rolls into the room and yells. 'Good morning, family!' That's when I knew there was life again. Shelia's example got me going."

And going. Today Williams is driving, studying social work, walking with a cane and working as a counselor for the center.

And Baby Makes Two

Starks's newest challenge has nothing to do with a wheelchair. Meet Staci, her three-year-old daughter.

Starks says being pregnant with Staci proves that yes, people in wheelchairs have sex, though for her the sensation is not as intense as it once was. She had a normal pregnancy and delivery and didn't need painkillers because she felt few labor pains.

After Staci's birth, Starks's mother, Peggy, moved in to help Starks care for the baby. And while the baby's father, an able-bodied man with whom Shelia had had a relationship for four years, is no longer romantically involved with Shelia, he is active in Staci's life, spending time with her and providing child support. She says, "I have a child to raise, so I have to go on."

And on she fights, refusing to lie down, collect disability and wither away: Starks's mom says her daughter is so active that she can hardly keep up. In 1992 Starks competed in the Miss Wheelchair contest and rolled away with the Miss Michigan title. She's taking classes at Wayne State University to become a rehab counselor, and she appears in a United Way video to help the nonprofit agency raise money for the disadvantaged.

"Regardless of the weather, honey, she's gone," says Peggy Starks, 68. "She doesn't have any time to be depressed."

Talk with Starks about her injury, and the conversation returns to where it started: abusive men and self-loathing.

"So many women aren't alive to tell their stories," says Starks. "That's why I tell women 'If he calls you a bitch once, he'll do it again. You have to respect yourself and leave. Don't let him treat you like dog meat, my sister. You're worth more.'"

Besides speaking to domestic-violence victims, she tries to keep teens away from guns. She cofounded Pioneers for Peace, an antiviolence program for youths.

"My shooting happened so that I can spend my life as an advocate," Starks says. "If I can keep tragedy from happening, I'll do that with everything in me. That's why I'm here."

67

Recovering Our Sense of Value after Being Labeled Mentally Ill

Patricia E. Deegan

In the final decade of this millennium, after centuries of being so fundamentally and brutally devalued by our culture, there is a glimmer of hope that people who have been labeled with mental illness can reclaim their dignity, can be viewed by others as being people of worth, and can begin to achieve valued roles. There is no doubt that the landmark piece of civil rights legislation, the Americans with Disabilities Act, will help to remove many of the barriers that have historically prevented those of us with psychiatric disabilities from achieving valued roles in this society. We are all charged with the valued role of carrying a new message of hope, of healing, and of recovery back into the communities where we live, love, work, and worship.

A Retrospect

As I was preparing this article, I found myself wondering how those of us who have experienced being profoundly devalued as a result of being labeled with a mental illness move from thinking we have little or no value, to discovering our own unique value. How do we reclaim and recover our sense of worth and value when we have been devalued and dehumanized? In the course of my reflections I found myself thinking back to the days when I was an adolescent and was first diagnosed with major mental illness. I was thinking about my first two hospitalizations and how I was labeled with schizophrenia and three months later, at my second hospital admission, I was labeled with chronic schizophrenia.

I was told I had a disease that was like diabetes, and if I continued to take neuroleptic medications for the rest of my life and avoided stress, I might be able to cope. I remember that as these words were spoken to me by my psychiatrist it felt as if my whole teenage world—in which I aspired to dreams of being a valued person in valued roles, of playing lacrosse for the U.S. Women's Team or maybe joining the Peace Corps—began to crumble and shatter. It felt as if these parts of my identity were being stripped from me. I was beginning to undergo that radically dehumanizing and devaluing transformation from being a person to being an illness; from being Pat Deegan to being "a schizophrenic."

As I look back on those days I am struck by how all alone I was. This profound sense of being all alone only served to compound my sense of feeling worthless and of having no value. Granted, people gave me medications, people monitored my blood pressure, people did art therapy, psychotherapy, occupational therapy, and recreational therapy with me. But in a very fundamental way I experienced myself as being all alone, adrift on a nameless sea without compass or bearing. And that deep sense of loneliness came from the fact that although many people were talking to me about my symptoms, no one was talking to me about how I was doing. No one came to me and said, "Hey, I know you're going through hell right now. I know you feel totally lost in some nightmare. I know you can't see a way out right now. But I've been where you are today. I got labeled with schizophrenia and a whole bunch of other things too. And I'm here to tell you that there is a way out and that your life doesn't have to be about being in mental institutions. I'm around if you want to talk."

No one ever came to me and said those words. All I knew were the stereotypes I had seen on television or in the movies. To me, mental illness meant Dr. Jekyll and Mr. Hyde, psychopathic serial killers, loony bins, morons, schizos, fruitcakes, nuts, straight jackets, and raving lunatics. They were all I knew about mental illness, and what terrified me was that professionals were saying I was one of them. It would have greatly helped to have had someone come and talk to me about surviving mental illness—as well as the possibility of recovering, of healing, and of building a new life for myself. It would have been good to have role models. Someone I could look up to who had experienced what I was going through—people who had found a good job, or who were in love, or who had an apartment or a house on their own, or who were making a valuable contribution to society. But as I said, this did not happen for me in those early years.

So today I want to take the opportunity to say the things that no one ever said to me back then. I want to talk with the seventeen-year-old girl that I once was. I want to talk to her about what I know now but didn't know then. I want to talk to her and in so doing peak to all of us who have been labeled with mental illness, who have suffered deeply, who have known despair, who have been told that we have no value and who have felt alone, abandoned, and adrift on a dead and silent sea.

A Bleak, Monotonous Existence

I turn my gaze back over the twenty-one-year span of time that separates me from that seventeen year old girl. I am trying to see her; it's difficult to look at her. I can see the yellow, nicotine-stained fingers. I can see her shuffled, stiff, drugged walk. Her eyes do not glance. The dancer has collapsed and her eyes are dark and they stare endlessly into nowhere. It is the time between the first and second hospitalization and she is back living at her parents' home. She forces herself out of bed at eight o'clock in the morning. In a drugged daze she sits in a chair, the same chair every day. She is smoking cigarettes. Cigarette after cigarette. Cigarettes mark the passing of time. Cigarettes are proof that time is passing and that fact, at least, is a relief. From nine A.M. to noon she sits and smokes and stares. Then she has lunch. At one P.M. she goes back to bed to sleep until three P.M.. At that time she returns to the chair and sits and smokes and stares. Then she has dinner. She returns to the chair at six P.M.. Finally, it is eight o'clock in the evening, the long-awaited hour, the time to go back to bed and to collapse into a drugged and dreamless sleep.

This same scenario unfolds the next day, and then the next, and then the next, until the months pass by in numbing succession, marked only by the next cigarette and then the next. . . .

And as I watch her, I know it is not so much mental illness that I am observing. I am witnessing the flame of a human spirit faltering. She is losing the will to live. She is not suicidal but she wants to die because nothing seems worth living for. Her hopes, her dreams, and her aspirations have been shattered. She sees no way to achieve the valued roles she had once dreamed of. Her future has been reduced to the prognosis of doom she had been given. Her past is slipping away like a dream that belonged to someone else.

Her present is empty but for the pungent cigarette smoke that fills the void like a veiled specter. No, this is not mental illness I am seeing. I am seeing a young woman whose hope for living a full and valuable life has been shattered. She feels herself to be among the living dead and her spirit is wavering under the weight of it all.

What I Wish I Could Tell Her

I walk into the room and sit near her. I want to talk to her. Just the thought of it makes me want to start to cry. What should I say to her? I lean towards her as she sits smoking in her chair.

"Patricia . . . I'm worried about you. I can see that you are suffering deeply. Your suffering is not invisible to me. I know that the professionals have been very busy observing you treating your symptoms and trying to rehabilitate you; but no one has addressed the way you are suffering. The fact that you have felt so alone in your suffering doesn't mean there's something bad or shameful about you. Try to understand that most professionals—in fact most people—are afraid to sit quietly and to be with a person who is suffering. It's the same sort of thing that happens at a funeral—when people line up to console the person who is bereaved they get all anxious and awkward and don't know what to say.

"People find it frightening to just spend time with people who are in great pain. You see a person who is in great anguish is crying out. Even if they are totally silent like you are, way down deep I can hear you crying out. Thus, to be with a person who is anguished is to risk experiencing the cry that is way down deep inside each of us. That is why the professionals have been so busy doing things to you, rather than being with you. Granted, it's their job, but it's also true that staying busy by doing things to you helps keep their anxiety under control, which in turn helps to distance them from the cry that your suffering might evoke in them.

"I also hear anger in your suffering. You are angry because you have been diagnosed with a major mental illness. You feel angry because all your friends are doing normal stuff like going to school, going on dates, and dreaming their dreams. You feel 'Why me. Why has this happened to me?' I don't know the answer to that question. I don't know why you were dealt this hand of cards. But what I do know is this: You may have been diagnosed with a mental illness but you are not an illness. You are a human being whose life is precious and is of infinite value.

"You are at a critical juncture, a very important time. The professionals are telling you that you are a schizophrenic. Your family and friends are beginning to refer to you as 'a schizophrenic.' It is as if the whole world has put on a pair of warped glasses that blind them to the person you are and leaves them seeing you as an illness. . . .

"Almost everything you do gets understood in reference to your illness.

"You used to feel sad sometimes but now you are said to be depressed. You used to disagree sometimes but now you are told you lack insight. You used to act independently but now you are told that your independence means you are uncooperative, noncompliant, and treatment resistant. . . .

"But now that you have been labeled with a mental illness the dignity of risk and the right to failure have been taken from you. No wonder you get angry.

"But this is a critical time for you because there is the great danger that you might succumb to the messages you are being given. You might slowly find yourself putting on those same warped glasses and viewing yourself as others are seeing you. The great danger is that you might undergo that radically devaluing and dehumanizing transformation from being a person to being an illness; from being Patricia to being 'a schizophrenic' (or 'a bipolar' or 'a multiple'). . . .

"Once you and the illness become one then there is no one left inside of you to take on the work of recovering of healing of rebuilding the life you want to live. Once you come to believe that you are a mental illness you give away all your power—and others take responsibility for you and for your life.

"That is why I say that this is a critical and dangerous time. It is important that you resist the efforts however unintentional they might, be to transform you into an illness. In this regard let your anger, especially your angry indignation be your guide.

"Your anger is not a symptom of mental illness. Your angry indignation is a sane response to the situation that you are facing. You are resisting the messages you are being given. In and through your fiery indignation your dignity is saying, 'No, I am not an illness. I am first and foremost a human being. I will not be reduced to being an illness or a thing. I will keep my power and save a part of myself that will, in time, be able to take a stand toward my distress and begin the process of recovery and healing. . . .

"One of the biggest lessons I have had to accept is that recovery is not the same thing as being cured. After twenty-one years of living with this thing it still hasn't gone away. So I figure I'm never going to be cured but I can be in recovery. Recovery is a process, not an end point or a destination. . . .

"To me recovery means I try to stay in the driver's seat of my life. I don't let my illness run me. Over the years I have worked hard to become an expert in my own self-care. For me, being in recovery means I don't just take medications. Just taking medications is a passive stance. Rather I use medications as part of my recovery process. In the same way I don't just go to the hospital. Just 'going to the hospital' is a passive stance. Rather, I use the hospital when I need to. Over the years I have learned different ways of helping myself. Sometimes I use medications, therapy, self-help and mutual support groups, friends, my relationship with God, work, exercise, spending time in nature—all these measures help me remain whole and healthy, even though I have a disability. . . .

"I have found that although my symptoms may seem the same or even worse, relapsing while in recovery is not the same thing as 'having a breakdown.' When I relapse in recovery, I'm not breaking down; rather I am breaking out or breaking through. It may mean I am breaking out of some prison or fear-filled place where I have been trapped inside of myself. It may mean I am breaking through to new ways of trusting people and myself. So you see, when I have a relapse within the context of my recovery, I try not to see it as a failure. It means I am growing, breaking out of old fears and breaking through into new worlds—like learning to make friends and keep them, to trust people, and to love people. . . .

"It is important to understand that we are faced with recovering not just from mental illness, but also from the effects of being labeled mentally ill. I believe many of us emerge from mental institutions with full-blown post-traumatic stress disorders that are a direct result of the trauma and abuse we may have experienced or witnessed in mental institutions or in community based programs. We are also faced with recovering from the process of internalizing the stigma we are surrounded with; as well as the effects of discrimination, poverty, and second-class citizenship. Indeed, there's no doubt that the label of mental illness comes as a 'package plan' that too often includes poverty, trauma, dehumanization, degradation, being disenfranchised, and being unemployed. Many of us find that the recovery process goes hand in hand with the empowerment process. We find that recovery means becoming politicized and aware of the social, economic, and human injustices we have had to endure. We find that empowerment and recovery means finding our collective voice, our collective pride, and our collective power, and challenging and changing the injustices we face.

"Finally, Patricia, I want to mention one other thing that can happen and that you must guard against during these early years of being in the mental health system. You might hear professionals referring to you or other people as being 'high functioning' or

The LIE

'low functioning.' Whether you get labeled high functioning or low functioning, don't fall into the trap of believing it. These are not attributes that exist inside a person. They are value judgments that are put on a person. All these words really mean is that there are those people whose actions or talents or gifts we value and there are those people in which we find no value. There are no high-functioning or low-functioning people. There are people whose contribution we are able to see and value and there are those whose gifts we have failed to see and have failed to value. When you hear a mental health worker say that someone is low functioning, say to yourself, 'That person is not low functioning. It's just that the mental health worker has failed to see and value the gifts and special talents of that person.'

"The real challenge in all this is to somehow learn to value yourself. That can seem like such an impossible task because you get bombarded with messages and images that are so negative and degrading. How is it, when we are surrounded by such messages of despair, that we can begin to value ourselves? That's a difficult question to answer. I am twenty-one years older and I am still working on really valuing myself—but somehow when I look back at you, Patricia, as I watch you smoking and staring, when I see the way you are suffering and are all alone, somehow, despite all they have said about you, I see you and a tenderness fills my heart. You are precious and good. You are not trash to be discarded or a broken object that must be fixed. You are not insane. You do not belong in institutions for the rest of your life. You don't belong on the streets. And even though they tie us down in four-point restraints and though they lock us up against our will like animals, you are not an animal. You are a human being. You carry within you a precious flame, a spark of the divine.

"Patricia, if I could reach back through the years I would hold you. I would say you are beautiful. I would say don't listen to the prognosis of doom. You are more than all their words. There is a place for you. There is a reason. This is not suffering for the sake of just more pain. A new life can be born of this labor. A water that is life giving can be found in this desert. Don't give up. Although there is no magic answer, no magic drug, and no magic cure, I would hold you now. I would tell you I love you. I would want to protect you. I would want to rescue you, but I know that I couldn't. It's not about being rescued. It's about taking up your journey of recovery, finding good people who will accompany you on that journey and then following your journey to wherever it leads you.

"They may tell you that your goal should be to become normal and to achieve valued roles. But a role is empty and valueless unless you fill it with your meaning and your purpose. Don't become normal. Our task is not to become normal. You have the wondrously terrifying task of becoming who you are called to be. And you are not called to be an inhuman thing. You are not called to be a mental illness. You were born into this world for a reason and only you can discover what that reason is. You were born into this world to grow and it is possible to grow into a whole, healthy person who also has a psychiatric disability. Your life and your dreams may have been shattered—but from such ruins you can build a new life full of value and purpose.

"The task is not to become normal. The task is to take up your journey of recovery and to become who you are called to be. You were born to love and to be loved. That's your birthright. Mental illness cannot take that from you. Nobody can take that from you. Patricia, become who you are called to be. Do what you do with love. Loving and being loved is what matters. That is the value."

68

Equal Opportunities— Yes, Please

Sally French

In 1967, I enrolled in my local further education college for a one-year GCE O level course. The college had never taken a visually impaired student before but after much deliberation and anxious discussion they decided to accept me provided I could manage without any extra help or support.

This turned out to be one of the most positive learning experiences of my life. My 'special school' had done very little to encourage my academic side and I was determined to succeed. Despite the harsh conditions attached, their attitude was easy to cope with because it was, at least, honest and direct. It was not unusual for staff to congratulate me for managing as well as the fully sighted students! The rhetoric of equal opportunities policies had not yet touched this institution and there were no attempts to make me 'just like everyone else'. There were of course pressures to minimise my disability, not to rock the boat, but no one pretended that I was *equal* or that I could be made *normal*.

Despite their pronouncements that no one would assist me, many staff proved eager to help on an individual basis. The English teacher wrote all her comments with a thick black pen so that I could read them, the biology teacher gave me duplicate diagrams of those she drew on the blackboard and the history teacher, whose enthusiasm for the subject would have made anyone's lack of access entirely intolerable to him, abandoned visual aids altogether. Extra time was arranged in the examinations and my papers were enlarged and printed on white paper rather than beige, with the minimum of fuss. My self-esteem began to grow, I felt relaxed and valued.

Not everyone was helpful, but the modest assistance I was given then was greater than anything I have since received despite all the guidelines and policy documents which have been produced in the name of Equal Opportunities.

For more than twenty years I studied and worked in educational institutions. My experience as a disabled woman has led me to believe that equal opportunities policies in such places offer, at best, tokenist help such as a piece of equipment, but also allow for enormous complacency and hypocrisy. There is a lot of pressure on employers to be seen to be 'doing something' but the 'solutions' adopted often take no account of the individual needs of disabled people.

A visually impaired person may, for example, be given a special piece of equipment like a computer. This may enable them to do the job but also has the effect of others assuming that all the problems are now solved. The computer was very expensive so this person must now be *equal* and they must be *normal*. They must ask for nothing more. Technology is often used as a substitute for human help, although for many disabled people it is the quick and flexible assistance of colleagues which is most useful. We are not supposed to query the benefits of such technology or to suggest that, however much it cost, there are still difficulties for us at work.

I had a very hard time at work when I said that I could not see sufficiently to use the on-site computers. With a lot of aggression and resentment, I was told that a blind colleague had not had any of these problems. There was no recognition of our differing impairments, working methods, or roles within the organization. It seemed to be assumed that I was using my disability as a tactic to avoid work. I still don't know how to resolve the intense anger I feel about this.

The advantages of technological solutions to non-disabled people are that they look more impressive, usually cost less and don't interfere with their lives. Electronic 'talking signposts' are at this moment being considered for installation in the grounds of the university where I work, because, it is said, they will assist visually impaired people to find their way around. They are triggered by a hand-held transmitter and it was proposed that a spare transmitter should be made available for visitors until I pointed out that this would be extraordinarily unhelpful and unfriendly, especially as even sighted visitors are often escorted round the grounds!

These signposts might satisfy the creative talents of their inventors, they certainly don't satisfy my needs. What I need, of course, are pavements and corridors which are free of obstacles, and people with the time and patience to show me around (and to do so more than once). Twenty years ago, before equal opportunities were thought of, I found this happened automatically, but lately it has stopped. Perhaps the arguments about the rights of disabled people have made others nervous of offering help. Perhaps it is because the organizations I have worked in have become larger and more impersonal. I don't know.

Administrators seem unwilling to understand how different the needs of visually impaired people can be. Large print is a case in point. Some visually impaired people find it very useful but for others it reduces their visual field to a word or even part of a word and for them, the density, colour and style of print may be more important. When I try to discuss these issues with my colleagues I can feel them switching off. I am constantly asking people to write clearly or not to give me microprint but, even if they comply, they rarely do so more than once. If I reject their 'help' or ask for some change, I sometimes feel that I am seen as ungrateful and unfriendly. . . .

Equal opportunity policies for disabled people, where they exist, often go no deeper than the idea of saying that they should employ more of us. Once they get a disabled person in the building it is convenient and cheap for employers to believe that we want to be treated 'just like anyone else'. A friend of mine who queried the delay of a vital piece of equipment was told by her disdainful manager 'I have worked with many blind people and they all wanted to be treated normally'.

The employers of disabled people need to acknowledge that along with the skills for which we have been employed we may also have particular needs and requirements and it is the responsibility of the employer to meet these needs. That is what equal opportunities practice should mean. My own attempts at work to collude with the expectations that I should be just like everyone else mean that I always try to minimize the difficulties I face at work. I do it to get the work I want but in doing so I have to deny who I really am.

When I have received recognition regarding my needs at work, this has sometimes been seen by the giver as a charitable act for which I should be grateful and beholden. I cannot see to read or write if the sun shines on my page, yet in one job I had to fight to get a curtain put up at my window. I was frequently reminded of the cost and once it was up, people didn't seem to be able to pass my desk without enquiring whether I was pleased with it or telling me how great it was that I'd got it. I was being given two distinct messages; first, that I had been granted a very special 'favor' and second, that I must ask for nothing more.

Expressing gratitude for a kind or thoughtful act is something I do willingly. Expressing gratitude when I receive what should be my right is a dangerous move. A colleague recently attended a degree ceremony as a spectator and later wrote to complain about the inaccessibility for some disabled graduates. The reply she received was short and curt with no apology. Enclosed were photocopies of letters from four disabled students expressing their extreme gratitude for attending the ceremony at all. If we expect little, we get nothing.

In these more enlightened days, I am often asked to educate everyone else on all matters relating to disability. 'We know nothing about it, you must teach us,' they say. This may be progress but I don't know 'all about it' and, although I have a clear perspective on what should be the rights of disabled people at work, I am not an expert on the individual needs of other disabled colleagues. No formal structures have been developed in which this process of educating my colleagues can take place and sometimes it feels that, although I am asked endless questions about disability, I am rarely taken seriously and what I do say is forgotten or ignored.

I am becoming increasingly wary of involvement in discussions which are stressful and make me feel that I am viewed by others as a problem, but which do not change anything. If organizations were really committed to understanding disability they would put as much thought and resources into acquiring the necessary knowledge and skills as they do into numerous other matters deemed to be important. Continually arguing and campaigning for our rights as lone disabled people with little or no support from others is exhausting. The fear of being labeled 'difficult', with all the implications for references and promotion in the very competitive academic world, leads many disabled people, myself included, to remain passive. I am not happy working like this but sometimes I am too tired and too frustrated to be any different.

I am on the Equal Opportunities Committee at work but I do not know what equal opportunities means. We spend our time writing guidelines, monitoring policies, or investigating interview practice but it has been hard to interest anyone in talking about how we might facilitate others or create opportunities for disabled employees. Not long ago, I sat in a meeting while the head of the Equal Opportunities Unit, who knows of my disability, presented all his information on the overhead projector with microscopic tables to illustrate the difficulties faced by students from ethnic minority groups with few academic qualifications. The meeting was entirely inaccessible to me. When my own rights are so blatantly ignored, it is hard to empathize with other marginalized people, and this makes me feel selfish, paltry, and ill-suited to my role.

Equal opportunity policies in organizations like the one in which I work are overwhelmingly about gender and race, with disability issues being 'tagged on' almost as an afterthought. In my own experience the notion that such policies exist has raised expectations with little result. Equality must be part of the very fabric of the organizations in which we work. This has considerable resource implications and it will mean radical changes to the social, physical and political structures of work.

Until this happens, it is important to remove the empty and dishonest rhetoric even if it means returning to the bluntness and ruthlessness of the bad old days. I found it a whole lot easier when I was told I could expect nothing and sometimes found there was something after all.

Next Steps and Action

69

Friendships and Depression

Laura Epstein Rosen
Xavier Francisco Amador

When a friend is depressed, a special set of problems arises. Generally it is not uncommon for someone to show less of her unattractive side to a friend than to a relative. Similarly, friends are often less likely to confront one another with "failings" than are people who are related to one another. The reason is that friendships tend to be more fragile than blood relationships. . . .

The problem with the relative impermanence of friendships is that friends are less willing to expose themselves. With less openness, misunderstandings are more common when a friend becomes depressed. . . .

The Importance of Social Support

Social support can work as a vaccine against coming down with depression. Research studies have shown that people with fewer close relationships, a smaller social network, and less supportive relationships are more likely to become depressed. People who report less social support are thirteen times more likely to meet criteria for major depression than persons who report higher levels of social support. There has also been a suggestion that the quality of one's closest relationships is most crucial; support from other relationships does not make up for deficiencies in intimate relationships. You might be asking yourself what the cause and the effect are here. Do depressed people have fewer good relationships? Or is it that they had fewer good relationships to begin with and that is part of the reason they were vulnerable to depression? The answer to both questions is yes. Some studies have shown that even before they became depressed, depressed people had less social support than nondepressed people did. The point is that social support can serve as both a vaccine and a medicine for depression.

Social support can be very helpful in the fight against depression. The problem is that people with depression can be difficult to spend any time with, especially quality time. Their distress leads to difficult interpersonal relations over time. Studies even show that the concern and good intentions of family members can be stressful. Some researchers have proposed that having social support may be more a matter of freedom from conflict and negative interactions than anything else. They suggest that coping with a stressful life event in the context of a conflictual relationship may be more difficult than not having a relationship at all.

Given the connection between social support and depression, you can see how important it is to establish a constructive, trouble-free (or nearly so) relationship with your depressed friend. In the next section, we will show you ways to avoid the vicious cycle of depression and how to optimize your ability to give the social support your friend will need to fight effectively against the depression.

Giving Social Support

The depression of a friend can have a big impact on your own mood. How you feel and react can also have an effect on your ability to help your friend. Your own anger, sadness, or worry will have a negative impact on your reactions, and then your friend may respond in a way that only perpetuates the depressive dance. . . .

When communicating negative feelings, there are several ways to increase the odds that the discussion will result in a constructive outcome. First, consider the costs and benefits of talking about how you are feeling. Ask yourself whether *not* talking about your feelings is making you less interested in spending time with her. If the answer is yes, then given everything we have talked about up to this point, the next step should be obvious: You need to talk with your friend about how her depression has affected you and your relationship with her. Here are some guidelines to keep in mind when you talk about your negative feelings.

Wait to Talk about How You Are Feeling

The first time you realize you are angry, say to yourself, "I can always tell him later. I don't have to do it right now." Give yourself the time to sort through what you are feeling and to think about how you want to talk about it. Give yourself and your friend the benefit of the doubt. If you have not yet established a pattern of constructive communication about negative feelings, then try *not* to talk about your negative feelings the moment you identify them. Trust that you can always talk about it tomorrow. . . .

Reassure Your Friend

Explain that you are telling her about your negative feelings because you want to feel good about the time you spend together and because you want to help her. One of the major symptoms of depression is an increased sense of worthlessness. Someone who is depressed is prone to interpret the opinions of others negatively. Consequently, when talking about how her depression makes you feel, you need to reassure her that you value your friendship with her. You are speaking up because you feel she is worth the trouble. . . .

Separate the Depression from Your Friend

Depression can be a tricky illness. Unlike other illnesses, where the symptoms are clearly separate from your impression of the person's personality, such as sneezing and watery eyes during allergy season, depressive symptoms can easily be mistaken for personality traits. A pervasive lack of interest in people and activities that usually give pleasure is often interpreted as something personal by people unfamiliar with the symptom of anhedonia. . . .

Don't Play the Blaming Game

Invite your friend to see the depression as the cause of the trouble in your friendship rather than as you or he being at fault. Whenever we feel badly, our natural reflex is to try to determine who or what is to blame. After all, something must be making you, or your friend, feel blue, irritable, or guilty. Someone must be at fault. . . .

There are two problems with blaming one person for the way another one feels. One is that it puts people on the defensive and usually results in increased distance and less collaboration. The second is that blaming one person for a problem in a relationship is usually a gross oversimplification of what is really going on.

The remedy to the first problem is simple: Don't blame yourself or the other person. Blame only breeds defensiveness and guilt, and neither will help matters. Human emotions and interactions are amazingly complex. To jump to the conclusion that you feel angry solely because your depressed friend ignored your needs is too simplistic. Some people are quick to feel angry in situations, while others would never feel anything more than mild frustration. The reasons for this variability are many. Your individual sensitivity to being ignored, the quality of the previous interactions with your friend, and the degree of patience you possess can all affect how you feel. Try to say to yourself, "I know what I am feeling and what triggered it, but there may be more here than meets the eye." Give yourself the time and space to explore the possibilities. You may be surprised by what you learn about why you are feeling the way you do.

Use "I" Rather Than "You"

For example, say, "I feel angry" rather than "You make me angry." This wording helps to minimize your friend's defensiveness and keeps the focus on solving the problem as a team rather than suggesting that it is entirely your friend's responsibility to fix it. This is an especially important guideline; it conveys that you are not out to blame your friend for how you are feeling. Using *I* rather than *you* implies that you have not jumped to any conclusions, that you are open to exploring the possibilities for why you feel the way you do, and that you want to resolve the trouble *with* your friend.

70

Learning Accommodations for ADD Students

Anne McCormick in collaboration with Faith Leonard

Learning accommodations for individuals with attention deficit disorder, or ADD, at the college level are as unique as the types and severity of ADD symptoms themselves. Nevertheless, there are two keys to being sure that the necessary adaptations for *your* learning style are provided at the college of your choice. First, the college learning center should be a well established one, with a history of serving students with learning disabilities. This strong foundation should indicate that wisdom of experience prevails and that unique learning accommodations will be welcomed with assurance and understanding.

The program's longevity may also ensure that the staff is properly trained in the field of special education.

As college programs for students with learning disabilities have grown, a shortage of well-trained and experienced learning specialists has developed. Students with ADD should be able to feel confident that basic accommodations, such as untimed testing, can be provided for them. Indeed, when the mechanisms for providing adaptations are securely in place and the learning specialists are experienced, the process for obtaining accommodations is not only simplified, but assured.

The other key to guaranteeing individualized accommodations is the student's self-knowledge and acceptance of the ADD. The first step to advocacy is a thorough understanding of how your disability affects your ability to demonstrate intellectual capability, which can be masked by the many symptoms of ADD. In turn, this can create inaccurate measures of your actual ability.

The emotional overlay of a disability and a lack of self-knowledge is frequently more difficult to surmount than the hierarchical ladder you may need to negotiate to secure accommodations. All too often, students with learning disabilities and ADD come to college with the idea of beginning with a "clean slate." In fact, it is still common for students with these disabilities to have received information assuring them and their families that they will outgrow the learning disability or ADD. Therefore, they see college as a chance to start anew without the traditional supports (tutoring, even medication) that some have had for 10 or more years. Though the emotional high of starting college may mask low self-esteem issues, years of repeated frustrations, both personal and academic, make individuals with ADD incredibly vulnerable to the social and academic struggles that lie ahead. This fragile emotional profile leaves students prone to a crisis surrounding accommodations that some do not even want to admit are needed. Staff who coordinate specialized testing programs for learning-disabled students are often faced with students' last-minute acceptance of the need for learning accommodations. In order to secure proper space and proctoring for specialized testing, advance notice to the professor and learning center staff is necessary. Students who belatedly decide that they need help create their own crises by arriving unannounced to take an untimed test. It is difficult to provide the accommodations without prior notice that would allow the student to perform at his or her level of competence.

You can be your own best advocate by knowing who you are and what learning accommodations will assist you in revealing your capabilities, both personal and academic. While an individual with ADD may be well prepared for college, he or she may not have the expertise needed to design accommodations that will highlight his or her capabilities. The Center for Psychological and Learning Services at The American University has compiled a list of common learning problems students at the college level may have. They are categorized into academic and emotional difficulties. No student will exhibit all of the characteristics listed here. The degree to which these characteristics are manifest will also vary greatly depending on each individual's profile of strengths and weaknesses.

Academic Difficulties

■ Organization of time and place is a major problem for many students at the college level and beyond. Frequently, it is the very freedom from structured time craved by the student that becomes a nemesis. People with ADD can become so consumed by the complexity of getting everything done that they do nothing.

■ Reading problems for persons with ADD frequently center around difficulty in persevering with the task over a length of time. Frequently, when tested for reading problems, these students do much better when time constraints are lifted. In addition, students with ADD may not be able to remember what they read because of attention deficits.

- Mathematics is an area of concern for students with ADD, again because of attention problems. Problem solving requires close attention and time. The longer the task takes, the more difficult the task can become. In addition, as time passes and anxiety mounts, visual distortions or reversals can sabotage even basic calculations.

- Note taking may be an impossible task for some students with ADD because two skills are called upon simultaneously, listening and writing. In addition, retaining information, even momentarily, can be very difficult, thus causing frustration, which then increases anxiety and interferes with processing information. Also, students with ADD can be so intent on getting everything down that, in the end, it is difficult to organize or even make sense of the notes taken.

- Writing for students with ADD can be difficult from two perspectives: it requires both sustained attention and organizational skills, which are frequently the areas affected by their disability.

- Verbal skills can be subject to word choice or word retrieval problems as the language skills for conversation or presentation are compromised by the concomitant anxiety of an attention deficit disorder.

- Foreign language studies can also be difficult for some who have language or auditory processing problems.

Emotional Difficulties

- An uneasy relationship with the disability can sabotage the process of securing accommodations.

- High levels of frustration are easily triggered by anxiety.

- Inappropriate social skills or impulsivity and manipulation can affect interactions with professors and others.

- Confusion about goals and the future can hinder attempts to persevere with academic challenges.

All students wrestle with academic and emotional struggles in college but for students with ADD the problems are often more severe and longer lasting. However, with determination and accommodations, students with disabilities can succeed at the college level. You can start by consulting with professors at the beginning of the semester regarding the types of modifications that you may require, given that ADD affects every student differently and to a different degree. Although special modifications in classroom procedures may be needed, academic standards remain the same. Academic ability is not the issue; it is the methods of meeting academic standards that may differ from those of other students.

Common Accommodations

Lecture Classes

During lecture classes, the ADD student may

- need to copy the notes of another student in class and may ask the professor's assistance in finding a note taker

- need to sit in the front of the room
- benefit from the use of visual aids, handouts, and the blackboard
- need to use a laptop computer

Writing Papers

When writing papers, ADD students may:

- need to meet with professors for clarification of writing assignments
- wish to have rough drafts evaluated
- require extra time to complete writing assignments
- use an editor for papers before submitting final drafts

Examinations

During exams, ADD students may:

- need extended time to complete exams and/or administration in an environment free of distraction
- need to alter the response format of a test
- need to take exams over a period of time in short intervals

Auxiliary Aids

ADD students may also:

- need to record lectures
- need to use a calculator
- need to use a computer for writing assignments
- need to order textbooks on tape from the Recordings for the Blind (a process that requires getting a book list well in advance of the course)

Other Accommodations

We have also compiled a few (nonstandard) adaptions that students have designed to accommodate their unique learning styles.

Lecture Classes

ADD students may need to arrange with the professor to sit by the door so that after a half an hour he or she can quietly leave and walk around for two or three minutes.

Writing

The ADD student may find it helpful to write and pass in papers in stages.

Examinations

ADD students may do better on take home exams or if they record exams and pass the tape in as a final copy.

Reading

ADD students may find it helpful to break the reading into manageable chunks over a number of reading sessions. (Skimming the entire assignment should be done first and a verbal review should be done after the reading is finished.)

Auxiliary Aids

ADD students may find some or all of the following to be useful.

- "white noise" machines
- earplugs
- daily planning calendars
- cognitive or self-regulatory skills such as reminders to work slowly
- proofreaders
- support groups
- taking an extra year to complete college

Finally, as an example, a student who has ADD and who has graduated from college has proved that accessing learning accommodations can assist individuals to perform at an academic level commensurate with their ability. After struggling for three years of college with a 2.0 grade point average, she sought help, was tested for ADD, and took untimed tests in an environment free from distractions. She raised her GPA to 3.19 and her self-esteem to "above average." She tells us that ADD is not a "life sentence," but part of a "life style" that requires some adaptations to direct her life toward achievable, realistic goals. You can do it, too.

71

Computers and Disability

Mark Nagler and Adam Nagler

Introduction

The Internet has revolutionized the way information is disseminated in our society. The World Wide Web has emerged as a massive storehouse of information that allows anyone to perform research on virtually any topic in a matter of minutes. Information that used to be available only to experts is now available to the general public at the click of a button.

The Internet offers people with disabilities ready access to the latest information (and misinformation) concerning their conditions. For example, people living with chronic conditions such as diabetes or fibromyalgia can find out about the latest experimental techniques that are being developed to treat their conditions. This chapter includes case studies of two Internet searches by people who were recently diagnosed with a disability. These searches illustrate how to use the Internet to gain the information needed to make educated decisions about your plan of care. The case studies are not designed as step-by-step manuals for information gathering, but rather to illustrate the possibilities of the Internet as a research tool. . . .

You may be well served by beginning your search at a Web site created by or affiliated with a major and reputable organization in your area of interest. For example, someone from Toronto who had just suffered a mild stroke may decide to start looking for information at the Heart and Stroke Foundation of Canada Web site (www.hsf.ca). No matter where you begin, confirm the integrity of your source before you pursue any of the strategies you find.

Support over the Internet

One of the most helpful features on the Internet is the availability of interactive on-line discussion groups, including list-servs, newsgroups, and chat rooms. These forums allow individuals to share information, coping strategies, and emotional support with people who have similar concerns. A list-serv is a distributed e-mail list on which members send a message to a central computer, and a copy is sent to all subscribers of the list. Newsgroups consist of messages posted to a central forum, where they can be read and responded to by anyone who visits the site, and chat rooms are live discussions (typed) in which anyone who logs on to a site can "talk" to someone in real time. You can post messages that outline your concerns or pose questions about your disability. Your message will be read by medical specialists and people from all over the world who share your disability, and who may be able to offer support or assistance. Typically, listservs are the most likely to be used or monitored by professionals, and chat rooms are the least likely.

The Internet is a unique resource for individuals who have conditions that occur so infrequently that support groups for them do not exist. If you have a very rare condition, posting messages to major disability sites can help you get in touch with people who share your situation. Some Web sites are dedicated to rare conditions, and may be of particular assistance.

Gaining Access to the Internet

If you don't own your own computer, you can gain access to the Internet from libraries, Internet cafés, universities and colleges, elementary schools, high schools, computer stores, a friend's computer, and Internet service providers (ISPs). National ISPs include America Online, Compuserve, Prodigy, and Sympatico, and there are many ISPs at the local level as well. Full Internet access can cost as little as ten dollars per month. Paying for a couple of hours of access each month may be a worthwhile investment. . . .

Case Study: Fibromyalgia and the Internet

This is the story of how a man named Jerry used the Internet to help develop an alternate course of treatment for his disability.

In April 1997 I was diagnosed with fibromyalgia. I was told by my doctor, as well as by a few people I knew, that I would have this debilitating disease for the rest of my life—that fibromyalgia could not be cured. I chose not to accept such a dire prediction. There were many avenues I pursued in my quest for information, and one that was most helpful was searching on the Internet. This allowed me to connect with other people who suffered from the disease, as well as with a wide assortment of health-care practitioners and professionals.

Using the AltaVista search engine, I typed in "fibromyalgia" and punched the search button. There are many other excellent search engines, such as Lycos, Dejanews, Yahoo, and Web Crawler. Within moments, more than four thousand hits on the disease were placed at my disposal. Some of the references were worthless, but many contained various first-person accounts of successful methods being used to combat the disease. In many instances, you could communicate directly with the individual whose story was posted on the Net.

My approach to evaluating their descriptions was based in part on whether they were selling something. If they were, I tended to dismiss their claims. If they were not, I continued "talking" to them via the Internet.

A large number of scholarly and not-so-scholarly articles were also placed at my disposal. I read many of these articles, though I tended to be somewhat more accepting of those that appeared in mainstream journals, and less accepting of those that appeared in one-time-only newsletters. Many of the latter were seeking to sell some miracle cure.

I would discuss with my doctor those articles that I found to be of merit. Fortunately, my doctor was open to naturopathic and homeopathic remedies. I cannot say that I am now permanently cured—perhaps the disease is only in remission, and I still have a way to go to rebuild my muscle strength—but the healing process is in full swing.

Case Study: Computers and Quadriplegia

This is the story of a woman named Vicki who has used computers extensively to help her cope with her disability.

I started using on-line services back in the days of 300 baud modems and monochrome screens. E-mail was not a household word and the Internet was still a government pet project. I was eleven or twelve then, and I found this means of communication fascinating. Here I was, in a distant suburb of Washington, D.C., talking to people in Wyoming, Alaska, and Germany—all at once.

My interest in computers kept growing. I taught myself what I could because PCs weren't quite mainstream and there weren't many classes available to young people. When I was in a car accident that left me with quadriplegia at the age of seventeen, however, computers quickly took over my life. They were no longer a hobby, but a necessary piece of equipment I needed to accomplish everyday tasks.

Now my computer is specifically adapted to my needs, with special software, voice activation, a headset mouse, and a smaller keyboard for typing with a mouth stick. I can use my computer and the Internet independently, as easily as those who operate a computer with their hands. I am now in college, studying English and creative writing. With my adapted system, I can navigate the Internet with ease, looking up information for research papers or downloading software to help me with my studies. E-mail plays a key role in helping me communicate with people when I am otherwise unable. If I am sick or run into complications (which so frequently haunt those of us with disabilities), I can e-mail my professors an explanation for my absence, or send them my completed assignments. Classmates use e-mail to keep me caught up with notes and assignments.

On-line communication is a great way to meet people. In the virtual world, you are faceless, ageless, sexless, and perhaps most important, without a disability. You are judged by your personality, not your looks or disability. E-mail keeps me in touch with family and friends. Here at college, I can talk to my family or my boyfriend whenever I want (and avoid the high phone bills).

I've even obtained a job via the Internet. I write reviews and news for the Baltimore section of MTV On-line. Since MTV is based in New York City, I communicate with my supervisor entirely through e-mail. Plus, my work is published on the Web. It's a great opportunity for an aspiring writer. Many company Web sites list their job openings. A good place to start is at the New Mobility Jobline at http:/www.newmobility.com.

The Internet keeps me in touch with the world around me. Since my accident, I have had great difficulty reading the newspaper. The Internet has services (InfoBeat is a personal favorite) that e-mail the latest news, sports, entertainment, and weather right to your desktop. Reading by scrolling down a screen is much easier than trying to flip those large newspaper pages with a mouth stick. On-line communication and the Internet substantially lessen my day-to-day difficulties, and those seemingly insurmountable obstacles are more easily overcome.

Conclusion

Computers and the Internet provide vast opportunities for people both with and without disabilities to learn about health issues. The Internet has fed the public's growing demand for information about health and wellness issues, and it probably contains more raw material than any other source. This explosion in the amount of information available at the touch of a button has helped thousands of people with disabilities and their loved ones to become informed, proactive consumers of care.

The Internet is an important resource for anyone who wants to become more knowledgeable about her condition. It can help to relieve uncertainty after an initial diagnosis, it can put you in touch with a warm and caring support network, and it can keep you up-to-date on recent medical advances. The Internet can complement any protection plan, and can help you take control of your care.

The Internet can also provide you with confidence. The Internet provides access to unlimited amounts of information, which you can use to build expertise on your condition. Developing an understanding of your condition and your options is one of the best ways to become more comfortable with your disability. Knowledge can minimize uncertainty and bring you the power to seek out new ideas and options, and to actively participate in your own care.

72

Invisible and On Center Stage: Who Do We Think We Are, Anyway?

Susan E. Brown, Debra Connors,
and Nanci Stern

We are each made up of a myriad of identities forged through our interactions with other people. Disabled women experience a lack of role models, especially positive ones through which to form our own identities. We are apt to be invisible to others or seen only as our disabilities.

We develop strategies for maintaining positive self concepts when vital parts of our selves are unacceptable to those around us. Withdrawal, passing and disclosing our identities are all ways we work to be ourselves and be O.K. with ourselves. Sometimes it is safer to withdraw from interaction with others than disclose our vulnerabilities to a hostile audience. At other times we may choose to interact, but pass ourselves off as able-bodied. Those of us with invisible disabilities can do this to the extreme, whereas visibly disabled women may have no choice about sharing some aspects of our disabilities. On rare and special occasions we feel safe and are totally open and sharing about our issues.

We may bounce back and forth among these ways of presenting ourselves. There are costs and rewards involved in using each. Withdrawal, while protecting us from negativity also insulates us from all that is positive and life sustaining in relating to other people. In a vacuum, we may feel very alone and isolated and may never come to know who we really are. We may internalize negative attitudes about ourselves and feel ashamed and embarassed about being disabled. Passing as able-bodied may allow us to avoid being seen as only our disabilities, and feel, if for only a short time "normal," a part of a world designed for the able-bodied. But the risks are heavy. We may come to dislike ourselves for being less than honest about who we are. We may endanger our physical health rather than admit we need the cooperation of others to meet our disability needs. By acting as if we have no needs, we may perpetuate a "super-crip" image—disabled people can do anything we want if we only try hard enough. We may exhaust ourselves trying and come to believe that we are better than other disabled people who have not accomplished as much. This can separate us from a very important resource in developing whole self concepts—other disabled women. As disabled women, we may also fit the social expectation for disabled women by appearing dependent, compliant and pitiful.

Sharing our disabilities with others makes it clear where we can and where we cannot get the support we need. Some people refuse to discuss our disabilities, or blame us for our condition. They have a hard time believing we are really disabled. We can choose to associate with people who acknowledge and accept all of who we are. Through this process, we begin to incorporate our disabilities into realistic and positive conceptions of ourselves. Holding onto our positive self images is a more difficult task if we are also old, lesbian, or women of color. Each of these identities needs nourishment to grow.

Our bodies and our abilities are an integral part of our identities. We need visible, available role models of other disabled women who can share with us realistic pictures of their lives. We need a shift in societal values, so that these genuine pictures are allowed to be seen instead of only images that offer false reassurance to able-bodied and disabled people alike. Our disabilities need not dominate our lives and identities if the individual differences of all people are valued and accommodated.

Classism

Introduction by Maurianne Adams

Persistent inequality on the basis of social and economic class seems especially difficult to acknowledge in the United States, possibly because of our belief in meritocracy (that hard work and talent will be rewarded), possibly because we equate our system of political equality with equality of economic opportunity. Yet the contemporary data, some of it presented in this section, point both to increasing economic inequality and to increasing inequality of economic opportunity. Recent newspaper reports note that the rich/poor gap in the United States has more than doubled since 1977; that race still plays a powerful role in one's chances for economic success; that "the richest fifth accounts for 86 percent of private consumption"; that Muscogee Indians who have rights to oil-rich land in eastern Oklahoma cannot get an accounting of what is owed them by the government or by the oil companies; that Blacks find cycles of poverty difficult to break; that the children of the poor fight a baffling surge in asthma; that poor women on Medicaid are overcharged by hospitals for procedures to stop pain in childbirth; and that although rising incomes are lifting 1.1 million people out of poverty, the Census Bureau is now having to revise *downward* its poverty threshold in order to accurately reflect current economic realities.* In the light of these prospects, it is difficult if not impossible to maintain that poverty can be solved solely by meritocracy or social mobility alone (that is, the Horatio Alger myth of pulling oneself up by one's bootstraps—as if everyone had boots), or that the poor and unemployed are to blame for their condition.

---

*These statements appear in newspaper articles carried in the *San Diego Union-Tribune*, September 5, 1999; *Daily Hampshire Gazette*,October 2, 1999; *New York Times International Sunday*, September 13, 1998; and *New York Times*, March 8 and 9; and October 1, 5, and 18, 1999.

This section takes the position that social class is a largely self-perpetuating category marked by persistent and pervasive inequalities of income, wealth, status, and social power, and that classism (like sexism or racism) constitutes a form of oppression that is structural, maintained by practices that constitute "business as usual," and played out at the individual, institutional, and cultural levels (Yeskel and Leondar-Wright 1997). An analysis of the growing gap between the rich and the poor in the United States illustrated by many of the chapters in this section points to three of the factors that Iris Marion Young includes among her "Five Faces of Oppression" (chapter 5 of this volume): namely, economic *exploitation* in the workplace; *marginalization* of people of color, women, the very young and the very old from useful participation in the nation's economic life; and the relative *powerlessness* of the nonprofessional, menial, service workforce and of those outside the labor force (class factors that Young ties to social status, power, and respectability).

Readings in This Section

This section includes a number of selections that document the increasing divide between the very rich and all others (Brouwer, Heintz and Folbe, Langston), and that help us understand the fundamental difference between inherited wealth and income, a distinction that also enables us to see some of the ways in which the legacy of racism interacts with classism (Oliver and Shapiro). The impossibility of extricating the multiple effects of racism, sexism, and classism is amply documented by many of the selections here, such as the journalistic account by Glenn Omatsu (and similarly, by Marc Cooper in the earlier chapter 12). The first-person narratives of Gwendolyn Lewis, Patricia Holland, and Kathleen Kelly; of Rosemary Bray and of Melanie Scheller all describe in detail the consequences of multiple oppressions in daily life and in limiting one's future life chances. The experiences recounted by Lewis, Holland and Kelly, and the approach taken by John Larew's description of college admissions, raise the question of whether we can consider the educational system to be a fair and equitable vehicle for getting ahead regardless of family class background, or whether it is a vehicle through which advantages and disadvantages are passed along from parents to children (Ogbu 1988, McMurrer and Sawhill 1998, Levine and Nidiffer 1996). Larew turns the current college admissions debate on its head, by asking why wealthy and privileged "unqualified, unprepared kids" are getting into college.

Two selections in this section illustrate how multiple dimensions of social oppression (on the basis of class, race, or gender) interact in the daily lives of specific people, but also can be abstracted as sociological models. Thus, Donna Langston elaborates upon the complexities resulting from the interactions of class with race and gender, while H. Edward Ransford presents a theoretical model to help us make sense of these interactions. These selections, and selections in other sections in this volume (Bowman and Burford in chapter 66, for example, or Patricia Hill Collins in chapter 87) illustrate the extent to which classism is deeply implicated in racism, sexism, and ableism so that it is often difficult to disentangle the consequences of race, gender, or other forms of oppression from those of social class. All have to do with fair and equitable life opportunities: where one lives, whom one lives with, the educational and occupational opportunities for oneself and one's family, and ultimately, the quality of one's own life and the lives of those who belong to one's community and family.

In "Next Steps and Action," a social class questionnaire provides a systematic set of questions to help us think about our own social class roots and their effects upon our current attitudes and values. The welfare reform program proposed by Barbara

Bergmann and Heidi Hartmann suggests one possible solution to the issues of poverty, welfare, lack of child care, and poor educational opportunities described in the earlier pieces by James S. Heintz and Nancy Folbre, Donna Langston, and Rosemary Bray. The selection from a much longer, more detailed and documented monograph by Peter B. Edelman urges an approach to poverty that is multilayered, and that includes all levels of government as well as the private sector.

The Further Resources section at the end of this volume explores other issues of importance, such as the direct causal linkage between segregated residential patterns, unequal schooling, and unequal job opportunities (Wilson 1987, Ogbu 1988, Albelda, Folbre and the Center for Popular Economics 1996, Levine and Nidiffer 1996). Although Scheller, and Lewis, Holland and Kelly in this section (and Bernice Mennis, earlier, in chapter 29) describe the painful consequences on identity of internalized classism, there is also a growing literature that specifically addresses class identity (for example, Zandy 1996, or Wray and Newitz 1997). There is an important history of classism and the history of resistance to class inequality (union organizing as well as armed rebellion), suggested in the piece by Omatsu (for further information, see Zinn 1995). And the impact of federal policy upon wealth and income redistribution, touched on by Steve Brouwer, by Melvin L. Oliver and Thomas M. Shapiro, and by Peter B. Edelman, is further explored in Barlett and Steele 1992.

There is a considerable sociological literature that analyzes the changing hierarchies of social and economic stratification and inequality (as in Rothman 1999) and describes the current scope and dimensions of inequality in America (see Dalphin 1989, Rothman 1999, as supplements to the selection by H. Edward Ransford). Many agendas have been put forward for eliminating poverty and increasing life chances for everyone, as in the further references to Demko and Jackson 1995, and to Herzenberg, Alic and Wial 1998. And finally, given the pervasiveness of class and its interactions with the other social justice issues identified in this book, the "Next Steps and Action" subsections within each of the preceding five sections, and of section 8 that follows, can be read as parts of a much larger picture that extend well beyond the covers of this volume.

References

Albelda, R., N. Folbre, and the Center for Popular Economics (1996). *The War on the Poor: A Defense Manual.* New York: The New Press.

Barlett, D. L. and J. B. Steele. (1992). *America: What Went Wrong?* Kansas City, Mo.: Andrews and McMeel.

Dalphin, J. (1987). *The Persistence of Social Inequality in America.* Rochester, Vt.: Schenkman Books.

Demko, G. J.and M. C. Jackson. (1995). *Populations at Risk in America: Vulnerable Groups at the End of the Twentieth Century.* New York: Westview Press.

Herzenberg, S. A., J. A. Alic,, and H. Wial. (1998). *New Rules for a New Economy: Employment and Opportunity in Postindustrial America.* Ithaca, N.Y.: Cornell University Press.

Levine, A., and J, Nidiffer, Jana (1996). *Beating the Odds: How the Poor Get to College.* San Franciso: Jossey-Bass.

McMurrer, D. P and I. V Sawhill, Isabel V. (1998). "Education and Opportunity." In *Getting Ahead: Economic and Social Mobility in America.* Washington, D.C.: Urban Institute Press.

Ogbu, J. U. (1988). "Class Stratification, Racial Stratification, and Schooling." In L. Weis, ed., *Class, Race, and Gender in American Education.* Albany, N.Y.: State University of New York Press.

Rothman, R. A. (1999). *Inequality and Stratification: Race, Class, and Gender.* Upper Saddle River, N.J.: Prentice-Hall.

Wilson, W. J. (1987). *The Truly Disadvantaged: The Inner City, The Underclass, and Public Policy.* Chicago: University of Chicago Press.

Wray, M., and A. Newitz. (1997). *White Trash: Race and Class in America.* New York: Routledge.

Yeskel, F., and B. Leondar-Wright. (1997). "Classism Curriculum Design." In Adams, M., L. A. Bell, and P. Griffin, eds., *Teaching for Diversity and Social Justice: A Sourcebook.* New York: Routledge.

Zandy, J. (1996). "Decloaking Class: Why Class Identity and Consciousness Count." *Race, Gender, and Class* 4, no. 1, 7–23.

Zinn, H. (1995). *A People's History of the United States,* updated and rev. ed. New York: Harper and Row.

Contexts

73

Sharing the Pie

Steve Brouwer

The distribution of wealth in the United States today is terribly unequal. The richest Americans, the top 1 percent, own almost half of the financial assets in our country. The affluent members of the upper middle class who make up the next 9 percent of the population own slightly more than one third of the wealth. That leaves only about one sixth to be divided among everyone else. A rich person, on average, has about 230 times more wealth than a member of the huge majority of Americans, the 90 percent who own very little at all. The pie is divided up like this:

Ownership of Financial Assets[1]	
The Very Rich (1% of the population)	46%
The Affluent (the next 9%)	36%
The Rest of Us (90% of the population)	18%

First of all, the only momentous economic growth in the United States in the mid-1990s was in the stock market, which was fed by a long-term speculative binge that primarily benefited very rich investors, Wall Street traders, and the largest businesses. The profits of giant corporations jumped 58 percent from 1992 to 1997, but this increase was not accompanied by any gains in wages and salaries for ordinary workers. The number of decently paying corporate jobs was on the decline, even at the middle-management levels. . . .

Hogging the Pie

The United States is not the world leader in many economic categories these days, but we are still the champions at making a few people very rich. As you can see by the figures that begin this chapter, wealthy people are not just slightly richer than the rest of us—they are hogging the whole pie.

There are three ways we can look at the division of total individual net wealth (that is, all assets owned minus all kinds of debt). One way is to consider everything owned by *1,* every citizen:

Total Wealth Owned[2]

Average Wealth per Household		Group Share of all U.S. Wealth
$9,000,000	**The Very Rich (the top 1%)**	37%
$950,000	**The Affluent (the next 9%)**	35%
$75,000*	**The Rest of Us (the bottom 90%)**	28%

*For the bottom 90%, most wealth consists of possessions—cars, household goods, and equity built up in homes—that are utilized in everyday life. Almost half of these people, the bottom 40%, have a net worth approaching zero, because their debts cancel out any property or assets they may own.

A second way to compare wealth is to look at ownership of financial assets. By *2,* subtracting out the value of such things as automobiles, house furnishings, and residences, we get a truer measure of usable wealth, the kind of ownership that gives a person distinct advantages in a capitalist society. Because most people have invested more in household assets and cars than in financial holdings, the share of wealth held by the bottom 90 percent of the population falls to just 18 percent when only financial assets are considered. The share of the affluent upper-middle class stays about the same, but the share of the very rich, who own almost half of all financial assets, jumps up sharply to 46 percent.

There is a third way of looking at accumulated wealth that reveals even greater *3,* inequality. When we focus on the ownership of our economic system itself—the stocks and bonds of corporations, the privately held business assets, and the large trust funds and investment portfolios that are managed by banks—we find that total control is in the hands of the richest 1 percent:

Corporate and Business Assets Owned[3]

	Business Assets	Stocks	Bonds	Trusts
The Richest (1%)	61.6%	49.6%	62.4%	52.9%
The Next 9%	29.5%	36.7%	28.9%	35.1%
The Rest of Us (90%)	8.9%	13.6%	8.70%	12.0%

This kind of wealth, which gives real economic power to a tiny fraction of our population, also reveals the truly undemocratic side of our society. Some scholars who carefully follow the patterns of ownership and financial control have found that the real wealth that translates into social and political power is held by a fraction of the very rich. In

1978 Maurice Zeitlin identified a group of 55,400 households, just one-twentieth of 1 percent of the population, who owned 20 percent of all corporate stock, 66 percent of all state and local bonds, and 40 percent of all other bonds and notes.[4] In the mid-1980s economist Lester Thurow reviewed the survey data for the richest four hundred individuals in the United States and eighty-two additional family groups who held extraordinary wealth. He estimated that through their ties to corporate ownership this tiny band of people had direct and indirect control over business assets amounting to more than $2 trillion, or "40% of all fixed nonresidential capital in the United States." With this kind of wealth, said Thurow, "it is hard to maintain the equality of influence that is the backbone of democracy."[5]

G. William Domhoff has argued convincingly that there is a core of wealthy people "who rule America," that they form a true upper class from which a minority gravitate toward prominent positions in business and government.[6] But this class is not stagnant. New people are always moving up to join the ranks of the very rich; occasionally an aggressive millionaire financier or entrepreneur attains billionaire status. Within the elite ranks are the people who manage the big corporations, those who hold high positions in the banks and law firms that simultaneously serve Wall Street and Washington, and those passively rich families who collect the dividends from the largest personal fortunes. All in all, these families not only control the majority of corporate wealth, but they also self-consciously nurture upper-class tastes and elite private education, as well as the next generation of financiers and presidential cabinet members.

The Billionaires Binge

Of course, there have always been some very rich people in the United States, and they have wielded tremendous political power. During the period between 1865 and 1929— the era of the Robber Barons, the railroad trusts, and the oil monopolies—the richest citizens exercised unchallenged control over the economy and many other aspects of American life. Then, following the Great Depression and the economic reforms of the New Deal, ownership of wealth became more equal from the mid-1940s through the mid-1970s.[7] Millionaires had by no means disappeared, but the very rich held only about half as much of the nation's wealth as they had before the Depression. This trend reversed itself in the late 1970s as the wealthy reasserted their economic dominance and inequality accelerated rapidly. By the 1980s, the country's financial assets were being transferred to the rich at a phenomenal rate.

The analysis of Edward N. Wolff, professor of economics at New York University and the editor of the *Review of Income and Wealth*, demonstrated that the richest 1 percent gained control of 5.4 percent of the nation's financial assets in just six years, from 1983 to 1989;[8] this transfer of wealth was worth approximately $2.5 trillion. This sudden shift was especially unsettling because it came at the expense of the bottom 90 percent of the population. Particularly hard-hit, according to Wolff, were the poorest 40 percent of Americans—more than 100 million people—who suffered "an absolute decline in their average wealth holdings." They lost about $300 billion in assets, which meant their already meager net worth was rapidly approaching zero.[9]

The richest 1 percent of Americans pigged out throughout the 1980s, accumulating 61.6 percent of all wealth created in that period.[10] After a deep recession followed by very slow growth from 1989 to 1995, the U.S. economy began to grow again, but at a modest rate. Wealth was once again created in ways that benefited the rich, most spectacularly in the huge run-up in stock prices between the middle of 1994 and the middle of 1997. Since the richest 1 percent of Americans owned nearly half of the stock they only had to sit back and watch the market.[11] The overall value of publicly traded stocks increased from approximately $3 trillion in 1988, to $5 trillion in 1992, to well over $10 trillion in 1997.

One way to exemplify the astounding multiplication of the biggest fortunes is to look at the annual incomes they can generate. Andrew Hacker, in his book *Money: Who Has How Much and Why*, examined the people who reported incomes of over $1 million per year to the Internal Revenue Service. Their number, even after adjusting for inflation, had increased dramatically in fifteen years, from 13,505 in 1979 to 68,064 in 1994.[12]

The degree of inequality in the United States is now so extreme that we have returned to the ignominious levels of the 1920s.

Percentage of Wealth (Total Net Worth) Held by the Top 1% of Americans[13]					
1929	**1949**	**1969**	**1979**	**1989**	**1995**
44.2%	27.1%	31.1%	20.5%	35.7%	40%

The Sinking Majority

How did the rich manage to get even richer? We know, having watched *Lifestyles of the Rich and Famous*, that the wealthy are not misers who put every penny they earn into their piggy banks. One reason the rich have been hogging the wealth is that they keep finding ways to earn more while the rest of us earn less.

From 1977 to 1994, real salaries and wages declined steadily for most people. For the 73 million Americans who work as private-sector employees—their ranks would include such people as nurses, truckers, office workers, retail clerks, machinists, construction workers, computer programmers, waiters, and miners—the average hourly pay fell by 13.1 percent.[14]

This steady downward trend was an unexpected blow to American families who had grown up in an age of prosperity. For thirty-two years after World War II, the median family income grew very handsomely, increasing by 111 percent between 1947 and 1979. Since then the median income has remained stagnant, rising ever so slightly from 1979 to 1989, then sinking 3.4 percent between 1989 and 1995.

Median Family Income (in Inflation-Adjusted Dollars)[15]				
1947	**1967**	**1979**	**1989**	**1995**
$19,088	$33,305	$40,339	$42,049	$40,611

The only reason the median family income did not fall precipitously in the 1980s and early 1990s was that more people in each household, and women in particular, went to work. By 1996 women comprised almost half, or 46 percent, of the labor force. This increased the percentage of working-age people who were active in the labor force from 61.2 percent in 1975 to 67.3 percent in 1997. As a result of this trend, the overall number of hours worked per capita increased by 12 percent.

By the mid-1990s this intensive work effort had more or less stabilized, yet average families and single workers had little or nothing to show for all their effort. No matter how much they worked, people entering the labor force had trouble saving because they were earning much less than an equivalent worker would have earned a generation earlier. This was especially true for high school graduates with one to five years of work experience. In 1993 young men in this category were earning 30 percent less than their counterparts did in 1973, young women about 20 percent less. Young people with more education fared better, but not much. Even college graduates with one to five years of work experience had to settle for less; men's and women's wages were 8.5 percent and 7.3 percent respectively below those of comparable grads in 1973.[16]

The situation was also getting worse for more established households, such as married couples with children. At the median level for this group, family income grew from $46,476 in 1979 to $48,093 in 1994. In order to achieve this meager 3.5 percent increase in the face of declining wages, these husbands and wives had to work 17 percent more hours in 1994 than they did in 1979.

The Downward Pressure on the Working Class

When Americans refer to the "middle class" they are generally referring to middle-income people who might be more accurately described as "the decently paid portion of the working class." Most of us (90 percent of the population) are wage-earning people who do not have an independent profession or small business (much less a private fortune) and are dependent on steady wages and salaries for our survival and the well-being of our families. The overall downward trends in income affected most wage earners, not just those at the very bottom:

Hourly Wages of Middle-Income Workers[17]

	1979	1989	1994	
30th Percentile	$ 8.11	$ 7.50	$ 7.22	down 11%
50th Percentile	$10.70	$10.30	$ 9.98	down 7%
70th Percentile	$14.56	$14.19	$14.00	down 4%

(The 30th percentile represents the level at which 30% of the population earned less and 70% earned more; the 70th percentile is the level at which 70% earned less and only 30% earned more.)

These wages were modest even in 1979, producing incomes between $15,000 and $30,000 per year. Most families needed two full-time wage-earners working harder than ever if they were going to be close to the median income of $40,611 in 1995. Some didn't have a chance: the wages of the lowest income men fell from $6.80 to $5.49 at the tenth percentile, and from $8.73 to $6.93 at the twentieth percentile; the situation for women was worse, for their wages fell to $4.84 from $5.82 at the tenth percentile and to $5.77 from $6.31 at the twentieth percentile. Male workers were losing the most ground:

18 percent at the twentieth percentile, 12 percent at the sixtieth, and 5 percent at the eightieth (women made some modest gains as gender bias diminished somewhat and new job categories opened up). Even at the high end, at the ninetieth percentile of all workers, where men earned almost $25 per hour, earnings did not go up at all.[18]

What's happening? Are we in the middle of an old-fashioned economic depression?

Not really, but there is ample reason for working people to be confused, discouraged, and, well . . . depressed. Wages have been falling even though labor productivity continues to rise and the workforce is much better educated than it was in the past. Average years of school completed by workers increased from 9.8 years in 1948 to 13.4 years in 1994. Cumulative productivity gains—the growth in the average amount of economic production per hour of work—totaled 25 percent from 1973 to 1995.[19] Since more Americans are now contributing more hours of labor than ever before, hours of work per capita have risen 12 percent in the last thirty years. If American incomes were really linked to the productivity of workers and the extra amount of work time expended—or to any possible combination of skill, education, and effort—median family incomes should have gone up 30 to 35 percent, rather than staying absolutely flat.

Sorting Out the Winners

In fact, overall income did keep growing in the United States over the past two decades—the average family income increased by 12 percent from 1979 to 1994—but all of the gains went to the top 20 percent of families. This was in stark contrast to the three previous decades, 1947 through 1979, when different segments of the population shared equally in exceptional income gains.

Changes in Family Incomes[20]				
	1947–79	Gain or loss per year	1979–94	Gain or loss per year
Bottom Fifth:	+138%	+4.3%	-12%	-0.8%
Second Fifth:	+98%	+3.1%	-10%	-0.7%
Middle Fifth:	+106%	+3.3%	-4%	-0.3%
Fourth Fifth:	+114%	+3.6%	+4%	+0.3%
Top Fifth:	+99%	+3.1%	+31%	+2.1%

It would be misleading, however, to say that most people in the top 20 percent of the population were the big winners in the recent period from 1979 to 1994. After all, the top 20 percent is a very large number of people, over 50 million. More detailed analysis of this group suggests that only the top 1 percent made inordinate gains, while the rest received more reasonable increases in their incomes:

Increases in Income among the Top 20% of American Families[21]				
	1979	1994	% Gain	Gain per year
81st to 90th Percentiles	$72,210	$79,386	10%	+0.7%
91st to 99th Percentiles	$112,476	$141,433	26%	+1.7%
Top 1%	$279,122	$560,090	101%	+6.7%

The gains made by the families between the 81st and 90th percentiles did not quite meet the modest level of overall growth in incomes (12 percent) generated by the American economy, while those in the next 9 percent (91st to 99th percentiles) did better than the average. Only the truly rich, the top 1 percent, made out like bandits. In fact, according to Edward N. Wolff, who calculates the unreported income of the rich more carefully than most other economists, the top 1 percent of households earned considerably more than the amount listed above, which is derived from U.S. census data that regularly understate the amount of property income collected.[22]

Probably only the tax lawyers and accountants know for sure how much income has increased for the very wealthiest individuals. And the job of those accountants is to make pre-tax income look as low as possible. For example, while Wolff calculated that the average income of the top 1 percent was $672,000 in 1992, the average tax return for that group filed with the IRS in 1992 showed reported earnings of only $464,800.[23]

If we assume that the very rich took in roughly the same share of personal income in 1997 as they did in 1992 (a safe bet given the huge gains that were made in the stock market), then their average income was more than $800,000. The following figures illustrate the striking disparities that now exist among the three main income groups:

Average Annual Earnings per Household, 1997[24]	
The Very Rich (the top 1%)	$825,000
The Affluent (the next 9%)	$150,000
The Rest of Us (the bottom 90%)	$35,000

Where Does It Come From?

Did the richest Americans, a little over a million households, really steal income away from the rest of the country?

Not exactly. But most of them certainly did not earn it by the sweat of their brows. Instead, they made money on their capital investments. The 1994 tax returns of 68,064 Americans showed incomes of more than $1 million. They also revealed the following: their ownership of stocks and bonds, other dividend and interest-producing investments, and sale of capital assets provided 38 percent of the income of such people; another 29 percent came via payouts from partnerships and personally held businesses; and finally, 33 percent came from salaries generated by business or professional employment.[25] Employment of the very rich can mean different things to different people; a few are the highest paid corporate CEOs and a small number are highly paid entertainers, including sports stars. However, many other wealthy people draw salaries from businesses they own, even if they don't contribute their labor.

When we note that the incomes of the wealthiest have increased so much faster than those of the rest of the population, it is futile to look for the explanation in changes in the structure of jobs, or in the increased education levels of a particular part of the population. It is not accurate to blame the inadequacies of the American family, as do some apologists for the status quo, for dragging the majority of the population down; nor is there much evidence that those few at the top have achieved their gains by playing according to the rules of a meritocracy.

In effect, wealthy Americans have been appropriating part of the national income, about 10 percent, that used to go to other citizens. And their gain has been spectacular indeed: about $700 billion a year in income that once went to others in the form of higher wages for their labor is now being transferred to the very rich each year.

In the 1990s, there were at least two kinds of big gainers. The most noticeable were the tiny minority made up of the corporate CEOs who run American business. In 1995 they delivered the goods to their corporations—the highest rates of profit ever—and they reaped the benefits. *Business Week* announced in the spring of 1996: "CEO Pay Up 30% at the Fortune 500 Corporations in 1995. Total compensation averages $3,746,392."[26]

In part these men at the top were being rewarded for their efforts to drive down the wages of ordinary Americans. The consequences of such efforts were dramatic. By 1995 the average American factory worker only earned 67 percent of the median family income, far below the 89 percent average of 1955. The worker in retail sales fared even worse, dropping from 57 percent of median family earnings to just 29 percent over forty years. Add the two together and the results are sobering. A working class couple in 1955, one laboring full-time in manufacturing and the other in retail, could do very well. Their combined pay averaged well above—about 146 percent—the median family income. In 1995 the situation was grim: two full-time workers in these same occupations could not even make it to the median.[27]

If the income generated by our growing economy was not rewarding labor, then it had to be multiplying the holdings of capital. The largest income gains in this category, less visible than CEO salaries, were enjoyed by the majority of the rich. Their earnings have almost no relation to their work but directly correlate with their economic assets. In 1996 some of the long-term major stockholders in America's corporations were choosing to cash in on their huge successes in the stock market. Charles Dorrance, who had inherited his wealth through the Campbell soup family, traded in 9 million shares of company stock on Halloween of 1996 and "earned" a treat of $740 million.

Other capitalists sat back and enjoyed the thought of unprecedented, yet-to-be-realized capital gains. For Warren Buffet, the renowned investor, the stock ticker noted that another $10.6 billion was added to his fortune over a period of twenty-four months; his total wealth doubled to $21 billion.[28] He was a beneficiary of the largesse produced by our giant political economy, and his good fortune illustrates why the United States has returned to a level of inequality not seen since 1929. All the gains won by the working classes in the middle of the twentieth century, and sustained through the 1950s, 1960s, and 1970s, have been lost. Is it possible that the 1990s will end up even more unfair than the 1920s?

Notes

1. Edward N. Wolff, *Top Heavy: A Study of the Increasing Inequality of Wealth in America*, New York: The New Press, 1996, and "Trends in Household Wealth in the United States During the 1980s," *Review of Income and Wealth*, June 1994, series 40, no. 2, table 4. Wolff's rigorous studies are based in part on the Surveys of Consumer Finances (SCFs) conducted by the Federal Reserve Board; these, combined with a number of other studies on private fortunes, estate taxes, and inheritances, yield more accurate information than census data. The financial assets compared here come from the analysis of 1992 Federal Reserve statistics made by Wolff *(Top Heavy)* and by James M. Poterba and Andrew A. Samnick ("Stock Ownership Patterns, Stock Market Fluctuations, and Consumption," *Brookings Papers on Economic Activity*, vol. 2 (1995). The 1992 figures were the most recent available as of this writing; most likely they are conservative (that is, showing a smaller share for the very rich) compared with the actual share of financial assets owned in 1997, since the holdings of the rich ought to have been inflated the most by the stock market boom of the mid-1990s.
2. Percentages of each group are based on Wolff, *Top Heavy*, 67; I have modified his categories slightly: he used top 1 percent, next 19 percent, and bottom 80 percent, whereas I use top 1 percent, next 9 percent, and bottom 90 percent; in doing so I am relying on Wolff's more

detailed categories in "Trends in Household Wealth in the United States, 1962–1983 and 1983–1989" (1994), and on Poterba and Samnick, "Stock Ownership Patterns, Stock Market Fluctuations, and Consumption" (1995).

I label the "affluent" as the "next 9 percent" that come after the "very rich," because I think this more accurately depicts the number of upper-middle class Americans who are not truly rich themselves but nevertheless have benefited from the growing disparities of income and wealth.

The figures for the average household wealth in dollars are my own, using the percentages of Wolff, Poterba, and Samnick and applying them to the U.S. economy in 1997 and conservatively reflecting some growth in the stock market and other economic assets. Although the dollar amounts are approximations, they accurately show the immense wealth disparities between each group.

3. Wolff, *Top Heavy*, 64.
4. Maurice Zeitlin, "Who Owns America?" *The Progressive*, June 1978, 5.
5. Lester Thurow, quoted in Andrew Winnick, *Toward Two Societies: The Changing Distribution of Income and Wealth in the U.S. Since 1960*, New York: Praeger, 1989, 184–85.
6. G. William Domhoff, *Who Rules America Now?* Englewood Cliffs, N.J.: Prentice-Hall, 1983.
7. Wolff, "Trends in Household Wealth in the United States During the 1980s," *Review of Income and Wealth*, June 1994, series 40, no. 2, 171.
8. Ibid., 153. In 1989, the share of financial wealth held by the very rich was 48.3 percent, as opposed to the slightly lower figure for 1992, 46 percent. The 1992 number was generated at the end of an economic downturn when some sources of wealth—real estate values, business assets, interest-bearing accounts—declined in value temporarily. The stock market boom of the mid-1990s pushed the financial assets of the rich back up; by 1997 it would be safe to assume that those assets were equal to or greater than the 48.3 percent share the wealthy held in 1989. In any case, the lower 1992 figure is quite sufficient to demonstrate the overwhelming inequality that exists in the United States.
9. Ibid.
10. Lawrence Mishel and Jared Bernstein, *The State of Working America*, Armonk, N.Y.: M. E. Sharpe, 1994, 248.
11. Poterba and Samnick, "Stock Ownership Patterns," 326.
12. Andrew Hacker, *Money: Who Has How Much and Why*, New York: Scribner, 1997, 73.
13. Wolff, *Top Heavy*, 78–96; and Ravi Batra, *The Great American Deception*, New York: Wiley, 1997, 172.
14. Batra, *The Great American Deception*, 9.
15. Lawrence Mishel, Jared Bernstein, and John Schmitt, "The State of American Workers," *Challenge*, November–December 1996, 41. The median refers to the family that is exactly halfway, at the 50th percentile, between the very top and the very bottom. Because all the overall income gains in the past twenty years have gone to the top, it is possible for the median to stay stagnant even though the average of all household incomes has increased by 12 percent.
16. Mishel, Bernstein, and Schmitt, 1997, 176.
17. Jared Bernstein, "Anxiety Over Wages Is Justified," *Challenge*, July-August 1996, 60. Since 1994 there has been no appreciable change in wages, according to the government statistics issued in *Economic Indicators*; this was in spite of the fact that the United States was in a period of cyclical economic upturn, a time when workers used to make substantial gains in earnings.
18. Mishel, Bernstein, and Schmitt, 1997, 143–44.
19. Mishel, Bernstein, and Schmitt, 1997, 33.
20. Campaign for America's Future, "Here We Go Again," *The Nation*, September 2, 1996, 18–19. Numbers are based on analysis by Mishel, Bernstein, and Schmitt in *The State of Working America*, 1997.
21. Derived from Mishel, Bernstein, and Schmitt, *The State of Working America*, 1997, 60–61. The reader will find no better data and analysis on income change and the reasons for falling wages and salaries than this study provides; the authors update the book every two years.
22. Wolff, *Top Heavy*, 1996.
23. Donald L. Barlett and James B. Steele, *America: Who Stole the Dream?* Kansas City: Andrews and McMeel, 1996, 6.

24. These are my approximations, which apply to the total personal income for 1997, and based on the proportions calculated by Wolff for 1992. Since in-depth analysis of incomes in the mid-to-late 1990s is not yet available, it is possible that my estimates are off by a few thousand dollars; however, the numbers should accurately portray the astounding disparities in incomes that separate the three groups. If anything they will underestimate the huge gains made by the richest citizens through the financial speculation that was rampant between 1993 and 1997.

25. Andrew Hacker, *Money: Who Has How Much and Why*, New York: Scribner's, 1997, 82.

26. "How High Can CEO Pay Go?," *Business Week*, April 22, 1996, 101.

27. Barlett and Steele, *America: Who Stole the Dream?* 123.

28. *New York Times*, August 18, 1996, Business section, 2, and *Forbes*, October 1997.

74

Who Owns How Much?

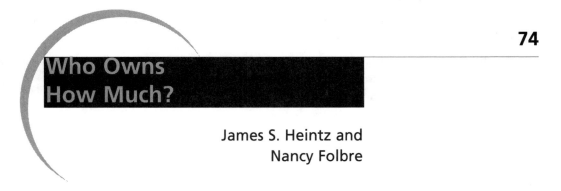

James S. Heintz and Nancy Folbre

"The rich are different from you and me," said F. Scott Fitzgerald. "Yes," replied Ernest Hemingway. "They have more money." More specifically, they have more wealth, an accumulation of money and other assets.

In the U.S., a small fraction of the people control most of the wealth. In 1997, the richest one-tenth of households owned 83 percent of the country's financial assets. The bottom four-fifths owned only 8 percent.

It's nice to be wealthy. Income arrives whether or not you work. A nice cushion protects you from the ups and downs of the business cycle. If we were to sketch a portrait of the richest households in America, what would it look like? In 1995, of the top 1 percent of wealth-holders, 95 percent were white, 72 percent were between the ages of forty-five and seventy-four, 88 percent reported good to excellent health, and about 70 percent had been to college.

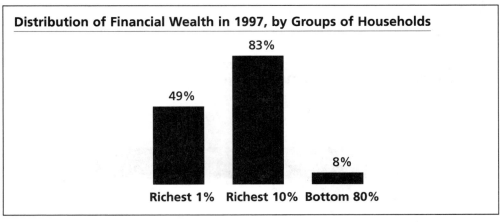

Distribution of Financial Wealth in 1997, by Groups of Households

Richest 1%: 49% Richest 10%: 83% Bottom 80%: 8%

What the Wealthy Own

It's not *if* you own, it's *how much* you own. While 41 percent of all households held some stock in 1995, most didn't have very much. The richest 10 percent of households controlled 88 percent of all stocks, 92 percent of business equity, and 90 percent of financial securities.

The fact that stock ownership has recently become more common doesn't mean that financial wealth is distributed more evenly. Most of the wealth of the middle-class is concentrated in houses and cars. The relatively small amount of stocks they own are often held indirectly in retirement and mutual funds.

Home ownership provides many families with some wealth; however, large mortgages reduce the net amount people actually own. In 1983, mortgage debt comprised 21 percent of the value of an average home, but jumped up to 36 percent by 1995.

Distribution of Wealth in 1995, by Households

The richest 1 percent held:
      51 percent of all stocks and mutual funds
      70 percent of all business equity
      66 percent of all financial securities

The richest 10 percent held:
      88 percent of all stocks and mutual funds
      92 percent of all business equity
      90 percent of all financial securities

The Color of Wealth

If a Ford Escort represents the average financial wealth of an African-American household, you would need a stretch limousine three hundred yards long to show the average for a white household. In fact, for many African Americans, net wealth is negative; people owe more than they own.

In times of stress, wealth makes a crucial difference. A sudden loss of income because of job loss, illness, or family breakup can mean poverty. When things get tough, white households use their wealth to keep their heads above water. With far fewer reserves, African-American families are more likely to go under.

Wealth passed from generation to generation explains much of this disparity. In 1995, 24 percent of white households reported that they had received inheritances at some time: the average value was $115,000. Only 11 percent of African Americans had received inheritances, averaging $32,000.

Median Financial Wealth of Households in 1995

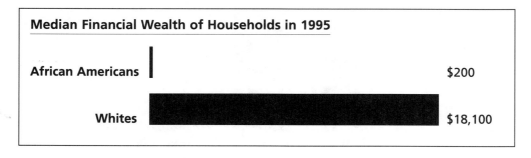

African Americans $200

Whites $18,100

Scraping By

Many people live from paycheck to paycheck, year after year, without much to show for it. When income flows just cover the basic costs of living, building up even small amounts of wealth becomes impossible.

In 1997, the one-fifth of households with the smallest earnings scraped by with an average income of just $8,872. On the other side of the tracks, the top one-fifth enjoyed an average of $122,764. Things aren't getting any more equal. Between 1990 and 1997, income at the bottom virtually stagnated while the top one-fifth of earners got a 15 percent boost.

Income and wealth are related in two ways. People with high incomes can accumulate wealth, and those with wealth get income from the assets they own. But for most people outside this elite circle, income is just a means of surviving.

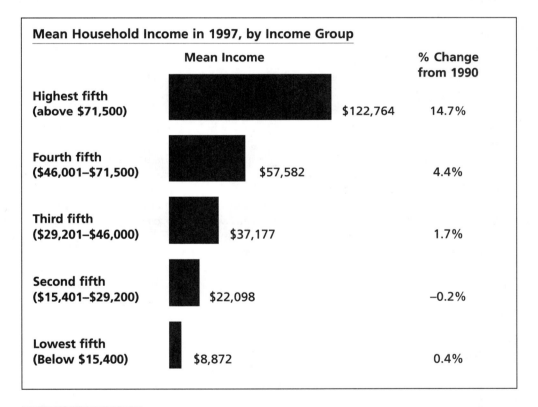

Mean Household Income in 1997, by Income Group

	Mean Income	% Change from 1990
Highest fifth (above $71,500)	$122,764	14.7%
Fourth fifth ($46,001–$71,500)	$57,582	4.4%
Third fifth ($29,201–$46,000)	$37,177	1.7%
Second fifth ($15,401–$29,200)	$22,098	–0.2%
Lowest fifth (Below $15,400)	$8,872	0.4%

Skimpy Paychecks

Paying rent and buying groceries chews up more of a weekly paycheck than it did in the past. While many people have compensated for low hourly earnings by working more, median weekly earnings of full-time workers have deteriorated since the 1970s.

Earnings can be measured in a variety of ways, but the take-home message remains pretty much the same. Both average hourly wages and weekly earnings are lower today than in 1973. Also, racial and ethnic differences in earnings have become more extreme in recent years.

The U.S. Census Bureau did not publish distinct statistics on African-Americans and Latinos until 1979, making long-term comparisons difficult. But people of color narrowed the pay gap with whites between 1970 and 1978. After 1979, that gap increased.

Median Weekly Earnings of Full-Time Workers, 1970–97 ($1997)

Jobless in 1998

There's an old saying: if your neighbor can't find a job, the economy is suffering a recession, but if *you're* the one who can't find a job, it's a depression.

Some groups experience permanent depression. In 1998, the unemployment rate for whites reached a historically low 3.9 percent. African-Americans were more than twice as likely to be unemployed, at a rate of 9.1 percent.

Teen-agers are particularly vulnerable with an unemployment rate of 14.6 percent. Even for those aged twenty to twenty-four, the rate was far above average.

Being out of work is hard on people. Studies show that it contributes to problems like alcoholism, child abuse, and mental illness. Unemployment also means the economy is functioning below its potential. Putting more people to work can increase output and growth.

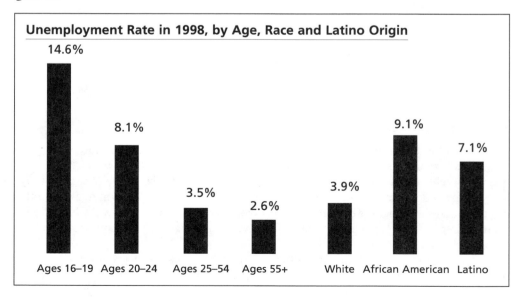

Unemployment Rate in 1998, by Age, Race and Latino Origin

Nice Work if You Can Get It

More women are climbing the professional job ladder. In the 1950s and 1960s, they were often blocked from entering fields such as engineering and medicine. But in the 1970s, a militant women's movement helped open the door. Affirmative action programs were particularly effective at improving women's opportunities to pursue advanced educational degrees.

By 1997, women accounted for 9 percent of all engineers, 28 percent of all lawyers and judges, 45 percent of all managers, and 23 percent of all doctors. While this trend strengthened the women's movement, putting more women into positions of power, it also intensified the divisive impact of class and race differences among women. Nice work if you can get it, but it helps to come from a family that can help pay the bills for college and graduate school.

Women in Professions, as a Percentage of Total in Those Occupations

	1960	1970	1980	1990	1990
Engineers	1%	2%	5%	8%	11%
Lawyers and Judges	3%	5%	14%	19%	30%
Managers	15%	18%	30%	41%	45%
Doctors	6%	8%	12%	18%	24%

The Demand for Child Care

Mothers in our society are now expected to work for pay. They are not eligible for public assistance unless they do. But good child care is hard to find and expensive. In dual-earner families, spouses help one another out. Even among this group, however, child care centers and other forms of non-relative care are indispensable.

Half of American parents with young children earn less than $35,000 per year. Yet unsubsidized child care costs between $4,000 and $10,000 annually for a single child. Many low-income working families cannot find subsidized care. New York state, for instance, provides subsidies to only one in ten eligible children. Some states, like Georgia and California, are moving toward public provision of preschool education of four and five-year olds.

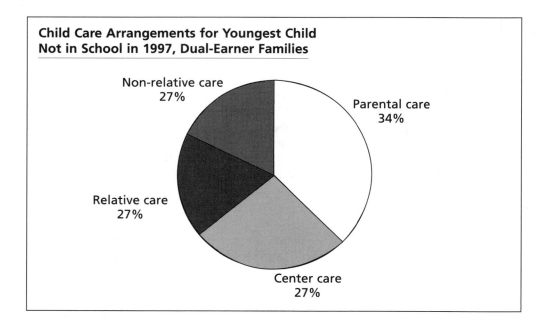

Child Care Arrangements for Youngest Child Not in School in 1997, Dual-Earner Families

- Non-relative care 27%
- Parental care 34%
- Relative care 27%
- Center care 27%

Family Policies in Europe

The parental leave and child care benefits given to working families in the United States are the least generous in the industrialized world.

- About 80 percent of (industrialized) countries offer paid maternity leave to women workers. Canada gives seventeen weeks. In the U.S., all we have is the Family and Medical Leave Act of 1993, which permits up to twelve weeks of unpaid leave.

- In Sweden, parental leaves can be shared or used by one parent, but one nontransferable month is reserved for the father and one for the mother, to encourage sharing. During their child's first year, more than one-half of fathers use some leave. Fathers use nearly one-third of all paid temporary leave to stay home and care for sick children under twelve.

- Family allowances (regular payments to help support children) are offered by most countries of Western Europe. The U.S. allows parents to deduct money from their taxable income for children as dependents. But the value of this deduction as a percentage of family income has declined over time. Tripling the current deduction would restore the relative value it had in 1948.

75

Tired of Playing Monopoly?

Donna Langston

I. Magnin, Nordstrom, The Bon, Sears, Penneys, Kmart, Goodwill, Salvation Army. If the order of this list of stores makes any sense to you, then we've begun to deal with the first question that inevitably arises in any discussion of class here in the United States—huh? Unlike our European allies, we in the United States are reluctant to recognize class differences. This denial of class divisions functions to reinforce ruling-class control and domination. America is, after all, the supposed land of equal opportunity where, if you just work hard enough, you can get ahead, pull yourself up by your bootstraps. What the old bootstraps theory overlooks is that some were born with silver shoe horns. Female-headed households, communities of color, the elderly, the disabled, and children find themselves disproportionately living in poverty. If hard work were the sole determinant of your ability to support yourself and your family, surely we'd have a different outcome for many in our society. We also, however, believe in luck and, on closer examination, it certainly is quite a coincidence that the "unlucky" come from certain race, gender, and class backgrounds. In order to perpetuate racist, sexist, and classist outcomes, we also have to believe that the current economic distribution is unchangeable, has always existed, and probably exists in this form throughout the known universe, that it's "natural." Some people explain or try to account for poverty or class position by focusing on the personal and moral merits of an individual. If people are poor, then it's something they did or didn't do: they were lazy, unlucky, didn't try hard enough, and so on. This has the familiar ring of blaming the victims. Alternative explanations focus on the ways in which poverty and class position are due to structural, systematic, institutionalized economic and political power relations. These power relations are based firmly on dynamics such as race, gender, and class.

In the myth of the classless society, ambition and intelligence alone are responsible for success. The myth conceals the existence of a class society, which serves many functions. One of the main ways it keeps the working-class and poor locked into a class-based system in a position of servitude is by cruelly creating false hope. It perpetuates the false hope among the working-class and poor that they can have different opportunities in life, the hope that they can escape the fate that awaits them due to the class position they were born into. Another way the rags-to-riches myth is perpetuated is by creating enough visible tokens so that oppressed persons believe they, too, can get ahead. The creation of hope through tokenism keeps a hierarchical structure in place and lays the blame for not succeeding on those who don't. This keeps us from resisting and changing the class-based system. Instead, we accept it as inevitable, something we just have to live with. If oppressed people believe in equality of opportunity, then they won't develop class consciousness and will <u>internalize the blame</u> for their economic position. If the working-class and poor do not recognize the way false hope is used to control them, they won't get a chance to control their lives by acknowledging their class position, by claiming that identity and taking action as a group.

The myth also keeps the middle and upper classes entrenched in the privileges awarded in a class-based system. It reinforces <u>middle- and upper-class beliefs</u> in their <u>own superiority</u>. If we believe that anyone in society really can get ahead, then middle- and upper-class status and privileges must be deserved, due to personal merits, and enjoyed—and defended at all costs. According to this viewpoint, <u>poverty is regrettable but acceptable</u>, just the outcome of a fair game: "There have always been poor people, and there always will be."

Class is more than just the amount of money you have; it's also the presence of <u>economic security</u>. For the working class and poor, working and eating are matters of survival, not taste. However, while one's class status can be defined in important ways in terms of monetary income, class is also a whole lot more—specifically, class is also culture. As a result of the class you are born into and raised in, <u>class is your understanding of the world</u> and where you fit in; it's composed of ideas, behavior, attitudes, values, and language; class is how you think, feel, act, look, dress, talk, move, walk; class is what stores you shop at, restaurants you eat in; class is the schools you attend, the education you attain; class is the very jobs you will work at throughout your adult life. Class even determines when we marry and become mothers. Working-class women become mothers long before middle-class women receive their bachelor's degrees. We experience class at every level of our lives; class is who our friends are, where we live and work, even what kind of car we drive, if we own one, and what kind of health care we receive, if any. Have I left anything out? In other words, class is socially constructed and all-encompassing. When we experience classism, it will be because of our lack of money (i.e., choices and power in this society) and because of the way we talk, think, act, or move—because of our culture.

<u>Class affects what we perceive</u>—and <u>what we have available to us</u>—as choices. Upon graduation from high school, I was awarded a scholarship to attend any college, private or public, in the state of California. Yet it never occurred to me or my family that it made any difference which college you went to. I ended up just going to a small college in my town. It never would have occurred to me to move away from my family for school, because no one ever had and no one would. I was the first person in my family to go to college. I had to figure out from reading college catalogs how to apply—no one in my family could have sat down and said, "Well, you take this test and then you really should think about. . . ." Although tests and high school performance had shown I had the ability to pick up white middle-class lingo, I still had quite an adjustment to make—it was lonely and isolating in college. I lost my friends from high school—they were at the community college, vocational/technical school, working, or married. I lasted a year and a half in this foreign environment before I quit college, married a factory worker, had a baby and resumed living in a community I knew. One middle-class friend in college had asked if I'd like to travel to Europe with her. Her father was a college professor and people in her family had actually traveled there. My family had seldom been able to take a vacation at all. A couple of times my parents were able—by saving all year—to take the family over to the coast on their annual two-week vacation. I'd seen the time and energy my parents invested in trying to take a family vacation to some place a few hours away; how anybody ever got to Europe was beyond me. . . .

Contrary to our stereotype of the working class—white guys in overalls—it is not homogeneous in terms of race or gender. If you are a person of color, if you live in a female-headed household, you are much more likely to be working-class or poor. The experience of Black, Latino, American Indian or Asian American working classes will differ significantly from the white working classes, which have traditionally been able to rely on white privilege to provide a more elite position within their class. Working-class people are often grouped together and stereotyped, but distinctions can be made among the working-class, working-poor and poor. Many working-class families are supported by unionized workers who possess marketable skills. Most working-poor families are supported by non-unionized, unskilled men and women. Many poor families are dependent on welfare for their income.

Attacks on the welfare system and those who live on welfare are a good example of classism in action. We have a "dual welfare" system in this country whereby welfare for the rich in the form of tax-free capital gain, guaranteed loans, oil depletion allowances, and so on, is not recognized as welfare. Almost everyone in America is on some type of welfare, but if you're rich, it's in the form of tax deductions for "business" meals and entertainment, and if you're poor, it's in the form of food stamps. The difference is the stigma and humiliation connected to welfare for the poor, as compared to welfare for the rich, which is called "incentive." Ninety-three percent of AFDC (Aid to Families with Dependent Children, our traditional concept of welfare) recipients are women and children. Eighty percent of food stamp recipients are single mothers, children, the elderly, and the disabled. Average AFDC payments are ninety-three dollars per person per month. Payments are so low nationwide that in only three states do AFDC benefits plus food stamps bring a household *up to* the poverty level. Food stamp benefits average ten dollars per person per week. A common focal point for complaints about "welfare" is the belief that most welfare recipients are cheaters—goodness knows there are no middle-class income tax cheaters out there. Imagine focusing the same anger and energy on the way corporations and big business cheat on their tax revenues. Now, there would be some dollars worth quibbling about. The "dual welfare" system also assigns a different degree of stigma to programs that benefit women and children, such as AFDC, and programs whose recipients are primarily male, such as those of veterans' benefits. The implicit assumption is that mothers who raise children do not work and therefore are not deserving of their daily bread crumbs.

Anti-union attitudes are another prime example of classism in action. At best, unions have been a very progressive force for workers, women, and people of color. At worst, unions have reflected the same regressive attitudes which are out there in other social structures: classism, racism, and sexism. Classism exists within the working class. The aristocracy of the working class—unionized, skilled workers—have mainly been white and male and have viewed themselves as being better than unskilled workers, the unemployed and poor who are mostly women and people of color. The white working class must commit itself to a cultural and ideological transformation of racist attitudes. The history of working people, and the ways we've resisted many types of oppressions, are not something we're taught in school. Missing from our education is information about workers and their resistance.

Working-class women's critiques have focused on the following issues:

Education. White middle-class professionals have used academic jargon to rationalize and justify classism. The whole structure of education is a classist system. Schools in every town reflect class divisions. Like the store list at the beginning of this article, you can list schools in your town by what classes of kids attend, and in most cities you can also list by race. The classist system is perpetuated in schools with the tracking system, whereby the "dumbs" are tracked into homemaking, shop courses and vocational school futures while the "smarts" end up in advanced math, science, literature, and college-prep courses. If we examine these groups carefully, the coincidence of poor and working-class backgrounds with "dumbs" is rather alarming. The standard measurement of supposed intelligence is white, middle-class English. If you're other than white and middle-class, you have to become bilingual to succeed in the educational system. If you're white middle-class, you only need the language and writing skills you were raised with, since they're the standard. To do well in society presupposes middle-class background, experiences, and learning for everyone. The tracking system separates those from the working class who can potentially assimilate to the middle class from all our friends, and labels us "college bound."

After high school, you go on to vocational school, community college, or college—public or private—according to your class position. Apart from the few who break into middle-class schools, the classist stereotyping of the working class as being dumb and inarticulate tracks most into vocational schools and low-skilled jobs. A few of us are allowed to slip through to reinforce the idea that equal opportunity exists. But for most, class position is destiny—determining our educational attainment and employment. Since we must overall abide by middle-class rules to succeed, the assumption is that we go to college in order to "better ourselves"—to become more like "them." I suppose it's assumed we have "yuppie envy" and desire nothing more than to be upwardly mobile individuals; it's assumed that we want to fit into "their" world. But many of us remain connected to our communities and families. Becoming college-educated doesn't mean we have to, or want to, erase our first and natural language and value system. It's important for many of us to remain in and return to our communities to work, live, and stay sane.

Jobs. Middle-class people have the privilege of choosing careers. They can decide which jobs they want, according to their moral or political commitments, needs for challenge, or creativity. This is a privilege denied the working-class and poor, whose work is a means of survival, not choice. Working-class women have seldom had the luxury of choosing between work in the home or market. We've generally done both, with little ability to purchase services to help with this double burden. Middle- and upper-class women can often hire other women to clean their houses, take care of their children, and cook their meals. Guess what class and race those "other" women are? Working a double or triple day is common for working-class women. Only middle-class women have an array of choices such as: parents put you through school, then you choose a career, then you choose when and if to have babies, then you choose a support system of working-class women to take care of your kids and house if you choose to resume your career. After the birth of my second child, I was working two part-time jobs—one loading trucks at night—and going to school during the days. While I was quite privileged because I could take my colicky infant with me to classes and the day-time job, I was in a state of continuous semiconsciousness. I had to work to support my family; the only choice I had was between school or sleep. Sleep became a privilege. A white middle-class feminist instructor at the university suggested to me, quite sympathetically, that I ought to hire someone to clean my house and watch the baby. Her suggestion was totally out of my reality both economically and socially. I'd worked for years cleaning *other* peoples' houses. Hiring a working-class woman to do the shit work is a middle-class woman's solution to any dilemma that privileges such as a career may present her.

Mothering. The feminist critique of families and the oppressive role of mothering has focused on white middle-class nuclear families. This may not be an appropriate model for communities of class and color. Mothering and families may hold a different importance for working-class women. Within this context, the issue of coming out can be a very painful process for working-class lesbians. . . .

Individualism. Preoccupation with one's self—one's body, looks, relationships—is a luxury working-class women can't afford. Making an occupation out of taking care of yourself through therapy, aerobics, jogging, dressing for success, gourmet meals and proper nutrition, and the like, may be responses that are directly rooted in privilege. The middle-class have the leisure time to be preoccupied with their own problems, such as their waistlines, planning their vacations, coordinating their wardrobes, or dealing with what their mother said to them when they were five—my! . . .

Women who have backgrounds other than the white middle-class often experience compounded, simultaneous oppressions. We can't so easily separate our experiences by categories of gender, or race, or class: "I remember it well: on Saturday, June 3, I was experiencing class oppression, but by Tuesday, June 6, I was caught up in race oppression, then all day Friday, June 9, I was in the middle of gender oppression. What a week!" Sometimes, for example, gender and class reinforce each other. When I returned to college as a single parent after a few years of having kids and working crummy jobs, I went in for vocational testing. Even before I was tested, the white middle-class male vocational counselor looked at me, a welfare mother in my best selection from the Salvation Army racks, and suggested I quit college, go to vocational/technical school and become a *grocery clerk*; this was probably the highest paying female working-class occupation he could think of. The vocational test results suggested I become an attorney. I did end up quitting college once again, not because of his suggestion, but because I was tired of supporting my children in ungenteel poverty. I entered vocational/technical school for training as an electrician and, as one of the first women in a nontraditional field, was able to earn a living wage at a job that had traditionally been reserved for white working-class males. But this is a story for another day. Let's return to our little vocational counselor example: Was he suggesting the occupational choice of grocery clerk to me because of my gender, or my class? Probably both. . . .

How to Challenge Classism

If you're middle-class you can begin to challenge classism with the following:

1. Confront classist behavior in yourself, others and society. Use and share the privileges, like time or money, that you do have.

2. Make demands on working-class and poor communities' issues—anti-racism, poverty, unions, public housing, public transportation, literacy and day care.

3. Learn from the skills and strength of working people—study working and poor people's history; take some labor studies, ethnic studies, women studies classes. Challenge elitism. There are many different types of intelligence, white, middle-class, academic, professional intellectualism being one of them (reportedly). Finally, educate yourself, take responsibility and take action.

If you're working-class, here are some general suggestions. They're cheaper than therapy—(free, less time-consuming, and I won't ask you about what your mother said to you when you were five):

1. Face your racism! Educate yourself and others, your family, community, any organizations you belong to; take responsibility and take action. Face your classism, sexism, heterosexism, ageism, ableism, adultism. . . .

2. Claim your identity. Learn all you can about your history and the history and experience of all working and poor peoples. Raise your children to be anti-racist, anti-sexist and anti-classist. Teach them the language and culture of working peoples. Learn to survive with a fair amount of anger and lots of humor, which can be tough when this stuff isn't even funny.

3. Work on issues that will benefit your community. Consider remaining in or returning to your communities. If you live and work in white middle-class environments,

look for working-class allies to help you survive with your humor and wits intact. How do working-class people spot each other? We have antenna.

We need not deny or erase the differences of working-class cultures but can embrace their richness, their variety, their moral and intellectual heritage. We're not at the point yet where we can celebrate differences—not having money for a prescription for your child is nothing to celebrate. It's not time yet to party with the white middle class, because we'd be the entertainment ("Aren't they quaint? Just *love* their workboots and uniforms and the way they cuss!"). We need to overcome divisions among working people, not by ignoring the multiple oppressions many of us encounter, or by oppressing each other, but by becoming committed allies on all issues that affect working people: racism, sexism, classism, and so on. An injury to one is an injury to all. Don't play by ruling-class rules, hoping that maybe you can live on Connecticut Avenue instead of Baltic, or that you as an individual can make it to Park Place and Boardwalk. Tired of Monopoly? Always ending up on Mediterranean Avenue? How about changing the game?

76

A Sociology of Wealth and Racial Inequality

Melvin L. Oliver and
Thomas M. Shapiro

Each year two highly publicized news reports capture the attention and imagination of Americans. One lists the year's highest income earners. Predictably, they include glamorous and highly publicized entertainment, sport, and business personalities. For the past decade that list has included many African Americans: musical artists such as Michael Jackson, entertainers such as Bill Cosby and Oprah Winfrey, and sports figures such as Michael Jordan and Magic Johnson. During the recent past as many as half of the "top ten" in this highly exclusive rank have been African Americans.

Another highly publicized list, by contrast, documents the nation's wealthiest Americans. The famous *Forbes* magazine profile of the nation's wealthiest four hundred focuses not on income, but on wealth. This list includes those people whose assets—or command over monetary resources—place them at the top of the American economic hierarchy. Even though this group is often ten times larger than the top earners list, it contains few if any African Americans. An examination of these two lists creates two very different perceptions of the well-being of America's black community on the eve of the twenty-first century. The large number of blacks on the top income list generates an optimistic view of how black Americans have progressed economically in American society. The near absence of blacks in the *Forbes* listing, by contrast, presents a much more pessimistic outlook on blacks' economic progress. . . .

The basis of our analysis is the distinction between wealth and other traditional measures of economic status, of how people are "making it" in America (for example, income, occupation, and education). Wealth is a particularly important indicator of individual and family access to life chances. *Income* refers to a flow of money over time, like a rate per hour, week, or year; *wealth* is a stock of assets owned at a particular time. Wealth is what people own, while income is what people receive for work, retirement, or social welfare. Wealth signifies the command over financial resources that a family has accumulated over its lifetime along with those resources that have been inherited across generations. Such resources, when combined with income, can create the opportunity to secure the "good life" in whatever form is needed—education, business, training, justice, health, comfort, and so on. Wealth is a special form of money not used to purchase milk and shoes and other life necessities. More often it is used to create opportunities, secure a desired stature and standard of living, or pass class status along to one's children. In this sense the command over resources that wealth entails is more encompassing than is income or education, and closer in meaning and theoretical significance to our traditional notions of economic well-being and access to life chances.

More important, wealth taps not only contemporary resources but material assets that have historic origins. Private wealth thus captures inequality that is the product of the past, often passed down from generation to generation. Given this attribute, in attempting to understand the economic status of blacks, a focus on wealth helps us avoid the either/or view of a march toward progress or a trail of despair. Conceptualizing racial inequality through wealth revolutionizes our conception of its nature and magnitude, and of whether it is declining or increasing. While most recent analyses have concluded that contemporary class-based factors are most important in understanding the sources of continuing racial inequality, our focus on wealth sheds light on both the historical and the contemporary impacts not only of class but of race. . . .

We develop three concepts to provide a sociologically grounded approach to understanding racial differentials in wealth accumulation. These concepts highlight the ways in which this opportunity structure has disadvantaged blacks and helped contribute to massive wealth inequalities between the races.

1. Our first concept, *racialization of state policy*, refers to how state policy has impaired the ability of many black Americans to accumulate wealth—and discouraged them from doing so—from the beginning of slavery throughout American history. From the first codified decision to enslave African Americans, to the local ordinances that barred blacks from certain occupations, to the welfare state policies of today that discourage wealth accumulation, the state has erected major barriers to black economic self-sufficiency. In particular, state policy has structured the context within which it has been possible to acquire land, build community, and generate wealth. Historically, policies and actions of the United States government have promoted homesteading, land acquisition, home ownership, retirement, pensions, education, and asset accumulation for some sectors of the population and not for others. Poor people—blacks in particular—generally have been excluded from participation in these state-sponsored opportunities. In this way, the distinctive relationship between whites and blacks has been woven into the fabric of state actions. The modern welfare state has racialized citizenship, social organization, and economic status while consigning blacks to a relentlessly impoverished and subordinate position within it.

2. Our second focus, on the *economic detour*, helps us understand the relatively low level of entrepreneurship among, and the small scale of the businesses owned by, black Americans. While blacks have historically sought out opportunities for self-employment, they have traditionally faced an environment, especially from the postbellum period to the middle of the twentieth century, in which they were restricted by law from participation in business in the open market. Explicit state and local policies restricted the rights of blacks as free economic agents. These policies had a devastating impact on the ability

of blacks to build and maintain successful enterprises. While blacks were limited to a restricted African American market to which others (for example, whites and other ethnics) also had easy access, they were unable to tap the more lucrative and expansive mainstream white markets. Blacks thus had fewer opportunities to develop successful businesses. When businesses were developed that competed in size and scope with white businesses, intimidation—and ultimately, in some cases, violence—was used to curtail their expansion or get rid of them altogether. The lack of important assets and indigenous community development has thus played a crucial role in limiting the wealth-accumulating ability of African Americans.

The third concept we develop is synthetic in nature. The notion embodied in the _sedimentation of racial inequality_ is that in central ways the cumulative effects of the past have seemingly cemented blacks to the bottom of society's economic hierarchy. A history of low wages, poor schooling, and segregation affected not one or two generations of blacks but practically all African Americans well into the middle of the twentieth century. Our argument is that the best indicator of the sedimentation of racial inequality is wealth. Wealth is one indicator of material disparity that captures the historical legacy of low wages, personal and organizational discrimination, and institutionalized racism. The low levels of wealth accumulation evidenced by current generations of black Americans best represent the economic status of blacks in the American social structure.

To argue that blacks form the sediment of the American stratificational order is to recognize the extent to which they began at the bottom of the hierarchy during slavery, and the cumulative and reinforcing effects of Jim Crow and de facto segregation through the mid-twentieth century. Generation after generation of blacks remained anchored to the lowest economic status in American society. The effect of this inherited poverty and economic scarcity for the accumulation of wealth has been to "sediment" inequality into the social structure. The sedimentation of inequality occurred because the investment opportunity that blacks faced worked against their quest for material self-sufficiency. In contrast, whites in general, but well-off whites in particular, were able to amass assets and use their secure financial status to pass their wealth from generation to generation. What is often not acknowledged is that the same social system that fosters the accumulation of private wealth for many whites denies it to blacks, thus forging an intimate connection between white wealth accumulation and black poverty. Just as blacks have had "cumulative disadvantages," many whites have had "cumulative advantages." Since wealth builds over a lifetime and is then passed along to kin, it is, from our perspective, an essential indicator of black economic well-being. By focusing on wealth we discover how black's socioeconomic status results from a socially layered accumulation of disadvantages passed on from generation to generation. In this sense we uncover a racial wealth tax. . . .

Kevin, a seventy-five-year-old retired homeowner interviewed for this study, captures the dilemma of unearned inheritance, saying, "You heard that saying about the guy with a rich father? The kid goes through life thinking that he hit a triple. But really he was born on third base. He didn't hit no triple at all, but he'll go around telling everyone he banged the fucking ball and it was a triple. He was born there!"

Inherited wealth is a very special kind of money imbued with the shadows of race. Racial difference in inheritance is a key feature of our story. For the most part, blacks will not partake in divvying up the baby boom bounty. America's racist legacy is shutting them out. The grandparents and parents of blacks under the age of forty toiled under segregation, where education and access to decent jobs and wages were severely restricted. Racialized state policy and the economic detour constrained their ability to enter the post–World War II housing market. Segregation created an extreme situation in which earlier generations were unable to build up much, if any, wealth. We see how the average black family headed by a person over the age of sixty-five has no net financial assets to pass down to its children. Until the late 1960s there were few older African Americans with the ability to save much at all, much less invest. And no savings and no inheritance meant no wealth.

The most consistent and strongest common theme to emerge in interviews conducted with white and black families was that family assets expand choices, horizons, and opportunities for children while lack of assets limit opportunities. Because parents want to give their children whatever advantages they can, we wondered about the ability of the average American household to expend assets on their children. We found that the lack of private assets intrudes on the dreams that many Americans have for their children. Extreme resource deficiency characterizes several groups. It may surprise some to learn that 62 percent of households headed by single parents are without savings or other financial assets, or that two of every five households without a high school degree lack a financial nest egg. Nearly one-third of all households—and 61 percent of all black households—are without financial resources. These statistics lead to our focus on the most resource-deficient households in our study—African Americans.

We argue that, materially, whites and blacks constitute two nations. One of the analytic centerpieces of this work tells a tale of two middle classes, one white and one black. Most significant, the claim made by blacks to middle-class status depends on income and not assets. In contrast, a wealth pillar supports the white middle class in its drive for middle-class opportunities and a middle-class standard of living. Middle-class blacks, for example, earn seventy cents for every dollar earned by middle-class whites but they possess only fifteen cents for every dollar of wealth held by middle-class whites. For the most part, the economic foundation of the black middle class lacks one of the pillars that provide stability and security to middle-class whites—assets. The black middle class position is precarious and fragile with insubstantial wealth resources. This analysis means it is entirely premature to celebrate the rise of the black middle class. The glass is both half empty and half full, because the wealth data reveal the paradoxical situation in which blacks' wealth has grown while at the same time falling farther behind that of whites.

The social distribution of wealth discloses a fresh and formidable dimension of racial inequality. Blacks' achievement at any given level not only requires that greater effort be expended on fewer opportunities but also bestows substantially diminished rewards. Examining blacks and whites who share similar socioeconomic characteristics brings to light persistent and vast wealth discrepancies. Take education as one prime example: the most equality we found was among the college educated, but even here at the pinnacle of achievement whites control four times as much wealth as blacks with the same degrees. This predicament manifests a disturbing break in the link between achievement and results that is essential for democracy and social equality.

The central question of this study is, Why do the wealth portfolios of blacks and whites vary so drastically? The answer is not simply that blacks have inferior remunerable human capital endowments—substandard education, jobs, and skills, for example—or do not display the characteristics most associated with higher income and wealth. We are able to demonstrate that even when blacks and whites display similar characteristics—for example, are on a par educationally and occupationally—a potent difference of $43,143 in home equity and financial assets still remains. Likewise, giving the average black household the same attributes as the average white household leaves a $25,794 racial gap in financial assets alone.

The extent of discrimination in institutions and social policy provides a persuasive index of bias that undergirds the drastic differences between blacks and whites. We show that skewed access to mortgage and housing markets and the racial valuing of neighborhoods on the basis of segregated markets result in enormous racial wealth disparity.

Banks turn down qualified blacks much more often for home loans than they do similarly qualified whites. Blacks who do qualify, moreover, pay higher interest rates on home mortgages than whites. Residential segregation persists into the 1990s, and we found that the great rise in housing values is color-coded. Why should the mean value of the average white home appreciate at a dramatically higher rate than the average black home? Home ownership is without question the single most important means of accumulating assets. The lower values of black homes adversely affect the ability of blacks to utilize their residences as collateral for obtaining personal, business, or educational loans. We estimate that institutional biases in the residential arena have cost the current generation of blacks about $82 billion. Passing inequality along from one generation to the next casts another racially stratified shadow on the making of American inequality. Institutional discrimination in housing and lending markets extends into the future the effects of historical discrimination within other institutions.

Placing these findings in the larger context of public policy discussions about racial and social justice adds new dimensions to these discussions. A focus on wealth changes our thinking about racial inequality. The more one learns about wealth differences, the more mistaken current policies appear. To take these findings seriously, as we do, means not shirking the responsibility of seeking alternative policy ideas with which to address issues of inequality. We might even need to think about social justice in new ways. In some key respects our analysis of disparities in wealth between blacks and whites forms an agenda for the future, the key principle of which is to link opportunity structures to policies promoting asset formation that begin to close the racial wealth gap.

Closing the racial gap means that we have to target policies at two levels. First, we need policies that directly address the situations of African Americans. Such policies are necessary to speak to the historically generated disadvantages and the current racially based policies that have limited the ability of blacks, as a group, to accumulate wealth resources.

Second, we need policies that directly promote asset opportunities for those on the bottom of the social structure, both black and white, who are locked out of the wealth accumulation process. More generally, our analysis clearly suggests the need for massive redistributional policies in order to reforge the links between achievement, reward, social equality, and democracy. These policies must take aim at the gross inequality generated by those at the very top of the wealth distribution. Policies of this type are the most difficult ones on which to gain consensus but the most important in creating a more just society.

77

Racism or Solidarity? Unions and Asian Immigrant Workers

Glenn Omatsu

At labor rallies, I have heard workers —White, Black, and sometimes Latino—tell moving stories about the central place of unions in their lives. I have heard stories about parents and grandparents who organized strikes, walked picket lines, and carried out sympathy strikes to help other workers. I have heard stories about hardships, sacrifices, and community solidarity—all on behalf of unions.

I have no such stories to tell.

My grandparents never joined unions. They—like thousands of other immigrants from Asia—came to California in the early twentieth century. They worked hard all their lives: as farm laborers and later as tenant farmers. My parents also worked hard all their lives. My father toiled in the produce industry and various small factories. My mother took all the standard jobs of Asian American women: farm laborer, domestic worker, and office clerk. My father never joined a union and my mother became our family's first union member only a few years before her retirement as a Los Angeles County office worker. It was not that my parents and grandparents shunned unions; rather, the unions shunned them. They were not the kind of workers that unions wanted as members. . . .

Racism has always been a pervasive force in American history, and anti-Asian racism has been a defining feature of American labor history. Just as we can only understand American history by knowing about the enslavement of African Americans, so can we only understand the development of American unions by knowing the legacy of racism against Asian Americans.

American unions were built on a foundation of racism. In the late nineteenth century, the American Federation of Labor (AFL) rose to national prominence with its campaign to "protect American jobs" and uphold the "purity of American society" by expelling all Chinese and Japanese immigrants. During the next one hundred years, union leaders—with very few exceptions—united with politicians and other chauvinists to ban all immigration from Asia, to bar remaining immigrants from joining unions, and to lead mobs to beat, and sometimes kill, those who could not be banned, barred, or expelled. Even as recently as World War II, union leaders—again with very few exceptions—agitated for the internment of Japanese Americans.

Historically, then, Asian Americans have been excluded from the mainstream labor movement. But it would be wrong to conclude that because of this exclusion Asian Americans lack a tradition of labor militancy. Like all other racial and ethnic groups in America, Asian Americans have engaged in strikes, organized unions, and created networks of solidarity with other workers. However, because Asian American labor activism emerged against the backdrop of anti-Asian racism and outside the main line of development of American unions, this history is not widely known.

Asian-American History Is a Working-Class History

Asian-American history is essentially a working-class history. Large numbers of Asian immigrants—predominantly men—first came to the United States in the late nineteenth century as a source of cheap labor for agricultural and industrial barons in Hawaii, California, and other areas of the West. Generally, historians describe this immigration in terms of ethnic waves: first the Chinese, then the Japanese, and later the Filipinos. Interspersed were smaller waves of Punjabis and Koreans.

Chinese workers came to Hawaii and the Pacific Coast to toil in the agricultural fields, to build the railroads, and to work in the mines. By the 1870s, the Chinese constituted over one-quarter of the population of San Francisco.

Aside from enduring severe exploitation at their jobs, Chinese laborers and other Asians who followed them faced racist hostility. This racism restricted where they could live and what occupations they could pursue. Thus, the Chinese, who were expelled from several communities throughout California and the Pacific Northwest, congregated in China-towns and worked in sewing factories, in agriculturally-related jobs, and also as laundry-men and seamen. The Japanese concentrated in agriculture as tenant farmers and truck farmers and in produce-related occupations such as retail clerking. The Filipinos worked as migrant farm laborers and in food processing, such as canning factories.

So it was under these conditions that Asian-American labor history developed, under the pressure of white racism—restricting Asian immigrants to certain types of occupations. It developed under the hostility of leaders of American unions, who called for the expulsion of Asians from America. And it developed under the harsh exploitation of employers, who continued to define the Asian worker as in a subhuman category—a source of cheap labor.

Under these difficult conditions, the labor struggles that emerged were truly remarkable. They were struggles with four key themes, and these themes continue to define the kind of labor movements we see in today's Asian American communities:

(1) Due to the racism, Asian-American labor history is characterized by struggles that go beyond workplace demands. Most of these struggles have embraced larger community concerns—issues of justice and equality for Asian peoples throughout America. And most of these struggles have been built around extensive community support networks.

(2) Due to the hostile attitude of American union leaders, Asian American labor history is characterized by struggles initiated by immigrant workers themselves at the grass-roots level. Thus, these struggles have stressed important rank-and-file concerns, such as democratic control of unions and accountability of union leaders.

(3) Due to the immigrant nature of Asian American labor history, many labor struggles have been linked to democratic movements in former homelands. In the late nineteenth and early twentieth centuries, many Asian nations were under foreign domination or military dictatorship. Thus, Asian immigrants often saw their labor movement as part of a broader democratic struggle and raised their workplace demands in the context of fighting for self-determination and liberation for their former homelands.

(4) Despite the hostile attitude of union leaders, Asian-American labor history is characterized by repeated attempts by Asian-American workers to unite with American unions. Immigrant workers have consistently put forward strategies for cross-racial alliances.

To more fully explain these themes, I will focus on five examples: the historic Oxnard sugar beet strike in 1903; labor organizing during the 1930s in San Francisco's Chinatown; union reform efforts in Seattle in the early 1970s; efforts to unionize California farmworkers, and the militancy of Asian women garment workers in the San Francisco Bay Area.

The Oxnard Sugar Beet Strike of 1903

In Oxnard, California, in 1903, some two thousand immigrant Japanese and Mexican sugar beet workers joined in solidarity in a strike for higher wages and union recognition. The strike, lasting several months, challenged the growing power of agribusiness in California. And it challenged unions as well, specifically the AFL's policy of refusing to admit Asian immigrants as members.

To carry out the strike, the workers formed the Sugar Beet and Farm Laborers Union of Oxnard, elected Japanese and Mexican officers, and held rallies and marches. They also battled scabs brought in by growers, resulting in the death of one striker.

Eventually, through militancy and solidarity, the workers won their strike. But when they wrote to AFL president Samuel Gompers for admission into the union, Gompers replied, "Your union must guarantee that it will under no circumstances accept membership of any Chinese or Japanese." The Oxnard workers rejected Gompers's conditions and chose to remain outside the AFL.

The Oxnard strike thus illustrates the two faces of American labor history: on the one hand, the efforts of workers to build multiethnic alliances at the grassroots level; and, on the other hand, the policies of union leaders promoting racism and exclusion.

The Chinese Workers' Mutual Aid Association of the 1930s

The Chinese Workers' Mutual Aid Association was officially established in San Francisco's Chinatown in 1937. Its aim was to unite Chinese workers and through this unity to raise their status in labor unions and improve their working conditions.

The mutual aid association had its roots in Alaskan salmon canneries where Asians had fought for the right to unionize in the mid-1930s. As an aftermath of the victory, a group of Chinese workers on a ship returning from seasonal canning discussed forming a workers' association in San Francisco.

The center began as a gathering place for returning cannery workers but soon broadened its scope, encouraging Chinese workers to join unions. Within two years, it had a membership of six hundred, drawn from restaurants, sewing trades, farms, and seafaring trades.

The association held labor history classes, English classes, and singing classes. In the singing classes, the members learned songs about China's war of resistance against Japan.

Members participated in a Workers' Movement Study Group to learn organizing strategies. They also built close ties with the American labor movement, especially with the International Dock Workers Union, Seafarers Union, and Dishwashers Union.

Thus, the work of the mutual aid association illustrates several key characteristics of

Asian American labor history: the close linkage between community and labor issues, the relationship between the immigrant labor movement and the national democratic movement in their former homeland, and the repeated attempts of Asian workers to build solidarity with the larger American labor movement.

The Alaska Cannery Workers Union in Seattle in the 1970s

The Alaska Cannery Workers Union draws from a rich legacy. It has its roots in the Industrial Workers of the World Local 283 in 1913; in Local 18257 of the Cannery Workers' and Farm Laborers' Union (AFL) in 1932; and in the United Cannery, Agricultural, Packing and Allied Workers of America union of the Congress of Industrial Organizations (CIO) in the late 1930s. The Alaska Cannery Workers Union has a long tradition of internal union democracy and rank-and-file power. It has an important history of active involvement by Asian workers, having been founded by Filipino, Chinese, and Japanese cannery workers.

However, by the late 1960s the Seattle local—affiliated with the ILWU (International Longshoremen and Warehouseworkers Union)—had been taken over by a corrupt leadership that refused to enforce seniority rules and assigned jobs through bribes. Moreover, the union president, a Filipino, maintained close ties with the dictator Ferdinand Marcos in the Philippines.

It was under these conditions that a rank-and-file movement emerged to reform the union. Two leaders—Gene Viernes and Silme Domingo—were elected secretary/treasurer and chief dispatcher of the local. They quickly began to implement fair assignment of jobs and to enforce seniority rules.

Domingo and Viernes were also members of the Union of Democratic Filipinos and promoted solidarity between their union and the anti-Marcos movement in the Philippines. In 1981, Viernes visited the Philippines, where he met with representatives of the largest grassroots labor alliance. One month later, Domingo and Viernes attended the ILWU national convention and succeeded in having delegates pass a resolution to send a labor delegation to the Philippines to study oppressive conditions.

Shortly thereafter, Viernes and Domingo were assassinated by gang members who used a gun owned by the former union president. However, it would take a decade of concerted community efforts to secure justice for the murdered men, and to fully reveal the web of espionage and corruption linking the former union president to the "hit men" and funds supplied by the Marcos dictatorship.

The campaign for justice for Domingo and Viernes encapsulates basic themes in Asian American labor history: the link between immigrant labor struggles and democratic movements in former homelands, as well as the long tradition of rank-and-file initiative by Asian American workers and their broad concerns for justice and equality.

Organizing Farmworkers in Central California

With the recent death of César Chávez, many have recalled the heroic efforts of the United Farm Workers (UFW) to organize California agricultural laborers in the 1960s and its impact on the political consciousness of the Chicano community. Many have celebrated the leadership of Chávez and the militancy of Mexican immigrants in creating this important new chapter in the American labor movement. However, in the process of honoring Chávez, many have forgotten the contributions of other co-founders of the UFW: Filipino immigrants.

In 1965, it was Filipino immigrants who first sat down in the Coachella vineyards of

Central California, launching a movement that culminated in the formation of the UFW. Filipino labor leaders such as Philip Vera Cruz joined with Chávez to forge a multiethnic UFW that became powerful enough to take on California agribusiness.

Until his resignation in 1977, Vera Cruz served as a UFW vice president. He left the union due to personal differences with the UFW's leadership relating to the issues of internal democracy and the union's treatment of its Filipino members. He was also highly critical of Chávez for traveling to the Philippines in 1977 and politically embracing the Marcos dictatorship.

Following a long life devoted to activism and social justice, Philip Vera Cruz passed away at age eighty-nine in June 1994. His life embodied the basic themes in Asian American labor history. For over half a century, he promoted the rights of working people, championed rank-and-file democracy within unions, and articulated the concerns of Filipino immigrants while at the same time forging cross-racial alliances for the advancement of all. For his entire life, he fought in solidarity with all who face oppression throughout the world.

Asian Immigrant Women Take On the Garment Industry

Historically, the garment industry has been a site of sweatshops and exploitation of immigrant women. In the early part of the twentieth century, garment workers in American cities were young immigrant women from Europe. Today, the garment workforce still consists of immigrant women, but most are from Latin America and Asia.

In 1992 in the San Francisco Bay Area, Chinese seamstresses began an important campaign to hold garment manufacturers and retailers responsible for flagrant labor abuses in the industry. The specific grievance—denial of pay by a contractor—is rooted in the particular structure of the industry.

The garment industry in the San Francisco Bay Area is the nation's third largest—following those in New York and Los Angeles—and employs some 20,000 seamstresses, 85 percent of them Asian immigrants. The structure of the industry is a pyramid with retailers and manufacturers on the top, contractors in the middle, and immigrant women working at the bottom. Manufacturers make the main share of profits in the industry; they set the price for contractors. Meanwhile, immigrant women work under sweatshop conditions.

For their campaign, the seamstresses contacted Asian Immigrant Women's Advocates (AIWA) for help. AIWA is not a union. In fact, scholars in Labor Studies and union officials label community formations such as AIWA as "pre-union." However, as AIWA staff member Miriam Ching Louie perceptively notes, it may be more accurate to describe these groups as "post-union"—given the drastic decline in union membership during the past two decades. Moreover, AIWA's strategy of addressing labor issues through community-based organizing challenges unions to adapt to today's changing workforce—a workforce consisting of growing numbers of immigrants, women, and people of color.

In their campaign, AIWA and the seamstresses initially confronted the contractor for the back pay. When they discovered that the contractor owed a number of creditors, they took the unusual step of holding the garment manufacturer, Jessica McClintock, accountable for the unpaid wages. McClintock operates ten boutiques and sells dresses through department stores. The dresses —which garment workers are paid $5 to make—retail in stores for $175. AIWA and the workers conducted their campaign through a series of high-profile demonstrations at McClintock boutiques, including picket lines and rallies in ten cities by supporters. AIWA designed these demonstrations not only to put pressure on McClintock and educate others about inequities in the structure of the garment industry but also to serve as vehicles for empowerment for the immigrant women participating in the campaign.

Thus, this campaign illustrates several themes we have encountered from our earlier examples: an emphasis on worker-initiated struggles, in contrast to those initiated top-down by union officials; an emphasis on community-based labor strategies; and an emphasis on building a campaign that embraces broad concerns for justice and equality for all immigrant workers.

78

Two Hierarchies

M. Edward Ransford

Our basic perspective is that racial-ethnic qualities and socioeconomic characteristics result in two distinct but interacting hierarchies. Although there are significant differences between these two orders, they share a common basis—both determine access to power, economic privilege, and social honor. The basic assumption of ethnic stratification is that *physical* and/or *cultural* distinction from the dominant ethnic stratum results in power inequality and limited access to important rewards. Quite apart from one's wealth or education, membership in an ethnic group per se determines to some extent one's life chances. This is especially the case when the ethnic minority has gone through a longstanding paternalistic relationship in which beliefs of inherent inferiority have developed and in which unequal power has become highly institutionalized. In contrast, the socioeconomic hierarchy deals with the economic earnings, education, and occupational status of persons.

A given socioeconomic stratum (often used interchangeably with social class in our discussion) refers to a category of people with roughly comparable levels of occupational attainment, education, and income. One sometimes finds the term "achieved rank" used when referring to socioeconomic status, or SES (as opposed to ascribed rank, in the case of race). But SES is not always entirely "achieved," since initiative, effort, and ability are not the only determinants.

Equally important are inherited wealth and privilege. Upper-middle-class children typically inherit not only material wealth and possessions, but a high achievement motivation from their home environment. They also attend the best schools, and have parental connections with the most influence. Diagramatically, the two-hierarchy perspective would look like figure 78.1.

Until recently, the correlation between race (black, Chicano, Native Americans), and low socioeconomic position was so consistent that the two categories were rarely separated. That is, it was assumed that practically all blacks, Mexican Americans, and Indians were lower class. Though the poverty rate is still high for all three groups, increasingly large numbers of urban blacks and Mexican Americans have attained better socio-

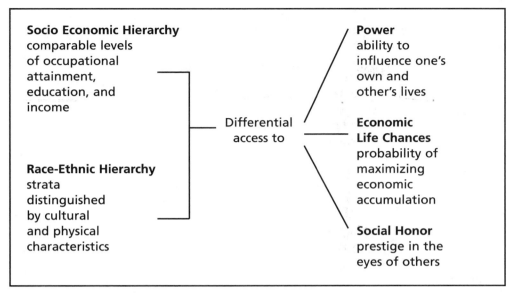

Figure 78.1

economic positions in the last thirty years. The 1990 census indicates that somewhere between 30 percent and 40 percent of the employed black and Latino/a populations (depending upon region of the country, and the age and sex of the respondent) are either in skilled blue-collar positions (craftsmen or foremen) or white-collar occupations. As one would expect, minority persons in white-collar positions tend to come from stable working-class or middle-class homes, rather than from poverty backgrounds. The child who faces the dual barrier of poverty and race has limited chances for substantial socioeconomic advancement, while minority children from stable working-class or middle-class homes do inherit some advantages.

The point is that in black, Chicano, and Indian populations the correlation between "race" and lower-class status is no longer .95 (as it would be under a paternalistic system) but has dropped to something like a moderate .50. This means that race and class increasingly interact in complex and interesting ways. A middle-class African American may have very different outlooks and battles to fight than those of a lower-class black. The dual-hierarchy model allows for the possibility of a middle- or upper-class black person having greater power, wealth, and prestige than a lower-class white person. However, before examining these interaction possibilities, the ethnic-race hierarchy needs to be more clearly defined.

There are many excellent discussions of social class ranking in the United States, but ethnic and racial ranking are less commonly viewed as hierarchical. In particular, blacks, Mexican Americans, and American Indians have not been commonly distinguished from other ethnic groups in hierarchical conceptions. Accordingly, a more extensive discussion of the ethnic-race hierarchy is presented below, followed by some important comparisons between race and class stratification.

Racial-Ethnic Stratification

The term race is used to include groups distinguished primarily by visible physical criteria such as skin color (e.g., blacks and Asians). By contrast, ethnic group usually refers to cultural populations distinguished by language, heritage, or special traditions (e.g.,

American Jews). The three groups discussed most in this chapter—blacks, Mexican Americans, and American Indians—have either a high degree of visibility or a combination of physical and cultural characterisitics. To separate clearly the *conquered minorities* from white ethnic groups we will frequently use the term *race* when referring to blacks, Mexican Americans, and Native Americans.

We view *power inequality* as the key variable for distinguishing strata in an ethnic-race hierarchy. That is, power inequality comes first, is the prime mover of the system, and determines the distribution of economic privileges and/or prestige (social honor). From this viewpoint, improvements in economic privileges and/or prestige for minority persons are only likely to occur when basic institutional arrangements are changed by the exertion of power. As Olsen puts it, "If racial inequality is in fact largely a consequence of power exertion by whites, it follows that *blacks seeking to change the situation so as to gain greater equality of privileges and prestige must in turn exercise power against the dominant whites.*[1] Similarly, prejudice is viewed as the result or outcome of power inequality institutionalized (e.g., segregation). Olsen argues that racial prejudice is far more likely to be reduced by minority power action that affects these institutions (eliminates segregation) than by education or persuasion. In terms of power inequality and differential access to rewards, a racial-ethnic stratification order in the United States would look like figure 78.2.

Descending the scale in figure 78.2, we find increasing degrees of political powerlessness, economic oppression, and social exclusion. Historically, White Anglo Saxon Protestants (WASPs) were the dominant group in the early American colonies. English language, law, and literature prevailed. Later arriving groups were judged according to their fit within this WASP model. White ethnics (e.g., Italians, Jews, Poles, Greeks) arrived in the United States during the later waves of immigration from 1880 to1920. The term *white ethnic* refers especially to immigrants from southeastern Europe. These groups faced a moderate amount of prejudice and discrimination. White ethnics were often judged as backward and boorish because of their lack of urban-industrial skills, their differences in religion, and their inability to speak English well.

Despite these handicaps, white ethnics had major advantages over racial minorities. First, they entered the United States voluntarily; they were not conquered groups. Second, white ethnics were able to set up enclaves or communities in which they could practice their traditions and religion. Thus, within the Italian, Greek, or Jewish areas of the city one finds separate support groups, newspapers, restaurants, churches and synagogues.

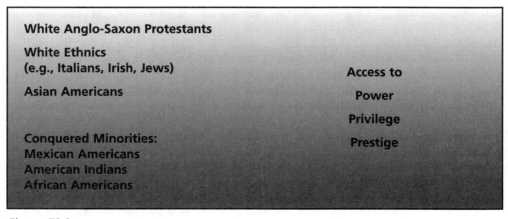

Figure 78.2

These were communities of choice and they provided members with an alternative source of connection and self esteem.[2] Third, these groups were white and blended in physically with the majority group, allowing for more rapid accultration and assimilation.

Asian Americans represent an interesting intermediate stratum between the WASPs and the most oppressed minorities. Though they are certainly physically visible—they are technically a racial minority—and currently face some degree of social exclusion,[3] their cultural stress on personal achievement, duty to the community, emphasis on long-range goals, and so forth, is highly compatible with that of the dominant culture. Further, Japanese and Chinese Americans did not enter this country as a conquered people. . . . Though legal controls against them have often been harsh (the "Gentleman's Agreement," "Yellow Peril," and the Acts of Oriental Exclusion), and though relocation during World War II was one of the most extreme temporary forms of total control that the white majority has exerted on a racial minority, Asian Americans have not experienced the long-range powerlessness of the three "conquered minorities."

From the perspectives of unequal power and differential access to scarce rewards, one finds blacks, Indians, and Chicanos at the lowest end of the ethnic hierarchy. Not only were all three groups conquered, but the unequal power relationship became institutionalized. All three groups experienced some version of a long-lasting paternalistic relationship with the white power structure (slavery, total control by the Bureau of Indian Affairs, the use of Mexicans as a commodity for farm labor). Such unequal power was not just a historical fact but continues to a large extent today, with the low degree of power and autonomy in many ghetto, barrio, and reservation communities (i.e., externally manipulated colonies). However, there are differences between blacks, Mexicans, and Indians on this dimension of differential access to scarce rewards. Mexican Americans and Native Americans face victimization due to cultural factors; blacks face discrimination mainly due to visibility and negative stereotypes attached to color.

Some segments of the Mexican-American and Indian populations have a distinctive culture that is at wide variance with the dominant culture. For example, Spanish language, greater emphasis on family cohesion, and less stress on individualistic achievement separates to some degree Anglo and Mexican-American outlooks. (However, the differences between Anglos and third-generation urban Mexican Americans on these dimensions are probably very small). Moreover, these cultural differences are not neutral or without consequence.

Moore notes that there has typically been a gross and insensitive reaction to Mexican language and culture in most Anglo institutions.[4] In the schools, Mexican-American culture is often viewed as inferior in the sense that it causes bilingualism (assumed to be detrimental to education) and a lack of motivation. Federal financial assistance to schools in barrio communities is often based on the assumption that we must "help Mexican-American children compensate for certain inadequacies they display compared to a 'standard' middle-class child."[5] Such efforts are aimed at changing the child rather than changing the system. Cultural differences in the case of Chicanos and American Indians have become further means of limiting opportunities and enacting oppression.

Blacks, in contrast to Chicanos and Indians, have fewer cultural differences in language and values but are more "locked in" by physical visibility, and by the ideologies attached to that color. Though the extreme racist ideologies that developed during slavery and the era of Jim Crow segregation (blacks were defined as biologically inferior and were assessed as three-fifths of a man for determining the number of seats a state got in Congress) have subsided, many white Americans now embrace an ideology of differential effort. Current surveys show that many white Americans subscribe to an ideology of free will and lack of effort.[6] From this view, whites believe that blacks have a higher poverty rate and lower socioeconomic status because they have not extended the necessary effort. Such a view completely ignores patterns of racism in institutions and places all of the blame for black disadvantage on blacks themselves. Racial stratification that is tied to visibility and beliefs in differential effort is likely to be especially rigid, making upward mobility much more difficult. In contrast, skin color and physical features in the Mexican American group are more variable, and hence there is more inconsistency in status assignments based on visibility. Mexican Americans lighter in skin color, or with a more classical Spanish appearance, may experience slightly less prejudice than darker skinned Latinos. However, visibility for Mexican Americans has not been as historically connected to ideologies of racial inferiority as it has been for blacks. In the sense of the permeability of a color line, upwardly mobile Mexican Americans and American Indians have more options for mobility than African Americans.

In sum, blacks, Mexican Americans, and Indians are lowest on the ethnic hierarchy (having the least access to scarce rewards) because of a combination of the following factors:

- pronounced cultural differences (especially for Mexican Americans and Indians);
- high visibility (especially for blacks);
- conquered status and long-lasting paternalistic relationship with the white majority;
- relatively powerless communities controlled and manipulated by white society;
- highly crystallized ideologies of inferiority or belief that the minority group has not invested necessary efforts for achievement.

Individual versus Institutional Racism

When speaking of a race-ethnic stratification order, it is important to distinguish between individual racism and discrimination. An employer who discriminates against a minority applicant because he/she believes that members of that group are inferior or lazy or non-productive is holding individual racist beliefs and engaging in individual discrimination. However, racism may be embedded in the system. Everyday "business as usual" routines, procedures, and policies may appear neutral yet impact harmful consequences on minority persons. Often there is no individual racist bigotry involved. That is, the policies appear to be benign, but in fact are discriminatory toward minority persons. Until very recently in California, black elementary school age children were classified in mental ability according to standardized IQ test scores. Research in the 1970s uncovered the fact that many of these tests are intrinsically racist in that they are based on white middle-class experiences. The test designers, and teachers and counselors who administer the test are not racist in attitude; the problem is in the measuring instrument and in the system of using that instrument.

Not all forms of institutional racism and discrimination are so impersonal; in some cases there is a focus on racial characteristics. Experimental studies of discrimination in housing find that when black and white couples with identical economic profiles (education, work experience, salary, etc.) approach real estate agents, black couples are less likely to get to see a house, and are more likely to be "steered" toward areas of black concentration. Diana Pearce refers to this as institutional discrimination, because there is a consensus among real estate agents as to which areas are to remain all white that goes beyond individual instances of discrimination.[7] In this particular example, the motivation to steer black families away from exclusive white neighborhoods may be economic, to provide ease of sales for incoming white buyers. Whatever the motivation, the discrimination involves organizational agreements and patterned inequalities that go beyond individual actions of particular persons. African Americans, Mexican Americans, and American Indians have, in particular, experienced both individual and institutional racism and discrimination.

Dominant White Stratum or Power Elite?

As we talk about power inequality being the essential fact of a racial stratification order, it is important to clarify several points dealing with the dispersal of power in the white population and in the minorities. Who has the power in this country? A widely held theory is that a small group of people (men, primarily) at the top of major institutions make things move. . . . However, from the perspective of this essay, a group of whites much larger than a power elite have controlled the destinies of black, Chicano, and Indian peoples. Systems of racial inequality initiated by a small group of powerful whites (as in colonialism or the doctrine of Manifest Destiny) allowed for a wide dispersal of authority resulting in middle-class, working-class, and, to some degree, poor whites acting out the racial order. Consider C. Vann Woodward's statement about the wide dispersal of power occasioned by Jim Crow laws:

> The Jim Crow laws put the authority of the state or city in the voice of the street car conductor, the railway brakeman, the bus driver, the theater usher, and also into the voice of the hoodlums of the public parks and playgrounds. They gave free rein and the majesty of the law to mass agressions that might otherwise have been curbed, blunted, or deflected.[8]

Currently, many whites of modest status and economic attainment have prevented black encroachment in their trade unions and neighborhoods. Indeed, it is commonly noted that the white working class has most rigidly acted out the discrimination norms of the old caste order, since they face the greatest status threat and economic competition from an upwardly mobile black population. Sociologists having an internal colonization perspective also emphasize the fact that white agents (e.g., the white police) of powerful ruling groups enforce the system of inequality.[9] Thus, large numbers of whites far in excess of the power elite have been and continue to be involved in racial discrimination. But to refer to the white population as dominant in power and the conquered minority populations as subordinate in power is only partially accurate. One exception worth noting is that some segments of the white majority have identified with the ethnic liberation movements and actively participated in them (one of the major support groups in César Chávez's farmworker movement is white and middle class). The white majority group cannot be viewed as one homogeneous oppressor. Another very important fact is that increasingly some members of the minority populations have more personal influence and control over their environment than some whites. Not all whites are dominant over all blacks.

Two Kinds of Power

If power is defined as control over major institutions and, in particular, control over the economy, then few minority persons have such top power when compared with whites. Even at upper middle levels of institutional power (for example, mayors or senators) whites have far more representation and influence than blacks, Chicanos, and Indians. However, if power is thought of in more personal terms as the probability of exerting control over one's own life, then middle-class blacks often have more control than working-and lower-class whites. That is, middle-class blacks, in contrast to lower-class whites, typically have more money, influence in the context of their jobs, knowledge of redress channels when they face inequities, and general life chances. The terminology of dominant and subordinate racial strata completely misses this possibility.

Notes

1. Marvin E. Olsen, "Power Perspectives on Stratification and Race Relations," in Marvin E. Olsen, ed. *Power in Societies* (New York: Macmillan, 1970), 302.
2. See Robert Blauner, *Racial Oppression in America* (New York: Harper and Row, 1972), the chapter "Colonized and Immigrant Minorities."
3. See Harry L. Kitano, *Japanese Americans: The Evolution of a Subculture* (Englewood Cliffs, N.J.: Prentice-Hall, 1969), 50–51.
4. Joan W. Moore, *Mexican Americans* (Englewood Cliffs, N.J.: Prentice-Hall, 1970), 81.
5. Ibid., 81.
6. See James R. Kluegel, "Trends in Whites' Explanations of the Black-White Gap in Socioeconomic Status, 19779–1989," *American Sociological* Review 55 (1990), 512–25; J. R. Kluegel and E. R. Smith, *Beliefs about Equality: Americans' Views of What Is and What Ought to Be* (New York: Aldine de Gruyter, 1986); and Howard Schuman, "Free Will and Determinism in Beliefs about Race," in Norman R. Yetman and C. Hoy Steele, eds., *Majority and Minority: The Dynamics of Racial and Ethnic* Relations (Boston: Allyn and Bacon, 1971).
7. Diana M. Pearce, "Gatekeepers and Homeseekers: Institutional Factors in Racial Steering," *Social Problems* 26 (1979), 325–42.
8. C. Vann Woodward, *The Strange Career of Jim Crow* (New York: Oxford University Press, 1957), 93.
9. Robert Blauner, *Racial Oppression in America*, 97–99.

79

Why Are Droves of Unqualified, Unprepared Kids Getting into Our Top Colleges? Because Their Dads Are Alumni.

John Larew

Growing up, she heard a hundred Harvard stories. In high school, she put the college squarely in her sights. But when judgment day came in the winter of 1988, the Harvard admissions guys were frankly unimpressed. Her academic record was solid—not special. Extracurriculars, interview, recommendations? Above average, but not by much. "Nothing really stands out," one admissions officer scribbled on her application folder. Wrote another, "Harvard not really the right place."

At the hyperselective Harvard University, where high school valedictorians, National Merit Scholarship finalists, musical prodigies—eleven thousand ambitious kids in all— are rejected annually, this young woman didn't seem to have much of a chance. Thanks to Harvard's largest affirmative action program, she got in anyway. No, she wasn't poor, black, disabled, Hispanic, native American, or even Aleutian. She got in because her mom went to Harvard. . . .

This past fall, after two years of study, the U.S. Department of Education's Office for Civil Rights (OCR) found that, far from being more qualified or even equally qualified, the average admitted legacy student at Harvard between 1981 and 1988 was significantly *less* qualified than the average admitted nonlegacy student. Examining admissions office ratings on academics, extracurriculars, personal qualities, recommendations, and other categories, the OCR concluded that "with the exception of the athletic rating, [admitted] nonlegacies scored better than legacies in *all* areas of comparison."

Exceptionally high admittance rates, lowered academic standards, preferential treatment. . . . These sound like the cries heard in the growing fury over affirmative action for racial minorities in America's elite universities. Yet no one is outraged about legacies. . . .

At most elite universities during the 1980s, the legacy was by far the biggest piece of the preferential pie. At Harvard, a legacy is about twice as likely to be admitted as a black or Hispanic student. As sociologists Jerome Karabel and David Karen point out, if alumni children were admitted to Harvard at the same rate as other applicants, their numbers in the class of 1992 would have been reduced by about 200. Instead, those 200 marginally qualified legacies outnumbered all black, Mexican-American, Native American, and Puerto Rican enrollees put together. . . .

Unfortunately, the extent of the legacy privilege in elite American colleges suggests something more than the occasional tie-breaking tip. Forget meritocracy. When 20 percent of Harvard's student body gets a legacy preference, *aristocracy* is the word that comes to mind. . . .

Of course, the existence of the legacy preference in this fierce career competition isn't exactly news. According to historians, it was a direct result of the influx of Jews into the Ivy League during the 1920s. Until then, Harvard, Princeton, and Yale had admitted anyone who could pass their entrance exams, but suddenly Jewish kids were outscoring the White Anglo-Saxon Protestants (WASPs). So the schools began to use nonacademic criteria—"character," "solidity," and, eventually, lineage—to justify accepting low-scoring blue bloods over their peers. Yale implemented its legacy preference first, in 1925—spelling it out in a memo four years later. The school would admit "Yale sons of good character and reasonably good record . . . regardless of the number of applicants and the superiority of outside competitors." Harvard and Princeton followed shortly thereafter.

Despite its ignoble origins, the legacy preference has only sporadically come under fire, most notably in 1978's affirmative action decision, *University of California Board of Regents v. Bakke.* In his concurrence, Justice Harry Blackmun observed, "It is somewhat ironic to have us so deeply disturbed over a program where race is an element of consciousness, and yet to be aware of the fact, as we are, that institutions of higher learning . . . have given conceded preferences to the children of alumni."

If people are, in fact, aware of the legacy preference, why has it been spared the scrutiny given other preferential policies? One reason is public ignorance of the scope and scale of those preferences—an ignorance carefully cultivated by America's elite institutions. It's easy to maintain the fiction that your legacies get in strictly on merit as long as your admissions bureaucracy controls all access to student data. Information on Harvard's legacies became publicly available not because of any fit of disclosure by the university, but because a few civil rights types noted that the school had a suspiciously low rate of admission for Asian-Americans, who are statistically stronger than other racial groups in academics.

While the ensuing OCR inquiry found no evidence of illegal racial discrimination by Harvard, it did turn up some embarrassing information about how much weight the "legacy" label gives an otherwise flimsy file. Take these comments scrawled by admissions officers on applicant folders:

- "Double lineage who chose the right parents."

- "Dad's [deleted] connections signify lineage of more than usual weight. That counted into the equation makes this a case which (assuming positive TRs [teacher recommendations] and Alum IV [alumnus interview]) is well worth doing."

- "Lineage is main thing."

- "Not quite strong enough to get the clean tip."

- "Classical case that would be hard to explain to dad."

- "Double lineage but lots of problems."

- "Not a great profile, but just strong enough #'s and grades to get the tip from lineage."

- "Without lineage, there would be little case. With it, we'll keep looking."

In every one of these cases, the applicant was admitted.

Of course, Harvard's not doing anything other schools aren't. The practice of playing favorites with alumni children is nearly universal among private colleges and isn't unheard of at public institutions, either. The rate of admission for Stanford's alumni children is "almost twice the general population," according to a spokesman for the admissions office. Notre Dame reserves 25 percent of each freshman class for legacies. At the University of Virginia, where native Virginians make up two-thirds of each class, alumni children are automatically treated as Virginians even if they live out of state—giving them a whopping competitive edge. The same is true of the University of California at Berkeley. At many schools, Harvard included, all legacy applications are guaranteed a read by the dean of admissions—a privilege nonlegacies don't get. . . .

If the test scores of admitted legacies are a mystery, the reason colleges accept so many is not. They're afraid the alumni parents of rejected children will stop giving to the colleges' unending fund-raising campaigns. "Our survival as an institution depends on having support from alumni," says Richard Steele, director of undergraduate admissions at Duke University, "so according advantages to alumni kids is just a given."

In fact, the OCR exonerated Harvard's legacy preference precisely because legacies bring in money. (OCR cited a federal district court ruling that a state university could favor the children of out-of-state alumni because "defendants showed that the alumni provide monetary support for the university"). And there's no question that alumni provide significant support to Harvard. Last year, they raised $20 million for the scholarship fund alone. . . .

Heir Cut

When justice dictates that ordinary kids should have as fair a shot as the children of America's elite, couldn't Harvard and its sister institutions trouble themselves to "get the message out" again? Of course they could. But virtually no one—liberal or conservative—is pushing them to do so.

"There must be no goals or quotas for any special group or category of applicants," reads an advertisement in the right-wing *Dartmouth Review*. "Equal opportunity must be the guiding policy. Males, females, blacks, whites, Native Americans, Hispanics . . . can all be given equal chance to matriculate, survive, and prosper based solely on individual performance."

Noble sentiments from the Ernest Martin Hopkins Institute, an organization of conservative Dartmouth alumni. Reading on, though, we find these "concerned alumni" aren't sacrificing *their* young to the cause. "Alumni sons and daughters," notes the ad further down, "should receive some special consideration." . . .

At America's elite universities, you'd expect a somewhat higher standard of fairness than that—especially when money is the driving force behind the concept. And many Ivy League types *do* advocate for more just and lofty ideals. One of them, as it happens, is Derek Bok. In one of Harvard's annual reports, he warned that the modern university is slowly turning from a truth-seeking enterprise into a money-grubbing corporation—at the expense of the loyalty of its alumni. "Such an institution may still evoke pride and respect because of its intellectual achievements," he said rightly. "But the feelings it engenders will not be quite the same as those produced by an institution that is prepared to forgo income, if need be, to preserve values of a nobler kind."

Forgo income to preserve values of a nobler kind—it's an excellent idea. Embrace the preferences for the poor and disadvantaged. Wean alumni from the idea of the legacy edge. And above all, stop the hypocrisy that begrudges the great unwashed a place at Harvard while happily making room for the less qualified sons and daughters of alums.

After seventy years, it won't be easy to wrest the legacy preference away from the alumni. But the long-term payoff is as much a matter of message as money. When the sons and daughters of today's college kids fill out *their* applications, the legacy preference should seem not a birthright, but a long-gone relic from the Ivy League's inequitable past.

Personal Voices

80

Working-Class Students Speak Out

Gwendolyn Lewis, Patricia Holland, and Kathleen Kelly

A diverse group of students from the University of Massachusetts/Boston presented a panel on October 5, 1990, at a national three-day conference on "Class Bias in Higher Education: Equity Issues of the 1990s" sponsored by the Center for Labor and Society at Queens College. Pamela Annas and Esther Kingston-Mann served as faculty advisors. The student panel included Patricia Holland, Kathleen Kelly, Saveth Noun, Juan Manuel Carlo, Gwendolyn Lewis, and Robert Terrell.

Each of the UMass participants, in five-minute presentations, gave examples of obstacles, incentives, and challenges to the college experience. Obstacles included a sense of inadequacy or disconnectedness to the college environment; discouragement by cultural and language barriers; and intimidation by the concept of higher education. Incentives included the sacrifice of previous generations for the privilege to attend college; the unalienable right to be in college; and gaining support through mentoring or other networks. Challenges included being first of their respective families to seek higher education; perseverence; the need to craft an education that is relative to one's community and world.

Gwendolyn Lewis

I am on a journey called *education* that did not begin with my entrance into the University of Massachusetts nor will it end with my baccalaureate exercises.

Once, when I was speaking to a doctor about the difficulties I was experiencing in studying, he related that by his observation of my situation, I had had no role models in education on which to imitate a career. Even as a single, self-supporting woman, I was far from the "norm" in the footstep-following mode. He told me that in his household, both he and his wife had received higher education and that for his children there was no question that they would be attending college at the proper time also. For this particular family, college education was a given. The only given I was aware of as a youngster was the necessity to work.

Raised in a household headed by my paternal grandmother, whose formal education ended in the fourth term of the British system in the small West Indian island of Montserrat, I had no aspirations of higher education beyond high school. Attending college was a luxury—a dream set beyond my scope. In my home, gaining a job and contributing to the household income was of utmost importance. In fact, during the late 1950s, for many poor black families, pursuing a college education (especially for females) was viewed as futile or wasteful. as so many doors were closed to blacks.

Today I am a student at the University of Massachusetts having entered college thirty years after my graduation from high school. I would like to tell you how I personally came to this status.

Although going on to higher education was something that I had secretly longed for, I did not believe that I had the means or support necessary to make education a priority. I was afraid to make a commitment to something that I did not know whether I would be able to complete. I had had good marks in school, but that was years ago. I knew that my study habits were poor. I was also worried about going to school and at the same time working full time. How would I make it? When I learned of a unique program at the University of Massachusetts's College of Public and Community Service in which a degree could be gained by mingling prior learning experiences along with basic disciplines, I still hesitated. Feeling a sense of low self-esteem, I doubted the worth of my life's experiences.

Fortunately, I had a friend, one who believed in education and who took me seriously when I said I wanted to go back to school some day. She dared me to do something positive about my desire. My friend took it upon herself to encourage me into college. She regularly asked me about getting an application, if and when I had filled it out, and what questions I had had problems with. When the application was finally filled out, she nagged me to actually mail it. When I received my approval letter, my friend took me out to dinner as a reward.

I can smile now because that episode, while it seems so simple, was so significant. It was necessary for me to overcome my fears and intimidation about going to college. My friend used elementary measures to coax me to overcome my largest obstacle to college—namely, *getting there.*

The campus that I am a part of is unique in that many of the student body are people like myself who have been out of school for a while and have careers, families, and other responsibilities. We also share fears and worries. As such, we are able to encourage one another to keep on hanging in there. With my own experience of supportive friendship, I try to offer the same kind of specific assistance that I received.

I cannot stress strongly enough the need for applied assistance and encouragement. It is important to find out where each person is coming from, meet them at that point, and help them to move on. I still meet obstacles while in college, but I know that I am not alone in facing them, that help is available, and that I am overcoming them—one by one.

Patricia Holland

My name is Patricia Holland, and I am the daughter of two Irish immigrant parents. My mother has the equivalent of a ninth-grade education, and my father, a fifth-grade education.

I feel very honored to be asked to speak here today; it gave me the opportunity to have a very special conversation with my father last weekend. (It's not often that I get to be alone with my father since I have five brothers and sisters.) Since I needed information for this talk, I asked him about the level of education he received in Ireland, and what his experience around this was like.

He told me that he had had five years of school and that he had repeated his last year. He then quit school. Later he moved to England with his brothers. He said that he would buy a newspaper and go to the top of the double-decker buses while his brothers smoked below. He would pull out the paper and try to make sense of the words. He did not know how to read. He said to me, "I can't tell you the humiliation I felt being a grown man of twenty-one and not being able to read." He then told me that I will be fortunate when I marry and have children. "When they go to college you will be able to help them. After the fourth grade, you kids had passed me educationally. I couldn't be of any help to you," my father said.

This huge gap in my parents' and my education left me feeling quite alone in my pursuit of an education. I often felt quite conflicted and pulled between wanting to be like them and wanting to have a better education. Each new year of college that I have completed has created a further widening of the educational gap between us.

I have been attending UMass/Boston for seven years, on and off, part- and full-time. In my family, I could not get the support I consider necessary to successfully complete a college degree. My parents didn't have it to give.

I believe that there are more students on campus who have an educational and/or cultural gap. Here are some suggestions I would like to make to universities:

1. Mentor students. Each professor could have six or so students they would be assigned to mentor their first year at the university. This would help students feel connected and supported around questions or concerns they might have.

2. When a professor sees a student having trouble in a class—or leaving the university suddenly—please reach out and try to get involved with this student. You may be the only support she has.

3. Professors could assign readings on the subject of how others have handled upward mobility.

Kathleen Kelly

My name is Kathleen Kelly and I am a senior at UMass/Boston. I came here today to talk about class differences. As I thought about this task, I realized it might be a difficult one because I've been told we live in a classless society. For some reason, people don't like to talk about social class in our society. Maybe there is a good reason for this that I just don't know about. If so, please excuse my ignorance, because I would still like to talk about this issue.

For me, entering school was like entering a whole new world. It was as if I had entered a foreign country and did not know the customs, the language, or the people. And yet, I felt I *should* know these things. This feeling was reinforced by others' expectations of me. But because I grew up in the projects, the closest I had ever come to college was to drive by one. Growing up I had no opportunities to learn the university culture. I did not know the difference between a bachelor's degree and an associate's degree. I did not know what *matriculate* meant. I did not know what it meant to declare a major, or what a major *was* for that matter. And I had no one who could teach me these things.

College was not something I generally aspired to as a child. I, like most people who grow up poor in our society, never seriously considered college a realistic option. I learned that people like us didn't go to college. People used to laugh when I told them I wanted to be a lawyer when I grew up. I didn't know then that kids from the projects didn't grow up to be lawyers. I was still innocent enough to believe that if you worked hard enough you could be anything you wanted. I soon learned the reality of my situation and gave up thoughts of college and of high school as well. I dropped out of school in the tenth grade.

Soon after, I had a child and realized I could not support her on a tenth grade education. After years of trying to survive as a single mother on welfare, I decided to get a high school diploma. I obtained my GED (general equivalency diploma] and for the first time in my life I seriously considered going to college. This is when, with the help of a former "welfare mother," I applied to UMass and was accepted into the Developmental Studies Program.

I've been a student at UMass for five years now. When I started college I was totally unprepared, both socially and academically. Luckily, I didn't know at the time what I was facing or I might never have begun. I began my college career in a program which was set up for students who did not have traditional preparation for college. This includes ESL [English as a Second Language] students as well as students from disadvantaged backgrounds. I would like to say that without the DSP program I *never* would have survived here at UMass.

One of the things that saved me during my first year of college was meeting a teacher in the DSP program who sensed I needed help. She validated my feelings by telling me that I had indeed entered a whole new world. She told me that while at times it might be frightening and disorienting, it could also be exciting. By offering me encouragement and helping me learn ways of filling in the gaps, this teacher helped me to realize that getting an education might be possible. During this time, I often had to study high school books and college texts at the same time. But just the fact that a college professor was taking time out for me was something that helped a lot.

Still, there were times when things were not very easy. I used to sit in class not understanding what was going on and wondering what I was doing there. I *often* felt as if I didn't belong. I seldom saw my reality reflected in the classroom. What we talked about in class had little bearing upon my life. It seemed so distant from anything I had ever known. Sometimes I felt really stupid. As time went on, however, I became more educated and learned that I was not stupid, just "culturally illiterate." For a while I liked this term; I thought it sounded better than stupid. Yet, soon I came to feel that *culturally illiterate* wasn't right either; after all, I knew my culture. It was this *new* culture I was having trouble with. I finally concluded that maybe, in some ways, we are all culturally illiterate.

I guess my advice for those here today would be to try to understand and value the diversity of the students they interact with. Help us to realize our potential and let us know that we, too, have something to contribute. Putting students down by saying things like, "You should have learned that in high school" or "If you have to work full-time you shouldn't be here" accomplishes little other than to lower self-esteem and increase feelings of inferiority. Few of us can learn effectively under such conditions.

Students from socially and economically disadvantaged backgrounds have overcome social, cultural, and economic barriers to try and get an education. Yet they stand on very shaky ground. I have seen many students make it this far only to drop out. When I started at UMass, I made friends with two women who were from backgrounds similar to my own. In June of this year, I will receive my diploma and neither of these women will graduate with me. I am saddened by this. I consider it a great loss, not only to the two women who have been denied the freedom which accompanies an education, but also to UMass and the entire society. We will never know what these women may have offered us. I still remember my friend saying to me the day she left college, "I don't belong here, I'm way out of my league." No one should feel this way. I hope in the future, a college education will be within everyone's league.

81

So How Did I Get Here?

Rosemary Bray

Growing up on welfare was a story I had planned to tell a long time from now, when I had children of my own. My childhood on Aid to Families with Dependent Children (AFDC) was going to be one of those stories I would tell my kids about the bad old days, an urban legend equivalent to Abe Lincoln studying by firelight. But I know now I cannot wait, because in spite of a wealth of evidence about the true nature of welfare and poverty in America, the debate has turned ugly, vicious, and racist. The "welfare question" has become the race question and the woman question in disguise, and so far the answers bode well for no one.

In both blunt and coded terms, comfortable Americans more and more often bemoan the waste of their tax money on lazy black women with a love of copulation, a horror of birth control, and a lack of interest in marriage. Were it not for the experiences of half my life, were I not black and female and of a certain age, perhaps I would be like so many people who blindly accept the lies and distortions, half-truths, and wrongheaded notions about welfare. But for better or for worse, I do know better. I know more than I want to know about being poor. I know that the welfare system is designed to be inadequate, to leave its constituents on the edge of survival. I know because I've been there.

And finally, I know that perhaps even more dependent on welfare than its recipients are the large number of Americans who would rather accept this patchwork of economic horrors than fully address the real needs of real people.

My mother came to Chicago in 1947 with a fourth-grade education, cut short by working in the Mississippi fields. She pressed shirts in a laundry for a while and later waited tables in a restaurant, where she met my father. Mercurial and independent, with a sixth-grade education, my Arkansas-born father worked at whatever came to hand. He owned a lunch wagon for a time and prepared food for hours in our kitchen on the nights before he took the wagon out. Sometimes he hauled junk and sold it in the open-air markets of Maxwell Street on Sunday mornings. Eight years after they met—seven years after they married—I was born. My father made my mother quit her job; her work, he told her, was taking care of me. By the time I was four, I had a sister, a brother, and another brother on the way. My parents, like most other American couples of the 1950s, had their own American dream—a husband who worked, a wife who stayed home, a family of smiling children. But as was true for so many African-American couples, their American dream was an illusion.

The house on the corner of Berkeley Avenue and 45th Street is long gone. The other houses still stand, but today the neighborhood is an emptier, bleaker place. When we moved there, it was a street of old limestones with beveled-glass windows, all falling into vague disrepair. Home was a four-room apartment on the first floor, in what must have been the public rooms of a formerly grand house. The rent was $110 a month. All of us kids slept in the big front room. Because I was the oldest, I had a bed of my own, near a big plate-glass window.

My mother and father had been married for several years before she realized he was a gambler who would never stay away from the track. By the time we moved to Berkeley Avenue, Daddy was spending more time gambling, and bringing home less and less money and more and more anger. Mama's simplest requests were met with rage. They fought once for hours when she asked for money to buy a tube of lipstick. It didn't help that I always seemed to need a doctor. I had allergies and bronchitis so severe that I nearly died one Sunday after church when I was about three.

It was around this time that my mother decided to sign up for AFDC. She explained to the caseworker that Daddy wasn't home much, and when he was he didn't have any money. Daddy was furious; Mama was adamant. "There were times when we hardly had a loaf of bread in here," she told me years later. "It was close. I wasn't going to let you all go hungry."

Going on welfare closed a door between my parents that never reopened. She joined the ranks of unskilled women who were forced to turn to the state for the security their men could not provide. In the sterile relationship between herself and the State of Illinois, Mama found an autonomy denied her by my father. It was she who could decide, at last, some part of her own fate and ours. AFDC relegated marginally productive men like my father to the ranks of failed patriarchs who no longer controlled the destiny of their families. Like so many of his peers, he could no longer afford the luxury of a woman who did as she was told because her economic life depended on it. Daddy became one of the shadow men who walked out back doors as caseworkers came in through the front. Why did he acquiesce? For all his anger, for all his frightening brutality, he loved us, so much that he swallowed his pride and periodically ceased to exist so that we might survive.

In 1960, the year my mother went on public aid, the poverty threshold for a family of five in the United States was $3,560, and the monthly payment to a family of five from the State of Illinois was $182.56, a total of $2,190.72 a year. Once the $110 rent was paid, Mama was left with $72.56 a month to take care of all the other expenses. By any standard, we were poor. All our lives were proscribed by the narrow line between not quite and just enough.

What did it take to live?

It took the kindness of friends as well as strangers, the charity of churches, low expectations, deprivation, and patience. I can't begin to count the hours spent in long lines, long waits, long walks in pursuit of basic things. A visit to a local clinic (one housing doctors, a dentist, and a pharmacy in an incredibly crowded series of rooms) invariably took the better part of a day; I never saw the same doctor twice.

It took, as well, a turning of our collective backs on the letter of a law that required reporting even a small and important miracle like a present of five dollars. All families have their secrets, but I remember the weight of an extra burden. In a world where caseworkers were empowered to probe into every nook and cranny of our lives, silence became defense. Even now, there are things I will not publicly discuss because I cannot shake the fear that we might be hounded by the state, eager to prosecute us for the crime of survival.

All my memories of our years on AFDC are seasoned with unease. It's painful to remember how much every penny counted, how even a gap of twenty-five cents could make a difference in any given week. Few people understand how precarious life is from welfare check to welfare check, how the word *extra* has no meaning. Late mail, a bureaucratic mix-up . . . and a carefully planned method of survival lies in tatters.

What made our lives work as well as they did was my mother's genius at making do— worn into her by a childhood of rural poverty—along with her vivid imagination. She worked at home endlessly, shopped ruthlessly, bargained, cajoled, charmed. Her food store of choice was the one that stocked pork and beans, creamed corn, sardines, Vienna sausages, and potted meat all at 10 cents a can. Clothing was the stuff of rummage sales, Goodwill, and bargain basements, where thin cotton and polyester reigned supreme. Our shoes came from a discount store that sold two pairs for five dollars. . . .

My life on welfare ended on June 4, 1976—a month after my twenty-first birthday, two weeks after I graduated from Yale. My father, eaten up with cancer and rage, lived just long enough to know the oldest two of us had graduated from college and were on our own. Before the decade ended, all of us had left the welfare rolls. The eldest of my brothers worked at the post office, assumed support of my mother (who also went to work, as a companion to an elderly woman), and earned his master's degree at night. My sister married and got a job at a bank. My baby brother parked cars and found a wife. Mama's biggest job was done at last; the investment made in our lives by the State of Illinois had come to fruition. Five people on welfare for eighteen years had become five working, taxpaying adults. Three of us went to college, two of us finished; one of us has an advanced degree; all of us can take care of ourselves.

Ours was a best-case phenomenon, based on the synergy of church and state, the government and the private sector, and the thousand points of light that we called friends and neighbors. Yet there was something more: what fueled our dreams and fired our belief that our lives could change for the better was the promise of the civil rights movement and the war on poverty—for millions of African-Americans the defining events of the 1960s. Caught up in the heady atmosphere of imminent change, our world was filled not only with issues and ideas but with amazing images of black people engaged in the struggle for long-denied rights and freedoms. We knew other people lived differently than we did, we knew we didn't have much, but we didn't mind, because we knew it wouldn't be long. My mother borrowed a phrase I had read to her once from Dick Gregory's autobiography: "Not poor, just broke." She would repeat it often, as often as she sang hymns in the kitchen. She loved to sing a spiritual Mahalia Jackson had made famous: "Move On Up a Little Higher." Like so many others, Mama was singing about earth as well as heaven.

These are the things I remember every time I read another article outlining America's welfare crisis. The rage I feel about the welfare debate comes from listening to a host of lies, distortions, and exaggerations—and taking them personally. . . .

So how did I get here?

Despite attempts to misconstrue and discredit the social programs and policies that changed—even saved—my life, certain facts remain. Poverty was reduced by 39 percent between 1960 and 1990, according to the U.S. Census Bureau, from 22.2 percent to 13.5 percent of the nation's population. That is far too many poor people, but the rate is considerably lower than it might have been if we had thrown up our hands and reminded ourselves that the poor will always be with us. Of black women considered "highly dependent," that is, on welfare for more than seven years, 81 percent of their daughters grow up to live productive lives off the welfare rolls, a 1992 Congressional report stated; the 19 percent who become second-generation welfare recipients can hardly be said to constitute an epidemic of welfare dependency. The vast majority of African-Americans are now working class or middle class, an achievement that occurred in the past thirty years, most specifically between 1960 and 1973, the years of expansion in the very same social programs that it is so popular now to savage. Those were the same years in which I changed from girl to woman; learned to read and think; graduated from high school and college; came to be a working woman, a taxpayer, a citizen.

In spite of all the successes we know of, in spite of the reality that the typical welfare recipient is a white woman with young children, ideologues have continued to fashion from whole cloth the specter of the mythical black welfare mother, complete with a prodigious reproductive capacity and a galling laziness, accompanied by the uncaring and equally lazy black man in her life who will not work, will not marry her, and will not support his family.

Why has this myth been promoted by some of the best (and the worst) people in government, academia, journalism, and industry? One explanation may be that the constant presence of poverty frustrates even the best-intentioned among us. It may also be because the myth allows for denial about who the poor in America really are and for denial about the depth and intransigence of racism regardless of economic status. And because getting tough on welfare is for some a first-class career move—what better way to win a position in the next administration than to trash those people least able to respond? And, finally, because it serves to assure white Americans that lazy black people aren't getting away with anything.

Many of these prescriptions for saving America from the welfare plague not only reflect an insistent, if sometimes unconscious, racism but rest on the bedrock of patriarchy. They are rooted in the fantasy of a male presence as a path to social and economic salvation and in its corollary—the image of woman as passive chattel, constitutionally so afflicted by her condition that the only recourse is to transfer her care from the hands of the state to the hands of a man with a job. The largely ineffectual plans to create jobs for men in communities ravaged by disinvestment, the state-sponsored dragnets for men who cannot or will not support their children, the exhortations for women on welfare to find themselves a man and get married, all are the institutional expressions of the same worn cultural illusion—that women and children without a man are fundamentally damaged goods. Men are such a boon, the reasoning goes, because they make more money than women do.

Were we truly serious about an end to poverty among women and children, we would take the logical next step. We would figure out how to make sure women who did a dollar's worth of work got a dollar's worth of pay. We would make sure that women could go to work with their minds at ease, knowing their children were well cared for. What women on welfare need, in large measure, are the things key to the life of every adult woman: economic security and autonomy. Women need the skills and the legitimate opportunity to earn a living for ourselves as well as for people who may rely on us; we need the freedom to make choices to improve our own lives and the lives of those dear to us. . . .

Welfare has become a code word now, one that enables white Americans to mask their sometimes malignant, sometimes benign racism behind false concerns about the suffering ghetto poor and their negative impact on the rest of us. It has become the vehicle many so-called tough thinkers use to undermine compassionate policy and engineer the reduction of social programs.

So how *did* I get here?

I kept my drawers up and my dress down, to quote my mother. I didn't end up pregnant because I had better things to do. I knew I did because my uneducated, Southern-born parents told me so. . . . Most important, my family and I had every reason to believe that I had better things to do and that when I got older I would be able to do them. I had a mission, a calling, work to do that only I could do. And that is knowledge transmitted not just by parents, school, or churches. It is a palpable thing, available by osmosis from the culture of the neighborhood and the world at large.

Add to this formula a whopping dose of dumb luck. It was my sixth-grade teacher, Sister Maria Sarto, who identified in me the first signs of a stifling boredom and told my mother that I needed a tougher, more challenging curriculum than her school could provide. It was she who then tracked down the private Francis W. Parker School, which agreed to give me a scholarship if I passed the admissions test.

Had I been born a few years earlier, or a decade later, I might now be living on welfare in the Robert Taylor Homes or working as a hospital nurse's aide for $6.67 an hour. People who think such things could never have happened to me haven't met enough poor people to know better. The avenue of escape can be very narrow indeed. The hope and energy of the 1960s—fueled not only by a growing economy but by all the passions of a great national quest—is long gone. The sense of possibility I knew has been replaced with the popular cultural currency that money and those who have it are everything and those without are nothing. . . .

When I walk down the streets of my Harlem neighborhood, I see women like my mother hustling, struggling, walking their children to school, and walking them back home. And I also see women who have lost both energy and faith, talking loud, hanging out. I see the shadow of men of a new generation, floating by with a few dollars and a toy, then drifting away to the shelters they call home. And I see, a dozen times a day, the little girls my sister and I used to be, the little boys my brothers once were.

Even the grudging, inadequate public help I once had is fading fast for them. The time and patience they will need to recreate themselves is vanishing under pressure for the big, quick fix and the crushing load of blame being heaped upon them. In the big cities and the small towns of America, we have let theory, ideology, and mythology about welfare and poverty overtake these children and their parents.

82

On the Meaning of Plumbing and Poverty

Melanie Scheller

If any one thing proves what bad shape this country is in, it is the growing number of children who live in poverty. In 1969, following the Kennedy and Johnson administrations, 9.7 million children, or 14 percent of all persons under age eighteen, were living in poverty. Twenty years later, at the end of the Reagan era, that figure had jumped to 12.6 million. One-fifth of all U.S. children are now living in poverty. We're all aware of the physical problems poverty creates—hunger, cold, and illness, to name just a few—but only those who have experienced it can tell us about an insidious long-lasting psychological consequence: shame.

Several years ago I spent some time as a volunteer on the geriatric ward of a psychiatric hospital. I was fascinated by the behavior of one of the patients, an elderly woman who shuffled at regular intervals to the bathroom, where she methodically flushed the toilet. Again and again she carried out her sacred mission as if summoned by some supernatural force, until the flush of the toilet became a rhythmic counterpoint for the ward's activity. If someone blocked her path or if, God forbid, the bathroom was in use when she reached it, she became agitated and confused.

Obviously, that elderly patient was a sick woman. And yet I felt a certain kinship with her, for I too have suffered from an obsession with toilets. I spent much of my childhood living in houses without indoor plumbing and, while I don't feel compelled to flush a toilet at regular intervals, I sometimes feel that toilets, or the lack thereof, have shaped my identity in ways that are painful to admit.

I'm not a child of the Depression, but I grew up in an area of the South that had changed little since the days of the New Deal. My mother was a widow with six children to support, not an easy task under any circumstances, but especially difficult in rural North Carolina during the 1960s. To her credit, we were never seriously in danger of going hungry. Our vegetable garden kept us stocked with tomatoes and string beans. We kept a few chickens and sometimes a cow. Blackberries were free for the picking in the fields nearby. Neighbors did their good Christian duty by bringing us donations of fresh fruit and candy at Christmastime. But a roof over our heads—that wasn't so easily improvised.

Like rural Southern gypsies, we moved from one dilapidated Southern farmhouse to another in a constant search for a decent place to live. Sometimes we moved when the rent increased beyond the thirty or forty dollars my mother could afford. Or the house burned down, not an unusual occurrence in substandard housing. One year, when we were gathered together for Thanksgiving dinner, a stranger walked in without knocking and announced that we were being evicted. The house had been sold without our knowledge and the new owner wanted to start remodeling immediately. We tried to finish our meal with an attitude of thanksgiving while he worked around us with his tape measure.

Usually, we rented from farm families who'd moved from the old home place to one of the brick boxes that are now the standard in rural Southern architecture. The old farmhouse wasn't worth fixing up with a septic tank and flush toilet, but it was good enough to rent for a few dollars a month to families like mine. The idea of tenants' rights hadn't trickled down yet from the far reaches of the liberal North. It never occurred to us to demand improvements in the facilities. The ethic of the land said we should take what we could get and be grateful for it.

Without indoor plumbing, getting clean is a tiring and time-consuming ritual. At one point, I lived in a five-room house with six or more people, all of whom congregated in the one heated room to eat, do homework, watch television, dress and undress, argue, wash dishes. During cold weather we dragged mattresses from the unheated rooms and slept huddled together on the floor by the woodstove. For my bathing routine, I first pinned a sheet to a piece of twine strung across the kitchen. That gave me some degree of privacy from the six other people in the room. At that time, our house had an indoor cold-water faucet, from which I filled a pot of water to heat on the kitchen stove. It took several pots of hot water to fill the metal washtub we used. . . .

In the South of my childhood, not having indoor plumbing was the indelible mark of poor white trash. The phrase "so poor they didn't have a pot to piss in" said it all. Poor white trash were viciously stereotyped, and never more viciously than on the playground. White-trash children had cooties—everybody knew that. They had ringworm and pinkeye—don't get near them or you might catch it. They picked their noses. They messed in their pants. If a white-trash child made the mistake of catching a softball during recess, the other children made an elaborate show of wiping it clean before they would touch it.

Once a story circulated at school about a family whose infant daughter had fallen into the "slop jar" and drowned. When I saw the smirks and heard the laughter with which the story was told, I felt sick and afraid in the pit of my stomach. A little girl had died, but people were laughing. What had she done to deserve that laughter? I could only assume that using a chamber pot was something so disgusting, so shameful, that it made a person less than human.

My family was visibly and undeniably poor. My clothes were obviously hand-me-downs. I got free lunches at school. I went to the health department for immunizations. Surely it was equally obvious that we didn't have a flush toilet. But, like an alcoholic who believes no one will know he has a problem as long as he doesn't drink in public, I convinced myself that no one knew my family's little secret. It was a form of denial that would color my relationships with the outside world for years to come.

Having a friend from school spend the night at my house was out of the question. Better to be friendless than to have my classmates know my shameful secret. Home visits from teachers or ministers left me in a dither of anticipatory anxiety. As they chattered on and on with Southern small talk about tomato plants and relish recipes, I sat on the edge of my seat, tensed against the dreaded words, "May I use your bathroom, please?" When I began dating in high school, I'd lie in wait behind the front door, ready to dash out as soon as my date pulled in the driveway, never giving him a chance to hear the call of nature while on our property.

With the help of a scholarship I was able to go away to college, where I could choose from dozens of dormitory toilets and take as many hot showers as I wanted, but I could never openly express my joy in using the facilities. My roommates, each a pampered only child from a well-to-do family, whined and complained about having to share a bathroom. I knew that if I expressed delight in simply *having* a bathroom I would immediately be labeled as a hick. The need to conceal my real self by stifling my emotions created a barrier around me, and I spent my college years in a vacuum of isolation.

Almost twenty years have passed since I first tried to leave my family's chamber pot behind. For many of those years, it followed behind me—the ghost of chamber pots past—clanging and banging and threatening to spill its humiliating contents at any moment. I was convinced that everyone could see it, could smell it even. No college degree or job title seemed capable of banishing it.

If finances had permitted, I might have become an Elvis Presley or a Tammy Faye Bakker, easing the pain of remembered poverty with gold-plated bathtub fixtures and leopard-skin toilet seats. I feel blessed that gradually, ever so gradually, the shame of poverty has begun to fade. The pleasures of the present now take priority over where a long-ago bowel movement did or did not take place. But, for many Southerners, chamber pots and outhouses are more than just memories.

In North Carolina alone, 200,000 people still live without indoor plumbing. People who haul their drinking water home from a neighbor's house or catch rainwater in barrels. People who can't wash their hands before handling food, the way restaurant employees are required by state law to do. People who sneak into public restrooms every day to wash, shave, and brush their teeth before going to work or to school. People who sacrifice their dignity and self-respect when forced to choose between going homeless and going to an outhouse. People whose children think they deserve the conditions in which they live and hold their heads low to hide the shame. But they're not the ones who should feel ashamed. No, they're not the ones who should feel ashamed.

Next Steps and Action

83

Social Class Questionnaire

This questionnaire was used in an undergraduate introductory course in American Civilization titled "Basic Issues in American Culture," taught at Brown University by Professor Susan Smulyan, 1990–1991 and 1991–1992. The course used Janet Zandy's anthology (1990) *Calling Home: Working-Class Women's Writing* (New Brunswick, N.J.: Rutgers University Press). Teachers may be interested in duplicating and using this questionnaire in class.

Please respond to the following questions about social class:

1. How would you characterize your family's socioeconomic background? (For example: poor, working class, lower middle class, middle class, upper middle class, upper class, ruling class).

   What tells you this?

2. What was/is your father's occupation (if applicable)?

   What was/is your mother's occupation (if applicable)?

3. How would you characterize the socioeconomic nature of the neighborhood(s) you grow up in?

   Of the larger community you grew up in?

4. Select, from the list below, five values/expectations/orientations that seem to be most valued in your family. Then select five that seem to be least valued or important. Do these most valued or least valued lists characterize class values?

Least   Family

X

     getting by   Mine

                                                      X

     making a moderate living   X

     making a very good living

     gaining social status or prominence

     open communication among family members   X

   X going to a place of worship

     keeping up with the neighbors

     being physically fit or athletic

     working out psychological issues through therapy   X

     helping others   X

     getting married and having children

     respecting law and order

     defending one's country

     staying out of trouble with the law

     being politically or socially aware

X   recognition

   X community service   X

     saving money

     making your money work for you

     enjoying your money

     getting a high school degree

   X getting a college degree

     getting an advanced or professional degree   X

X   learning a trade

Least   Family   *Mine*

helping to advance the cause of one's racial, religious- cultural group

physical appearance

✗   being a professional

being an entrepreneur

✗   owning a home

being patriotic

going to private school

not being wasteful

having good etiquette.

Others: _____

5. Think of one or two people who you perceive to be from a different social class from you (someone from high school, from a job, from your university). What class would you say they belong to? What tells you this?

   Besides money, what do you see as distinguishing them from you (or your family from their family)?

   How would you characterize their values or their family's values?

   How are their values the same or different from yours?

6. What do you appreciate/have you gained from your class background experience?

7. What has been hard for you being from your class background?

8. What would you like never to hear said about people from your class background?

9. What impact does your class background have on your current attitudes, behaviors, and feelings (about money, work, relationships with people from the same class/from a different class, your sense of self, expectations about life, your politics, etc.)?

84

A Welfare Reform Program Based on Help for Working Parents

Barbara Bergmann and Heidi Hartmann

We should enact a welfare reform that encourages job-holding and sustains working parents and their children in decency; it would be based on the concept of Help for Working

Parents (HWP). The two keys to such a reform are help with health insurance and child care. Those now on Aid to Families with Dependent Children (AFDC) get their health insurance and child care needs provided for. It is brutally difficult for families with access only to low-wage jobs to survive on welfare unless these two are provided. If they are provided, then a year-round, full-time job at the minimum wage would support a mother and two children, if supplemented by the Earned Income Tax Credit and Food Stamp programs we already have, as well as an expanded housing assistance program, especially for families in high-rent areas.

From where Data suggest that many women currently receiving welfare want to work. With the assistance proposed here, they would be able to get a fair share of the jobs that do exist (even if the unemployment rate increases as more women enter the labor market). Most already have a high-school diploma and several years of work experience; but inadequate child care and inadequate health care benefits on the jobs they can get have slowed their progress. Data also show that women who have jobs want fewer births than women who stay home. Through working, these mothers can provide a higher standard of living for the children they already have.

Under the HWP program, low-income two-parent families would get the same help as single-parent families, and families would not have to go on welfare to qualify. There would be a fallback package of benefits and cash assistance for parents out of jobs. Research suggests that a considerable proportion of single parents would leave AFDC in response to the new possibility of living decently without welfare, but those whose employability problems are too severe would continue to need long-term income support.

The cost of this program would depend on how many welfare clients became employed. If 60 percent of them did, the program would cost $86 billion a year in new spending, which could be financed by shifting funds from now-superfluous defense activities, the CIA, and agricultural subsidies to wealthy farmers. Alternatively, taxes on the better-off could be raised to provide the needed revenue.

We advocate a Help for Working Parents (HWP) welfare reform package that would:

1. guarantee health insurance to all families with children (additional cost: $29 billion; would cover all currently uninsured families with children);

2. provide child care for preschool children and after-school care for older children at no cost to families in the bottom 20 percent and at sliding scale fees to middle-class families. These facilities should get children ready for school, and should teach nonviolence, tolerance, honesty, and self-reliance (additional cost: $54 billion; assumes money currently spent on half-day programs would be used to fund some of the full-day costs);

3. provide more housing assistance to families with children, especially in high-rent areas (additional cost: $8.2 billion);

4. maintain current cash assistance (equivalent to AFDC) for single parents who do not work, and extend and expand it to all low-income parents who are out of the labor force or unemployed as a cash fallback (savings over current AFDC and food stamp costs, based on 60 percent shift to the labor market: $19.6 billion).

Other costs of the program would result from increases in the cost of the Earned Income Tax Credit and Unemployment Insurance, as the number of working families receiving help grows.

Additional revenue both to the government and to families could come from more rigorous enforcement of child support obligations, under a Child Support Assurance program for mothers willing to establish paternity. We have not, however, calculated the costs of generating this revenue; we believe the increased collection effort would more than pay for itself through increased revenues.

85

Responsibility for Reducing Poverty

Peter B. Edelman

Looking Forward

We have learned an enormous amount since the 1960s about what steps would be effective in reducing poverty, although we are far from fully applying those lessons to public policy. In too many cases we continue to listen to the age-old refrain of "blame the victim," a simple tune, the words and music of which are far easier to master than the costlier, more complex harmony of sounds involved in a three-dimensional assault on the problem. Any new policies must draw on the lessons of the Great Society and the 1970s and 1980s: that the provision of opportunity is critical and that any antipoverty policy must be created with an eye on labor market problems and employment policy if it is to be successful.

The politics of the 1980s featured an all-out assault on the antipoverty stance of the 1960s, reframing the facts about the earlier period to justify the policy approaches of the latter time. Policies for the 1990s must be responsive insofar as the critics of the 1980s hit upon partial truths in building their politics.

The first piece of revisionism leveled was that the 1960s had featured a totally misplaced reliance on government as the sole source of answers to poverty. This was coupled with a contemporaneous new myth to justify inaction—the representation that government has no role at all to play in reducing poverty. Hence the famous suggestion by President Ronald Reagan in his first inaugural address that government is the enemy.[1] . . .

The second piece of revisionism that came during the 1980s was that sixties antipoverty proponents thought money grew on trees—that they believed there were unlimited resources, and that the only thing lacking was the political will to spend enough of the cornucopia on fighting poverty. The new counterpart myth, nourished by David Stockman's destruction of the federal revenue base and the massive and pervasive success of the antitax propaganda juggernaut, was that no money was available for anything but strengthening the military. . . .

The third piece of revisionism was that the poverty fighters of the 1960s were social engineers who believed that, like Thomas Edison tinkering at his laboratory bench, they would invent some single, magic solution to poverty. The replacement myth to justify the policy thrust of the 1980s was that nothing works, that beyond the ideology of total reliance on the market and a belief in complete laissez-faire government, no program or policy that government could think of or do can possibly make a difference, so there is thus no point in even trying. . . .

The third piece of revisionism was that the poverty fighters of the 1960s were social engineers who believed that, like Thomas Edison tinkering at his laboratory bench, they would invent some single, magic solution to poverty. The replacement myth to justify the policy thrust of the 1980s was that nothing works, that beyond the ideology of total reliance on the market and a belief in complete laissez-faire government, no program or policy that government could think of or do can possibly make a difference, so there is thus no point in even trying. . . .   *To Reduce Poverty:*

The lessons for the new century are threefold: (1) a recognition that poverty will not be significantly reduced unless responsibility for action is undertaken by a wide array of entities and actors, including but not limited to government; (2) a recognition that resources are limited, that the overall health of the economy is critical, and that choices of a sometimes excruciating nature will have to be made along the way to providing funding that, at least in the short run, will be more limited than many would prefer; and (3) a recognition that different solutions apply for different people, and that some among the poor imperatively need interconnected multiple policies that simultaneously attack an array of difficulties. Indeed, the theme of multidimensionality pervades the discussion in the remainder of this article.

If these are the broad outlines of an approach for the next century, what are some details—still somewhat thematic, still overarching—that can help guide policy formation as the decade unfolds with the new opportunities that a change in administration affords? The remainder of this article is devoted to a number of suggestions of perspective and framework that may be helpful to policymakers as new initiatives are considered and undertaken.

Responsibility for Ameliorating Poverty Must Be Undertaken by a Wide Array of Actors, Including the Poor Themselves

Government at all levels; the business community and trade unions, foundations and churches, civic leaders and ordinary citizens, and poor people themselves all have a role and a responsibility in reducing poverty.

The Federal Government

The federal role has been tragically and cynically inadequate in terms of all three dimensions—leadership, funding, and standard-setting. The president, however, can provide leadership to set a positive tone, and the federal government can alter priorities to provide increased funding, basic guidelines, and adequate standards.

A key point to remember is that insofar as government is the institution needed to carry out and implement some of the policies, local and state governments are primarily the ones to do this, and it will often be the case that private, generally nonprofit, entities should be the ones that actually deliver services financed in part with public funds. (The private sector in all of its manifestations must also play a greatly enhanced role.) Other than through the Social Security Administration, the Veterans Administration, and some aspects of agriculture policy, the federal government has never delivered services directly to the general public. Conservatives continue to attack proposals for partial federal financing of activities as efforts to create a massive new federal bureaucracy—when no one is suggesting anything of the kind.[2]

State Government

One major change that has occurred since the 1960s is the revitalization of state government. The states in Lyndon Johnson's time were still suffering the effects of decades of legislative malapportionment. They were still in the thrall of the rural interests that had controlled the legislatures for so long, and they were managed like the mom-and-pop stores of small rural towns.

While nirvana has surely not arrived, the states today are far more competently staffed and managed, and are in general relatively more responsive to their urban citizens. This is not so evident at the moment, with earlier recessions having forced state after state to cut budgets that have long since been cut past fat. The budget cuts have resulted in the decimation of work forces to the point that the states are severely crippled in their ability to deliver some basic services. States today do, however, have the capacity to play a very different role in poverty-related initiatives than they did in the 1960s, when they were bypassed by many programs, especially those administered by the Office of Economic Opportunity and the Departments of Housing and Urban Development and Labor.

Public Funds and the Role of Private Nonprofit Organizations

Another significant change is the public sector's role, which is still evolving; the change concerns the extent to which publicly funded services are delivered by private, generally nonprofit organizations.[3] To some extent, there is less here than meets the eye, because America has always had an active and extensive nonprofit sector that delivers services of various kinds, especially health and welfare services. Yet increasingly, questions are being asked about the efficacy of public service delivery by public employees. Critics are troubled by the moribundity and unresponsiveness that seem to attend delivery of services by people with civil service job protection, especially delivery of services to constituencies with very little political power. Public employee unions are understandably quite concerned about this line of questioning, which implies that replacement of unionized civil service workers by nonunion, nontenured private workers would be appropriate. The trend toward additional privatization will most likely continue unless public sector managers and union leaders can find ways to demonstrate that they can improve productivity and responsiveness.

At the same time, privatization contains significant pitfalls, even when confined largely to nonprofit entities. While private organizations do not face the barriers created by civil service laws in discharging unsatisfactory workers, quality control of the performance of service deliverers who work for private groups is difficult to achieve. Hard as it is for a central office, or even a regional or district office, to know what is going on in a series of decentralized offices or sites among employees who are all directly on the public payroll, it is even more difficult to monitor the performance of groups that are separately incorporated and organized.

Running a holistic system in which people are successfully referred for different kinds of required assistance is another challenge that is made more difficult by utilizing private agencies to deliver services that need to be part of a larger system. Difficult as it is to get people who all work for the same government to coordinate and cooperate with one another, it is vastly more difficult to get agencies that are chartered for only one or even a number of limited purposes to work actively as part of a genuine system of service delivery.

The Business Community

The business community has increasingly come to see that it has a role to play in reducing poverty in America. Concerned about the labor force of the future, the corporate community in the 1980s began to speak out nationally on the need for policies and programs to develop and educate children to the fullness of their potential. Locally, in city after city, businesses began to get involved in school improvement efforts, and often participated in blue-ribbon commissions to diagnose school systems' problems and propose remedies. In some states and communities, businesses have stayed with the process to help press for implementation of proposed reforms, including adequate funding to make change occur.

These efforts have been largely confined to the corporate sector of the business community, and they have been, as implied, mainly limited to "prevention" policies such as child development, prenatal care, and education. A major challenge for the next century is to interest a larger portion of the business community in the poverty problem, and to broaden topics of interest, particularly to add a focus on employment and immediate preparation for employment. Self-sufficiency will not be forthcoming for any significant number of the poor without the availability of jobs; and, even when jobs are available, proactive steps need to be taken to ensure that low-income people are ready to perform in those jobs and are given a chance to apply. The business community needs to play a role in publicizing available jobs and in helping people, especially young people with no experience in the labor market, to understand what is involved in pursuing employment.

A particular agenda item for the business community (as well as for law enforcement) concerns employment discrimination, which is still widespread and operates to intensify poverty for people of color. Both nationally and in particular locales, business leaders can work with civil rights advocates and with public agencies charged with enforcing antidiscrimination laws to foster public understanding about the degree to which widespread employment discrimination continues to exist.

Foundations

Foundations have undertaken major new initiatives against poverty over the past decade, particularly in designing new services for families and children in low-income neighborhoods, and also in funding studies to sort out which policies work and which do not. There is an unprecedented level of sophistication about poverty issues in the foundation world at this time. With the advent in Washington of a more responsive administration, there is a possibility of translating the foundation initiatives of recent years into public policy, and of new foundation-government partnerships leveraging greater resources into various demonstrations and initiatives.

Religious Institutions

Religious institutions must become more deeply involved in reducing poverty. Some individual churches have played a critical role for a long time, delivering services to families, running Head Start programs, sponsoring mentoring programs, and building low-income and elderly housing. Many denominations have been outstanding in their national commitment to public action.

These efforts, both local and national, need to be expanded, but a new dimension of activity is needed as well. There is a moral breakdown in the inner city. Violence, drugs, and unduly early pregnancy involve issues of economics, law enforcement, and public health, but they are also moral questions. The long-term answers to these questions may lie in greater economic opportunity and in social, economic, and racial justice. The short-term answers may include incarceration and community policing, drug treatment, and prenatal care and family preservation services. Additionally, a message needs to be sent about values and personal responsibility, the importance of marriage and family, the avoidance of out-of-wedlock pregnancy, abstinence from drug use (and drug dealing), and the value of work at a legal job. These messages can do little good without accompanying public policy, but they are crucial messages all the same, and we need religious and spiritual leaders to make an extra effort to join in sending them. We have had a poli-

[handwritten margin notes: "This is all top-down 'fix it' solutions. What do those in poverty want for themselves?"]

tics of values about the poor for some time (for centuries, in fact), but in recent years this has involved using values as weapons to divide rather than as tools to teach and build.

Individuals

This leads to the last point on the issue of who must take responsibility; *individuals must take responsibility for themselves and their families*. Children need to hear that the counterpart of opportunity is responsibility and that, with all the barriers that confront them if they are poor, and even more so if they are poor and of color, there exists no substitute for their own effort. The message needs especially to be repeated through the years of adolescence and young adulthood.

That individuals must take responsibility is a message that must be understood carefully by those who send it and those who make policy based on it—it is hard for a person to take responsibility who cannot find a job and it is hard for a person to take responsibility who has no way to pay rent or buy food. There are millions of the poor who are not disabled within the legal definition of that term, but who are nonetheless so damaged by the ravages of life that they are simply not in a position to take responsibility. Asking people to take responsibility for themselves who are unable to do so is not wise public policy. Nonetheless, if the responsibility of all is a basic tenet of antipoverty strategy in the 1990s, it must be extended to the poor themselves.

Appropriate Strategies Used to Attack Poverty Are Complex and Multifaceted—They Begin with the Overall Health of the Economy and Extend Through a Broad Array of Structural and Targeted Policies

There is a tendency, in political rhetoric at least, to treat "welfare reform" as not just one antipoverty strategy, but as *the* antipoverty strategy. Welfare reform used to mean transforming cash assistance into a guaranteed annual income. Now it means finding ways ranging from kind to cruel to help welfare recipients become self-sufficient, or at least free from dependence on state largesse. It has always been the case, however, that making welfare reform the heart of an antipoverty strategy is exactly backwards. Welfare should be our provision for people for whom all else has failed. Our antipoverty strategy should be our "all else," and our concomitant aim should be to minimize the number of people for whom all else fails. We should certainly want to "reform" welfare, both to make it adequate for survival and to help (or even shove) people to get off of it. But we should work even harder to prevent people from ever having to depend on welfare in the first place. . . .

The complexity of a genuine antipoverty strategy is awe inspiring. It would include, although not be limited to (1) structural economic policy to create economic activity and jobs in specific locations or jobs targeted at specifically needed tasks; (2) job creation targeted to give work experience, perhaps in community service, to tide over low-income young people through what is otherwise a period of utterly predictable long-term unemployment and to assist them in seeking unsubsidized employment; (3) low-income housing policies to stabilize family residential situations, including geographic strategies to enable low-income people to reside on a scatter-site basis throughout metropolitan areas; (4) health coverage, for its intrinsic value and to enable people to work without losing the health coverage afforded by Medicaid;[4] (5) child care and Head Start, for both child development and poverty prevention purposes and to enable parents to work;[5] (6) decent education for all poor children;[6] (7) tough antidiscrimination laws to ensure that no one is kept out of employment for unacceptable reasons; (8) family support and family preservation services (and legal services) to help low-income families cope with some of the problems and forces that buffet and beset their lives; (9) substance abuse treatment services; (10) effective law enforcement, to make the mean streets safe; (11) strong child support enforcement to require noncustodial parents to fulfill their responsibilities and to provide a more adequate income floor for female-headed families that are so disproportionately poor; and (12) adequate income support and supplementation policies for people who work and do not earn enough to escape poverty, and for people who are unable to function in the labor market or cannot find work.

As complex and lengthy as the foregoing list is, it fails to take account of a number of specific issues and concerns, which are the subject of the rest of this article.

Antipoverty Strategy Must Take Account of Place— Where People Live and Their Preferred Places of Living

The fact of place is central to understanding poverty. The rural poor, for example, must cope with a dearth of employment opportunities and minimal government assistance. Severe declines in traditionally rural industries have depleted jobs in rural regions, while the relatively low educational and skill levels of rural residents have deterred new industries from locating in rural areas. Rural unemployment rates are higher and rural wages lower than in metropolitan areas, although rural living costs are about the same as urban costs; as a result, a higher proportion of rural residents are vulnerable to poverty.

Place is an equally important factor in shaping the circumstances of the urban poor. Concentrated poverty means concentrations of people who have dropped out of school, had children too young, do not have jobs, and depend on welfare. Concentrated poverty means few role models of success by legal means and few peers headed for college and professional careers. Concentrated poverty means crime, violence, drugs, and premature death.[7]

We need to think more broadly. There are two possible solutions, not mutually exclusive, to the problem of place: changing the conditions of life in the inner city, and making it possible for people to live elsewhere. Neither solution is easy, either substantively or politically, but both are essential if we are to have any chance of making serious headway.

The best solution would be for people to acquire the economic wherewithal to be able to choose where they want to live, free from any constraint on that choice. If they wanted, they could then move out of the inner city without any need for continuing subsidy. This pattern of upward economic mobility and suburban settlement has been the time-honored course for wave after wave of new Americans—Irish, Italians, Poles, Germans, Jews, and countless others, including the black middle class. Ironically, the inner city exists in its current form for a disproportionate number of African Americans,[8] in significant part because the traditional black middle class—the doctors, the lawyers, the preachers, and the teachers, joined by the new middle class that emerged in the wake of the 1960s—moved out in droves.

Yet the movement—both upward and outward—has stopped. The people left behind in the inner city are extremely poor, unemployed, and on welfare. If they, or at least their children, are going to be enabled to choose whether to leave the inner city on their own steam they need a sense of possibility, a jump start that does not now exist. It is as though they live at the end of a bridge that lacks an approach ramp. There may be a way out but, as things are, they cannot even get to it. To build the approach ramp, life in the inner city has to change significantly. There need to be schools that teach. Children need to be safe going to and from school as well as in school itself. They need to live in housing that is both safe and adequate.[9] They need access to decent health care. There need to be at least the basic elements of commercial life so families can buy food and clothing and obtain basic necessary services—fewer liquor stores and more grocery stores would be one way to say it. Without these basic conditions, it is simply unrealistic to expect the inner-city poor to lift themselves out of poverty.

To some the goal is transforming a neighborhood so that it becomes a real community in which people can live safely and stably for the long run, one that includes a new middle class that has developed within and even some who have been lured back by the revitalization. To others the aim is to make the inner city a launching pad for people to move elsewhere. Either way, multidimensional initiatives are necessary in the inner city. The need is for total and comprehensive approaches to inner-city vitalization, which encompass the physical, educational, economic, and service needs of the people. The need is for place-specific strategies that go well beyond enterprise zones in their breadth.

Antipoverty Strategy Must Recognize That Poverty Is a Function of Both Race and Class in the United States

There is a tendency among poverty "warriors" to talk about policies that are race-neutral: Head Start, compensatory education, job training, and so on. Thinking race-neutrally about poverty is as sterile as thinking in class-neutral and place-neutral terms. African Americans, Latinos, and Native Americans are disproportionately poor. In fact, the issues of race, class, and place are intertwined. In the preceding discussion about place, the suggestion was that even though the condition of the African-American inner city might appear related predominantly or significantly to race because of the racial homogeneity of the population, the problem is significantly one of class. The hypothesis was that class isolation is a major cause, particularly for children, of a lack of peer models and role models and a consequent lack of expectations. Yet the isolation is surely connected to race as well. One reason why dispersal solutions are bitterly opposed is not so much the opposition to having low-income people in a predominantly middle-income area, but to having low-income black people. Breaking down the isolation of the black lower class means, in part, combatting discrimination against lower-income black people in the field of low-income housing.

Another aspect of the disproportionate poverty of African Americans, Latinos, and Native Americans is the continuing, pervasive racial discrimination in America. This is particularly true in employment and housing. The question of the plain old garden-variety ugly race discrimination has gotten lost in the more arcane niceties of the affirmative action debate. The unspoken assumption in recent years has been that, of course, no one discriminates in the one-by-one hiring of employees or the one-by-one selling or rental of houses or apartments to those who can afford to pay. The only problem, it has implicitly been said, is the attempt to force the pace, to require hiring of "unqualified" or less well-qualified people by reference to fixed numerical objectives.

The opponents of affirmative action succeeded incidentally and effectively in drawing attention away from the pervasive employment (and housing) discrimination that was going on all the while. Discrimination in entry-level hiring is difficult to detect. People apply for a job and are not hired. As long as they are not told blatantly that "we don't hire your kind," they never find out why they were not hired. They simply assume that they lost out to someone better qualified.

In recent years, though, the concept of employment testing has been developed and applied, and has demonstrated with all too spectacular success that, in fact, vast numbers of employers routinely engage in discrimination based on race and ethnicity. Two testers, one African American and the other white, or one Latino and the other Anglo, with matched résumés, approach an employer for an advertised job (or go to an employment agency to seek assistance in finding a job). About one time in five, a blatant difference in treatment occurs: the white tester is offered the advertised job and the black tester is not even interviewed or is perhaps considered only for a menial job.[10] Among other facts about which we have buried our national head in the sand for twelve years, the pervasive racial discrimination that affects millions of hiring decisions in our country every year stands near the top of the list.

Priority Attention Should Be Given to Focusing on Age Groups with Which There Is a Particular Chance of Success

If place, race, and class are essential elements of policy, so is age. The transition from youth to adulthood is an especially critical time. This is the time of entry (or not) into the labor market and of decisions whether to stay in school, have a child, or marry. These decisions are interrelated. Young people who drop out of school are less likely to find a job, more likely to have a child, and less likely to marry after they have the child. Young people who cannot find work are more likely to possess the other interrelated characteristics. The same holds for young people who have a child in their teens, and so forth. Young women who have children in their teens without finishing school or getting married are disproportionate candidates for long spells on welfare. An intervention that successfully attacks any of the four variables will affect the others, and interventions that operate in multiple fashion are even more promising. Initiatives that target young mothers can be designed to target their small children at the same time, and can therefore have a simultaneous two-generation payoff. . . .

The Ideas of Building Community and Empowering People Are Intertwined Qualitative Aims That Are Essential Elements in Approaches to Reducing Poverty

Community is a kind of mirage—an attractive if vague aim pursued by all who would enhance the functioning of our democracy at all levels, but not there to grasp tangibly. Similarly, empowerment is a buzzword often heard in both liberal and conservative statements of poverty policy. Yet both ideas are critical. The massive problems faced by the poor are not simply the sum of thousands of failures of individual responsibility by the people involved. They are failures of community. As we have perpetuated the idea that this nation provides opportunity to each of us as individuals, that each of us needs only to grasp the opportunity to achieve success, we have seldom acknowledged that without membership in a community, success is much more difficult to attain. There are, as there have been throughout history, some who do succeed against all odds. But most of us need good schooling, decent housing, safe streets, and role models and mentors of various kinds in order to do our best. Most of us need to be part of a community to succeed. Poverty strategies, then, must recognize the importance of community—of shared responsibility and security—if efforts that require responsible and productive behavior by individuals are to succeed.

Equally important is the goal of empowerment, as our society's strong emphasis on the value of work illustrates. Without romanticizing lousy jobs, for most people there is satisfaction in earning an income, or at least there is more satisfaction in bringing home a paycheck than there is in depending on the dole. Earning an income is empowering. Empowerment means self-esteem, a sense of control over one's life. Parents who feel empowered are more likely to raise children who have a will to succeed.[11]

Parental involvement in the schools is another empowerment and community-building strategy.[12] At its simplest and least controversial, parental involvement for low-income parents means only the kind of concern and activity that other parents engage in as a matter of course. The point here is that school authorities need to reach out and take special steps to involve low-income parents.[13] . . .

Personal Safety and Security Are Critical to Any Comprehensive Antipoverty Strategy

Individual economic security is a necessary, but not sufficient, aim of policy. If place and community are elements of policy, physical safety, and security are elements of policies of place and community. A sense of community cannot be built without safety.[14] If conservatives have pursued law enforcement and incarceration to the exclusion of economic security and prevention of crime, liberals have tended to underplay public safety as an element of policy. The violence, crime, and rampant drug use will not shrink to manageable levels unless there is a sense of movement on a larger agenda of opportunity and change, but that larger agenda will be difficult to pursue with any optimism so long as children are being gunned down in the street and people are so habituated to crack cocaine that they neglect basic parental responsibilities. Immediate stress on law enforcement and drug education and treatment is an indispensable element in a total strategy.

Self-Sufficiency Will Not Be Attainable for Everyone, Even in the Long Run; Income Maintenance Must Continue to Be Part of Antipoverty Policy

The working poor are likely to be with us for the long run. We have become more conscious in recent years of the number of people who try their hardest and "play by the rules," and still do not earn enough to escape poverty. Two policy mechanisms available to assist them are the Earned Income Tax Credit (EITC), and the minimum wage. The EITC and the minimum wage are complementary strategies, in part because they have differing disadvantages that will be minimized if both are pursued. Making the EITC more adequate costs the taxpayers money and, while it may actually increase employment, it may do so by letting employers pay less than a living wage (although it could also save consumers money in the cost of the goods or services that the employer provides). Increasing the minimum wage may cause employers to let some workers go (or cause an increase in the price of the employer's goods or services, if demand is sufficiently inelastic to allow the employer to pass the increase on).[15]

Using work experience as a training device and a concomitant way to provide income support to someone on a temporary basis is another component of the antipoverty framework. Hence the proposal to create limited-term community service opportunities for young people who are in an age category that experiences massive unemployment, and who might be tided over and learn something valuable by participating in a youth corps type community service program. Programs that provide transitional work experience and training make sense as part of an antipoverty strategy. . . .

Conclusion: What an Appropriate Antipoverty Policy Is Will Mean Different Things for Different People— Moving beyond The Silver Bullet

Some of the poor are children who will be helped out of poverty by prevention and education programs that break the cycle of poverty. Some are low-income workers who will be helped out of poverty by income supplementation. Another group are women on welfare who would go to work tomorrow if they could find affordable child care for their children and would not lose the health coverage they have under Medicaid. Others are substance abusers who would pursue employment if they could obtain treatment. Some of the poor do not live in areas of concentrated poverty, making place-oriented strategies irrelevant for them. In addition, there are some who are not members of groups that have historically been the subject of discrimination, and they will not be helped by antidiscrimination policies.

The comprehensiveness of the strategy called for in this article is not a comprehensiveness for each individual in poverty. It is comprehensive because of the significant differences in the situation of various groups among the poor. Some individuals will escape poverty as a consequence of the application of one particular policy; some will escape poverty by participating in a certain program. Others, though, are themselves candidates for comprehensiveness because of the complexity of their own situation: their race or other status, the place where they live, a multiplicity of problems in their family, or a multiplicity of their individual needs for help.

When the Lone Ranger and Tonto had finished solving the problem of the week's radio or TV program, the Lone Ranger always left behind a silver bullet. For those who remember the Lone Ranger, the silver bullet represented the national symbol of the simple, magic solution to a problem. If we ever did believe that a silver bullet solution to poverty might be found, that time is over. There are solutions to poverty, but they are different for different people, and multifaceted for some. It is time to get beyond the silver bullet.

Notes

1. As Ronald Reagan explained,

   > In this present crisis, government is not the solution to our problem. . . . It is no coincidence that our present troubles parallel and are proportionate to the intervention and intrusion in our lives that result from unnecessary and excessive growth of government. . . .
   >
   > It is time to check and reverse the growth of government which shows signs of having grown beyond the consent of the governed.
   >
   > Ronald Reagan, Inaugural Address (Jan. 20, 1981),
   > reprinted in Joint Congressional Committee On Inaugural Ceremonies,
   > *Inaugural Addresses of the United States* (1989), 331, 332–34.

2. For example, during debate over the child care legislation enacted by Congress in 1990, conservatives argued that expanded federal involvement in child care would simply create an expensive federal bureaucracy that would interfere with local and state child care efforts when in fact nothing in any pending proposals would have created any vast new federal bureaucracy. See Martin Tolchin, "Deep Divisions Emerge in Congress on Ways to Expand Aid for Child Care," *New York Times*, Nov. 11, 1989, A12.

3. For a generally positive assessment of privatization at the local and state levels, see David Osborne and Ted Gaebler, *Reinventing Government* (1992), 45–48, 76–107.

4. In 1991, 35.4 million Americans lacked any form of health insurance coverage, 800,000 more than in 1990.

5. Although more than two-thirds of all mothers with children under eighteen were in the labor force in 1991, existing child care resources are simply inadequate. Because of high costs, inadequate supply, and poor quality care, many children lack adequate and safe supervision and do not receive the stimulation necessary for healthy development. Only 30 percent of all eligible children were served by Head Start in 1992, although Congress has authorized expansion to serve all eligible children by 1994. See Children's Defense Fund, *The State Of America's Children 1992* (1992), 17–24.

6. Educational testing data indicate that a significant number of children fail to learn critical academic skills. Less than half of all high school seniors read at levels considered necessary for even moderately complex tasks. Only 17 percent of eighth graders show proficiency in mathematics. See National Education Goals Panel, *The National Education Goals Report: Building A Nation of Leaders 1991* (1991), 46. Minority students tend to score even lower; by middle school, minorities perform a full year behind their white schoolmates.

7. A black male child born and living in Harlem has a shorter life span than his cohort in Bangladesh, one of the world's poorest nations. See Gale Scott, "Harlem's '3rd World' Life Expectancy," *Newsday*, Jan. 18, 1990, 6.

8. Some urban areas have become so segregated that population experts have coined the term *hypersegregation* to capture its extent. See Isabel Wilkerson, "Study Finds Segregation Worse Than Scientists Imagined," *New York Times*, Aug. 5, 1989, sec. 1, p. 6. Indeed, the researcher who invented that term argues elsewhere that racial segregation has been the primary cause

of the increase in the concentration of poverty. See Douglas S. Massey, "American Apartheid: Segregation and the Making of the Underclass," *Am. J. Soc.* 96 (1990), 329, 331–36.

9. In 1984, some 2,380,600 children between the ages of six months and five years were exposed to lead levels that exceeded ceilings set by the Environmental Protection Agency. Children of black families with low incomes were those hardest hit. Lead exposure was also more prevalent in urban than in rural areas. See Dana Hughes et al., *Children's Defense Fund, The Health of America's Children* (1989), 34-35. Poor families often live in deficient, overcrowded, and unaffordable housing. In 1987, more than two-thirds of all families in poverty lived in substandard housing and many paid more than half of their income for housing, although most state and federal standards suggest no more than 30 percent of family income should be spent on housing. See Twentieth Century Fund, *More Housing, More Fairly: Report of the Twentieth Century Fund Task Force on Affordable Housing* 8 (1991).

10. For a study of employment bias in Washington, D.C., and the use of paired testers to detect its prevalence, see Marc Bendick Jr. et al., "Measuring Employment Discrimination Through Controlled Experiments" (Jan. 1993); unpublished manuscript, on file with the *Georgetown Law Journal*. In this study, testers were "closely paired in terms of age, personal appearance, articulateness, and manner" (5). The testers trained and rehearsed and were given fictional biographies that, across a particular pair, were similar in terms of education, skills, and experience. The study found that black testers were treated significantly worse than their white partners 24 percent of the time; Latino testers were treated worse than their Anglo partners 22 percent of the time (37). In this study, employment bias took five general forms: whites were more likely to be interviewed than nonwhites; whites were more likely to receive a job offer or referral than nonwhites; when both test partners received job offers, the white's compensation was, on average, higher than the nonwhite's; nonwhites were more likely to be steered into positions lower than those for which they had applied; and whites were more likely to be considered for unadvertised job vacancies than were their partners (13–14).

11. On the other hand, parents who experience external pressures on their family life are more likely to believe their children will face a wide range of problems, including violence, drug use, teen pregnancy, inadequate education, and underemployment. See National Commission on Children, *Speaking of Kids* (1991), 21, 31 (comparing beliefs of single parents to parents in intact family units, and comparing beliefs by incomes).

12. Parental involvement may increase academic performance, motivate teachers and students, improve school curricula, and increase accountability. See Ann Bastian et al., *Choosing Quality: The Case for Democratic Schooling* (1986), 94-95.

13. Many low-income parents may be discouraged from taking an active role in their child's education because the parents themselves may have had a poor experience with, or bad memories of, their own schooling; they may be intimidated by an institution that they associate with failure. Moreover, economic survival may present a barrier to parental involvement of low-income families: "[E]ven the expense of child care and travel to attend school meetings are real factors limiting parent inclinations to activism" (National Commission on children, *Speaking of Kids* [1991], 95). However, several foundation initiatives that facilitate the participation of low-income parents in their children's education have enjoyed a measure of success at the community level.

14. In addition to posing a physical threat to children and families, violence also impedes children's healthy development; recent research indicates that living in an unsafe environment significantly increases children's anxiety levels. Almost one in every six children worries that someone on drugs will harm him; poor children and those in urban areas report even higher levels of fear about their security and well-being. See National Commission on Children, *Speaking of Kids* (1991), 28, 33–34.

15. See Charles Brown, "Minimum Wage Laws: Are They Overrated?" *J. Econ. Persp.* (1988), 132, 144–45 (suggesting that both critics and supporters of minimum wage laws overstate their economic impact).

Section 8

Working for Social Justice: Visions and Strategies for Change

Introduction by Ximena Zúñiga

One of the fundamental questions of our day is whether the tradition of struggle can be preserved and expanded. I refer to the struggle for decency and dignity, the struggle for freedom and democracy.

—Cornel West, "The Moral Obligations
of Living in a Democratic Society"

As a democratic relationship, dialogue is the opportunity available to me to open up to the thinking of others, and thereby not wither away in isolation.

—Paulo Freire, *Pedagogy of Hope*

Change means growth, and growth can be painful. But we sharpen self-definition by exposing the self in work and struggle together with those whom we define as different from ourselves, although sharing the same goals.

—Audre Lorde, *Sister Outsider*

Throughout this volume we take the view that developing an awareness of and knowledge about the systemic and interlocking qualities of social oppression are critical steps that must be taken for personal and social change. Alternative perspectives about what is possible and strategies for making a difference are generated, at least in part, by how we examine an issue or problem. That is why so much of this book focuses on analyzing the systemic and interlocking quality of all systems of oppression, how they manifest themselves at the institutional and cultural levels, and impact individual lives. At the same time, we take the view that it is important for each of us to believe that there are steps we can take to effect change as individuals or in concerted efforts with other individuals or groups. Like Beverly Daniel Tatum (1992), we believe that it is unethical to critically examine issues of social oppression in the classroom without offering hope, a vision for the future, and practical tools for change. Otherwise, our well-intended efforts become "a pre-scription for despair" (1992, 24).

In his essay "The Moral Obligations of Living in a Democratic Society," Cornel West (1999) argues that hope is part of the democratic tradition. In his own words, "to be part of the democratic tradition is to be a prisoner of hope" (p. 12). West suggests that you cannot have hope without engaging in some form of struggle against the social, political, and economic systems that target and disenfranchise those who are most vulnerable and provide a disproportionate amount of wealth, power and influence to the wealthy. Hence, hope and struggle for social justice are inextricably linked, and both are necessary for actualizing the promise of democra-cy. However, collective struggle without vision can also be a prescription for despair. We need individual *and* collective visions to sustain us and move us to take action against social injustice.

Readings in This Section

The selections herein offer direction for developing a vision for working toward social justice and suggest strategies for personal and collective action. In the first selection, Suzanne Pharr reminds us that "a truly democratic society is always in the process of redefining itself" and that struggles for liberation are an essential part of that process. She suggests that liberation requires a struggle against all forms of discrimination and against all those barriers that keep large portions of the population from attaining economic and social justice, from participating fully in decisions affecting their lives, and from having the rights and responsibilities of living in a free society. In Pharr's thinking it is not enough to be critically aware of the historical and social context of oppression and its manifestations at the cultur-al, institutional and personal levels, or even to have the ideological commitment to struggle against social injustice. We also need to be willing to engage with our hearts, build and honor relationships across differences, hear other perspectives, lend support where there is pain and loss, develop individual and institutional integrity, and redefine and share power.

In the second selection, Patricia Hill Collins suggests that those who wish to engage in multi-issue social change efforts with people different from themselves need to learn how to transcend barriers created by their own experiences with race, class and gender oppression in order to build the types of coalitions essential for social change. Hill-Collins identifies three major challenges that need to be addressed: (1) recognizing that differing experiences with oppression create prob-lems in relationships; (2) learning how to build relationships and coalitions around common causes with people of different races, genders, and socio-economic sta-tuses; and (3) developing the capacity for empathy for the experiences of individu-als and groups different from ourselves.

Probably the biggest challenge faced by people who want to work for social jus-tice is where to begin. The process of becoming increasingly aware and confident of one's ability to effect change at the personal, institutional and cultural levels has been broadly defined as *empowerment.* This process involves a range of per-sonal and collective actions that enable people from dominant and subordinate groups to work together to dismantle oppression and generate visions and prac-tices for a more socially just future. Bobbie Harro describes a cyclical path for individual empowerment that she calls the "Cycle of Liberation." This conceptual tool maps the process individuals may follow as they "take themselves toward empowerment or liberation." Harro identifies seven points of entry in the path toward personal empowerment, including getting ready, reaching out, joining others to dialogue, building community, and participating or forming coalitions to create change. Barbara J. Love, on the other hand, discusses the concept of liberatory consciousness, and identifies four critical elements in its development: awareness, analysis, action, and accountability/ally-ship. In her view, the development of liberatory consciousness is a crucial step for individuals who are committed to struggling for greater equity and social justice. A liberatory consciousness enables us to live our lives "in oppressive systems and institutions with awareness and intentionality, rather than on the basis of the socialization to which we have been subjected." It also enables us to remain hopeful and not give up to despair.

The selections in this concluding section offer specific strategies or approaches that people working alone or together can use to bring about social change. Mary McClintock outlines a framework for individuals who wish to begin to interrupt oppressive behaviors and take actions toward social justice, which she refers to as the *action continuum*. In discussing this framework, she identifies five actions individuals can take to interrupt oppression: educate yourself; interrupt the oppressive behavior; interrupt and educate; support others' efforts to educate and take action that promotes understanding of differences; and initiate actions that promote understanding and value cultural differences. Cooper Thompson writes about his own struggle as a white heterosexual man to become increasingly aware of racism, sexism, and heterosexism, and its impact on his life and the lives of others. Ricky Sherover-Marcuse outlines a set of working assumptions and guidelines for alliance building for people from both dominant and subordinate groups who wish to collaborate across differences. And Gloria Anzaldúa discusses the concept of "allies," and what it takes "to help each other heal," using her own experiences as a Chicana, Mexican, lesbian activist, and writer.

Building alliances across differences requires dialogue and developing and sustaining relationships. Our last two selections include an article by Ximena Zúñiga and Todd D. Sevig that focuses on student-led intergroup dialogues aimed at consciousness-raising and the bridging of differences. These dialogues allow student participants to engage in conversation about "taboo" topics to explore conflicts and common ground. In the concluding selection, John Anner offers examples of how people can learn to work together across differences. After describing the experiences of several grass-roots organizations, Anner lists strategies for building successful multicultural organizations committed to social justice. He reminds us that we can sustain our vision and remain hopeful by working together for social justice, bridging differences, educating ourselves, engaging in dialogue and solidarity work, interrupting bigoted behavior, and confronting racism and other forms oppression.

References

Freire, P. (1994). *Pedagogy of Hope*. New York: Continuum.

Lorde, A. (1984). *Sister Outsider*. Freedom: Calif: Crossing Press.

Tatum B.D (1992). "Talking about Race, Learning about Racism: The Application of Racial Identity Development Theory in the Classroom." Harvard Educational Review 62 (1), 1–24.

West, C. (1999). "The Moral Obligations of Living in a Democratic Society." In D. Batstone and E. Mendieta, eds., *The Good Citizen*. New York: Routledge.

Contexts

86

Reflections on
Liberation

Suzanne Pharr

These political times call for renewed dialogue about and commitment to the politics of liberation. Because a truly democratic society is always in the process of redefining itself, its evolution is fueled by struggles for liberation on the part of everyone wishing to participate in the development of the institutions and policies that govern our lives. Liberation requires a struggle against discrimination based on race, class, gender, sexual identity, ableism and age—those barriers that keep large portions of the population from having access to economic and social justice, from being able to participate fully in the decisions affecting our lives, from having a full share of both the rights and responsibilities of living in a free society. . . .

This is the challenge for all of us. The work of liberation politics is to change hearts and minds, develop empathy with and sympathy for other people, and help each other discover how we are inextricably linked together for our common good and our survival on this planet.

Like power, liberation cannot be given; it must be created. Liberation politics requires

- helping individuals to fulfill their greatest potential by providing truthful information along with the tools and skills for using it, supporting their autonomy and self-government, and connecting them to life in community with others;

- fostering both individual freedom and mutual responsibility for others;

- recognizing that freedom demands people always be able to make their own choices about their lives;

- creating a politic of *shared power* rather than *power over*;

- learning the non-violent skills of compromise and mediation in the sometimes difficult collective lives of family and community—in organizations, the workplace, and governing bodies;

- developing integrity in relationships through understanding that the same communal values—generosity and fairness, responsibility and freedom, forgiveness and atonement—must be maintained not just in personal relationships but in the workplace, social groups, and governing bodies;

- treating everyone as a valued whole person, not as someone to be used or controlled;

- maintaining civility in our relationships and being accountable for our behavior;

- seeing cultural differences as life-enhancing, as expanding possibilities;

- placing a broad definition of human rights at the center of our values: ensuring that every person has food, shelter, clothing, safety, education, health care, and a livable income. . . .

We are seeking ways to bring people together to work on common causes across differences. If, indeed, all oppressions are connected, then it follows that the targets of this oppression are connected as well as their solution. This interconnection leads us to the idea of collaborative efforts to create democratic values, discourse, and institutions.

We believe that we will succeed when we collectively create a vision that in practice offers a way of life so attractive that people will not be able to resist it. As progressive people across this country we are working to create a multi-issue, multiracial and multicultural liberation movement; we are trying to redefine our work and bring more integrity to it; we are engaged in developing a clearer, more compelling vision, building stronger relationships among justice-seeking people, and including more people in the process of creating a democracy that works for all of us. . . .

Transformational Organizing and Building Community

For whatever reasons, progressive people have not always talked a great deal about the strong moral convictions underlying why we do this work of social justice. *It is because we believe every person counts, has human dignity, and deserves respect, equality and justice.* This morality is the basis for our vision, and when we do our best vision-based organizing (as opposed to response-based or expediency-based), all our work flows from this basic belief.

Ours is a noble history. Because progressive people believe in the inclusion of everyone in the cause of justice and equality, we have struggled for civil rights for people of color, for women, for people with disabilities, and now for lesbians and gay men. We have worked to save the environment; to provide women autonomy and choice concerning our bodies; to end unjust wars; to end homelessness, hunger, and poverty; to create safe workplaces, decent wages, and fair labor practices; to honor treaty rights; to eliminate HIV and improve health care; to eliminate bias crime and violence against women and children. We share broad principles of inclusion, fairness, and justice. We must not forget what provides the fire for our work, what connects us in the struggle for freedom and equality.

We are living in a time in which people are crying out for something to believe in—for a moral sense, for purpose, for answers that will bring some calm to the chaos they feel in their lives. As progressive people, we have not always offered up our vision of the world, our activities for justice, as a moral vision. When we have, as during the civil rights movement, people working together for a common good have felt whole.

I believe it is our moral imperative to help each other make connections, to show how everyone is interrelated and belongs in community, or as it is currently expressed, "We all came on different ships but we're in the same boat now." It is at our peril if we do work that increases alienation and robs meaning from life. Today's expressions of violence, hatred, and bigotry are directly related to the levels of alienation and disconnection felt by people. For our very survival, we must develop a sense of common humanity.

It may be that our most important political work is figuring out how to make the full human connection, how to engage our hearts as well as our minds, how to heal the injuries we have suffered, how to do organizing that transforms people as well as institutions. With these as goals, we need to rethink our strategies and tactics.

We have to think about our vision of change. Are we involved in a struggle for power that requires forces and resources on each side and a confrontational showdown in which only one side wins? If we are in a shoot-out, then the progressive side has already lost, for certainly there are more resources on the Right at this moment. In other cases where we can organize the most resources, such as the 1992 "No on 9" campaign in Oregon, what is the nature and permanency of the win? The antigay and lesbian constitutional amendment was defeated, but in general, people did not have a sense of ecstatic victory. I think there were two primary reasons: (1) the Right immediately announced its intention to take the fight to local rural communities and to build a string of victories in areas where it had developed support, indicating that this is indeed a long struggle for the hearts and souls of Oregonians; and (2) the campaign did not facilitate the building of lasting relationships, of communities, of progressive institutions—because it did not see itself as part of a movement. At the end, I believe people felt a warlike atmosphere had been created, but that the language and tactics of war had failed them. In the months that followed the election victory, people seemed fatigued, wary, often dispirited and in retreat. Rather than being transformed into new politics and relationships by their experience, they seemed battered by it.

Transformational Organizing

There is something to be learned when victory feels like defeat. Somehow, people did not emerge from the Oregon experience with a sense of vitality, of wholeness, of connection. Justice-seeking people must call into question our methods of organizing. Often we have thought that effective organizing is simply being able to move people as a group, sometimes through manipulation, to act in a particular way to achieve a goal. Too often the end has justified the means, and we have failed to follow Gandhi's belief that every step toward liberation must have liberation embedded within it. By concentrating on moving people to action, we have often failed to hear the voice of their spirit, their need for connection and wholeness—not for someday after the goal has been gained, but in the very process of gaining it.

I am not arguing that we should give up direct action, civil disobedience, issue campaigns, political education, confrontation, or membership and voter drives. We need to do these things and much more. I am suggesting that we rethink the meaning of social change and learn how to include the long-term work of transforming people as we work for social justice. We must redefine *winning*. Our social change has to be more than amassing resources and shifting power from the hands of one group to another; we must seek a true shift in consciousness, one that forges vision, goals, and strategies from belief, not just from expediency, and allows us to become a strong political force.

The definition of *transformational politics* is fairly simple: it is political work that changes the hearts and minds of people, supports personal and group growth in ways that create healthy, whole people, organizations, and communities, and is based on a vision of a society where people—across lines of race, gender, class and sexuality—are supported by institutions and communities to live their best lives.

Among many possibilities, I want to suggest one way to do transformational work: through building community that is based on our moral vision.

Building Community, Making Connections

Where do we build community? Should it be geographic, consisting of everyone who lives in the same neighborhood? Based on identity, such as one's racial identity, sexual identity, orrganizational or work identity? Where are the places that community happens?

It seems to me that community can be created in a vast number of places and ways. What is more important is the *how* of building community. To get to the *how*, we first have to define *what* community is. Community is people in any configuration (geographic, identity, etc.) bonded together over time through common interest and concern, through responsibility and accountability to one another, and at its best, through commitment, friendship, and love.

To live in authentic community requires a deeper level of caring and interaction than many of us currently exhibit in our drive for individualism and self-fulfillment. That is, it calls for living with communal values. And we face a daunting challenge here because we all live in a culture that glorifies individualism. For example, what the Right calls "traditional family values" actually works against the often-quoted African proverb, "It takes a village to raise a child," which speaks to the communal value of the importance of every child in the life of the community, present and future. Such values point to very different solutions than those currently suggested for the problems of youth alienation, crime, and violence. Rather than increasing police forces and building more jails, with these shared values we would look toward more ways for the community as a whole to be responsible for and accountable to children. We would seek ways to support and nurture their lives. All of us would be teachers, parents and friends for every child.

Creating community requires seeing the whole, not just the parts, and understanding how they interrelate. However, the difficult part is learning how to honor the needs of the individual as well as those of the group, without denying the importance of either. It requires a balance between identity and freedom on the one hand and the collective good and public responsibility on the other. It requires ritual, celebration, and collective ways to grieve and show anger; it requires a commitment to resolve conflict.

Most of all, it requires authenticity in relationships between and among whole people. This means that each of us has to be able to bring all of who we are to the relationship, neighbor to neighbor, friend to friend, worker to worker. Bringing all of who we are to community requires working across great differences in culture, in lifestyle, in belief. It demands that we look beyond our own lives to understand the lives of others. It demands that we interact with the lives of others. It requires understanding the connections among people's lives and then seeking comprehensive solutions to multi-issue, multifaceted problems. If we allow only certain parts of people to surface, and if we silence, reject or exclude basic pieces of their essential selves, then we begin designing systems of oppression. Community becomes based on power and nonconsensual authority: those who have the most power and privilege dictate the community norms and their enforcement.

One of the goals of every political activity we engage in should be to move beyond superficial interactions to the building of relationships and community. Much of this work is simple, not difficult or complex; it merely requires redefining our values and how we spend our political time. For example, far too often I go to meetings, frequently held in sterile hotel conference rooms, where introductions are limited to people giving their names or, at best, what work they do. Building relationships—whether those of neighbor, friend, lover, work partner—requires that we ask *Who are you?* In rural communities in the South and on American Indian reservations, people spend a lot of time talking about who their people are, how they are connected to people and place. Women activists in the housing projects in New Orleans get to know each other by telling their life lines, the major events that shaped them along the way. It is almost ritual for lesbians to get to know each other by telling their coming out stories—when and how they first experienced their lesbianism.

Building connection and relationship requires that we give it time, not just in meetings but in informal opportunities surrounding meetings, structured and unstructured. For instance, when I did political education on oppression issues within the battered women's movement, there was always a dramatic difference in the relationships that were built when we stayed in retreat centers or self-contained places away from distracting outside activities rather than in city hotels. So much of what happened in people's growth and understanding came from living, sleeping, and eating together in an atmosphere that encouraged interaction.

As a way to think about building community, we can ask ourselves these questions:

- In what settings with other people have I felt most whole? What is it that makes me feel known and accepted as who I am?

- What conditions make me most able to work well in partnership with other people? What makes me feel connected rather than alienated?

- What are communal values? What are the practices that support them?

- Where are the places where community is occurring? (For example, in care teams for people living with AIDS, in youth gangs, in certain churches or neighborhoods, in AA groups?) What are the characteristics of these communities?

- Who is being excluded from community? What barriers are there to participation?

- What are the qualities of an inclusive community as opposed to an exclusive community?

- What makes a community democratic?

Our communities are where our moral values are expressed. It is here that we are called upon to share our connection to others, our interdependence, our deepest belief in what it means to be part of the human condition, where people's lives touch one another, for good or for bad. It is here where the rhetoric of belief is forced into the reality of living. It is from this collection of people, holding within it smaller units called families, that we build and live democracy. Or, without care and nurturance, where we detach from one another and destroy our hope for survival.

Political Integrity and Multi-Issue Politics

It is one thing for us to talk about liberation politics; it is of course another to live them. We lack political integrity when we demand liberation for one cause or one group of people and act out oppression or exploitation toward others. If we do not have an integrated analysis and a commitment to sharing power, it is easy to act out politics that simply reflect a hierarchy of domination.

In our social change organizations in particular we can find ourselves in this dangerous position where we are demanding, for example, liberation from sexism but within the organization we act out racism, economic injustice, and homophobia. Each is reflected in who is allowed to lead, who makes the highest and lowest salaries, who is allowed to participate in the major decision making, who decides how the resources are used. If the organization does not have a vision and a strategy that also include the elimination of racism, sexism, economic injustice, and homophobia (as well as oppressions relating to age, physical ability, etc.), then internal conflict is inevitable. People cannot single out just one oppression from their lives to bring to their work for liberation: they bring their whole selves.

Creating a multiracial, multicultural, multi-issue vision of liberation is no easy task. It is much easier to stay within the framework of oppression where our women's organizations' leadership is primarily white, middle-class women, heterosexual or closeted lesbians; our civil rights organizations are male-dominated; our gay/lesbian/bisexual/transgender organizations are controlled by white gay men and/or white lesbians. And where the agendas for change reflect the values of those who dominate the leadership.

It is easier to talk about "diversity" than about shared power. Or to use a belief in identity politics to justify not including others in a vision for change. I do not believe in either diversity or identity politics as they are currently practiced.

First, diversity politics seem to focus on the necessity for having everyone (across gender, race, class, age, religion, physical ability) present and treated well in any given setting or organization. A core premise is that everyone is oppressed and all oppressions are equal. Since the publication of the report "Workforce 2000" that predicted the U.S. workforce would be made up of 80 percent women and people of color by the year 2000, a veritable growth industry of "diversity consultants" has arisen to teach corporations how to "manage" diversity. With integration and productivity as goals, they focus on issues of sensitivity and inclusion—a human relations approach—with acceptance and comfort as high priorities. Popular images of diversity politics show people holding hands around America, singing "We Are the World." People are generally reassured that they do not have to give up anything when they diversify their workplace. They simply have to include other people and become more sensitive to differences.

Because the history of oppression is one of excluding, of silencing, of rendering people invisible, I have great appreciation for the part of diversity work that concentrates on making sure everyone is included. However, our diversity work fails if it does not deal with the power dynamics of difference and go straight to the heart of shifting the balance of power among individuals and within institutions. A danger of diversity politics lies in the possibility that it may become a tool of oppression by creating the illusion of participation when in fact there is no shared power. Having a presence within an organization or institution means very little if one does not have the power of decision making, an adequate share of the resources, and participation in the development of the workplan or agenda. We as oppressed people must demand much more than acceptance. Tolerance, sympathy and understanding are not enough, though they soften the impact of oppression by making people feel better in the face of it. Our job is not just to soften blows but to make change, fundamental and far-reaching.

Identity politics, on the other hand, rather than trying to include everyone, brings together people who share a single common identity such as sexual orientation, gender, or race. Generally, it focuses on the elimination of a single oppression, the one that is based on the common identity—for example, homophobia/heterosexism, sexism, racism. However, this can be a limited, hierarchical approach, reducing people of multiple identities to a single identity. Which identity should a lesbian of color choose as a priority—gender, race or sexual identity? And does choosing one necessitate leaving the other two at home? What do we say to bisexual or biracial people? Do we tell them to *choose*? Our multiple identities allow us to develop a politic that is broad in scope because it is grounded in a wide range of experiences.

There are positive aspects of organizing along identity lines: clarity of single focus in tactics and strategies, self-examination and education apart from the dominant culture, development of solidarity and group bonding. Creating organizations based on identity allows us to have visibility and collective power, to advance concerns that otherwise would never be recognized because of our marginalization within the dominant society.

However, identity politics often suffers from the failure to acknowledge that the same multiplicity of oppressions, a similar imbalance of power, exists within identity groups as within the larger society. People who group together on the basis of their sexual identity still find within these groups sexism and racism that have to be dealt with—or if gathering on the basis of race, there is still sexism and homophobia to be confronted. Whole, not partial, people come to identity groups, carrying several identities. Some of liberation movements' major barriers to building a unified and cohesive strategy, I believe, come from our refusal to work directly on the oppressions—those fundamental issues of power—within our own groups. A successful liberation movement cannot be built on the effort to liberate only a few or only a piece of who we are.

Diversity and identity politics are responses to oppression. In confronting oppressions we must always remember that they mean more than people just not being nice to one another. They are systemic, based in institutions and in general society, where one group of people is allowed to exert power and control over members of another group, denying it fundamental rights. Also, we must remember that oppressions are interconnected, operating in similar ways, and that many people experience more than one oppression. . . .

The question, as ever, is, What to do? I do not believe that either a diversity or identity politics approach will work unless they are changed to incorporate a multi-issue analysis and strategy that combine the politics of inclusion with shared power. But, one might say, it will spread us too thin if we try to work on everyone's issue, and ours will fall by the wayside. In our external work (doing women's antiviolence work, working against police brutality in people of color communities, seeking government funding for AIDS research), we do not have to work on "everybody's issue"—we *can* be focused. But how can we achieve true social change unless we look at all within our constituency who are affected by our particular issue? People who have AIDS are of every race, class, age, gender, geographic location, but when research and services are sought, it is women, people of color, and poor people who are most overlooked. The HIV virus rages on because those in power think that the people who contract it are dispensable. Are we to be like them? To understand why police brutality is so much more extreme in communities of people of color than in white communities, we have to understand also why, even within these communities, it is even greater against *poor* people of color, women who are prostitutes, and gay men and lesbians of color. To leave any group out leaves a hole for everyone's freedoms and rights to fall through. It becomes an issue of "acceptable" and "unacceptable" people, deserving and undeserving of rights, legitimate and illegitimate, deserving of recognition as fully human or dismissable as something less.

Identity politics offers a strong, vital place for bonding, for developing political analysis. With each other we struggle to understand our relationship to a world that says that we are no more than our identity, and simultaneously denies that there is oppression based on race, gender, or sexual identity. Our challenge is to learn how to use the experiences of our many identities to forge an inclusive social change politic. The question that faces us is how to undertake multi-issue coalition building from an identity base. The hope for a multiracial, multi-issue movement rests in large part on the answer to this question.

Our linkages can create a movement, and our divisions can destroy us. Each point of linkage is our strongest defense and also holds the most possibility for long-lasting social change.

If our organizations are not committed internally to the inclusion and shared power of all those who share our issue, how can we with any integrity demand inclusion and shared power in society at large? If women, lesbians and gay men are treated as people undeserving of equality within civil rights organizations, how can those orgarnizations demand equality? If women of color and poor women are marginalized in women's rights organizations, how can those organizations argue that women as a class should be moved into full participation in the mainstream? If lesbian and gay organizations are not feminist and antiracist in all their practices, what hope is there for the elimination of homophobia and heterosexism in a racist, sexist society? It is an issue of integrity.

In the larger social change community our failure to connect issues prevents us from being able to do strong coalition and alliance work with one another. Most frequently, coalitions and alliances are created to meet crisis issues which threaten all of us. Made up of groups that experience injustice, they should have common ground. They most frequently fall apart, I believe, because of failure in relationships. As in all human relationships, it is difficult to solve the issue of the moment without a history of trust, common struggle, and reciprocity. Homophobia, for example, has kept us "quiet" and invisible in our antiracist work; racism has kept us "quiet" in our lesbian and gay work. We need to be *visible* in our work on all fronts. Working shoulder to shoulder on each other's issues enables us to get to know each other's humanity, to understand the broad sweep of issues, to build trust and solidarity.

Our separateness, by identity and by issue, prevents the building of a progressive movement. When we grasp the value and interconnectedness of our liberation issues, then we will at last be able to make true coalition and begin building a common agenda that eliminates oppression and brings forth a vision of diversity that shares both power and resources.

87

Toward a New Vision: Race, Class, and Gender as Categories of Analysis and Connection

Patricia Hill Collins

How Can We Transcend the Barriers Created by Our Experiences with Race, Class, and Gender Oppression in Order to Build the Types of Coalitions Essential for Social Change?

Reconceptualizing oppression and seeing the barriers created by race, class, and gender as interlocking categories of analysis is a vital first step. But we must transcend these barriers by moving toward race, class, and gender as categories of connection by building relationships and coalitions that will bring about social change. What are some of the issues involved in doing this?

Differences in Power and Privilege

First, we must recognize that our differing experiences with oppression create problems in the relationships among us. Each of us lives within a system that vests us with varying levels of power and privilege. These differences in power, whether structured along axes of race, class, gender, age, or sexual orientation, frame our relationships. African-American writer June Jordan describes her discomfort on a Caribbean vacation with Olive, the Black woman who cleaned her room, "Even though both 'Olive' and 'I' live inside a conflict neither one of us created, and even though both of us therefore hurt inside that conflict, I may be one of the monsters she needs to eliminate from her universe and, in a sense, she may be one of the monsters in mine" (1985, 47).

Differences in power constrain our ability to connect with one another even when we think we are engaged in dialogue across differences. Let me give you an example. One year, the students in my course Sociology of the Black Community got into a heated discussion about the reasons for the upsurge of racial incidents on college campuses. Black students complained vehemently about the apathy and resistance they felt most White students expressed about examining their own racism. Mark, a White male student, found their comments particularly unsettling. After claiming that all the Black people he had ever known had expressed no such beliefs to him, he questioned how representative the view points of his fellow students actually were. When pushed further, Mark revealed that he had participated in conversations over the years with the Black domestic worker employed by his family. Since she had never expressed such strong feelings about White racism, Mark was genuinely shocked by class discussions. Ask yourself whether that domestic worker was in a position to speak freely. Would it have been wise for her to do so in a situation where the power between the two parties was so unequal?

In extreme cases, members of privileged groups can erase the very presence of the less privileged. When I first moved to Cincinnati, my family and I went on a picnic at a local park. Picnicking next to us was a family of White Appalachians. When I went to push my daughter on the swings, several of the children came over. They had missing, yellowed, and broken teeth; they wore old clothing, and their poverty was evident. I was shocked. Growing up in a large eastern city, I had never seen such awful poverty among Whites. The segregated neighborhoods in which I grew up made White poverty all but invisible. More importantly, the privileges attached to my newly acquired social class position allowed me to ignore and minimize the poverty among Whites that I did encounter. My reactions to those children made me realize how confining phrases such as "well, at least they're not Black," had become for me. In learning to grant human subjectivity to the Black victims of poverty, I had simultaneously learned to demand White victims of poverty. By applying categories of race to the objective conditions confronting me, I was quantifying and ranking oppressions and missing the very real suffering which, in fact, is the real issue.

One common pattern of relationships across differences in power is one that I label *voyeurism*. From the perspective of the privileged, the lives of people of color, of the poor, and of women are interesting for their entertainment value. The privileged become voyeurs, passive onlookers who do not relate to the less powerful, but who are interested in seeing how the "different" live. Over the years, I have heard numerous African-American students complain about professors who never call on them except when a so-called Black issue is being discussed. The students' interest in discussing race, or qualifications for doing so, appear unimportant to the professor's efforts to use Black students' experiences as stories to make the material come alive for the White student audience. Asking Black students to perform on cue and provide a Black experience for their White classmates can be seen as voyeurism at its worst.

Members of subordinate groups do not willingly participate in such exchanges but often do so because members of dominant groups control the institutional and symbolic apparatuses of oppression. Racial/ethnic groups, women, and the poor have never had the luxury of being voyeurs of the lives of the privileged. Our ability to survive in hostile settings has hinged on our ability to learn intricate details about the behavior and worldview of the powerful and adjust our behavior accordingly. I need only point to the difference in perception of those men and women in abusive relationships. Where men can view their girlfriends and wives as sex objects, helpmates, and a collection of stereotyped categories of voyeurism—women must be attuned to every nuance of their partners' behavior. Are women "naturally" better in relating to people with more power than themselves, or have circumstances mandated that men and women develop different skills? Another pattern in relationships among people of unequal power concerns a different form of exploitation. In scholarly enterprises, relationships among students and teachers, among researchers and their subjects, and even among us as colleagues in teaching and scholarship can contain elements of academic colonialism. Years ago, a Black coworker of mine in the Roxbury section of Boston described the academic colonialism he saw among the teachers and scholars in that African-American community. "The people with notebooks from Harvard come around here and study us. They don't get to know us because they really don't want to and we don't want to let them. They see what they want to see, go back and write their books and get famous off of our problems."

Under academic colonialism, more powerful groups see their subordinates as people that they perceive as subordinate to them, not as entertainment as was the case in voyeurism, but as a resource to be benignly exploited for their own purposes.

The long-standing effort to "colorize" feminist theory by inserting the experiences of women of color, represents at best, genuine efforts to reduce bias in women's studies. But at its worst, colorization also contains elements of both voyeurism and academic colonialism. As a result of new technologies and perceived profitability, we can now watch black and white movie classics in color. While the tinted images we are offered may be more palatable to the modern viewer, we are still watching the same old movie that was offered to us before. Movie colorization adds little of substance—its contributions remain cosmetic. Similarly, women of color allegedly can teach White feminists nothing about feminism, but must confine ourselves to "colorizing" preexisting feminist theory. Rather than seeing women of color as fully human individuals, we are treated as the additive sum of our categories.

In the academy, patterns of relationships among those of unequal power such as voyeurism and academic colonialism foster reformist postures toward social change. While reformists may aim to make the movie more fun to watch by colorizing their scholarship and teaching via increased lip service to diversity, reformists typically insist on retaining their power to determine what is seen, and by whom. In contrast, transformation involves rethinking these differences in power and privilege via dialogues among individuals from diverse groups.

Coming from a tradition where most relationships across difference are squarely rooted in relations of domination and subordination, we have much less experience relating to people as different but equal. The classroom is potentially one powerful and safe space where dialogues among individuals of unequal power relationships can occur. The relationship between Mark, the student in my class, and the domestic worker is typical of a whole series of relationships that people have when they relate across differences in power and privilege. The relationship among Mark and his classmates represents the power of the classroom to minimize those differences so that people of different levels of power can use race, class, and gender as categories of analysis in order to generate meaningful dialogues. In this case, the classroom equalized racial difference so that Black students who normally felt silenced spoke out. White students like Mark, generally unaware of how they had been privileged by their whiteness, lost that privilege in the classroom and thus became open to genuine dialogue.

Reconceptualizing course syllabi represents a comparable process of determining which groups are privileged by our current research and pedagogical techniques and which groups are penalized. Reforming these existing techniques can be a critical first step in moving toward a transformed curriculum reflecting race, class, and gender as interlocking categories of analysis. But while reform may be effective as a short-term strategy, it is unlikely to bring about fundamental transformation in the long term. To me, social transformations, whether of college curricula or of the communities in which we live and work, require moving outside our areas of specialization and groups of interest in order to build coalitions across differences.

Coalitions Around Common Causes

A second issue in building relationships and coalitions essential for social change concerns knowing the real reasons for coalition. Just what brings people together? One powerful catalyst fostering group solidarity is the presence of a common enemy. African-American, Hispanic, Asian-American, and women's studies all share the common intellectual heritage of challenging what passes for certified knowledge in the academy. But politically expedient relationships and coalitions like these are fragile because, as June Jordan points out, "Much organizational grief could be avoided if people understood that partnership in misery does not necessarily provide for partnership for change: When we get the monsters off our backs all of us may want to run in very different directions" (1985, 47).

Sharing a common cause assists individuals and groups in maintaining relationships that transcend their differences. Building effective coalitions involves struggling to hear one another and developing empathy for each other's points of view. The coalitions that I have been involved in that lasted and that worked have been those where commitment to a specific issue mandated collaboration as the best strategy for addressing the issue at hand.

Several years ago, masters degree in hand, I chose to teach in an inner city, parochial school in danger of closing. The money was awful, the conditions were poor, but the need was great. In my job, I had to work with a range of individuals who, on the surface, had very little in common. We had White nuns, Black middle class graduate students, Blacks from the "community," some of whom had been incarcerated and/or were affiliated with a range of federal antipoverty programs. Parents formed another part of this community, Harvard faculty another, and a few well-meaning White liberals from Colorado were sprinkled in for good measure.

As you might imagine, tension was high. Initially, our differences seemed insurmountable. But as time passed, we found a common bond that we each brought to the school. In spite of profound differences in our personal biographies, differences that in other settings would have hampered our ability to relate to one another, we found that we were all deeply committed to the education of Black children. By learning to value each other's commitment and by recognizing that we each had different skills that were essential to actualizing that commitment, we built an effective coalition around a common cause. Our school was successful, and the children we taught benefited from the diversity we offered them.

I think that the process of curriculum transformation will require a process comparable to that of political organizing around common causes. None of us alone has a comprehensive vision of how race, class, and gender operate as categories of analysis or how they might be used as categories of connection. Our personal biographies offer us partial views. Few of us can manage to study race, class, *and* gender simultaneously. Instead, we each know more about some dimensions of this larger story and less about others. While we each may be committed to an inclusive, transformed curriculum, the task of building one is necessarily a collective effort. Just as the members of the school had special skills to offer to the task of building the school, we have areas of specialization and expertise, whether scholarly, theoretical, pedagogical, or within areas of race, class, or gender. We do not all have to do the same thing in the same way. Instead, we must support each other's efforts, realizing that they are all part of the larger enterprise of bringing about social change.

Building Empathy

A third issue involved in building the types of relationships and coalitions essential for social change concerns the issue of individual accountability. Race, class, and gender oppression form the structural backdrop against which we frame our relationship—these are the forces that encourage us to substitute voyeurism and academic colonialism for fully human relationships. But while we may not have created this situation, we are each responsible for making individual, personal choices concerning which elements of race, class, and gender oppression we will accept and which we will work to change.

One essential component of this accountability involves developing empathy for the experiences of individuals and groups different from ourselves. Empathy begins with taking an interest in the facts of other people lives, both as individuals and as groups. If you care about me, you should want to know not only the details of my personal biography but a sense of how race, class, and gender as categories of analysis created the institutional and symbolic backdrop for my personal biography. How can you hope to assess my character without knowing the details of the circumstances I face?

Moreover, by taking a theoretical stance that we have all been affected by race, class, and gender as categories of analysis that have structured our treatment, we open up possibilities for using those same constructs as categories of connection in building empathy. For example, I have a good White woman friend with whom I share common interests and beliefs. We know that our racial differences have provided us with different experiences. So we talk about them. We do not assume that because I am Black, race has only affected me and not her or that because I am a Black woman, race neutralizes the effect of gender in my life while accenting it in hers. We take those same categories of analysis that have created cleavages in our lives—in this case, categories of race and gender—and use them as categories of connection in building empathy for each other's experiences.

Finding common causes and building empathy is difficult, no matter which side of privilege we inhabit. Building empathy from the dominant side of privilege is difficult, simply because individuals from privileged backgrounds are not encouraged to do so. For example, in order for those of you who are White to develop empathy for the experiences of people of color, you must grapple with how your white skin has privileged you. This is difficult to do, because it not only entails the intellectual process of seeing how whiteness is elevated in institutions and symbols, but it also involves the often painful process of seeing how your whiteness has shaped your personal biography. Intellectual stances against the institutional and symbolic dimensions of racism are generally easier to maintain than sustained self-reflection about how racism has shaped all of our individual biographies. Were your fathers, uncles, and grandfathers really more capable than mine, or can their accomplishments be explained in part by the racism members of my family experienced? Did your mothers stand silently by and watch all this happen? More important, how have they passed on the benefits of their whiteness to you?

These are difficult questions, and I have tremendous respect for my colleagues and students who are trying to answer them. Since there is no compelling reason to examine the source and meaning of one's own privilege, I know that those who do so have freely chosen this stance. They are making conscious efforts to root out the piece of the oppressor planted within them. To me, they are entitled to the support of people of color in their efforts. Men who declare themselves feminists, members of the middle class who ally themselves with anti-poverty struggles, heterosexuals who support gays and lesbians are all trying to grow, and their efforts place them far ahead of the majority who never think of engaging in such important struggles.

Building empathy from the subordinate side of privilege is also difficult, but for different reasons. Members of subordinate groups are understandably reluctant to abandon a basic mistrust of members of powerful groups because this basic mistrust has traditionally been central to their survival. As a Black woman, it would be foolish for me to assume that White women, or Black men, or White men or any other group with a history of exploiting African-American women have my best interests at heart. These groups enjoy varying amounts of privilege over me and therefore I must carefully watch them and be prepared for a relation of domination and subordination.

Like the privileged, members of subordinate groups must also work toward replacing judgments by category with new ways of thinking and acting. Refusing to do so stifles prospects for effective coalition and social change. Let me use another example from my own experiences. When I was an undergraduate, I had little time or patience for the theorizing of the privileged. My initial years at a private, elite institution were difficult, not because the coursework was challenging (it was, but that wasn't what distracted me) or because I had to work while my classmates lived on family allowances (I was used to work). The adjustment was difficult because I was surrounded by so many people who took their privilege for granted. Most of them felt entitled to their wealth. That astounded me.

I remember one incident of watching a White woman down the hall in my dormitory try to pick out which sweater to wear. The sweaters were piled up on her bed in all the colors of the rainbow, sweater after sweater. She asked my advice in a way that let me know that choosing a sweater was one of the most important decisions she had to make on a daily basis. Standing knee-deep in her sweaters, I realized how different our lives were. She did not have to worry about maintaining a solid academic average so that she could receive financial aid. Because she was in the majority, she was not treated as a representative of her race. She did not have to consider how her classroom comments or basic existence on campus contributed to the treatment her group would receive. Her allowance protected her from having to work, so she was free to spend her time studying, partying, or in her case, worrying about which sweater to wear. The degree of inequality in our lives and her unquestioned sense of entitlement concerning that inequality offended me. For a while, I categorized all affluent White women as being superficial, arrogant, overly concerned with material possessions, and part of my problem. But had I continued to classify people in this way, I would have missed out on making some very good friends whose discomfort with their inherited or acquired social class privileges pushed them to examine their position.

Since I opened with the words of Audre Lorde, it seems appropriate to close with another of her ideas. As we go forth to the remaining activities of this workshop, and beyond this workshop, we might do well to consider Lorde's perspective:

> Each of us is called upon to take a stand. So in these days ahead, as we examine ourselves and each other, our works, our fears, our differences, our sisterhood and survivals, I urge you to tackle what is most difficult for us all, self-scrutiny of our complacencies, the idea that since each of us believes she is on the side of right, she need not examine her position. (1985, n.p.)

I urge you to examine your position.

References

Lorde, Audre. 1985. "Sisterhood and Survival." Keynote address, conference on the Black Woman Writer and the Diaspora, Michigan State University.

Jordan, June. 1985. *On Call: Political Essays.* Boston. South End Press.

88

The Cycle of Liberation

Bobbie Harro

As people come to a critical level of understanding of the nature of oppression and their roles in this systemic phenomenon, they seek new paths for creating social change and taking themselves toward empowerment or liberation. In my years as a social justice educator, it became increasingly clear that most socially conscious people truly want to "do something about" the injustices that they see and they recognize that simple, personal level changes are not enough. They want to know how to make system-level change manageable and within their grasp, and they often become frustrated since so little has been written about the process of liberation.

As more students asked, "How do we make a dent in this thing that seems so big?" I began to think about how we might consciously transform the Cycle of Socialization (see chapter 2 of this volume). The cycle "teaches" us how to play our roles in oppression, and how to revere the existing systems that shape our thinking, leading us to blame uncontrollable forces, other people, or ourselves for the existence of oppression. If there is an identifiable pattern of events that repeats itself, becomes self-fulfilling, and leads us to a state of unconsciousness about issues of oppression, then there may be another identifiable pattern of events that leads us toward liberation from that thinking. I began to read about and study efforts to eliminate oppression on a systemic level, and discovered that indeed, some paths were successful at actually creating the kind of lasting change that addressed the root causes of the oppression, and people's roles in it, while other paths were not. These paths were not always the same, and certainly were not linear, but they had in common the same cycle-like traits that characterized the socialization process that teaches us our roles in oppression. There were certain skills and processes, certain ways of thinking and acting in the world, certain seemingly necessary ingredients that were present in every successful liberation effort.

I am defining *liberation* as "critical transformation," in the language and thinking of Paulo Freire (1968). By this I mean that one must "name the problem" in terms of *systemic* assumptions, structures, rules, or roles that are flawed. Significant social change cannot happen until we are thinking on a systemic level. Many people who want to overcome oppression do not start in the critical transforming stage, but as they proceed in their efforts, it becomes necessary for them to move to that level for success.

The following model describes patterns of events common to successful liberation efforts. Its purpose is to organize and name a process that may otherwise be elusive, with the goal of helping people to find their pathway to liberation. It could be characterized as a map of changing terrain where not everyone goes in the same direction or to the same destination or at the same speed, so it should be taken not as a "how to," but rather as a description of what has worked for some.

Cycle of Liberation

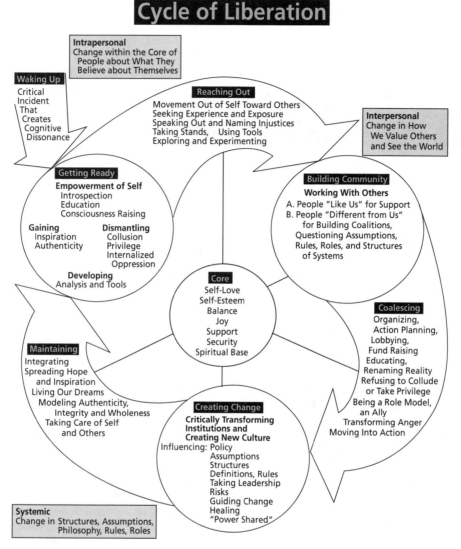

Intrapersonal
Change within the Core of People about What They Believe about Themselves

Waking Up
Critical Incident That Creates Cognitive Dissonance

Reaching Out
Movement Out of Self Toward Others
Seeking Experience and Exposure
Speaking Out and Naming Injustices
Taking Stands,   Using Tools
Exploring and Experimenting

Interpersonal
Change in How We Value Others and See the World

Getting Ready
Empowerment of Self
Introspection
Education
Consciousness Raising

Gaining
Inspiration
Authenticity

Dismantling
Collusion
Privilege
Internalized Oppression

Developing
Analysis and Tools

Building Community
Working With Others
A. People "Like Us" for Support
B. People "Different from Us" for Building Coalitions, Questioning Assumptions, Rules, Roles, and Structures of Systems

Core
Self-Love
Self-Esteem
Balance
Joy
Support
Security
Spiritual Base

Coalescing
Organizing,
Action Planning,
Lobbying,
Fund Raising
Educating,
Renaming Reality
Refusing to Collude or Take Privilege
Being a Role Model, an Ally
Transforming Anger
Moving Into Action

Maintaining
Integrating
Spreading Hope and Inspiration
Living Our Dreams
Modeling Authenticity, Integrity and Wholeness
Taking Care of Self and Others

Creating Change
Critically Transforming Institutions and Creating New Culture
Influencing: Policy
Assumptions
Structures
Definitions, Rules
Taking Leadership
Risks
Guiding Change
Healing
"Power Shared"

Systemic
Change in Structures, Assumptions, Philosophy, Rules, Roles

Figure 88.1   The Cycle of Socialization

The Model

The model described in this chapter combines theory, analysis, and practical experience (see fig. 88.1). It describes a cyclical process that seems to occur in most successful social change efforts, leading to some degree of liberation from oppression for those involved, regardless of their roles. It is important to note that one can enter the cycle at any point, through slow evolution or a critical incident, and will repeat or recycle many times in the process. There is no specific beginning or end point, just as one is never "done" working to end oppression. Although there is not a specific sequence of events in the cycle, it is somewhat predictable that all of the levels (intrapersonal, interpersonal and systemic) will occur at some point.

Waking Up

Often liberation begins when a person begins to experience herself differently in the world than s/he has in the past. It is marked by an intrapersonal change: a change in the core of someone about what s/he believes about her/himself. This may be the result of a critical incident or a long slow evolutionary process that shifts our worldviews. I refer to this phase as the *waking up* phase. We may experience some form of cognitive dissonance, where something that used to make sense to us (or that we never questioned), ceases to makes sense. Perhaps a white mother adopts a child who is Puerto Rican and in dealing with her expectations for the child suddenly realizes that she has more deeply based racist attitudes than she thought she did. Perhaps a heterosexual woman who has a gay coworker recognizes that the longer she works with him, the more "ordinary" he becomes to her, and the more she gets angry when people make antigay remarks. Perhaps a welfare recipient begins to get angry that she is often treated with disrespect by service providers and the general public, and begins to see the disrespect as a pattern of how poorer people are treated in the United States. Any of these examples could mark the beginning of the Cycle of Liberation.

Getting Ready

Once we know something, we can't *not* know it anymore. The process may not begin immediately, but odds are that it will begin at some point. Often the first part of the process involves a *getting ready* phase. This involves consciously dismantling and building aspects of ourselves and our worldviews based on our new perspectives. Processes that are central to this first part of liberation are introspection, education, and consciousness raising. We become introspective to identify which aspects of our beliefs, attitudes, and behaviors need to be challenged. We tend to pay attention to and inventory thoughts, language, and actions to see if they are consistent with our newly recognized beliefs, or if they need to be dismantled. We may discover that we need to educate ourselves: read more, talk to people, bounce ideas and views around with others, begin listening to the news with new ears, seek expertise. We may begin to "make sense" of our experiences differently and seek out more chances to explore what we thought we knew, and how it compares to the reality. We may start exercising our questioning and challenging skills to expand our conscious understanding of the world.

This *getting ready* phase is composed of dismantling our wrong or diminishing beliefs (stereotypes, ignorance or misinformation), our discriminatory or privileged attitudes (superiority or inferiority), and behaviors that limit ourselves or others (collusion, oppressive language, or resignation). It also involves developing a consistency among what we believe, how we want to live our lives, and the way we actually do it. We move toward gaining authenticity and coherence between our worldview and how we live. We begin to see connections among all of the aspects of our lives and move toward integrity. Part of this phase also includes developing a coherent analysis of oppression and building a repertoire of skills and tools that will serve us throughout the rest of the process. We begin to take steps to empower ourselves.

The mother of the Puerto Rican child might decide to read about Puerto Rican history and cultures, talk to her Puerto Rican coworker, trace the origins of her assumptions and expectations about her child, or begin to catch herself when she makes excuses for her child's behavior. The heterosexual coworker may take a course on the gay rights movement, or pick up a copy of a gay newspaper, or ask her gay coworker to dinner. The woman on welfare may read a book on welfare rights, or start listening to the economic news, or start to keep a list of examples of "corporate welfare" totaling how much money goes from the federal government to large corporations when they are in financial trouble.

Reaching Out

Almost inevitably, as we are getting ready, it becomes necessary for us to seek experiences outside ourselves in order to check our reality and to expose ourselves to a wider range of difference than we had before. We need to practice using our skills and tools with others, and experiment with expressing our new views, and speaking out when we disagree, instead of staying silent. This *reaching out* phase provides us with feedback about how our new worldviews will be met by others. We may get pressure from some to stop making waves, and accept the status quo (and this may arrest some people's progress for a while), and we may get encouragement and new friends as a result of taking a stand on something that we were quiet about before.

The adoptive mother may change social workers so she can talk to a Puerto Rican social worker about her child. She may suggest to her partner that they take a class in Spanish, or attend a local Puerto Rican festival. The heterosexual coworker may disclose in a conversation with friends that she supports the domestic partnership clause in their benefit package, or she may have a talk with her kids about not using the term *gay* to mean something bad. She may invite her gay coworker *and his partner* to dinner, or draw comparisons between her primary relationship and his. The woman on welfare may attend her first welfare rights meeting. She may object assertively when she is treated with disdain for using food stamps by the person behind her in the checkout line. She may decide to share her list of examples of corporate welfare with two friends also on welfare. All of these actions mark the transition from intrapersonal to interpersonal liberation.

Building Community

The Interpersonal phase of the liberation process is marked by a change in how we value others and interact with them on a regular basis. It is the phase of *building community*, and consists of two steps: dialoguing with *people who are like us* for support (people who have the same social identities as we do, with regard to this issue of oppression), and dialoguing with *people who are different from us* for gaining understanding and building coalitions. This phase is characterized by the creation of an ongoing dialogue, where views are exchanged, people are listened to and valued, and we begin to view each others' points of view as making sense and having integrity, even if they are very different from our own.

In the first step, building community with people who are like us, we seek out people who may have similar experiences to our own, and talk with them to see how they have made sense of their experiences and what we can learn from them. This often begins happening informally, and even sometimes unconsciously: two mothers with adopted children meet in the pediatricians waiting room and start comparing notes, or two neighbors who both receive welfare benefits talk in the laundry about their frustrations, or two friends going for a hike begin discussing "the gay people" who work with both of them. With increased knowledge and consciousness, these people might start looking for more organized forms of support discussions. These dialogues serve to prove to people that they are not alone in their situation, that there is a bigger "system" operating, that others have faced and are facing similar situations as our own, and that there are more strategies, ideas, and options than we had initially thought. We feel confirmed, and like we are part of a group that wants to change its role with regard to oppression.

A large part of this interpersonal step also involves dialoguing about how we see the "other" group (those with power if we are disempowered, or the disempowered if we possess power and/or privilege), and beginning to identify things that we may mutually have in common. We have moved out of stereotyping the "other" and have discovered those "others" who are more like us than different from us. We may begin to see that the "other" is no more to blame for the oppression than we are—that, in fact, we are both victims of a larger system that pushed us into roles. With this realization, a new level of analysis begins, and it becomes inevitable and necessary to expand our dialogue to include "others."

It's important to note that both privileged groups and targeted groups need to find this support step. We can't change *our* roles only; we must address changing the roles of *everyone* involved, as well as the assumptions and structures of the entire system, and we cannot do that alone. Coalitions are a necessity, and dialoguing across differences is the first step to building coalitions. We will never be able to focus on the real challenge—changing the system—until the barriers and boundaries that divide us are minimized. They will not be eliminated, but they can be significantly diminished in potency and clarified through the dialogue process.

This is not to say that creating dialogues about and across differences is easy. An integral part of this dialogue is exploring our differences, clarifying them, erasing assumptions, and replacing them with firsthand contact and good listening. That means that we must talk about our differences in a civil manner. It is useful, even desirable, to create together some guidelines for how our dialogues across differences will take place, and some principles to guide the process. These are best negotiated by all the parties who will participate.

Our mission is to question and challenge assumptions, structures and rules of the system of oppression, and to clarify our different needs, perceptions, strengths, resources, and skills in the process. Done well, these dialogues result in a deeper and richer repertoire of options and opportunities for changing the system. We are enhanced in many ways: our energy, our resources, our inspiration, our understanding, our compassion, our empathy, our humanness, and our motivation are all expanded in this process. We discover and are sustained by inspirations that we have not met before. With these new springboards, we move into the coalescing phase.

Coalescing

Having minimized our barriers, joined with allies, and fortified our resolve, we are ready to move into action to interrupt the oppressive system. We may organize, plan actions, lobby, do fund raising, educate and motivate members of the uninvolved public. We coalesce and discover that we have more power as a coalition. This gives us encouragement and confidence. We may find ourselves taking more overt stands, expressing ourselves more assertively, rallying people to support us as we respond to overt oppression. We have begun to "see our reality" differently, and are naming ourselves differently. We are a "we" now, rather than adversaries. We are on the same side as those in our coalition, and that often surprises and confuses the system. We are refusing to "play our roles" and "stay in our places" as we had done before. We are refusing to collude in oppression, and to participate in self-fulfilling prophesies. We are refusing to accept privileges, and we are acting as role models and allies for others. We are interrupting the status quo, by speaking out calmly and with self-confidence. In this process, we have transformed our energy away from anger, frustration, guilt, and mistrust, and toward hope, shared power, trust, and optimism. We begin to see evidence that, working together, and organizing, we can make a difference. This doesn't mean that we will be successful at everything we try, but our likelihood of creating change is greatly enhanced.

Creating Change

The parameters of this phase of the cycle of liberation include using our critical analysis of the assumptions, structures, rules, and roles of the existing system of oppression, and our coalition power, to begin transforming the system. This means creating anew a culture that reflects our coalition's collective identity: new assumptions, new structures, new roles, and new rules consistent with a more socially just and equitable philosophy. It includes operating from a shifted worldview, where the values of a diverse and united community shape the system. It involves forming partnerships across differences to increase shared power. This manifests in influencing structure, policy, and management of organizations and systems of which we are a part. It involves taking leadership, taking risks, and guiding change. We must continue to heal from past differences by sharing power and by redefining power as collective power, power within, and power created through cooperation. In this phase, the very essence of the system is transformed, and nothing can remain the same after the transformation.

People experience this kind of transformation on a personal level, when, for example they or someone in their family is diagnosed with a terminal illness. Priorities shift, and what is important becomes totally different. With regard to oppression, some examples of critical transformation have occurred when psychiatric facilities began to appoint consumers to their boards of directors, or when community funding agencies began to be run by community constituents rather than elected officials. Critical transformation may take place when an organization decides to use only consensus decision making for all policy decisions, or to use a flat collaborative management structure rather than hierarchical.

Critical transformation in our examples might happen like this. The heterosexual coworker and the gay coworker might organize a human rights committee in their workplace; conduct dialogues among employees and a public awareness campaign; design a new domestic partners' benefits amendment and a new policy protecting gay, lesbian, bisexual, and transgendered people from discrimination in the workplace. The person receiving welfare benefits might join a welfare rights coalition that lobbies local legislators, speak at a hearing in the state capital, and propose a referendum that for every dollar spent on "corporate welfare" in their state a dollar must also be spent on domestic welfare. The white mother of the Puerto Rican child might join a local Puerto Rican political action committee working to reform curriculum to include relevant Puerto Rican history, literature, famous people, and current events in her child's school. The committee might also be working to reform policies on bilingual education district-wide, so that her child can study and learn in both Spanish and English.

Efforts to critically transform systems are greatly enhanced by a wide range of resources, perspectives and creativity being brought to bear on a commonly defined problem. If good dialogue has taken place and the coalitions are as inclusive of every perspective as possible, systemic change becomes the logical outcome rather than an unlikely or unattainable goal. Making transformation happen is not, however, the last step. Creative new structures, assumptions, rules and roles must be maintained and nurtured.

Maintaining

In order to succeed, change needs to be strengthened, monitored, and integrated into the ritual of daily life. Just like anything new, it needs to be taken care of, learned about, "debugged," and modified as needed. It's rare if not impossible that new structures, assumptions, rules and roles are perfect or all-inclusive. It is imperative that a diverse group of "maintainers" work together to keep the change efforts aimed at their goals, and provided with resources. It's also necessary to celebrate successful change efforts. This process says to the larger world, "Look, this can work. You can change things by dialoguing and working together." It spreads hope and inspiration, and provides a model for others.

When a diverse group of people have worked to understand one another, and have created critical transformation together, we teach the lesson of hope and peace. It becomes increasingly possible that we can live our dream of equality and justice for all people. We become more human, more whole, more authentic, more integrated, and by living this way, we increase the likelihood that the human species will survive.

The Core of the Cycle of Liberation

At the core of the cycle of liberation is a set of qualities or states of being that hold it together. Some of these are present when people first begin the cycle, and they are nurtured, elaborated on, filled out, and matured as we proceed through the various phases. They exist and operate on both the individual and collective levels throughout the process of liberation. They are made stronger with each phase and with each human connection we make. Liberation is *the practice of love*. It is developing a sense of self that we can love, and learning to love others with their differences from us. Liberation is *finding balance* in our individual lives and in the agendas of our coalitions. Balance keeps us upright and oriented, moving toward our goals. Liberation is the *development of competence*, the ability to make something happen consistent with a goal. It is taking charge of our own destiny and creating the world we want to live in, together with all the others we need to survive. Liberation is the *belief that we can succeed*, a sense of confidence in ourselves and in our collective efforts. Liberation is *joy* at our collective efficacy and at surviving in a world that sometimes tries to kill us. Liberation is the knowledge that *we are not alone*. It is mutual support, encouragement, and trust that others will be there if we fall, and that we need to be there for others. Liberation is *commitment* to the effort of critical transformation, to the people in our community, to the goal of equity and justice, and to love. Liberation is *passion and compassion*, those strong and motivating feelings that we must live by our hearts as well as our minds. Liberation is based in something far bigger than me as an individual, or us as a coalition, or our organization as a community, or any one nation, or any particular world. It's about that force that connects us all to one another as living beings, that force that is defined differently by every spiritual belief system but which binds us by the vision that there can be a better world and we can help to create it.

References

This model is the product of the thinking of several colleagues, specifically Felice Yeskel and Jerry Koch-Gonzales and myself, and the version described here is my latest adaptation.

Freire, P. (1968). *Pedagogy of the Oppressed*, trans. Myra B. Ramos. New York: Seabury Press.

Harro, R. L. (1983). "Heterosexism 101: The Content of an Educational Experience." Unpublished doctoral manuscript. Amherst, Mass.: University of Massachusetts.

Harro, R. L. (1997). "The Cycle of Socialization Diagram." In M. Adams, L. A. Bell, and P. Griffin, eds., *Teaching for Diversity and Social Justice: A Sourcebook.* New York: Routledge.

89

Developing a Liberatory Consciousness

Barbara J. Love

All members of society play a role in keeping a "dis-equal" system in place, whether the system works to their benefit or to their disadvantage. Through the socialization process, every member of society learns the attitudes, language, behaviors and skills that are necessary to function effectively in the existing society. This socialization prepares individuals to play roles of dominant or subordinant in systems of oppression.[1] For example, men are assigned the role of dominant and women are assigned the role of subordinant in the system of dis-equality based on gender. Whites are assigned to play the role of dominant and People of Color are assigned the role of subordinant in the system of dis-equality based on race. The socialization process of the society works to insure that each person learns what they need to know to behave in ways that contribute to the maintenance and perpetuation of the existing system, independent of their belief in its fairness or efficacy.

No single human can be charged with the creation of the oppressive systems in operation today. All humans now living have internalized the attitudes, understandings, and patterns of thoughts that allow them to function in and collaborate with these systems of oppression, whether they benefit from them or are placed at a disadvantage by them. The patterns of thought and behaviors that support and help to maintain racism, sexism, classism and other manifestations of oppression are not natural or inherent to any human. They are learned through this socialization process.

Many members of society, both those who benefit from oppression as well as those who are placed at disadvantage, want to work for social change to reduce inequity and bring about greater justice, yet continue to behave in ways that preserve and perpetuate the existing system. This happens because humans are products of their socialization and follow the habits of mind and thought that have been instilled in them. The institutions in which we live reward and reinforce behaviors that perpetuate existing systems and resist efforts toward change.

To be effective as a liberation worker—that is, one who is committed to changing systems and institutions characterized by oppression to create greater equity and social justice—a crucial step is the development of a liberatory consciousness. A liberatory consciousness enables humans to live their lives in oppressive systems and institutions with awareness and intentionality, rather than on the basis of the socialization to which they have been subjected. A liberatory consciousness enables humans to maintain an awareness of the dynamics of oppression characterizing society without giving in to despair and hopelessness about that condition, to maintain an awareness of the role played by each individual in the maintenance of the system without blaming them for the roles they play, and at the same time practice intentionality about changing the systems of oppression. A liberatory consciousness enables humans to live "outside" the patterns of thought and behavior learned through the socialization process that helps to perpetuate oppressive systems.

Elements of a Liberatory Consciousness

The process for developing a liberatory consciousness has been discussed by many educators working for social change and social justice. Paulo Freire, the Brazilian educator, described it as developing critical consciousness. Carter G. Woodson described it as changing the "miseducation of the Negro." Michael Albert's humanist vision and bell hooks's feminist critical consciousness are examples of other ways that a liberatory consciousness has been discussed.

Four elements in developing a liberatory consciousness are described here. They include awareness, analysis, acting, and accountability/ally-ship. The labeling of these four components in the development of a liberatory consciousness is meant to serve as reminders in our daily living that the development and practice of a liberatory consciousness is neither mysterious nor difficult, static nor fixed, or something that some people have and others do not. It is to be continually practiced event by event, each time we are faced with a situation in which oppression or internalized oppression is evident. These labels remind us that every human can acquire the skill to become a liberation worker.

Awareness, the first part of the task, includes practicing awareness or noticing what is happening. The second part includes analyzing what is happening from a stance of awareness along with the possibilities for action. The third part of the task includes deciding on the basis of that analysis what needs to be done, and seeing to it that the action is accomplished. The fourth part may be the most troublesome part for it requires that individuals accept accountability to self and community for the consequences of the action that has been taken or not taken.

With a liberatory consciousness, every person gets a chance to theorize about issues of equity and social justice, to analyze events related to equity and social justice, and to act in responsible ways to transform the society.

Awareness

The awareness component of a liberatory consciousness involves developing the capacity to notice, to give our attention to our daily lives, our language, our behaviors, and even our thoughts. It means making the decision to live our lives from a waking position. It means giving up the numbness and dullness with which we have been lulled into going through life. For some, facing life with awareness may at first seem painful. One student, in a class examining oppression, declared with dismay, "You have taken the fun out of going to the movies. Now I can't watch stupid movies and laugh anymore." This student had observed that even while watching "stupid movies" certain attitudes were being instilled in his consciousness. He noticed that some of these were attitudes and ideas that he would reject if he were consciously paying attention.

Living with awareness means noticing what happens in the world around you. If a salesperson reaches around you to serve the person in line behind you, a liberatory consciousness means taking notice of this act rather than ignoring it, pretending that it did not happen, or thinking it is of little consequence. If disparaging remarks about people of a different group are made in your presence, awareness requires taking note that an event has occurred that effects the maintenance or elimination of oppression. It means noticing that the remark was made, and not pretending that the remark is harmless.

Analysis

A liberatory consciousness requires every individual to not only notice what is going on in the world around her or him, but to think about it and theorize about it—that is, to get information and develop his or her own explanation for what is happening, why it is happening, and what needs to be done about it.

The analysis component of a liberatory consciousness includes the activity of thinking about what needs to be done in a given situation. Every human has the capacity to examine any situation in order to determine what seems to be true about that situation. Awareness coupled with analysis of that situation becomes the basis for determining whether change is required, and if it is, the nature of the change needed.

If what we observe to be true about a given situation seems consistent with our values of an equitable society, then the analysis will conclude that the situation is fine exactly as is. If, on the other hand, the observation leads to the conclusion that the situation is unjust, then a conclusion that the situation needs to be changed is reached.

Analysis will reveal a range of possible courses of action. Each possibility will be examined to determine what results are likely to be produced. Some possible activities will produce results that are consistent with our goals of justice and fairness while some will not. Analysis means considering the range of possible activities and the results that each of them is likely to produce.

Action

The action component of a liberatory consciousness proceeds from recognition that awareness and analysis alone are not enough. There can be no division between those who think and those who put thinking into action. The action component of a liberatory consciousness is based on the assumption that the participation of each of us in the liberation project provides the best possibility of gaining liberation for any of us.

The action component of a liberatory consciousness includes deciding what needs to be done, and then seeing to it that action is taken. Sometimes it means taking individual initiative to follow a course of action. Sometimes it means encouraging others to take action. Sometimes it means organizing and supporting other people to feel empowered to take the action that the situation requires. And sometimes, locating the resources that empower another person to act with agency is required. In still other cases, reminding others that they are right for the task, and that they know enough and are powerful enough to take on the challenge of seeing that the task is completed will be the action that is required. In any event, the liberatory consciousness requires each human to take some action in every situation when the opportunity to transform the society and move toward a more just world presents itself.

Accountable/Ally-ship

The socialization to which we have been subjected results in our thinking and behaving in very role-specific ways. We have been socialized into roles of dominant and subordinant. One result is that our vision of possibilities for change is limited by our confinement in the roles to which we have been assigned. Many white people flounder in their efforts to extricate themselves from racist conditioning. They become stuck while working on racism because their socialization to the role of dominant provides very little opportunity to understand what life might be like outside that role. A Person of Color will often have a perspective or "window of understanding" that is unavailable to a white person because of the latter's socialization into whiteness. Left alone in their struggle, some individual white people do eventually figure the difficulty out; many do not. When a Person of Color chooses to share her or his "window of understanding," the growth and development of a white person, away from racist conditioning, can be significantly enhanced and quickened.

Similarly, a Person of Color can become stuck in patterns of internalized racism and left alone to struggle. A white person can hold a perspective that is outside the socialization into racial subordination that, when shared, boosts the efforts of a Person of Color to eliminate patterns of internalized racism. The same holds true for men addressing sexism and for women addressing internalized sexism, as well as for "owning-class" people, those raised poor, and working-class people who are concerned with classism.

People raised on one end of patterns of gender, race, and class subordination or domination can provide a different perspective for people raised on the other end. At the same time, people within role groups can assist other members of their own role group to recognize and eliminate those patterns of thought and behavior that originate in internalized subordination or domination. For example, women, People of Color, those raised poor, and working-class people can help each other better understand the ways that our automatic responses help to perpetuate and maintain our own oppression.

The accountability element of a liberatory consciousness is concerned with how we understand and manage this opportunity and possibility for perspective sharing and allyship in liberation work. Individuals engaged in liberation work can have confidence that, left to their own struggles, others will eventually figure out what they need to know to disentangle thought and behavior patterns from the internalized oppression, either internalized domination or internalized subordination. But working in connection and collaboration with each other, across and within "role" groups, we can make progress in ways that are not apparent when working in isolation and in separate communities.

In our liberation work, many of us have taken the position that is it is not the responsibility of members of the subordinant group to teach or help to educate members of the dominant group. This is a reasonable and essentially "righteous" position. Those people who bear the brunt of the oppression should not be required to also take responsibility for eliminating it. At the same time, it is self-evident that people in the subordinant group can take the lead in setting the world right. For one thing, if people in the dominant group had access to and were able to hold a perspective that allowed them to change systems and patterns of domination, they would have done so already. Members of the subordinant group can wait for members of the dominant group to recognize that their language or behavior is oppressive, or they can share their perspective in every place where it could make a difference, including in the lives of members of the dominant group. In the end, it is in their best interest to do so.

This does not mean that members of groups who have been socialized into roles of subordination should focus their attention outward on the dominant group, or that members of dominant groups should be focused on the subordinant group. It is to suggest that when the perspective of the other group can serve as the critical energy to move things forward, liberation will be hampered if we hold our thinking and perspectives back from each other. Concomitantly, it also suggests that individual members of dominant and subordinant groups offer their perspective to other members of their role group in the effort to move forward.

As liberation workers, it is axiomatic that we will make mistakes. Rather than self-condemnation or blame from others, it will be important to have the opportunity and the openness to hear an analysis from others that allows us to reevaluate problematic behaviors or positions. If a Black person notices another Black person acting out of internalized racism, a liberatory consciousness requires considering the usefulness of sharing a viewpoint that enables that person to explore the implications of internalized racism for their behavior. While we do not take responsibility for another's thinking or behavior, accountability means that we support each other to learn more about the ways that the internalized domination and internalized subordination manifests itself in our lives, and agree with each other that we will act to interrupt it.

Accepting accountability to self and community for the consequences of actions taken or not taken can be an elusive concept for a people steeped in the ideology of individualism. Multiplicities of experiences and points of view contribute to problematizing the concept of accountability as well. None of us can claim for ourselves the right to tell another that her analysis is retrogressive. Recent discussions of "political correctness" can also prove troubling in the effort to grasp the idea of accountability and make it a workable concept.

There will be no easy answers here. The significance of a liberatory consciousness is that we will always question, explore, and interrogate ourselves about possibilities for supporting the efforts of others to come to grips with our conditioning into oppression, and give each other a hand in moving outside of our assigned roles. The accountability element of a liberatory consciousness requires us to develop new agreements regarding our interactions with each other. As a beginning, we get to decide the extent to which we will make ourselves available to interrupt language and behavior patterns that, in our best analysis, originate in an internalization of the ideology of domination and subordination.

Summary

In the end, institutions and systems respond to the initiatives of individuals and groups of individuals. Systems do not perpetuate themselves; they are perpetuated by the actions of people who act automatically on the basis of their socialization. If we all acted on the basis of values and beliefs of our own choosing, systems and institutions would show greater flexibility and propensity for change. As it now stands, most of us act on the basis of values and beliefs instilled in us through the socialization process, designed to prepare us to act in ways that insure the perpetuation of existing systems of oppression.

The development of a liberatory consciousness would allow us the opportunity to reclaim choice in our values and attitudes and consequently, in our response patterns. It would enable us to move from an automatic response system grounded in our socialization, to the capacity to act on a range of responses based on our own awareness, analysis and decision making, and the opportunities we have to learn from our colleagues and other who are themselves embarked on a journey to liberation.

Notes

Adapted from a chapter in a forthcoming book titled, *Internalized Oppression and the Life Experience of Black People in the United States.*
1. I prefer the spelling *subordinant* because: (1) *subordinant* is a noun; *subordinate* is an adjective, modifying the noun; (2) *subordinant* parallels *dominant*, but *subordinate* describes what is done to the subordinants; (3) if we were to parallel *subordinate*, then we need to write *dominate*; and (4) using the modifying adjective to refer to groups of people seems to further objectify and reduce.

References

Albert, Michael, et al., 1986. *Liberating Theory.* Boston: South End Press.
Freire, Paulo, 1973. *Education for Critical Consciousness.* New York: Seabury Press.
hooks, bell. 1994. *Feminist Theory: From Margin to Center.* Boston: South End Press.
Jackins, Harvey, 1972. *The Human Side of Human Beings.* Seattle: Rational Island.
Woodson, Carter G., 1933. *The Mis-Education of The Negro.* Washington D.C.: Associated Publishers

Personal Voices

90

Allies

Gloria E. Anzaldúa

Interviewed in Santa Cruz, California,
November 26, 1993

Becoming allies means helping each other heal. It can be hard to expose yourself and your wounds to a stranger who could be an ally or an enemy. But if you and I were to do good alliance work together, be good allies to each other, I would have to expose my wounds to you and you would have to expose your wounds to me and then we could start from a place of openness. During our alliance work, doors will close and we'll have to open them up again. People who engage in alliances and are working toward certain goals want to keep their personal feelings out of it, but you can't. You have to work out your personal problems while you are working out the problems of this particular community or this particular culture.

When you are doing alliance work it is very important to say who you are. For example, I am a Chicana, Mexicana, dyke, whatever. I come from a *campesina* background but I have now put one foot into middle-classness. I belong to the *inteligencia,* the intelligence class, the artistic class as an artist, and I am speaking today to you as all these people, but primarily as a Chicana or as a "dyke," et cetera. You must situate yourself and tell what your stance is on particular things, so other allies know exactly where you are coming from. And they can later say, "Oh, you say that you are talking from a working-class perspective but you have a house, you have a car, you have these privileges, you are a professor, or a salaried publisher, a privileged writer, et cetera." Allies might challenge some of your positions as a first step in finding out whether you are a real potential ally. Then you can get a sense of whether you can trust this person or not. And you go with your gut feeling. You go with how you feel, because sometimes they will say all the politically correct rhetoric, but you just know that they are trying to put one over on you.

I have edited three books, *This Bridge Called My Back, Haciendo Caras,* and *Signs: Theorizing Lesbian Experience.* In the first two books I consider anthologizing as my way of making alliances with women of color. In *Signs* it was more (or less) white women wanting to make alliances with lesbians of color. Many lesbians of color I asked to submit work didn't, because they didn't trust *Signs* because they know it to be elitist, esoteric and racist.

In the books that other people anthologize me in, some editors are very genuine and want to diversify their community. Then there are the anthologizers that call on me so that dykes of color will not call them and say, "You have one contributor of color and ninety white contributors, this is racist!" So they attempt to tokenize me, or they try to pull a fast one on their readers, by tokenizing in general. Some of my work is hard to assimilate and I consider assimilation in white culture like an amoeba trying to swallow me. But it is hard for them to assimilate me in that manner because of language and because of the way that I write. They can ignore some issues that I bring out, but because of my writing style, there are things they must confront. I don't write like a white person. I don't write like an academic or follow those rules. I break them.

If they can't assimilate my writing, what they try and do is assimilate me, by tokenizing me. They bring me into their book, or into their conference, or into their alliance in a way that will acknowledge the easy stuff I raise, but ignore the more dangerous stuff. They try to do this to me all the time, so then I have to respond back, either on the phone or in a letter, and say, why? One anthology that asked for my work was called *Growing Up Latino.* Before I agreed to publish in it, I had this whole dialogue with one of the editors, and talked about naming the book *Latino* and not *Chicano.* I asked "How many Chicanos/Chicanas are in your book? How many are Latina and how do they identify themselves?" Once the magazine *New Chicano Writing* asked me to sit on their board. I called and voiced my objections to the editor before I agreed to join: I objected having Chican*o* writers but not Chican*a* in the title, and furthermore told them that the groundbreaking writing being done in the Chicano/Chicana community was by women. I also objected to their project only accepting work written in English. So the editor went home and thought about the issues and later called me and said, "I've changed the title of the magazine to *New Chicana/Chicano Writing,* and people can write in Spanish, they can do bilingual, and they can do *Tex Mex.*" Then I felt like the editor was open to me, and I agreed to be on their editorial board.

The biggest risk in forming alliances is betrayal. When you are betrayed you feel shitty. When I have been betrayed I have felt stupid, like, Why did I trust this person and allow this person to stab me in the back, it's all my fault—you know, the victim syndrome. Betrayal—especially with Chicanas—betrayal is a big thing, because we were betrayed as women, as Indians, as a *minority* in this country, everything. We have been stabbed in the back by all of these various people. And betrayal makes you feel like less of a person—you feel shame, it reduces your self-esteem. It is politically deadening and dangerous; it's disempowering. When you lose your self-esteem you no longer trust yourself to make value judgments about other people; you lose confidence in yourself and your values. When a whole person is slowly destroyed, and this is what women of color are suffering from, their personhood is destroyed.

At first I felt really good belonging to the lesbian community, even though it was mostly white. It made me feel like where I had no home, I now had a new one. But after two or three or four years, I started looking at power, and who had power and who was trying to define for me what I was as a Chicana lesbian. I realized how my voice was silent and how my history was ignored and that drove me into looking at my roots, my queer roots in my own culture. I had to get a positive sense of being queer from my culture, not just from the white culture. Now I am in a place where I can look at both the white lesbian community and my own culture that is only beginning to have groups of lesbians organizing. *Ellas San Antonio* is a group of Chicana dykes, *Amigas y Que,* in Houston and Austin. But they were not in place when I was coming out. Chicana dyke organizations are just now coming into their power.

Now I look at my culture and white culture and the whole planet. I look at other nationalities and how they deal with their queer people; I'm getting a global perspective on being a queer person. And sometimes I feel very comfortable with a bunch of white dykes and other times I feel totally invisible, ignored. I feel that they only see the queer part of me. They don't see the Chicana part of me or the working-class part of me. As long as I leave my class and culture outside the door when I enter a room full of white dykes I am okay, but if I bring in my race or class, then my role as educator starts.

I think that most white dykes really want a community that is diversified. And sometimes they want it so badly that they want to put everybody under this queer umbrella and say, We are all in this together and we are all equal. But we are not equal. In their thirst and hunger for this diversity the issues of class and race are issues that they don't even want to examine, because they feel like they're divisive. So they are hungry for being political- ly correct and having women of color in their organizations, in their syllabi, and as per- formers, singers, writers, and lovers. But a lot of times in order to bring us under the queer umbrella they will ignore or collapse the differences, not really deal with the issues. When it comes down to the numbers of who has power or *how many* dykes of color are getting in this anthology and how many don't—in terms of the real work, they fail. I mean the ideas are good, like the greater numbers/the greater strength kind of thing but they want us to leave our race and our class in the check room when we enter their space.

As a group, I think dykes are more progressively political than any other group because of feminism, and because of being (at least) doubly oppressed. Because they have been oppressed as dykes, I believe white lesbians are more apt to recognize the oppression of women of color. So they have a true wanting of multicultural groups. And there are always the false ones, of course, there are always the ones that do want it to be white. But there is some honest motivation about wanting to be allies and in this they still have a lot of work to do. For example, one of the things they often don't contend with is the unconscious motivation of doing it out of guilt. But I am very hopeful and I think that I am one of the very few people. I think that most people of my age or younger have been burned out and disillusioned and feel like it's the pits right now. Much younger people than me have no hope, do not see alliances working, do not see white people reaching out or doing their work, and do not see the possibility of white people changing perspec- tives. Or allowing change to come into their lives, but I do.

91

Can White Heterosexual Men Understand Oppression?

Cooper Thompson

I am a white heterosexual man. For years I have struggled to understand oppression and its impact on my life and the lives of others. For the past twelve years I've been leading workshops on sexism, homophobia, and racism for white heterosexual men. It is clear to me that these men have a difficult time accepting the notion that systemic oppression is real and has an impact on all people. I believe that I understand some of our resistance to coming to terms with oppression. (*Our, us,* and *we* in this article refer to heterosexual white men). In this article I'm going to use my own experience in learning about oppression to explore some of the barriers heterosexual white men come up against in opening themselves to the meaning of oppression.

My Encounters with Feminism

I met my first outspoken feminist, a coworker, in 1975. Like many men I refused to accept her words and experience as valid. With other men at my side, I teased her when she called attention to the sexism in our workplace. I didn't understand what she was saying. I thought that I knew what was true in the world, and her version of the truth was different from mine. I was angry that she wanted a set of rules different from the one by which I had so carefully lived my life as a man. I also suspect that I was afraid of what she was proposing.

I liked this woman, and in the process of spending time together I began to question my assumptions about the world. One day we were rock climbing. She was able to complete a climb, while I got stuck below the difficult part of the rock face. I had always assumed that *I* would teach *her* about rock climbing; instead, I had to confront the fact that I needed *her* to teach *me*, to get me out of a tough spot. Over the next few years the process continued. As I allowed her experiences to sink in, they began to make sense to me, and I began to make connections between the oppression she experienced and my masculinity. I realized that my participation in sexism was restricting me as well as oppressing her. I began to feel angry about the ways in which I was limited to a particular set of human qualities that the society had arbitrarily labeled "masculine."

Connecting Homophobia and Racism

In time my questioning led me to think about the impact of homophobia and racism on my life and other men's lives. Why was I so afraid of other men? Why did I work so hard to avoid the "feminine" part of myself? Why did I know so little about racism? Why was I afraid of people of color? I was also afraid that I might do or say something that would be racist or homophobic! I struggled to do the right thing, to say what was politically correct; I was still stuck in having to be in control. I found myself afraid of being in new situations with lesbian and gay people or people of color. I feared that I would not know how to behave "appropriately." For many years I either avoided such contact, or in situations where I did make contact I tried to be the expert on homophobia and racism. Both strategies prevented me from telling who I was and listening to who they were.

During these years, I began to hear and read about the privileges I get as a man, as a white person and as a heterosexual. I was able to see how oppressed persons—particularly women, people of color, and lesbians and gay men—are denied some of the rights I have. Yet it was difficult to translate that into the day-to-day experiences in which I benefited from the oppression. It was easier to see the ways in which the system was unfair to me; I had to be willing to stretch my perspective to see the ways in which I was privileged.

Barriers to Change

From my experiences I have identified four barriers that kept me—and that I believe keep many of us—from understanding oppression.

Barrier #1: Lack of information about the experience of oppression. As a child, and even as a young adult, I received little or no direct education about the oppression of women, lesbians and gay men, or people of color. No one ever consciously sat me down and explained what oppression means, what it looks like, what it feels like. Rather, in many subtle and overt ways I had been taught that "anyone" could be successful in this egalitarian society, if only they worked hard enough. If they didn't succeed, they had no one to blame but themselves. At the same time, through "jokes" told by family and friends, I learned that people of color, women, and gay men were "less than" heterosexual white men. I seldom got information to counter the stereotypes.

How, then, could I as an adult believe the claims of the oppressed? Even if I believed that there were some "legitimate" cases of oppression—like slavery!—I could easily see them as isolated, extreme and belonging to another era and another place. Or I could blame the oppressed for their oppression, saying that the injustice was due to something they had done. I saw myself as a well-intentioned person who would not knowingly hurt another person. How could I be an oppressor?

I believe that many, perhaps most heterosexual white men have similar perspectives grounded in what we learned and experienced as children and young adults. Ironically, most of us were oppressed as children through the impact of adultism. But because we were males, most of us were taught to deny our feelings and get on with the business of life. If we can't feel our own pain, how can we acknowledge others' pain?

Barrier #2: Belief that we, the dominant group, have a market on the truth. Although I was never told directly that heterosexual white men are the bearers and protectors of truth in the world, I could not believe otherwise. God, political leaders, philosophers, judges, sports heroes, my father—all were white men. The result was a skepticism about the validity of other people's perspectives. Could we believe what women were telling us? Weren't we smarter? Could we believe what lesbians and gay men were telling us? How could they be objective when we suspected they had another agenda? Could we believe people of color? What were they trying to pull on us?

Heterosexual white men in this society tend to have a dualistic view of the world: we are either right or wrong, winners or losers. There is only one truth, and we will fight with one another to determine whose truth is right. To understand oppression requires that we accept others' experiences as truthful, even though they may be very different from ours. To live with equality in a diverse, pluralistic society, we have to accept the fact that all groups and individuals have a legitimate claim to what is true and real for them.

Barrier #3: Fear of offending members of oppressed groups and fear of their anger. I was raised to be polite. I was taught that it was inappropriate to say mean things about other people in their presence. In my family it was inappropriate to be angry at all. I had little preparation, therefore, for hearing the anger of the oppressed, particularly when I didn't believe that I was a bigot. I didn't say those mean things; why were they angry at me?

Many heterosexual white men raised with similar values are honestly confused about the anger that is directed toward us. We don't understand that this anger comes from many sources; our privilege and our failure to recognize the oppression that seems so obvious to others; our willingness to stand back and quietly watch the oppression unfold without using our privilege and power to challenge it; our belief that we can't do anything about the oppression; and, of course, intentional and overt prejudice. When anger comes our way, we often unintentionally intensify and contribute to it by our defensiveness. Instead of listening, we plead our innocence.

On a very practical level, one of the results of "trying not to offend" members of oppressed groups is that heterosexual white men find it difficult to join any dialog about oppression when members of oppressed groups are present. We become extraordinarily cautious about what we say, for fear of being called racist, sexist, or homophobic. We fear others' anger should we "accidentally" say the wrong thing. Although we may behave this way for good reason—self-protection—the result is that we remove ourselves from contact with the oppression and the oppressed. If we keep it up, we sabotage our own learning.

Barrier #4: Belief that being white, heterosexual and male is better than being a person of color, homosexual, or female. Throughout my life, culture has bombarded me with information about the accomplishments of white heterosexual men and the deficiencies of people of color, gay people, and women. Furthermore, my parents taught me to be grateful for what I had and to pity those who were not as fortunate. Even when, as an adult, I began to understand the nature of oppression, my attitude was still one of pity. My antioppression work was tied to "bettering" the oppressed.

The notion that our lives might be improved by egalitarian relationships with people of color, lesbians, and gay men, and women is difficult for us to understand and accept. We don't see ourselves deficient or needing help. We can't imagine them teaching us anything. We tend to focus on the ways in which we will have to give up control and share scarce resources if greater numbers of people are to participate in all aspects of our society. In workshops, for example, I sometimes ask white men to describe some of the ways we are hurt by racism. Their responses include comments about job loss due to "reverse discrimination" and feelings of increased tension in the workplace as more people of color join the workforce at managerial levels. Curiously, these responses are examples of the ways that we are affected by attempts to reduce institutional racism, not racism itself.

Beyond Denial

The workforce is changing in profound ways. Heterosexual white men will soon be a numerical minority, if we aren't already. (On a worldwide scale, we are definitely the minority.) We realize that women and people of color are requesting—or demanding—a place in the power structure, but frankly we don't know much about power sharing. I've heard men describe how they believe that power is finite: sharing it with others is equivalent to losing it.

I believe that it takes a leap of faith for us to even speculate on the benefits to us for ending oppression. We have to first be willing to admit that all is not well with the way that we have constructed reality and lived our lives: we die sooner than women; we experience tremendous amounts of stress; we are cut off from intimate relationships with our parents, peers, and children; we have an understanding of the world based only on the perceptions of other white men; and we live in a society that professes—but does not deliver—a commitment to freedom and equality. As I watch white men interact with one another, I sense that some of us have lost our spirit. We seem disconnected to ourselves, our colleagues, and the world around us.

Yet, many of us choose to avoid contact with people from different cultures by living in white communities, socializing with other white people, competing in sports with other men, and working with other white men. Consequently, we don't know what we're missing by continuing to live in a monocultural environment.

The benefits to us for living in a multicultural society, and ending oppression, are real. We need the creative talents of all people—women and men, people of color and white people, lesbians, gay men, and heterosexuals—to solve the problems facing our world. The world is a richer and more exciting place for me as I take in information based on others' realities. Options for how I can live my life are increased when others' lives are valued. I can be free from deep and crippling feelings of guilt for creating and perpetuating a system of oppression. Having to be responsible for the welfare of others is not fun; living with the anxiety that the oppressed will rise up in anger against me is not pleasant.

An Effective Educational Program

I believe that carefully designed and gently led educational programs on oppression can help heterosexual white men understand the reality and impacts of oppression. "Educating" people about oppression must not be a euphemism for forcing someone to accept the party line. Education can be a process in which learners willing to engage with one another and the material at hand, in ways that are helpful to them. I have used the following guidelines and approaches in my work with heterosexual white men and have found them helpful:

1. *We can listen to one another, and understand our histories, rather than judging one another for our oppressive attitudes and behaviors.* Racism, sexism, and homophobia are learned early. Regardless of how much I might want to rid myself of prejudicial thoughts, I find it nearly impossible to do so. I have felt guilty at times about my prejudices, but this guild has tended to make me want to deny the prejudices rather than come to terms with them. Therefore, it's critical that we not blame one another for being prejudiced. I've often felt relief sweep over the room at the beginning of a workshop when I've made it clear that I won't allow blaming in the group. I offer the possibility that we can't help but be prejudiced in this society, and I offer my own prejudices as an example. We explore the ways in which we learned about "the other," and I encourage participants to take responsibility for their behavior given their new awarenesses of themselves and others.

2. *We can speak for ourselves and from our own experiences.* When heterosexual white men are encouraged to speak about our past, we often recall painful memories of witnessing the oppression of others or being hurt ourselves. Ironically, this telling of one's own story creates space for hearing others' stories. A colleague of mine believes that many white men are unable to hear others' pain or recognize their own privilege until their pain has been acknowledged.

    In a recent workshop on racism, I noticed how the white men seemed unable to appreciate the anger felt by the women and people of color in attendance who described how they were locked out of certain jobs with real power to create change. The white men lamented the fact that those men with "real power" weren't in attendance. Yet this group of men included a university president, a chief of police, and several corporate presidents and vice-presidents. I encouraged them to talk about the sacrifices they had made to get where they were. They believed that they had given up a great deal for these jobs, and now felt insecure about their positions, wondering who was "gunning" for them. Eventually, they were able to recognize that they did have power and that their opportunities to move up, as well as to create change in their current positions, were generally far greater than those of the women or people of color in the workshop.

3. *We can recognize and appreciate our differences as well as the ways in which we are similar.* Even among a seemingly homogeneous group of heterosexual white men, there are profound differences in values, abilities, and life experiences. These can be used as a basis for exploring other cultural differences. Recognizing and appreciating these differences is crucial, even though many of us—including myself—were taught to treat everyone as if they were the same. I've seem many white people get nervous when I

simply call attention to the fact that there are African-American people in the room. Unless we recognize, and then appreciate differences across race, gender and sexual orientation, we will not see others for who they are. And if women, people of color, and lesbian and gay people can't bring their culture to their work then they are leaving much of themselves outside the door. Recognizing and appreciating differences will bring all of our creative talent to the task, not just those which are valued by white male culture.

4. *We can encourage feeling as well as thinking.* As a white man, I have been taught that knowledge comes from cognition, that the search for truth is an intellectual process. Yet in my work on oppression I have also come to value emotion as a powerful tool for learning. In many cases, my heart knows as much as my head, and if I can bring both to my work, I will have a broader base from which to make decisions. I've often noticed how as white men we can talk our way into thinking that women or people of color deserved the treatment they got. Yet if we are willing to feel the pain and fear associated with prejudice, harassment, and discrimination, then we may be able to understand the impact of oppression.

5. *We can identify the ways oppression has hurt us and how we will benefit from ending oppression.* It may take us a while to understand how oppression has hurt *us*, the oppressors. With enough time, and safety, I have seen other men begin to claim, at a very personal level, how they are tired of the stress and responsibility of being in a position of power; how they do want justice for all people; and how they want true freedom in their own lives. In the long run, those of us who are motivated to end oppression out of our self-interest will be more honest with ourselves and others and less prone to burnout. Guilt does not sustain us as agents of change nor does it lead to sound decisions about resource and power sharing which will truly benefit the oppressed.

Lingering Questions

Even after 12 years I still have many questions about my identity and my work. Will I have satisfying relationships with other heterosexual white men? I sometimes feel isolated from other heterosexual white men; my friends are largely women, lesbians and gay men, and people of color. One colleague, in his work on sexism, has described this as a sense that he has betrayed other men, and so he feels rejected by them.

Will I stay committed to this work, knowing that I can walk away at any time from the day-to-day reality of oppression? I know that in most parts of the United States. I can live comfortably without having to struggle against sexism, homophobia and racism. Will my self-interest be strong enough to keep me doing this work?

Will I be patient with the ways I am distrusted by members of oppressed groups? Although I understand that the distrust is both historical and functional in the present— there are many heterosexual white men who knowingly perpetuate the oppression—I can get defensive about questions of my integrity.

And finally, will I be optimistic enough to continue this work? When working with heterosexual white men, I sometimes find myself flipping back and forth between despair and hopefulness. My despair comes from the fear that those with power to affect systemic oppression will never find the reasons or courage to do so. My hopefulness comes from the experience of watching people get insights that lead to positive action. My goal is to learn more about my despair and remember my moments of hope. I believe that it is the possibility of change, and the excitement of watching people reach their potential, that will sustain me.

Next Steps and Action

92

How to Interrupt Oppressive Behavior

Mary McClintock

- Jokes that made fun of Helen Keller's disabilities were very popular one summer at a camp run by a local social service agency.

- After the first week of the camp season, two girls were sent home. They were the only two black campers in a camp of one hundred white campers. The camp director said that they "weren't adjusting well," and that they wouldn't like it at that camp.

What do these incidents have in common? They're experiences I had during my years as a camper and staff member at a variety of camps. Name-calling, jokes, stereotyping, and discrimination against campers or staff are examples of ways that societal attitudes about particular groups of people are acted out as individual behaviors.

Prior to celebrating diversity, we must first eliminate intolerance. No matter what form it takes or who does it, we must all take action to stop intolerance when it happens. Working toward a celebration of diversity implies working for social justice—the elimination of all forms of social oppression.

Camps reflect the social injustice that is prevalent in North American society. Even though many camps are in idyllic physical settings away from the environmental problems of the cities, the social problems come to camp with the staff and campers. Social injustice takes many forms. It can be injustice based on a person's gender, race, ethnicity, religion, sexual orientation, physical or mental ability, or economic class.

While there are differences among forms of social injustice, there are also a number of commonalities. Some of those commonalities include a power differential between groups of people, the use of stereotyping to limit people, and the exclusion of the disempowered group.

In order to work for social justice in the world, we need to confront all forms of social injustice. What do we do when a camper tells a Helen Keller joke or a camp director excludes a camper based on his race? *First and foremost, it is important to confront the behavior.*

This chapter focuses on summer camp settings. However, the Action Continuum described within this chapter can be applied to many other contexts.

When I experience oppressive behavior, it is helpful for me to think about having a whole range of possible responses — what I think of as an *action continuum*.

In any situation, one can choose a range of actions—from participating in the oppressive behavior to working to prevent oppressive behavior on an organizational level.

Works Against Social Justice		Works Toward Social Justice				
Actively Join in Behavior	No Response	Educate Oneself	Interrupt the Behavior	Interrupt and Educate	Support Others' Proactive Response	Initiate Proactive Response

Now, let's apply the continuum to the incidents described at the beginning of the article.

Actions That Work against Social Justice

Actively Joining in the Oppressive Behavior

To actively join in oppressive behavior means doing something that supports the oppressive behavior rather than interrupting it.
Examples:

- laughing at the Helen Keller joke and sharing another of your own;

- saying, "I'm glad the director sent those girls home. This camp isn't for black people."

Having No Response:

Having no response means not responding to the behavior. Examples:

- not laughing at the joke;

- not saying something in response to the black campers being sent home.

Actions That Work toward Social Justice

Educating Yourself

To educate yourself means to learn more about what is behind the oppressive behavior. Examples:

- reading about the accomplishments of people with disabilities in the face of discrimination;

- reading about ways camps have been exclusive in the past and now welcome campers from a range of ethnic and racial backgrounds.

Interrupting the Behavior

To interrupt the behavior means expressing your disapproval of the behavior. Possible responses:

- "I don't think that joke is funny."

- "I don't think those campers should be sent home."

Interrupt and Educate

To interrupt any educate means expressing your disapproval of the behavior *and* explaining what is oppressive about the behavior. Possible responses:

- "I don't think jokes that make fun of someone's disabilities are funny because they assume that someone with a disability is not worthy of respect."

- "I don't think it is appropriate to send the black girls home. People of color have a long history of being unfairly excluded from all-white organizations in this country. We should not perpetuate that exclusion."

Supporting Others' Proactive Responses

To support the proactive responses of others means supporting the efforts of other people to educate or take action that promotes understanding of differences. Examples:

- encouraging the campers who are telling jokes about Helen Keller to go to the campfire program that includes a puppet show about kids with disabilities;

- supporting the camp board of directors' efforts to investigate ways to welcome campers and staff from various racial and ethnic backgrounds.

Initiating a Proactive Response

Initiating a proactive response means taking some kind of action that promotes understanding and valuing of cultural differences in camp settings. Examples:

- planning a series of events that focus on understanding and valuing people who have a wide range of abilities;

- organizing a seminar for the camp staff on working with campers from various racial and ethnic backgrounds.

Taking action to stop oppressive behavior can be difficult. It is easy to feel awkward or caught off guard. This action continuum can be used to think about different situations one might encounter. One can then mentally rehearse possible responses to situations that might occur. It also gives an individual the opportunity to choose an action that will be best suited to the situation and to the goal of promoting social justice.

Factors in deciding which response to make include the level of risk for yourself and others, your power in the situation, and your understanding of this form of social injustice. I recommend that you think about situations you have encountered and think about the range of possible responses you could have to each situation. You will then be better prepared the next time someone around you makes an oppressive comment or does something that creates a barrier to celebrating diversity. This action continuum can also be used during staff training as the basis for a discussion on dealing with oppressive behavior.

If everyone makes a commitment to respond appropriately to oppressive behavior, the ground work will be lain for creating settings in which diversity is truly celebrated.

93

Working Assumptions and Guidelines for Alliance Building

Ricky Sherover-Marcuse

Since, under present world conditions, everyone either is now, or has been, or will be at some time a *target* of social oppression, and since everyone is now, or has been, or will be in a *non-target group* in relation to some other group's oppression, alliance building is for everyone. Everyone of us needs allies, and everyone of us can take the role of an ally for someone else. The following guidelines are based on this premise. They should be equally applicable from the perspective of the target and the non-target group.

I. Strategies for Winning Allies

1. Assume that your group and that *you in particular* deserve allies.

2. Assume that your liberation issues are *justifiably* of concern to all people outside your group;

3. Assume that people in other groups are your *natural allies*; assume that all people outside your group *want* to be allies for you and that it is in *their* interest for them to do so.

4. Assume that it is only other people's own oppression and internalized oppression that prevents them (temporarily) from being effective allies to you at all times.

5. Assume that your allies are doing the best they can at the present time, given their own oppression and internalized oppression. Assume that they can and will do better.

6. Assume that you are the expert on your own experience and that you have information which other people need to hear.

7. Speak from your own experience without comparing your oppression to theirs.

8. Assume that your experience is also an experience of victories; be sure to share these as well as the stories of how things are hard.

9. Expect perfection from your allies; expect them to be able to deal with the "difficult issues" in your struggle. Assume that allies make mistakes; be prepared to be disappointed, and *continue to expect the best from them*.

10. Assume that you have a perfect right to assist your allies to become more effective for you. Assume that you can *choose* to do this at any time. Take full pride in your ability to do this.

2. Strategies for Being an Effective Ally

1. Assume that all people in your own group including yourself want to be allies to people in other groups. Assume that *you in particular* are good enough and smart enough to be an effective ally. (This does not mean that you have nothing more to learn—see #6 below.)

2. Assume that you have a perfect right to be concerned with other people's liberation issues, and that it is in your own interest to do so and to be an ally.

3. Assume that all people in the target group want members of your group and *you in particular* as an ally. Assume that they recognize you as such—at least potentially.

4. Assume that any appearances to the contrary (any apparent rejections of you as an ally) are the result of target groups people's experience of oppression and internalized oppression.

5. Assume that people in the target group are already communicating to you in the best way they can at the present time. Assume that they can and will do better. Think about how to assist them in this without making your support dependent upon their "improving" in any way. (Hint: think about what has been helpful for you when you were in the target group position.)

6. Assume that target group people are experts on their own experience, and that you have much to learn from them. Use your own intelligence and your own experience as a target group member to think about what the target group people might find useful.

7. Recognize that as a non-target person you are an expert on the experience of having been conditioned to take the oppressor role. This means that you know the content of the lies which target group people have internalized. Don't let timidity force you into pretended ignorance.

8. Assume that target group people are survivors and that they have a long history of resistance. Become an expert on this history and assist target group people to take full pride in it.

9. Become an expert on all the issues which are of concern to people in the target group, especially the issues which are most closely tied in to their internalized oppression. Assume that making mistakes is part of the learning process of being an ever more effective ally. Be prepared for flare-ups of disappointment and criticism. Acknowledge and apologize for mistakes; learn from them, *but don't retreat.*

10. Recognize that people in the target group can spot "oppressor-role conditioning;" do not bother with trying to "convince" them that this conditioning did not happen to you. Don't attempt to convince target group people that you "are on their side"; just be there.

11. Do not expect "gratitude" from people in the target group; thoughtfully interrupt if it is offered to you. Remember, being an ally is a matter of your choice. It is not an obligation; it is something you get to do;

12. Be a 100% ally; no deals; no strings attached: "I'll oppose your oppression if you oppose mine." Everyone's oppression needs to be opposed unconditionally.

94

Bridging the "Us/Them" Divide: Intergroup Dialogue and Peer Leadership

Ximena Zúñiga and Todd D. Sevig

Our meetings served as a forum where questions could be asked, no matter how ignorant or insensitive they might have been, and be answered honestly. It was strange to be able to ask those questions that were bottled up inside you forever and not be afraid of what kind of reaction you might receive.

—African-American man, black/white dialogue

This has been a great place for me to learn to work with women of color. . . . [It has] deepened my commitment to multiculturalism and given me renewed hope and energy. . . . Seeing how little and how much we could do in seven weeks helped me understand more thoroughly how entrenched racism is and how important is change at the personal level.

—White woman, white women/women of color dialogue

I have felt very isolated and ignored as a Latina (and a minority) on this campus. Through the dialogue I've come to find that I do not stand alone with this feeling . . . ; [I found here] support and encouragement . . . and a group of individuals that are head strong and very brave. . . . I never realized how important increasing intergroup [contact] can be to survival.

—Latina, black/Latino(a) dialogue

Higher education in the United States is at a historical juncture. In spite of the efforts to attend to diversity issues in faculty hiring, student recruitment and retention, and the college curriculum, the prevailing campus climate is not conducive to substantial conversations across race and other social-group boundaries or to understanding the bases for the tensions between groups that lead to intergroup conflict. Students often leave diversity discussions angry, defensive, and confused by the inability of faculty, staff, and administrators to provide competent leadership in these areas.[1] . . .

In this article, we describe a peer-facilitated intergroup dialogue program at the University of Michigan that is attempting to help in this process. . . .

An *intergroup dialogue* is defined as a face-to-face meeting between students from two or more social identity groups that have a history of conflict or potential conflict. These groups are broadly defined by ethnicity, race, gender, sexual orientation, mental and/or physical ability, socioeconomic class, religion, and/or other social characteristics.

Some examples of dialogue groupings include the following: women and men; lesbians, gay men, bisexuals, and heterosexual people; white people and people of color; women of color and white women; blacks and whites; Christians, Muslims, and Jews; Latinos and Asian Americans; people with disabilities and people without disabilities; and international students and U.S. students. The groups are ideally composed of ten to sixteen participants, with roughly equal numbers from each social identity group participating in the dialogue.

The goals of the intergroup dialogues are as follows:

- to develop awareness as members of social groups in the context of systems of privilege and oppression;

- to explore similarities and differences between and among participants and link these differences to issues of oppression at the cultural and institutional levels;

- to develop skills in intergroup communication, constructive use of conflict, alliance building, and social change;

- to examine the origins of beliefs, attitudes and behaviors at individual, cultural and institutional levels;

- to challenge ignorance, misinformation, biases, and oppression through reflective learning, honest feedback, critical analysis of issues, and input from facilitators; and

- to identify actions that facilitate alliances and coalitions in order to work toward just social change.

The dialogues are cofacilitated by two trained peer facilitators—one from each of the participating groups.[2] Student facilitators make a two-semester commitment to the program. In the first semester they receive intensive training; in the second semester they facilitate at least one credit-bearing intergroup dialogue.

The cofacilitation model is a blend of traditional group-facilitation practices, transformative models of conflict intervention, and group-building models for creating and maintaining alliances. The cofacilitation teams work closely with a group of consultants who assist them with agenda planning and design issues, and with learning the skills required to facilitate dialogue and conflict and confront difficult group dynamics. . . .

Student Learning

Throughout the period during which the dialogues have been held, ongoing research and evaluation has provided information that allowed us both to track progress and to improve the model. An analysis of the findings shows that the learning outcomes fall into the following categories.[3]

Challenging Misconceptions, Biases, and Stereotypes

The dialogue experience helps students realize that "not all people from this particular group" fit their preconceptions of the group. As students learn to ask difficult questions of each other they begin to challenge their misconceptions and their prejudices. A combination of readings about the social groups involved in the dialogue in addition to more experiential, "here and now," work is often helpful to reach this end.

An African-American woman observed, "I had always thought that the skin-color issue was one relevant only to blacks. It was very interesting to discover how the issues of skin color figure into the lives of Latinos and Latinas."

A white man stated, "My original stereotypes were that the people of color would be easily set off by a comment that a white person would make, and would become hostile to every white person in the group. I thought the people of color would just sit and talk about oppression. The dialogue experience made me rethink my stereotypes."

Personal Awareness of Self as a Member of Social Identity Groups

Understanding the concept of "social identity group" and how one's membership in a group impacts construction of self-in-relation-to-others is an important but often difficult task. White students, especially, often struggle with the idea that they have a social group or collective identity, and that this group identity as "white" grants them unearned privileges not available to members of other racial groups, and with the ramification of these privileges upon their self-definition.

A white woman stated, "No one ever explained to me what it meant to be white. . . . Instead of saying that it was I who had privilege, I thought it was they who were oppressed. I could only see one side of the whole thing. . . . I didn't know the important side of me that I need to see in order to gain better understanding of racism."

Students of color are more aware of the impact of their race/ethnic social-group membership on their social identity in a predominantly white campus and society, but are not often aware of the layers and complexities of identity that may unfold as they engage in dialogues about "race" with their peers—white students and students of color.

An African-American woman, in a white women/women of color dialogue, observed, "In discussing with these women [now I see] a constellation of things that constitute my social identity—I am a dark-skinned African-American woman. To be black in America means to be deprived of basic human rights and liberties. To be a woman in America means to be condescended [to] and disrespected more times than you care to remember. [To be] a dark-skinned woman means that we cannot find ourselves represented anywhere. We are not on TV, in magazines or billboards. . . . [W]hen instances of discrimination occur I can never tell if it is because I am black or because I'm a woman—or maybe because I'm dark. . . . [Before this class] I would never have believed that all of these things could, simultaneously, contribute to a single racist or sexist incident."

Developing More Complex Ways of Thinking

Recognizing and analyzing some of the complexities of "identity," "race," and "intergroup relations" is critical in striving toward a more realistic and complete analysis of intergroup conflicts, and in engaging in dialogue across differences. In so doing, students enhance their critical-thinking and intercultural skills.

An Asian-American woman, in a white women/women of color dialogue, explained, "Through the dialogue process I realized that while there are many forces that divide women, women do not and cannot compartmentalize their lives. [We] cannot neatly separate our experiences into distinct categories and label some *racial* and some *gender.*

A white woman stated, "For me, being a woman is my primary source of identity. It is what I struggle with when I am deciding how to act or react in most situations. However, the dialogue group taught me that the reason I think this way is because I never had to think about how race shaped the body image issues I faced as a woman. I began to realize that the reason I didn't think my struggles with body image were connected to my race was because I saw white women everywhere I looked."

The face-to-face setting of dialogues provides students the opportunity to learn actively about the complex facets of social life and intergroup relations, in the "here and now."

A Latina in a black/Latino(a) group observed, "I was surprised to see some of us disagreeing with each other. I had made the assumption that people who are in the same social identity group also shared the same thoughts but I was soon proven wrong. Members of the other group also disagreed with each other. That also surprised me because I went to the dialogue thinking that black people always agree with each other."

Developing a More Positive Approach to Conflict and Difficult Dialogues

Learning to work through conflicts is one of the most difficult but often the most rewarding outcomes students talk about. Once students learn to move beyond their initial caution and anxiety about conflict, they develop skills to intervene to keep dialogue going, even when it is difficult.

One white woman said, "Before this dialogue I had tended to avoid conflict, and think that conflict only led to anger and hate. However, now I realize this is not the case. Through our discussions, which did contain conflict, issues were brought out into the open and could no longer be ignored in the name of comfort. Yes, at times I have felt uncomfortable, just as I had initially feared, but that discomfort also resulted in learning and increased understanding and awareness."

An African-American man stated, "The dialogue effectively showed how constant communication helps us resolve such conflict not by necessarily agreeing on everything, but in better understanding and respecting one another's feelings and experiences."

Identifying Ways of Taking Actions That Address Social Injustices

Students generally come to recognize that they are all "part of the solution." This can involve two dimensions: first, gaining a new "mindset" regarding ally work or coalitional actions (for example, new conceptions of working together), and second, taking specific actions (using sensitive language, confronting members of one's "own" group about issues of oppression, and becoming involved in student organizations which address diversity issues).

An African-American woman said, "The most valuable thing I am taking away from this experience is the realization that blacks and Jews are very concerned about survival, even though this means different things to each group. . . . I hope to work toward bridging the gap that seems to separate us."

A Latina woman noted, "Even though the twelve of us in the group, alone, cannot make the changes that are needed . . . we have definitely learned how to bond and work together to make a difference."

A white woman said, "Though I cannot and will not end racism by this action alone, it is a powerful thing for each of us to have sat together and talked. . . . I hope to be able to practice [what I've learned] as a diversity facilitator [and work] toward practicing and living in nonoppressive spaces."

Design Ingredients

Participants and facilitators often report that the dialogue process has a kind of "magic" in its impact. Over the years we have identified the following ingredients as key to this powerful transformative effect.

The Personalized Peer-Learning Structure

For nearly all participants, the dialogues represent their first opportunity to sit down and talk openly with each other across race and other social-group boundaries. Students value participating in a nonjudgmental peer environment where they can ask taboo questions and explore their perspectives and experiences. Having adequate time set aside, meeting regularly, and paying attention to both "intellectual and emotional selves" are cited as critical ingredients. Students also found the dialogues more helpful than traditional classroom experiences in moving them toward thinking for themselves.

> An African-American woman put it this way: "Being in an open space like this made me feel like people (both white people and people of color) were actually listening to everything that I had to say. They also provided me with alternative outlooks to each issue we discussed. This is one part of the dialogue that initially shocked me because I was expecting everyone to have one-track minds like the open forums [I watch] on TV."

> A white man stated, "Our discussions were thought-provoking and the communication in the groups was very good. [We] were able to ask questions and speak our minds without being judged."

> A biracial woman observed, "There were no 'right' answers, no 'narrow view' or 'particular theory,' we were studying. We were actively learning from each other."

The Size and Diversity of the Group

The small-group design and the balanced group composition were frequently cited by students as evidence that this experience was going to be "for real." They commented on the supportive environment of the dialogue group in comparison with the "chilly climate" of the classroom as a critical ingredient for success.

> A biracial woman, in a white people/people of color dialogue, highlighted the value of the diverse composition of the group in relation to the status of minorities on campus: "I think the topics discussed and the racial composition of our group took away a lot of the white privilege found in other places on campus."

The Opportunity to Work across Differences

Being able to explore, in coalition with each other, difficult questions and issues without ignoring or eliminating difference is identified by participants as a critical ingredient in the success of a dialogue.

> A white woman reported, "The dialogues have been an ideal place in which to learn about the tenuous relationship between white women and women of color, which is indicative of race relations in the United States. It is so rare that there is a special place and time created to work on problems that play themselves out on every level of life."

For people of color, the dialogue experience provides a rare opportunity to communicate and address differences without the "pressure to perform" of the predominantly white classroom.

A Latina said of her participation in a black/Latino(a) dialogue, "The dialogue has been unique because we, as blacks and Latinos, could discuss sensitive issues without always having to educate or give historical explanations about our thinking. In the predominantly white classroom we represent the 'other' point of view. Our knowledge is often questioned, misunderstood or disrespected."

The Emphasis on Communication and Constructive Use of Conflict

Attention to issues of group development and coalitional group facilitation is at the center of the intergroup dialogue pedagogy. Working through initial feelings of caution, mistrust, and defensiveness takes time and hard work, but is essential if the process is to succeed. Many students describe moments in which they experienced real communication and a sense of safety that encouraged risk taking. They also recognize that such opportunities are not often available in other settings.

An Asian-American woman put it this way: "The more I listened the more I was able to understand things from the other women's points of view. For example, how each felt about issues of body image and sexual assault. The communication in the group gradually improved as members were willing to listen to someone else before jumping to conclusions or being easily offended. The more we felt comfortable expressing our honest opinions and experiences, the more we got to know each other at a personal level. [Early on] we decided to abolish 'political correctness' from our vocabulary, which gave us more leeway for communication." . . .

In sum, the "magic" of the design suggests that the peer orientation, the diverse composition of the groups, and the careful attention to group process are critical ingredients in the success of the intergroup dialogue process. In addition, the academic structure enhances the quality and depth of learning through reading and writing. . . .

Notes

Many of the ideas presented in this article were developed in collaboration with our colleagues at Intergroup Relations and Conflict (IGRC) over the years. We especially appreciate our discussions with Ratnesh Nagda, Andrea Monroe-Fowler, Pamela Motoike, Mark Chesler, Luis Sfeir-Younis, Carolyn M. Vasques, Diane Kardia, Monita Thompson, Pat Gurin and David Schoem. We also thank Mark Chesler for his encouragement and helpful feedback on the preparation of this article.

1. For context, see *The Diversity Factor* (Fall, 1996), for a review of diversity issues on campus.
2. The design and training model has been described in more detail in B. A. Nagda, Ximena Zúñiga, and Todd D. Sevig, "Bridging Differences in Peer Facilitated Intergroup Dialogues," in L. Sherry Hatcher, ed., *Peer Programs on the College Campus* (San Jose, Calif.: Resource Publications, 1995).
3. The "lessons" presented here are extrapolated from a paper by Ximena Zúñiga, Carolyn M. Vasques, Todd D. Sevig, and B. A. Nagda presented at the American Educational Research Association, New York (April 1996), and a paper by Zúñiga, Nagda, Sevig, Monita Thompson and Eric Dey presented at the annual meeting of the Association for Higher Education, Orlando, Fla. (November 1995).

95

Having the Tools at Hand: Building Successful Multicultural Social Justice Organizations

John Anner

There is no mystery to building effective multicultural social justice organizations, say many activists and organizers. A variety of organizations provide training and consultations, and, as this chapter indicates, there are specific methods available to activists and organizers. "What matters most of all," says diversity trainer Guadalupe Guajardo, of Technical Assistance for Community Services in Portland, Oregon, "is being able to listen and learn, and having the tools at hand to make changes."

This chapter focuses on the specific tactics and strategies that social justice organizers use to build multicultural organizations. Organizers can begin to confront the larger economic and political forces devastating low- and middle-income communities by building social justice organizations that can adapt to rapid changes in the demographic and cultural environment. While these organizations may not lead a national social justice movement if and when it develops, they will train its political leaders, provide models of effective organizing methods, educate and develop memberships, keep people involved on a regular basis in community work, and test the local power structure for weak points. . . .

The models and mechanisms being used to build successful multicultural social justice organizations include

- building personal relationships between members from different backgrounds;

- actively engaging in solidarity campaigns, actions, and activities with social justice organizations in other communities;

- challenging bigoted statements and attitudes when they arise;

- holding regular discussions, forums, "educationals," and workshops to enhance people's understandings of other communities and individuals;

- working to change the culture of the organization so that members see themselves as "members of the community" first instead of members of a particular part of the community;

- developing issues, tactics, and campaigns that are relevant to different communities and that reveal fundamental areas of common interest;

- conducting antiracism training to get people to confront and deal with their biases;

- examining and changing the organization's practices in order to hire, promote, and develop people of color;

- confronting white privilege and nationalism; and

- hiring, recruiting, and training more people of color for leadership positions.

It Doesn't Just Happen

Elsa Barboza is an organizer with South Los Angeles-based Action for Grassroots Empowerment and Neighborhood Development Alternatives (AGENDA), which has generally focused on the African-American community. In 1994, says Barboza, "We wanted to [make AGENDA] an authentic multicultural organization, but we learned an important lesson: It doesn't just happen." . . .

One way to create an authentic multicultural organization is to define issues and campaigns so as to make them relevant to all members of the organization, . . . working to research and develop campaigns that are of particular concern to [all their] members. AGENDA is conducting what they call "educationals" with all their African-American members to "demystify" the changing demographics of Los Angeles, and show how low-income communities of color face similar challenges and problems. . . .

In the Heat of the Struggle

Perhaps the most common way that multicultural groups deal with diversity in their memberships is through a political ideology that emphasizes how the struggle at hand transcends differences of race, age, gender, or sexuality. The Committee against Anti-Asian Violence (CAAAV) is a New York-based community group that has been active and visible on issues ranging from hate crimes to police brutality and economic exploitation. The group's 2,500 members are diverse, but all Asian. . . . Although it is certainly true that there is a good deal of mutual dislike and often active hostility among the large variety of immigrant communities that have found themselves living side by side in urban America, it does seem to be the case that these differences can be set aside in the heat of the struggle. . . .

On the other hand, says Saliem Osman, a CAAAV staff organizer, working in coalition with other groups requires a lot of internal education: "Our members, who are taxi drivers, garment workers, and vendors mostly, need to be challenged to look at [their prejudices]." Prejudice against Latinos and African Americans among CAAAV members was clearly revealed during city council hearings on a bill that would have granted taxi drivers the right to refuse to pick up any individual based on their appearance. CAAAV organizers knew that drivers were supportive of the bill because it gave them the right to refuse rides to African-American men.

"We had to do a lot of work with the members on that one," says Osman. "That was a law aimed directly at African-Americans. So we said, 'No, we won't support it because it's racist.' But first we put together a video and used it to educate the drivers" in day-long training sessions.

CAAAV then took the issue one step further, appearing at public hearings to argue against the law, sometimes surprising African-American civil rights groups. "The best way to overcome prejudices between [communities of color]," says Osman, "is to work together in solidarity with each other to build unity." For this reason, CAAAV has actively sought to build a working relationship with Puerto Rican and African-American groups active in the fight against police brutality. . . .

The anti-AIDS activist group ACT UP and the gay visibility network Queer Nation also started to come apart at the seams in the mid-1990s, in part because of their inability to cope with demands by members of color that the particular needs of their communities receive greater attention. Similarly, at the 1995 National People's Action (NPA) conference in Washington, D.C., a group of Latino delegates stormed the stage and took over the microphone from executive director Gale Cinotta. Led by Juan Mireles, they demanded that the NPA start translating meetings and conference plenaries into Spanish and that a minimum of 25 percent of the delegates to the next year's convention be Latino. Mireles told freelance writer Daniel Cordes that part of the problem is that the NPA—as a predominantly white and African-American organization—doesn't see the need to organize around issues of particular concern to Latinos or to figure out mechanisms to bring in a more diverse membership.

For both NPA and NTC [National Toxics Coalition], shared concerns among the membership about declining neighborhoods, redlining, and economic justice were not enough to paper over conflicts among staff and/or members of different races. Some formal mechanism is needed for "surfacing" these conflicts, letting them come out into the open, and resolving them as a group.

This can be as simple as not letting bigoted comments pass without comment. When prejudices are aired openly in a meeting or other event, say organizers, it can poison relations unless it is dealt with openly. "I remember one time at a meeting where we had whites, Blacks, and three or four Mexican members," says San Francisco Anglers for Environmental Rights (SAFER) organizer Wendell Chin, "and an outspoken white leader commented that she was glad that [the anti-immigrant California ballot initiative] Proposition 187 had passed because of the problems too many immigrants were causing. I looked over at the Mexican [members] and they weren't saying anything. So I had to step in and intervene." . . .

Sometimes a more involved process is required. When tensions surfaced between Asian and Black participants in a year-long program called A New Collaboration for Hands-On Relationships (ANCHOR), program director Rinku Sen decided to skip the actual program for that week and hold a series of discussions about the differences between the two communities. "Just because we call ourselves people of color doesn't mean we have the same backgrounds," says Sen. "Someone who was born in Cambodia and moved into a Black neighborhood in Oakland might experience racism as a daily fact of life. But that experience itself might be different than it would be for a Black person, and of course it is filtered through their history and current expectations."

Speaking My Language

Multicultural organizations are usually multilingual. People for a Better Oakland (PUEBLO), Direct Action for Rights and Equality (DARE), and other community groups have invested in a number of simultaneous translating machines. "They are a costly but highly effective tool," says PUEBLO lead organizer Rosi Reyes. The machines allow members to be seated anywhere in the room, instead of being segregated in one area, while the translator speaks quietly into a transmitter worn over the head. Receivers are smaller than a pack of cigarettes, with tiny earphones. . . .

Most organizers warn, however, that translation demands more than simply literally transcribing what is being said. In order to transmit the real meaning and invite participation, says Peter Cervantes-Gautschi, director of the Portland, Oregon, Workers Organizing Committee, "the critical thing is that the [translator] has to be into the movement. Because if [that person] doesn't really understand what we're trying to accomplish, then they are not going to get it right."

From White to Rainbow

"There are two main obstacles to building multiracial social justice movements," says Libero Della Piana, who edits *Race File* at the Applied Research Center, "nationalism and white racism." Although many barriers divide people of color from each other, diversifying white organizations presents a different and more difficult set of challenges. "People of color generally understand racism as institutional," says Guadalupe Guajardo, "while to white people white privilege is virtually invisible, and they see prejudice as being something personal." . . .

When working with an all-white group that wants to become multicultural, TACS trainers lay out five concrete areas to examine and consider changing: (1) the recruitment process, including where it is done and what the qualification requirements are; (2) planning, that is, who is at the table when plans are being made; (3) decision making, that is, who is involved when decisions are made, both in formal and informal settings; (4) resource allocation, including money, access, and power; and (5) promotion and leadership. Promoting people of color to leadership positions is vital, but only if these individuals have a base of support, are going to be given power and resources, and are held accountable. . . .

Changing the Mix

A criticism frequently directed at national community organizing networks is that the staff organizers and directors are mostly white, while the people they organize are predominantly people of color. . . . There are more people of color working at the average metropolitan daily newspaper than at all the left-wing magazines in the country combined.

This situation—at least on the community organizing side of things—is responsible for at least three significant trends in grassroots social justice organizing that appeared in the 1980s and developed throughout the 1990s. First is the rapid growth of independent organizations in communities of color not connected to any of the community organizing networks or unions, including many of the groups described in this book.

Second is the formation of organizer training programs specifically designed to train organizers of color to work in community and labor organizations comprised of people of color. Of these, by far the most prominent is the Center for Third World Organizing (CTWO), which has trained several hundred organizers of color through ten years of programs such as the Minority Activist Apprenticeship Program (MAAP) and the Community Partnership Program. Along with the organizer training programs, CTWO has also developed a model of community organizing that relies on organizers of color.

Finally, many emerging social justice organizations have made an explicit commitment to leadership diversity. The New Party constitution, for example, states that 50 percent or more of the leaders of local chapters must be people of color and 50 percent must be women. Greater diversity in the organizing staff can bring immediate rewards for community and labor organizations; it is now pretty much accepted by labor leaders that white men are the least effective organizers.

Teamsters Local 175 in Seattle, Washington wanted to organize Asian women working in private postal facilities. The notion that these women could not be organized, says organizer Michael Laslett, was partly due to the fact that nobody had ever tried, and partly due to the expected barriers of culture, race, and language. He brought on two Asian-American interns from the AFL-CIO Organizing Institute to go into one particular shop, which resulted in a victorious union drive. "Having Asian organizers is what made organizing this company possible," he said. . . .

Fluid Identities

The strategies for diversifying that work with this generation may not work with the next, however. In fact, say some youth organizers, most of what has been outlined above is based on strict definitions that don't fit with the mixed identities and intensely multicultural lives of urban youth. These young people don't need to be taught how to get along with other cultures, nor do they necessarily identify with the racial categories that guide the previous generation.

"It's pretty wild," says Next Generation co-director Mike Perez, who used to work at the Oakland-based youth program Encampment for Citizenship. "Race and class intersect in different ways for young people than they do for their parents." Many young people believe they can choose their racial identity based on how they feel. "I didn't have enough attitude to be a Black girl," one white high school student told *YO!* editor Nell Bernstein, explaining why she dressed like a *cholita*, or Latina gansta girl.

"You have white kids coming in saying they are just as much a 'nigga' as any Black kid since they come from the same 'hood," says Perez. "You have Asian kids dressing hip-hop and talking [African-American dialect]. Other Black kids talk and act white, in the eyes of their friends. Identities are very fluid, but it's what being young is about now." . . .

It is probably true, as some youth organizers argue, that the intense problems that race, gender, and sexuality caused for older political groups and movements will not be as much in evidence as younger people start to move into leadership positions in social justice organizations. Perhaps "the fire next time" will burn brightly in rainbow patterns. But if we want social justice organizing to move beyond the limitations of identity struggles into an enlightened next phase, with justice, community, democracy, and true solidarity on the top of the agenda, we would do well to remember what Elsa Barboza said: It doesn't just happen.

Further Print and Video Resources

Section 1: Conceptual Frameworks

Print Resources

Adams, M., L.A. Bell, and P. Griffin, eds. (1997). *Teaching for Diversity and Social Justice: A Sourcebook.* New York: Routledge.

Andrzejewski, J., ed. (1996). *Oppression and Social Justice: Critical Frameworks,* 5th ed. New York: Simon and Schuster.

Bell, L. A. (1997). "Theoretical Foundations for Social Justice Education." In M. Adams, L. A. Bell, and P. Griffin, eds., *Teaching for Diversity and Social Justice: A Sourcebook.* New York: Routledge.

Frye, M. (1983). "Oppression." In *The Politics of Reality: Essays in Feminist Theory.* Freedom, Calif.: The Crossing Press.

Griffin, P. (1997). "Introductory Module for the Single Issues Courses." In M. Adams, L. A. Bell, and P. Griffin, eds., *Teaching for Diversity and Social Justice: A Sourcebook.* New York: Routledge.

Hardiman, R., and B. W. Jackson. (1997). "Conceptual Foundations for Social Justice Courses." In M. Adams, L. A. Bell, and P. Griffin, eds., *Teaching for Diversity and Social Justice: A Sourcebook.* New York: Routledge.

Lorde, A. (1983). "There Is No Hierarchy of Oppressions." *International Books for Children Bulletin* 14.

Miller, J. B. (1976). *Toward a New Psychology of Women.* Boston: Beacon Press.

Pharr, S. (1988). "Common Elements of Oppressions." In *Homophobia: A Weapon of Sexism.* Inverness, Calif.: Chardon Press.

Rothenberg, P. S., ed. (1996). *Race, Class, and Gender in the United States: An Integrated Study,* 4th ed. New York: St. Martin's Press.

Steinberg, S. (1989). *The Ethnic Myth: Race, Ethnicity, and Class in America,* updated ed. Boston: Beacon Press.

Takaki, R. (1993). *A Different Mirror: A History of Multicultural America.* Boston: Little, Brown.

Wildman, S. M. (1996). *Privilege Revealed: How Invisible Preference Undermines America.* New York: New York University Press.

Zinn, H. (1995). *A People's History of the United States, 1492–Present,* rev. and updated ed. New York: Harper and Row.

Videotapes

A Tale of "O": On Being Different (user's manual included) (1993). [videotape (two versions, 0:27 full and 0:18 training)]: Goodmeasure, Inc., One Memorial Drive, Cambridge, MA 02142.

A Class Divided: Then and Now (videotape, facilitator's guide, and book set). (1985). [videotape, 0:60]: PBS Video, 1320 Braddock Place, Alexandria, VA 22314-1698; 800-344-3337; book: Peters, W. (1987). *A Class Divided: Then and Now,* exp. ed. New Haven, Conn.: Yale University Press.

Breaking Through Stereotypes (1994). [videotape, 0:15]: Educational Video Center, 55 East 25th Street, suite 407, New York, NY 10010; 212-725-3534 ext. 103; fax: 212-725-6501, attn. Stephanie.

Distorted Image: Stereotypes and Caricature in America: Popular graphics. (1973). [Videotape, 0:28]: ADL, 823 United Nations Plaza, New York, NY 10014; 212-490-2525.

Facing Difference: Living Together on Campus. (1990). [videotape, 0:10]: ADL, 823 United Nations Plaza, New York, NY 10014; 212-490-2525.

Names Can Really Hurt Us (Teens Talk about Their Experiences of Prejudice). (1994). [videotape, 0:26]: ADL, 823 United Nations Plaza, New York, NY 10014; 212-490-2525.

Section 2: Racism

Print Resources

Anzaldúa, G., ed. (1990). *Making Face, Making Soul: Haciendo Caras.* San Francisco: Aunt Lute Foundation Books.

Lipsitz, G. (1998). *The Possessive Investment in Whiteness: How White People Profit from Identity Politics.* Philadelphia: Temple University Press.

Marable, M. (1995). *Beyond Black and White: Transforming African American Politics.* London: Verso.

O'Hearn, C. C. (1998). *Half and Half: Writers on Growing Up Biracial and Bicultural.* New York: Pantheon Books.

Orfield, G and E. Miller. (1998). *Chilling Admissions: The Affirmative Action Crisis and the Search for Alternatives.* Cambridge, Mass.: Harvard Education Publishing.

Perea, J. F., ed. (1997). *Immigrants Out! The New Nativism and Anti-Immigrant Impulse in the United States.* New York: New York University.

Pincus, F. L. and H. J. Ehrlich. (1999). *Race and Ethnic Conflict: Contending Views on Prejudice, Discrimination, and Ethnoviolence.* Boulder, Colo.: Westview Press.

Reed, I., ed. (1997). *Multi-America: Essays on Cultural Wars and Cultural Peace.* New York: Penguin Books.

Reskin, B. F. (1998). *The Realities of Affirmative Action in Employment.* Washington, D.C.: American Sociological Association.

Smedley, A. (1999). *Race in North America: Origin and Evolution of a Worldview,* 2nd. ed. Boulder, Colo.: Westview Press.

Urciuoli, B. (1996). *Exposing Prejudice: Puerto Rican Experiences of Language, Race and Class.* Boulder, Colo.: Westview Press.

Wong, P., ed. (1999). *Race, Ethnicity and Nationality in the United States.* Boulder, Colo.: Westview Press.

Zack, N. (1998). *Thinking About Race.* Belmont, Calif.: Wadsworth.

Videotapes

Blue-eyed. (1995). [videotape, 0:93]: California Newsreel, 149 9th Street, #410, San Francisco, CA 94103; 415-621-6196, fax: 415-621-6522.

Chicano! (four videotapes) (1996). [videotape, 0:60 each]: National Latino Communication Center, P.O. Box 39A60, Los Angeles, CA 90039; 800-722-9982.

Domino: Interracial People and the Search for Identity. (1995). [videotape, 0:44]: Films for the Humanities, P.O. Box 2053, Princeton, NJ 08543.

Eyes on the Prize I: America's Civil Rights Years 1954–1965 (six videotapes). (1986). [videotape, 0:60 each]: PBS Video, 1320 Braddock Place, Alexandria, VA 22314-1698; 800-344-3337.

Eyes on the Prize II: America at the Racial Crossroads 1965–1985 (eight videotapes). (1990). [videotape, 0:60 each]: PBS Video, 1320 Braddock Place, Alexandria, VA 22314-1698; 800-344-3337. Study guide: *Eyes on the Prize: America at the Racial Crossroads: 1965–1985. A viewer's guide to the series.* Blackside, Inc., 486 Shawmut Ave., Boston, MA 02118.

In the White Man's Image. (1991). [videotape, 0:60]: PBS Video, 1320 Braddock Place, Alexandria, VA 22314-1698; 800-344-3337.

In Whose Honor? (1997). [videotape, 0:46]: Community Media Production Group, Inc., New Day Films, 22-D Hollywood Ave., Hohokus, NJ 07423; 888-367-9154, fax: 201-652-1973.

Skin Deep (includes study guide and instructor's manual; excerpts appear separately as *Talking About Race,* parts 1 and 2, 12 minutes each). (1995). [videotape, 0:53]: Iris Film Library, 22-D Hollywood Avenue, Hohokus, NJ 07423; 800-343-5540, fax: 201-652-1973.

Slaying the Dragon. (1987). [videotape, 0:60]: Women Make Movies, Inc., 462 Broadway, suite 500, New York, NY 10013; 212-925-0606, fax: 510-419-3934.

Tales from Arab Detroit (includes study guide). (1995). [videotape, 0:45]: Community Media Production Group, Inc., New Day Films, 22-D Hollywood Ave., Hohokus, NJ 07423; 888-367-9154, fax: 201-652-1973.

True Colors (Black and White testers reveal racism in every day life). (1991). [videotape, 0:17]: ABC Prime Time, MTI Film and Video, 420 Academy Drive, Northbrook, IL 60062; 888-777-8100.

Voices in Exile: Immigrants and the First Amendment. (1990). [videotape, 0:30]: Community Media Production Group, Inc., New Day Films, 22-D Hollywood Ave., Hohokus, NJ 07423; 888-367-9154, fax: 201-652-1973.

Section 3: Antisemitism

Print Resources

Adams, M., and J. Bracey, eds. (1999). *Strangers and Neighbors: Relations between Blacks and Jews in the United States.* Amherst, Mass.: University of Massachusetts Press.

Brodkin, K. (1998). *How Jews Became White Folks and What That Says about Race in America.* New Brunswick, N.J.: Rutgers University Press.

Dinnerstein, L. (1994). *Anti-semitism in America.* New York: Oxford University Press.

Falbel, R., I. Klepfisz, and D. Nevel, eds. (1990). *Jewish Women's Call for Peace: A Handbook for Women on the Israeli/Palestinian Conflict.* Ithaca, N.Y.: Firebrand Books.

Fernea, E. W., and M. W. Hocking, eds. (1992). *The Struggle for Peace: Israelis and Palestinians.* Austin: University of Texas Press.

Hilberg, Raul (1961). *The Destruction of the European Jews.* New York: Harper.

Lerner, M. (1992). *The Socialism of Fools: Anti-Semitism on the Left.* Oakland, Calif.: Tikkun Books.

Mosse, G. L. (1985). *Toward the Final Solution: A History of European Racism.* Madison: University of Wisconsin Press.

Pedersen, W. (1997). "Who Is a Jew?" In *Ethnicity Counts.* New Brunswick, N.J.: Transaction Publishers.

Sachar, H. M. (1992). *A History of the Jews in America.* New York: Vintage.

Shepherd, N. (1993). *A Price below Rubies: Jewish Women as Rebels and Radicals.* Cambridge, Mass.: Harvard University Press.

Svonkin, S. (1997). *Jews against Prejudice: American Jews and the Fight for Civil Liberties.* New York: Columbia University Press.

Weinberg, M. (1986). *Because They Were Jews: A History of Antisemitism.* Westport, Conn.: Greenwood Press.

Weinstein, G. and D. Mellen. (1997). "Antisemitism Curriculum Design." In Adams, M., L. A. Bell, and P. Griffin, eds. *Teaching for Diversity and Social Justice: A Sourcebook.* New York: Routledge.

Wistrich, R. S. (1991). *Antisemitism: The Longest Hatred.* New York: Pantheon Books.

Videotapes

America and the Holocaust: Deceit and Indifference. (1994). [videotape, 1:30]: PBS Video, 1320 Braddock Place, Alexandria,VA 22314-1698; 800-344-3337.

Backgrounds: A Brief History of Israel and the Arab/Palestinian Conflict. (1992). [videotape, 0.29]: First Run/Icarus Films, 153 Waverly Place, New York 100114; 212-727-1711.

Blacks and Jews: Point of View (July 29, 1997). [videotape, 1:26]: California Newsreel, 149 9th St, #420, San Francisco, CA 94103; 415-621-6196.

The Courage to Care. (1986). [videotape, 0:28]: Zenger Video, 10200 Jefferson Blvd., Room 902, P.O. Box 802, Culver City, CA 90232

Genocide 1941–1945, part 20 from the *World at War* series. (1982). [videotape, 0:52]: A and H Home Video, P.O. Box 2284, South Burlington, VT 05407.

Gentleman's Agreement. (1947). [videotape, 1:18]: Critics' Choice Video, P.O. Box 749, Itasca, IL 60143-0749; 800-367-7765.

Heritage: Civilization and the Jews. (1984). (9 videotapes) [videotape, 1:00 each]: Films Inc., 5547 North Ravenswood, Chicago, IL 60640. 312-878-2600 ext. 43. Book series: Eban, Abba.

(1984). *Heritage: Civilization and the Jews* (New York: Summit Books); titles: *A People Is Born: 3500 B.C.–6th Century B.C.; Power of the Word: 6th–2nd Century B.C.; The Shaping of Traditions: 1st–9th Century; The Crucible of Europe: 9th–15th Century; The Search for Deliverance: 1492–1789; Roads from the Ghetto: 1789–1917; Golden Land; Out of the Ashes; Into the Future.*

The Long Way Home. (1997). [videotape, 1:20]: Bonneville World Wide Entertainment Broadcast House, 55 N. 300 West, suite 315, Salt Lake City, Utah, 84110-1160; 1-801-575-3680; www.bwwe.com.

Not in Our Town. (n.d.). [videotape, 0.27]: KQED Books and Videos, 5959 Triumph Street, Commerce, CA; 800-358-3000; 800-422-9993.

Weapons of the Spirit (classroom version with study guide). (1987). [videotape, 0.28]: Zenger Video, 10200 Jefferson Blvd., room 902, Culver City, CA 90232, or Friends of Le Chambon, 8033 Sunset Blvd., #784, Los Angeles, CA 90046; 213-650-1174.

Section 4: Sexism

Print Resources

Anzaldúa, G., C. Moraga, and T. Bambara. (1984). *This Bridge Called My Back.* Watertown, Mass.: Persephone Press.

Bass, E., and L. Davis. (1994). *The Courage to Care,* 3rd ed. New York: Harper-Perennial.

Boston Women's Health Book Collective. (1984). *Our Bodies, Ourselves.* New York: Simon and Schuster.

Faludi, S. (1991). *Backlash: The Undeclared War against American Women.* New York: Doubleday.

Feinberg, L. (1993). *Stone Butch Blues.* Ithaca, N.Y.: Firebrand.

Kimmel, M. (1996). *Manhood in America: A Cultural History.* New York: Free Press.

Ms. Magazine. New York: Matilda Publications.

Pipher, M. (1994). *Reviving Ophelia: Saving the Selves of Adolescent Girls.* New York: Putnam.

Tannen, D. (1991). *You Just Don't Understand: Women and Men in Conversation.* New York: Morrow.

Wolf, N. (1991). *The Beauty Myth: How Images of Beauty are Used against Women.* New York: Doubleday.

Videotapes

bell hooks: Cultural Criticism and Transformation. (1997). [videotape, 1:06]: Media Education Foundation, 26 Center Street, Northampton, MA 01060; 800-897-0089.

Date Rape Backlash: Media and the Denial of Rape. (1994). [videotape, 0:57]: Media Education Foundation, 26 Center Street, Northampton, MA 01060; 800-897-0089.

Dreamworlds 2: Desire, Sex, Power in Music Video. (1995). [videotape, 0:56]: Media Education Foundation, 26 Center Street, Northampton, MA 01060; 800-897-0089.

The Fairer Sex (male and female testers reveal sexism in everyday life). (1993). [videotape, 0:25]: ABC Primetime; ABC News Videos, P.O. Box 2249, Livonia, MI 48151; 800-913-3434.

Game Over: Gender, Race, and Violence in Video Games. (1999). [videotape, 0:35]: Media Education Foundation, 26 Center Street, Northampton, MA 01060; 800-897-0089.

Playing the Game: A Video On Date Rape. (1993). [videotape, 0:16]: InterMedia, 1300 Dexter Ave. N, Seattle, WA 98109; 800-553-8336.

Reviving Ophelia: Saving the Selves of Adolescent Girls. (1998). [videotape, 0:38]: Media Education Foundation, 26 Center Street, Northampton, MA 01060; 800-897-0089.

Slim Hopes: Advertising and the Obsession with Thinness. (1995). [videotape, 0:30]: Media Education Foundation, 26 Center Street, Northampton, MA 01060; 800-897-0089.

Still Killing Us Softly III: Advertising's Image of Women. (2000). [videotape, 0:30]: Media Education Foundation, 26 Center Street, Northampton, MA 01060; 800-897-0089.

Tough Guise: Media Images and the Crisis of Masculinity. (1999). [videotape, 0:57 or 1:22]: Media Education Foundation, 26 Center Street, Northampton, MA 01060; 800-897-0089.

Section 5: Heterosexism

Print Resources

Beam, J., ed. (1986). *In the Life: A Black Gay Anthology.* Los Angeles: Alyson.

Blumenfeld, W. J., ed. (1992). *Homophobia: How We All Pay the Price.* Boston: Beacon Press.

Bornstein, K. (1994). *Gender Outlaw: On Men, Women, and the Rest of Us.* New York: Routledge.

Eng, D. L., and A. Y. Hom, eds. (1998). *Q&A: Queer in Asian America.* Philadelphia: Temple University Press.

Faderman, L. (1991). *Odd Girls and Twilight Lovers: A History of Lesbian Life in 20th-Century America.* New York: Penguin.

Feinberg, L. (1996). *Transgender Warriors: Making History from Joan of Arc to RuPaul.* Boston: Beacon Press.

Hutchins, L. and L. Ka'ahumanu, eds. (1991). *Bi Any Other Name: Bisexual People Speak Out.* Los Angeles: Alyson.

Miller, N. (1995). *Out of the Past: Gay and Lesbian History from 1869 to the Present.* New York: Vintage.

Trujillo, C., ed. (1991). *Chicana Lesbians: The Girls Our Mothers Warned Us About.* Berkeley: Third Woman Press.

Vaid, U. (1995). *Virtual Equality: The Mainstreaming of Gay and Lesbian Liberation.* New York: Anchor.

Videotapes

After Stonewall: From the Riots to the Millennium. (1999). [videotape, 1:25]: Cinema Guild, 1697 Broadway, suite 802, New York, NY 10019.

Before Stonewall: The Making of a Gay and Lesbian Community. (1984) [videotape, 1:27]: Cinema Guild, 1697 Broadway, suite 802, New York, NY 10019.

Gay Youth. (1992). [videotape, 0:40]: Wolfe Video, P.O. Box 64, New Almaden, CA 95042.

Pink Triangles: A Study of Prejudice against Lesbians and Gays. (1982) [videotape, 0:34]: Cambridge Documentary Films, P.O. Box 385, Cambridge, MA 02139.

It's Elementary: Talking About Gay Issues in Schools. (1996). [videotape, 1:18 and 0:37]: Women's Educational Media, 2180 Bryant Street, suite 203, San Francisco, CA 94110.

The Celluloid Closet. (1996). [videotape, 1:42]: Columbia Tristar Home Video, 10202 W. Washington Blvd, Culver City, CA 90232-3195.

The Question of Equality. (4 videotapes) (1995). [videotape, 0:55 each]: Wolfe Video, P.O. Box 64, New Almaden, CA 95042.

Out of the Past: The Struggle for Gay and Lesbian Rights in America. (1997). [videotape, 1:10]: Wolfe Video, P.O. Box 64, New Almaden, CA 95042.

Out: Stories of Lesbian and Gay Youth. (1993). [videotape, 1:19]: National Film Board of Canada, P.O. Box 6100, Station A, Montreal, Quebec H3C 3H5, Canada.

Tongues Untied. (1989). [videotape, 0:55]: Frameline Distribution, 346 Ninth Street, San Francisco, CA 94103

Section 6: Ableism

Print Resources

Association on Higher Education and Disability. (1999). "Being Sensitive to Culture." In *Expanding Postsecondary Options for Minority Students with Disabilities.* Columbus, Ohio: AHEAD.

Barton, L., ed. . (1996). *Disability and Society: Emerging Issues and Insights.* London: Longman.

Baynton, D. (1996). *Forbidden Signs: American Culture and the Campaign against Sign Language.* Chicago: University of Chicago Press.

Christensen, C., and F. Rizvi, eds. . (1996). *Disability and the Dilemmas of Education and Justice.* Philadelphia: Open University Press.

Davis, L. J. (1995). *Enforcing Normalcy: Disability, Deafness and the Body.* New York: Verso.

———, ed. . (1997). *The Disability Studies Reader.* New York: Routledge.

Hurford, D. M. (1998). *To Read or Not to Read: Answers to All Your Questions about Dyslexia*. New York: Scribner.

Linton, S. (1998). *Claiming Disability: Knowledge and Identity*. New York: New York University Press.

Oliver, M. (1996). *Understanding Disability: From Theory to Practice*. New York: St. Martin's Press.

Palka, F. (1997). *The Disability Rights Movement*. Santa Barbara, Calif.: ABC-CLIO.

Project Staff for Grey House Publishing. *The Complete Directory for People with Disabilities: A One Stop Source Book for Individuals and Professionals*. (1998/99). Lakeville, Conn.: Grey House.

Rudner, A. (1992, May/June). "Chronic Fatigue Syndrome: Searching for the Answers." *Ms.*, 33–36.

Shapiro, J. P. (1991). *No Pity: People with Disabilities Forging a New Civil Rights Movement*. New York: Random House.

Stone, K. G. (1997). *Awakening to Disability: Nothing About Us Without Us*. Volcano, California: Volcano Press.

Wendell, S. (1996). *The Rejected Body: Feminist Philosophical Reflections on Disability*. New York: Routledge.

Videotapes

Disabled Women: Voices and Visions. (1996). [videotape, 0:13]: Program Development Associates, 5620 Business Avenue, suite B, Cicero, NY 13039; 800-543-2119.

How Difficult Can This Be? A Learning Disabilities Workshop (The F.A.T. City Workshop; includes teacher's guide). (1989). [videotape, 1:10]: PBS Video, 1320 Braddock Place, Alexandria, VA 22314-1698; 800-344-3337.

Just Friends, The Road You Take Is Yours, and *A Different Way of Learning* (3 videotapes) (1997). [videotape, 0:22, 0:19, 0:10]: Program Development Associates, 5620 Business Avenue, suite B, Cicero, NY 13039; 800-543-2119.

Learning Disabilities and Self-Esteem: Look What You've Done! (parent and teacher versions) (1997). [videotape, 0:66, 0:65]: PBS Video, 1320 Braddock Place, Alexandria, VA 22314-1698; 800-344-3337.

A Little History Worth Knowing. (1998). [videotape, 0:23]: Program Development Associates, 5620 Business Avenue, suite B, Cicero, NY 13039; 800-543-2119.

Positive Images: Portraits of Women with Disabilities. (1989). [videotape, 0:58]: New York: Women Make Movies, 462 Broadway, suite 501, New York, NY 10013; 212-925-0606.

When Billy Broke His Head. (1994). [videotape, 0:57]: Fanlight Productions, 47 Halifax St., Boston, MA 02130; 800-937-4113; fax 617-524-8838.

When the Chips Are Down (1997). [videotape, 0:62]: PBS Video, 1320 Braddock Place, Alexandria, VA 22314-1698; 800-344-3337.

Withstanding Ovation . . . the Emphasis Is on Capability (1993). [videotape, 0:24]: Fanlight Production, 47 Halifax Street, Boston, MA 02130; 800-937-4113.

Section 7: Classism

Print Resources

Albelda, R., N. Folbre, and the Center for Popular Economics (1996). *The War on the Poor: A Defense Manual*. New York: The New Press.

Barlett, D. L., and J. B. Steele. (1992). *America: What Went Wrong?* Kansas City, Mo.: Andrews and McMeel.

Dalphin, J. (1987). *The Persistence of Social Inequality in America*. Rochester, Vt.: Schenkman Books.

Demko, G. J., and M. C. Jackson. (1995). *Populations at Risk in America: Vulnerable Groups at the End of the Twentieth Century*. New York: Westview Press.

Herzenberg, S. A., J. A. Alic, and H. Wial. (1998). *New Rules for a New Economy: Employment and Opportunity in Postindustrial America*. Ithaca, N.Y.: Cornell University Press.

Levine, A., and J. Nidiffer. (1996). *Beating the Odds: How the Poor Get to College*. San Franciso: Jossey-Bass.

McMurrer, D. P., and I. V. Sawhill. (1998). "Education and Opportunity." In *Getting Ahead: Economic and Social Mobility in America*. Washington, D.C.: Urban Institute Press.

Ogbu, J. U. (1988). "Class Stratification, Racial Stratification, and Schooling." In L. Weis, ed., *Class, Race, and Gender in American Education.* Albany, N.Y.: State University of New York Press.

Rothman, R. A. (1999). *Inequality and Stratification: Race, Class, and Gender.* Upper Saddle River, N.J.: Prentice-Hall.

Wilson, W. J. (1987). *The Truly Disadvantaged: The Inner City, The Underclass, and Public Policy.* Chicago: University of Chicago Press.

Wray, M., and A. Newitz. (1997). *White Trash: Race and Class in America.* New York: Routledge.

Yeskel, F., and B. Leondar-Wright. (1997). "Classism Curriculum Design." In Adams, M., L. A. Bell, and P. Griffin, eds., *Teaching for Diversity and Social Justice: A Sourcebook.* New York: Routledge.

Zandy, J. (1996). "Decloaking Class: Why Class Identity and Consciousness Count." *Race, Gender, and Class* 4, no. 1, 7–23.

———. (1995). *Liberating Memory: Our Work and Our Working-Class Consciousness.* New Brunswick, N.J.: Rutgers University Press.

Zinn, H. (1995). *A People's History of the United States,* updated and rev. ed. New York: Harper and Row.

Videotapes

America: What Went Wrong? (Bill Moyers' *Listening to America;* 2 videotapes) (1992). [videotape, 1:00 each]: PBS Video, 1320 Braddock Place, Alexandria, VA 22314-1698; 800-344-3337. Book: Barlett, D. L. and J. B. Steel. (1992). *America: What Went Wrong?* Kansas City, Mo.: Andrews and McMeel.)

America's War on Poverty (5 videotapes) (1995). [videotape, 1:00 each]: PBS Video, 1320 Braddock Place, Alexandria, VA 22314-1698; 800-344-3337.

Down and Out in America. (1985). [videotape, 0:57]: MPI Home Video, Dept. 1500, 15825 Robroy Drive, Oak Forest, IL 60452; 800-777-2223.

The Global Assembly Line. (1986). [videotape, 0:58]: New Day Films, 121 W. 27th St., New York, NY 10001; 212-645-8210.

The Great Depression (7 videotapes). (1993). [videotape, 1:00 each]: PBS Video, 1320 Braddock Place, Alexandria, VA 22314-1698; 800-344-3337.

Social Class (Two high school girls). (1991). [videotape, 0:30]: Insight Media, TSI-114, 2162 Broadway, New York, NY 10024.

Section 8: Working for Social Justice: Visions and Strategies for Change

Print Resources

Allen, R. L. (1995). "Stopping Sexual Harrassment: A Challenge for Community Education." In A. F. Hill and E. C. Jordan, eds., *Race, Gender and Power in America: The Legacy of the Hill-Thomas Hearings.* New York: Oxford University Press.

Albrecht, L., and L. Brewer, eds. (1990). *Bridges of Power: Women's Multicultural Alliances.* Philadelphia: New Society.

Brecher, J., and T. Costello, eds. (1990). *Building Bridges: The Emerging Grassroots Coalition of Labor and Community.* New York: Monthly Review Press.

Bunch, C. (1993). "Going Public with Our Vision: Transformational Politics and Practical Visions." In V. Cyrus, ed., *Experiencing Race, Class and Gender in the U.S.* Mountain View, Calif.: Mayfield.

Charlton, J. I. (1998). "Empowered Consciousness and the Philosophy of Empowerment." In *Nothing About Us Without Us: Disability Oppression and Empowerment.* Berkeley and Los Angeles: University of California Press.

Du Bois, P. M., and J. Hudson. (1997). *Bridging the Racial Divide—A Report on Interracial Dialogue in America.* Brattleboro, Vt.: Center for Living Democracy.

hooks, b. (1984). "Men: Comrades in Struggle." In *Feminist Theory: From Margin to Center.* Boston: South End Press.

Lorde, A. (1987). "I Am Your Sister: Black Women Organizing Across Sexualities." Freedom Organizing Pamphlet Series no. 3. New York: Kitchen Table/Women of Color Press.

Marable, M. (1995). "Beyond Racial Identity Politics: Toward a Liberation Theory for Multicultural Democracy." In *Beyond Black and White.* London: Verso.

Minkowitz, D. (1989). "Why Heterosexuals Need to Support Gay Rights." *Village Voice,* June 27.

Naples, N. (1998). *Community Activism and Feminist Politics: Organizing across Race, Class and Gender.* New York: Routledge

Stout, L. (1997). *Bridging the Class Divide and other Lesson for Grassroots Organizing.* Boston: Beacon Press.

Statham, M.A., ed. (1997). *Interracial Dialogue Groups across America: A Directory.* Brattleboro, Vt.: Center of Living Democracy.

Videotapes

Carved From the Heart: A Portrait of Grief, Healing and Community. (1999). [videotape, 0:30]: New Day Films, 22D Hollywood Ave., Hohokus, NJ 07423; 201-652-6590; fax, 201-652-1973.

Fundi: The Story of Ella Baker. (1986). [videotape, 0:36]: First Run, Icarus Films, 153 Waverly Place, Sixth Floor, New York, NY 10014; 212-727-1711.

Healing the Heart of America. (1993). [videotape, 0:27]: Hope in the Cities/MRA Inc. Available from Grosvenor Books USA, 3735 Cherry Ave., NE, Salem, OR 97303; 503-393-2172.

Holding Ground: The Rebirth of Dudley Street. (1996). [videotape: 0:58]: New Day Films, 22D Hollywood Ave., Hohokus, NJ 07423; 201-652-6590; fax, 201-652-1973. .

Forgotten Fires. (1998). [video: 1:00]: Independent Television Series, P.O. Box 78008, San Francisco, CA 94107-8008; 415-356-8383. www.itvs.org.

A Town of Hope. (1995). [videotape, 0:46]: Films for the Humanities and Sciences, P.O. Box 2053, Princeton, NJ 08543-2053; 800-257-5126, fax: 609-275-3767. www.films.com.

Intergroup Dialogues. (1997). [videotape, 0:30]. Intergroup Relations, Conflict and Community Program, The University of Michigan, 3000 Michigan Union, Ann Arbor, MI 48105; 734-936-1875.

The Way Home. (1999). [videotape, 1:32]: World Trust, 5920 San Pablo Ave., Oakland, CA 94608; 800-343-5540; fax: 201-652-1973.

Yuri Kochiyama: Passion for Justice. (1994). [videotape:0:58]: Women Make Movies, 462 Broadway, Ste. 501, New York, NY 10013; 212-925-0606.

Watts, Then and Now, 1965–1991. (1998). [videotape:0:47]: Films for the Humanities and Sciences, P.O. Box 2053, Princeton, NJ 08543-2053; 800-257-5126, fax: 609-275-3767. www.films.com.

Welfare Warriors. (1997). [videotape, 0:36]: Vision Quest Film and Video Production, P.O. Box 278, Huntington, NY 11743; 631-385-7459.

Thematic Table of Contents

Social Identity

Oppression and Liberation

Historical Contexts

Stereotypes

The Dominants' Experiences

The Targets' Experiences

The Body

Institutions: Educational, Political, Social, Economic

Permission Acknowledgments

The following essays were previously published. Permission to reprint is gratefully acknowledged here.

Anner, John, 1996, excerpts from "Having the Tools at Hand: Building Successful Multicultural Social Justice Organizations," from *Beyond Identity Politics*, ed. John Anner. Reprinted by permission of the Institute for Social and Cultural Change, South End Press.

Anzaldúa, Gloria, excerpts from "Interview," from *Sinister Wisdom* 52 (Spring/Summer 1994), 47–52. Reprinted by permission of Gloria Anzaldúa.

The Associated Press, excerpts from "Menorah Light Banishes Hate," from *Newsday*, December 13, 1996, A4. Copyright © 1996, the Associated Press. Reprinted by permission of the Associated Press.

The Association for Higher Education and Disability (n.d.). "Understanding Disability Issues," from *Expanding Postsecondary Options for Minority Students*. Reprinted by permission of the Association for Higher Education and Disability. (AHEAD).

Bem, Sandra Lipsitz, excerpts from "The Conundrum of Difference," from *The Lenses of Gender* by Sandra Lipsitz Bem. Copyright © 1993 by Yale University Press. Reprinted by permission of Yale University Press.

Bergmann, Barbara, and Heidi Hartmann, excerpts from "A Welfare Reform Program Based on Help for Working Parents," from *The War on the Poor: A Defense Manual*, by Randy Albeda, Nancy Folbre, and The Center for Popular Economics. Copyright © 1996 Reprinted by permission of The New Press.

Bernards, Reena, excerpts from "Pioneers in Dialogue: Jews Building Bridges," from *The Narrow Bridge: Jewish Views on Multiculturalism*, ed. Marla Brettschneider, 1996, Rutgers University Press. Reprinted by permission of Reena Bernards.

Blumenfeld, Warren J., excerpts from "How Homophobia Hurts Everyone," from *Homophobia* by Warren J. Blumenfeld. Copyright © 1992 by Warren J. Blumenfeld. Reprinted by permission of Beacon Press and Warren J. Blumenfeld.

Blumenfeld, Warren J., and Diane Raymond, excerpts from "Prejudice and Discrimination," from *Looking at Gay and Lesbian Life* by Warren J. Blumenfeld and Diane Raymond, 1988, Beacon Press. Reprinted by permission of Warren J. Blumenfeld and Diane Raymond.

Bornstein, Kate, excerpts from *Gender Outlaw*. Copyright © 1994 by Kate Bornstein. Reproduced by permission of Taylor and Francis/Routledge, Inc.

Bowman, Elizabeth Atkins, and Michelle Burford, excerpts from "Wheel Power," from *Essence*, September 1998, 144–46. Reprinted by permission of the publisher.

Bray, Rosemary, excerpts from "So How Did I Get Here?" Reprinted from *The New York Times Magazine*, November 8, 1992. Reprinted by permission of Rosemary Bray. Copyright © 1992. All rights reserved.

Brouwer, Steve, excerpts from "Sharing the Pie," and from The Sinking Majority," from *Sharing the Pie* by Steve Brouwer. Copyright © 1998 by Steve Brouwer. Reprinted by permission of Henry Holt and Company, LLC.

Browne, Susan E, Debra Connors, and Nanci Stern, excerpts from "Invisible and on Center Stage (Who Do We Think We Are, Anyway?)," from *With the Power of Each Breath: A Disabled Women's Anthology*, ed. Susan E. Browne, Debra Connors and Nanci Stern (1985). Copyright © 1985, Cleis Press, San Francisco. Reprinted by permission of the publisher.

Bryan, Willie V., excerpts from "The Disability Rights Movement," from *In Search of Freedom: How Persons with Disabilities Have Been Disenfranchised from the Mainstream of American Society*, 1996. Reprinted courtesy of Charles C. Thomas, Publisher, Ltd., Springfield, Illinois.

Burns, William David, excerpts from " Why Don't Gay People Just Keep Quiet?" from *Empathy* 2, no. 1 (1989/1990), 22–23. Reprinted with permission of the ONE Institute/International Gay and Lesbian Archives, Southern Studies Collection.

Chernick, Abra Fortune, excerpts from "The Body Politic." Copyright © 1995 by Abra Fortune Chernick. Reprinted from *Listen Up: Voices from the Next Feminist Generation*, ed. Barbara Findlen and published by Seal Press. Reprinted with permission of Seal Press.

Childs, John Brown, excerpts from "Red Clay, Blue Hills: In Honor of My Ancestors," printed with permission of John Brown Childs.

Collins, Patricia Hill, excerpts from "Toward a New Vision: Race, Class and Gender as Categories of Analysis and Connection," from *Race, Gender and Class* 1, no. 1 (1993), 36–45. Reprinted by permission of the publisher.

Cooper, Marc, excerpts from "The Heartland's Raw Deal," from the February 3, 1997 issue of *The Nation*. Reprinted by permission of the publisher.

Davidson, Ellen and Nancy Schniedewind, excerpts from "Linguicism," from *Open Minds to Equality: A Sourcebook of Learning Activities to Affirm Diversity and Promote Equity*, 2nd. ed. Copyright © 1998 by Allyn and Bacon. Reprinted by permission of the publisher.

Deacon, F. Jay, excerpts from "What Does the Bible Say About Homosexuality?" from *The Welcoming Congregation Handbook*, 2nd ed. Universalist Association of Congregations.

Deegan, Patricia, excerpts from "Recovering Our Sense of Value after Being Labeled Mentally Ill," from *Journal of Psychosocial Nursing and Mental Health Services* 31, no. 4 (1993), 7–11. Reprinted by permission of the publisher.

Diehl, Marcia, and Robyn Ochs, excerpts from "Biphobia," from *Empathy* 2, no. 1 (1989/90), 15–19. Reprinted by permission of ONE Institute/International Gay and Lesbian Archives, Southern Studies Collection and the authors.

Dinnerstein, Leonard, excerpts from "Prologue," from *Antisemitism in America* by Leonard Dinnerstein. Copyright © 1995 by Oxford University Press, Inc. Reprinted by permission of Oxford University Press, Inc.

Edelman, Peter B., excerpts from "Toward a Comprehensive Antipoverty Strategy: Getting Beyond the Silver Bullet," from *Georgetown Law Journal* 81, no. 5 (1993), 1726–1732. Copyright © 1993. Reprinted by permission of Georgetown University and *Georgetown Law Journal*.

Edgington, Amy, excerpts from "Moving Beyond White Guilt," from *Transformation* 13, no. 3 (1998), 5–7. Copyright © 1998 by the Women's Project. Reprinted by permission of the Women's Project, 2224 Main St., Little Rock, AR 72206.

Feagin, Joe R., excerpts from "The Continuing Significance of Race: Antiblack Discrimination in Public Places," from *American Sociological Review* 56 (February, 1991), 102, 103, 105, 106, 107, 108, 109, 110, 114. Reprinted by permission of the American Sociological Association and the author.

Fine, Michelle, and Adrienne Asch, excerpts from "Disability Beyond Stigma: Social Interaction, Discrimination, and Activism," from *Journal of Social Issues* 44, no. 1 (1988), 3-21. Reprinted by permission of Blackwell Publishers.

Ford, Clyde W., excerpts from "Developing Cross-Cultural Communication," from *We Can All Get Along*, by Clyde W. Ford, 1984, Dell. Reprinted by permission of the author.

French, Sally, excerpts from "Equal Opportunities—Yes, Please," from *"What Happened to You?" Writings by Disabled Women*, ed. Lois Keith. Copyright © 1996. Reprinted by permission of The New Press.

Fry, Varian, excerpts from "The Massacre of the Jews," from *The New Republic* 107, no. 25 (1942), 816–19. Reprinted by permission of the publisher.

Gilbert, Martin, maps from *The Holocaust: Maps and Photographs*, by Martin Gilbert. © 1994, Martin Gilbert, Anti-Defamation League. Reprinted by permission of Sir Martin Gilbert.

Harro, Bobbie, "The Cycle of Socialization." Copyright © 1997. From *Teaching for Diversity and Social Justice: A Sourcebook*, ed. Maurianne Adams, Lee Anne Bell, and Pat Griffin. Reproduced by permission of Taylor and Francis/Routledge, Inc.

Harro, Bobbie, "The Cycle of Liberation." Copyright © 2000 by Bobbie Harro. Published by permission of the author.

Haubegger, Christy, excerpts from "I'm Not Fat, I'm Latina," from *Essence* 25, no. 8 (December, 1994). Reprinted by permission of the publisher.

Heintz, James, Nancy Folbre, and the Center for Popular Economics, "Who Owns How Much," from *The Ultimate Field Guide to the U.S. Economy* by James Heintz, Nancy Folbre, and The Center For Popular Economics, 2000, The New Press. Reprinted by permission of Nancy Folbre.

Herek, Gregory, "Internalized Homophobia Among Gay Men and Lesbians," is reprinted from chapter 7, "Heterosexism and Homophobia," from *Textbook of Homosexuality and Mental Health* ed. Robert B. Cavaj and Terry S. Stein, 1996, American Psychiatric Press. Reprinted by permission of American Psychiatric Press.

hooks, bell, excerpts from "Feminism: A Movement to End Sexist Oppression," from *Feminist Theory: From Margin to Center*, by bell hooks, 1984, South End Press. Reprinted by permission of South End Press.

hooks, bell, excerpts from "Homophobia in Black Communities," from *Talking Back: Thinking Feminist, Thinking Black* by bell hooks, 1989, South End Press. Reprinted by permission of South End Press.

"International Bill of Gender Rights" from the International Conference on Transgender Law and Employment Policy (ICTLEP), 1995. Reprinted by permission of ICTLEP, ictlephdq@aol.com.

Katz, Jackson, excerpts from "Pornography and Men's Consciousness: Rethinking Private Pleasure," from *Empathy* 3, no. 2 (1992/93), 47–49. Reprinted by permission of the author.

Kaye/Kantrowitz, Melanie, excerpts from "Jews in the U.S.," Copyright © 1996. from *Names We Call Home*, ed. Becky Thompson and Sangeeta Tyagi. Reproduced by permission of Taylor and Francis/ Routledge, Inc.

Kimmel, Michael S., excerpts from "Masculinity as Homophobia," from *Theorizing Masculinities*, ed. Harry Brod and Michael Kaufman. Copyright © 1994 by Sage Publications, Inc. Reprinted by permission of Sage Publications, Inc.

Krebs, Jennifer, excerpts from "Short Black Hair," from *Naming the Waves: Contemporary Lesbian Poetry*, 1988, London: Virago Press. Reprinted by permission of Jennifer Krebs.

Langman, Peter F., excerpts from "Including Jews in Multiculturalism," from *Journal of Multicultural Counseling and Development* 23, no. 4 (October 1995), 222–36. Copyright © American Counseling Association. Reprinted with permission; no further reproduction authorized without written permission of the American Counseling Association.

Langston, Donna, excerpts from "Tired of Playing Monopoly," from *Changing Our Power: An Introduction to Women's Studies*, ed. Jo Whitehorse Cochrane, Donna Langston, and Carolyn Woodward, 1988, Kendall-Hunt. Reprinted by permission of Donna Langston.

Omi, Michael, excerpts from "Racial Identity and the State: Contesting the Federal Standards for Classification," Copyright © 1999. From *Race, Ethnicity and Nationality in the United States*, edited by Paul Wong, Westview Press. Reprinted by permission of the publisher.

Padden, Carol, excerpts from "The Deaf Community and the Culture of Deaf People," from *Sign Language and the Deaf Community: Essays in Honor of William C. Stokoe*, 1980, National Association of the Deaf. Reprinted by permission of the National Association of the Deaf.

Pharr, Suzanne, excerpts from "Reflections on Liberation," from *In the Time of the Right: Reflections on Liberation* by Suzanne Pharr, 1996, Chardon Press, distributed by the Women's Project, 2224 Main St., Little Rock, AR, 72206. Reprinted by permission of the author.

Pincus, Fred L., excerpts from "Discrimination Comes in Many Forms: Individual, Institutional, and Structural," from *American Behavioral Scientist* 40, no. 2, (1996) 186–95. Copyright © 1996 by Sage Publications, Inc. Reprinted by permission of Sage Publications, Inc.

Plant, Richard, excerpts from "The Men with the Pink Triangles," from *Christopher Street*, February, 1977, 4–10.

Ransford, H. Edward, excerpts from "The Interaction Between Race and Class," from *Race and Class in American Society: Black, Latino, Anglo* by H. Edward Ransford, 1994, Schenkman. Reprinted by permission of the publisher.

Rodriquez, Richard, excerpts from "Complexion," from *Hunger of Memory* by Richard Rodriguez. Reprinted by permission of David R. Godine, Publisher, Inc. Copyright © 1982 by Richard Rodriguez.

Root, Maria P. P., excerpts from "A Bill of Rights for Racially Mixed People," from *The Multiracial Experience*, ed. Maria P.P. Root. Copyright © 1996 by Sage Publications, Inc. Reprinted by permission of Sage Publications, Inc.

Rosen, Larua Epstein, and Xavier Amador, abridgement of chapter 6, from *When Someone You Love Is Depressed: How to Help Your Loved One without Losing Yourself.* Copyright © 1996 by Laura Epstein Rosen and Xavier Amador. Reprinted with permission of The Free Press, a Division of Simon and Schuster, Inc.

Scheller, Melanie, excerpts from "On the Meaning of Plumbing and Poverty," from *The Independent Weekly*, (Durham, North Carolina) January 4, 1990. Reprinted by permission of Melanie Scheller.

Scott, Linda M., excerpts from "Fresh Lipstick: Rethinking Images of Women in Advertising," from *Media Studies Journal* 7, Nos. 1-2 (1993), 141–55. Reprinted by permission of the publisher.

Shapiro, Joseph P., excerpts from "A Separate and Unequal Education for Minorities with Learning Disabilities," from *Learning Disabilities: Lifelong Issues*, ed. S. C. Cramer and W. Ellis, 1996, Paul H. Brookes. Reprinted by permission of Paul H. Brookes Publishing Co. and Joseph P. Shapiro.

Smith, Sally, excerpts from "The Hidden Dimension of Learning: Time and Space," from *Their World*, 1998/1999, 43–45, National Center for Learning Disabilities. Reprinted by permission of the publisher.

"Social Class Questionnaire," from *Radical Teacher* 46 (Spring, 1995), 19. Reprinted by permission of the publisher.

Steinem, Gloria, excerpts from "Revving Up for the Next 25 Years," from *Ms.* 8, no. 2, (September/October, 1997), 82–84. Reprinted by permission of Gloria Steinem.

Takaki, Ronald, excerpts from "A History of Multicultural America," from *A Different Mirror: A History of Multicultural America* by Ronald Takaki. Copyright © 1993 by Ronald Takaki. Reprinted by permission of Little, Brown and Company.

Tatum, Beverly Daniel, excerpts from "The Complexity of Identity: "Who am I?" from *Why Are All the Black Kids Sitting Together in the Cafeteria?* by Beverly Daniel Tatum. Copyright © 1997 by Beverly Daniel Tatum. Reprinted by permission of Basic Books, a member of Perseus Books, L.L.C.

About the Editors

Maurianne Adams is Chair of the Social Justice Education Program at the School of Education, University of Massachusetts/Amherst. She has co-edited *Strangers and Neighbors: Relations between Blacks and Jews in the United States* (UMass Press, 2000), *Teaching for Diversity and Social Justice: A Sourcebook* (Routledge, 1997), and edited *Promoting Diversity in the College Classroom* (Jossey-Bass, 1992). Dr. Adams has published book chapters, delivered papers, and conducted workshops on faculty leadership and student development in relation to social justice education on college campuses. She teaches graduate courses on foundations of social justice education, models of social identity development, multicultural adult development, and undergraduate courses on social diversity in education and on the historical relations of Blacks and Jews in the United States.

Warren J. Blumenfeld is co-author of *Looking at Gay and Lesbian Life* (Beacon Press, 1988, 1993), *AIDS and Your Religious Community* (Unitarian Universalist Press, 1991), and editor of *Homophobia: How We All Pay the Price* (Beacon Press, 1992) and of the quarterly *International Journal of Sexuality and Gender Studies* (Kluwer Academic/Human Sciences Press). He has written a Massachusetts Governor's commission report on making colleges and universities safe, and *Gay/Straight Alliances: A Student Guide,* co-produced the documentary film "Pink Triangles" (Cambridge Documentary Films), and founded the National Queer Student Coalition of the U.S. Student Association. He teaches courses on social issues in education, heterosexism, antisemitism, and Black-Jewish relations at the University of Massachusetts/Amherst, where he is a doctoral candidate completing his dissertation in the Social Justice Education Program.

Carmelita (Rosie) Castañeda is a Staff Trainer and Organizational Development Intern in the Office of Training and Development at the University of Massachusetts/Amherst, where she is a doctoral candidate completing her dissertation in the Social Justice Education Program. She teaches courses on social diversity in education, with emphasis on issues of race, ethnicity, sexual orientation, and oppression related to physical and mental ability. She also consults with organizations on the design and delivery of training programs, organizational interventions, and workshop sessions related to multicultural issues and team development. A national aerobic champion, Rosie was an international fitness consultant and one of three authors of the college textbook *Creative Aerobic Fitness* (Kendall/Hunt, 1998).

Heather W. Hackman is currently conducting research on educator power dynamics in the college classroom and has developed a teacher education/faculty development model designed to effectively assist educators in reflecting on their power. She has presented this material at several national conferences including the National Association of Multicultural Education, an organization in which she is a state board member. She has taught Education and Women's Studies courses at the University of Massachusetts, Human Services courses at Springfield College, and Multicultural Education courses at Westfield State College. She is currently completing her doctoral degree in the Social Justice Education Program at the University of Massachusetts.

Madeline L. Peters is the Director of Disability Services at the University of Massachusetts/Amherst, where she is a doctoral student in the Social Justice Education Program. She has worked in the field of disability for twelve years and in Student Affairs for seventeen years. She holds a Masters degree that focuses on organizational development, human services and social justice education. She has taught classes in social justice education and a range of social justice issues, presented her work at national conferences, and facilitated workshops on disability, diversity, and social justice. Her areas of specialty are people with disabilities, women, and people of color, to build leadership, empowerment, and self-esteem.

Ximena Zúñiga is a faculty member in the Social Justice Education Program at the School of Education, University of Massachusetts/Amherst. She has co-edited *Multicultural Teaching in the University* (Praeger, 1993) and published book chapters and journal articles on teaching about conflict in the diverse classroom, dialogues across race and other social group boundaries, and student development in social justice education. She teaches graduate and undergraduate courses on multicultural group processes, racism in the United States, social justice education teaching and facilitation, and dialogues across differences.

Teaching for Diversity and Social Justice: A Sourcebook

Edited by Maurianne Adams, Lee Ann Bell, and Pat Griffin

Readings for Diversity and Social Justice was inspired by the highly successful, *Teaching for Diversity and Social Justice: A Sourcebook*, a much-needed resource for social justice teaching. *Readings for Diversity and Social Justice* can be used as a companion to the sourcebook or as a stand-alone text. Using an integrated approach to oppression and social justice, *Teaching for Diversity and Social Justice* presents theoretical foundations and frameworks for social justice teaching practice. It includes extended illustrative samples of classroom and workshop activities, with print and video resources. The sourcebook is written for both novice and experienced faculty and trainers in higher education, adult formal and non-formal education, and workplace diversity and staff development programs.

Teaching for Diversity and Social Justice is also published by Routledge. For information on ordering the sourcebook or to receive an exam copy, please contact our Customer Service Department at 1-800-634-7064. Fax: 1-800-248-4724.

ISBN: 0-415-91057-9